T0049115

Handbook for Treatment of Attachment-Trauma Problems in Children

Beverly James

THE FREE PRESS
New York

THE FREE PRESS
A Division of Simon & Schuster Inc.
1230 Avenue of the Americas
New York, N.Y. 10020

Manufactured in the United States of America

10

Library of Congress Cataloging-in-Publication Data

James, Beverly
Handbook for treatment of attachment-trauma problems in children / Beverly James.
p. cm.
Includes bibliographical references and index.
ISBN 0-02-916005-7
1. Psychic trauma in children. 2. Attachment behavior in children. I. Title.
RA506.P66J35 1994
618.92'8521—dc20 94-21395
CIP

ISBN: 978-1-4391-43001
ISBN: 1439143005

Contents

Acknowledgments

My deepest appreciation goes to Stephen Gross whose support and editorial skills midwifed this book into being. I am grateful to the many colleagues, children, and families whose contributions added depth and breadth to this work. Discussions with my friend and colleague Patricia Dixon contributed to the development of concepts integrating attachment and trauma theory. Mary-Lou Carson, Karen Sittlerle, and Molly Romer Whitten generously shared their clinical expertise and personal support throughout the writing of the manuscript. Joyce Mills added spirit. Margaret Zusky of Lexington Books provided guidance that is much appreciated. Nourishment and "hanging in there" were steadfastly provided by my family and friends when I displayed many of the symptoms described in attachment-trauma disturbances.

Aloha nui loa and mahalo to you all.

Introduction

The Children Belong to All of Us

Lush brown bodies shaking with laughter, the grandmothers slowly nodded their collective heads while looking at me as if I were a naive child questioning the obvious. They struggled to explain to me a Micronesian custom that was so inherent, so natural, so right, that none of them had ever considered why it was done that way. I had asked this circle of Micronesian women what to me seemed a simple question: Why is it that the grandmothers, and not the mothers, care for the babies all the time?

These women gathered together daily, sitting on their mats under the trees to "talk story" while holding, cuddling, nuzzling, and talking to their grandbabies. They enjoyed the novelty of my being there with them, and I felt honored to be invited. I was thinking that this intimate circle, this woman-bonding, could be taking place anywhere in the world. With just a change of hats, dress, and skin tone, I could have been in India, Peru, Thailand, or Swaziland. Or even some communities in the United States.

The island grandmothers, not the mothers, are traditionally the children's primary caregivers from the time of birth. Some of the mothers were my students in high school. Some had left the island to attend college, leaving behind several young children. These mothers did not seem to yearn for their babies even when separated from them for a long time. I could not, as a parent myself, imagine being at ease leaving my young children for months or years, even with the best of caregivers. What happened to maternal instinct? What about attachment? I wanted to understand this different way of being in the world.

The women, amused and patient, gave me their collective answer through Auntie Nani. "The mothers are too . . . too . . ." She searched for the right words and, passionately pressing the center of her large body with both hands, said, "They are too full of *Life* to sit and be with babies all day. And the mothers are too stupid. They don't know what to do with babies yet. They will care for their babies' babies." The aunties sighed in unison, "Yes, that's it." Then they had a question for me.

"Why is it that in your country you sell babies?"

"Oh God," I thought, "what 1940s movie has come to the islands now that I have to explain?" They waited eagerly for my response. Clearly Americans selling babies had been discussed before, and this was not a spontaneous question.

"Can you tell me what you know about this so I can understand?" I asked in my best English-as-a-Second-Language voice.

Subtle body adjustments on the woven mats suggested the women were settling in for a long juicy talk. There was a chorus of excited voices between them. Auntie Farita, whose voice overpowered all the others', said, "Yes, yes, we know. In your country no one takes care of the babies if they have no mother." Heads nodded around the circle. "If parents die in one car crash, you sell the baby. In your country the relatives do not want to take care of them."

"Adoption," I thought. "How do I explain adoption to these women who live in a world where children are cherished and cared for by the clan? Where children naturally expect all the adults in their large extended families to enjoy providing them with affection, food, limits, and playful attention?"

"We do not sell children," I began explaining in my storytelling-cum-teaching mode. I spoke of nuclear family life and the process of adoption. I talked about how some people wanted to care for children who didn't have homes.

"Ah, so you give one baby or some children to someone who does not have one."

"Yes."

"And they give money for this child?"

I sighed. I could see where this was going, and I didn't know how I'd get out of it. "The money is to pay for the lawyer's work and the doctor's work." I couldn't bring myself to mention the paperwork.

"You pay money, you get one child. This is selling," Auntie said firmly. "We could not do this."

No, they could not do this. An unwanted child was beyond their comprehension.

And that is where my interest in attachment began.

I spent the early 1970s in Micronesia. Since then, I have studied, taught at various universities, and performed clinical work for governmental agencies; at times I have maintained a clinical private practice, lectured, and consulted. My work has concentrated on the treatment of trauma and abuse and their impact on present and future attachment relationships. Throughout this professional life, I have passionately focused on empowering children and their families.

My work takes me to other countries where I train mental health practitioners, and I always learn from those I teach. Cross-cultural and multidisciplinary experiences influence my theoretical approach and clinical interventions, as do a feminist perspective, training and practice as a clinical social worker and family therapist, and, finally, the multidisciplinary and collegial nurturance and challenges I've experienced working in the arenas of trauma and attachment.

I've observed firsthand and wondered at the remarkable resiliency of children who survive war, poverty, and disaster. They may not come through completely unscathed, but with good, consistent family care they are often able to cope, and their scars can be few. Their deeper wounds, the ones that sometimes do not heal, are those related to attachment relationships—actual or threatened loss of family, significant disruptions to family contact, or the profound betrayal a child experiences when abused or not protected from abuse by a caregiver.

Professional wisdom related to attachment, trauma, and children's emotional development has grown significantly in the past twenty years. The good news is that specialized multidisciplinary organizations have been established in each of these interest areas to study the issues in depth and to share experiences via professional networks and journals. The bad news is that the knowledge gained within these specialties has not been readily integrated between the groups.

While reviewing the many contributions for this book, I was again moved by the grit of the young survivors, the tenacity and skill of their caregivers, and the wisdom and creativity of their therapists. Heroes all. The work is difficult, heartrending, often thankless, and usually accomplished in the face of insufficient resources.

Mental health resources for children, which were already shamefully scarce, are now being reduced even further. I am frequently asked how to help children in ten clinical sessions, or in six, or without seeing the parents, because this is all the time that is available. The help needed by these children and their families cannot be provided in brief therapy or, usually, in therapy alone—the problem is too great.

One child psychiatrist who works in an inner-city children's mental health clinic likened her work to that of a photographer in a war zone: documenting the damage and unable to offer help.

The work needed to help the future generations of our global village is everyone's problem and must be addressed on all levels. We must recognize that children's mental health issues are a priority for their survival and for ours.

This book provides an overview of important concepts from the attachment, trauma, and child development arenas. It offers an integrated theoretical blueprint for working with trauma-related attachment disturbances, which may include such situations as a child's frightening loss of or separation from a parent; maladaptive parenting; chaotic, arbitrary changes of caregivers; and persistent patterns of intimacy avoidance by parent or child. Practical guidelines for assessment and treatment that can be adapted to meet the unique needs of the children and their caregivers are included.

Several chapters are devoted to contributions from many people—professionals, parents, other caregivers, and the children themselves. Contributions come from colleagues working in various countries, thus reinforcing the universality of the problem; one chapter addresses the issues of attachment disturbances affecting thousands of children who are victims of war and government policy.

Three chapters are written by professionals whose unique healing approaches have much to offer for those of us who struggle with issues of traumatic attachment disturbance. Two chapters were generously provided by the Jasper Mountain's Residential Treatment Program, a program specifically designed to meet the long-term treatment needs of children with severe attachment disorders and to provide clinical support and guidance for the adoptive families who eventually care for these children. These contributions add spice, richness, hope, and proof that work with severe attachment disturbances in children and families is viable. This chorus of voices speaks for those children who have no voice.

The last chapter indulges some of my fantasies and wishes—to which readers are invited to add their wishes and suggestions—for creative and interesting ways we can support and nurture the well-being of children and families. The problems of children's severe attachment disturbances and trauma-related disorders are too big and too important to be relegated to the care of the mental health community alone. We need help from everyone. The children need to belong, and they do—to all of us.

1

Human Attachments and Trauma

Intimate attachments to other human beings are the hub around which a person's life revolves, not only when he is an infant or a toddler or a schoolchild but throughout his adolescence and his years of maturity as well, and on to old age. From these intimate attachments a person draws his strength and enjoyment of life and, through what he contributes, he gives strength and enjoyment to others.

Bowlby, 1980

As the fetus must be in the womb to survive, so must a child have a human attachment relationship in which to develop, feel protected, be nurtured, and become that which is human.

The attachment relationship is typically established within the context of a family, be it single-parented, adoptive, foster, tribal, or nuclear. But it *is* a family—it is the matrix that provides the child with the necessary feelings of safety and a place in which to grow. It is every child's birthright (*Fraiberg, et. al. 1975*).

Serious attachment disturbances and trauma coexist in the lives of many children and families; each may be the originating event giving rise to the other. Loss of a primary attachment relationship can be traumatizing to any age child. Traumatizing events in a family can result in serious attachment disturbances between parent and child. Clinicians and caregivers charged with helping children and families deal with severe attachment problems or traumatizing events venture into an arena that is complex, highly specialized and replete with uncharted territory. This chapter presents basic concepts in attachment and trauma on which is built an integrated treatment framework presented in subsequent chapters. The concepts are gleaned from the professional literature and from the clinical and caregiver experiences of those who work intimately and intensively with child and family attachment-trauma problems.

What Is Attachment?

An attachment relationship, hereafter referred to as attachment, has various definitions. The most useful to me as a clinician is that *an attachment is a reciprocal, enduring, emotional, and physical affiliation between a child and a caregiver*. The child receives what she needs to live and grow through this relationship, and the caregiver meets her need to provide sustenance and guidance.

Infants and very young children usually develop a *preferred*, or *primary, attachment*. This is the person selectively sought by the child when there is need for comforting and reassurance. Although other attachments are formed as the child matures, the primary attachment typically remains with the parents, usually the mother. The primary attachment figure may call on others to assist in meeting the child's parenting needs but maintains his role as primary provider of the child's comfort and security through consistency and quality of relationship.

The *caregiver*, or parenting person, is the one who provides ongoing care. The caregiver may be the youngster's biological parents, an older sibling, a grandparent, a foster or adoptive parent, a childcare worker, or someone else.

The mission of the primary attachment person is threefold, and each mission bears its own message:

- *As protector*: "Everything will be OK. I'll take care of you, set limits, and keep you safe."
- *As provider*: "I'm the source of food, love, shelter, excitement, soothing, and play."
- *As guide*: "This is who you are and who I am. This is how the world works."

Attachment provides the building blocks of children's development. Youngsters learn to modulate affect, soothe themselves, and relate to others through these relationships. Attachment is the base from which children explore their physical and social environments; their early attachment experiences form their concepts of self, others, and the world.

Formation of Attachments

Primary attachments are most optimally formed when baby and caregiver are ready, willing, and able to do so. The caregiver and child each bring to the relationship varying abilities, forms of expression, needs, and temperament. The connection is formed and reinforced through sensorial contact—gazing, smelling, tasting, hearing, touching, rocking, feeding, playing, vocalizing. A secure attachment grows for caregiver and baby when both experience their relationship as emotionally and physically gratifying. The child comes to perceive the caregiver as the source of joy, surprise, loving warmth, and relief from pain. The caregiver experiences the child's unfolding development as a source of satisfaction.

Attachment-seeking behaviors start when the infant cries for the parent and become more complex as the child develops. The cry of alarm or discomfort of an infant or young child cues a caregiving response in the adult. The parenting response can provide relief for the child in distress as well as provide a sense of competency and well-being for the parenting person. Other attachment behaviors include proximity-seeking and attention-getting on the part of the child. A child experiencing stress increases her attachment behaviors. We see this when children are frightened or injured. The primary attachment person becomes a conditioned, instant source of comfort over time and is perhaps best exemplified by the mother whose healing kiss on a minor injury makes the pain disappear and allows the child to resume play. This attachment, once formed, persists even though the primary attachment person may be absent.

Barriers to Attachment

Barriers to early attachment formation include the physical or emotional unavailability of the parent or baby and can be partial or complete. Unavailability can result from a child's or caregiver's physical pain, illness, drug addiction, or developmental disability, among other things. Chronic emotional disturbances, such as depression, dissociation, extreme shame, and distorted perceptions, can interfere with attachment formation.

In our clinical practices we often see barriers to later attachment formation among people who have suffered loss and disruption of earlier primary attachments. Forming a new relationship can represent an act of disloyalty, loss of hope, lack of love, or the sealing of one's fate if the act is perceived as guaranteeing that the person with whom one has an attachment will no longer love them. The child or adult who lives apart from an attachment figure may be unable or unwilling to form an intimate relationship with another person because doing so may represent a threat to the existing but unavailable attachment. For example, some divorced parents who no longer live with their birth children resist forming attachments with stepchildren because doing so would make them feel disloyal. A child living apart from a birth parent may resist forming a new attachment because she believes that any positive relationship with another adult will ensure the estranged parent will not return.

Someone who has experienced parental maltreatment may have considerable difficulty forming later attachment relationships because the child, the parent, or both do not know how to relate to another person in an intimate, reciprocal relationship. This is sometimes seen in parents who have histories of attachment disturbances and in abused children who have been placed in out-of-home care. Trust, a needed ingredient for attachment formation, may not be possible or come easily to these parents and children. Or the experience of intimacy in an attachment relationship may be intolerable because it leads to feelings of vulnerability and danger. Clinicians often find such dynamics in newly formed adoptive, foster, and stepparent relationships.

Dance of Development

Attunement, or harmony, in attachment relationships will naturally fluctuate—it is affected by changes in mood, availability, awareness, and interest of child and caregiver, among other things. A serious, chronic lack of attunement between child and parent can negatively affect a child's development. While there are other important developmental lines—motor, cognitive, and linguistic, for example—attachment is most central and essential for the survival of the infant.

As with most love relationships, both child and caregiver experience stimulation, interest, pleasure, delight, and satisfaction when they are emotionally and physically attuned to each other and the needs of both are being met. The attachment dance between parent and child is always in motion. The dance may be graceful, with each person responsive to his or her own and to the other's varying rhythms over time. Constricted or jarring choreography may reflect confusion over who is leading and who should follow, with attachment partners continually stepping on each other's toes or becoming preoccupied in doing their own solo and thus being unresponsive to the other.

The needs and abilities of both caregiver and child are in a continuous state of change, constantly influenced by the growth of child and parent and the surrounding world. The general tendency toward independence exhibited by the youngster as she develops toward adulthood needs to be matched by the caregiver's willingness to let go. The child needs to learn to cope with emotional tension, make decisions, protect, and care for herself as her parents let go of their caregiving functions. Clinical experience with interdependent extended families and tribal and clan systems suggests that children's attachment needs may be met through consistent, quality care provided by multiple attachment relationships.

The toddler's biological development and the security provided by attachment facilitate exploration and learning in a larger social world. The child will often have attachments with extended family members or other adults who augment the functions of the primary attachment. These relationships can provide support for the parent-child attachment and mitigate possible relationship problems.

The youngster's entrance into an expanded environment during the school years provides more challenges and opportunities whereby she can compare herself with others. The functions of the attachment are gradually internalized by the child as she develops autonomy and views herself both as a part of the family and as a member of the community.

The functions of the primary attachment—protection, limit-setting, nurturance, and guidance—recede in primacy during adolescence as they shift to the youngster herself, to peers, and to other adults in the community. The adolescent practices adult functioning, while the attachment relationship provides a safety net. Adolescent attachment with peers and adults outside the family is interdependent and characterized by shared attachment functions.

Adulthood brings attachment functioning full cycle with the development of mature attachment relationships with family, marriage partner, and one's own children.

Adaptations to the Attachment Relationship

Children of all ages—infants to adolescents—alter their behavior in service of preserving attachment relationships when their parenting needs are not met. Such alterations are necessary for their survival and are often wise and creative but not necessarily healthy. Thus we see children suppressing spontaneous thoughts, feelings, and wishes and instead playing adaptive roles in order to stimulate caregiving behavior in their parents. All children do this from time to time; however, it becomes a serious problem when the child must assume a role in order to obtain basic care. It then becomes an attachment dance of disturbed patterned behavior. Children's adaptive roles include being overly compliant with abusive parents, being entertainers with distracted parents, being minicaregivers with needy parents, being demanding bullies with nonresponsive parents, or being manipulators with neglectful, withholding parents.

The children's adaptive behavior is reinforced by the parent's eventual response to their needs. The youngster's sense of worth becomes wedded to the role that elicits adult caring. A child who must ignore her authentic thoughts and feelings in exchange for parental care and attention will identify with the role she must play and not have a real sense of self, or she can develop a sense of self that she believes is unacceptable to society and perhaps to herself, since her selfhood was not acceptable to her own parents.

Categories of Attachment Problems

Problems within the parent-child attachment relationship can seriously disrupt a youngster's development. These problems can generally be placed into three categories:

- Disturbed attachment
- Attachment trauma
- Trauma-related attachment problems

Disturbed Attachment

Attachment security is related to the quality and consistency of the parent's response to the child's expressions of physiological, emotional, and social needs. In the absence of problems that interfere with the process, parents have compelling desires to respond positively to children's basic needs. Children too are neurologically "wired" from birth to be responsive; the child is very much attuned to the manner, timing, and frequency of the caregiver's response to her signals. Attachment disturbances develop when there is an ongoing lack of attunement, or mismatch, between parent and child. This disharmony can have several causes, including impairment of child or parent functioning that interferes with the sending of, recognition of, or response to attachment signals; difficulties adapting to temperament differences; inadequate parenting skills; or inconsistent, disruptive parenting.

Greenspan and Lieberman's (1988) review includes studies of physiological and neurochemical reactions to disturbances in attachment that reveal the interactive nature of biological and behavioral systems. They cite examples showing that it is possible for caregivers to alter early constitutional patterns of infants in a favorable manner.

Attachment Trauma

Loss of the primary attachment figure represents a loss of everything to a child—loss of love, safety, protection, even life itself, and prolonged unavailability of the primary attachment is the same as total loss for a young child. This was graphically brought to the attention of the public by Spitz's (1947) haunting pictures of children in orphanages and by Robertson's (1957) film of a child's traumatizing separation from her parent during an eight-day hospitalization. These candid portrayals of children's suffering resulted in both professional awareness and changes in social policy regarding children's attachment needs.

Children experience their primary attachment figure as necessary for survival—he or she is the person whose presence provides protection and whose actions reduce the child's terror to manageable size and enable the youngster to cope with changing situations (Spitz,

1945). Other adults can provide some comfort when the child's worries are minor, but a child's deep fears can be alleviated only by the presence of an attachment relationship. The loss of the attachment figure evokes a fear that cannot be assuaged, depression and despair that are inconsolable, because the source of safety and love is gone.

The child abused by a primary attachment figure suffers in multiple and complex ways. There is the pain, confusion, and fear of the abuse itself; there is the mind-boggling experience of having the source of danger and the source of protection residing in one person. Most terrifying of all is the fear of loss of the attachment relationship, a loss children often believe is likely to happen if they try to protect themselves from being abused by a parent.

Children adapt to these situations by engaging in protective practices, such as dissociating, anesthetizing themselves physically, and muting sensory awareness. They commonly deal with the need to maintain a relationship with an abusive parent by blaming themselves for the abuse. This directs rage away from the abuser and frees the child to seek love and protection from that person, thus preserving the essential attachment relationship.

Trauma-Related Attachment Problems

The urgent and life-threatening aspects of traumatic events and family difficulties arising in the wake of trauma can obscure the serious attachment problems between parent and child that are generated by the traumatizing event. Single-incident traumatic events, such as injuries, severe illness, or catastrophes, can result in impaired functioning, prolonged separation, fear, anxiety, and misinterpretation of behavior. Any of these happenings can lead to patterns of child or parent behavior that seriously interferes with the attachment relationship. The parent might not be able to recognize or respond adequately to the child's needs; the child might not be able to adequately express needs or respond to the adult. A family member who avoids contact with a child because contact stimulates painful memories for either the child or the parent exhibits trauma-related impaired functioning. Parents who emotionally smother a child because they fear the consequences of not doing so also exhibit impaired functioning. Should such behaviors continue past an initial crisis stage, significant attachment problems may develop.

Chronic and repeated traumatizing events likewise impact attachment relationships. A child traumatized by an abusive parent, for example, can develop a severe disturbance in her attachment relationship with the nonabusive parent—she may believe she was not protected because she was unworthy or unlovable. An abusive parent may deliberately drive a wedge between the child and the other parent with lies and threats to both. A child's attachment relationship can be seriously compromised by a nonprotective or coercive parent or by a parent who has an investment in the child forgiving the abusive parent.

Life in a violent home or in a violent community can create attachment disturbances because children believe their parents cannot protect them. Youngsters might look for power and strength in peer groups rather than in parent relationships. Their parents then become restrictive and punitive, and the children perceive that behavior as unloving.

Integration of Attachment and Trauma Dynamics

Serious attachment disturbances and traumatizing experiences often coexist in children's lives. Both can be perceived as threats to survival. Both the attachment process and traumatizing experiences affect children biologically, psychologically, and behaviorally; both influence a child's self-concept and how future relationships and events are experienced. Treating attachment problems and treating child trauma require an understanding of the interrelatedness of both, respect for the inherent complexities associated with children's development, knowledge and skills in both fields, and the ability to weave together treatment aspects of both when they coexist in the life of a child and his caregivers. And treating these problems requires a robust and playful way of being in the world.

What Is Trauma?

Psychological trauma occurs when an actual or perceived threat of danger overwhelms a person's usual coping ability. Many situations that are generally highly stressful to children might not be traumatizing to a particular child; some are able to cope and, even if the situation is repeated or chronic, are not developmentally challenged. The diagnosis of traumatization should be based on the context and meaning of the child's experience, not just on the event alone. What may appear to be a relatively benign experience from an adult perspective—such as a child getting "lost" for several hours during a family outing—can be traumatizing to a youngster. Conversely, a child held hostage with her family at gunpoint might not comprehend the danger and feel relatively safe.

We can hypothesize that certain events may or may not be traumatizing to a child, but to accurately evaluate a child's experience the clinician or caregiver must take into account the meaning of the event to the child. The meaning is influenced by the child's biopsychosocial history, temperament, level of development, and preparation, and by the context in which the event occurred and the support that was available from attachment figures. A child who screams for help when frightened by a situation, for instance, is soothed and protected by her parents. For one child, this means that she is powerful, her parents love her and will protect her, and the attachment relationship is reinforced as available, loving, and necessary. Another child may feel responsible for the event, ashamed of needing her parents' help, and unworthy of protection, and this evidence of neediness weakens the attachment relationship.

A simple and common example of meaning being the marker, not the event, is parental divorce: The meanings for children can include safety, relief, vulnerability, shame, or terror, to name just a few.

A disastrous traumatic experience for the entire family might not have any negative impact on attachment. Children take their cues from significant adults as to what is dangerous. A family that can look at the destruction of their home as a chance to begin anew and can express gratefulness at not having been injured are unlikely to have attachment problems related to that event.

Unique Issues of Childhood Trauma

Children's responses to trauma are complex and are different from those of adults because of the vulnerabilities and the needs of childhood. Children's traumatizing experiences, particularly when chronic, can compromise all areas of childhood development, including identity formation, cognitive processing, experience of body integrity, ability to manage behavior, affect tolerance, spiritual and moral development, and ability to trust self and others.

Children's coping skills are determined by age, verbal abilities, strength, mobility, freedom, experience, and availability of attachment figures. The child's primary source of safety and ability to cope is the attachment figure, whose absence or presence can influence the child's experience of danger.

Regressive behavior is a common reaction to trauma; children return to a more helpless state, which can then restimulate the traumatizing experience of helplessness and terror. Such adaptive responses as needing to be in control, avoidance of intimacy, and provocative behaviors are significant barriers to forming or rehabilitating attachment relationships. Symptoms of trauma, such as flashbacks, hyperreactivity, and dissociation, not only interfere with children's learning but are often not recognized as such; they can be mislabeled as conduct disorder, oppositional and defiant behavior, lying, and disrespect for or not loving the parent.

Consequences of Trauma

Childhood traumatizing experiences, particularly from repeated and chronic experiences, have a neurodevelopmental, physiological, emotional, social, and behavioral impact.

Children's interrelated and complex symptoms arising from the impact of trauma fall into four major categories and range from mild to severe:

- Persistent fear state
- Disorder of memory
- Dysregulation of affect
- Avoidance of intimacy

Persistent Fear State

Perry (1993) describes emerging medical research concerning the neurological effects of repeated and chronic traumatic life experiences on children. A key principle in developmental neurobiology is that the brain develops and organizes as a reflection of experience. The neurophysiological activation seen during acute stress in a child is usually rapid and reversible. According to Perry, "When the stressful event is of a sufficient duration, intensity, or frequency, however, the brain is altered. . . . The experience of the traumatized child is fear, threat, unpredictability, frustration, chaos, hunger, and pain. . . . The traumatized child's template for brain organization is the stress response (p. 14)."

Fight, flight, and freeze are immediate and automatic survival responses to acute trauma that serve to protect the organism from harm. They are total body responses to fear, mediated in large part by the primitive brain. Perry correlates adult fight-flight-freeze behaviors with equivalent behaviors in children as follows:

- The fight response of the young is to cry and thus alert a caregiver who will defend and protect them. Regressive tantrums and aggressive behaviors may also be fight equivalents for a terrorized child.
- Physical flight is often not possible for children. The most common equivalent is dissociation.
- Freezing occurs when a dangerous event is perceived as inevitable. Freezing provides camouflage and time to process and evaluate a situation. Adults often respond to a child's psychological and physiological freezing with threats and demands that result in the child experiencing increased fear. The child's freezing behavior is commonly perceived as oppositional-defiant.

These automatic, primitive brain responses to fear can be restimulated when children are exposed to reminders of the traumatizing event, leading to a persistent fear state. Responsive behaviors include hypervigilance, heightened startle response, increased irritability, anxiety, physical hyperactivity, and extreme regressive behaviors.

Disorder of Memory

Severe traumatizing experiences are not processed and stored in memory in the same manner as other events. Instead of being integrated with past experiences, they appear to remain separate and are partly or fully out of conscious awareness. Intense recollections can intrude unbidden into awareness and be experienced as if occurring in present time. The intrusion into awareness can occur during a waking state or as a vivid nightmare that awakens the sleeping person.

A sudden, spontaneous reexperiencing of all or part of a traumatizing event is commonly called a flashback. Flashbacks can be physiological sensations, affective experiences, behavioral reenactments, or horrific images that intrude into a person's awareness. They are stimulated by associative cues—similar affective states, such as fear combined with helplessness; sensory experiences, such as a smell or a loud voice; behavioral interactions, such as a whispered threat or a spanking; or specific objects in the environment, such as a knife or a beer can.

Flashbacks in infants are most often seen as somatic reactions to a stimulus—an infant who suddenly vomits when held by an abusive mother, or a medically traumatized infant who becomes wildly agitated or dissociative in response to a hospital smell.

Flashbacks in young children are reported by parents as sudden, out-of-context, intense affective-behavioral episodes that the child does not remember having. The driven, repetitive behavioral reenactments of trauma observed in child treatment (Terr, 1981; van der Kolk, 1989) might be flashback experiences.

Protective dissociation is another disturbance of memory. Dissociation is a sudden, temporary alteration in the integrative function of consciousness wherein one's experience is separated from one's conscious awareness. This involuntary, natural mechanism is present in infancy and continues throughout adulthood. Everyday dissociative responses occur when a person is absorbed in play, listening to a story, or driving a car and, for a time, is not consciously aware of self or aspects of the environment. Dissociation protects trauma survivors from overwhelming emotions, thoughts, and sensations and allows them to function in their environment. Children's chronic use of protective dissociation can become an automatic, habitual response to any and all stressors that can interfere with functioning and development. A dissociative disorder may seriously impede a child's development by fostering fragmentation of personality and problems with self-identity.

Symptoms of trauma-related memory disorganization can be easily misinterpreted when seen in children as lying, unexplained aggression, withdrawal, or weird or spacey behavior.

Dysregulation of Affect

Trauma survivors experience significant problems with modulation of affect. They often have intrusive, spontaneous, affective recollections of trauma that they attempt to control or prevent by numbing and affect avoidance. Affect dysregulation is commonly described as an all-or-nothing emotional style. Adult survivors say they feel as if they are about to burst with emotion and would lose control and overwhelm themselves and others with uncontrollable expressions of emotion if allowed to experience or express even a small amount of what they feel. The child version of this experience is seen in the play of traumatized children, which is severely constricted in affect (verbalizations, movement, and fantasy productions) and interspersed with out-of-control affective storms unrelated to play. The developmental tragedy is the disruption of a child's ability to learn to regulate affect and the interference with the freedom and creativity of play that helps children learn about themselves and the world.

Alexithymia is a disturbance in which one is aware only of the physiological aspects of affect, such as increased heart rate, perspiration, and dry mouth, and is unable to name or give symbolic representation to an emotional experience. The capacity to understand and identify emotions is present, as evidenced by an ability to describe, for example, how another child might feel if she were unjustly punished, but the alexithymic child cannot describe or predict her own affective experience except for the physiological aspects. Alexithymia inhibits learning from one's emotional experiences.

Krystal (1988) considers alexithymia to be related to early childhood trauma. Clinicians and caregivers sometimes fail to recognize the presence of alexithymia in young trauma survivors who exhibit constricted behavior and flat affect.

Intense affect related to trauma inhibits and blocks the ability to verbally communicate one's experience. Traumatizing experiences appear to be encoded in the primitive, nonverbal part of the brain, thus explaining the inhibition or inability to verbalize the experience. Our language reflects this phenomenom when we refer to "unspeakable acts," being "struck dumb," and being "mute with terror."

Children's behaviors related to dysregulation of affect include oppositional, defiant, uncooperative, anxious, depressed, impulse-ridden, and unpredictable behavior. These youngsters can be learning disabled and often misinterpret verbal or nonverbal cues.

Avoidance of Intimacy

Intimacy is commonly avoided by adult and child trauma survivors because the inherent emotional closeness leads to feelings of vulnerability and feelings of loss of control, and both of these feelings are intolerable to victims of violent abuse and other trauma. Intimacy represents a threat, not safety. It is extremely difficult to parent children who engage in behaviors related to a persistent fear response, disordered memory, and affect dysregulation; it feels impossible to parent children who actively avoid intimacy and who mightily resist dependency, both of which are inherent parts of primary attachment relationships.

Intimacy avoidance is an adaptive response in children who have been hurt by adults or who have witnessed adult violence. A single-incident trauma may not result in this behavior, or the behavior may be of such short duration that it does not interfere with the attachment relationship. Clingy behavior, hyperactivity, avoidance of eye contact, withdrawal, oppositional behavior, and disgusting personal habits can all be in service of avoiding intimacy.

Clinicians and caregivers often see simultaneous approach and avoidant behaviors when traumatized children relate to caregivers; this is a potent example of conflicting developmental needs. Examples of getting their needs met include a toddler walking backward to approach the parent, a child screaming to be held but allowing it only if facing away from the parent, a little one who can be fed only if he does not look at the caregiver, and children who get their affectional needs met through their fantasy-embellished relationship with their pet dog. Intimacy avoidance is not usually limited to those who are the source of the trauma; the behavior often extends to other adults as well.

Other behaviors of children avoiding intimacy include an inability to trust adults and an aversion to physical or emotional closeness. These children can be guarded, hyperactive, or controlling and often exhibit pseudomaturity.

Summary

An attachment relationship is a reciprocal, enduring emotional and physical affiliation between a child and caregivers, typically the parents. Attachment provides the base from which a child learns to explore her world, and the intensity and elements of the attachment change as the youngster develops. Various traumatic experiences interfere with attachment and create problems that can generally be categorized as disturbed attachment, attachment trauma, and trauma-related attachment problems. Traumatic events and attachment disorders often coexist in the lives of children and their caregivers. Clinicians and caregivers need to be able to understand and integrate the concepts from both of these specialized arenas to develop a coherent treatment and healing experience.

2

The Alarm/Numbing Response

In situations of terror, people spontaneously seek their first source of comfort and protection.

Herman, 1992

The Alarm/Numbing Response Model proposed in this chapter integrates the arousal/numbing cycle cited in the trauma literature with the provocative behaviors commonly seen in children with attachment problems. In this model, the child appears to seek out negative and dangerous situations and responds to positive and neutral events with provocative, destructive behavior. These behaviors in turn provide relief from the unbearable, escalating anxiety associated with trauma that the child cannot otherwise attain *because the child has no available, viable attachment relationship.* Background information is presented, followed by the description of three primary components—the alarm response, the numbing response, and provocative behavior. These are then brought together in the model and followed by a summary of treatment implications.

Background

A key symptom arising from psychologically traumatizing experiences is biphasic oscillation from extreme arousal to numbing—extreme arousal in response to intrusive reminders of the trauma and numbing as an attempt to manage the overwhelming arousal experiences (Horowitz, 1976; Lindemann, 1944; van der Kolk, 1987).

Children's arousal and numbing patterns related to trauma are obscured by adults' focus on children's behavior and adults' resistance to knowing the suffering children experience. These youngsters are often incorrectly diagnosed as conduct-disordered, with the goal of treatment identified as behavior change.

Management of emotional and physical arousal is limited by children's development and may be compromised by their attachment relationships. Children gradually learn to modulate arousal through the experience of being physically and emotionally cared for by the primary attachment figure(s). The experience enables the child to internalize how to self-soothe and self-protect, as well as the right to be cared for and safe.

Let us examine some of the provocative behaviors of children with histories of trauma and attachment problems and the current explanations for them. An exasperating and puzzling behavior often seen in the children placed in out-of-home care is their extreme negative reaction to apparently positive experiences. Veteran professional caregivers can predict with incredible accuracy the length of time before a child damages a new item of clothing or gift he has received. They know that a child who has just had a good time on a family outing will be asking for punishment by the end of the day, or they await with dread the predictable aftermath when the youngster played well on the soccer team. These negative responses to positive happenings are often explained as a feature of the child's low self-esteem; that is, the child simply does not believe he deserves anything good and needs to ruin things and sabotage positive experiences.

Other puzzling behaviors are those which are dangerous and can result in harm to the child or to others. These behaviors include mutilating self, hurting animals, physically or sexually assaulting children, eating disorders, destroying property and provoking abuse from others. We explain these behaviors as attempts to live out a negative self-image, or to somehow master a past traumatic experience.

The Alarm Response

Feelings of terror and helplessness can be restimulated by cues identified with traumatizing events, including sights, sounds, smells, tastes, or objects. Less recognized but equally potent are the associations a child makes between his present internal state and past traumatizing experiences. The traumatized child may become extremely fearful if, for example, he hears someone yelling at him. His internal state of fear cues and restimulates feelings of terror and helplessness related to a bygone traumatic event.

Along these lines, a child with an alexithymic condition cannot distinguish between positive and negative emotions, since he is aware only of the physiological component of affect. He cannot differentiate between excitement and fear—both feel the same, and he does not have the cognitive labels to discriminate between the two. The physiological manifestations can be similar whether positive, neutral, or negative. Play, for instance, can trigger alarm because the somatic experiences of excitement and terror are the same. The alexithymic child, however, does not know *why* he experiences alarm and anxiety; alarm cues more alarm, his heart beats faster, his arousal (alarm) increases. He is caught in a cycle of escalating alarm until something breaks it.

The Numbing Response

An event perceived as dangerous and inescapable is mitigated by emotional and physiological numbing. Other forms of relief similar to numbing are provided by dissociation, depression, emotional and kinetic constriction, social withdrawal, intense concentration, and avoidance of tactile-emotional stimulation. The general phrase "numbing response" refers to any of the above. Basically, the person overwhelmed by terror from within sends out the message "Leave me alone!" and needs to sit motionless, holding her breath, praying that what feels like an internal explosive device will not detonate.

The numbing response interrupts the escalation of alarm in the only way available to those who cannot modulate affect arousal. The escalation of their anxiety is too intense, too fast, and too overwhelming. Children have not yet developed the ability to modulate intense affect; those who would help them are often not available; and the usual means of mastering an experience—symbolizing, fantasizing, and desensitizing through play—is an unnatural act when the aspects to be dealt with are horrific and life-threatening.

Numbing responses can be paired or associated with perceived danger or other threats and thereby become automatic. The smell of liquor, a loud voice, violence portrayed on television, or a strange pet may produce fear that escalates and automatically triggers a numbing response in a child who has been traumatized by violence. Another example is a twenty-month-old child's instant reaction to seeing a jar of Vaseline: She rolled back her eyes and, in a trance state, spread her legs apart, pounded her groin with her fists, and began ritually chanting. Subsequent medical findings identified the child as a rape victim.

A child might automatically respond to experienced danger by an immediate numbing even if the perceived danger is only her own physiological arousal. If the environment is seen as continuously dangerous, the numbing response may be maintained for a prolonged time. At some point, however, the numbing effect ceases and the child is again open to an alarm response.

Provocative Behavior

Children who experience physiological arousal as terror and cannot or do not experience relief through protective numbing may up the ante. Their behaviors are in service of escalating the internal alarm *in order to trigger their own numbing response and thus gain relief* from their unbearable anxiety. Provocative behaviors will typically include those involving risk of severe punishment, self-harm, and harm to others. Whatever the act, it is so emotionally charged that it triggers a self-numbing response.

Adults commonly use alcohol and drugs in service of numbing anxiety that causes alarm. Children will do the same, if they have access, or will invoke aberrant behaviors to accomplish the same goal.

The Alarm/Numbing Response Model

Affective reactions to a frightening event have emotional, physiological, and cognitive components. A nontraumatized child processes the experience in all three domains and uses coping mechanisms to relieve distress. He will seek help from the primary attachment figure or will rely on his own resources. He has no need to invoke a numbing response when frightened.

The traumatized child responds to any frightening event with an escalating alarm response. The child becomes anxious when cues, including his own internal state, are similar to circumstances experienced during trauma. The child's fear leads to increased fear, and arousal accelerates. Hypervigilance, a normal consequence of alarm, can alert him to other signs of danger and thus exposes him to even more alarm stimuli. The child interrupts the alarm by invoking a numbing response or engaging in provocative behaviors.

The alexithymic child follows much the same pattern except that the triggering stimulus is the physiological component of affect alone; emotional and cognitive components are blocked from awareness. As a result of this inability to differentiate affect or to provide emotional labels, the child experiences excitement, surprise, and joy, for example, as cues of potential danger and helplessness. Any stimulus that produces somatic responses similar to those experienced during trauma can initiate a chain of escalating anxiety and numbing or provocative behavior that interrupts the escalation process.

Typical responses by nontraumatized, traumatized and alexithymic children to a disturbing event are summarized in the figure on page 22.

Van der Kolk (1989) offers a neurophysiological perspective suggesting that some people may be physiologically addicted to traumatic reexperiencing of events or thrill-seeking behavior. His work with people traumatized as adults suggests that "re-exposure to situations reminiscent of the trauma evokes an endogenous opioid response analogous to that of animals exposed to mild shock subsequent to inescapable shock" (p 401). Thus people may reexpose themselves as a form of self-medication to induce a "narcotic" relief.

The Alarm/Numbing Response Model elaborates on van der Kolk's work by positing that the intent of negative and provocative behaviors in traumatized children, whether conscious or not, is to obtain relief from unbearable anxiety.

Clinical focus on specific trauma-reactive behaviors has in many instances developed into specialty areas of study, such as self-mutilation, destructive behaviors, eating disorders, and child-perpetrated sexual and physical abuse. I believe this model provides a common foundation for these behaviors and has important clinical implications. Treatment should focus on helping children learn to

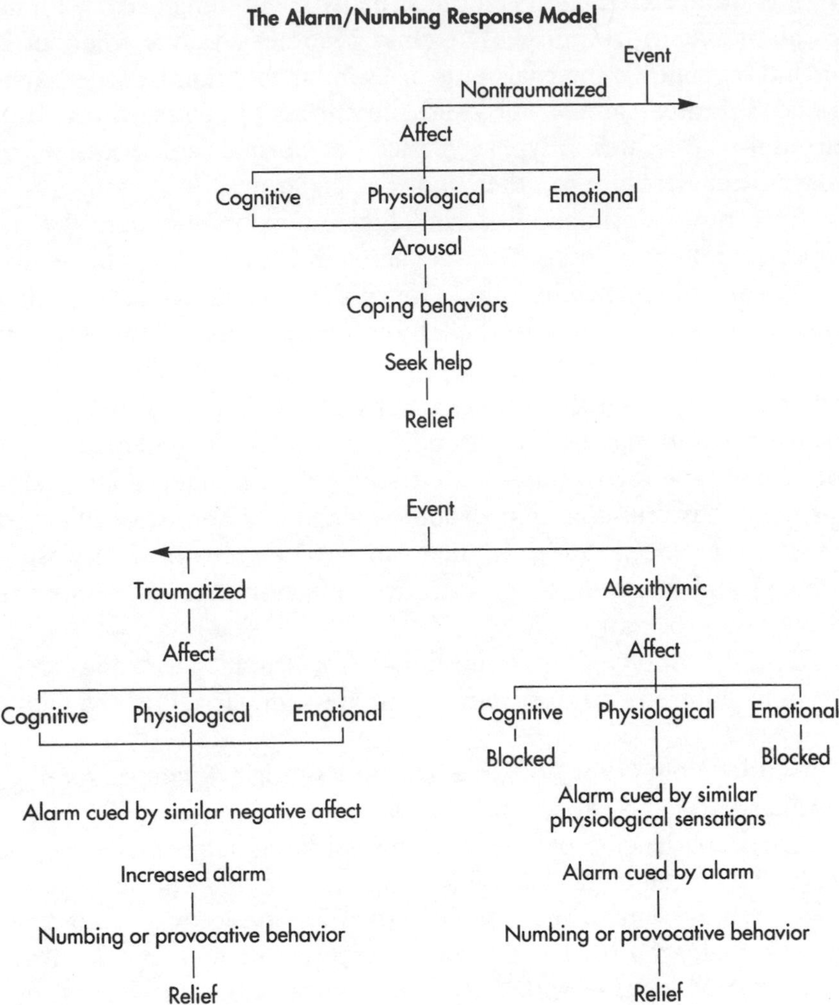

identify affective cues, modulate and tolerate affect, and understand the personal meaning of their affective experiences.

Summary

The Alarm/Numbing Response Model proposes that many of the puzzling behaviors seen in children with attachment disturbances serve the function of helping them to cope with intolerable anxiety. An alarmed child consciously or unconsciously engages in provocative or otherwise dangerous behaviors in order to increase his state of anxiety to the level where a numbing response is automatically invoked. The numbing response provides relief that cannot otherwise be attained. Effective treatment focuses on affect modulation and tolerance, identification of cues that raise anxiety, and understanding of the meaning of affective experiences.

This model provides a clinical framework that has helped me to understand some of the worrisome behaviors of attachment-disturbed and traumatized children and, more importantly, provides a foundation and direction for treating problems related to these behaviors. I invite suggestions, critical thoughts, stories, and support from colleagues, caregivers, and children.

3

Attachment vs. Trauma Bonds

There are two powerful sources of reinforcement [of an abusive Relationship]: the "arousal-jag" or excitement before the violence and the peace of surrender afterwards. Both of these responses, placed at appropriate intervals, reinforce the Traumatic bond between victim and abuser.

van der Kolk, 1989

Children with secure attachments and children who are trauma-bonded to adult caregivers perceive their relationships as necessary for survival and cling fiercely to their respective caregivers in similar ways. The dynamics of each of these relationships, however, and their impact on the child's development are very different. It is crucial that we distinguish between the two.

A secure attachment is a love relationship that is caring, is reciprocal, and develops over time. Attachment provides the nurturance and guidance that foster gradual and appropriate self-reliance, leading to mastery and autonomy.

Trauma-bonding is a relationship based on terror. The goals of submission and obedience can be reached almost immediately. Trauma-bonded persons commonly experience their abuser as being in total control and feel their lives are in danger. The relief victims experience when not killed is often expressed as gratitude toward the perpetrator.

We know that children seek increased contact with a primary caregiver when they are frightened or experience danger or pain; we commonly see and understand this behavior. The child cries out and the parent responds. Less seen and understood is the behavior of adults and children who cling to those who abuse them, be they assaultive parents, adult partners, cult leaders, or hostage takers in war or peace.

Van der Kolk (1989) has examined the phenomenon of intensified attachment in the face of danger. He brings together supportive research to describe the behavioral, emotional, and neuroendocrine factors related to the persistence of traumatic bonding. I draw on his work here.

The strength and endurance of trauma bonds are related to the increase in attachment-seeking behaviors frequently seen in man-made and natural disasters. The child victim perceives outside help as unavailable; the dominant person strengthens the bond by alternating between terroristic and nurturing behaviors. The child's responses—dissociation, numbing, or self-blame, among others—lead to a confusion of pain and love that interferes with judgment and allows the victim's need for attachment to overcome his fears. At the same time, increased physiological arousal resulting from fear activates production of endogenous opioids, which alleviate stress and intensify the trauma bond.

Children subjected to parental assault are hostages, held captive by virtue of their relationship, development, and lack of alternatives. Their survival is dependent on those who abuse them; they believe no one else can help them. Logic suggests that when removed from such a situation, victims would not want to return. But they do. Adults and children alike literally cannot imagine survival without their abusers, for the abusers have granted them life. This is learned helplessness, supported by cognitive distortion.

An evaluator may confuse attachment and trauma-bond relationships. There is a tendency to see attachment and trauma-bonding as extremes of an attachment continuum rather than as the two distinct processes they really are, each with its own specific etiology and outcomes. The figure on page 26 illustrates the complex dynamics associated with each process.

There are variations in the strength and features of trauma bonds, just as there are variations in the strength and quality of attachments. A child-parent relationship must not be evaluated on the strength of the connection alone; the connection may be a strong trauma bond and not a secure attachment relationship. We must look at the quality and function of the relationship before

Characteristics of Attachment and Trauma-Bond Relationships

Attachment	*Trauma-Bond*
Love	Terror
Takes time	Instantaneous
Reciprocity and caring	Domination and fear
Person is experienced as essential for survival	Person is experienced as essential for survival
Proximity → safety (pleasure)	Proximity → conflict (alarm/numbing)
Separate person dependent	Not separate person, extension of other's need
Self-mastery	Mastery by others
Autonomy-individuation	Obedient to will of other

making a judgment about its nature and influence on the child's development. Children have been allowed to remain in psychologically and physically dangerous living situations because of their stated wishes and/or perceived needs, not necessarily because we have considered the kind or quality of the relationship. A trauma bond is potentially dangerous, and we should place no more reliance on a youngster's stated desire to remain in that situation than we would on a child's stated desire to be in any other dangerous situation.

Children's expressed wishes for parental contact may not reflect their actual desires. Their statements might have been made under threat or coercion by a parent or can represent what the child understands the interviewer wants to hear. The child's wishes and emotional needs must be carefully assessed on the basis of clinical observation, a comprehensive review of the family's history and dynamics, and a thorough understanding of child development, attachment, and trauma-bonding.

The major complicating factor in dealing with a trauma bond is the child's experienced need for the person with whom he or she has the relationship. Separation from that person can itself be traumatizing and thus intensify the bond, increase idealization of the relationship, and result in an inability to form another primary relationship. Decisions and interventions in such complex situations must be made with exquisite sensitivity to the child's well-being. We must use adult wisdom as we see through the eyes of the child, and we must take responsible, immediate action to protect the child while providing time for the youngster to experience safety in a new situation. It might be appropriate, for instance, to remove the child from the direct care of the parent and provide supervised parental contact that is emotionally and physically safe in order to temper the wrenching separation experience for the child.

Summary

There are important differences between attachment and trauma-bonding: One is based in love and the other in terror; one enhances child development and the other is potentially harmful. Therapists need to carefully assess the quality and function of a child's relationship with a caregiver before determining the appropriate intervention. How to assess these two different processes is outlined in the next chapter.

4

Assessment of Attachment in Traumatized Children

Molly Romer Whitten

Thirty or forty years ago the term *attachment* had a very explicit meaning that was understood only by infant researchers and those interested in infant development. It originally referred to that set of behaviors characterized by infants and young children moving closer to their parents or primary caregivers for security whenever their anxiety is heightened. It took on another meaning as research about attachment filtered down to clinicians and educators, expanding to the actual difficulties encountered when infants and toddlers were separated from their caregivers. Most recently, as the concepts of the attachment literature have been applied in cases of developmental psychopathology, it has taken on a third meaning and now encompasses the development of human relationships. We can most easily work with attachment issues of traumatized children if we first integrate these different angles of attachment and thus provide a coherent focus to our observations. Without this focus, we can learn little about the child's clinical needs in order to help the child; nor can we say with any accuracy whether the child's safety is in jeopardy.

This chapter is organized into four sections, the first of which presents a brief history of attachment theory. The second section discusses the differences between those behaviors and behavior patterns that represent a child's attachment system and those that represent a child's response to traumatic interactions with others. The third section deals with assessment instruments and activities. The final section provides a case study illustrating how variables can be combined to create attachment assessment processes that reflect the child's unique situation.

History of the Concept of Attachment

In its first conceptualization, attachment referred to a set of behaviors, a dance that occurs between every baby and its mother, father, or primary caregiver. The steps of the dance seem to be hardwired into both the baby's and the parent's nervous systems (Bowlby, 1969). The purpose of the dance is to facilitate the infant's ever increasing ability to explore and learn about the world without falling prey to any of the dangers that, in its immaturity, it is unable to avoid.

John Bowlby, while not the first researcher to contemplate such an innate protective system, completed the first seminal work in the area of attachment when he described the nature and development of human relationships during infancy. His conclusions allowed psychologists, developmentalists, and others to understand the baby's behavior toward its mother long before the child could tell us in words what was happening. Bowlby observed four complementary behavioral patterns available to an ambulatory toddler: exploration, fear/wariness, attachment, and affiliation. He acknowledged that children create a flexible balance between their yearnings to explore and move into the world and their desire to stay connected to others, especially to their most intimate caregivers. This balance changes as a function of the child's experiences, developmental growth, and family environment.

Mary Ainsworth and her colleagues furthered our knowledge by creating a paradigm for studying the attachment process. Her work expanded our understanding of the balance inherent in the attachment process:

> All of these considerations suggest that the relative balance between exploratory and attachment behavior and thus the way in which an infant uses his mother as a secure base from which to explore, are influenced by a variety of circumstances—including the size of the room; the length of the observational session; the nature, diversity, and complexity of the stimuli that activate and maintain exploration; the orienta-

> tion and behavior of the mother; as well as the internal condition of the infant and the influence his previous experience has on his expectations of his mother's accessibility and responsiveness.
>
> (Ainsworth et. al., 1978, pp. 259–260)

Ainsworth identified three situations in which attachment behavior could be observed:

- When the child explores the environment using his mother as a secure base
- In the child's characteristic response to the introduction of a novel stimulus, often a stranger, into the exploration space
- In response to separation from the primary attachment figure

She formulated a classification system using the paradigm of safety in the child's primary attachment relationship. This paradigm postulated that most infants fall into three categories with regard to their attachment behavior. The classification system is based on observations of "effectiveness" of a child's ability to use her primary caretaker as a source of security and protection.

Group B

Group B infants demonstrate a secure attachment to the mother. According to Ainsworth, "These babies tend to be more readily socialized, that is, they are more cooperative and willing to comply with mothers' commands and requests. They have been found to be more positively outgoing to and cooperative with relatively unfamiliar adult figures than is true for babies in the other two groups. Group B babies explore more effectively and more positively, and thus they have a head start in learning about the salient features of the environment. They are more enthusiastic, affectively positive and persistent as well as less easily frustrated in problem solving tasks" (Ainsworth, 1978, p. 166).

Group A

Group A babies demonstrate a second type of attachment behavior. Babies in this group are characterized by frequent distress at separation. They seem to avoid using their mother as a secure base when presented with new situations or strangers, and after separations from their primary attachment figure they do not show the intense activation of the attachment system that Group B babies demonstrate. This behavior on the part of the infant is matched by observations that mothers of group A babies responded to their infants in a rejecting way by denying the infant's request for close bodily contact. Long-term consequences of this type of attachment include deficiencies in exploratory behavior and cooperativeness and difficulties with inappropriate aggression and establishing of empathetic interaction with other people (Ainsworth, 1978, p. 166).

Group C

These babies demonstrate behavior

> somewhere between the fully positive picture of group B babies and the approach-avoidance conflict of the group A babies. They demonstrate an ambivalence about physical contact with their mothers, although they do seek it appropriately. They are slower to be soothed, demonstrate many more instances of expressing anger with their mothers, and seem sensitized to separation from their mothers. They advance the slowest cognitively, were easily frustrated, over reliant on their mothers and generally incompetent in problem-solving situations.
>
> (Ainsworth, 1978, p. 315)

Ainsworth was quick to qualify her results and cautioned against a direct translation of the behaviors she observed to clinical settings. In a decisive manner she stated that no single behavior could be identified as "attachment behavior" because the phenomenon of attachment

> is defined as a class of behaviors that have the predictable outcome of gaining or maintaining proximity to a caregiver or later to an attachment figure. . . . It is only with consideration of the context—both environmental and behavioral—in which the behavior appears that we can assert that the behavior in question is operating in the service of the attachment system or in the service of some other behavioral system at the time it is observed. To demand that the label "attachment behavior" be reserved for a discrete action that is displayed exclusively or

even more frequently toward an attachment figure rather than toward others is to distort our understanding of the function of attachment behavior.

(Ainsworth, 1978, p. 315)

Ainsworth's attachment paradigm has been applied and expanded to clinical populations and expanded to children above the age of three (the original sample cutoff age).

A fourth pattern, also of insecure attachment, observed in populations of abused children has resulted from this research. Youngsters in this group respond to the strange situation research paradigm by seeking proximity to their mothers in ineffective ways. A child may, for example, begin to approach her mother only to stop halfway there and fall to the floor crying so that the mother must finish the rejoining process. Another variant is for the child to acknowledge the mother's return but not make any movement toward reuniting physically with her.

Research into the etiology and effects of child maltreatment has also helped form our conceptualization of attachment. Crittenden and Ainsworth (1989) made a number of observations with respect to the behavior of maltreated children:

- Maltreated children form anxious attachments to parents that are characterized by either oppositionality or compulsive compliance.
- Anxious attachments will provoke conflicting impulses within the child that lead to behavior that seems to be paradoxical. This situation occurs when the child demonstrates both avoidance and anger with the parent and yet behaves in a clingy, overly intimate manner.
- There is an observable difference between the way an abused child responds to a parent—typically resistant or overly compliant—and the way a neglected child responds to a parent—without expectation that the parent will respond. A neglected child assumes she is incapable of communicating her own needs and does not expect maternal cooperation. She may reverse roles and become caregiver to her mother, or she may be precociously independent and unconcerned with what her mother thinks. She thus surmounts the unavailability of the parent.

- Difficulties in relating to the parent are reflected in the maltreated child's ability to effectively explore her environment. "Because maltreated children are neither protected adequately by proximity to the mother nor secure in the belief that she will be available, their ability to explore safely and effectively would be expected to be impaired" (Crittenden and Ainsworth, 1989, p. 453).
- Socially, maltreated children tend to engage in aggression to a greater extent than other children, demonstrate greater vigilance in interaction with peers, or become victims in peer aggression.
- Maltreated/abused children tend to develop manipulative interpersonal styles resulting from their attempts to contain or control their mother's behavior. The styles include excessive social vigilance, superficial compliance, and inhibited anger.
- Maltreated/neglected children do not learn strategies for engaging successfully with others, for actively exploring the environment, or for developing strategies to appropriately search out stimulation. These children may therefore become loners, socially inept, or accident-prone.

Clinicians have developed observational indices with which to describe the interaction between a mother and child by examining the aspects of mother-child interactions that are more or less functional or perturbed as measured by cognitive, interpersonal (dyadic), and social characteristics. The level of dysfunction observed in the attachment system or, more specifically, in a child's interactions with her primary caregiver can be distinguished along a number of characteristics, including (1) intensity of conflict, (2) duration of disturbance, (3) generalizability of dysfunction, (4) level of dysfunction in learning capacity, (5) existence of oppositional behavior, (6) negativism in response to requests, (7) passivity in interaction, (8) overly compliant behavior, and (9) ineffectiveness and lack of persistence in problem-solving behavior.

Differentiation between Attachment Behaviors and Trauma-Influenced Interaction Patterns

A youngster usually moves further and further from using her attachment figure or parent as a safe base. She can do this because she keeps a memory of the safety provided by the caretaker. When the child assesses risk, she makes decisions based on expectations developed in relation to that attachment figure. The more competent the child becomes at acknowledging risk and assessing it accurately, the further afield she will travel from her original attachment figure into the social surroundings. As previously described, in a disturbed attachment the child does not become competent at risk assessment or problem solving. Rather, she characteristically takes extravagant risks and rarely uses the attachment relationship to provide security and nurture, or she remains very close to the attachment figure and develops a clingy, nonexploratory style of learning and, as a result, suffers cognitive limitations.

Children who experience abuse often respond as if they have disturbed attachment patterns; that is, they demonstrate the defiant and/or clingy behavior observed in children whose attachment system has developed ineffectively. Herman eloquently described this trauma bond in the following way:

> The child trapped in an abusive environment is faced with formidable tasks of adaptation. She must find a way to preserve a sense of trust in people who are untrustworthy, safety in a situation that is unsafe, control in a situation that is terrifyingly unpredictable, power in a situation of helplessness. Unable to care for or protect herself, she must compensate for the failures of adult care and protection with the only means at her disposal, an immature system of psychological defenses.
>
> (Herman, 1992, p. 96)

The literature regarding trauma responses in children is replete with references to a form of interaction termed a "trauma bond." Hindman (1989, p. 229) described the trauma bond as "habits of the hurt, . . . the habits [that are] specifically designed as coping skills used for survival." Attachment theory and research contributed to expanding the concept of the trauma bond so that it came to represent the entire relationship between the child and the abusive caretaker system in which the child existed. Object relations theory, as well as Stern's (1985) theory on internal representations, and the concept of the evoked other, helped to clarify the process by which a child develops an effective relationship with an abusive adult.

Theoretically, then, a trauma bond is also the internalized set of expectations a child develops regarding interactions with an abusive adult that allows the child to feel and sometimes remain safe. In an abusive interaction the child, unable to prevent the abuse, forms a set of internal cues to warn of or ward off potentially abusive interactions (Herman, 1992). These cues in turn motivate the child to behave in ways that placate the abusive adult or reflect the behavior that the abusive adult allows as acceptable. The child does not concern herself with learning about the environment, developing more and more sophisticated ways of maintaining interpersonal connections, or learning about her own psychological self. Her focus on the needs, wants, and emotional state of the abusive adult is her best shot at maintaining safety for herself.

The behavior patterns that characterize this disturbed relationship pattern include cognitive constriction, dull affect or emotions, pre-emptive compliance, and extremes of interpersonal closeness (clinginess) or physical distance (high activity level without focus).

The child often responds to adult cues with automatic compliance, more than the normal give-and-take of childhood compliance. Because the child experiences a chronically high level of anxiety, she restricts her perception in order to limit the painful anxiety of wondering when the next abuse will come. This restriction prevents her from using all the stimuli that could enhance her cognitive functioning and thus provokes perceptual and cognitive constriction.

Also, when she limits perception of her own tension she must limit her perception of the many other feelings that may fleetingly get connected to an experience of tension and the result is she develops a dull style of interaction. Sometimes unknowing adults misinterpret this dull style and/or inability to see what's going on around her as low intelligence. If the child developed a habit of being a moving target (rather than a sitting duck), this habit might seem like hyperactivity, or high distractibility.

The assessment process must discover and distinguish between trauma-bond-related behavior and attachment behavior. This can be very difficult because so many of the behaviors characteristic of the trauma bond are inherent in disturbed attachment behavior. The distinction becomes even more important when one is deciding whether the child should remain in foster placement or be returned to the care of a previously abusive adult. The evaluator must develop a set of criteria both for observing the quality of the attachment and for defining the behaviors that constitute the trauma bond. It helps in this endeavor to remember the purposes of each type of behavior pattern.

Attachment behavior patterns have as goals safety, exploration, avoidance of danger, and affiliation. Consequently, a child who engages in behaviors for the purpose of maintaining an attachment will demonstrate exploratory behavior, a full range of expression of feelings, periodic checking back with the attachment figure, and participation in affectionate behavior that is age-appropriate. These behaviors will occur even if the child is considered disturbed or demonstrates dysfunctional coping in some situations.

The goals of trauma bond behavior, however, have as objectives the adult's well-being, regulation of the intensity of feeling, limited interaction, and safety. Behaviors that reflect trauma bonds include spontaneous or complete and unwavering obedience, clinging behavior, little expression of feeling or exaggerated expressions of feeling that reflect the adult's need-state, and limited cognitive functioning.

Several factors influence the quality of both the trauma bond and the attachment patterns. Some of these factors include number of placements, length of placement, regularity and quality of interaction with the abusive noncustodial parents, the child's developmental stage, the therapeutic intervention that has already occurred, the emotional availability of the temporary caretakers, and the child's sense of safety in out-of-home placement. The evaluator must consider these parameters when drawing inferences in the assessment process. These factors determine the meaning of observed behaviors.

The evaluator must assess the quality and nature of the child's trauma-related interaction patterns in order to adequately and accurately assess the quality and nature of a traumatized child's attachment behavior patterns. This assessment of both types of interaction patterns clarifies whether the child's behavior with the previously abusive parent demonstrates goals consistent with attachment or goals related only to maintenance of safety. The evaluator will then be in a better position to gauge whether foster or other temporary parents can establish effective attachment patterns with the child and whether the child can move beyond the reenactment of traumatic relationships with authentically nurturing adults.

A partial set of questions that reflect these subtle but important distinctions include at least the following:

- Under what conditions is the child compliant?
- Who regulates the intensity of feelings in the interaction between adult and child?
- Does the adult help the child function more independently or dependently? How does the adult achieve this support?
- To what extent are the boundaries between adult behavior and child behavior maintained or blurred? How are these boundaries established?
- Under what conditions does the child engage in exploration? Does the child use the adult to enhance her ability to explore? Does the adult take over and dictate what the child should do? To what extent does the adult coach the child regarding possible solutions to problems?
- If the child has a high activity level, under what observable conditions does this activity level change?
- Does the child's behavior regress during interactions with the adult? If so, in what ways is this regression observable? Is the regression appropriate to the situation?
- Does the child show anxiety when the adult must leave the room? If so, how? What is the child's response to the adult's return?

Assessment Instruments and Activities

Given these parameters or characteristics, assessment of attachment becomes a matter of collecting data that reflect the various aspects of parent-child or caretaker-child interaction. There are basically three different ways to obtain these data:

- Adult report and/or child self-report checklists
- Direct observation
- Projective techniques

Multiple samples of behavior are used as a means of concurrent validation. It is probably most accurate if all three types of data are collected. Cross-checks are built into the assessment process to verify any given set of data.

Assessment of attachment must provide for an open-ended sample of behavior, since no single discrete interaction is likely to demonstrate the quality and fullness of attachment. The behavior sample must be structured in content so that individual differences in process from caretaker to caretaker can emerge. These differences are the basis for comparing the quality of attachment with various caretakers.

Jernberg and Booth (1979) adapted and published the Marschach Interaction Method (MIM) to distinguish "affection-giving" from "direction-giving" parental patterns. The MIM tasks are categorized according to the child's developmental level: neonate, infant, toddler, preschooler, latency-age child, or adolescent. Tasks are grouped within each level according to four dimensions:

- Nurturing activities, such as applying lotion to each other
- Structuring tasks, such as simple teaching tasks
- Intrusive activities, such as hide-and-seek games
- Challenging activities, such as engaging the child in successive games of skill or physical power

Seven to ten activities are chosen from a list and are presented in written form on instruction cards to the parents. They are told to read the card silently and then carry out the task.

The observer, as unobtrusively as possible, records the concrete actions making up the interactive process that occurs between the two individuals. By reviewing the interactions between a child and various caretakers, the observer can determine characteristics of the child's attachment-enhancing behaviors, deviant or paradoxical actions, and overall ability to respond effectively to any specific adult. Often this set of activities will projectively enact the parent's assumptions about the child. Both the child's working model of interaction and the parent's assumptions about his or her own role as well as expectations about the child can be elicited using this method.

The Early Relational Assessment (Clark, 1985) is another measure of parent-child interaction that allows an observer to elicit characteristic interaction patterns:

> The purpose of the Early Relational Assessment is to attempt to capture

> the infant/child's experience of the parent, the parent's experience of the child, the affective and behavioral characteristics that each brings to the interaction and the quality or tone of the relationship. This is an assessment of the areas of strength and areas of concern in the parent, the child and the dyad. . . . For the purpose of observing the parent-child interaction and to assist in assessing current relationship issues in the dyad, parents and children are videotaped together for four 5-minute segments of 1) feeding, 2) structured task, 3) free play and 4) separation/reunion.
>
> (Clark, 1985, p. 2)

This instrument is used primarily for children under the age of five years.

Checklists and Self-Report Forms

Three types of checklists exist for use in the assessment of attachment. One group asks parents to catalog the child's behaviors; self-report checklists deal with adult functioning; and the third consists of checklists and observational inventories for use by the assessing professional.

The Child Behavior Checklist (Achenbach & Edelbrock, 1979), Conner's Behavior Rating Scales (Conners, 1973), and any other child behavior inventory are examples of this category of assessment instrument. Self-report inventories are useful for uncovering the child's behavioral repertoire.

The point of the assessment, however, is to discern not only the child's behavior but the interaction between the child and the adult. It is therefore extremely important to gather information about the adult's functioning also. Adult self-report forms, such as the Brief Symptom Inventory or the Symptom-Checklist-90-Revised (Derogatis 1990, 1992), are useful for putting the adult's observed behavior in context. Depression inventories may also be useful, as may scales of adaptive functioning. Self-report inventories that examine or measure the likelihood of substance use are important to include in the assessment if substance abuse is suspected. While theoretically it should be possible to use other extensive personality inventories, the sheer magnitude of these instruments limits their usefulness within the context of interaction assessment.

Instruments and evaluator use tend to be classified by guild considerations. The Nursing Child Assessment Satellite Training (BARNARD, 1988) which requires training for reliability, was originally devised for nursing professionals to complete. Several instruments aimed for diagnosticians achieve reliability by their restricted use; an example is the Parent-Infant Relationship Global Assessment of Functioning Scale (PIR-GAS). There also exist pediatric checklists that primary health care professionals complete during a routine physical examination. The utility of these checklists lie in their ease of administration and their brief time requirements for data collection.

If the child is old enough to use coloring markers, completing the Kinetic Family Drawings (Knoff & Prout, 1989), the Draw-a-Person (Buck, 1966), or the House-Tree-Person (Harris, 1963) drawings can yield useful projective information. Children who are not oppositional or resistant seem to enjoy these activities and will often spontaneously volunteer important information as they draw. Other forms of projective assessment can provide useful information. The more ambiguous the stimuli, however, the less the diagnostician can extrapolate specifically about the nature and quality of interaction between the child and any given adult.

Clinical Example of a Completed Evaluation

Relationship report for Jill. Age: three years, ten months.

Identifying information and reason for referral. Jill is a three-year, ten-month-old girl who was referred for an assessment of her relationship status with both her biological mother and her foster mother. A complete diagnostic evaluation report was submitted to the court in December. (For a complete developmental and social history, please refer to university hospital documents.)

The summary of that report, submitted by a licensed psychologist, stated in part that "Jill's development in the areas of gross- and fine-motor skills and social skills is within the normal range for a child her age. Her expressive language abilities, however, fall significantly below expected levels, greater than 2 standard deviations below average. Her receptive comprehension, although better developed than her expressive skills, is also an area of relative weakness for her, falling 1.5 standard deviations below average." The rest of the university report, written by a psychiatrist, stated in its summary that "Jill's primary attachment is with her foster mother. In the past three months we have seen the disruptive effects of Jill's removal and the disruption of this attachment become evident. . . . We have seen Jill's regression, her self-injurious behavior, and the failure to resolve these behaviors over the past three months." Since the time of that report, Jill has been placed back in the care of her foster father and foster mother, and her behavior has again changed. The purpose of this assessment is to clarify the present quality of attachment that Jill has developed with her biological mother and with her foster mother.

Instruments used

Marshach Interaction Method (MIM), (Jemberg & Booth, 1979), with first the biological mother and then the foster mother
Achenbach Child Behavior Checklist (CBCL), (Achenbach & Edelbrock, 1979) completed by both the biological mother and the foster mother
Symptom-Checklist-90-Revised (SCL-90R), (Derogadis, 1990) completed by both the biological mother and the foster mother
Diagnostic play session prior to the evaluation
Kinetic Family Drawings, (Knoff & Prout, 1989) completed by Jill with both biological mother and foster mother
House-Tree-Person Drawings, (Harris, 1963) completed by Jill with both biological mother and foster mother

Behavioral observations: During the first session Jill was accompanied by her foster mother, her foster sister, and a same-age female child for whom the foster mother provides daycare. The foster mother stated that this daycare child is HIV positive. During this session Jill was initially cautious and then eager to play with the toys in the playroom with her two companions. She used her foster mother appropriately to help her navigate frustrations and squabbles that arose among the three girls. Jill demonstrated that she enjoys playing with other children her age. She entered into age-appropriate fantasies with the other two, and at other times she went off by herself and played out fantasies and reenactments (memories of past traumatic events). She demonstrated appropriate skill at playing interactive motor games with the other children, as well as an ability to handle externally imposed structure. The foster mother reported that Jill did not go to preschool last year but that she would go this coming school year. Jill seemed to use her foster mother for emotional refueling and was aware of her foster mother's whereabouts at all times.

During the second session the foster mother brought Jill for a 10:00 A.M. appointment with her biological mother. The biological mother, however, seemed confused about the time of the appointment and eventually was able to come at 3:00 P.M. Jill spent the entire day downtown with her foster mother. By the time her appointment with her biological mother, Jill was tired and in need of a nap. Nevertheless, she participated enthusiastically in the activities of the MIM and projective drawings with her biological mother. She separated easily from her foster mother at the beginning of the session, and she separated easily again from her biological mother at the end of the session.

By the third session Jill recognized me immediately and came enthusiastically to play with her foster mother. But during this session—in which Jill completed the MIM and projective drawings with her foster mother—Jill seemed fearful that her foster mother would leave. Her behavior seemed more dependent and clingy than it had been the two previous times, although she was age-appropriate throughout the evaluation. Also, during this last session Jill engaged in free play with dolls at the end of the session. During her free play she acted out sexual acts with the dolls, undressing them and placing a male and female doll together to "go to bed." She seemed interested in sticking her finger in the various orifices of the dolls, put one doll on top of the other, and made remarks indicating sexual activity. The examiner engaged in no exploration of her behavior or remarks. During this play Jill was observed to be in an agitated state. She had difficulty leaving the dolls and seemed engrossed in acting out some play sequence over and over, suggesting that she was engaging in reenactment of unresolved traumatic experiences.

During all three sessions Jill demonstrated a demand for reassurance and emotional nurture, as well as a basic unmet neediness. This neediness took the form of having little ability to delay gratification or the resolution of action, an inability to share food with others, periods of agitated whininess, and difficulty with transitions. Her foster mother encouraged her at the tough points to find something to do that would make her feel better. During the session with her biological mother, Jill seemed to regress as a result of the moody periods. Her biological mother responded to Jill's agitated state by allowing Jill to lie across her and kiss her all over. This interaction also helped Jill recover from her moods, but not in an independent manner—rather, in a manner that made her more dependent on her biological mother for appropriate functioning.

MIM observations, projective drawings, and inventories with the biological mother. The MIM is a semistructured set of activities in which an adult and a child engage in specific interactions together. These interactions fall into four categories: (1) nurturing, (2) challenging or stress inducing, (3) structuring, and (4) intrusive. Observations of the different interactions allow an examiner to assess which, if any, types of typical parent-child activity present problems for the pair.

The biological mother seemed to have an excellent ability to keep Jill engaged, and she reported that she enjoyed the activities with her daughter. She demonstrated good skill at structuring activities and at helping Jill orient to different characteristics of the environment. She encouraged Jill to use modeling and passive imitation to complete performance activities, such as drawing, playing interactively with toys, and listening to stories. She had more difficulty carrying out challenging activities that induced stress in Jill. For these activities, she seemed to abdicate her parenting role whenever Jill resisted, insisted on her own way, or began to regress to whiny behavior. The biological mother seemed to have a limited repertoire of methods for helping Jill maintain age-appropriate behavior during these activities. During nurturing activities especially, there were times when Jill and her biological mother seemed to be competing with each other for who would receive nurturing first. For example, during the candy-sharing activity the biological mother initially gave Jill the first candy but then insisted that Jill give her a candy before she would give Jill another one. She began to tease Jill with the candy, changing a nurturing activity that was meant to be low-stress into a high-stress activity. As the activity progressed,

Jill became possessive about taking all the candies for herself, and her biological mother sternly took the candies away from Jill and told her she couldn't have anymore until Jill fed her mother. During the MIM, when Jill became agitated her biological mother responded by increasing the interpersonal stimulation to Jill, not helping Jill reduce it. Jill's response was to become emotionally younger (regressed) or to stop the activity and interaction altogether and attempt to physically distance herself from her mother. The biological mother responded to these cues, and at the times Jill was not functioning well she attempted to help her daughter recover.

During the separation activity of the MIM, Jill looked after her biological mother, sat quietly for a moment, and then occupied herself until her mother came back. Initially she protested her mother's leaving, but then she accepted it with resignation. She had a concerned look on her face, looked from one observer to the other for reassurance, and then became engaged in exploring the contents of her mother's handbag. When the biological mother announced she was leaving the room, Jill begged to go with her. After the biological mother left the room, however, Jill's behavior became more exploratory, inquisitive, and age-appropriate than it had been previously during the assessment. When her biological mother returned, Jill showed an inclination to ignore her mother and to become resistant by refusing to give the handbag back. Jill focused her energy on resisting Mom's efforts to get her purse back. The biological mother won out by snatching the purse. When the biological mother took it, Jill grinned happily and reengaged. The stress in this activity seemed to be modulated by Jill, not between Jill and her biological mother.

Jill's drawings with her biological mother of a house, tree, person, and her "family doing something together" were developmentally at approximately a two-and-a-half-year level. She insisted that her biological mother complete the drawings first. The biological mother complied with Jill's request but asked her for details as to what she should draw. In this way the biological mother allowed Jill to imitate her passively, although she did allow Jill to express her own internal structure. When invited to draw a picture of her family doing something together, Jill drew her foster sisters and foster parents, not her biological mother or half-sister.

At the time of the MIM observation, the biological mother completed the SCL-90R, a self-report inventory of symptoms experienced during the last seven days. Her responses to the questions on this inventory indicated that at the time of the MIM activities, the biological mother experienced slightly elevated scores on six of the nine scales of symptoms. Her scores did not demonstrate clear statistically significant evidence of any identifiable pathological syndrome.

Three weeks after the MIM observation, the biological mother filled out the CBCL, a parent report of child behaviors and symptoms. Her responses to that instrument indicated that she perceived Jill as being within the normal range in all aspects of her behavior. The biological mother stated that her only concern at this time was whether Jill was going to contract AIDS as a result of playing with the child who has tested HIV positive and is cared for by the foster mother during the day. When asked if she identified any difficulties between Jill and her, the biological mother demonstrated no insight into the conflicts observed in the nurturing, challenging, and intrusive tasks of the MIM. She stated that she felt her relationship with Jill was appropriate and without difficulty. She also stated that while Jill can become willful and oppositional, it is clear that Jill wants to please the adults who are important to her and that she is an obedient child when she is with her. The biological mother further stated that Jill plays exceptionally well with her younger half-sister and that this makes her very proud of her daughter.

MIM observations, projective drawings, and inventories with the foster mother: The Foster mother seemed to have an excellent ability to keep Jill engaged. She demonstrated good skill at all four types of activities. She encouraged Jill to use cognitive modulation of her affect, creative expression, and modeling and imitation to complete performance activities, such as drawing, playing interactively with toys, and listening to stories. Whenever Jill resisted, insisted on her own way, or began to regress to whiny behavior, the foster mother reflected back to Jill her behavior and seemed to give her choices as to how she might cope with the situation. During nurturing activities the foster mother clearly maintained a parental role, allowing Jill to dance all over the room with the candies, eventually eating most of them herself. It seemed that the foster mother was unthreatened by Jill's clear neediness to have the candies for herself. Eventually Jill did give her foster mother some of the candies. Jill became agitated during this activity, and the foster mother helped her to calm down and lower the stress Jill seemed to experience.

During the separation activity of the MIM, Jill became distraught when her foster mother went to leave. The foster mother initiated leaving while Jill was crying loudly and frantically. Eventually the foster mother was unable to leave Jill in such an uncontrolled state, and she took Jill to the bathroom with her. The foster mother reported that at home Jill will allow her to go off easily; she thought Jill was being fearful because the office in which the assessment took place was relatively unfamiliar to Jill. This activity was an impetus for both foster mother and Jill to reminisce about when Jill had lived with her biological mother for three months. The foster mother related that Jill sometimes has nightmares in which she wakes up and makes her foster mother promise not to let her go anywhere else. Jill also spoke briefly about not wanting to go away. As soon as the pair came back from the bathroom, the observer questioned whether Jill might be scared of her, and Jill nodded affirmatively while sitting in her foster mother's lap. She stated, while nodding, "No, not when my mommy is here."

Jill's drawings with her foster mother of a house, tree, person, and her "family doing something together" was developmentally at approximately a three-and-a-half-year level. Although Jill insisted that her foster mother complete the drawings first, her foster mother encouraged her to do the drawings first, promising to do them after Jill did them. In this way the foster mother helped Jill to express her own internal structure without becoming an interpreter. When invited to draw a picture of her family doing something together, Jill drew her foster sisters and foster parents, as well as the pets in the household.

At the time of the MIM observation, the foster mother completed the SCL-9OR, a self-report inventory of symptoms experienced during the last seven days. Her responses to the questions on this inventory indicated that at the time of the MIM activities, her scores did not demonstrate clear, statistically significant, evidence of any identifiable pathological syndrome. Her scores were not elevated or in the clinical range at all. The foster mother filled out the CBCL, a parent report of child behaviors and symptoms in relationship to Jill, just as the biological mother had. Her responses to that instrument indicated that she perceived Jill as being within the borderline clinical range for having an internalizing coping style. The foster mother stated that her major concerns at this time are that Jill seems to have increased acting-out behaviors after visits with her biological mother and that Jill has difficulty modulating her moods in an age-appropriate way. When asked if she identified any difficulties between Jill and her, the foster mother spoke of having difficulty calming Jill down after visits with her biological mother and of having difficulty when Jill gets aggressive with other children, has temper tantrums, throws herself on the floor, or bites. The foster mother stated that sometimes she felt Jill went off into her own world and that it was then difficult to reach her to help her understand what was being required of her, especially if Jill was scared. Overall, the foster mother stated that Jill is a very loving and caring child.

Summary. Jill, a three-year, ten-month-old girl who has been in foster placement since she was three months of age, was seen for three 90-minute sessions to assess the quality of attachment between her and her foster mother and her and her biological mother. Previous evaluations have established that her cognitive, social, and motor functioning is within normal limits and that she has both an expressive and a receptive language delay. A moderate articulation disorder was observed during the present assessment. (For a complete developmental and social history, please refer to university hospital documents.)

One function of attachment behavior is to keep the immature infant and child safe from danger. Jill's behavior demonstrates, by its greater range and higher functioning level, that she feels most safe with her foster mother. It is clear that Jill enjoys her time with her biological mother and that the biological mother is very important to her. When Jill is with her biological mother, however, she is more constricted in her repertoire of behavior, seems to behave in those ways sanctioned by her biological mother, and does not express her own internal structure, based on her own perceptions, but instead tries to copy her biological mother. It was also observed that when Jill and her biological mother began to have difficulty negotiating, the biological mother encouraged Jill to become developmentally younger, regress, become dependent, and thereby accept the biological mother's structure. This method of achieving compromise influenced Jill to function at a younger age than necessary and to use avoidance coping strategies, and it did not encourage her to develop approach coping mechanisms.

It is quite evident that Jill has strong relationships with both women; however, her responses to nurturing, separation, and exploratory situations indicate that her primary attachment is to her foster mother. With her foster mother Jill showed a greater range of affect and functioned at a more age-appropriate level than with her biological mother, both in actual interaction and when drawing. With her foster mother Jill gleefully, joyfully, and sometimes impertinently expresses her own opinions and perceptions, even if the foster mother is not always happy with those views.

Recommendations

1. If Jill's placement is based on her psychological well-being, then this assessment supports the notion that Jill needs to maintain her placement with the foster family. She behaves as though she were one of the family and acts out her relationships with that family when given the opportunity. It is clear from her behavior in four typical parent-child interactions—nurturing, challenging, structuring, and intrusive—that Jill feels safer to explore and take cognitive and emotional risks when with her foster mother.
2. It is also important that Jill's relationship with her biological mother be supported and nurtured. There is much strength in that relationship, and the biological mother and Jill should be referred for dyadic psychotherapy with a qualified, licensed clinical psychologist, psychiatrist, or social worker who can address the relationship problems noted in this and previous evaluations.
3. Jill should be referred to the Board of Education for preschool educational and speech evaluation in order to adequately resolve the language-based disability she now demonstrates.

Summary

The purpose of this chapter has been to highlight the various perspectives that go into an assessment of attachment behavior. The assessment of attachment entails an assessment of the interaction between a child and her caretakers. No single set of behaviors or situations constitutes an intrinsic part of such an assessment. Rather, in order to assess the relationship the child's behavior needs to be observed across a series of situations and interactions. Additionally, the caregivers' behavior patterns are as important to observe and understand as the child's. A number of different assessment instruments, including self-report, observation, and projective tools, should be used and their results integrated so that an adequate sample of behavior can be developed.

The assessment of interactions will necessarily include both attachment behaviors and trauma-bonding interactions. The only way to discriminate between these two types of interaction patterns is to carefully observe the child within the context of interaction with the important adults in her life.

5

Relationship-Based Treatment Categories

Deep uncertainty about one's right to exist and one's right to a separate identity leads to a terror of being in close contact with others.
McDougall, 1982

Reminding ourselves of the obvious is sometimes helpful. We cannot create recipes for treating children with emotional disturbances. Each child and family situation brings its own unique combination of ingredients. A recipe book that included all possible combinations would be too voluminous to be useful or so basic that it would not be used and the wisdom therein discarded. What is presented here is a mixture of treatment basics—categories, needs, focus, and process, that serve as the core of treatment; one must then add "season to taste" options that meet the specific needs of the child and family.

Attachment relationships can be divided into five categories based on the quality or nature of the relationship: good enough, maladaptive with potential for change, maladaptive without potential for change, new primary caregiver, and nonprimary supplemental attachment. Using relationship-based categories of treatment helps the clinician to stay focused on the core issue of treatment: the attachment relationship.

Clinical focus is essential in this work, which is characterized by complex issues that are shrieking for attention; dynamics that are hidden, elusive, and denied; child and parent needs and concerns that are conflictual; and all sorts of people involved who can be simultaneously demanding and resistant.

A clinician relationship with a child, caregiver, and whenever possible, both, will continually focus, with varying intensity, on the attachment relationship. This may involve enriching the present one, saying goodbye or hello again to the old one, or helping create a new one, such as in an adoptive family wherein the clinician must find time and room for everyone's considerable "baggage." Although it is most favorable to have the option of any and all family members present when the clinician wants them there, that is rarely the case; however, *unavailability does not prohibit working with important relationship issues related to that person.*

Good Enough Attachment

A good enough attachment is a relationship between a caregiver and a child that meets the needs of both (Winnicott, 1960). Problems arise when a good enough attachment is interrupted by the prolonged emotional or physical unavailability of the attachment figure, as by illness of the child or parent, disaster, divorce, or death. The frightened child, dependent on the attachment figure for soothing and protection, becomes overwhelmed and traumatized by the parent's absence.

A child's sense of time is such that the feeling of terror accompanying the loss can seem unending, and the feeling cannot be assuaged because the source of soothing is not there. The meaning of the parent's absence to the child can be that he is not loved or that he has done something wrong. An important aspect of therapy is to determine, when possible, the meaning of the parental absence in order to correct the child's misperceptions.

Insecurity and fright can continue after parent and child are reunited if the child believes the parent might leave again. The parent's absence created a lack of trust in the child, and his subsequent behavior can prohibit or delay reestablishment of a trusting relationship. The parent, who feels rebuffed by the child's rage or withdrawal, becomes confused and does not know how to deal with the behavior.

Treatment emphasis is twofold: (1) understanding and accepting the circumstances that caused the unavailability of the parent and (2) helping the child and caregiver reestablish trust in their relationship.

Maladaptive Attachment Relationship with Potential for Change

The maladaptive attachment relationship does not adequately provide the child with the security and care needed for development. The presenting circumstances can usually be related to the caregiver's failure to protect the child, to inadequate or abusive parenting, and/or to disturbing child behaviors. It is crucial for the well-being of the child, parent, and the attachment relationship, as well as for the success of treatment, that the clinician carefully assess the history, circumstances, and context of the behaviors related to the maladaptive parenting and the strengths within the relationship. Questions to be answered might include the following: Is the child's behavior related to allergies? To other medical problems? Are the child and mother locked into a dysfunctional dance? Is the mother scapegoating the child? How can we explain the mother's secure attachment with sibs?

The key feature is a potential for long-term positive change determined by the child's and parent's demonstrated abilities and willingness to change. This language, developed by the courts, evolved from many bitter experiences of caregivers stating that they wanted to provide safe and loving homes for their children when they were not willing or able to do so. Thus evaluators must balance what parents say they want with what they show they are willing to do. Demonstrated abilities and willingness are usually assessed by current behavior and track record. Evaluators *must* consider cultural values and practices, as well as a parent's present and past circumstances. For example, current stressors, personal crises, meaning and purpose of the current evaluation, and shame or rage will all influence the parents' functioning and may not accurately portray their usual way of relating to the child, to each other, and to community people.

The child's behaviors are typified by clinginess, withdrawal, a focus on the parent's well-being, and an unwillingness to explore the environment. The youngster goes to anyone or to no one for soothing, and he is unable to soothe himself. This maladaptive relationship is likely to have a negative impact on the child's development and, without intervention, might place the child at risk for maltreatment or for serious dysfunction in forming and maintaining relationships. The treatment focus for child and family is on examining the current and past attachment functioning and traumatizing experiences of both child and parent. Child-parent dyad therapy and, where appropriate, family therapy will work directly with ingrained, dysfunctional patterns of interactions that have developed in the attachment relationship. Modifications of the attachment relationship will require ongoing support, consultation, and monitoring to ensure they become securely integrated into the family behavior pattern.

The child's work is to learn to cope with and master the traumatizing experience of the past and the resultant negative adaptive behaviors. Child therapy can include individual or group sessions and sessions in which the parent is invited to observe or participate.

The work for the parents is psychodynamic and psychoeducational. Psychodynamic work helps the parents understand the genesis of their behavior and deal more effectively with issues from their own childhood, including an understanding of how these issues may reemerge in their present parenting. Remediating the maladaptive parenting practices utilizes psychoeducational modalities, such as direct teaching, demonstration, and practicing positive parenting skills in group and/or couples therapy.

The clinician will usually need to coordinate with people from other agencies and learn to clarify roles and share power. The clinical work needed will take longer than anyone imagines it will.

Maladaptive Attachment Relationship without Potential for Change

This category includes the same or worse maladaptive patterns seen in the previous category, but here it is not possible or likely that the child will again live with his or her parents. These situations include abandonment, a long-term jail sentence, incapacity of the parent, or patterns of severe child abuse that clearly endanger the physical safety of the child. These are situations where remediation is not possible and parental rights have been or will be terminated.

The plan for the child can be placement in permanent out-of-home care while maintaining a visiting or extended family relationship with the primary attachment figure. Or his relationship with the parents can be terminated, with plans that the child be raised in an adoptive home where he will develop a new primary attachment.

Treatment will initially focus on strengthening the child, helping the child feel safe in a new environment, and, beginning in the initial phase and continuing throughout treatment, helping the child develop a positive sense of self so he can cope with the losses and changes in his life.

An essential part of the later clinical work is helping the child cope with the partial or total loss of the primary attachment figure. The child is then prepared and invited to work on accepting the realities of past traumatizing experiences.

The youngster will need the assistance of both old (if available) and new family to adjust to the restructured relationship and to mourn the loss of old relationships. The mourning process happens over time and includes protesting the loss, internalizing the relationship, saying goodbye, and grieving. The treatment might include work with the child's parents alone, child-parent dyad therapy, and work with the present caregivers.

New Primary Caregiver

We must help children and caregivers establish new primary attachments when children have permanently lost their primary attachment figure or when no attachment has existed previously, as with a newborn. This is not to say that all new mothers need therapy; however, a new mother who is in a vulnerable situation, such as with a seriously ill or special-needs child, or who herself has limited function or ability may need supportive prevention work, education, and/or assistance in developing a healthy attachment relationship with her child.

New attachments can be potentially permanent or can be recognized from the outset as an interim measure. Potentially permanent attachments can be between mother and infant, with long-term foster parents, with stepparents, or with adoptive parents. Interim attachment can be appropriately promoted between a child and a foster parent or residential caregiver or with the therapeutic person, who might be the only constant figure in the child's life at the time.

The goal is relationship building, and it is accomplished through teaching, guidance, support, modeling, and practice. The new relationship may fall apart and have to be rebuilt several times, especially when confounding elements have not been resolved, as when a youngster has not finished grieving the loss of a primary attachment. Ongoing support, consultation, and monitoring are essential.

Nonprimary Supplemental Attachment

Extended family members, short-term foster parents, therapists, case managers, daycare providers, and group therapy peers, among others, may provide the essential supportive attachment relationships needed to maintain a primary attachment. A supplemental relationship is needed when the primary attachment is jeopardized, such as by parental disability, inadequacy, or current unavailability or when the child's behavior is so horrific or his needs so overwhelming that it is not possible for parents to meet the needs of the child without significant ongoing assistance.

Clinical work is directed toward supporting the child's primary attachment figure and eliciting that same support from the child's supportive attachments. Role clarification is integral and ongoing to prevent good guy/bad guy jealousies and resentments that can sabotage needed support for the child. The clinician does therapy with the child and consults with the supportive attachment person as clinical work proceeds.

Relationship based treatment categories, situations that may need clinical attention, and treatment focus are illustrated in the figure shown on page 56.

Integration of Relationship Categories and Types of Attachment Problems

Treatment will address issues in various attachment relationship categories (good, bad, awful, old, new, ending, beginning) and will also deal with past and present issues in the attachment problem categories described in Chapter 1, which include (1) disturbed attachment, in which the existing attachment is compromised; (2) attachment trauma related to loss or unavailability of a primary attachment; or (3) trauma-related attachment problems arising from

Categories: Attachment Therapy

Relationship	*Possible Situations*	*Treatment Focus*
Good enough	Disrupted, disturbed primary attachment	Reestablish attachment
Maladaptive—potential for long-term positive change	Failure to protect Inadequate/abusive parenting Disturbing child behavior	Trauma work Modification of attachment
Maladaptive—not likely to change	Abuse Parental dysfunction Abandonment Death	Resolution of loss Trauma work Prepare child for new or restructured relationship
New primary	Special-needs child Compromised infant-mother relationship Loss of primary caregiver	Facilitate mourning Relationship building
Nonprimary supplemental relationship	Child's primary relationship at risk without support	Support primary relationship Clarify roles Relationship building

a traumatizing event that compromised the attachment relationship. Examples incorporating both attachment relationship and attachment problem categorizations together are as follows:

1. *Good enough attachment relationship with trauma-related attachment problems.* A seven-year-old has a life-threatening illness. Her mother copes by denying the seriousness of the situation. Her father, who states he will be supportive of the child, plans to divorce the mother.
2. *Maladaptive attachment relationship without potential for change with attachment trauma.* A ten-year-old has an insecure emotional relationship with her neglectful, distracted mother who has recently been convicted of a murder that the daughter witnessed. The child is in foster care. Neither father nor other relatives are available.
3. *Maladaptive relationship with potential for change with disturbed attachment.* A twelve-year-old has an insecure attachment with his father and no history with his absent mother. The father's pattern of emotionally abusing the child appears

to be alcohol related, and he is in a rehabilitation program that includes parenting classes. The father and child live with the paternal grandparents.

4. *New primary attachment relationship with attachment trauma*. A five-year-old adopted child has a history of an enmeshed, insecure attachment with birth parents. He was chronically abused in his birth home and had several traumatizing foster placements. The adoptive parents are robust, experienced, and willing to work with therapist. The birth parents are available and willing to facilitate child's "saying goodbye" so he can be helped to form a new primary attachment.
5. *Nonprimary supplemental relationship with trauma-related attachment problem*. A fire at home injured the mother and destroyed the home and all family possessions. No father or extended family is available. The ten- and thirteen-year-old children have strong, positive attachments with their mother. They have been struggling to care for her and themselves for the past year, but are becoming emotionally overwhelmed.

Summary

Treatment of attachment disorders vary with, among other things, the nature of the attachment relationship. It is helpful to think about five categories of attachment relationships that are seen in clinical practice: good enough, maladaptive with potential for change, maladaptive without potential for change, new primary caregiver, and nonprimary supplemental attachment.

Treatment goals for each are different, as are the work involved and the focus. Some attachments need to be strengthened, as when an event has caused disruption. Others will require intensive work to help change the maladaptive and destructive nature of parent-child interactions. Clearly treatment will deal with mourning the loss of a relationship, with its accompanying loss of security and safety in the world, and, when needed, will focus on supporting the formation of new attachments.

6

Treatment Essentials

If I don't see you anymore, will there still be Mondays?
Five-year-old to therapist

Five conditions—safety, a protecting environment, therapeutic parenting, appropriate clinical skills, and a therapeutic relationship—must be in place before serious treatment work begins. These conditions must remain intact throughout treatment and must be periodically assessed to ensure their continuance and strength.

Safety

A safe environment is one in which the child is protected from threatened or actual harm to herself and is kept from harming others. An abusive family member or a caregiver who threatens the child not to divulge critical information is a safety threat. So are violent, impulsive parents; a child's risk-taking behaviors; and lack of emotional support and supervision.

We assess safety by evaluating information obtained from records, reviewing the child's history, interviewing caregivers and others who know the child, and obtaining information from the child herself. Her safety needs are then met through supervision, environmental control, and ongoing evaluation.

Protecting Environment

A protecting environment is one in which the youngster feels safe enough emotionally to explore events or issues that are frightening, such as the loss of a parent. The protecting environment initially substitutes for a trusting personal relationship, which is the foundation of treatment in most therapy models. Given, however, that attachment-trauma problems invariably include an inability to trust and that intimate relationships are often the source of the trauma, we cannot expect all children to easily develop a trusting clinical relationship. Children and adults who are intimacy-avoidant and untrusting will be wary, perhaps frightened, by a therapist's or new caregiver's warmth and familiarity.

A safe therapeutic alliance can be achieved when the process of therapy—its purpose, structure, and methods—are understandable, consistent, and predictable. Trusting the process will eventually lead to trusting the therapist or new caregivers, and a relationship is then possible.

The clinician promotes reliance on the therapeutic process by

- exhibiting a professional demeanor that exudes confidence, hope, and empathic warm distance;
- clarifying roles;
- discussing rules;
- explaining why treatment is needed and how it works;
- describing what assessment will entail, encouraging the active participation of child and caregiver in the assessment process, and providing verbal and written results of assessment; and
- encouraging child and family input into the treatment plan.

Therapeutic Parenting

Individual child therapy by itself is inadequate for treating attachment problems. We must recognize the child's attachment needs—not to do so is irresponsible and may be dangerous. Treatment must pervade the child's total environment because the child's disturbed behavior, emotional distress, and fear that adults will not protect and care for her may not emerge during weekly therapy sessions. If the child's difficulties do show during clinical sessions, these problems cannot be sufficiently addressed within that limited period of the treatment session. The therapeutic milieu—be it home, group facility, or hospital—provides daily, ongoing care for the child and can thus be referred to as therapeutic parenting. Those with whom the child spends significant periods of time—teachers, visiting parents, or extended family—are ideally also involved in the treatment program in order to provide consistent care.

Therapeutic parenting requires better-than-average parenting skills. A partial list of necessary caregiver attributes includes

- the ability to consider issues that underlie children's behaviors;
- the ability to acknowledge, recognize, and bear witness to the child's pain;
- the skill to recognize and appropriately intervene when disturbed emotions and behaviors surface;
- self-perception, which allows recognition of one's own maladaptive response patterns to the child;
- an understanding of a child's need to process and integrate painful past experiences;
- a willingness to participate in the child's therapy and appropriately use clinical guidance;
- a willingness to work as part of the treatment team and to report good, bad, and ugly interactions in the home;
- sufficient self-awareness to be able to seek and use personal support or therapy when needed; and
- a life beyond therapeutic parenting.

Some caregivers may legitimately not be available to participate in the child's treatment. We know in our secret heart of hearts, however, that we may choose not to work with parents for other reasons, and so we readily accept their statements that they are unable to participate in the child's therapy. We must be willing to seduce parents, as Fraiberg, et. al. (1975) suggest, despite the following realities:

- Some parents are easy to hate because of what they did to the child, and, with robust countertransference going for us, we know we can love the child back to happiness.
- Parents can be troublesome and uncooperative.
- If a placement is fragile and the caretaker is not fully committed and willing, his or her participation may jeopardize the placement.
- We hesitate to ask overworked foster parents and childcare workers to extend themselves further and to give even more to the child.

- Parent work requires that we explain what we are doing and why we are doing it. We may be too uncertain, muddled, and confused to be able to do this.

Clinical Skills

Therapists need a basic understanding of attachment and child development and of the impact of trauma and attachment disruption on the child's cognitive, emotional, and behavioral development and treatment needs. We need to be skilled in child and family therapy, know and understand parenting skills, be able to provide consultation, and be able to work as part of a team with parents and other professionals. We must be especially aware of how we are affected by the child's and family's pain, so that our responses do not interfere with clinical decisions. Support and consultation from peers are generally necessary when we work with these complex and intensely emotional issues.

Therapeutic Relationship

Psychotherapy dealing with most trauma and with the development, dysfunction, or loss of an attachment figure must be practiced within the context of a clinical relationship. Work related to core survival issues that may be painful and frightening requires not only skill but the emotional support and protection provided by such a relationship. The child may need to rely on the protective environment for his initial experience of safety in therapy, as stated earlier, but developing a trusting relationship is needed to accomplish deeper work.

Children who have learned not to trust adults and who are intimacy-avoidant may not show signs of relationship development with the therapist for many months. It is a fairly common occurrence in work with attachment disturbance that the clinician becomes suddenly, rather than gradually, aware that the child experiences sufficient relational support to begin deeper work. This sudden "opening up" may be understood as the child responding to a specific clinical intervention or technique, rather than as the child having developed emotional readiness.

It is an error, though tempting, to consider such a clinical occurrence a "breakthrough." The phenomenom may appear to be an instant shift caused by a specific action or event: a wall of "resistance" that the child or therapist shatters, splits apart, bursts through. The process leading to children being able to trust their therapists, allowing themselves to be vulnerable and revealing tender feelings can be likened to the slow, complex development of a critical mass of emotional safety, not a sudden breakthrough.

There are serious risks in adopting "breakthrough" ideology: The clinical focus becomes the search for the perfect, clever intervention; the relationship with the child becomes less valued and in some cases ignored; the clinician's professional self-esteem becomes eroded by lack of success; and such beliefs reinforce and support the procrustean policy of ruthless conformity to brief therapy for children.

Summary

Safety, a protecting environment, therapeutic parenting, appropriate clinical skills, and a therapeutic relationship must be in place before serious work with attachment-disturbed children is begun. Safety is emotional and physical. The protecting environment fostered by the therapist promotes a clinical alliance with the child until a relationship is possible. Therapeutic parenting is offered by the therapeutic milieu and the total environment, not just an individual caregiver. The necessary clinical skills are specialized, and one cannot treat relationship problems without first establishing a therapeutic relationship.

7

Treatment Process

It is loving that saves us, not loss that destroys us; just as it is the people who stay in our lives that drive us mad, not the ones who leave.
Valliant, 1985

Treatment of attachment- and trauma-related problems is exacting, laborious, and often lengthy, reflecting the severity and complexity of these disturbances. In order to do this kind of treatment successfully, five areas must be continuously addressed:

- Education
- Developing Self-identity
- Affect tolerance and modulation
- Relationship building
- Mastering behavior

Clinical work in two additional areas takes place *only* when the child has developed sufficient security in the relationships with the clinician and present caregivers that will allow her to begin to address these issues without becoming overwhelmed. These issue are:

- Exploring trauma
- Mourning losses

It is a clinical error to move too quickly—an error that will retraumatize the child, damage the clinical relationship, and reinforce beliefs the child may hold that adults cannot be trusted to provide protection.

The proportion of time spent in each of the five areas—indeed, whether or not a specific area will be addressed—will vary according to the nature of the trauma and the quality of the primary attachment relationship.

The treatment process for children blossoms in a play therapy context, and sometimes adults alone or with their children benefit from play therapy. Creative therapeutic ideas for family play therapy directed toward promotion of the attachment relationship will be found in Harvey's contribution (Chapter 16). Body work, stories, art, adventure activities, puppet play, sandtray work, and music can be used extensively. Children who have attachment difficulties and have been intensely frightened or in life-threatening circumstances need help in learning to play freely and spontaneously. In some instances, such as children living in prolonged threatening circumstances, the children have never learned to play. These children must be taught *how* to play. Young children who have been emotionally deprived or who have experienced serious trauma, such as young victims of severe burns or of rape or witnesses to parental murder, are often inhibited in their abilities to engage in symbolic play or fantasy. Under normal circumstances play is naturally healing; it enables the child to creatively master ordinary frightening situations—normal challenges and stresses—and satisfies needs through fantasy. Play facilitates expression of overwhelming emotion that is most easily accomplished nonverbally. Also, children do not have the verbal skills needed for full verbal expression. Therapy needs to have elements of fun to balance the difficult times and to promote the child's interest in continuing therapy.

Clinical work with parents and their infants to promote secure attachment will include many of the same objectives described in this chapter. The clinician works with the parent individually and with the parent-infant dyad. Examples of this work are described in Chapter 10 in brief vignettes by Sheets, who describes her work with a streetwise mother in recovery and her infant, and by Isles, who works with an adolescent mother and her newborn.

Education

Direct and indirect clinical teaching is a part of each area of therapy. Education and information are empowering to individuals who feel overwhelmed and helpless. The teaching focus during the initial phase of therapy is on basic information about the nature of attachment and of traumatizing events, and their effects on children and families. It is an approach that is less emotionally charged than some others, provides time for the child to develop comfort in the treatment setting, and furnishes tools the child and family can use in therapy. Specifically, body work, art, and other forms of play can be used to teach the names of emotions and how they are experienced in the body, or they can be used to teach communication and social skills.

The initial teaching phase has two primary goals: (1) to provide a framework within which the child is able to sort out, understand, and normalize his experience and (2) to provide specific information about the traumatic situation this child and family has experienced.

Children and family members are empowered when they learn the dynamics of attachment and trauma. They become better able to understand and cope with their experience when they know how relationships form, what happens when overwhelming and life-threatening circumstances interfere with this formation process, and how thinking, feeling, behavior, and relationships are affected by trauma. Children and teens are comforted when they know that even courageous astronauts and police officers can be frightened, shake and tremble, wet their pants, and sometimes feel no one can protect them.

Therapy participants may need information pertinent to their specific situation, such as discussions about policies and procedures related to adoption, divorce, death, surgery, abuse, court, jail, or anything else that is relevant. These discussions open the way to further dialogue in which misperceptions and cognitive distortions can be identified and addressed.

Clinicians will often teach therapeutic parenting and behavior management as well as provide ongoing consultation to the significant adults who care for the child. This teaching addresses usual parenting issues and also the complex needs of disturbed children, such as those of an older child who has not learned skills in an earlier stage of development or those of a youngster who is pseudomature and needs to be convinced that being a child can be safe and fun.

Education goes beyond the simple process of providing information. It empowers caregivers at a time when they feel helpless. Caregivers need support as they develop self-awareness so that they can look at their own reactions and responses to the child. Clinicians draw on the caregiver's experience, creativity, and wisdom in their work with the child, and they welcome the caregiver as a partner in the child's therapy. The strength and quality of the partnership depends on the parent's abilities and relationship with the child and the therapist's willingness to include the parent.

Therapists can teach many parenting skills by modeling and direct instruction during therapy sessions with child and caregiver (Fraiberg, 1980). One of the more important skills a therapist can model for the parent is acknowledging her own mistakes and asking for help.

Time should always be allocated to practice what has been learned. While practice is continuous throughout treatment, it should be the primary focus of certain sessions, usually at the conclusion of coverage of a therapy area. Practice provides a time in which to guide, model, cheer on the skills and knowledge attained, and experience success.

Children, families, and therapist need practice time to consolidate the gains they have made and to allow their relationship to grow and to strengthen. This helps prepare the child and parent for the next period of intensive work.

The Blueprint for Attachment Therapy in the figure shown on page 67 outlines basic areas that usually require significant clinical attention in attachment-trauma therapy: developing self-identity, affect tolerance and modulation, relationship building and mastering behavior. Issues of safety and creating a protective environment must be addressed first. Exploring past trauma and mourning losses are embedded in the continuing work when some progress has been made in therapy. Gains are consolidated after specific clinical objectives have been met. The depicted therapy process is simplified to help us remember our plan, it is not meant to imply that the process is simple and tidy. The issues are complex and therapy must be constantly adjusted to delays, stoppages, the discovery of hidden strengths and vulnerabilities, and all of the other confounding variables and unanticipated consequences that are typical in this work.

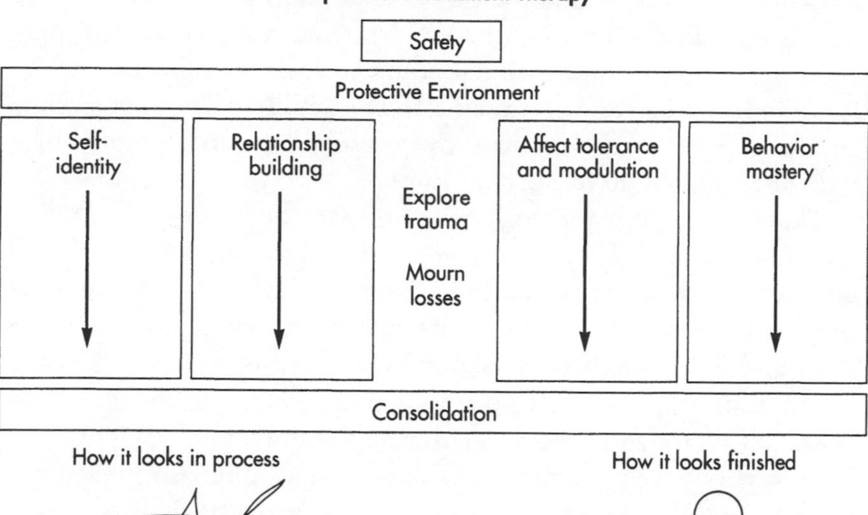

Developing Self-Identity

A child's sense of self develops and blooms in the attachment relationship. Ideally a child learns who she is through thousands of repeated interactions between herself and the attachment partner. Ideally she learns she is competent, worthy, interesting, fun to be with, and able to communicate needs and influence another person. When there are problems in the attachment relationship, such as limitations of one of the attachment partners, significant temperament mismatch, or serious traumatizing influences on the relationship, there is a failure in this area of development.

Children who experience chaotic or dysfunctional early parenting sometimes develop a survival self in which their adaptive behaviors and cognitive distortions override and block the development or awareness of a sense of authentic self.

The word *survival* is used so often in this work that it can slide right by without our resonating to its profound and literal truth for the children with whom we work. It is important to understand how deep into the marrow of a child's being is the need to display whatever emotions and behaviors are necessary to be fed, to be loved, to not be injured or killed. The children learn how they should act—how to anticipate by means of the most subtle cues what they should do in the next minute.

These little survival-beings have not had the luxury of knowing an authentic self. They hide and disown their thoughts, feelings, and behaviors, for it is unsafe to have them. If it is unclear how they must behave, the children are masters at mimicking the emotions and behavior of those around them. Caregivers say they are phony, unfeeling, unreal, or manipulative and find it difficult or impossible to have an intimate relationship with them.

How do we help a child build a sense of self? First we teach her there is such a thing, that it is safe to have one, that she has a right to have one. And then all the adults in the milieu nest of her existence midwife it into being.

A child must be seen and heard before he can build a core identity. Caregivers, teachers, and therapist need to frequently see and comment on the child's uniqueness, from the shape of his ear to the special way he puts peanut butter on his sandwich. Brody's work, described in Chapter 17, focuses on helping children develop a core self and feeling truly seen by others.

Early developmental issues may need to be worked through with youngsters of any age; work with infants and toddlers is described in Chapters 12 (Hewitt) and 13 (Barone). Those who live with traumatized youngsters commonly find that the children have anesthetized or dissociated awareness of all or part of their bodies. The caregiver and child may be helped by understanding the alarm/numbing response described in Chapter 2.

Clinical experience with child trauma survivors has taught us that they anesthetize or mute their senses. It may be that to touch, to smell, to see, or to hear is to invite the awakening of sensory traumatic memory and so is avoided. We can teach them it is safe now to experience their environment. We begin tiptoeing into the sensory world, and, as the child is able to tolerate the gradual progression, we advance to sensory wallowing.

Stimulating and sharing—delight paired with sensory arousal—this is the function of attachment. This area of work clearly integrates attachment and trauma treatment. How do we do it? Boxes of textured materials, such as sandpaper, satin, and squishy things; small film containers of cotton balls scented with various aromas, lotions, and powder; oranges and small containers of chocolate pudding—all are props for games, play, and contests that wake up and stimulate the senses. Find a preschool teacher to consult with; find a child; try what was fun for you as a child. In Chapter 9, Glass briefly describes using movement to help a youngster return to himself. Music, dance, and movement can teach children to wake up, shake out, and reclaim their bodies. Basically the children must learn that it is safe to feel, to live, and to know who they are.

Self-identity work is a continuous part of treatment in clinical sessions and within the therapeutic parenting relationship. Soliciting opinions about the youngster's feelings, thoughts, body experience, food, play, clothing, and music likes and dislikes can fit in almost anytime. Physical care of the child can also provide opportunities to identify and respect the child's uniqueness—hair color and texture, teeth, and body shape are subjects for comment. In-depth discussions about the child's preferences in color, texture, and sound or about his curly hair and brown skin promote a sense of self. It is in this way that the child begins to learn who he is, what is important to him, how he is different from other kids, and how he wants others to view him. Again we are attachment-functioning here: helping the child to learn about his uniqueness and what is special about himself.

Virtually any situation provides an opportunity to teach the youngster that each person is unique and everyone experiences situations differently. The therapist (and other adults in the milieu) models awareness of self by explaining her experience of an event—her feelings, thoughts, and fantasies. Then she explains that everyone is different and invites the child to tell about his experience. The Basket of Feelings exercise is fun and effective for this work with all ages (James, 1989).

The same work continues with the child in a more concentrated, structured manner that identifies, respects, and celebrates a child's uniqueness of mind, body, behavior and spirit. Fantasy and creativity can be stretched, and the lesson practiced, by the child and therapist speculating how ants, aliens, dogs, a potato, or a video recorder might experience an event. The youngster begins to learn who he is and to respect himself by having his uniqueness seen, heard, and honored. He learns about personal boundaries—respect for his own and for others'. Creating a "Me" book that tells all about that child with drawings, collages, writings, and photos is also a useful tool for solidifying a sense of identity (see Bauer, Chapter 11).

Some youngsters have fragmented identities. They disown unacceptable aspects of themselves through simple disclaimers, splitting, or dissociation. The task with these children is to identify the disowned parts and make them user-friendly. Dramatic play and discussions help children learn about feelings and behaviors commonly experienced by others. They see and feel the therapist's acceptance of children (or bunnies or police officer puppets) as they are, and they learn that bad thoughts are not the same as being bad. This process, together with the self-confidence gained during the course of therapy within a trusting relationship with the therapist, helps the child identify and eventually accept and own his experience.

Affect Tolerance and Modulation

Dysregulation of affect is an issue for many children with trauma-related attachment problems. Their experiences often produce overwhelming and out-of-control emotional states, which in turn can create feelings of shame and guilt. Their attempts to cope range from destructive behavior to withdrawal emotionally in an attempt to feel nothing. Hornstein (1989) describes children with severe dissociative disorders as affect-phobic. We see, then, that an important and ongoing part of therapy is to help the child tolerate and modulate affect.

Krystal (1988, p. 30) says, "The greatest obstacle to our clinical and therapeutic conceptions has been metaphors that refer to the 'discharge' of emotions. . . . [A]lthough expression of one's emotions still often implies riddance, the only real help patients can obtain is to increase their tolerance and management of their emotions." The best approach to this work is general education—to help the child and parents identify a range of different affective states and practice emotional expression using various media before doing any specific work with the child's own traumatizing emotional experiences.

Various techniques are suitable for affect work. Detective work is enjoyed by children and is very effective; the child and therapist "search" together for the what, why, when, and how of feelings common to all children. They discover clues, such as what may be going on when the intensity of the feeling gets out of sync with the "now" and thus messes up their power to make decisions.

Weather is a great metaphor for affect. Weather, like emotion, is always present. You can't make it go away, and you really wouldn't want to, because it makes life interesting. The child can understand that we can deal with any amount of weather if our house is good and strong but that even a small rainstorm can be uncomfortable if we are not used to it or are caught unaware. Children talk about preparation and coping, and such discussion always includes asking for help when needed. They learn to notice not only the hurricane but also what happens before, during, and after the storm; they learn the elegant signals our feelings are designed to convey.

Or play scientist. Simple diagrams about neurotransmitters in the brain intrigue youngsters. They delight in knowing that hairs inside the ears can stand at attention when people are startled. They make the connection with all the physiological signs related to what is going on with themselves. Older children can be given assignments, such as finding out why people get dry mouths when they are frightened or discovering the origin and meaning of having "cold feet."

The possibilities around body work are limited only by the imagination. A child can demonstrate with her body how an infant shows anger, how an action-movie hero would show loneliness, or how a little old lady shows love.

Stories and drama allow children to practice the feelings of young animals and astronauts and everything in between. Art projects provide a means for them to start showing their own feelings in a concrete way. Sandtray work and puppets help them relate important events in their lives, with the child giving specific directions about how the characters feel and express emotions.

A school counselor, Mike Phimister, teaches Slo-Mo to aggressive young students. They learn to express their emotions in exaggerated slow motion, to call out their insulting words and make gestures over seconds, even minutes. What they learn is how to control their aggressive behaviors.

Chapters 16, Dynamic Play Therapy, and 18, Playback Theatre in this book illustrate creative ways to help children begin to tolerate expressions of emotion. In safe and respectful ways, without the need for the child's testimony, children have their unspeakable acts acknowledged, witnessed, and honored by their parents and community. This shows them the way and extends the invitation for them to respect and honor their survival.

Verbalizing feelings can restore personal power and control; it helps children learn to identify the "thought" part of the feeling and its personal meaning for them. Ten-year-old Lydia said that the thought part of tender feelings was that she was very little and could be badly hurt. Calvin, age three, told his mom that his "idea" is that he is bad when he is mad.

Children readily learn to employ self-soothing "power" techniques when we characterize the techniques as being used by whoever might be heroic to the child—firefighters, Olympic champions, or teenagers. They readily learn imaging, meditation, breathing techniques, self-statements, and more. Biofeedback devices for children are very popular, especially those which hook up to a monitor. A therapist recently told me about two brothers who use tandem biofeedback with monitors. They practice competitive relaxation—the one who can relax the best is the winner.

Learning to tolerate and modulate feelings assists children in exploring past experiences in therapy and helps them cope more effectively with current life events. They learn to exercise feelings as bodybuilders learn to exercise muscles: They keep at it, look at themselves to see what they have accomplished, and either work on new muscle groups or fine-tune what they have developed. Then the children are prepared to examine traumatic painful experiences, in manageable segments, so they are not retraumatized.

Relationship Building

While relationship building is continuous throughout therapy, two specific treatment areas need to be addressed during the relationship-building process: exploring unresolved trauma issues and saying goodbye to lost relationships. These two treatment issues cannot be addressed unless and until there has been sufficient consolidation in relationship building to provide adequate support for the child.

It is essential, even with the support in place, that therapist and caregivers be prepared for the attachment crisis that commonly occurs during this time. Youngsters often respond to the intensity and stress of this work with regressive behaviors or other hard-to-live-with behaviors. Relationship building may appear to have been a waste of time to everyone as the child seems to take a backward leap and may turn away from caregivers. Caregivers need advance warning, then support and help, to understand that all is not lost and that these behaviors will not last forever.

Intimacy and closeness in relationships generate feelings of vulnerability and loss of control that can restimulate feelings of helplessness and fear related to the child's past trauma. Acceptance of a new relationship is developed in carefully paced steps that are non-threatening. Ideally the youngster comes to acknowledge that he wants the relationship to happen and is not being forced into it.

Myriad small acts of protection and kindness are needed to erode a child's negative stereotype of adult caregiving from previous traumatic experiences. The family and therapist can promote relationship building by sharing positive and negative intimate experiences with the child—experiences of mind, such as going to a science museum, discussing some intriguing phenomenon, and then building a project together; emotional experiences, such as seeing a heartfelt movie together or sharing pet care intimacy; and spiritual experiences, shared under the stars, in nature, in the church.

Relationship building will usually begin between the child and therapeutic parents, be they birth, adoptive, extended family, group home staff, or hospital staff. If a child is functioning adequately within a temporary home environment, the therapist may be the person with whom the child needs to form an attachment that can function as a stabilizing force until he is placed in a long-term living situation.

Relationship building can involve the child and his future therapeutic parents, as when the child is returning to his parents' home after a long separation due to foster placement or custodial changes made by the court, for instance, or when placement in a specific adoptive home is planned. The Jasper Mountain Center describes its Adoption Courtship Model for children with attachment disturbances in Chapter 20.

Family Identity

Children with attachment and trauma problems need help in connecting to families, be they original families in which big changes have occurred and everyone is awkward or families in which rehabilitation is needed because the relationships were horrible. Perhaps the child is joining a new family, in which case we want to open up and restructure the system so the child is an integral part of it, not an add-on that may or may not stick.

Families benefit from and enjoy sorting out "who we are" as a group. Structured family work using such activities as play, detective work, and dramatic reenactment of family stories can help develop an awareness of family history, values, and culture—a family identity.

Part of the family work is to sort out how things are done in the family. For example, what are the rules about privacy and personal boundaries? How does the family deal with feelings like sadness or anger? How and when do family members work and play? What is the family's spiritual source, if any? How is discipline maintained? When and how do family members touch? How different can a person be and still fit into the family? This work can culminate in an "Our Family" album or video composed of pictures, stories, drawings, and research documents.

The family identification process provides an opportunity to see where maintenance or change may be needed. The family and therapist work together to determine which issues will be handled within the family; which ones should involve others, such as extended family members or a spiritual adviser; and which ones should be addressed in therapy.

Claiming

Claiming is what new parents do when they sniff their babies, taste them (yes, they do), count their toes, look at their entire naked bodies, and rub up against them. With older children who have not been claimed or who have been disposed of, theoretically it might be a fine idea for the new or rehabilitated family to do all that nice primitive connecting, demonstrating unequivocally "You are mine!" But such behavior would probably upset or frighten a newcomer to the family; the family would be unlikely to have such urges right away and would probably also be upset and frightened by the suggestion. Moreover, such behavior would create turmoil for the authorities charged with placing the child. Claiming is a necessary part of attachment, but we must approach the healing of wounded bonds with less gusto and more delicacy.

Families that engage in claiming behaviors help a child enter or reconnect with the family, whether the child is brand-new, eight years old, or an adolescent. Claiming can begin immediately on entry into the family or at some later point. Constant but subtle verbal references tying the child to the family enhance the child's feelings of belonging. For example, the child and parents might take a new family picture and together place it in a position of honor in the home or display the child's artwork in the home. Or they might select the child's special place at the table, go on a family shopping trip to purchase a special gift for the youngster's room, or prepare a formal welcoming meal with song and testimony. Ritual and ceremonial activities can also help to reinforce acceptance and belonging.

The therapist can in turn support this process of enhancing family cohesion and belonging by reenacting claiming behaviors during clinical sessions. Doll play is very effective; children who have been abused often reenact horrible scenes with dolls, providing an opportunity for the therapist to later make appropriate comments and show how the doll is precious and needs care. Creating stories and acting them out in the sandtray, with puppets, or by dramatic reenactment produce similar opportunities. The therapist may also want to include stories about searching for and finding lost or new families who may look different and not be what is expected. A charming story effectively used in therapy is about an abandoned tiger cub who searches for a mother; after several adventures with other types of animals, the tiger cub realizes what mothering really is and eventually decides that a bird could mother him.

Touching

Skin touching is a human need; it is a requirement for healthy development and helps relationships grow. Attachment- and trauma-related problems often involve past negative experiences with touching, and children who have these problems must learn through experiencing it that intimate touching can be a safe and pleasurable means of communication as well as intrinsically rewarding. New parents of any age child may feel awkward about touching and need encouragement and guidance to initiate intimate touching behaviors.

Professionals may need similar education and guidance. Nurses in an intensive care nursery were disturbed when a foster mother insisted on taking the infant she would be caring for to the "Kangarooing" room where moms sit and rock their infants, skin to skin, when the little ones must stay in the hospital. The nurses promoted this interaction between birth and adoptive mothers but lost sight of the infant-caregiver needs and considered the foster mom's action an unnatural act.

Children with histories of hurtful or inappropriate body contact are especially in need of positive intimate physical touch. The settings and structures for touching these children need to have clarity and be such that the child is not confused. Young teens are particularly awkward about being touched, although touch and the positive validation of their body that touch provides are deeply felt needs for most. It is a bit of a challenge to find ways to comfortably touch and snuggle with these youngsters.

Family touching behaviors can be developed and become routines. They can be explained to the child, involve several family members, occur at times and places that are not likely to raise the child's anxiety, and include grooming behaviors, such as shampooing, cutting, and styling hair or trimming and painting toenails; foot, shoulder, or sports massage; rocking-chair times; or physical games.

New parents and parents who have been estranged from their children sometimes feel hurt by a child's startle response to or withdrawal from touching, and they withdraw in turn. A therapy homework exercise that helps parents and older children overcome initial awkwardness is a prescribed ten minutes of physical touching twice a day for a few weeks. The family decides on the activity, which can be something like snuggling with the parent while watching television, the daughter putting makeup on Mom, or the parent giving the child a foot massage. The youngsters will initially fuss and complain that the therapist is "making us do this ridiculous exercise," but they invariably report, with relief and pleasure, that spontaneous touching has become a part of their relationship.

Nesting

Nesting behaviors are those cozy times when families bunch together and experience physical intimacy. Therapists can support and encourage nesting behavior in the family and can bring it into the therapy session with play, drawings, stories of the events, and discussions about the experience. Storytelling in the parent's bed and sharing a tent while camping provide excellent nesting sites. One adoptive mom who disliked outdoor experiences arranged monthly out-of-town trips during which the family bunched together in a hotel room.

Cohesive Shared Experience

Shared intense emotional experiences—singing together at home or in a choir; attending religious services; playing music together; attending sporting events; playing games; looking at the stars; creating food, art, or building projects together; helping people less fortunate—build important family memories while emphasizing the cohesiveness of the family.

Mastering Behavior

Children's persistent negative behavioral patterns, whether clingy or rebellious, compliant or frightening, intentional or unintentional, interfere with forming and maintaining positive intimate relationships. Almost always, behavioral issues related to attachment problems exist for child and caregivers. The child usually begins, and the other responds, in ways that reinforce the problem, thus creating a negative cycle. Changing these negative behavior patterns requires a ready, willing, patient, and able caregiver who uses appropriate interventions and understands the psychological meaning and function of the child's noxious behavior.

Behavior change begins by abandoning the search for the magic key that will unlock the door to immediate success. Disruptive behavior changes over time with understanding, motivation, learning, and practice. If the child's behavior is dangerous or frightening, preventive measures, such as supervision and environmental control, must be imposed while the child's behavior is in the process of change.

Understanding the Meaning and Function of Behavior

Recognizing attachment- and trauma-related behaviors such as those described in Chapter 1 helps caregivers and children with troublesome affect. Flashbacks, hypervigilence, withdrawal, rage, and intimacy avoidance in children are some of the behaviors often interpreted by some caregivers and therapists as simply disturbing or bad, and their underlying conflicts and fears are not understood.

Caregivers and therapists might not recognize negative adaptive behaviors the child employs to survive and to avoid pain. Negative, unexplainable, or strange behaviors are many times driven by direct and immediate fear or are automatic responses to situations the child associates with fear and prior trauma. The underlying fears and their survival value to the child, however, may not easily be identified, because of the following:

- The behavior does not appear to avoid pain or danger, since it is itself dangerous or distances the child from a caregiver who could provide protection and comfort.
- It is not obvious that the situation might engender fear in the child.
- The behavior seems manipulative and volitional.
- The child is unable to give reasons for his behavior. It is long past the time of the trauma, and the child usually behaves as if all is well.
- Parents and therapists block or minimize awareness of the child's fear in order to protect themselves emotionally. It is painful to witness how deeply fearful, terrorized, and damaged these children really are.

The persistent fear state described in Chapter 1 and the alarm/numbing response pattern described in Chapter 2 suggest that some of these behaviors become automatic, are biologically based, and serve to protect the child from what is or once was perceived as danger. The clinical implication is that we cannot limit our attention to only eliminating the objectionable behavior; we must also help the youngster feel safe and learn affect modulation. Self-calming techniques, such as meditation, focused breathing, and biofeedback, can be used. Psychopharmacological treatment may sometimes be needed. Some of the antidepressants targeting the serotonin system have been found to be helpful.

We must be careful to look for current issues, not only past experiences, as causes of behavior. A youngster may displace rage felt toward a parent onto siblings, for example.

Staying in Charge

Caregivers must learn the fine art of staying in control and not allowing themselves to be manipulated or controlled by the children in their care. These youngsters commonly employ manipulative, controlling behavior because control helps them to feel safe and serves to avoid intimacy. At first glance this may appear paradoxical: If controlling behavior provides a feeling of safety and the child must feel safe before real work can begin, why change the situation? The answer: because the child's perception of safety does not convey actual safety but in fact often provokes those around the child to be abusive. The child's behavior is also maddening to live with and distances the child from the attachment that provides real safety.

Some behaviors do not at first appear to be controlling, as when a child is clingy and demanding of adult attention. Living with such a child, however, should convince almost anyone that clinginess and demanding behavior are not at all an act of intimacy. It is dynamically somewhat like a boxer's clinch: It holds you up and keeps you so close that the other person can't hit you.

Weaning a child from controlling behavior is arduous and exhausting. The parent must give the child considerable reassurance and opportunities to make some choices. This imparts a sense of control and empowerment to the child but does so within a safe structure that is controlled by the important adults in the child's life. Structure, constant feedback, repeatedly telling the child what is expected of her—these reassure her that control is being maintained and that intense feelings will not get out of hand. The caregiver must firmly claim and hold the role of powerful, loving, in-control parent. Failure to do so reinforces the child's controlling behavior and does not allay fears. Exhaustion, pity for the child, and losing sight of the goal to foster positive attachment are common reasons why many parents are unable to consistently stay in charge.

Parents can set limits in ways that teach children self-caring and self-empathy. Limits can be frightening to the child because they represent loss of control/safety. The issue is to let the child know the adult can be trusted to protect her. The mother can say, for example, that she will put the child's skates away for three days because she loves the child and wants to be sure that she is safe. The child learns to love and care for herself, in part, by following safety rules, knowing Mom will continue to provide supervision and control until the child is more self-protective.

Parents frequently need help and support to maintain firm control, anticipate and block manipulative behavior, avoid power struggles, and implement solid behavior management. *Tough, tender*, and *patient* are key words for caregivers. Therapeutic behavior management is an ongoing process of learning, practicing, celebrating all the small gains.

Not surprisingly, caregivers need to be able to ventilate their frustrations and concerns. They deserve and need enormous support. Sometimes they have to have custom-designed, specific suggestions. Child behavior management books and typical parenting classes are not adequate to meet the needs of these parents but can be useful when combined with regular consultation with the therapist. A support group of other parents who have dealt with similar issues can also be valuable.

Adult Behavior

Parents are biologically programmed to protect their young and, when unable to do so, become frustrated and agitated and feel like failures. Intense primitive emotion such as displayed by children can be contagious, especially with long exposure, and when it is negative, we just want it to stop. Adults' own childhood pain and fears may be restimulated when caring for children, causing them to feel overwhelmed, helpless, and perhaps numb.

Caregivers who parented a child during a period of trauma or who themselves were traumatized by the same situation may experience restimulation of the traumatic event when they relate to the child and witness the youngster's pain and distress. Such caregivers may need to believe the child was unaffected and interpret the youngster's disturbed behaviors as unrelated to the trauma, in order to avoid their own restimulation. A restimulated parent usually feels helpless and fearful, and perhaps guilty for not having protected the child. The parent's feelings are so overwhelming that he or she is unable to take care of the child. This situation is especially difficult when the parent has in fact contributed either directly or indirectly, through negligence, to the child's trauma. This reaction can lead to avoidance, making it extremely difficult to be intimate with the child or to maintain firm parental controls. This parental behavior can inadvertently give the message that the child is not to express feelings related to the awful, horrible things that happened.

Foster and adoptive parents must learn to deal with the child's displays of hostility, resentment, and ingratitude when they have offered only love. These parents need to brace themselves for awareness of extreme cruelty and ignorance related to the child's situation, awareness that can easily become overwhelming. These caregivers need massive amounts of hope, reasonable expectations, deep reserves of patience, and abundant support from others.

Birth parents trying to pick up the pieces of their relationship with their child—such as when a child has been in out-of-home care for a considerable time—may, like the child, be enormously needy but unable to ask for help or to use what is provided. A parent may feel ashamed because her child has suffered so much or may become jealous of the youngster's positive relationship with the therapist and other adults. These parents can become so vulnerable that they protect themselves with rage and uncooperative behavior. Clinicians and substitute caregivers must be able to consider that the parent's rage can be healthy and appropriate.

Foster and adoptive parents and other caregivers can be bombarded by feelings of resentment, anger, betrayal, and hurt when the child sucks up the caregiver's energy, disrupts the whole family, and repays sensitive caregiving by flaunting idealized perceptions of absent birth parents and projecting hostility onto the caregiver. Love, at this juncture, may feel like an unnatural act.

Therapists, too, experience all of the above.

Belonging

Many children shun the parenting and sense of belonging they need because accepting them is experienced as disloyalty to an absent parent. These youngsters feel it is unacceptable to have a positive experience while being cared for by another; they believe allowing pleasurable caregiving ensures that they will lose the absent parent and will not be loved by him or her—or, if the missing parent was unable to care for them, are convinced no one else could do so. These deeply rooted beliefs represent survival to the child, and changing them is a complex task that will take considerable time and effort.

The therapist may be able to gain the cooperation of the absent parent by explaining the situation and having the parent formally, in therapy sessions with the child, give the child permission to love and be cared for by other adults. Carson's story of Michael in Chapter 9 gives a poignant example of this process. The child needs assurance that she will still be loved by the absent parent whether or not she cares for her placement caregivers, and that her behavior with the caregiver will not affect the outcome of her placement. Support from the absent parent may be by letter, videotape, or phone call received in the therapist's office, where it can be processed with the child.

The active caregiver must create an environment in which the child is not only free to love the absent parent but is also encouraged not to abandon her feelings even when she screams vicious and defamatory statements about the absent parent. It is a mistake to assume the child does not have loving feelings for the absent parent, and the caregiver falls into a trap by supporting the negative expressions of the child as if they were all she feels. The child may be voicing what she considers to be socially or morally acceptable views of an abusive parent while secretly longing for contact; she may be expressing rage over being abandoned; or she may be expressing only one aspect of a complex assortment of feelings. She may indeed feel only hatred, but we cannot assume that is so and must leave room for the child to express different feelings as they emerge over time.

Children with attachment disturbances resist feelings of belonging and being cared for because the feelings and the care can generate anxiety, depression, and feelings of loss and uncertainty, especially when the birth parents were unable to protect them from danger or when the children are placed with unknown parenting figures. Children will move slowly, in fits and starts, and vary in the arenas in which they allow themselves to relax, be parented, and eventually belong in a family.

The therapist and new caregiver can facilitate the process by a thousand micro-acts that demonstrate the caregiver can be trusted. A parent might notice, for example, that a youngster is hesitant when a cat approaches. She says, "I see you don't like that cat being here. I'm going to put him outside. I want you to feel safe, and I am here to protect you every way I can." Or, with a teenager, "It looks to me like you're just a little nervous about playing in the game Friday night. I'd like to support you because you're a fine kid and a good athlete. How about us going down to where the game will be? I've heard about some things professional athletes do before a game that help get rid of the jitters." We need to demonstrate over and over again that parenting can be strengthening even if dependence happens.

The youngsters not only need to experience safety; they must believe they are worthy of care, and, finally, they must understand why someone wants to parent them. They "get it" that there is pleasure inherent in caring for others when they themselves experience pleasure in giving to others. Opportunities abound for such experiences—participating in a supervised family or church project to help others, helping build housing for the homeless, making clothing for needy children, creating a community garden for the elderly.

The child's progressive acceptance of belonging can be easily monitored by using the Parenting the Attachment-Disturbed Child chart shown in the figure on page 84. This chart lists the critical dimen-

Parenting the Attachment-Disturbed Child

Parent Provides	*Child's Response*			
	Allowing	Accepting	Seeking	Owning
Basic food, shelter				
Protection				
Support				
Limits				
Guidance				
Affection				

sions of parenting on one axis and the youngster's response, which progresses from allowing to accepting to seeking and finally to owning, on the other. The chart also serves to remind us that there are steps and gradations between belonging and not belonging.

Parents must endlessly repeat, by words and deeds, "I won't hurt you. You are safe. You are worthy and deserving. I like to do this. I am available." This type of parenting is difficult to sustain in any situation, even more so when the child gives no evidence of belonging even though it may be happening. Then one day, when the parent least expects it, there is a small breakthrough. But it comes only after the parent has been tested and tested and tested. It helps to remind parents that regular kids do the same thing, but with less drama and less damage to psyche and property. It takes a lot for these youngsters to really believe all they are experiencing and learning.

Exploring Trauma

Sometime during the relationship-building process, the child will feel secure and connected in the relationship to the point where he is able to cope with exploring traumatizing events.

Forcing children to face their terrors is dangerous, antithetical to all we know about trauma, and cruel. Children must not be pushed to deal with their fears, but trauma and attachment disturbances are too close to the bone, too frightening, for children to bring up by themselves. Even big tough combat veterans have trouble initiating discussions about past pain. In the interest of not pushing and not waiting forever, we do the following: create safety and acceptance in the clinical setting, have play materials that draw the child into creative interactions, and, if a particular child indicates readiness through relationship and confidence, gently invite the child to explore. And the child may not be ready and we still do the work. We cannot lose sight of the primary goals: secure relationship and empowerment, not finding out everything and processing it.

Debriefing children who have experienced single-incident trauma, such as a catastrophic accident or a disaster, will be approached quite differently. Research and clinical experience related to single incident trauma has led to the development of expertise (Hamada, 1993; Pynoos & Eth, 1986; Pynoos & NADER, 1988; Vernberg & Vogel, 1993). This is an area of expertise that cannot adequately be addressed here.

Children and their caregivers need to understand the reasons for the child to tell his story and go through the gory details: to gain power, to accept what really happened without maximizing or minimizing the experience, to have the child's experiences witnessed and legitimized, and to be able to put it away in memory.

Exploration of traumatizing events must be tightly structured and controlled by the therapist and paced so that the child does not become overwhelmed and reexperience his helplessness and fears. One way to do this is to structure ten-minute midtherapy sessions to "do our work," with time before and after focused on nondirective activities. The child learns that affect can be regulated through structuring.

Caregivers need guidance and support from the clinician so they can understand the child and be prepared to deal with the distressing behaviors that can emerge as the youngster acknowledges her pain. We might see regressive behaviors, nightmares, difficulty concentrating in school, or frightening behaviors.

Regressive behaviors will not last forever, and children readily give them up when they are no longer needed. Some parents become very concerned that supporting regressive behaviors is highly reinforcing and not in the best interests of the child. This is a sensitive area, and careful discussions with the parents is in order because half-hearted participation on their part will sabotage the work and create troubles in the clinical relationship. We need to normalize regressive behaviors for the parents. That is, we remind them we all regress when under significant stress. Adults regress after divorce, following car accidents, during income tax preparation; we whine, don't take good care of ourselves, get clingy. We usually don't pee in the bed and suck our thumbs and such, but the process is normal and we need to trust that children have an inner drive to thrive and mature. When they are "filled up" emotionally, they will get back on track. See Carson's work with the foster mother and her child related to severe regressive behaviors (Chapter 9). The parents may not believe you completely, but be willing to give the work an honest effort.

It is helpful, and helps the parents, to limit and structure regressive behaviors. You can tell the child, for example, that it's fine to want to be a little kid for a while. Then you can suggest that the parents, each evening after dinner, wrap the child in a blanket for a half-hour and rock and sing to her or read her a story. And if the child needs to be a little kid at other times, she just needs to ask.

We can aid children in their trauma exploration by creating play scenes that invite them to show their experience through metaphor—stories told through sandtray work, art, drama, body movement, or music. See, for example, Gil's vignette in Chapter 11, in which a very young child portrays her experience of severe neglect through sandtray metaphor.

Many children are able to take the next step of shifting out of metaphor to explore directly what happened through drawing, sandtray, and discussion. Anchoring, legitimizing the child's experience, and accepting reality come from the therapist and others, witnessing and honoring the child's portrayed experience. The child can be directed to describe exactly what the experience was like (sights, smells, tastes, sounds, thoughts, wishes, prayers, body sensations, and reactions) before, during, and after the traumatizing experience. Special focus should be given to how relationships in the family were upset and changed.

Some youngsters who feel supported by the therapist will spontaneously create a heroic, perhaps vengeful ending to the trauma in play. This act allows the child to cope and to feel a bit more powerful. But other children need help. We do not to just leave them with telling their story. It is important to take it one step further to empower them. One technique is to ask them questions like these: How are you different now? How are you stronger? How will you be able to handle this difficult situation in the future? Where is your hero self? Another method is to invite the child to create an ending by saying, for instance, "Let's think up something magical that could make things different at the end." These new endings should simply be witnessed without comment. An adult who describes what really happened or who points out that the child was "just little and helpless and couldn't have really done anything" is not helpful and interferes with a natural healing process. Integrating techniques of dramatic play, art, and body movement help the child acknowledge her history rather than distort or disown it.

Terr (1981) teaches clinicians to be alert for secret hidden behaviors that may last for years. We know that children may have dissociative experiences, demonstrate sexualized and/or violent behavior, or engage in hurting or humiliating behaviors to self and others. These are not usually disclosed until well into the treatment process, if at all. The clinician must therefore be alert to these behaviors and periodically issue an invitation for the child to make disclosures.

This is a time to again present the child's-level review of trauma and attachment concepts, with explanations of how and why people think, feel, and behave as they do during and after trauma. This normalizes the trauma experience and the reactions children have to overwhelming horrible events and is a natural time for the therapist to bring up the topic of secret things children sometimes do after traumatizing life experiences and invite the child to reveal his hidden behavior. The child may not want to reveal at that point but will be reassured by knowing that he is not alone and that when he is ready, the therapist will be understanding and able to help. These children often ask the therapist to talk more about "those other kids."

The child who has integrated his experience sometimes "forgets" or pretends the trauma did not occur. The therapist needs to gently tell the child, and clearly tell the parent, that part of childhood is magic and pretending, fantasy and wishes—that children need their energy to grow and that it is sometimes less of a burden to pretend that something awful did not happen. The child will generally acknowledge that his statement was a wish. The therapist can say that she too wishes it had not happened and that it is fine to pretend, play, and wish—that's what kids are supposed to do.

The trauma mastery piece is difficult, delicate work and intertwines with mourning losses, discussed next, which also requires that a clinician have a good supply of emotional resiliency and be both tough and tender. Ideally the child, family, and therapist would delay working with this material for a while so everyone has time to regroup after the trauma work.

During the interim, therapy would focus on the other continuing areas, such as identity and affect tolerance.

Mourning Losses

Children need to mourn their losses, and they need adult help to do so. They are not able to let go of a wounded bond, no matter how dysfunctional, unless they have something with which to replace it, something to hang onto. But they cannot find something else to hang onto as long as their emotional focus and energy are on maintaining ties to the attachment. Asking these children to let go of this tie is like asking ship wreck victims in the middle of a storm-tossed ocean to let go of the piece of wood they are clinging desperately to. They see we have a rope, but are compelled to hang onto what they have. Often what we may see is that these disturbed children pretend they have let go of their attachment yearnings and may even go through the motions of disavowing their parents. These children are survivors and have learned what caregivers want them to say and do. Their behavior, however, sometimes tells us they are still hoping all will work out with their lost family. We may learn of their reunion fantasies.

Children can say goodbye to a primary attachment after they have formed at least a limited connection with other significant adults and believe they will receive adequate, consistent care. The present caregiver, usually a foster or adoptive parent, will be significantly burdened by the child's raw pain, inconsolable grief, and disorganized behavior as the child lets go. It will sometimes appear that relationship gains have disappeared and will not be regained, but the caregiver must understand and trust that the child would not be able to grieve so unless the core of a relationship existed.

Clinical experience shows that the steps necessary for acceptance of the loss of a relationship are to protest the loss, internalize the person who is lost, say goodbye and commemorate the event, grieve, and create meaning with a ritual closing ceremony. See the contributions by Carson (Chapter 9) and Archibeque and Bauer (Chapter 11), who discuss saying a formal goodbye to birth parents.

The therapist's role is to be steady as a rock for all to lean on. The therapist will need to schedule extra clinical time to support and guide the therapeutic parents and, for the child, create an environment for protest behavior and invite it if the child appears emotionally immobilized. The therapist may arrange for a series of goodbye meetings with the departing parents. The work for the child during this time with the leaving parent is to remember and internalize family stories and events. "Grief work is remembering, not forgetting; it is a process of internalizing, not extruding. Attachment, if properly treated, provides us strength forever" (Valliant, 1985). It can be very helpful for the child and the family to have a ceremonial goodbye at their last meeting. Grieving happens in waves of overwhelming pain, interspersed with periods of respite. Caregivers cannot hurry it up or cut it off, lest the mourning process go underground, still ever present but unseen.

Consolidation

The consolidation phase is a period of time in which the child, family, and therapist can review the gains made in treatment and celebrate the growth of the family relationship. This can be a time for the family to explore issues that may emerge for themselves and for the child in the future.

They can use psychodrama, family sculpting, or discussion to put forth problems that might appear when the child becomes a teenager or when the parents become grandparents, and then practice problem solving as a family. Exercises such as these are fun, convey a sense of the future together, and underscore and consolidate the skills learned during the therapeutic process.

The intensive work related to attachment is usually best accomplished using a developmentally sequenced model (James, 1989). This approach is based on maintaining an ongoing consultation relationship with the family after a course of therapy is completed.

The therapist is able to provide guidance when new issues arise or when those once resolved in treatment reemerge at later stages of the child's development. Different issues and insights related to past attachment trauma arise at different times, and the family may need guidance or assistance in therapy. This model empowers the family and leaves the door open for further therapy that may involve a few problem-solving sessions or a short course of therapy for one or more family members.

When the first phase of the therapy has come to a close, a graduation celebration—planned by the family and entailing food, music, small gifts, pictures, extended family members, and commemorative speeches—honors everyone for work well done.

Treatment Failures

Sometimes attachment does not happen. We do not want to acknowledge treatment failure, but it occurs, is painful, and is demoralizing. As clinicians committed to healing, we work hard and sometimes it still does not work! We beat ourselves up emotionally after having done the best we could. We remember the times we were not at our best, when we did not care but instead were happy and relieved that an appointment was canceled. We blame treatment failure on a time when we ignored or mistreated the child or reflected back the hate the child directed toward us.

Some of the children with whom we work are so damaged that they are not ready or able to form a relationship. They take and take and take, and nothing seems to change. This does not mean that these children will be unable to make changes at a later time or that they cannot live meaningful lives and contribute to society. It helps to remind ourselves that there are people who make positive connections with their work, or with a group, and seem to get along without intimate relationships. Perhaps in our clinical work we have planted seeds that will blossom. Perhaps not.

Summary

Treating attachment problems in families is both simple and complex. The simple part is establishing goals; the complex part is reaching them. We know, for instance, that a major goal is to establish trust so that love between child and parent can grow. The child, the caregiver, or both must often overcome deeply held beliefs and alter automatic survival behaviors that prohibit what they most need and desire—a trusting, loving parent-child relationship.

This is not traditional child or traditional family therapy. Attachment work attends to three entities: the attachment relationship, the child, and the parents, of which there may be many. We need to combine child and family work in a milieu that (1) provides ongoing support and guidance to build a sense of identity and family relationship, (2) deals with traumatic life experiences that have led to dysfunctional behavior and an impaired ability to trust others, (3) provides safety and guidance for grieving lost relationships, and (4) establishes a protective environment in which to create and maintain new relationships. The milieu may be a combination of outpatient therapy with therapeutic parenting in the home and school, or it may be a residential or institutional treatment program that provides a strong transitional bridge between the residential setting and the child's home.

8

A Brief Treatise on Coercive Holding

Immobilizing, Tickling, Prodding, Poking, and Intimidating Children into Submission

Of all tyrannies, a tyranny exercised for the good of its victims may be the most oppressive. Those who torment us for our own good will torment us without end, for they do so with the approval of their own conscience.
Lewis, 1952

Children and caregivers who deal with serious attachment problems are desperate for professional help and are often vulnerable to quick-fix solutions. Fear and desperation can lead parents as well as trained clinicians to try radical techniques that have no place in child therapy. Several approaches have been developed that practioners claim are the only way to cure attachment disordered children. Their methods include:

- prolonged restraint other than for the protection of the child;
- prolonged noxious stimulation; and
- interference with body functions, such as vision and breathing.

These coercive interventions are variously called holding therapy, attachment therapy, and rage therapy, among other things. Some therapists employ these same names for noncoercive techniques and actually use other methods. It is thus prudent to talk about the actual techniques, and not the name given to the technique. I believe the phrase "coercive techniques" accurately describes the listed procedures.

Prolonged restraint as used by coercive therapists is unrelated to the child's immediate behavior. The intervention is arranged by appointment, usually continues for several hours, and often is repeated daily for weeks. The child is held immobile by one to six adults who may include the parents. The clinician typically places his or her face, bearing a deliberately angry expression, within inches of the child's face. In a harsh, angry voice he or she repeatedly yells at the youngster, stimulating him to a high level of arousal. The youngster fights against the restraint and anger; he screams and cries; and he may experience uncontrollable urination. The child, still being restrained, might be momentarily soothed, rocked, given sips of water, and told he is "doing a good job" before the coercive holding resumes.

Some practitioners also advocate prolonged noxious stimulation while the child is restrained. This includes such actions as poking the child's ribs, continuously tapping the youngster's chest or the bottom of his feet, tickling, pulling toes, or continuously moving the child's head from side to side.

In addition, the child's eyes might be covered and his nose pinched for more control. The practitioner yells at him to breathe through his mouth, then covers his mouth and yells at him to breathe through his nose.

Practitioners of these techniques often claim they are treating "attachment disorders," explaining that the child's repressed rage interferes with formation of an attachment and that prolonged restraint, noxious stimulation, and interference with body functions release the rage and tell the youngster that adults can and will control him. When the child totally surrenders, he is placed in the arms of the parents, and the practitioners claim that the child instantly attaches to the parent, now free of rage.

Children subjected to coercive techniques often have histories of severe abuse, neglect, multiple out-of-home placements, and adoption. Practitioners of coercive therapy often tell desperate, frustrated, and frightened parents these methods are the only ones that will work to keep their child from becoming a serial murderer or sociopath.

I believe these coercive techniques are cruel, unethical, and potentially dangerous and must not be used unless and until they are shown to be safe. Heart rate and blood pressure are elevated during arousal. Incidents of cardiac arrest in children undergoing painful and frightening medical procedures are well documented. While it may be impossible to directly attribute the arrests to pain and fright, common sense advises against taking such a risk in the absence of compelling documentation of their safety and effectiveness.

We have already been shown that there are long-lasting, enduring neurological changes in children who experience prolonged stress and psychological trauma (Perry, 1993). It is also not unusual for children to dissociate when faced with inescapable frightening situations (Terr, 1981). We know that people with a history of abuse and traumatic losses are more sensitized to traumatic experiences and retraumatization when exposed to stimuli or physical coercion that is likely to remind them of the original abusive situation.

Coercive therapy is terroristic and abusive as well as dangerous. Literature confirms that similar techniques are used in brainwashing: The subject is degraded, belittled, may be physically abused, is told it is for his benefit, and is thus coerced to consent. Hacker (1976), an acknowledged expert in terrorism, writes, "Coercion, having obscured its brutal origins, is then at its most triumphant when the victims are compelled to experience submission as a voluntary decision. This is rape of the mind (p. 94)."

We would not be permitted to use these methods on prisoners of war or convicted felons, but we permit it for our children—children who have no voice.

Coercive techniques are antithetical to all we know about helping survivors of trauma. Trauma treatment is intended to empower survivors—not to frighten them, have them give up control, and make them assume a submissive posture. Coercive techniques foster the development of trauma bonds based in terror; they do not facilitate healthy attachment.

We have an ethical obligation to take a strong, well-voiced position against coercive techniques. We are responsible for the wellbeing of our children. These techniques have no place in our clinical armamentarium for treating wounded children.

9

Comprehensive Case Descriptions

If I'm so good, why don't they love me?
Seven-year-old to therapist

The first of the following case descriptions depicts work with a very young child whose severe disturbance was based in an attachment disruption. The work included individual child therapy, coordinated with family guidance and support. Carson describes the child's gradual ability to form a relationship with her and gain enough trust in his relationship with his adoptive parents to be able to build a sense of self and eventually say goodbye to his birth mother and grieve the loss of that connection. This allowed the child to accept the realities of his severe early abuse. His parents, school, and therapist created a protecting environment that enabled the little boy to feel safe enough to allow himself to belong to a family.

The second case describes a team approach in a hospital setting. The clinical team coordinated the use of several creative modalities to facilitate transformation and healing in a boy who experienced severe disruption in his attachment capabilities. Eight months of intensive treatment in the hospital included sound, dance, movement, art, and adventure therapies to foster emotional strength and establishment of boundaries, enabling the youngster to feel less threatened and to eventually face his abuse history. The support and guidance of the treatment team helped the child to reconnect with other people and with life.

The Story of Michael*

This vignette illustrates the treatment of trauma-related attachment problems, cases that are common within the child welfare system. It is crucial to concurrently treat both the issues related to abuse and the issues related to attachment. Treating one and not the other does not provide the child and family with the significant tools they need to understand and claim each other.

The attachment disorder in this vignette manifested as reckless and danger-seeking behaviors in a very young child. Such behaviors are often signs of a resistance and avoidance to attachment. The disorder was directly related to the trauma inflicted on the child during the first two years of his life: He was physically and sexually abused by one parent and not protected by the other.

This little boy's first experience of adult protection came after placement with a foster family. He rejected the mother's overtures of caring and love because they were unfamiliar and frightening. He expected to be hurt by caregivers, so he kept his distance and sought danger himself—a defensive strategy to cope with a world of overwhelming terror.

The treatment key was development of an attachment relationship between the child and his new family. The parents needed support and instruction for managing the child's behavior—he needed to feel more managed, and they needed to feel they could manage him successfully. Only then could his attachment behaviors and signals begin to change.

The child had to grieve the loss of the birth parents before the new attachment could begin to solidify. As the attachment relationship deepened, the trauma work could begin. When the youngster began to experience safety, and could rely on it, he could begin to give voice—literally and symbolically—to his terror and could disclose the horror of his abusive past.

Teamwork between the family and the therapist was crucial. The parents needed and deserved as much support as the child. They lived with the child and the difficult behaviors for twenty-four hours a day—no easy task.

Michael, not quite three years old, bolted into my office for his

---

*Contributed by Marylou Carson, Napa, California.

first visit. He showed no curiosity or fear about me and didn't seem to notice when I asked his foster mother to wait outside. He rushed around the room, grabbing at toys and throwing them on the floor. His exploration was totally random and without any apparent pleasure. It was accompanied by a high-pitched wail that could have turned into a sob at any moment but never did.

During the first three sessions, I never saw Michael's eyes. In fact, it took my total attention to see anything more than his jet black hair flying about as he roamed the room, picking up toys and hurling them all over. He literally walked over me several times as I sat cross-legged on the floor.

Michael's foster parents brought him to see me after he had been in their home only a few months. They were worried about his behaviors and responses. Michael had an intense fear of the dark. He screamed hysterically if anything was put over his head; he could not tolerate being in a room alone if the door was closed; and he had a sleep disturbance that included night terrors. He had serious temper tantrums several times each day.

Discipline and consequences had virtually no impact on Michael. He appeared not to care when he was "in trouble." He preferred candy or objects to being held. He was hard to comfort and would pull away, arch his back, kick, scream, and scratch when his foster mother would try to hold him. Michael threw himself on the floor and banged his head when he was angry. He would hide from his foster parents and place himself in dangerous situations, such as running away from the foster parents into the middle of a busy street. At times Michael seemed spacey, withdrawn, and out of contact.

Michael's play themes in therapy were full of violence and destruction. Using the sandtray, he buried people figures and vehicles and never brought them back. He created terrible accident scenes and wrecks of catastrophic proportions. He took baby figures and hurled them down, to be devoured by monsters. His play disrupted often, and he would churn his hands in a circle as if he were mixing all of his internal turmoil together. One day he took a black marking pen and pounded it, screaming, "Michael's dead! Michael's dead!"

All this trouble in such a small boy! What had caused this? What had Michael experienced that caused him to be so frightened and so disturbed? We knew some of his early history, but we had to wait for Michael to tell us and show us more.

For the first two years of his life, Michael lived with his birth mother. She was seventeen when he was born and had abused substances for many years, as had her birth parents, from whom she was removed early in life. The birth mother had been adopted and on her own since running away at age thirteen. When she discovered she was pregnant, she married a man who turned out to be a registered sex offender. He abused both the mother and Michael.

After the first few sessions, Michael's behavior began to shift and he no longer ignored me but instead started coming to me with toys. He demanded more and more nurturing during the therapy sessions. We developed a bath ritual in which he delighted. He would splash and splash in his pretend bathtub, telling me all the while that, when the bath was over, I could wrap him in a big towel to dry him. He used a baby bottle, which became an important item. He would carry it around or demand that I "take care of it" until he needed it.

As Michael began settling into therapy, his behavior at home worsened. He lost bowel and bladder control; he virtually stopped sleeping at night; and his tantrums increased. He began abusing the family animals. I met with the foster parents at least once a month, and we spoke often on the telephone. They were frustrated and worn-out. They wondered what they had gotten themselves into.

Michael had arrived at his foster home fully toilet-trained and weaned from the bottle. I suggested to the parents that they offer him diapers and the bottle again. I explained that I believed Michael needed to go back to an earlier stage and experience it with his new, safe family. I stressed that the return to diapers needed to be handled in a nonpunitive way. Michael needed to sense that he had some control over what would happen next. Michael's family agreed to the plan. He was delighted to have diapers, especially when he was told that he could decide when he didn't want them anymore. He used the bottle for comfort at bedtime and during the day. Michael needed the diapers only for a few weeks. He got up one morning and announced that he was "done" with the diapers and wanted his "big-boy pants" back. He continued to use the bottle for transitions and comfort.

Visitation with Michael's birth mother during these months was erratic. She would request visits, then sometimes appear and sometimes not. Michael responded intensely both to the contact and to the disappointment. We planned together that Michael would have a therapy appointment right after a proposed visit, whether or not his birth mother came. When he saw her, he seemed relieved. He would tell me that he worried she might be dead.

Michael's tantrums and dangerous behaviors occurred more with his foster mother than with his foster father. He had an easier time allowing his foster father to nurture and manage him. His foster mother often felt rejected and inadequate, and she questioned her own responses to Michael. At the same time, in therapy I could see Michael's attachment to both parents deepening. He would cling to his foster mother in the waiting room and have difficulty separating from her. He talked more about his "new" mom and dad and their life together.

The family and I often spoke of Michael's need for them to protect him and to explain to him what they were doing. Children like Michael who have not been protected don't understand the concept of protection. Their internal model of relationships works on the premise that people who love you do not protect you and in fact are likely to abuse you. After all, Michael's birth mother could not protect herself or her son. Michael needed the adults in his life to keep him safe before he could give up his reckless and dangerous behaviors. He had to be taught that he was worth protecting. It was a daunting task, as Michael seemed constantly to seek danger. And it was the cornerstone of the developing attachment relationship.

I had been working with Michael and his family for five months when the Juvenile Court terminated the parental rights of his birth mother. I spoke with the birth mother and her attorney and suggested that we have three visits within a two-week period to process the goodbye. I told the birth mother that if she missed any of the visits, they would be stopped because Michael could not tolerate the disappointment. I tried to comfort her and tell her that she had a gift to give to her son, that gift being her permission to go on with his life and his new family. I told her that he needed her permission to love and be loved by his new mom and dad.

Michael's birth mother came to just one visit. It was all she could tolerate. It took place on her twentieth birthday. Michael and his foster mother painted her a T-shirt as a birthday and goodbye present. The foster mother sent a series of pictures for the birth mother. Michael sat in my lap for much of the visit, which took place away from the playroom so that the therapy would not be contaminated. His birth mother was able to tell him that it was OK with her that he live with this family, call them Mom and Dad, and love them. Michael wondered where the birth mother would live now that he had his "home." In her own way, she tried to assure him that she would be all right. He gave her a quick hug and kiss; the visit was over. Michael was three years, three months old.

The goodbye visit set off a grief reaction for Michael that was intense, profound, and lengthy. He stopped sleeping again at night. He rejected offers of love and nurturance from his foster mother. His cruelty toward the family pets resurfaced. Michael had long periods of time when he would literally "space out" and was unable to respond to either of his foster parents when they talked to him. He wept inconsolably, sometimes for as long as an hour. He wondered and worried about his birth mother and whether she was alive and where she would live.

During therapy we focused on the goodbye. We often spoke of the last visit and exactly what had happened and what had been said. Michael drew goodbye pictures and hid toys and told me not to bring them back out. He brought one of his favorite puppets from home and insisted that it stay with the playroom puppets. We screamed "goodbye" out the playroom window. This seemed to give Michael the most relief, and he would sometimes arrive for therapy and walk to the window and stand there quietly until he was ready to ask me to open it.

This was an exhausting time for Michael's family. It seemed that he had lost the gains he had made. The foster mother found it almost impossible to manage him. She felt rejected and abused by him, frustrated that she could not ease his pain, and angry that so much of his pain was projected onto her. There were times when she told me she did not like Michael and wasn't at all sure she could go on. The marital relationship suffered as Michael's pain became the focus of the family. It felt to all of us at times as though this little boy's grief was too big to be handled. The family would ask me, "How long will this last?" I didn't know, but I did know that unless Michael had a chance to really say goodbye to his birth mother through grieving his loss, he would never be able to truly allow himself to attach to his foster family.

As Michael processed his grief, other memories began to surface. He told me about the abuse he sustained both at the hands of his mother and by her husband. He told me about being hit, being unable to breathe when hands covered his mouth and nose to stop him from crying, and how he was physically injured by sexual abuse. Michael looked terribly sad as he told me the horrible things that had happened to him. He disclosed them slowly, over time, pacing himself and checking always to make sure that I could listen to him and that together we could manage the feelings that came up.

Michael and I developed therapy rituals that changed as he changed and grew. His favorite became the last ten minutes of the hour, when we would invite his mom into the room and we would all sit together on the couch and I would read to Michael. The connection between the three of us was crucial for him. Sometimes Michael would not look at his mom during this time, but he wanted her in the room. Leaving became a difficult transition, and often the session would end with a Michael tantrum and a harried mom and therapist.

A few months later it was time for Michael to start preschool. His parents were less than enraptured with the idea. What would Michael do? How would the children and the staff react to him? How could we keep him safe? The questions were valid, and I was not sure that I knew the answers. We all held our breaths. Michael loved it! He liked the children; he liked the teachers, and they liked him back. He loved the learning and could not wait to share what new song or piece of information he learned each week. He could not wait for his preschool days.

Nevertheless, Michael had horrible tantrums whenever Mom picked him up from school. He would get in the car full of smiles and within a block would fall apart. He would rage and cry and scream. Sometimes Mom was unable to safely drive the car and would have to pull over and hold him until he was calm enough for her to continue. I felt that Michael was experiencing a reenactment of his birth mother's abandonment, and that his tantrums were a protest at the separation from both his birth mother and his new mother. Nothing we could improvise helped for a while. Mother always reminded Michael that she would come back. She arrived at the preschool early so he could see her car. She gave him small items of hers to keep while he went to preschool. What seemed eventually to help was the routine and the fact that Michael's mother always kept her word—she always came back. The preschool staff was supportive of Michael and his difficulties with separation. Over time the tantrums decreased, but they reoccurred if there was any additional stress in Michael's life.

Michael became more and more expressive with words and symbols in therapy. One day he took the fire engine and the ambulance and started banging them together. He looked angry and intense. I asked what was happening, and he said, "This is the bad me [holding up one toy] and this is the good me [holding up the other toy]." When I asked him to tell me more, he said, "This is the good me, the me that did not get hurt. And this is the bad me. The me that got hurt. Really bad me." The banging continued at a ferocious rate until one of the toys shattered.

I began to talk quietly to Michael about the part of him that was hurt, the mad and sad part. I told him that when little kids got hurt by grownups, it was never the fault of the little kid, that it was always the fault of the grownup. I told Michael that the badness was in the hurting, not in him; that it was bad he got hurt, but he was not bad. He looked straight at me and said, "Tell me again." I did. While I knew that he did not believe me, that he couldn't take the information in that quickly, he was relieved. We talked about the badness often from then on. He would tell me when he needed to hear it again.

Eleven months after the goodbye with his birth mother, Michael was adopted by his foster parents. This was one transition that did not seem to bring a reaction from Michael. He was openly delighted to be Mommy and Daddy's little boy. He told me, "I can live with them forever and ever!"

Two months after the adoption, Michael and I said goodbye. He and his family moved to another state. He was four years, four months old. I had worked with Michael for just under one and a half years.

The termination was paced slowly. We began to talk together about Michael's move four or five months before it happened. Michael was excited about the move, but he was also sad about leaving his preschool friends and not seeing me anymore. I took photographs of Michael in the playroom and in my office. His mother took pictures of Michael and me together. I wrote him a story about our relationship and made a little book for him with the story and the pictures.

Not long before the goodbye, Michael took Play-Doh and made a caterpillar. He then took more Play-Doh and created a cocoon. He then broke open the cocoon and turned it into a butterfly. I was speechless. There was no need to say anything. Four-year-old Michael had just summarized his experience in therapy and in his new family.

I heard from Michael's mother a few months after they moved. She called to report the usual ups and downs. Under stress, he was very hard to handle. His tantrums continued; sometimes he hurt the family pets and sometimes was very rejecting of her. But all in all, things were going well. Michael told me about his new house and preschool, and then the following conversation took place:

MICHAEL: "MaryLou, where are you?"

MLC: "Michael, I'm in my office."

MICHAEL: "But where?"

MLC: "I'm sitting in the black chair."

MICHAEL: "Can you see the couch?"

MLC: "Yes, I can see the couch."

MICHAEL: "Can you see the toys in the playroom?"

MLC: "Yes, Michael, I can see the toys in the playroom."

MICHAEL: "OK, everything is still there, I can go now, I love you, goodbye."

Reflections

Working with Michael and his family was exhausting, challenging, frustrating, and delightful. I learned a great deal from them. Without the support of his parents, the therapy would not have progressed as rapidly as it did. To say the family was cooperative would be an understatement; they were a significant part of the treatment team. Many times I wondered if they would be able to go on caring for Michael. He was so hard to handle. I felt pressure at times to "fix" Michael. I think much of the pressure was my own, but I also did sense the frustration of the family wanting a "normal" little boy.

Michael will probably never be totally "normal." But this little boy who had such a horrible start in life is bright, is verbal, and has developed enough trust in adults that he has a reciprocal relationship with both his parents, two sets of grandparents, and schoolteachers. He could easily have given up. Michael's attachments are likely to be anxious and somewhat angry in tone. He will probably be controlling and quick to perceive rejection. On the other hand, he has a quirky sense of humor and the ability to explore and have fun in the process.

This is the sort of case therapists would like to follow for many years. I still hear from Michael's family every once in a while. His birth mother keeps in touch with me as well. She sends letters to him a few times a year. They, of course, cause a reaction in Michael. But he is always relieved to know that his birth mother is "OK." I think about Michael often and of the hours we spent together in the playroom. Sometimes when I'm really struggling with another case and feel like something just is not working, I think about Michael's Play-Doh butterfly. For whatever reason, it helps.

Transformation and Healing through the Creative Process*

John is an eight-year-old boy who was hospitalized for eight months with a history of severe and repeated physical, emotional, and sexual abuse by an adult male. John displayed disruptive behavior and temper tantrums, impulsively made animal noises, and sexually acted out. Once he placed a screwdriver between his legs and asked his mother if she wanted to be raped by him.

He has a history of poor sleep and appetite, nightmares about being abused with soda bottles, flashbacks, intrusive thoughts, poor

*Contributed by Stuart M. Silverman, Richard T. Gibson, Harriet Glass, and Judith E. Orodenker, Honolulu, Hawaii.

peer relations, and preoccupation with insects and reptiles. John would often attack his mother aggressively and pointed a knife threateningly at her. He was accident-prone and exhibited low self-esteem and vulnerability. He often tripped on his own feet and stepped on the feet of others.

Psychological testing revealed themes of violence and death, unstable relationships, and issues of abandonment. John displayed a need for nurturance as well as difficulty perceiving and trusting nurturance. It was difficult for him to relate to others and to feel comfortable in intimate relationships. He desired closeness but was quite afraid to trust. At times he dissociated, seemed disorganized, bizarre, and even psychotic. John would often make animal sounds when he was placed in the quiet room, usually secondary to aggressive behavior. On a few occasions I (S.S.) asked him why he made these sounds, and he replied that they helped calm him down. On other occasions I joined John in the quiet room and we made sounds together, or hummed. While John laughed at this, he participated, and the sounds allowed me to engage with him and produced a calming effect. This was a nonverbal means of reaching a child who experienced difficulty trusting and relating to others.

It became clear that John's main issues centered on trusting others, anger and aggression, and poor boundaries. These all affected his ability to attach to and engage with others. John was referred to participate in art therapy and dance/movement therapy with the hope of improving attachment abilities and fostering healing through creative expressive therapies.

In art therapy (J.O.) John was able to move from being in a disorganized and uncreative state to creating crude and primitive artwork and to finally channeling and expressing his inner world effectively. As this transformation unfolded, his ability to relate changed in flavor and quality. Hostility decreased, and his aptitude in making true connections with others increased. As John's boundaries became better defined and he began to feel empowered and better able to protect himself, he was able to experience others as less threatening and less intrusive. A key factor in John's healing process was his need and ability to learn to discharge, and then channel, anger and aggression into artistic expression. By learning to channel this energy into the creative process, he discovered he could express his rage in a safe and controlled manner. By releasing anger, other emotions became available for expression.

John began working with clay slowly, at first banging it on the table with his fist. Then he progressed to throwing it on the ground as hard as he could, using his large muscles. He began to make sounds, yelling loudly as he threw the clay. This became a ritual, occurring at the beginning of each session. Eventually the ritual became shorter, and John was able to immediately engage in more sophisticated creative expression.

His clay work initially consisted of different animals of prey, aggressive animals such as snakes, and benign clay turtles transformed into snapping turtles. Working through his issues of abuse, trickery, and deception, John defended himself by identifying with the aggressor. Many forms John created were phallic and sexual in shape and nature. Acts of penetration were mimicked, and John would place the forms in his mouth.

The use of color, which raises the emotional key, was initially lacking in John's work, as he appeared to be detached from emotion. This gave a depersonalized flavor to what he created, reflecting his own state as well as his experience of others.

As John learned he could handle and express rage and could face his own abuse, he explored ways of protecting and empowering himself. He created a special magic potion holder out of clay with a sign saying Do not touch. He also created many weapons with special magical features, as well as game boards with special pieces wherein he created the rules and was in control.

John eventually began working with color and created a human figure he called Operation Man. With the aid of an anatomy book, John fashioned all the internal organs, then created a shieldlike piece, the chest, which could be removed and served to protect the vulnerable organs. This figure seemed symbolic of John's increased sense of self and his more defined boundary structure. He could now allow others, including his mother, to get close without feeling violated. In later sessions John became much more engaging and wanted to socialize as well as create during sessions.

John initially appeared self-absorbed in dance/movement therapy (H.G.). He was preoccupied with danger and had a distorted body image. He could not stay vertical, walk a straight line, or stay in his own personal space. He was willing to follow limits with constant reminders that he could not hurt himself or the therapist. John first played by himself, watching the therapist vigilantly out of the corner of his eye. He was very self-protective, drew rigid boundaries, and would allow no touch unless it occurred accidentally during the movement process. John tended to be quite literal and concrete while using the padded equipment or games. No matter what activity he started, he interrupted himself by wildly and recklessly flailing himself against the equipment or impulsively reaching for something and throwing it at the equipment.

Interactive form emerged with a game of catch, the ball serving as a bridge of affective contact. John made loud and screaming sounds, with rhythms, sounds, and movements being mirrored by the therapist. John laughed, yelled, and pointed at the therapist, but he never stopped the interaction. John referred to an "angry ball spinning and screaming through the air," an apt metaphor for his behavior.

Respect for the body and self-protective behaviors were taught to John through the movement process. He was assisted on unsteady equipment so as not to crash into walls or fall on the floor. He was taught that it was acceptable to move and play with strong energy and to express angry feelings but that it was also important to protect the body and not destroy things in the environment. We were encouraged when John spontaneously set up soft cushioning on the floor and donned knee pads before a session.

After two months he began to creatively tease the therapist by mimicking his own behavior as it was reflected back to him. Spontaneous games were negotiated, with rules created and defined verbally and nonverbally to accompany the movement. Instead of the bizarre, screaming vocalizations of earlier sessions, laughter, humor, and a growing affection accompanied the strong movement play. The games emerged from some variety of fighting play: no-touch karate, fencing with sticks, hand-to-hand combat with large padded tubes, punching, kicking, or rebounding off the large padded equipment. John titled all the games: "Death and Healing," "Save Me, Don't Save Me," and "Kill the Bronco."

John displayed emotional investment by trying out new behaviors and new coping strategies in a context that provided immediate and active feedback. He could experiment with anger and aggression in a safe and trusting environment. Experiencing aggression, creatively channeling it, controlling it, and productively making games of it allowed anger to be mastered, transformed, and healed. The movement work with John invited and encouraged him to participate in a meaningful encounter on his terms. By using John's own metaphors in developing the movement process, the therapist did not need to focus on content but could become a supportive and facilitative partner. In the movement play a heightened synchrony developed between John and the therapist that strengthened the therapeutic bond. As trust increased, attachment deepened and John became less bossy, demanding, and controlling. From an initial position of rigid control, John gradually allowed himself a more inquisitive and indulging style of exploring and experimenting. He eventually allowed the therapist to rock him on the large padded equipment and to drag and roll him in the fabric tunnel. Now he could initiate as well as follow; he could yield as well as take charge.

The Child Psychiatry Fellow (R.G.) assigned to John fostered trust building, self-reliance, and body awareness through challenging activities, such as ocean kayaking and tree climbing. A creative opportunity emerged during an outing when John, spotting a dead rat on the hiking trail, mumbled, "I'd like to piss on the rat." His therapist sorted through the clinical advantages, the possible negative implications, and the developmental appropriateness of letting John fulfill his desire, and allowed him to do so after suggesting that John envision the rat as the person who had abused him. John later saw a centipede and spontaneously screamed at it, then sheepishly turned to the therapist and said, "I pretended it was [the guy who abused me]."

Anger and aggression were discharged and abuse mastered through such activities as urinating on a dead rat and screaming at a centipede, each of which was assigned the role of abuser.

In a combined music and art therapy group (S.S./J.O.), John was encouraged to express emotions through improvisational sounds, rhythms, and drawings that were created with art materials as instruments. Once a Tibetan bowl was utilized, producing harmonic sounds and vibrations that were soothing and calming.

In summary, John, a victim of abuse, experienced severe disruption in attachment capabilities, expressed as anger and rage, inability to trust, loss of control and power, vulnerability, and poor boundaries. John was unable to fully or appropriately express anger and rage, as he was overwhelmed and frightened by them and also feared retribution. He was unable to appropriately cope with or provide protection from intrusion by others, and he was quite intrusive himself. As a means of coping and as a defense, John dissociated and appeared bizarre, ungrounded, and out of touch with his body. Engaging John in various types of creative processes that were therapeutic, challenging, unconditionally accepting, supportive, nurturing, and fun allowed for a testing of the waters, an opportunity to let go, to feel powerful, to feel unconditionally accepted by another, to reconnect without danger, to feel safe enough to return "home." Inherent in the creative process is a transforming and a healing power that transcend logic and foster a profound connection and relationship within the deepest parts of ourselves and others.

10

Maladaptive Attachment Relationships

Maladaptive parental relationships are not commonly identified as presenting problems in referrals for treatment but rather are typically buried under urgent and alarming issues that can appear to be unrelated. Clinicians may fail to recognize maladaptive attachment relationships when their primary focus is the child's immediate behavior or when they are influenced by the pressures exerted by parents, school personnel, social services, and legal systems. Referring parties vary in their willingness to accept the premise that the genesis of the problems may lie in a poor parent-child relationship.

Identification of the problem determines how therapy is conducted. The inclusion or exclusion of various family members in the treatment sessions is a complex decision based on clinical needs, parental abilities and motivation, and availability or allocation of mental health resources.

A client whose disturbing behavior is rooted in a maladaptive parental attachment relationship will not get adequate help by attending education classes, self-esteem groups, or group therapy alone. Nor will that child or adult be adequately served by individual therapy unless the therapy is based on a secure, positive relationship with a therapist who, with exquisite sensitivity and timing, will directly work with the specific maladaptive relationship issues in addition to the myriad complexities of relationships in general.

The parent-therapist relationship is always important when

working with maladaptive parenting problems. How parents and clinician perceive their roles in relationship to each other influences both the style of treatment and the goals and issues it addresses and may determine its success or failure. The clinician may be seen as an adversarial enforcer of the social service system, the child's ally, a neutral professional consultant, or a therapist for the family. The parents may be perceived by the clinician as those who wounded the child and are thus unworthy of attention. They can also be seen as the youngster's primary attachment figures and therefore the ones who are in the best position to provide care and support for the youngster. Parents should always be seen as people who have their own individual needs, vulnerabilities, blind spots, and wishes, all of which can influence their attachment relationships with their children.

Developing a clinical relationship with caregivers in which the parenting relationship is a core issue is akin to a journey through an emotional minefield. Issues of parenting, authority, criticism, childhood pain, inadequacy, and helplessness bring forth intense, unresolved feelings from the past and the present for both clinician and caregivers. Time spent in self-reflection by the therapist and time spent clarifying roles with parents is time well spent.

Where does one begin in such complex cases? An obvious maxim, often forgotten under pressure, is to take time to do adequate assessments and to develop customized, flexible treatment plans. Failure to do so is like rushing off on a hiking trip and realizing, midjourney, that you have food and sleeping bags but have forgotten the map, compass, and first-aid kit. Your immediate needs can be resolved, but you don't know where you are going or how to get there, and you are not likely to be able to deal with an emergency.

The following group of vignettes describe clinical work with infants, school-age children, and adolescents. They are based on the child, the caregiver, or both developing a meaningful relationship with the therapist. This need for clinical relationship-building in treating attachment-related problems may seem obvious, but continued requests and demands for brief therapy suggest otherwise.

The clinicians in the first two vignettes worked primarily with the mothers of infants, focusing first on forming relationships wherein the mothers felt emotionally safe and experienced being seen, heard, and accepted as who they are rather than who they might be when "fixed." Both mothers, one a streetwise woman and the other a young teen, were then able to accept guidance and support in caring for their infants. The women not only gained insight into their concepts of self and mothering but also experienced some of what they had missed relationally in their own early childhoods. With treatment they were able to pass this on to their young infants.

Dramatic play therapy with a young girl who has more out-of-home placements than years of life, is described by her therapist. His sensitivity to the child's yearnings for human contact and fears of closeness allows her to take the lead in therapy. The therapist describes how the child copes with her pain.

Several brief examples of clinical work interpreting attachments are provided by French colleagues. The vignette about Patricia demonstrates parental involvement in the child's therapy in which the parents' relationship with their child significantly improved through less direct means. The child's parents, who were extremely limited in their functioning, were guided in altering their interactions with their daughter by the therapist teaching them how to assist the child with her speech difficulties. In the next case the parents developed understanding and insights into their son's behavior after being guided through an examination of familial circumstances and parental expectations. This led to significant changes in interactions. A youngster with unmanageable behavior was helped after the mother learned to express the difficulties she had in showing physical affection to her child. The last vignette in this series describes long-term clinical work with a boy and his family when attachment did not form in early childhood.

The next two authors provide case examples in which maladaptive parenting was an issue but the parents were not emotionally or physically available to participate in the child's therapy. We see here examples of children developing anchoring, safe relationships with their therapists that enabled them to deal with painful losses and eventually to connect with their parents. The clinicians utilized quite different means to help their respective clients, in one case, the therapist used advocacy and creative professional leadership to create a therapeutic milieux in the school setting. In another situation, a hospital-based clinician was finally able to establish a relationship with the girl nobody liked by simply being consistent and hanging in there.

The last contribution in this chapter provides an example of a crucial adjunct to the therapy, supervised parent-child visitation, which helped a terrified child and his estranged parent begin to reestablish a relationship.

Prison Mom*

Kim was referred to me by her parole officer. She was twenty-eight-years old and had given birth to a son, Alex, while in prison. She currently had custody of her son.

Kim lived in a large old San Francisco home that housed a halfway program for women who have shown they have the capacity to be assimilated back into the community. One goal of the program was to help women maintain custody of their children. About half of the women in the program had children with them.

Kim's history is not atypical of other halfway house residents. Her mother, father, stepfathers, and other family members repeatedly abused her as a child, physically and emotionally. She started running away as a young teenager and became addicted to the drugs she used to numb herself so that she could avoid feelings and memories that were too intense, painful, and horrible to experience. She supported her habit by theft and prostitution, for which she was frequently incarcerated. Regular jobs did not last long—Kim had few employable skills and was unable to comply with a regular employment schedule, and her needs were not met by her salary. She was raped while "in the life" and subsequently gave birth to Alex.

Kim wanted to keep her child but was woefully unprepared to assume a parenting position. Her role models were an abusive mother and women she met on the streets. She did not know the rudiments of childcare. Her own attachment to her mother was severely dysfunctional, and it followed that her child's attachment was likely to be similarly compromised.

Kim began counseling sessions with me without hesitation. She

*Contributed by Ruth Sheets, Oakland, California.

brought Alex with her during one of our early sessions, proud of her baby and proud of the fact that she had made it thus far. Kim spoke with delight about Alex's antics and tried to imagine what life would be like later on when he was older.

She was afraid to hold Alex. She believed he was so fragile that she would hurt him if she handled him too much. When she did hold him, he would be balanced on her crossed knee, facing her, so she could watch his face. Her movements were stiff and jerky, and she would hold her breath when she picked him up. Kisses and hugs were brief and usually given only once or twice a day, "so I won't spoil him."

Alex was born three months premature and was chronologically six months old at this time. He was cute and chunky, had lots of hair, and was the size of a three-month-old. Kim had many questions about Alex's development, especially because he seemed to be slow compared with other children in the house and because other parents commented that he might be retarded. Naturally she was frightened, but she was also eager to get information and thus became a willing pupil.

Kim and I worked on many personal issues relating to her early childhood. It was necessary that Kim have some basic information about role modeling and parenting in her home so that she could understand why she was so uncomfortable in her new role as a mother. She initially felt that, because of her history, she was just stupid and ignorant and didn't have the capacity to change. We worked on self-esteem and relationship issues. Kim also had a history of battering, so anger issues were an integral part of our work as well.

I really liked Kim and respected her for having survived all she had been through. My primary concern was whether she might physically hurt her baby. She had a history of physically abusing her adult partners. Her anger was instantaneous. When we began therapy, she seemed unable to modulate her feelings. I was also concerned that she and Alex form a healthy attachment.

While Kim was seeing me for individual therapy, she enrolled in a perinatal drug treatment program. This program had child care available, parenting classes, developmental testing, and relapse prevention, HIV education, and self-esteem groups. They also tested urine on a weekly basis, and she worked with a drug treatment counselor individually.

In the parenting classes Kim met other women who had similar experiences, thus decreasing her isolation. Each class was on a different topic relating to issues that parents were currently facing. Common topics included feeding and nutrition, discipline, toys and play, choosing and using a doctor, childhood illnesses and what to treat at home vs. when to go to the hospital or doctor, finding appropriate childcare, and dividing time between several children. A play group was available, facilitated by a staff member, to teach the parents how to play with their children.

The play group was probably one of the most important for Kim. For a long time she was afraid to hold and play with Alex. She was able to take excellent custodial care of him, but the warmth and closeness frightened her. After several weeks in the play group, Kim was significantly less afraid of Alex but still had difficulty being close. During an office session with Kim, I demonstrated step by step how to hold Alex close to the body, how to interact with him with and without a toy, how to give Alex time to respond both physically and verbally, and how to let him initiate an interaction. Eyes glistening, Kim said, "I really love him. I really want to be a good mom." Her assignment for the week was to go home and spend time with Alex, practicing everything we did in therapy.

Alex was developmentally tested and found to be within the normal range for his adjusted age and at age level in several tasks for his chronological age. The testing, while at first scary for Kim, turned out to be a source of relief and offered reassurance that Alex was "normal" and that she was doing well as a parent. An excellent self-esteem builder!

Kim has now developed a significant amount of self-confidence in her role as a parent. It was important for her to understand why, in the beginning, she had no idea how to do things or even recognize feelings related to her child. Once she developed some insight, she was able to take in basic information regarding parenting and begin to practice new skills. Once Kim was sure she knew what it was she needed to do and was given some reassurance that everything would be OK, she was able to move forward.

Kim and Alex have four more months in the halfway house, and then her parole will be finished. They will complete the drug treatment program, and Kim will decide about continuing ongoing therapy. She is making plans for independent living and returning to school. Some awesome task!

Adolescent Mom*

When working with single adolescent mothers, I attempt to balance the needs of mother and child to facilitate the building of their relationship. Incorporating attachment theory in identifying the developmental needs of the mother as an adolescent and those of the child helps to create a viable, trusting relationship between them. I promote the development of a secure base on which the mother can feel free to express herself, acknowledge past experiences, and, with my guidance and encouragement, focus on her relationship with her infant.

Tracy's grandmother had a dream in which she saw Tracy abusing her infant. She told her granddaughter about the dream, which upset Tracy. Tracy told me was afraid the dream might be a premonition. My purpose was to help her see that her grandmother's fears were her own, and not Tracy's. She needed to know that she was a separate person, with her own needs, before she could begin to see her infant as an individual with his own needs.

Tracy felt strongly that her mother was rejecting her and her son because she had repeated her mother's mistake, that is, she had borne a child as an adolescent. She felt unloved and abandoned, resulting in a sense of being alone and overburdened, with no one to support her or to help care for her infant. She was overwhelmed by the responsibility of parenthood and needed some relief so she could have time to herself. This in turn made her feel guilty, and she worried that she was a bad mother.

I represented an idealized mother who was accepting of Tracy and nonjudgmental. This modeled the proximity and accessibility needed to develop a secure attachment. Tracy eventually felt secure enough to talk to her grandmother about her dream and to state clearly that the dream was not a prediction that Tracy would abuse

---

*Contributed by Valerie Iles, Toronto, Ontario, Canada.

her infant but instead was about her grandmother's own roots and own past.

Although the infant was the identified patient, the focus of the work was with the mother and her developing relationship with her child. Tracy always appeared able to look after her son's physical needs but was easily frustrated by his demands and could not engage him in play at his level.

We dealt first with the original situation presented, namely, that the infant had a sleeping problem and that Tracy was unable to cope with it. What emerged from our sessions was that Tracy did not feel safe at night, a fear she communicated to her child. We examined Tracy's own insecurities, and this seemed to have a positive effect.

Tracy appeared cheerful at subsequent visits. Her son had been sleeping through the night, giving her the rest she needed. She was much more involved with her son. She had previously been more concerned with her own fears, complained that her son was fussy and always clinging, and related how frustrated she was by his neediness. As our visits continued and Tracy began to feel more secure, she began to look at her son as a separate being, with needs of his own that were different from hers.

The infant, at nine months, was beginning to explore his environment, but Tracy was still having difficulty entering into a playful relationship with him. I noted that when he moved away, he did not check back with his mother to confirm their connection; nor did Tracy make eye contact or otherwise interact with him during his play. Tracy said she would like to be able to interact more with her son, but it appeared she was trapped in her own space and unable to enter his.

Tracy and I agreed to spend six sessions at the clinic videotaping play sessions between her and her son. My only instructions were that Tracy follow her son's lead and actively engage with him in his activities. I would be in the room, but only as an observer. We would later review the videotapes together.

Tracy found it difficult to engage in her son's level of play. She followed him around, but they made very little eye contact and had almost no verbal interaction. Tracy, however, was very open to the process and was soon able to adapt more to her son. After several sessions they were sharing more and beginning to enjoy their time together. As we reviewed the tapes, Tracy began to take more delight in her son and to feel more confident in her ability to parent. She soon began to anticipate his needs. She was becoming more accessible, and the relationship between them was becoming more reciprocal—they were now more able to relate to and enjoy each other.

As Tracy began to respond to her son as an individual, it seemed to help in her own struggle to improve her relationship with her mother. Though still distressed by her mother's rejection, she began to understand the process and the need to avoid repeating her mother's pattern with her son. She understood that she could do it differently.

Tracy and her son have been able to begin building a more secure attachment to each other. Our weekly meetings will continue in order to consolidate the gains Tracy has made and to support her continued growth as a parent. As you know, it's all in the process: We inch forward, and there are no tidy conclusions.

Symbolic Dramatic Play*

My clinical journey with Susan was a process of using play therapy to facilitate a healthier attachment with her mother and to help her accept the loss of her relationship with her father.

Both parents actively abused drugs and alcohol during Susan's first three years of life, and she suffered multiple brief placements with family friends. Susan's father was reported for physically and sexually abusing her; he was imprisoned and never came back into her life. She was placed with her paternal grandmother, since her mother was unable to care for her due to continuing drug use. A year later her grandparents separated. The grandmother could not cope with the angry, oppositional, and controlling behaviors Susan was developing as a defense system, and the child entered the first of five different foster home placements.

Susan was referred to me for intensive therapy at age six. A psychological assessment showed she had developed a strong defense system in which she was attaching to pseudostructures of

---

*Contributed by Louis Lehman, Tacoma, Washington.

objects and roles rather than to persons. Seeking but fearing closeness, Susan defended herself through her demanding, aggressive, narcissistic, and controlling behaviors. Sexually reactive behavior with younger children had twice contributed to changes of foster placement.

A preliminary treatment plan was developed that would (1) meet Susan's regressive nurturance needs in environments where more positive ways of relating to others could be successfully learned and where her counterproductive defenses could be safely lowered, (2) allow her to experience appropriate and safe ways in which to seek and accept affection, (3) teach her to process and work through the many losses in her life, and (4) lead to successful reattachment to others, initially in preparation for adoption but later changing the goal to reunification with her mother when social service plans changed.

Susan moved quickly into her controlling defenses to distance from affective material. I was usually nondirective, as Susan had little reason to trust yet another person. After two weeks, however, she symbolically "gave" herself to me and began processing the pain of parental losses when she drew a face on a slab of Plasticine and said it was her own face on a birthday cake. She presented it to me, saying she wanted to live in my office, with me as her daddy, because she didn't have a daddy. "He did bad things to me. So did my mommy. It was her fault."

I reassured Susan that this would be a safe place for her to sort out the hurt of such losses by gently clarifying my role as therapist while validating her losses.

It was clear by the end of the third week that Susan favored dramatic play. She used controlling defenses to deal with an accumulated sense of powerlessness, often casting herself as parent or teacher and me as her child:

> SUSAN (as a stern and irritable mother): "If you keep on being bad, I'll send you to a foster home."

I responded as a tearful, worried child, whereupon Susan briefly dropped her controls and became a nurturing mother as she assured me that she loved me, made me "go to sleep," and sang lullabies. After the play I reassured her that little kids had a right to cry when sad.

The next week Susan meshed her roles by casting herself as a foster mother, this time with her mother's name. She was less bossy and directive, but she still distanced from affect as needed. I was again designated to be her child as she bluntly spoke of her father: "You don't have a daddy anymore. He 'aborshed' you."

In response to my inquiries about this, in my role as a child, Susan said, "I don't know why he left. He did bad things to you. You didn't do anything wrong. He loved you. I don't know why he did the bad things. I don't want to talk about it anymore."

Two weeks later Susan was differentiating her concepts of "good" and "bad" parents as she moved further toward symbolic reconnection to her mother while continuing to let go of her relationship with her father. She did this while continuing her emotional distancing, as illustrated in a session where I was again a child and Susan was a mother/foster mother who was alternatively punitive and comforting:

SUSAN: "If you're not good, you'll have to live in another foster home. You can't live with us forever."

THERAPIST (as child): "I'm scared."

SUSAN: "Don't talk about it."

THERAPIST (tearfully): "What am I supposed to do with my feelings?"

SUSAN: "Keep them inside. [Shifting to therapist role:] Pretend to dream about your dad."

THERAPIST (as frightened awakening child): "Oh, I had a scary dream about my dad. Help me!"

Now Susan became a soothing and comforting "new foster mother," announcing she was my "real-real-real mother": "I'm not the mother who did the drugs but a new 'real' mother. You have a new dad too—not the one who sex-abused you."

The next week Susan opened up with some of the pain underlying her rage when she tearfully said, "He was the best daddy I ever had until he did those bad things to me. Why did he do those things?"

Then she quickly retreated into her defense system. Because I had encouraged her to talk about her feelings, she made me stand in the corner while she resumed the symbolic reconnection to her mother by drawing a picture of "Mommy" with a large, sad face next to a smaller sad face, and then made a similar drawing of the same two faces, but now with smiles.

During the next six months, treatment focused more on the reunification goal. Susan and her mother were becoming increasingly reacquainted through visitations and family therapy, but her need for symbolic processing of the maternal renewed attachment and paternal loss of attachment continued.

Susan's coping with the loss of her father continued with further expressions of rage as she drew pictures of him and tore them up, molded and attacked clay representations of him, and persistently asked to change her surname to her mother's maiden name. Susan was extremely resistive to efforts to help her verbalize other feelings about her father. She reverted to her controlling defenses, changed subjects, and plugged her ears.

By now she had lowered many defensive behaviors in other areas. She readily cuddled with her mother in family therapy as they shared memories and hopes for the future.

Susan's need to reorganize people in her life, together with her anxiety about the future, emerged shortly before she was to return to her mother in a different community, where she would be transferred to another therapist. During this session she developed an elaborate tea party and directed me to open with a prayer. I expressed thanks for Susan's progress in dropping her angry and controlling behaviors and allowing herself to experience needed nurturing from her mother. Susan then moved to the sandtray, buried a "fairy godmother" doll in a corner, put in dollhouse furniture, and ceremoniously grouped all of the room's adult male dolls in the tray "by the father's bed" and all of the adult female dolls "by the mother's bed." She then placed all of the room's boy dolls with the man dolls and all of its girl dolls with the woman dolls. Finally she uncovered the fairy godmother and brought her into the center of the tray.

"She has a maid with her who cleans toilets but has to be in the middle because she needs to be watched."

The clear grouping of the males apart from the females was

striking in the context of Susan's anticipation that her family would consist only of her and her mother, with no plans for any significant inclusion of males. The pairing of the fairy godmother with the maid suggested her hopes and fears about how her mother might function in the future.

This brief clinical description focuses on how this six-year-old dealt with multiple attachment disturbances. Susan processed the pain of many attachment losses through play therapy and eventually was able to develop a renewed and healthier attachment with her mother, first in the world of play and then in real life. This little girl became empowered and better able to cope with life, although many unresolved issues remained at the conclusion of treatment.

I learned much from this incredibly imaginative and creative child. Susan made me very aware of the need to provide attachment-disturbed children with opportunities to practice both loss and emotional reconnection at their own pace. She did this through expressive play, storytelling, dramatics, art, imaginary companions, and substitutes such as therapists and foster families before developing a trusting relationship with her mother and accepting the loss of her relationship with her father.

Behavioral aspects of Susan's treatment have not been discussed in this brief vignette. Susan needed direct behavioral intervention as well as play therapy. The more I realized how powerless she had been regarding the attachment disturbances and losses in her life, the more I could understand and respect the reasons for her controlling defenses and her need to work so symbolically. The world of play provided the staging ground for this child's complicated work of attachment.

Interpreting Attachments*

Presenting facets of our practice that aim to the reconstruction of a loving relationship between parents and child is not an easy task and, within the limits of such a vague and simple notion as attachment, might well be an impossible job. In neither of our fields—psychoanalysis and school psychology—do we encounter simple situa-

*Contributed by Bernard W. Sigg and Edith Sigg-Piat, Ivry, France.

tions where the ways and means of bonding between two closely related persons can be described with a single word, in terms of yes or no. A large array of feelings, behaviors, and thoughts build up these relationships, from quasi-indifference to dependence, and with different degrees and qualities. Utmost complexity is the rule.

Closeness, for instance, as usually expected between mommy and toddler, could also imply distance, since fusion often leads to confusion. The intricacies of relational factors, the enmeshed currents of thought and affect, are some of the determinants that make it difficult to report these events—a difficulty that, when conveyed to the reader, exposes part of our daily reality.

Patricia; or, The Desire of Language

The specific human link is speech: Talking to one's child is an absolute necessity in order to humanize him or her. This was precisely what Mrs. Tr. did not know how to do so. She was an uneducated person from a western farmland who had been raised in a large family in which nobody had especially cared for her. She had been pregnant at least ten times and had borne eight children before Patricia. Not surprisingly, this last, quiet girl was of little importance in the midst of the family turmoil created mainly by the father's alcoholism and the elder son's behavioral and learning problems. Characteristically, Mrs. Tr. commonly called her "Katricia," mixing her surname with the one of her previous daughter, Kathryn.

Actually, the two sisters were very close to each other, Kathryn always anticipating her smaller sister's actions or gestures, playing with her and her toys, and polarizing adults' attention. Patricia could not yet talk at age two and a half. Most of her older brothers and sisters presented speech defects. I (E.S.) therefore proposed to the parents that we dedicate a session a week during the year for their participation in joined observation of their youngest daughter's speech acquisition. My aim was to create a privileged situation of communication between mother, father, and daughter, as well as secondarily between mother and father. In order to do that, I started with simple items from Patricia's daily life evocations; a children's picture book with a small bear, which I first showed to the little girl with adequate commentaries; an attractive two-piece puzzle; etc. Progressively the parents inaugurated every session with a description of similar activities at home, on their own, which made me think they had begun to take pleasure in such exchanges with their daughter.

Ten years later, by sheer luck, I met Patricia again. Her face lit up, and she greeted me with, "Do you remember the small bear? I have not forgotten!"

Nick; or, The Subject's Value

Nick was ten years old, the first child in a rather well-to-do and educated family; however, he usually did not speak to his parents, unless aggressively, and his scholarly achievements were more and more unsatisfactory to them. They had come to the opinion that he was indifferent to their attention, and they were increasingly irritated by his behavior. Recently, however, he had begun talking about suicide, and they were quite afraid, hence asking for an urgent appointment with me. I (B.S.) received them first separately, then the whole family together, and they stubbornly stuck to their claim of the sudden and totally unexplainable appearance of Nick's death wishes.

Then came a revelation: Nick's mother was discovered to have cancer about the same time Nick started to talk of suicide. Linking the two facts helped the parents to discover that their son could love *à la vie et à la mort*—for life and death. But how much talk it had required!

A second discovery was the father's. He realized he never took time to discuss things with Nick, nor did he allow Nick any of his own leisure time. When he started doing so, most of their relational difficulties vanished.

With this second example of a child's crucial need of lively speech exchanges with his or her parents, we reach another symbolic phenomenon: The young human subject wants to be recognized through her or his own name, to which is usually added the patronyme, which is nothing else than the name of the father, with its far-reaching significance.

Another aspect of this familial association could be perceived in Nick's case: acknowledgment of the child's self-esteem, or, more theoretically, his narcissism, by mediation of "confidence." This can be the result of a dialectical relationship, no self-confidence being possible as long as the child's parents do not show any confidence or trust in him or her.

Michael; or, The Parent's Expectations

Trouble may arise from an excess of trust, or, I (B.S.) would otherwise say, parents' expectations regarding their child's beauty, strength, sociability, and school achievements. If these expectations are so high and a belief in their realization so total that the child could not attain the expected height, deception is brought to both sides. The consequence is a weakening of the narcissistic ties, leading to estrangement.

Eight-year-old Michael was interested in nothing at all. His schoolteacher appreciated his kindness and helpfulness but confessed that he regularly succeeded in remaining unnoticed or forgotten. Sometimes he would dream or tell funny stories, for instance, that his father flew a plane at night. During interviews with me, Michael displayed an original personality with rather clever remarks. He came to the center with pleasure, talked freely, and seemed to reestablish a trusting relationship with an adult. He would mention the overtraining work of his parents and how Mommy was always busy with his baby brother. She eventually confirmed having no time to spend with her firstborn, who, paradoxically now, had earlier overpowered her with pride because he was a beautiful and lively baby.

How very disappointing was his later career at the elementary school, where he soon lost any interest in learning, as well as in toys and even TV. "He likes nothing," his mother repeated, and with her husband they started turning away from him. The forgotten mutual trust had placed poor Michael in a position of affective near-abandonment, and he tried to compensate with various imaginary productions.

In several interviews and with the teacher's contribution, I succeeded in partially restoring the parents' confidence in their son and helped them to understand their own need for gratification. It was then that the father discovered some resemblances, or identifying traits, between what he had been as a boy and how his son was.

Disappointment and decathexis (loss of investment) can go as far as turning into repulsion. I once met a self-conscious father who had made a quasi-slave of his son and beat him severely because he did not measure up to expectations. In another case the dad had been rendered furious and depressed by the encopresis of his small boy, too hastily separated from his mother; unconsciously he wanted to destroy his previously adored object, now turned into a filthy one.

In all those cases the parents' expectation had been twice spoiled, first because of the child's nonconformity and second because of their own failure to be good parents. My task was then to figure out the hidden or forgotten positive sides of both child and parents.

Hugh; or, The Unconscious Hugging

A flaw in the way of relating can exist at a much cruder level than what we identify as abstract or sophisticated bonds. Some parents, or some children, appear unable to touch tenderly. A Mrs. L., who claimed to have been deprived of affectionate parents, did not know how to cuddle, pat, or kiss her only son, Hugh, then four years old. On his side, he was becoming less and less bearable, destroying everything and displaying terrible fits of anger. Both his mother and his nursery school mistress were calling for help, saying similarly that he was now totally unmanageable.

I (B.S.) faced his opposition in our first visit. He sat silent, kicking my desk and ignoring toys and pencils as well as my various attempts to communicate with him. I then explained that his mother and I would talk about his behavior. Suddenly he darted toward the door, trying to rush out, and when I blocked his escape he became enraged and unmanageable. Without thinking, I seized him and sat down with my arms firmly around him. Ten minutes later he had stopped struggling, and as soon as he was quiet, to the great astonishment of his mother, I put an end to the interview.

To my surprise, he came joyfully to the next visit, and we three talked about what had happened. Bodily closeness, warmth, and physical security were our topics, the mother being able to express how she was and had been frustrated on this plane. In a few sessions she became able to take her much gentler son in her arms and on her knees. They then quit coming—quite prematurely, in my opinion.

Sergio; or, The Determinant Countertransference

Sergio, born while his father was imprisoned, lived his first year with a caring but absentminded mother. He thus had nobody to whom he could attach. The work we did later on, parents, son, and I, (B.S.) had to extend to all levels and through all mediums: touching, playing, picturing, talking, telling. Sixteen years later Sergio stopped seeing me. He was autonomous, knew how to read and write, and had friends. But he still has no real job, he confessed to me recently, during a short, informal visit.

We may now emphasize again the determining role of reciprocal confidence or trust. In Sergio's case he and his parents have always known that I was there, available, never distressing them with a fatal diagnosis (I avoided speaking and even thinking of psychosis during those several years). I always trusted their ability to love, to care, and to implement the many tasks supposed by our initial pact. Yes, we had somehow become attached to one another, but with rather clear rules and prohibitions.

Healing cooperation, as well as education or marriage, is never free of ambivalence and variations. Esteem and deceit, joy and anger, love and hate, always coexist. But owing to their verbal expression and a set of agreements about rules, they stay within acceptable limits. The power of desire is accepted, without its leading to incest, and that of anger is acknowledged, without its bringing destruction or death.

Sarah: Like Mother, Like Daughter*

Sarah was referred to me when she was eleven by her mother, by her fourth-grade teacher, and by the school nurse. Mrs. G., Sarah's mother, described Sarah as unmanageable, unpredictable, and unable to get along with anyone. She said her daughter's difficulties began when she was nine years old and was molested by a man in their neighborhood. The teacher noted that Sarah had great difficulty with peer relations and seemed unable to maintain any friendships, either smothering potential friends or driving them away

*Contributed by Peter H. Sturtevant, Kittery, Maine.

with spiteful, sometimes mean behavior. Sarah's progress in school was erratic, despite her known ability.

The school nurse reported Sarah as a "frequent flyer" who manifested many somatic complaints, often wanted to go home, and frequently insisted her mother be called so that she could speak with her.

Mrs. G.'s view that Sarah's troubles were of recent origin was not substantiated by the records. She had been enrolled in four different school systems in six years and referred for counseling at least six times. School records and reports from social workers, counselors, and other professionals suggested that Sarah had always behaved pretty much as described by her present teacher.

Sarah presented as a tall, slender youngster with large dark eyes and long dark hair. Her mother, age twenty-nine, was a near-twin to her daughter.

Sarah was quiet, seemingly uninterested, when her mother was present during our first session. As Mrs. G. was about to leave the session, Sarah became very animated, clinging to her mother, sobbing, and begging her not to go. Mrs. G. seemed embarrassed and offered to stay. I indicated it would be best if she did not do so, and she left over the loud and pleading objections of her daughter.

Sarah's behavior changed the instant her mother disappeared. She became angry and hurled spiteful insults in the direction of her mother's departure. She vented her rage for nearly ten minutes, then became suddenly calm and fairly cooperative.

This pattern prevailed during the first few visits; she exhibited the same smothering and rejecting behavior noted by others. Her boundaries were poor, in relation not only to others but also to her own person. She had no real sense of personal space, either for herself or for others. She was frequently flirtatious and provocative in an almost adult way. She exhibited a poor sense of personal modesty with respect to her dress and posture.

She could and frequently did express some insight into her own behavior. It was clear from the outset that her troubles were longstanding and that Mother's belief that her daughter's difficulty stemmed from having been molested at age nine was inaccurate.

A major part of Sarah's difficulties arose from her poor boundary system and from her inability to form any sort of attachment. A nagging reality in this case was the close parallel between Mrs. G.

and her daughter. Both would reach out to others but could not accept what was offered. I believed Mrs. G. needed intensive work to help her with her self-defeating behaviors. Expecting her to work on her relationship with Sarah could be likened to using the wounded to help the injured.

I felt it was important to engage Mrs. G. in the therapy, but I did not feel I could work with her and with her daughter at the same time. I referred Mrs. G. to a colleague, with a close collaboration as a planned approach. This referral and Mrs. G.'s subsequent behavior gave further insights into Sarah's behavior.

Because Sarah's behavior was so inhibiting of her social and academic progress, I chose to make some behavioral interventions while working toward a clearer understanding of her personality.

It seemed most appropriate to work with the school personnel who came in contact with Sarah. It was essential that they learn to view Sarah in a different, more positive way. They were more likely to be willing and able to maintain the consistent approach needed to help Sarah than her mother seemed capable of sustaining. Mrs. G.'s assistance was encouraged and supported, but it was not made the most important element of the program.

Specific behaviors were selected for modification over several months. I worked with Sarah to establish cognitive understanding of the behaviors that were identified as troubling. An important part of the process was gaining Sarah's acceptance of the behavior as problematic, such as her frequent need to call her mother from school so that she could talk with her. "Where's Mom?" seemed to preoccupy the child. The issue was framed as her need to know that her mother was available to her.

Although it was an administrative nightmare, we arranged that Sarah could use the telephone to call her mother at any time. I had been able to do this in the past with a few students who were agitated and anxious because their mothers were seriously ill.

It was tough to get Sarah's mother to cooperate, but, with some fits and starts, she was able to do so. She provided Sarah with phone numbers where she could be reached and agreed to always accept her calls.

Sarah was rewarded for a decreasing frequency of calls. Rewards were in two categories: (1) things within the school framework that staff could control and administer as appropriate and (2) things at home that Mother would agree to support. Sarah had no trouble filling either list—her wants seemed endless. In three months' time, with only a few lapses when Sarah was particularly stressed, the calls were nearly extinguished.

Sarah's native intelligence and her willingness to accept a specific behavior as problematic were keys to the success of this approach.

Everyone who worked with Sarah was solicited to treat her in essentially the same way, that is, to support and encourage her when she demonstrated appropriate respect for personal boundaries. When she behaved inappropriately, the behavior was immediately dealt with in a positive way, with clear messages that the "other" did not like that behavior but that she, Sarah, was cared for in any case. Again, this was much easier to manage with school personnel than with Sarah's mother.

Sarah was a bright youngster and often very insightful. Play therapy, drawing, and clay work helped her relax and have a little fun, although she would sometimes grin and say, "You just want me to draw so you can tell what I'm thinking." Stories and mutual storytelling were more useful. Sarah was most imaginative and willingly or unconsciously put much of herself into stories. On one occasion I read her *The Silver Boat*. It became one of her favorites. She purchased a copy of her own with some birthday money. Mrs. G. reported that Sarah would occasionally ask to have it read to her or would read it aloud herself. These and other similar pieces formed an important part of Sarah's journey toward self.

A real understanding of Sarah came only with a closer look at Mrs. G. My initial referral had been to a young woman I knew to be a particularly skillful therapist. Mrs. G. rejected her out of hand. A second and third colleague were also rejected after an initial visit. She finally settled on a choice of her own, a male therapist about fifty-five years old.

This therapist reported that Mrs. G.'s behaviors exactly paralleled those of her daughter during the first six months of their work together. He obtained a simple genogram, which helped unfold the entire picture.

Sarah's father married her mother about four months before Sarah was born and divorced her before the child was a year old. Mrs. G. was seventeen and Sarah's father was twenty-four at the time of the marriage. Within a year Sarah's mother married again, this time to a man who was thirty. That marriage lasted less than two years. There followed in rapid fashion relationships with a half-dozen men, each of whom was at least ten to fifteen years older than Mrs. G. None of the relationships lasted more than a year or two. Mrs. G.'s own father abandoned the family when she was between three and four years old, and her mother was largely unavailable to her for most of her early years of development.

Over the course of the next year in therapy, Mrs. G. was able to understand that her own failure to achieve appropriate attachment relationships had prevented her from relating to Sarah in healthy ways and from helping her daughter form necessary relational attachments for herself. She became better able to participate in Sarah's treatment as she gained increased insight into her own needs and motivations.

Sarah is now nearly fifteen, a beautiful young lady on her way to a healthier self. She and her mother have moved once again, but both seem more stable now. Sarah was able to deal with issues of sexual abuse that had taken place at age seven and that had never been revealed. The sexual abuse reported by Mrs. G. when Sarah was nine turned out to be an incident of a neighborhood early adolescent exposing himself to a group of youngsters—something of concern but in no way as serious as Sarah's earlier victimization by one of her mother's male companions. Mrs. G. possibly felt compelled to raise the issue because she knew but did not want to know. In any case both Sarah and Mrs. G. are making positive progress. They have a good relationship between themselves, and their ability to connect with others is much better.

The Child Nobody Liked*

Leslie was a cute, charming eight-year-old whose chronic lying, stealing, and disruptive behavior at home and at school finally exhausted the patience of her father and stepmother. Their efforts to control Leslie were unsuccessful and had resulted in a punitive, negative economy of criticism, withholding, spankings, and groundings. In fact, their attempts had finally escalated to the point

*Contributed by Karen Sitterle, Dallas, Texas.

where there was a question of physically abusive behavior. Attempts to manage this case on an outpatient basis had failed miserably, prompting Leslie's admission to an inpatient psychiatric children's unit for evaluation. I was asked to see this youngster in individual therapy as part of the multidisciplinary team evaluating this child.

Leslie's parents divorced when she was an infant, and she spent her first six years living with her mother, a fairly unstable, self-absorbed, and chaotic individual who had many antisocial features. She had been unable to hold a job for longer than a few months at a time, relying on financial assistance from her own parents, and in fact had spent six months in prison for embezzlement. Leslie's mother was seventeen when she gave birth to her daughter. Two years before the child came to the hospital, Leslie's mother had decided she wanted to be free of the responsibilities of motherhood and had taken off for California, leaving Leslie to live with her father. Leslie had virtually no contact with her mother and knew little about her whereabouts during that time.

The hospital evaluation revealed Leslie to be a self-absorbed youngster who projected the attitude of a "cool customer." On the surface she acted as if her hospitalization didn't bother her. Despite the unstable, chaotic nature of Leslie's attachment to her mother, the disruption in the relationship was clearly traumatic for this youngster. Added to this were her father's absence and lack of contact during the first six years of her life. When Leslie went to live with her father, she found a rigid, punitive, and withholding environment that lacked prior emotional commitment. Early attempts at closeness were painful and unsuccessful, leaving Leslie with a defensive pattern of disruptive, hostile behavior that interfered with her ability to form satisfactory relationships with others and became a blueprint for her future relationships.

Leslie developed a view of the world as depriving, rejecting, and withholding, leaving her with a clinging, dependent attitude, voracious neediness, and a demand for immediate gratification. Her attachments were distorted and she seemed motivated to fight and to take what she didn't get from her ungiving environment. She was determined to get what she wanted one way or another, even if it meant taking it. It appeared that Leslie maintained a superficial and exploitive attitude toward other people as a way of not becoming close or dependent, and she gave nothing in return. We felt this child would require intensive, long-term treatment in a safe, predictable, and reassuring milieu where she could begin to address her attachment and behavioral difficulties and begin the difficult work of mourning the loss of and separation from her mother and the lack of emotional involvement by her father.

Leslie quickly revealed herself to be a master manipulator. She forged staff signatures on her goal sheets, she constantly lied, and her every action seemed designed to raise the ire of those around her. She was initially very clinging and affectionate and used many physical complaints to seek attention from staff. She had difficulty accepting limits and was highly stubborn and defiant. She was superficially affectionate, saying "I love you" often, but especially after being confronted about her behavior. Leslie exhibited similar behavior with her peers and quickly earned the reputation of the most feared and disliked child. She used group as a whipping post for her peers and would verbally abuse them there.

In our therapy sessions Leslie presented as an engaging, silly, self-absorbed youngster who was very demanding of my attention. She often acted entitled, manipulative, and sneaky in her play. Issues around honesty, control, and trust surfaced almost immediately. Her play activities centered on choosing board games, and she avoided any play activities that had a potential for eliciting fantasy material. She blatantly cheated in her play and was intent on winning at all costs. But she wouldn't reveal anything about herself or her early traumatic experiences, nor would she look at her disruptive behavior on the unit. She tried to avoid, deny, or minimize her problematic behavior, preferring instead to play and to exaggerate how well things were going on the unit. While our relationship seemed important to her, Leslie used her dishonesty and sneakiness to keep me at arm's length and tested me to see how I would respond to her behavior.

A turning point came when I confronted Leslie about her sneaky behavior and her dishonesty—I refused to play games with her where she cheated. I said, "Leslie, I like you and spending time with you. But look, this game is no fun if you're going to cheat. If you want to play with me, you'll have to play straight. I'm sure your friends feel the same way." I felt it was important to provide Leslie with the experience that I would not tolerate her antisocial behavior while also communicating to her that I was interested in her and getting to know her. I also felt she was using the games to avoid revealing her underlying feelings, and the games were thus of limited therapeutic value in helping Leslie work with her painful feelings.

Our talk resulted in some slight progress—she began to talk about meaningful issues, such as her behavior on the unit. What she said, however, had a superficial and shallow quality to it. Leslie seemed to mimic comments she heard in groups or from her doctors; her comments were apparently designed to please us and to continue to avoid addressing her feelings. Her behavior in the hospital continued to try even the most patient and nurturing of our treatment team, and kept her peers at bay.

After about five months with little improvement, we decided to implement several changes in Leslie's treatment. The treatment team confronted her defensive behaviors more actively and also confronted her father and stepmother about their resistance to working with the treatment team, their undermining of Leslie's treatment, and their refusal to deal with Leslie's physical abuse prior to her admission. We found that they tended to be quite critical and punitive toward Leslie during home visits and were concerned only with her behavior rather than with the underlying emotional issues facing the child. We also made an aggressive attempt to deepen Leslie's mother's involvement in her treatment.

Although Leslie's parents slowly began to show more of a commitment to and involvement in her treatment, there was till the underlying issue of who wanted her and where she would live following her discharge. Each parent used this situation to express his or her hostility toward the other. Failure to resolve this issue offered Leslie little motivation to improve. This issue was at the fore of family therapy with both parents for the next couple of months and was clearly distressing to the child. Although Leslie acted as if it were no big deal, her disruptive behavior escalated, betraying the intense turmoil going on beneath the surface.

At about this time, Leslie directed more anger toward me in therapy. Sometimes she would give me the silent treatment, or tell me she'd rather stay on the unit to watch videos, or schedule another activity at the same time as her therapy time. She refused to talk about any of the events in her family therapy or her feelings about these events. It was my impression that Leslie was acting out her anger toward her parents with me and that therapy provided a safer environment for expressing these feelings than family therapy, where she feared pushing them away or prompting abandonment. Leslie's behavior intensified and continued over many months and was quite trying. Nevertheless, I felt it was important to communicate to Leslie that I would hang in there with her and not give up. My approach was to be tolerant and to continue to be supportive, constant, and interested in her and her feelings despite her well-designed attempts to push me away.

Leslie's mother eventually decided she wanted her daughter to live with her, and Leslie's father and stepmother dropped their efforts to pursue custody. Home visits with Mother were stepped up in an effort to see if Mother could provide Leslie with a nurturing home environment. Leslie showed a dramatic change in her behavior on the unit, toward me, and in her therapy. She was more willing to talk about going to live with her mother and about their visits. She also began talking more about her sadness and grief at not going to live with her father and stepmother. Not surprisingly, Leslie also had grave concerns that her father would be angry and withdraw from her again. She was more playful, open, and trusting, and she was able to talk more about her feelings of anger toward me in the past months and to relate her behavior to the difficulties going on in her family therapy. In the ensuing months our relationship deepened and Leslie showed more reciprocity in her play, an increased awareness of me as a person, and a willingness to let me know how important her therapy and our relationship was to her.

Over the next several months we addressed the difficult task of preparing Leslie for discharge from the hospital and moving home with her mother. We decided to take this slowly, as transitions in the past had always been sudden, unpredictable, and without explanation. Leslie was finally able to talk about her feelings of attachment to the hospital and how difficult it was for her to leave. She had clearly become attached to the staff, her doctors, peers, and myself—much more so than she had ever been able to openly let others know.

I continued to see Leslie in therapy following her discharge from the hospital. It was only then that she was able to begin addressing the painful feelings associated with the traumatic comings and going of the significant adults in her life. She began making friends at school, and her manipulative, hostile behavior gradually faded away. In looking back, it was apparent that there was no magic or single intervention that helped this child. Rather, it seemed that the treatment team's ability to hang in there, to not give up, particularly in the face of such noxious behavior and few emotional rewards, provided the healing ingredients.

Supervised Parent-Child Visitation*

For several years I have supervised parental contact at the direction of the court or attorneys when there is need for objective observations of parent-child interactions or when there is concern that the child may be at risk of harm or emotional distress without the supervision of a responsible adult. My role is often to assist in parent-child reunification through parental support and guidance and through recommendations to the court.

In the case of divorced or separated parents, the custodial parent may resent, deny, or be fearful of the child's emotional attachment to the absent parent. It may pose an attack, a threat. It may stir jealousy or rage. These same feelings may also be experienced by the absent parent who, in addition, is often emotionally needy and looks to the child to meet those needs as well as to make up for lost time.

The child's foster parents or guardians who are asked to help with the child's eventual reunification with absent parents may experience all of the above feelings and more.

These emotions all place a strain on the child, who resonates to the conflictual feelings. The child often tries to meet everyone's needs, his or her own needs often becoming lost in the process.

Reunification visits must be viewed and planned not only with the interests of the child in mind but with attention given to the needs and concerns of all adults involved as well, or it is unlikely to be successful.

The parents attempting to reunify must have no immediate be-

*Contributed by Claudia Gibson, Fairfax, California.

havioral expectations of the child; that is, they should not depend on reciprocal behavior. They should be able to put themselves at the child's disposal and nurture the child without expectations of return.

By removing the parental expectations from the situation, the child has a chance to sort out for himself how he feels and to act on his authentic feelings, dropping along the wayside the false self most children create to accommodate their parents.

There is a reward in allowing the child to drop his false self: When he is ready to peek out of his cocoon, he is being open—trusting and unafraid to take the risk of exposing his true self. This means he is in a safe place. The ability to reopen the hearts to an absent or abusive parent is a connection to life as well as to the parent. After all, isn't what we're talking about the gift of unconditional love—acceptance as is?

The goal of therapeutic visitation is to enable the child to carve out a niche of comfort with a parent who has been absent so that the child can deal with the ongoing contact and be supported and comforted as needed during the period of reunification and of allowing trust to evolve. For this goal to be met, it is important that the supervisor establish a relationship of safety and eventual trust with the child.

Following is a brief description of how supervised parental visitation was helpful in the reunification of three-and-a-half-year-old Brad and his father. The boy became speechless and encopretic after witnessing, and possibly experiencing directly, a series of violent domestic incidents between his parents. The last one was so egregious that he shattered emotionally.

We started parental contact with one hour a week. Brad ran the moment he saw his father. Not wishing to contain or control the boy, we ran along with the child until he stopped. This behavior continued for several visits, the running eventually giving way to walking, with the father trying to initiate a dialogue. Since the child was electively mute, I encouraged the father to just tell him about his day's work or tell a story, to have *no* expectations. Some weeks later, while walking in the woods, Brad, still in diapers, spontaneously burst into tears and ran off. He had soiled himself and was ashamed. I told the frantic father to just tell him that it was OK, they could go home and change—that Daddy wasn't angry; he was calm and wanted to help. The father did that, and he yelled, "I love you."

At first the child stayed hidden in the trees. But after the third time Dad reassured him, he stuck his head out from behind the tree, and then, as his Dad gently urged him to come back, he began to walk toward us. The father was so thrilled that he scooped him up in a great hug and told Brad how much he loved him. The boy spoke back, asking to go home and change.

Progress was relatively steady over the next year and a half. Brad regained bowel control, he began to communicate with words, and he and his father began to reformulate their relationship. Eventually the child was mainstreamed into regular classes at public school.

One day on the trail, Brad took a stick and drew a house in the dirt. There were his room, Dad's room, and *my* room.

The boy and his father were eventually reunited in a joint custody arrangement, went to conjoint therapy, and two years after that were released from the control of the court. The process took five years. At age eight the youngster appeared to have successfully reattached to the point where it was safe to be angry, it was safe to disagree, it was OK just to be.

Rituals and routines were agreed on, and there was a mutual level of comfort. Each allowed the other his own space and learned mutual respect. There were still problems, but the tools learned in therapy had made the two intact enough to deal with their ups and downs. Spontaneous displays of affection and ease of contact, the dramatic level of physical interaction, and the respect for boundaries, among other things, indicated the reattachment was successful.

11

Saying Goodbye to Lost Relationships

To lose someone whom we have loved and been loved by produces grief, not psychopathology; tears, not patienthood.

Valliant, 1985

How do we help a child say goodbye to a relationship that she needs, wants, and experiences as necessary for survival? Can a child form a new primary attachment when doing so represents betrayal and loss of another? This is a common dilemma faced by most of the children with whom we work in therapy and in out-of-home care. A child who has other significant attachment relationships available may be able to cope with the realities of parental loss and its attendant pain. Nevertheless, the most skillful and loving adults cannot provide for the emotional needs of the child experiencing profound loss unless the support, assurance and guidance occurs within the context of a trusting relationship.

In the absence of their attachment figures, children give themselves what they need to live: a viable relationship with the missing parent through idealization, splitting, bargaining, magical thinking, and various reunion fantasies. These youngsters find sustenance in crumbs of hope, cherishing past parenting relationships and creatively and actively resisting the efforts of numerous adults to have them deal with reality so they will "get better". We are left with a sense of respect, if not reverence, for their life force when we witness the efforts they make to provide for themselves. There comes a time when those survival skills interfere with these children's development and ability to receive, in actuality, what they are attempting to supply themselves with in fantasy and distorted thinking. The therapist helps by providing support, hope, and guidance to the caregivers; developing a relationship of safety through consistency and emotional closeness with the child; and working patiently at the child's pace. We know that most children have some awareness of the realities of their past and present situation; it is acceptance of reality that is resisted. Children grow in their ability to accept their personal realities when they experience safety and when they are ready. As with any growth, it cannot be hurried. All we can do is provide the environment that nurtures and sustains the process.

Children may invoke extreme avoidant defenses if they are forced to confront losses that are overwhelming to them, and in so doing they may alienate themselves from their present relationships. The process of coping with such losses is one of internalizing the lost attachment relationship in order to say goodbye, and then grieving in manageable segments.

All the vignettes in this chapter demonstrate how clinicians connect with youngsters in supportive, consistent relationships; meet their needs; and wait for them to indicate they are ready to begin dealing with their profound losses. These may sound like relatively simple tasks, but they are not. It requires extreme patience to accept the child's natural timing related to healing, trusting that it is in fact happening even when there are long stretches of time when there is no evidence that things are moving. We feel our clinical confidence draining away when we don't really know what to do besides "hang out" with the child and hope no one will ask specifically what we are doing and why. We hope there isn't something else we should be doing—this requires patience and wisdom.

The child is strengthened by the relationship formed with the therapist, and the therapist comes face to face with the pain, terror, and longings of the child that cannot be assuaged, only accepted. This is extremely difficult work for even the most seasoned therapists.

The first contribution in this chapter elegantly describes a child who worked through her profound early losses in the emotionally safe environment provided by her therapist. The author describes a crisis that restimulated abandonment fears and terror in the child two years later when there was an addition of another child in the family. This reminds us that these children have long-lasting, perhaps permanent vulnerabilities related to perceptions of loss and abandonment in relationships.

The youngster in the next vignette is touched by a story she hears, and reveals hidden feelings about her deceased parent. The child, after months of what appears to be not doing much of anything in counseling, begins to directly discuss painful past and present experiences. This is an example of an event cuing a child's response that had relational support as a prerequisite. A less experienced clinician might well have been discouraged by the lack of progress of the first four months; indeed, some might well have ended the child's treatment. The child was helped to share and honor hidden reminders of a deceased parent. The therapist's work with the child and the guidance he provides to her caregivers enable the child to accept the loss of both her parents.

Black high heels facilitate an intimate connection between a youngster and her therapist in the next contribution. The therapist describes how the child builds a sense of safe self in relation to others. Support, and clinical consultation with others who are important in the child's life, enable her to say both hello and goodbye to her birth parents.

In the last vignette a clinician reaches far and wide in her efforts to help a boy accept the loss of his mother and his dream of reunification. She gives us an example of how a lifebook and religious ritual was used to help the boy internalize and hold onto his past in order to "let it go" and move on in his life.

Working through Loss in Dramatic Play*

Niki was a then four-year-old girl who lived in foster care due to a history of severe deprivation and neglect. Her mother, twenty-year-old Tamara, was also severely neglected as a child and spent little time feeding, holding, nurturing, or caring for her child. This lack of nutritional and physical nurturing caused the baby to develop

*Contributed by Eliana Gil, Rockville, Maryland. This vignette, in a briefer form, originally appeared in E. Gil & T. C. Johnson, *Sexualized Children: Assessment and Treatment of Sexualized Children and Children Who Molest* (Rockville, Md.: Launch Press, 1993), and is reprinted here with permission.

nonorganic "failure to thrive." When Tamara took the child at age three to a physician because the baby was not toilet-trained, the child was immediately hospitalized. Niki was suffering from severe malnutrition and showed signs of minimal care: She had impetigo on her face and hands, a massive rash on her vaginal area, and lice in her hair. She was developmentally delayed in her language and expressive abilities. She could not walk, both from weakness and because her muscles were constricted from her having been mostly confined to her crib. She had never been immunized and had signs of untreated ear infections and tonsillitis. Tamara was charged with criminal neglect, and parental rights were terminated six months after Niki's hospitalization. When she was released from the hospital, Niki was referred both to a fost-adopt placement and for psychotherapeutic treatment.

The foster mother reported that Niki was lethargic and passive. She did not cry, even when soiled or hungry. She preferred to stay in one spot, apparently uncomfortable with being out of her crib. She didn't seem interested in toys and usually clutched her blanket in her hands. Niki flinched when the foster mother came into the room in the morning.

Niki was unresponsive in therapy as well. She did not play spontaneously and required stimulation to become interested in toys. I did parallel play with her to awaken her interest in various activities. Sitting next to her, I would make sure she watched as I rolled a ball, cut cardboard into shapes, played with water, built blocks, and did a variety of other things. She usually sat staring, with fingers of both hands in her mouth. She did not speak, and a special tutor was helping her develop linguistic skills.

The youngster remained unattached and reticent during the first four months of therapy, although she did become accustomed to the small playroom and my constancy. I would often introduce different toys to gauge her interest. She definitely liked playing with the sand in the sandtray, pouring sand from one cup into another and pouring water on the sand, watching it absorb and dry. She eventually focused on a mother pig with seven piglets and brought them into the sandtray. From this time forward her play took on different characteristics, becoming repetitive and exact. At every session for about three months, she buried the mother pig in the left-hand corner of the sandtray. The piglets were placed in the opposite corner, and they took turns trying to find the mother pig. The child said nothing during this play, yet appeared to be absorbed in what she was doing, frequently showing a low-range affective variance. The piglets would go looking for the mother and would alternately fall in water and drown, climb and fall off a tree, fall off a bridge, and be unable to climb fences, mountains, or other obstacles.

There was no variation in the play—The piglets followed a similar course each time. I sat next to Niki as she played, and from time to time I would comment, without interpretation, on what she had done. I would say, for example, "The mother pig is buried. The baby pig fell from the tree."

One day there was a major difference in Niki's repetitive scenario: None of the piglets drowned, fell down, or otherwise faced an overwhelming obstacle—they instead found and uncovered the mother pig! Niki stopped abruptly, almost surprised by what she had done, and quickly moved away from the sandtray, indicating she was done for that day.

During the following session one piglet began the "search for mother" ritual and found and uncovered her quickly. This time the child put the piglet next to the mother, looked up at me, and said, "Titty, no milk." She seemed genuinely sad, and her eyes watered up. I said, "No milk for the baby," and the child responded tearfully, "Baby sad." She held a big stuffed rabbit in her lap for the rest of the session and rocked it and fed it with a plastic bottle. From time to time a single tear would fall on her cheek.

The next session the child repeated the play—the piglet looked for the mother, found her, and was saddened by the mother's lack of milk. Niki then held her rabbit in her lap, stroking its head and feeding it for a while. When the piglet found no milk the third time Niki did this play, Niki reached over and placed a mother giraffe in the opposite corner of the tray. She then picked up the baby giraffe, and the baby giraffe and the piglet seemed to nestle together next to the mother giraffe. "This mommy gots milk!" the child exclaimed. She again held the rabbit and stroked its head, saying "There, there, . . . you awright."

Niki was working on her feelings of abandonment by her mother, as well as on her emerging sense of trust in and attachment to her foster mother, through symbolic play. The child verbalized very little, but her working-through had a positive impact on not only her relationship with her foster mother but her relationship with me, her therapist.

There were some visible changes after these sessions. Niki made more frequent eye contact, asked me questions, relaxed her hand on mine, laughed, and made spontaneous remarks, such as "You're always here when I come" and "You have good toys." She exhibited intermittent interest in the sandtray and was now more likely to choose other toys in the playroom. She particularly liked to prepare food in a play kitchen, making soups and breads. Her foster mother often encouraged Niki's help in the kitchen, and the child proudly showed me how to make real bread, using clay to simulate kneading dough.

The foster mother told me Niki seemed to have "come to life" at home. She now cried when she was unhappy or frustrated, and she told the foster mother when she was tired or hungry. She was beginning to sleep through the night, and her obsession with hoarding food was somewhat diminished. Niki had begun to attend a small preschool play group with three other children her age, and although she had felt very frightened at first, she was beginning to interact with the other children. The foster mother reported that Niki even wanted her to "hurry" to take her to her play group.

The tutor reported similar progress, and the foster mother initiated adoption procedures, reassuring Niki that she was going to be her new mother. Niki asked about the "other lady" from time to time, and her foster mother told her that she was fine and getting help for her problems.

Symbolic play had been effective in helping Niki address the issues of dependency, abandonment, and attachment. It was clear that she had to process some of her feelings about her biological mother before she could attach to the foster mother. By stroking and feeding the rabbit, she was in essence self-nurturing and accepting the fact that her mother had failed to provide the appropriate care. Once she allowed herself to feel the pain of longing for the nurturing parent who had not been there, she could shift her dependency to the nurturing parent who was available to her, as represented in her play by the giraffe figurine.

The therapy with this child continued beyond this point, and many other issues surfaced, including anger, acute dependency and separation anxiety, and distrust of men. Two years later the family went through a crisis when the foster mother took another child into the home. When Niki came to therapy, she again focused on the mother and baby giraffe, now having the piglet kill and destroy the baby giraffe. This transition phase was quite difficult, since Niki's fragile sense of security was threatened by the presence of the other child, who eventually was also adopted. The stability of her placement, her positive attachment to her foster mother and siblings, and the consistent availability of the therapy setting were major factors in Niki's recovery.

What I gained most in working with Niki was a respect for the child's capacity to self-repair. I found myself despairing at the situation she had endured and struggling to help find some way that she might begin to have a positive, healing experience. Niki clearly found her own way, her own symbolism. My job was to open as many windows as possible, patiently allowing her to see a range of symbols around her from which she might choose. My job was also to create a safe environment. This meant I had to give her physical and emotional space. She had not been nurtured in her early years, and she was still frightened when people looked at her, touched her, or focused too much on her. She would have to learn to tolerate others' attention, and I felt that I needed to proceed with caution, giving her no more attention than she could tolerate. This went against my instinct, which was to give her constant attention and nurturing. Once she found that the sandtray and the pig and piglets were her symbols, and she created a metaphor that challenged her to work through her deepest feelings, my job was to "get out of her way," allowing her to do what she needed, at her own pace, and within the metaphor she had created. At the same time, my comments were offered often enough for her to know she had my support and encouragement. I have never forgotten this child and her enormous ability to find her own way to heal herself.

Memories of Mom*

Terry was referred by her first-grade teacher because of some unusual acting-out behaviors and extreme difficulty in relating to her

*Contributed by Felix Sarubbi, Narraganset, Rhode Island.

peers and to school staff. We had been working together for sixteen weeks of half-hour sessions—a limitation imposed by our in-school counseling program's format—at the time of this session.

Terry was typically vague and avoidant when I picked her up from her classroom, and this day was no exception. Her greeting was inserted perfunctorily into a sort of play-by-play monologue she was reciting to herself as she put her things away and made ready to come along with me. "I won't be back till gym time," she said to no one in particular and, stuffed "kitty" in hand, hurried past me and down the corridor to the playroom.

Although we were making slight progress in our work together, Terry was having difficulty in tolerating any kind of intimacy and in making significant attachments following some traumatic disruptions in her life. Her parents had died within six months of each other when she was four and a half years old, and she had been adopted by her maternal uncle and aunt. She was struggling to adjust to her new environment—a new state and a rural town much different from her original surroundings, new parental attachment figures, and sibling stepbrothers where she had been an only child. In addition, it appeared that she had little assistance in grieving her tremendous losses. Her new family, though strong in many ways, was eager for her to be "over it," and her adoptive parents were having difficulty allowing her latitude when issues continued to resurface as she struggled to deal with them.

During our previous session, we had agreed to read *The Tenth Good Thing about Barney*. Given Terry's many issues and the complexities of her situation, this grieving piece, at least, seemed clear and strong and so a good place to begin.

We read the story, and then Terry wanted to draw. I introduced the idea of our writing a book together about her life. At first she hid her eyes from me with her hands. "I'm going to sit over here," she said as she moved her chair. With some distance between us, she told me that the story reminded her of the day her mommy had died.

"I did the exact same thing," she said. "I cried, and I couldn't eat as much as my appetite wanted me to. I just ate one little pea."

"Then what did you do?"

"I went to bed."

"What did you do there?"

"I read a book. It was my mother's. It was about God. It had pictures in it I could look at."

We drew as the session went on. She moved around the table and stood across from me, facing me. I asked, "Was there a funeral for your mom? Like there was for Barney?"

"Yes, but I didn't go. I wanted to go, but they wouldn't let me. They were scared, but I wasn't scared. I wanted to go."

We talked about how not being able to go to a funeral gives us the sense of not having been able to say goodbye to our loved ones. I introduced some ideas for activities we might be able to do together to deal with that feeling. I said that sometimes writing a person a letter to say the things we didn't get to say before he or she died can make us feel better. Terry asked how we could do that, and I said we could do it together.

She said, "At least I have a picture of her." She told me she had a "blankie" that her mom "used to cuddle up with too," and a sweater of her mom's. The blankie and the sweater still smell like her mom, and she keeps them in her bottom drawer, which is reserved for her most special, private things. She said she was big enough to wear the sweater now but wouldn't wear it to school, because she didn't want to get it dirty and have it "lose the smell." I reflected to her that it is comforting to have keepsakes of the people we love who are no longer here with us, and that I understood how important it was to have a special place to keep such things.

This session was significant because it was our first direct dialogue about her experience of her mother's death and the events immediately following. Terry's adoptive parents knew about the drawer of precious things, and I strongly supported them for their willingness to allow her this meaningful bit of privacy.

The olfactory aspect of comfort objects is extremely interesting to me; I think we often overlook this kind of self-comforting device used by those recovering from a traumatic experience. These kinds of details were unknown to Terry's adoptive parents through my discussions with them, and they became aware of how much Terry is still dealing with all that has happened to her.

This brief description of one session in Terry's counseling provides a look at the beginning of a course of deeper work related to her losses, a process that soon included her experience of the death of her father. The attachment to her adoptive parents and relationship with me grew in importance and comfort as we continued working with both past and present issues.

Black High Heels*

Naomi is the youngest of three siblings; she has two older sisters. Their parents were mere children themselves when they had children. One by one, these three children were removed from their home by Child Protective Services because of parental neglect, physical abuse, and allegations of sexual abuse. The children were also exposed to parental domestic violence and drug use. Parental rights were terminated when the parents were unable to demonstrate, over a period of several years, that they could provide a safe and adequate home life for their three small kids.

It was difficult to find a family able to take and handle all three children at the same time. Further, keeping the children together seemed to perpetuate chaotic interactions among them. They would sometimes act out aggressively and even sexually toward each other, reopening the confusion and trauma of their early childhood history of neglect, abuse, and dysfunction.

Naomi had extensive developmental delays and emotional and behavioral problems. She needed special education in her school setting, with curb-to-curb transportation, a small class size, and close supervision to manage her impulsive, disruptive, aggressive, and sometimes self-destructive behavior. She also needed close care and supervision in her foster placement. Most of all, she needed loving, creative, "get in the kid's skin" kinds of parents, teachers, caseworkers, and therapist.

Naomi sometimes felt that there was something stuck in her throat that gagged her, that she could neither throw up nor swallow. The foster mother and I thought this was an indicator of posttraumatic stress associated with sexual abuse. When Naomi was five, she made scratch marks about her neck area in an attempt to dislodge the "something stuck" in her throat. Not surprisingly, the foster parents were very concerned about her behavior.

---

* Contributed by T. Nalani Waiholua Archibeque, Maui, Hawaii.

Foster mother and therapist put their heads together to come up with an intervention to relieve Naomi's periodic and desperate emotional and throat discomfort. A suggestion and gestures to "throw it up" over the toilet bowl or a garbage can did not relieve the "stuck in the throat" symptoms. But a second suggestion by the foster mom to just let it pass through and "push it out" and eliminate it in the toilet did. What a relief! It was a stimulating challenge to understand the incredible symptomatology, or, if you will, metaphors, of this child's expression.

Instances of unusual change in Naomi's personality, voice quality, and character suggested there was fluid, dissociative splitting going on. Over time, given loving support and strong guidance, Naomi's sophisticated ability to engage in fantasy play helped to promote her healing. With her imaginary family and her "dolly" family, she evolved from being a verbally and physically abusive "parent" who engaged in name-calling, yelling, and hitting into becoming a kindly speaking, caring, more appropriately acting mother parent and father parent. This was fascinating to witness. It happened as her own real life provided what a child brought into this world deserves—safety, love, and decent parenting.

Naomi began working through her sense of maternal betrayal and maternal loss through fantasy play. For example, she pretended to roll up an imaginary parachute, which, she explained, came from her birth mother, who was dropping by Naomi's home. Naomi explained she was sending her birth mother back to where she came from. It seemed as though this child was saying she was settled now and OK. Naomi continued to create many more stories and facilitated mastery through her use of metaphor.

Ultimately, and very fortunately, Naomi was able, through her culturally and family-sensitive adoptive parents, to see her own parents, siblings, grandparents, and extended family; to ask the "why" questions that bothered her; to gather pictures for her scrapbook; and to say goodbye, cry, and grieve the loss of the family that couldn't be.

Her adoptive parents and the foster family who immediately preceded them were multicultural families of Asian, Caucasian, and Hawaiian backgrounds. Their life experience was to live and appreciate the diversity and uniqueness of culture and color. They were easily able to receive Naomi and her mixture of "local" (Hawaiian

Island) cultures. They also related well to the birth family, despite their grave deficiencies in parenting. This helped Naomi reengage with her birth parents and family and truly say "hello" before they said "goodbye."

Naomi began psychotherapy with me in 1990, she at age five, her therapist at age forty-five. At the beginning of our therapy relationship, Naomi would often arrive early and either open the door (often interrupting a session that had not been completed), as if ready to run into my office, or hide under one of the waiting room chairs, waiting to be coaxed to come out. Once we got started, she frequently got into everything that was not bolted down. She had a heck of a time settling down. She was often in one of the five A's—*a*nxious, *a*ngry, *a*fraid, *a*gitated, and, sometimes, momentarily *a*ffectionate. I would brace myself for Naomi's arrival, childproofing my office of car, cabinet, and bathroom keys, lipstick, crayons and Magic Markers—things that were small and easy for her to hide. It took a good part of the sixty-minute sessions for Naomi to settle down; then she'd become reluctant to leave, creating delay after delay.

A few weeks into treatment, Naomi discovered a pair of high heels I kept in the office. Instead of their being part of my uniform, they became part of her uniform every time she came in. She would put them on, walk around, and wear them through the session. I finally got smart and brought in an older pair of heels that I no longer used for her to wear. Somehow, getting into my shoes settled and focused her enough for us to engage. I saw it as her way of taking charge of herself in an uncertain experience with a "How can I trust you?" person. It was also a way for her to be intimate (nothing like wearing someone else's shoes) but not too intimate, and to create an attachment but not be too attached. Often at a loss about what to do or say, I followed and trusted this extraordinary child to show me the way to what she needed most.

Naomi created another ritual in our journey toward connection. She sat in my chair, a high-backed, pink, upholstered executive chair, and worked at my desk. She played teacher, therapist, mommy, daddy, and husband from the large chair behind the desk. As she played, these "adult" people became more real, more decent, more consistent, more trusting, and more enduring. Naomi's role play mirrored to me her internal process of rebuilding a self, a safe self in relationship to safe others. This was in dramatic contrast to her earlier world, which had fallen apart, where she had lost her whole family and way of life.

Whereas Naomi's creative coping/survival process had earlier taken her from fantasy to splitting and dissociation, we were able to change this process to one that went from fantasy to modeling of live situations and role playing. This redirection shifted her from potentially severe, massive impairment toward healing. Some scars are likely to remain, reminding her of the reality of her life history.

I think the Guardian Angel who looked after this child and me, in our attachment-ing, was a pair of old black leather high heels, size 8, medium width, and a well-worn armchair and desk around which Naomi *became* me before it was safe to be *with* me, and I became her, to know (to show) who she really was. It was a healthy, balanced attachment in that we were able to say our goodbyes, take pictures together, mark the event with a gift to her (a picture frame for photos of special times and people in her life), exchange addresses, and promise to remember each other.

I was in a small shopping center the weekend before Naomi and her adopted family moved to another community. I heard a child behind me yell my name, using the four distinct syllable pronunciation many adults have trouble with. Naomi ran up to me, we hugged, said hello, then said goodbye again. A few minutes later I was in the drugstore when Naomi appeared with her adoptive mom and dad and two of many siblings. She said, "I want you to meet my *family* [whom I had met before]. This is my dad. This is my mom. This is my sister. This is my brother," instructing each of us to shake each other's hand. The child had come such a long way in the two and a half years from the time Naomi and I had begun psychotherapy!

Naomi was able to say goodbye because she now belonged to a family she embraced as her family. She was graced by the universe to have two child-loving, child-knowing sets of parents: a single foster mom with children, then an adoptive mom and dad with many children. These wonderful, spiritually strong, culturally sensitive, child-loving, giving parents set Naomi on a path of healing and growth.

Lifebook and Rituals*

Lifebooks, those wonderful pieces of work we do with unattached and abandoned children, carry with them exciting possibilities for grief resolution and, in time, reattachment in relationships. The traditional lifebook is a collection of photos, when available, and children's drawings. It is a chronicle of their life story or life events up to the present. With imagination, curiosity, and a little extra time, this involvement with children can greatly assist them in not only putting together their past but also letting it go.

When Steve, a beautiful eight-year-old Hispanic child, arrived at the residential treatment center, his colossal losses were evident in his dark, troubled eyes, with only flashes of eye contact. His hopeless posture and somber expression were more characteristic of an elderly person who had tried to digest too many overwhelming losses in a brief period of time. His life had been a series of placements following abandonment by his mentally ill birth mother in a train station. His maternal grandparents pursued his custody vigorously but where deemed "too poor" to take him and lacked the resources to attempt a legal remedy.

Steve arrived in residential treatment with a near-obsession to find his birth mother. Traditional grief work was minimally effective; however, he grew more trusting and eventually expressed an interest in "having a family." An adoptive family was located. There was progression to a series of weekend visits over an extended period of time. These potential adoptive parents were wild about the child. They possessed all the strengths necessary to parent a child with Steve's vulnerabilities, but Steve could not break free of his deep desire to be reunited with his birth mother, and he would not settle for anything less. This unresolved grief resulted in serious property destruction at the adoptive family's home prior to his adoptive placement date. All parties agreed that this adoption was not workable.

During this time we continued to laboriously review the pieces of his early life and transfer them to paper in his lifebook. We also spent painful hours in therapy reviewing the impact of his life events. Sometimes therapy times were long rides in an agency vehi-

---

*Contributed by Sharon K. Bauer, Terre Haute, Indiana.

cle, where he could be more open and feel less inhibited in sharing feelings. There are no known reasons for this except that eye contact is less expected when riding than within an office.

Steve was encouraged to accept responsibility for his behavior, while all his wonderful strengths were supported. He was invited to learn from recent past events and then let go and look to his future hopefully. I loved this child very deeply, and I desperately wanted what was in his best interest and for him to have a happy life. This was a period of anguish and vulnerability, with no clear road map to resolution.

Work on his lifebook continued. Contact with former foster homes yielded no photos, but there were written pages, drawings, and reviews of events. One document was especially sought—a copy of his birth certificate. He was delighted to review this, and it gave him grounding in his heritage and beginnings. We asked the public relations department at the hospital in a distant city where he was born for a picture of the hospital. Steve was delighted when this was added to his growing collection of pieces of his history.

I contacted the Department of Human Services in the small town where he was born for possible photos of his early life with his birth family. I did this without his knowledge, to spare him further grief if the contact yielded no pertinent or helpful information. An employee there contacted me by phone; she knew his family and his mother! To my stunned disbelief, she revealed that Steve's mother had died in a boating accident several years earlier and that his maternal grandparents still lived in the area. She was willing to make contact with them to seek early photos and to write me a letter confirming the details of his mother's death.

I anxiously told Steve what I had learned and then gave him the letter and photos. It was a time of shock and deep sadness—it was the death of a dream, and dreams for little boys of being reunited with a missing mother die slowly and painfully. There were lots of discussions about properly grieving this awesome loss.

Steve identified with being Catholic; it was the faith practiced in his longest placement. We talked about contacting the local Catholic priest. Steve indicated he would like to meet with him. The young priest was most encouraging and helpful in arranging a memorial mass at the chapel of the residential center. This provided a ritual for mourning in a familiar surrounding. Steve invited staff and peers he wanted to attend. Following this touching ceremony, I took Steve out for dinner and then for another of our long rides. His growth was evident in his new openness to explore this painful grief and to begin letting go.

Some months following the completion of his lifebook and the walk through the agony of mourning the death of his mother, he was again linked with a potential adoptive family, one who joyously received him into their home.

This vignette underscores the need for adequate mourning of events and persons in order to promote attachment. Searching for information and providing support, rituals, and ongoing relationship building between therapist and child may also aid in the complicated task of mourning and attachment.

12

Connecting in New Attachment Relationships

And then there was the seeker of wisdom who, crawling, bloodied, and panting with exhaustion, reached his destination and humbly asked the guru, "How can we help these children transcend their pain and their fears and allow themselves to trust and to deeply love again?" Lightning and thunder burst across the skies, and the mighty words were spoken. Quivering, tears in his eyes, the seeker gathered together the shards of his faltering confidence and whispered, "That's it? You mean, that's the answer?" The earth trembled and the answer once more rang across the land—HANG IN THERE!

There are helpful things clinicians and caregivers can do for the children and for ourselves while we continue to hang in there and wait for attachments to grow. And the most important of these things is to support one another as we gather, share, and honor the wisdom we gain as we struggle with attachment problems. I find it exciting and a source of joy to translate complex research and clinical experiences into practical examples that clinicians, parents, and children can use to help accept the realities of their experiences and learn to love and play again. From discussions with veteran foster parents, I have learned much about how to live with children who have attachment problems. These adults have useful, creative suggestions for helping youngsters feel welcomed into new households, and we help each other plan ways to keep children from hurting themselves and others. Children and adults who have experienced out-of-home care are, of course, the experts in what it is like to be a child living in someone else's home, or to have new people in theirs. They have insights to share.

The clinical stories in this chapter are generally brief and have in common descriptions of children with severe attachment problems and the parents' struggles to help them learn to live in their family.

The first contribution relates a slow, cautious, lengthy clinical journey taken with a very young child. The clinician and parent work together and, with the help of careful use of tactile stimulation, teaching of play skills, behavior management, medical intervention, and large doses of love and patience, the child eventually allows the physical warmth of his foster mother to penetrate his armor.

"Can this child live in a family?" was the question ultimately answered by professionals seeking placement for a child one could only describe as feral. We are reminded that placement decisions are clinical decisions and, when carefully made, can reduce the multiple placement failures that are common among children with attachment disorders.

The parents who wrote the next two vignettes share their thoughts and feelings with poignant honesty. Their stories document the differences between working in a structured clinical setting and integrating these frightened, snarling, destructive, and avoidant youngsters into their lives. The impact of the children's behavior and their mute and vociferous suffering affect the marriage relationship, the other children, pets, and treasured family belongings. We learn of a boy's limitations in allowing closeness, and how an adolescent "tests the waters." In thinking more deeply about the metaphor of testing the waters, I considered how children who grow up in a family feel safe and test the waters thousands of times in small increments as they mature; young people entering a new family do not know it is safe, and they cannot trust verbal assurances. It may be obvious to us that the stream is safe, is shallow, and has a solid bottom, but that stream may appear treacherous to one who is unfamiliar with the terrain and who has had life-threatening experiences in similar situations.

Shanna, the now adult daughter described by her mother in the previous vignette, reflects on her experience as a newcomer to her family. Her reflections and insights help us understand that some exasperating behaviors are in service of avoiding pain and humiliation. Shanna and others who have formed new attachments in families not only teach us how it was for them but help us understand what is helpful and what is not, in the home, in the therapist's office, and at a policy level.

Warm Mother, Cold Boy*

A product of marital rape, Nick was rejected by his mother during the first three months of life. Then his mother gave him and his two-year-old brother to their grandmother for care. For the next nine months her care of him and his brother was not monitored. When Nick was twelve months of age and his brother thirty-six months, they were abruptly removed from the grandmother's care because of observed sexual abuse of the older boy by an adolescent aunt in the grandmother's home. Sexual abuse of Nick was suspected but never proved. For the next six months, critical periods in attachment formation, Nick and his brother were expelled from four foster homes.

Nick had a superficial smiling presentation. His behavior was unmanageable. He would disregard the rules, be unresponsive to adult authority, destroy home furnishings or goods, and commit impulsive and destructive acts. At eighteen months Nick and his brother were placed in a specialized foster home and have continued in placement there. Nick was remote and untouchable, unresponsive to caretakers, his brother, or other family members.

His hyperactivity became much more apparent at age two. He was clearly unable to sustain attention for any length of time and demanded constant watching because he would engage in treacherous and frightening behaviors, such as fearlessly jumping from tall heights, grabbing knives, running outdoors without clothing during the winter and putting his hand on hot burners. In sum, Nick appeared to be a very active, disconnected child whose impulses made him dangerous to himself and to others.

His destructive behavior took another turn at age two and a half, when he began killing animals. He killed four kittens during a four-month period by squeezing their necks or deliberately snapping their backs. He showed no apparent remorse and appeared pleased with

---

*Contributed by Sandra Hewitt, Minneapolis–St. Paul, Minnesota.

his actions. These incidents were initially regarded as accidents and not seen as deliberate aggressive behavior. As "accidents" continued to occur, they became markedly more prominent and alarming.

Three-and-a-half-year-old Nick was a most difficult child to work with in ongoing therapy. His current foster home was warm and nurturing. The experienced foster mother and father attempted to engage emotionally with Nick, but his self-contained behavior, gaze avoidance, and increasingly violent temper outbursts made this seem impossible.

The foster mother and I worked for several months on developing eye contact and gentle physical intrusions with tactile stimulation (rubbing his back, brushing his hair, stroking his face, and rocking and cuddling). Nick was slow to respond.

Continued attempts were made to engage Nick in relationships with people. His delayed language skills finally matured enough to allow him to communicate some of his feelings. We began to work on labeling feelings and stressing their communication.

Nick resisted identifying any feeling state that involved happiness or pleasure, acknowledging only anger until he was three and a half years old. At that time he admitted to feelings of fear and began to show some sense of missing his foster mother when she left him for family vacations or for occasional weekend respite care. This beginning awareness of feelings was markedly accelerated when Ritalin treatment was begun. The Ritalin calmed Nick so that he could have sustained contact with his foster mother. The increased relaxation allowed his foster mother and me to use a variety of methods to identify his feeling states.

Nick always had difficulty with sleep disturbance, often waking up three or four times a night. By about age three he began to allow his foster mother to cuddle him at night when he was disturbed, and this seemed to calm him somewhat.

The family dog was brought to a session in an attempt to intervene in Nick's cruelty to animals. The dog clearly became anxious when left in the room without the protective foster mother. The dog's anxiety and concern about the absence of the foster mother was pointed out to Nick and identified as similar to the feelings he had about his foster mother's absence. Nick denied any sense of shared emotion with the dog and resisted any attempt to identify the dog's feelings as fearful.

Nick began to allow nighttime snuggling and would even allow a little bit of it during the day. He did not associate daytime physical contact with meeting his needs.

Probably the most significant intervention facilitating attachment occurred serendipitously while the family was on vacation. Nick loved the lakefront cottage where the family vacationed and would often want to go into the water. The water and air temperatures were cold, chilling Nick until his teeth chattered and his small body was covered by a mass of goose bumps. The foster mother insisted on wrapping him up to warm him; he resisted being held on her lap. She continued to push him to remain on her lap, encouraging him to remain there until he was able to absorb some of her body heat. She would say, "I need to snuggle you until I can make you warm. You need to sit still and snuggle until we can get warm together." This contact between the cold young boy and the warm foster mother suddenly melted Nick's resistance to physical contact, and he began to relax in his foster mother's arms, melt in her lap, mold to her body, and absorb her warmth. Nick allowed her to repeat this many times during the family vacation. He even started coming to her in subsequent weeks, specifically asking for holding, snuggling, and warmth.

Nick is by no means cured of his attachment disorder. Progress in creating attachment is a slow, cautious journey, but the combination of increased language ability, carefully managed Ritalin usage, and the chance occurrence of a cold boy and a warm mother have helped create some inroads in the work with this very disturbed young boy.

Observations of a New Family*

Lani, an eighteen-month-old toddler, appeared to be sturdy, sober, self-assured, and mature for her age. It was my job to evaluate her progress in her preadoptive home of six months. My experience with this little one dramatically reinforced for me the importance of multiple observations and knowledge of both the child's history

---

*Contributed by Mark D. Everson, Chapel Hill, North Carolina. An abbreviated form of this vignette appeared in J. Garbarino et al., *What Children Can Tell Us* (San Francisco: Jossey-Bass, 1992).

and the ways abuse can influence patterns of behavior in future relationships.

I was troubled by my observations during my first home visit with Lani and her parents. Lani initiated few interactions with her parents, preferred me to them, sought my comfort when distressed, and protested my departure, expressing an interest in leaving with me. From my first observations of her, it seemed that either her current relationship with her parents was going poorly or she had been so damaged by the unstable and neglectful care she had received in the first year of life that she could not attach to them.

Observations a week later, during a second home visit, were consistent with those of the first. Lani again mostly ignored her parents, seeming to prefer my attention, and again cried when I departed. She did reveal another side of herself, however. Twice during this home visit she briefly panicked when she was startled—she lost her composure and self-assurance when faced with something she was unprepared for. Her armor was cracked.

My third visit came a week later. This time I observed a quite different little girl. She was clearly focused on her mother, initiated interactions with her, sought her attention, and related to me as a visitor in very appropriate ways. It therefore seemed that she was attached after all. I believed her initial reaction to me was counterphobic. She was actually fearful that I would take her away from her parents, in whom she was significantly invested, as she had been abruptly taken from previous parent figures by other visitors. She acted as if she wanted to leave with me as a way of gaining control over her fears. When she realized that I was only a visitor and not someone who was going to wrench her away from her attachment figures, she was able to relax and display that attachment in appropriate ways.

A week or so later I saw her in an office setting to conduct a Bayley (a standardized assessment of development). She was unable to concentrate on the testing, even though it was well within her abilities, because of the presence of a videotape operator. It seemed that it was important for Lani to know how each stranger she encountered fit into her world. After his departure she was able to focus on the task at hand and did quite well.

In the next few months it was encouraging to see Lani's relationship with her adoptive parents continue to develop, as she began to display her attachment in more obvious ways: proximity-seeking, especially in the presence of strangers; distress during separation; and clinginess at reunion.

The Feral Child*

Maria had the presence and movement of a battleship on a mission. She was a forty-two-year-old Italian "Mama" who had vigorously loved three birth children into adulthood and was determined to love Suzie, our feral child, into health.

Suzie came into our specialized evaluation program at age three after the police found her sixty-year-old biological father in the act of sexually assaulting her in a motel room. He told the officers that Suzie's mother had sold her to him, and Suzie had been moving around the state with him for most of her three years of life.

He had met his wife when she was fourteen and married her when she was eighteen. He described his wife as a drug-addicted teenager.

A seventeenth-century painting of a cherub—or a modern shampoo advertisement—describes Suzie. Floating blond hair framing her round face, translucent white skin, and dreamy large blue eyes were magnetizing attributes of this wild child. She would defecate anywhere. If unsupervised, she'd graze through garbage, eating spoiled food and nonfood items. Unsuspecting adults would find her climbing onto their laps, molding her body to theirs as she licked their faces and reached for their genitals. She was significantly delayed in language and made growling sounds when she felt threatened. The child was hypervigilent and at times dissociative. Maria, embodiment of motherhood, was resolute in her efforts to adopt this youngster.

Our evaluation center had been researching attachment problems between children and parents for three years. Suzie's ability to survive and her dysfunctional and traumatic attachment relationship were not only a mystery but a source of wonder. Our clinical team could only speculate as to how Suzie might be able to grow and develop, even given the best care available. The choices for her were limited. We believed that even a specialized foster home

*Contributed by Beverly James.

would be unable to adequately supervise her or meet her needs. Treatment group home settings were not available for a child as young as Suzie. Institutional care for three-year-old children was available only for pediatric psychiatric problems, not for bright, unsocialized three-year-old survivors of terrorizing abuse whose receptivity for attachment was unknown.

But we had Maria. Her determination never waned. In fact, it increased as I made attempts to present the realities of parenting Suzie. I watched Maria as she watched a videotape I'd made of Suzie's most disturbed behaviors. Maria's eyes glazed over, a woman in love. She patiently waited until I finished talking and repeated her mantra, "I know the pain she has suffered, and I know the work involved. I want to be Suzie's mother." The team decided to place Suzie with Maria and her husband. We thought the arrangement might be successful and reasoned that, should the placement fail, the impact for Suzie might not be overwhelming, given her history and apparent lack of attachment. She was given a fost-adopt placement whereby she would be eligible for adoption after a year in foster care with the family. Although psychotherapy could have been available for Suzie, the treatment she needed was therapeutic parenting, so she was not seen individually. Instead, professional consultation and support for the family were made available as needed, twenty-four hours a day.

In a year's time Maria's loving and aggressive nurturing, teaching, and guidance resulted in extraordinary positive changes in Suzie's behavior. What had not changed, however, and what Maria could no longer tolerate, was Suzie's attachment behavior: The child did not reciprocate emotionally—she did not seem to need her mother, and she did not spontaneously return affection. Maria had believed that she could tolerate that predicted behavior but found it to be more than she could bear. Her guilt, sadness, and relief were profound when she returned Suzie.

Our staff mirrored some of Maria's feelings. We struggled with how to help the child and where she could be placed. With all she had learned, it was clear that she should not be institutionalized. Yet we knew that this placement failure could be the first of many for this young child. We discussed what we knew theoretically and through clinical experience: that attachment is a *reciprocal* relationship. We knew that *both* parent and child need to be able to cope with and experience satisfaction with the attachment behaviors the other exhibits. We recognized that we often forget this piece of clinical wisdom when we are caught up in the drama/horror of a child's experiences and desperate needs. We then limit our thinking to the child's readiness and ability to attach, assuming, sometimes incorrectly, that motivated, well-functioning parents are all the same regarding attachment style.

Suzie went to a foster home containing what is most accurately described as a litter of children. Here four to five children of the same age are parented by a highly skilled foster mom who engages with these very damaged youngsters as a group. She does not need to have emotional responsiveness from the children in order to feel satisfied professionally or personally.

This type of placement worked for Suzie. She is now sixteen, still in the same foster home. She has been in psychotherapy off and on through her growing-up years, with early adolescence being particularly stormy. Her foster parents accept her just the way she is emotionally. Her relationships with her family and friends are functional but not close. Suzie does well in school and enjoys group recreational activities. She has a sense of who she is—her strengths and preferences (which some might call limitations). She plans to attend the local community college.

Our team's struggles in making placement decisions for Suzie mirror the struggles of parents whose children have physical or emotional limitations. We want to promote and support children's goals, but we grapple with not knowing what the children can realistically achieve. We do not want to promote unreachable goals that, when not achieved, can be disheartening for both child and caregiver, reinforcing for them self-concepts of inadequacy and feelings of helplessness. On the other hand, we do not want to unrealistically limit what can be accomplished. We are all familiar with amazing stories of people who have "dreamed the impossible dream" and made it come true despite all odds and predictions.

Just as mothers and fathers do not always know best, neither do professionals. Needing to believe that we do is a reflection of our insecurity, arrogance, ignorance, or combination thereof. Maintaining an attitude toward children and their caregivers that is respectful and humble and creating custom-made plans that are flexible are essential. The model of the wise, lone professional making independent decisions is not the best way to practice. We need to listen and learn from the children, their caregivers, and each other, and work in teams. Teams may be a formal structure or *ad hoc* consultations, but working collectively helps to mitigate the lone professional's limited knowledge and perceptions, generates more creative plans, suggests modification of plans when necessary, and helps us to tolerate negative outcomes and celebrate successes.

Connecting under the Stars*

Noah, my eleven-year-old foster son, chose to be the first one to camp out with me in our backyard. We lay quietly in our new tent on our newly purchased queen-size air mattress. What a life! I don't know who started the conversation about life five years before, when he and the other kids first came to live in our home. We spoke about the high fever he had for three weeks. I told him of the fear I had when the doctors didn't know what was wrong. They first suspected leukemia, then TB. We stopped talking, and the memories came back.

I vividly remember the panicked look on his face when I drove him to the medical center. I had told him we were going Christmas shopping—I couldn't bear to tell him he had to have yet another blood test done. I just didn't know what else to say.

The tears welled in my eyes as we walked in. He sat so bravely and so quietly, his slim dark body looking so vulnerable. I again relived the pain I had felt as I looked at his stoic face when the needle approached his arm. I knew it wasn't only the needle that brought tears to his face; it was also the entire last episode of his young life.

Noah is the oldest of four and was essentially the father figure in his birth family. The two younger ones were placed elsewhere, and Noah and his brother came to live with us, strangers. All four had been taken away from Grandma, whom Noah loved so much. He just doesn't understand why all this happened. Was it his fault? What was he supposed to do?

The blood test wasn't as painful as the others, and we got on with our Christmas shopping. A few days later the fever went away. No one really knows why. Or do we?

---

*Contributed by Lani Bowman, Hawi, Hawaii.

"So what was it?" I asked. "You know, the fever. Was it because you were afraid and didn't know what was happening?" I heard a faint "Yeah, I guess." I wanted so much to just hold him and allow both of us to know that it was OK to be afraid. Yet I knew that our type of bonding didn't allow that to happen. I did, however, tell him that he had every right to be afraid and confused. It was also OK to be mad. I added that it's OK, even now, to have these feelings. After all, we all had been through a lot. I ruffled his hair and said I loved him. We both drifted off. I don't know if it was to sleep or to seeking a deeper understanding of why things happen. I soon heard a slight snore and was thankful, at least for now, that his deeper understanding came with sleep.

As I gazed at the stars I have always loved, I thought about all we had been through and where our relationship had taken us. Noah was so different from his younger brother who lives with us and constantly longs for attention. I remembered his brother jumping on every person who entered our home. Noah, on the other hand, would stand back and speak only when spoken to. But it was different when his grandma and aunt came to visit—he would rush to the door and not leave their sides. He would hardly have anything to do with me during these visits. I used to watch them, envy their closeness, and ache because he and I couldn't have this.

I slowly began to understand why. His birth mom really wasn't there for him—she had her own problems. I knew she loved him, but, perhaps through circumstance, he was driven away from a mother figure. What figure am I now? I began to understand. I tried as best as I could not to take it personally. But I will never forget one day when Grandma and Aunty were leaving. I touched Noah's shoulder as he let go of them. He furiously pushed me away. It was like a knife piercing my heart. I couldn't take it anymore. I screamed out my hurt and pain to this seven-year-old. Through my tears I told him how much I loved him and asked why he couldn't think of my feelings. Then, of course, I felt guilty about my outburst. I apologized, and life went on.

He muttered something and rolled toward me. I looked at his handsome face. He truly is one heck of a kid—a great looker, a great athlete, and a great person. It is sad because I know inside that there is a lot of pain and that there remain unanswered questions.

Now, just when Noah was beginning to relax and be a kid, my husband left us. I remember the father role Noah immediately fell into. I had to remind him he wasn't the father. To be honest, I don't know what I would have done without him. It was during this time that our bond grew stronger.

The other night I sat in my dining room listening to him cry himself to sleep. We had gotten into an argument over something not too important and I overreacted. It hurt him and I knew it. I tried to apologize, but the pain was already there. As I listened to him sob, I thought, "It's not only about tonight. I know that cry. It's the cry of all the pain that he's felt, all the unfair things that have happened." I went up and rubbed his back. He didn't pull away, just continued to cry. So did I.

I wish there were a fairy tale ending to all of this, but there isn't. Our lives together have much more in store for both of us. There are, however, days when I get a quick hug or am even allowed to hold him. There are nights when I can kiss him goodnight without him first rolling away. There are also those days when either he or I feel like the matador in a bullfight. There are times when snide remarks are made merely to hurt the other.

A friend once said it takes a very mature person to deal with this type of relationship. She is right. I have to remind myself that, like it or not, I am the mother. I need to *really* remind myself that I may not always be right, loved, or appreciated. No mother really is.

I know the definition of unconditional love. I try as best as I am able to live this type of love. This type of love is tested throughout our lives, and Noah is one of those tests. Yet I also know how strong our unspoken bond is becoming. I know also that when he is older, he will have an understanding of the good person he is. He will succeed. I believe he will also do his best to live with unconditional love in his heart.

Frightening and Confusing Love: A Mom's View*

I am a child and family therapist. Eight years ago I had the opportunity (I can call it that now!) to experience just how hard it is for a child to live in a family that wants to provide her with love, struc-

---

*Contributed by Molly Reed, Eugene, Oregon.

ture, and security when those are the very things which most frighten and confuse the child. In 1985 my husband and I lived in a small town in Oregon. I had a four-year-old child, Sarah, and a newborn, Emily. I was volunteering for the Children's Services Department, the government agency responsible for foster children, in one of its treatment programs when I met Shanna, who had run away from her foster home. She was in the county lockup facility; no foster placements were available in our county, and it was decided she would be placed in a center for emotionally disturbed children in Portland until she was eighteen.

That was on Wednesday. By that Saturday she had moved into our home—which tells you how much thought and planning I put into the decision! All I knew was that this kid did not seem like the kind who needed that restrictive placement and that, for some reason, I wanted to be the alternative.

I will never forget the day she moved in. We went shopping for a few things immediately after I picked her up from detention, and then I brought her home to meet my family. As we all sat there, I began to comprehend the immensity of the decision to bring Shanna home, realizing I had absolutely no idea how to take care of a sixteen-year-old. I knew how to "do" four and under, but that was it.

We wanted to provide a home where Shanna could feel safe and accepted, experience some successes at school, and hopefully grow to love and accept us. Yeah, right! What we did provide was an environment different from anything she had experienced before, one that was unpredictable because it was so predictable, one that accepted her before she was ready to accept herself, and one that provided her with chances to fail and fail again.

I felt that my education and experience would carry me through this relationship. I found that, no matter what I had read or done, being a mother to this child would challenge everything I had taken for granted throughout my life. Her presence challenged my relationship with my husband, who felt that providing a safe home should be enough for Shanna to "get it together"; raised concerns about my younger children, who were getting less of my time and who were exposed to situations they would otherwise know nothing about; and certainly made me question my competency as mother and counselor.

Shanna was not used to doing well in school and often used humor or mild aggression to get out of tough situations, a coping skill that had stood her well in the past. Unfortunately, the behavior didn't stop the instant she was in a safe situation. On her first day of speech class, Shanna was asked to talk about her family. After a moment of panic she told about us, Molly and Dennis, and her two "sisters," Sarah and Emily. Easy. Next day she was asked to talk about growing up with her "family." Panic! Act out in class . . . get kicked out. Problem solved.

Taking her at face value, this was a kid who was disrespectful and trouble for sure. The reality was that this kid couldn't just say, "Well, actually, class, I was abused in my birth family and I know it was not my fault. I've been in a bunch of foster homes, ran away, almost got put in a psychiatric hospital, and now I'm living with another family and I am not really sure what they are all about. In fact, I just met them six weeks ago."

This is a classic example of what attachment-impaired kids do. Instead of taking what they do at face value, we need to try to interpret their behavior, to look at what it is they are feeling and/or trying to tell us.

Homework was another area we struggled with. When Shanna first moved in, she had trouble with her English assignments. She had been in so many grade schools that she never did learn basic grammar and writing skills. We spent many hours over the next few months writing and rewriting her homework. And then I discovered that she was finally completing assignments but not turning them in; they were ending up in the bottom drawer of her dresser. At face value, again, Shanna did not care about school and was still being rebellious. What I felt from her was that it was easier to get an F for not turning in the work than to get an F based on the work. Being judged on what you didn't do is easier than being judged on what you did do.

Even though I would have sworn that I was not doing this, I know now that I brought Shanna into my home to try to make up for what had happened to her in the past. I thought I was "the answer" for this kid. I so much wanted her to like me, to stay with us, to do well, to heal, and, yes, to help me feel like a success. I think a lot of foster and adoptive parents do not admit to this or even recognize it might be what they want. We feel everyone is watching us, judging our parenting, and waiting to let us know that they have made a mistake in letting us keep this child. We do not want to acknowledge that it is difficult to integrate a child into our families. And when the child does not thank us or make us feel that we are the best thing that ever happened to him or her, we may feel like giving up. And when a child appears to go out of his or her way to "get us," it can be very difficult to hang in there.

I remember a night when I was feeling particularly frustrated. It seemed that no matter what I did, this kid did not like me and wasn't going to like me. I went into her room and sat on a big pillow while she sat on the bed. I told her that I was not going to try anymore to prove to her that I loved her. We were both crying, and I told her that maybe she was going to have to live with us as a roommate—there would be no expectation to love us, to bond with us, or to care about us. I wasn't going to continue trying to make up for what had happened to her in the past, something she never actually asked me to do. I told her if she wanted more from us, we would be there for her, but not wanting us was also OK.

I felt a big improvement in our relationship following this conversation. Looking back now, I don't think she changed that much. It was more that I gave myself permission to let her be where she was and to not expect her to give more than she was ready to. I no longer felt the pressure to treat her as a "damaged child," but rather I came to treat her as a healing young woman.

Holidays were special times, Mother's Day in particular. I caught Shanna's anger and pain for all the things her mother had not done for her, for all the times she had not been there. I was Mother in this new house and the logical target; it was a struggle not to take it personally. I had to keep my expectations low for the day so when the sneak attack came I was at least a bit prepared. Like other times, it wasn't Shanna who needed to change; it was the responsibility of the adult to consider what the child was feeling and experiencing and to gauge responses accordingly. This does not mean that I allowed her to continue to disrupt this day for me. I just made sure that my need for her to accept me was not getting in the way.

At times kids are likely to display behaviors that are not socially acceptable. The stress of ordering wrong in a restaurant or of not knowing how to do something is sometimes so overwhelming that it is much easier to do anything just to be sent out of the restaurant or to be taken home. It may look like being a pain in the butt, but it seems much more likely that it is just survival behavior.

We were pretty good about letting Shanna know what the limits were and usually followed through with the consequences we had agreed on. She told us when she was twenty-two that she had always liked knowing just what our limits were, knowing that we were there to provide control when she felt she had none of her own. I told her it would have been so nice to know that, when she was pushing those limits, she actually thought it felt good.

And Shanna did test the limits, almost reaching them after being with us for a year when she decided to "borrow" the brand-new van for a drive to the lake. Not only didn't she have a driver's license, but she had never driven a car before. We purchased the van because we needed to room for the kids and were planning a trip to Disneyland in six weeks. The younger girls, Dennis, and I had gone with friends to a wedding, and Shanna stayed home. We noticed as soon as we got home that the driveway looked a little empty. We found the van a mile down the road, crashed into a telephone box. She hadn't made the corner. Luckily, no one was hurt.

Shanna wasn't there when we got home. She called a few times, testing the waters. When she did return, at 1:00 A.M., we placed a call to the police and she ran away. She returned on her own an hour later, talked to the police, and was taken to juvenile detention. We were all crying as they were leaving and Shanna asked for pictures of the little girls to take with her.

This was a very tough time for my husband and me. He said Shanna could not return to our home. I understood, but I felt we still needed to let her know we would hang in there with her.

Stealing the van was clearly a test, although I do not think she started out with that in mind. She felt that every family had a bottom line and that she may have just found ours.

After three days of "discussions" we decided to bring her back home with us, but we did not withdraw the theft charge. I will never forget walking into the little interview room to tell her that we still wanted her to live with us but that things were going to be a bit different. She was going to have to start from square one to allow us to rebuild our trust in her. She was going to have to attend school and maintain a certain level of performance. And she was going to have to "work off" the deductible on our insurance through jobs around the house.

The look on her face still brings tears to my eyes—there was so much relief and disbelief, all rolled into one. She had clearly believed that she was not coming home. I do not think until that week either she or I realized how much we meant to each other.

Although there were still some rocky times, this was a turning point for us. It was as if some invisible line had been crossed, and we were better off for it.

No One's Mashed Potatoes Are the Same Now: A Daughter's View*

When I went shopping for the first time, I didn't know what I was supposed to do. I felt like everyone knew that this was my first time shopping and that I didn't know what I was doing. I felt like I should have this confident feeling like the women on the commercials; they look like they feel so great and know exactly what they want and need. I don't think I really liked the clothes that I got. I think I was just glad that it was over, and it was nice to have new things. I might have acted like I didn't appreciate the clothes, but it was all so overwhelming for me.

I loved holidays and hated them all at once. Everyone was so cheery. No one tried to ruin the day by arguing and yelling. No one wanted to go home just as we were having fun and feeling that it was a good day. It was way too pleasant! It was very uncomfortable. It wasn't at all what I was used to, but I loved it too. I missed my family, and I hated my family for not giving this kind of life to me. I felt I would never get used to this. The day seemed to go on forever. I was glad it was over. I felt like everyone was faking the loving feelings everyone showed when they were together. This whole family thing had to be fake. No one's family could be this nice and be so close. The words "I love you" were not in my vocabulary, and it was really hard to believe someone could say them to

*Contributed by Shanna, a daughter.

me and really mean them. I felt like everyone was being nice to me because they had to, not because they really liked me.

Mother's Day was spent remembering about the other family. Not that they were missed, but I felt that I had to think of them. I didn't want to think of my birth family, and I didn't want my new family to act like they were my family. It took so much energy, and I usually tried to deal with it in a way that seemed hurtful. I didn't mean to, though; I just couldn't let myself feel those good feelings.

I had always felt like I didn't belong or fit in at school. Living in a family of seven, we didn't have the right clothes or "things." We were on the free lunch program. I was glad that it meant I was going to eat a good meal, but I felt like everyone knew I was a charity case. I used school as a safe place or a place where I could let loose and not have to be scared. Whatever the punishment was at school, it was nothing compared with what happened in my birth family. I grew up feeling that I could do anything I wanted to at school. It was hard to let that go. I didn't know how else to be. School was a safe place to be when I wasn't home. When I moved in to the Reeds' home, it was the same way. I didn't feel comfortable there, and it was just a matter of time before I would be somewhere else. I could not make myself do homework. The only thing I felt comfortable in was math class. All other classes meant I had to write and show everyone that I didn't know what I was doing. Sometimes it was just easier to not show them anything. I remember saying to my foster mom that I wasn't going to run away this time and saying to myself that it would only be a matter of time and I would have to move on. At the same time, I really wanted to believe I could make it work and that I would stay. I just could not picture myself fitting in anywhere.

I felt like I would never get close enough to start feeling I really cared about these people, because I always knew I would have to leave. Inside I knew they really wouldn't want me around. I knew it would just be a matter of time before I did something and they would send me away. I felt the reason they were trying to give me a home was that they were compensated by the state for their trouble.

Going to a restaurant for the first time was very scary and overwhelming. Having lived in a family of seven on welfare, we didn't dine out much. There were too many choices, and I didn't know how to order. When it came time for me to order, I felt like everyone was watching the kid who was bound to make a complete fool of herself by not being able to pronounce some item on the menu. I was sure they all knew that I had never done this before and that I probably should not have been brought this time.

How hard could it be to drive . . . just a little drive to the lake to see my friends, and the Reeds would never know the difference? I crashed their new van, and they gave me another chance! Ahhh! These were very brave people. Didn't they know that I was nothing but trouble? Once we signed a contract that I had to follow when I was brought home. I was really going to try.

All I had to do was not get any grades below a C (well, there were also progress reports and a small curfew change). Once I started doing all my assignments, I was getting A's and B's. I didn't want any less, and the Reeds were beginning to trust me and I was beginning to trust me. I think I even decided to stay.

Now . . . I love the Reeds (my family); I love myself. Thank God for their patience, their understanding, and their belief that there was some potential in that scared little girl.

I live in Seattle now and often spend holidays with my husband's family. I really miss My Family. There is no other way I want to spend the holidays. No one else's mashed potatoes are the same. It's just not home.

13

Recovering Self Shattered by Attachment Trauma

Some survivors are so shattered by early attachment trauma that therapy involves working with significant regressive behaviors; here mergings and dependencies can re-create feelings of fear and confusion in both client and clinician. The clinical work with children presented in this chapter did not include the caregivers until late in the child's treatment. The children's disorganization, their shattered sense of self, needed the intensity of one-to-one focus and relationship building with the therapist until well into treatment. In all of the cases presented, the clinicians followed the lead of the client and supported the natural healing process as it unfolded.

The first contribution illustrates work in which the therapist noted unmet early developmental needs through sensitive clinical observations. Her attunement to the child and her creative responses fostered the growth needed for the child to begin to relate to her.

The next clinician connects with a child in the only way the child can tolerate: being there while not being physically present. She describes a child who created the fantasy attachment relationships she needed to assuage her loneliness and to meet other needs. Children, like heat-seeking missiles, will find warmth and caring where they can. My observations in an evaluation program for children with multiple failed placements were that most of them rejected adults—some would be able to connect emotionally only with peers, others only with the house pet, and the most disturbed only with fantasy figures they created. One colleague told me that her own emotional survival as a youngster who had suffered extreme cruelty and toxic parenting came from years of reading and rereading the twenty-three Oz books and identifying with Dorothy, the main character.

Matthew's therapist fosters the development of a relationship through availability, through caring, and through helping him to understand his feelings and behavior by teaching him the basics of post traumatic stress disorder. The author reflects on her work with abused adolescents who attempt to form relationships with adults.

The last vignette tells of healing work with an adult who is creatively supported and guided in order to master an early attachment disturbance. The therapist shares thoughts about her own personal growth and issues, issues that resonate with our own, in this deep and moving work we do.

The Disposable Child*

Angel's life story is a mystery. No one, including Angel, knows her real birthday. She was thought to be five or six years of age when she came to therapy. Angel was born addicted to cocaine and was abandoned at birth by her mother. She spent the first four months of her life in a hospital nursery until her father could be located.

She was a disposable child. Her father would often go to the store for milk and not return for days, even weeks. Her father left her with neighbors, who handed her off to others when they had to go to work or tired of caring for her. What horror and hell she withstood growing up alone in the darkness of the inner-city streets. "I seen this man go after this guy with a knife, and there was blood everywhere. He killed him," she described with terror in her face.

Angel lived with her father and his many girlfriends until his death. "I seen my father die. He had AIDS. I was jumping on his chest trying to make him breathe. He was dead. And now I don't have a father anymore."

After her father's death Angel went to live with her father's brother and his wife. They were considering giving Angel up for

*Contributed by Blair Barone, Boston, Massachusetts

adoption because they felt overwhelmed trying to cope with her "bad manners." Angel stole anything she could get her hands on and hoarded enough food to feed an army. Her cousin had been selling M&M candies to raise money for a school trip; Angel ate forty boxes in two days.

I was quite surprised when I met Angel because she didn't present as the "crazy kid" her uncle and teacher described. Despite her relentless appetite, she was petite and waiflike. She looked unkempt, with dirty tattered clothes she had outgrown. While sucking her thumb, she was quick to give an ear-to-ear smile. The first thing she told me about herself was that she was named by her father. "He got my name from the Bible."

The impact of Angel's traumatic history of loss, abandonment, numerous caregivers, and neglect expressed itself in her inability to attach and relate to me in treatment. In no time it became clear that Angel had not developed object constancy or an evocative memory. When I greeted her each week in the waiting room, she always seemed reserved in her approach, as if confused by my presence. Even in the office she sat with her back facing me, as if I weren't there. I suspected that was how she was accustomed to relating to others. I understood more clearly when Angel greeted me in the waiting room before our session saying, "I didn't know that I was going to see you again. I thought you were dead." Her inability to hold onto my image between weekly sessions made me practically a stranger to her each week.

I realized that in order to facilitate treatment I would have to help her develop object constancy so that I would not need to reintroduce myself at the beginning of each session. Since it appeared that the time between weekly sessions was too long for her to hold onto my image, I increased her sessions from once a week to twice a week and this change made a marked difference. Instead of waiting in the waiting area, Angel would stand outside my office door, eager to greet me. She would often knock on my office door the minute she arrived for sessions, which was sometimes an hour early.

In addition to increasing the frequency of her appointments, I incorporated transitional objects into the treatment. I made it a point to send Angel home after each session with something we had made together that would remind her of our relationship and help her to internalize me as a caring, nurturing other who continued to exist even when not present.

With her developing object constancy and attachment, Angel added her own therapeutic intervention to the therapy. Each session she would bring an assortment of goodies to eat in my presence. The eating process would go on for almost the entire session. She would not talk during this time, but remained absorbed with eating her snack. Instead of sitting with her back to me, she would now sit facing me. She would often look over at me while eating, then smile and giggle and say, "I like it when you look at me." I realized that she was trying to create a corrective experience of the environment that had originally failed her. She was seeking the maternal preoccupation that she had always longed for and probably not experienced since her days in the hospital nursery. I could then see that, through her stealing and hoarding of food, she was attempting to self-cure and gain what she never had. Angel was driven by an insatiable hunger—for someone to love her.

Deidre and the Wind*

Deidre was brought to me, on the advice of a school counselor, when she was eleven years old. She had been truant from school a number of times, forging her parents' signatures on absent notes, and was stealing makeup and clothes to resell to older kids, sneaking out of the house at 3:00 A.M. to "hitchhike and meet boys," and using drugs and dressing provocatively. When I first saw her, she was wearing spiked high heels, black fishnet stockings, a leather miniskirt, and a halter top. Her makeup was heavy, and she looked much older than she was. Her appearance shocked me. This was an eleven-year-old! Why was she dressed this way? Didn't her parents see something wrong with this picture?

I introduced myself to Deidre, who made no eye contact. I asked her if she would like to meet with me alone or with her parents. She lowered her head and quickly walked right by me into my office/playroom. Her parents looked at me, smiled, and suggested that they remain where they were. They both looked so pleasant,

*Contributed by Charlene Winger, Toronto, Ontario, Canada.

so unaware. I followed Deidre into the room and sat down. She sat as far from me as she could and said nothing. I asked her why she thought she was here. She grumbled, "I don't know. I don't care."

She said and did nothing for the entire session. She virtually would not respond to me. I left for a few minutes, and when I returned I found her exploring the room. She stopped as soon as she saw me and returned to her corner. I reassured her that it was perfectly fine for her to look around, ask questions, and touch whatever she wanted to. She asked me to leave again, and I did.

When she came back the next week, she said she wanted to spend her time in the room alone again. I agreed but told her I would be in the viewing room doing some of my work and that she could come to me if she changed her mind or had any questions. I learned a lot about Deidre as I watched her paint and heard her talk aloud to "the Wind" about her favorite stories as she drew them. One of her favorite paintings was of a winged unicorn flying with the wind. I also obtained from her parents, sibs, and teachers information that helped me begin to understand Deidre.

Freckle-faced and cute in a homely sort of way, Deidre grew up in a family where her desperate attempts to be noticed and accepted by her family were mostly met with emotional rejection. She was ignored by her dissociative mother, kept in her room for hours at a time, and physically and emotionally abused by her equally rejecting sibs.

Why Deidre's older sisters were abusive and rejecting never became clear. Since the mother was only minimally available to the children emotionally, perhaps the older sibs fought harder for whatever was available and saw Deidre as a threat to their own survival. Sibling rivalry would thus be intense. Moreover, the mother's dissociativeness seemed to have perpetuated a lack of clear messages regarding boundaries. The children were unclear about what behaviors were appropriate and what were excessive, and they received ambivalent messages about expectations and what belonged to them.

Emotional abuse, neglect, and guilt-inducing messages were ongoing issues in the parenting of these children. While the mother and father were committed to caring for their children in the best way they knew how, the father was frequently absent and the mother was left feeling emotionally unsupported and unequipped to deal effectively with normal child development, behaviors, and emotional needs.

By the time Deidre was five, she had developed a creative way to experience the kind of meaningful and mutually rewarding and secure attachment relationship that was lacking in her life—she created "Horsey," a part of her who served in the development of her self in relation to others.

Horsey, of course, did not notice being ignored, because the world of people had little meaning to Horsey. Horsey did not worry about not being noticed or accepted in the world of people, because she was a horse and horses didn't need people. Horsey could run very fast and escape the physical dangers of the people world, and it was perfectly normal for her to run away whenever approached by an adult or child. When Horsey was hungry, she could eat grass. Horsey did not need people in her life.

By the time Deidre was eleven years old, she began to realize how lonely she was. She had made friends with the horses in the nearby fields, but she wanted more and had no idea how to develop friendships. She knew only how to avoid them, and she did so for two reasons. First, she believed people did not view her as a worthwhile person, and she could not imagine anyone wanting to get to know her. And even if someone did, Deidre believed the person would hate her and hurt her the way her sibs did. Second, Deidre was used to living by herself in her own world and was uncomfortable interacting with people.

Longing to be accepted by others but fearing the consequences, Deidre developed an important relationship with "the Winds"—the South Wind, the East Wind, the North Wind, and the West Wind. The Winds liked her and were her friends. She knew them by their strengths, "attitudes," and temperatures. They guided her with advice, accepted her completely for who she was, and were available to her whenever she needed them, and she, of course, had complete control over what they said to her. She went into the fields every day to meet and talk with the Winds. Deidre had created her own therapist.

Horsey, the Winds, and every cat and dog in the neighborhood were Deidre's friends. Living this way was comfortable and helped reduce her feelings of loneliness. The Winds were substitute parents, and Horsey helped her survive in a world where she felt either hated or alienated.

It was a long time before Deidre began to allow herself to be "seen" by other people. She felt every adult and child would reject her if given the chance. It was incredibly anxiety-provoking for her to be noticed for anything other than those behaviors which she believed were in keeping with the perceptions others held of her.

Because of these behaviors, which were comfortable for Deidre, she was ultimately rejected or ignored by others, including her piano teacher, schoolteachers, and Brownie leaders. She was not particularly disruptive in class or group, but she had very poor social skills, since she had never learned how to related positively with others. Her interactions with her family were usually negative experiences. Deidre had created a self-fulfilling prophecy.

She was sexually abused when she was eleven. What she learned from this was that she was worth something sexually to some people, and she began to behave and dress provocatively.

Deidre's initial treatment was basic. She was offered safe and supportive listening in a nonthreatening environment in an attempt to develop a positive relationship. Her safe environment meant no parents and no therapist—she had to be alone in the room. A therapist in the room paying attention to her was threatening. Deidre did not accept praise; reflective listening was overwhelming and anxiety-provoking.

Had Deidre's therapist been male, she might have reduced her anxiety by behaving the only way she knew might be of interest to males. Because I was female, Deidre did not know how to relate, except to ignore and try to be ignored. By staying out of the therapy room and behind the one-way mirror, I became the Wind, with whom Deidre could relate through fantasy, without the physical presence of another. This was Deidre's choice for a number of sessions. Her only contact with me was the neutral but warm greeting and goodbye before and after each session.

Eventually Deidre started coming into the viewing room to make sure I was still there, and even to ask a question or two. Then she invited me into the playroom with her to show her how to do something.

I shared with Deidre some questions on paper that another child I was seeing had left with me at that child's suggestion. The second youngster was curious about the experiences of other children. This was only after Deidre and I had developed a stronger relationship and I saw she was feeling comfortable with reflective listening. The youngsters began to leave questions for each other. Introducing this exchange was a risk, since I wasn't certain what was best for the children, but my instincts said it would be right. My goal was to help Deidre see that she was human and interesting to others.

During one of her final sessions, Deidre read me a story over and over about a lonely little girl who is rejected by all the children in the community until one day the Wind blows to her a special friend. I told Deidre that I understood how important the Wind was to her and that I was really glad Deidre had allowed me to be a part of her world too.

Deidre was eventually able to participate in sessions with her parents and with her sibs. The goals of these sessions were to help the family "see" Deidre and to help them develop and learn new ways of listening to and approaching one another.

Over time Deidre learned different ways to deal with her family. She became better able to identify her boundaries and strengthened her sense of self. While she continued to distance herself from her family for self-protection, she did develop support outside of the family—from me and from two close friends. She joined a riding club and showed an interest in working with children and animals.

Deidre's mother refused therapy for herself. She had difficulty trusting others, and therapy meant making herself vulnerable. She also believed that it was her job to be strong and that therapy meant she was somehow a failure as a parent and as a human being. Fortunately, we were able to do some family work through Deidre.

The Transcendence of Matthew*

Matthew, now eighteen, suffered almost unbearably from repeated traumatic relationships with adults. This boy is now making a remarkable recovery and inspires my current work with traumatized

*Contributed by Joyce Kennedy, Denver, Colorado.

teenagers. The labels he acquired throughout his eighteen years have been deleted from this story.

Matthew was subjected to early neglect, often being left at home with his brother, only two years older than he. His father, a violently aggressive man who had little respect for anyone, worked in a biker bar as a bouncer and part-time cook. Matthew once described a fight in which his father kept punching a bar patron until the man fell and became still. Matthew was unsure of the man's fate.

The youngster has only fleeting images of his mother—she was apparently not home much. He does remember that she took him to the hospital once because of injuries when his father, in a violent fit, threw him from a window. At another time his father shattered the bunk beds Matthew and his brother shared, then grabbed his brother and threw him across the room against the wall.

These were the rageful episodes. The mental and emotional cruelty displays were typified by Matthew's description of the time his father drove his dog to a parking lot and abandoned it.

Matthew was orphaned at age five or six. He ventured into the living room one night and saw empty liquor bottles scattered about. Knowing the signals, he became frightened and hid under the couch. His mother and father entered the room screaming at each other. Following several loud and ugly exchanges, a gun went off, and his mother dropped to the floor not far from the couch and lay in a pool of blood. After his father left the room, Matthew ran to the neighbors. Later in the evening he had to identify his mother's body, a task that crystallized the trauma already experienced. He then identified the body of his father in a back room.

Matthew remembers his first foster parents as an older couple who kept "dragging" him off to church. This was a transient placement for Matthew and his brother. They were subsequently placed with a neighbor to the family before the traumatic death of his parents. His first Christmas present was a stuffed bear that he received from his family. Unfortunately, things did not gel and Matthew's brother had to be placed in a children's home. Although Matthew has seen and visited his brother at times, he has never lived with him again.

Matthew was adopted three years later. He could now look forward, for the first time, to the joy of having a mother and a father who would be devoted to him. But he did not fit well into the family, and his dream did not come true. His memories are mostly of dreadful ballet lessons and dreaded spankings. He remembers becoming depressed and exhibiting aggressive behavior. His parents admitted him to a hospital and eventually placed him in a shelter; the adoption was relinquished.

There were more then ten placements over the next five years. Matthew became exceedingly depressed, angry, and aggressive. During one placement he pummeled a boy who harassed him. In a group home later on, he was molested by an older boy. His memories of the adults in charge in several placements were of alcoholics, drug addicts, and perverts. One male foster parent tickled Matthew inappropriately, in a way that might easily be considered abusive. The leader of a male group home was a cross-dresser.

Matthew was alexithymic by his midteens, having been severely traumatized by violently abusive, morally corrupted, and psychologically confused adults. He shut down, was psychologically numbed and barely communicative. He was diagnosed with post-traumatic stress disorder and hospitalized with haunting flashbacks of his mother's murder by his father.

Matthew's final foster placement came at fifteen; it represented the start of a three-year process of freeing this young man from a lifetime of horror. The new foster parents arranged for a therapist to work with Matthew. The critical intervention used was the building of an authentic connection.

The therapist relied on a multiexpression relationship with Matthew. She genuinely loved him and provided the first corrective and safe love he had ever experienced. She took him skiing and snowboarding, and she took him to play tennis. She taught him social skills and provided a foundation for ethical behavior he would need later in life. She helped him to tell his story in his own words, without pressure, letting him do it in his own time.

She parented Matthew, teaching him how to keep safe and stay connected. He knew her home telephone number, and she never left town without identifying a known, trusted colleague to back her up. The connection was not a traditional professional-patient relationship; nor was it focused on control, as are many adult-adolescent therapies. The relationship represented an equal partnership for recovery and growth.

The therapist respected Matthew and taught him about the

adaptive responses he had used to survive, such as numbing, hypervigilance, hyperarousal, and avoidance of adults. He was too young to have the ego strength to integrate the terror he experienced, so he needed to numb out. He did not have a nurtured, protected childhood, so he needed to be hypervigilant to compensate for it. Hyperarousal prepared him to ward off danger and mistreatment. Horrifying flashbacks kept alive feelings of helplessness until he was able to process them with his therapist and his peers. His despair slowly lessened. In his eyes, he needed to keep a safe distance from adults to stay alive.

The therapist understood that Matthew's behavior and lifestyle knew few limits, so she unconditionally accepted Matthew when he became so hyperaroused that he was in danger of assaulting someone. She understood and accepted him even when he became so psychologically numbed that he would cut himself, or send his fist through the wall in anger, not feeling the pain. She accepted him when he abused drugs, and when he became alcohol-dependent.

Much healing occurred at a Village Inn, an all-night restaurant, sometimes with his therapist but mostly with the good friends he cultivated over the three years. The therapist understood that, like the past itself, recovery was painful and the pain needed to be neutralized by good times and authentic, caring, stable relationships. Matthew still has some bridges to cross, but he's on a steady path toward making successful attachments to adults and to mental health professionals.

I often reflect on the decades during which I've watched teenagers painfully but courageously attempt to form effective relationships with adults who have historically betrayed, corrupted, neglected, and abused them. A new school of thought suggests these adolescents must separate emotionally and physically from such adults in order to survive; if they stay close to abusive adult caretakers, they are in harm's way.

These teenagers must maintain a safe distance in order to adapt to their environment. This distance does not imply they are incapable of attachment. It does imply it has not been safe for them to be close to adults in the past. Is it any wonder such teenagers seek out their own safety zones, which, ironically, can come from being armed with a gun, from becoming a "respected" member of the Crips or Bloods, or from seeking comfort within their control—

drugs and alcohol? Teenagers act out their suffering rather than sitting down and discussing it. Perhaps this is why adults become frustrated and are unaware of the deep feelings teenagers harbor and are unable to explain verbally.

Acting-out behaviors have, unfortunately, caused these youths social stigmatization. They are egregiously labeled and are treated as outcasts. It seems almost primitive. I have seen adolescents who have experienced extreme parental abuse, equivalent to holocaust proportion, act out and then be labeled as borderline personalities, or as having personality disorders featuring impulsive, delinquent, schizoid tendencies. They find themselves "branded" when these terms are keyed into a computer. It can be a long trip back, likened to a person who experiences bankruptcy and cannot get credit for the next ten years.

Special education teachers sometimes label these same adolescents as SED, or severely emotionally disturbed. Their focus of intervention is commonly behavior management rather than identifying the source of and current life circumstances maintaining the disturbance. If these adolescents run afoul of the courts or the juvenile system, they are labeled truants, delinquents, thieves, and on and on. Their dignity has been not only stripped away by parental figures but tossed off by the professionals trying to serve them.

Studies of young people who have experienced traumatic stress from neglectful and abusive relationships with adults have recently identified new directions for treatment. Evolving approaches adopt the need for humane treatment of the youths and the preservation of their self-esteem. New approaches validate the often heroic transcendence of the object terror these teenagers feel and support them to align with their own courage and power.

Resolving Old Attachment Trauma*

I'm working with a young woman whom I will call Agnes, who said her mother had abused her physically and emotionally when she was a child. Her mother "liked babies when they were little" but became abusive and violent when she felt opposed. Agnes had a

*Contributed by Katharine Stone Ayers, Kailua-Kona, Hawaii.

dream about a disemboweled doll who had blue batteries and was equipped with sword and boots. The doll in the dream gave an accurate representation of how Agnes felt in her relationship with her mother—disemboweled and like a doll rather than a human being.

Agnes describes her feet as cold and numb, as if wearing boots. During this session grief is surfacing about not being seen and being emotionally abandoned by her mother. She has pain in her throat and chest. She is trying to hold back tears by clamping down with her jaw, swallowing her tears, and holding against exhalation. It is often useful to me to consider the practice of Bodynamics in my therapeutic practice. With this in mind I hold her left hand, contacting the little-finger muscle that has to do with taking in nourishment in a deeply satisfying way. I ask her to sense the contact I'm making with her left hand. Anger and rage begin to surface. As she continues to rage, her hands make twisting motions. I ask her what her hands want to do. She begins to strangle a pillow. More rageful sounds come out of her mouth, interspersed with comments like "I hate you" and "How could you treat me that way?" She says later in the session that she was recalling being mistreated as a baby.

I direct her to sense her feet and the back of her legs and to use her calf muscles while kicking into a pillow and saying, "I want you to see me." More grief and crying surface. I again ask her to sense her feet. She says they are getting warm. She describes a feeling of pink fluff, like mohair, spreading from her feet to her knees, thighs, abdomen, head, eyes. She feels comforted and supported by this pink substance. She experiences it as a loving, supportive nest.

In Agnes's case her ability to attach, bond, merge, and/or separate or be autonomous in her adult life will be colored by her early childhood experiences, particularly her relationship with her mother. By moving through her childhood wounds and trauma and experiencing true support, security and love coming from within herself in the presence of a safe, supportive therapist, she has a new experience and imprint. If she carries this imprint/experience and sense of herself into her everyday life, her relationships will change. With ongoing therapy and practice in therapy sessions and in her life, she will be able to attach or separate and do what is appropriate to her everyday living situation.

It is important to me to be a professional who can provide a safe environment for clients to process whatever pain, anger, trauma, wounds, or disruptions that stem from their childhood. It is equally important to be there when the client expresses positive emotions such as love and joy, or attributes such as strength and enthusiasm.

My experience with adults who have had disruptions in the natural attachment process and with those who have formed toxic bonds, is that it is usually appropriate to physically or emotionally hold the client, to give the person the support he or she didn't have in childhood. I feel it is important to be present for whatever anguish, rage, grief, or negative concept the client is feeling.

I believe a therapist must be able to provide certain services to a client with attachment problems. While these services are not specific to attachment, they are especially important here.

1. Provide a safe space. If one can be truly present for one's client, whatever the client is feeling frequently transforms spontaneously into another state of being, often the very thing the child or person has needed all along—a feeling of comfort, support, being loved, or being at peace, among other things.
2. Be aware of one's own countertransference issues. This sounds simple enough, but for me it has taken, and continues to take, work toward my own growth to not interfere with the client's growth process but to allow it to happen naturally. My countertransference issues may create a tendency in me to collude with my client's pain, anguish, or trauma. If I am too merged or if my client's process triggers my own process, I may short-circuit the client's process by trying to fix it rather than allow it to be.
3. Be present to whatever the client is experiencing, and trust in the client's process. It may be difficult to just allow a client's process because of the intensity of the terror he or she experiences. This means being able to tolerate witnessing any pain, anguish, or trauma that the client is expressing. The intensity exists because attachment disorders often stem from infancy and early childhood, when emotions are especially intense. Abandonment issues may subjectively feel like dark abysses, like floating in space, or like being in prison forever. Not only is this difficult for clients to tolerate, but if it touches into unresolved issues of the therapist, he or she may try to rescue or distract the client from his or her distress. The clients may de-

> fend against these memories of early states of deprivation by acting big and strong, saying they don't need anyone or anything, or saying that they don't have any needs. Certainly if they have been abandoned in the past, it is difficult for them to be supported by anyone in the present, so they feign a kind of false autonomy.

I need to know inside myself that if the client is guided skillfully through the healing process, it will lead to a reclaiming of lost resources and repressed parts of the self. My experience is that states natural to our core self, such as love, support, strength, and peace, often emerge spontaneously after a client has worked through whatever issue is blocking that state.

Agnes, whose mother abused her, experienced a feeling of warmth, comfort, safety, and nurturance at the end of the session. This is what she needed from her mother as an infant, but her mother was not capable of giving it. Agnes had an object relation with her mother of feeling like a disemboweled doll with cold, bootlike feet. When Agnes began feeling her body sensations and experiencing her grief and her rage, the lifeless doll aspect of her personality transformed to that of a warm, pulsating, supported human being.

14

Wisdom from Those Who've Been There

Children and parents who have struggled, resolved, transcended, or failed in their work with attachment problems have wisdom to share. A foster mother taught me that a child deemed to be unreachable, a failure-to-thrive toddler, could form an attachment; she lay beside the child for hours a day, every day—touching the youngster's cheek, stroking her back, murmuring prayers of hope and love, and quietly singing lullabies—for months before the child responded to her new mother. Children in residential care show us they can survive emotionally by making deep emotional connections to each other when they can no longer trust that adults will not harm them.

Long before professionals considered trauma-reactive behavior in infants, caregivers told us about infants and toddlers who respond with extreme fear when cued by specific physical contact and sensory experiences. Children and caregivers described childhood dissociative disorders before the professional community recognized their existence. An important teaching for me has been to refrain from identifying parents and children by their problems. They do have problems—big ones—but they also joke, sing, do their work, clean the garage, and write poetry. We could learn much from each other in a forum for shared teaching and learning.

The contributions in this chapter are from child and adult veterans who have been on the front lines. The open letter from youngsters to parents and clinicians, and the poem, bear witness to children's dignity and hope. One of these girls, in the midst of her despair at the loss of her foster mother of five years, became totally absorbed in endlessly replaying the musical theme from a popular movie—Whitney Houston's "I'll Always Love You." This adult song, written about the loss of a lover, passionately declares love and yearning, begs for another chance, and proclaims lasting love. For the girl the song literally gave voice to her unspeakable pain at the loss of her mother. She suffered when she sang along with the song; it hurt and it provided release. I thought with sadness that along with everything else, she had to use an adult song, that there wasn't one for her. Then I realized that, of course, we don't expect mothers to leave children. I thought of popular children's music—how sweet and how unreal. We could use some child operas.

Another child contributor gained some degree of mastery over her challenging life by advocating for foster children's rights and by writing short stories and poems, one of which is presented here. The teenage dancer and healer is using her experience of assault and her creativity to help young children through a dance program she has developed. She plans to attend college and become a trained dance therapist.

Foster parent contributions include descriptions of some patenting difficulties that may not be considered by those who haven't lived with transplanted youngsters. They tell us about the toughness and the tenderness they developed from their experience and give useful survival tips for others.

An adoptive mother writes of the pain and confusion she experienced when attachment failed to form between herself and her young son. She speaks of her many attempts to adopt others' views that her son's behavior was not unusual for a very bright boy and of how alienated she felt from friends and professionals. She continues to hope that the experience will someday have meaning to her son. Her wish is that mothers with similar experiences will be helped by her story.

Open Letter to Foster Parents

Loved and Wanted, age 11, writes:

Dear Foster Parents,

I live in a home with my sister. Sometimes I think no one wants me or loves me. When I feel like this, I like to write, maybe in my diary or I write poems. I also enjoy playing piano when I feel like no one pays attention to me.

I tried calling my foster parents Mom and Dad in my new foster house, but it was hard to while thinking of my biological parents. It is like a lifelong tug-of-war, which I am trying to shrug off, forever fighting.

Also, when I talk about my other parents, I get uncomfortable. When I talk about love, I start squirming. Now, I won't do that as much.

Sincerely,

Loved and Wanted Age eleven
Sixth foster placement

Letters to Therapists

From Loved but Confused, age 10:

Dear Therapists,

I'm a kid, age ten. I found it hard to attach myself to any family because my new family was a nice family and I wasn't a nice kid then. Sooner or later I knew that I would attach myself to them. I would be inseparable because I knew they loved me a lot.

I needed good parents. The hardest time I have attaching myself to the family is when I get busted. It feels like they don't love you anymore, but they do. They are just trying to break you of old bad habits.

Loved but Confused, age 10

One year later, Loved but Confused writes:

Hi,

I'm a foster child who has been bounced around from home to home just like a Ping-Pong ball. I was abused by my dad and abandoned by my mom, who couldn't take care of me. At my eighth foster home something different finally happened. I stayed for more than a year. That is unusual because none of the other seven foster homes wanted me. My eighth home was a couple who really loved and cared for me (something different). I give credit to my social worker, who helped me with tough problems. My foster mom and dad gave me proper discipline and love, so I got quite attached to them.

After five years of living with them and calling them Aunty and Uncle, something wonderful happened. My therapist helped me get more and more attached to my foster parents by assigning us ten minutes each day for close physical touching of each other. She kept it up until one day she assigned me to call my foster mom "Mom" and my foster dad "Dad." At first it was difficult because I was ashamed that I hadn't already and because they did so much for me and I wasn't calling them Mom and Dad. So I started by only once a day calling my foster mom "Mom," and "Dad" came right after. By the time I had started calling mom "Mom" full-time, I had started calling dad "Dad" sometimes. And eventually full-time came. It was hard when I first started because if they got mad at me and yelled, I would get mad and call them Aunty or Uncle again. But I finally did it, and I was really very attached. I was very happy with my life and was hoping to stay there forever and ever. Then one day something terrible happened. My mom found out she had cancer. I cried and cried the day I found out, and I felt terrible. Since she had cancer, I would have to go to another home because she couldn't take care of me, and my dad had to watch over her. I cried and cried till the day I moved out. I didn't stop crying until a week after; even then I was feeling blue. I felt hurt and ripped off, and I expected them to still keep me even though she had cancer. But now I know she did it for her own good, and my good. A couple of months passed, and now I am living in another foster home. I will try my best to attach myself, but again, it is very hard. Thank you, and I hope you listened because you may have already experienced this.

Sincerely,
Loved and still confused,
one year later

Who? You!

The Following is from Poet, age twelve:

Misty eyes
and the wildest cries
you could ever hear.

Feeling sad
not a bit glad
and the sounds make you tear.

You know that
these sounds
will turn your heart
upside down.

A sickly little kid
trying with all his might
just to get rid of
all that fright.

A kid that's been abused
and nonetheless
been used
needs someone.

But who?
Who can it be?
Maybe you!!!

Dedicated to children like me who've been abused in one way or another and need to belong somewhere with someone.

Helping Others through Dance

The following is from The Dancer, age fifteen:

What is dance therapy?
Dance therapy is a number of things, not just one. Dance therapy is especially helpful for children four to eight, because they do not

have the words to describe what has happened to them. They can't just sit down and tell you what happened.

What do I hope to prove by dance therapy?
I do not want to prove anything. This is therapy. I do hope this will help the children.

How does it work?
It works like this: I say to them, "If your feelings have ever been hurt, let's take a little step. If you didn't like that feeling, let's take another little step. Then come the feelings that are deep. If you were told to do something to someone you love or loved and trusted, let's take a medium step, and if you didn't like that feeling, let's take another medium step. If you were touched in your private spots, where only you should be able to touch, let's take a BIG step! And if you didn't like that feeling, step as big as you can!"

You keep going through these steps, but you include clapping, jumping, stepping, and stamping.

All of this together is therapy. You can express your feelings through doing something healthy. Those who can't talk about it don't even have to say a word, only physically show it. It *releases stress* for all ages. The children now have a chance to show people what happened and don't have to be afraid of what people might say. It builds your self-esteem by being able to show yourself you can do something right. This is all a sense of communication. It lets out your anger and shows the children that they are not the only ones it happens to. This gives them the chance to see life isn't always bad, and expressing what has happened to them also isn't a bad thing.

Why do I feel this would work?
I feel this would work because as a young girl I was abused by my father and brother. I was raped at age fourteen, then again on Thanksgiving weekend at age fifteen. I know the hurt, the confusion, the guilt, and the anger these kids are going through! If I had had this physical way of explaining what happened, I would not have been so angry, guilty, hurt, and confused. This is a perfect way

for the little ones to let go of their hurt, a great way to let out anger because they can't hurt anyone because it's already physical. They can express themselves. Remember, these children don't have the words to say it like a young adult or an adult. Drawing pictures gets out feelings of guilt, not anger. Only being physical, very physical, burns off that energy. None of us wants any anger building up, and let's not let another child wreck her or his life because they don't have the words to say what they want.

Are there any rules?

Yes, there are. Anyone entered in this group will not have their names exposed.

I would like it better if the parents were not in the room, because the children would have the fear that their parents will not believe them and that is not the feeling we want the kids to have. The kids must be able to feel safe and trust everyone around them. There would be no making fun of each other and no wrong or absolute right way of doing the steps.

Anyone who wants to talk to me can. You can write me a letter.

The Dancer
c/o D. Kim Wilson
Family Sexual Abuse Program
2020 Halifax Street
Regina, Saskatchewan, Canada S4P 3V7

Embarrassing Moments while Foster Fathering

As I approached the football field to pick up Brad after practice, the coach called me aside. "Mr. Smith, I need to let you know that Brad's attitude toward his teammates is less than desirable. Today Brad called another guy a 'black nigger.' This is simply unacceptable behavior, and it's got to stop." My first internal reaction was an immediate need to let the coach—and the rest of the world—know this is not the kind of language that is ever used in our family, that our family is not racially prejudiced, that our birth children don't say such things, that Brad is a troubled foster child, that . . . that . . . that! After catching my breath and my embarrassment, I told the coach, "I will deal with this today. Please let me know if you have any other problems with Brad."

I was able to collect my thoughts and emotions and discuss with my wife where such outbursts might have come from. Brad's birth mother, who abused him, is now involved in a relationship with an abusive black man.

While Brad's anger may be psychologically justifiable, his behavior is socially intolerable. Brad's therapist is dealing with his anger. Our family is dealing with its embarrassment. We do inform certain authorities, such as teachers, that our child is a foster child who has emotional difficulties, but we are cautious not to give information to those who don't have a need to know, in order to protect his privacy. We don't want to stigmatize him by explaining his background to community members, but there is a cost: His behavior can be assumed to reflect our family's behavior and attitudes.

"Shut up!" "I'm not gonna do it!" "You can't make me!" "I'll tell my social worker!" Etc., etc., etc. As troublesome as these phrases (and similar or worse ones) are to foster parents, it is important for us to recognize the "warrior defense," the need to overcome the aggressor, in our foster child's effort to survive. This strength needs to be supported, but the words need to be tempered to reflect socially acceptable behavior.

The challenge for us foster parents is to step back from the heat of battle, identify the child's warrior strength, and then harness it, not extinguish it. Such harnessing comes as much in the foster parent's recognition of the source of the behavior as it does in the child's recognition of the difference between a life-threatening situation (e.g., sexual abuse) and a nuisance (e.g., "Clean up your room").

Together these two perspectives can change a hostile "I'm not gonna' do it" into a socially more acceptable "I feel angry when you make me clean my room, but I know it's really a fair request so I'll do it."

Ah . . . would that life were so wonderful with any child, foster or birth!

A foster Dad

A Foster Mother's Guidelines for Coping with Attachment Problems

1. The social worker cannot always tell you the important things about your foster child, such as what might remind him of a frightening past experience, or how much or how little demonstrations of affection are needed or wanted.
2. You will need to speak out for the child everywhere, being his advocate at home, in school, everyplace.
3. Be prepared to accept the reality that court procedures rarely reflect what you believe should actually be happening.
4. Parents need to individualize. Everyone—school, court, social worker—seems to need to categorize and pigeonhole the child to fit.
5. Foster parents should not discuss the child's circumstances or background with anyone in the community.
6. A foster parent needs to discuss her overwhelming feelings of confusion or frustration related to living with a disturbed child. Turning to those in the system may not be supportive. Commonly foster parents are often judged or diagnosed, and given advice instead of just being heard and supported.
7. Foster parents should have a good reputation before the child enters the home because their reputation may be questioned repeatedly afterward. Police and neighbors may blame the family for children's acting-out behaviors.
8. Foster parent marriages must be solid and united before the child enters the home. The child may attempt to reenact a disruptive, violent past with behaviors that separate parents.
9. Foster parents should have had the opportunity to raise other children so that they can reaffirm their self-esteem with memories of their other children when their parenting skills do not work with the newcomer.
10. Do not bring a foster child into a new, fragile home with good furnishings. Slamming doors and destructive behavior are common. A safe time-out room is necessary—soundproofing would be ideal!
11. If your motive for being a foster parent is to be thanked and appreciated, try another profession. You cannot please biologi-

cal parents, courts, lawyers, therapists, social workers, and/or the foster child.

12. Be prepared for a foster child's definition of love being fundamentally different from yours. He may think, for instance, that love means sharing a bed or giving pain.
13. Be prepared to experience feelings that you might never want to admit. You may never have even thought of hitting your own child but be strongly tempted to hit a foster child.
14. Be able to forget. The foster child will do many things that you will need to let go of and start again. This is not a place to hold grudges.
15. Remember the one genuine laugh the foster child may produce. It reminds us there is still hope.
16. Be flexible. The foster child comes with a lot of anger and needs permission to get it out. Outlets might include sports, cleaning, weeding, kneading, or even shredding paper. As with anger, the child probably comes with a lot of sadness that also needs permissible outlets—journal writing, singing, drawing, and crying provide appropriate avenues.
17. Be with the child. Pick him up. Take him wherever he needs to go. Listen to his hopes, dreams, and desires while providing transportation and when he's not talking. Play children's music that is fun and uplifting.
18. Whatever has happened to the foster child before coming to your home may not have helped him grow emotionally and socially. A five-year-old, for instance, needs to be seen as a negative 5 because it will take five years to get him to zero. When he is biologically twelve, he is emotionally only seven.
19. Appreciate that the foster child has a warrior personality. He has survival techniques that allowed him to persevere through severe abuse. Accept and respect his techniques while helping to give him healthier defense mechanisms.
20. When all else fails, laugh! Bring up the ridiculous or make something weird—anything—but help him laugh.

A foster Mother

Maxims, Myths, and Messages about Attachment: A Collection from Caregivers

Maxims

- It is important to teach the child that part of the work of healing is to accept the past, not hide from it.
- Invite expressions of experience through sound, movement, visual art, smell, taste, drama, song, and language. Exercise *all* the senses.
- Don't be overly impressed or frightened by emotional displays.
- Demonstrate and teach the ideas that we each have the right to feel and to say how we feel, that feelings are natural and we shouldn't put them down.
- Establish family traditions and rituals.
- Speak of the future.

Myths

- All they really need is love. (They also need limits, guidance, courage, time to heal and to accept the realities of their experience, and an enormous amount of parental patience.)
- They will appreciate what you're doing and will show it. (Children often react negatively to positive parenting. The experience may generate great anxiety in children simply because that style of parenting is unfamiliar. Good parenting can lead to worries that receiving or enjoying such care is disloyal to absent parents; it can generate sensations that may be experienced as dangerous; or it may mirror a child's past seduction or exploitation.)
- Children's early abuse histories will fade in memory if they are allowed to forget them. (Children don't just forget pain and terror. They may hide from their memories, but their behavior is often directed by unexpressed feelings. Ignoring what is known to be true about the child can lead the child to believe that her past is shameful or too overwhelming for even the adults to mention.)
- You'll like them. (Not always and, sometimes, not often.)
- You'll be rewarded. (Well, maybe . . . someday.)

- You will not think bad thoughts about the biological parents. (You may have rageful thoughts about and urges toward the parents, the social worker, the courts, and everyone and anyone else who may have had a hand in the child's predicament.)

Messages Children Need to Hear

You are likable.
You cannot overwhelm me.
Others have been there too.
There's hope.
You have choices.
You are needed.
You make a difference.
This is a safe place.
It's not your fault.
You are not a bad person.

David's Story*

It began in China.

With marriage I acquired not only a husband but also a son. Unlike in America, where we would all live together, in China our son, David, continued to live with his paternal grandmother.

"The cultures are so different," I'd tell myself. "Stepmothers in China are like the stepmothers in *Cinderella*. I'll show them I'm different." When I'd try to pick David up or play with him, I could feel his reserve toward me. Then someone in the family would suggest that I not bother myself with him. "He'll get you dirty," they would say. Grandmother would magically appear to the rescue and take David from me. "The cultures are so different," I'd tell myself.

My husband and I came to America without David and returned to China in 1989 to get our son. On a prearranged street in the middle of Guangzhou, China, my Chinese brother-in-law delivered David into my arms. When I heard David's high-pitched, three-

* Contributed by Carolyn Han, Hilo, Hawaii.

year-old Chinese voice say "Mama," tears streamed down my face. As I hugged him to me, I felt a limp, unresponsive child. "All that will change," I said aloud. "You just need to know me."

Our first day in America David refused to eat a sandwich and became angry. "Of course, it is understandable," I told myself. "He's tired. He has never seen a sandwich before in his life. Dinner will be different."

Dinner was different. For this meal David's father prepared Chinese food. We began. Chinese children are served by a parent placing food in their rice bowl. We kept to this tradition. David seemed happy and enjoyed his meal until I reached for a piece of broccoli with my chopsticks and placed it in my bowl. He let out a bloodcurdling scream that echoed around the room. At first I thought he had eaten a chili pepper, but then the look on his face revealed hate.

"You took his piece of broccoli," his father said.

"What do you mean *his* piece of broccoli?" I asked.

"He had his eye on it," he answered. "It's his."

"What do you mean he had his eye on it? How am I supposed to know that it was his piece of broccoli? Are you kidding me?" I asked.

"Give it to him," his father ordered.

"Not on your life," I answered, stuffing the broccoli into my mouth. I felt instantly foolish, and a little crazy, for behaving in such a childish way.

David, now even more incensed that I had eaten his broccoli, screamed louder, jumped off the chair, and ran into his bedroom.

"Now you've done it!" shouted his father. "You've ruined his first day in America!"

Not only was the first day ruined, but the door to David's room was ruined too. David kicked the bedroom door so hard and so many times that the hinges came loose and the side panel splintered.

"He's only frustrated," I told myself. "Everything is new. He can't understand or speak the language. That's why he is mad at me. I speak English. I'll just have to try harder."

Preschool was a blessing. David soon learned English, and even though his social skills with other children were slow to develop, he showed intellectual promise.

"He's just hyperactive and hypercritical," said his preschool teacher. "With all the changes he's been through, it's no wonder."

He wasn't hyperactive at home. He had the ability to sit alone in his room for hours, to write and draw. Sometimes when I hadn't heard from him, I'd check to see if he was OK. He would be bent over his desk, working on writing and rewriting the alphabet. It had to be perfect or he wasn't satisfied. His teacher was right about his being hypercritical. He had his own sense of perfection, and he'd become very upset if something did not meet his high standards. Many times he'd throw the work, or himself, on the ground and beat his fists and cry.

A month before his fifth birthday, I stood in the hallway outside his room with tears of joy running down my face, listening to him read his first book. David remembered facts and dates. He could see relationships in words and numbers. His mind never stopped. "He's brilliant. That's why he's temperamental and difficult at times. His anger is understandable," I'd tell myself. But I began to notice that he was never difficult or temperamental around other adults. He was delightful, engaging, responsive. Often I heard "What a wonderful child you have," or "You are so lucky to have such a special child."

I couldn't tell them this was his public, not his private, behavior. Instead I said, "Thank you. I am lucky." I loved David, my marvelous son.

I was not lucky in my marriage. David's father became more and more dissatisfied and finally returned to China. But before he left, I adopted David.

Single-parenting David wouldn't be easy. I knew that, but David was my son. After David's father left, I thought I could now give him the attention he needed, but he needed so much. He could never get enough. No matter how much I gave, he wanted more.

"He's like a sieve," I told the psychiatrist. "He never gets filled up. The only thing I know about his biological mother is that she left him when he was a tiny baby. I really don't know the full story. Now his dad is gone. I'm sure the issues of abandonment are part of the problem."

Over the next few weeks the psychiatrist spent several sessions playing "Candyland" with David and having him draw pictures.

When I met with the psychiatrist alone, he said that David was an extremely intelligent child and that he didn't feel I had anything to worry about. He reminded me that when I had left David alone with him, David was not anxious. "If he were worried about being abandoned," he went on, "David would have shown some concern when you left him."

As I drove home, I thought to myself that David never was disturbed if I left him or, for that matter, if anyone left him. The only emotion he ever showed was anger. But the doctor's evaluation reassured me that David was, after all, a normal boy.

Do normal boys steal? Do normal boys try to hurt pets? Do normal boys show intense anger and rage toward their mothers? "Of course," I'd tell myself, "boys must be boys."

David often came home from school with another child's belongings, but I couldn't call it stealing. My first awareness of David's stealing came when I picked him up from school and his teacher handed me a dollar, asking that I not send David to school with money. I hadn't.

"Well, it's my money," he told me when I asked where he got the dollar. He had taken the money from his piggy bank. "That's not too bad," I thought, and he quickly reminded me that you can't steal from yourself. When we arrived home, I checked the piggy bank and realized that more than eight dollars was gone. When I asked him where the other money was, he said that he had bought candy after school. He had spent it all except for the dollar I was still holding in my hand. "That's my money," he yelled as he grabbed for the dollar. Two weeks later he had another dollar, and this time he said a boy gave it to him, then later said he found it.

After dinner I explained that I was disappointed he hadn't told me where the money came from, and that he should return it. "Why did you take it?" I asked.

"I wanted it!" he shouted, and sullenly walked back to his room, leaving me sitting alone at the table.

One day I found David pushing our cat down into a trash can filled with water. "What are you doing?" I screamed. "Stop!"

"Nothing," he answered, then smiled.

Other times I'd look outside the window and catch David throwing stones at the cat, or poking him with sticks. "Leave the cat alone," I'd say. "How would you like it if someone bigger did that to you?"

David's behavior didn't change. It went underground. He became more sophisticated with age, and was better able to hide what he was doing. Soon I took the cat into the bathroom with me when I showered.

If David wanted something, he was the best child in the world. When his behavior was good, it was very, very good. And when it was bad, it was horrid. My hope was that the behavior could change from bad to good, and stay that way. This "too good to be true" behavior could last for up to two weeks at a time, but it always ended. His control of situations astounded me. David never functioned as a child—he was either an infant or an adult, never a little boy.

"Maybe after more time passed, David could learn to trust me," I'd tell myself. I could never say "love me," because I couldn't tell myself that he didn't. "It must be an issue of trust. His mother left him; his father left him. He probably thinks I'll leave him, so he's afraid to form a close bond," I'd tell myself.

David didn't have an easy time with other children. He had superficial friendships. No close or lasting relationships. As he matured, he became very adept at handling adults. Acquaintances and total strangers wanted to take him home. I'd think to myself, "If they could only see how he acts at home—when we shut the door."

Denial! I was in denial, and I didn't want anyone to know how much David disliked me. If my friends knew how David treated me, maybe they would think I deserved it. No one would believe that a child could have such ideas on his or her own. When I'd finally get enough courage to discuss his behavior with friends—the stealing, the lying, and the hate—they would say, "He's just a bright boy. You are being too emotional."

"He's no different from Jimmy or Bobby," I'd hear. "All children act that way. My child does the same thing, even worse." Of course, I knew there was a difference, but I let my friends invalidate, and undermine, my own assessment of the situation. I was living it; I felt crazy; but I let others tell me I was making it up.

I was wrong.

The worst part was that no one understood. I kept quiet. "Maybe I'm not a good mother," I began to believe. "Have patience," I'd remind myself with a pep talk. Then I'd reaffirm my commitment to being a good mother. The more I invested in an intimate, loving relationship with David, the more he withdrew. If I got too close, he would remind me that I was old, ugly, a terrible cook, or an awful person, but he'd do it in subtle ways.

"Mom, it's not that I don't like you, but I'd rather live with Sheila. I don't want to hurt your feelings, but if you died, could I live with her?" he'd ask. Then he'd question me about what happened to children who killed their parents. "Is there a kid's jail?"

"Paranoid. You are too paranoid," I'd tell myself as I put the scissors and knives on the top shelf of the cupboard.

David's second-grade teacher noticed his aggressive behavior toward his classmates and expressed her concern. "David told Lily that he was going to 'get her' because she didn't stay by the tree," his teacher confided in me. "Now Lily's terrified and has missed two days of school because she is sure David will hurt her." During the semester David's teacher felt his hostility toward her grow when she tried to correct him or suggest that he do something other than what he wanted.

Three weeks after the "Lily" incident, the principal called me to say that David had eaten another child's lunch and, when questioned, had answered, "I wanted it, so I ate it." That same week the art teacher spoke with me about David stealing her wool and selling it. "He didn't care about the stealing, only being found out," she said. "Like he didn't have a conscience." His piano teacher suggested stopping the lessons because, when she corrected him, he would begin kicking the piano. These events gave me the incentive to once again seek counseling for David.

This time the counselor understood her patient. She did not make excuses for David because of his brilliance. In the eight months David saw her, she also counseled me. At her suggestion I tried different techniques that would help David to bond with me.

In the past I had sent David to his room for time-out when he did something unkind or hurtful. Now I held him instead. I'd draw him toward me and gently hold him in my arms. This is the same tack you might use on an infant to redirect behavior. The first time I did this, David reverted to an infant. As I held him on my lap, his facial expressions changed. His smooth face became wrinkled and red; his fists tightened; and he wailed in a high-squealing baby cry for more than twenty minutes. He was angry and fought me, but I continued to talk to him soothingly, and gently held him in my arms while I rocked him back and forth. He finally quieted down, but he did not use language to communicate. He used grunts to express himself, and they later changed to cooing sounds. After holding him for twenty-five minutes, my arms became tired and I placed him on the carpet. I sat down beside him. He didn't use his legs to crawl, but scootched by pulling himself with his arms. My guess is that he reverted to an eight-or nine-month-old baby.

I used this holding technique for more than two months and saw some changes. At least, I felt like we were achieving some positive results. But I realized that it wasn't getting the desired outcome when he asked, "Mom, why don't you punish me anymore? Each time I do bad things, you hold me. I'll just keep doing bad things. You make it easy."

David's anger escalated. Sometimes when I'd be putting on makeup, he'd come up behind me and hit me in the back. "I'm only teasing," he'd say. "It wasn't teasing," I assured him, "and it hurt." He'd smile and walk away.

During the night David would wake up and scratch on the screens and windows to pretend that someone was breaking into the house. When I'd go into his room, he'd fake sleep, but finally acknowledge he'd done it. "Why?" I'd ask. "I want you to be afraid," he replied.

David was almost eight years old and growing into a big boy. How much longer could I physically control him? How much longer could I pretend there wasn't a problem?

The worst expression of his anger toward me did not occur on Mother's Day, but that day marked the most hurtful event. All the children, including David, made cards and gifts for their moms in class. David didn't bring his card or gifts home—he had thrown them away.

We had planned a Mother's Day picnic with a friend and her son. When they arrived, David ran up to the mother and threw his arms around her, singing out, "Happy Mother's Day!" As he continued hugging our friend, he looked back at me standing alone in the doorway, and he smiled his hate-filled smile.

After much counseling I came to realize that David wasn't responding—he just wasn't available. Intellectually I could deal with his anger, the horrid and sometimes frightening behaviors he exhibited. What I couldn't deal with was his emotional distance, his lack of attachment to me.

During one session I said to the counselor, "At one time in my life I thought anything was possible with love."

"Anything is possible with love," she assured me, "but the love has to be received."

Since the love wasn't reaching David, I began searching for alternatives. One suggestion was "Rage Reduction Therapy," but after reading about it and watching a video, this method seemed too fear-oriented and abusive to me. A foster family was out of the question, so at some point he might have to be placed in an institution. Unthinkable.

My only option was to return David to his father. On the long, lonely flight back across the Pacific Ocean, I looked at the empty seat beside me and knew what it was like to lose a son.

The story ends where it began. In China.

15

Lost Children

War, Torture, and Political Policy

A peak experience in my professional life came when I taught with colleagues at a particular gathering of child clinicians—the Children in War Conference in Israel—in 1990. Worldwide children's suffering was powerfully distilled in presentations from many countries. The testimony of dedicated professionals who described their work, and described the enduring spirit of the children they see, inspired hope. Cutting through barriers of political, cultural, and professional boundaries, we—Palestinians, Israelis, South Africans, Argentineans, Cambodians, Swedes, and Canadians; analysts, pediatricians, social workers, and psychologists; and participants from other countries and from other fields—spoke of *our* children. We talked about the young survivors who were child soldiers, refugees, street children, homeless, without families—children without attachments.

This chapter includes a sampling of what we've learned from young people who have suffered profound, traumatizing attachment disruptions stemming from war and government policy. The children's experiences of torture, kidnapping, and disruption, as well as the survival skills homeless children learn in street communities and refugee camps, are not so different from those of the children we see in our own clinical practices. They may in fact be a model from which we can learn.

The first contributor describes a school-based group therapy program for refugee children in Canada. The story of Ben underscores the reality of many children with attachment problems: Even though he lives with his parents, they are unable to provide the necessary emotional support or appropriate model for coping because of their own overwhelming needs and circumstances. Ben's dual-role behavior is commonly seen in children who perceive their parents as ineffectual and powerless. The child is drawn to power and identification with aggressive adults or older adolescents, and when realistic and age-appropriate fears emerge, the youngster's desires for comfort and tenderness result in feelings of self-loathing. This in turn reinforces the "value" of a powerful, aggressive role; power and aggression provide comfort and become an automatic response to feelings of vulnerability.

Group therapy for these children provides a forum for sharing horrific past experiences and present difficulties, as well as promoting the growth of relationships between group members. The support, comfort, and sharing of vulnerabilities provided by the program offer alternative models to violence and to parents who are perceived as ineffectual.

The next contributors share professional insights about necessary attachment vs. parental attachment, insights that grew from their work with the returned children and families of the Disappeared in Argentina. The authors describe the internal and external factors that bound the kidnapped children to the intense yet fragile attachment relationships they needed for survival, and the cost the children paid for feeling loved.

Gradual transition of the children from the parents who raised them to their true extended families was not a viable option, given the circumstances of murdered birth parents. Such information cannot be given or understood a little at a time; nor could this be done while the children were being cared for by those who were involved in the past horror. The shift was sudden for the children, though carefully planned and with considerable thought given to the children's emotional needs. The authors speak of the reality of the youngsters' traumatizing experience in having to deal with the total change of their objective world. The project provided considerable continuous clinical support for the children and their families, resulting in positive outcomes.

The authors' conceptualization of necessary attachment has many similarities to trauma-bonding as described in Chapter 3.

Their insights into the emotional and behavioral impact of such attachments on the children are directly applicable to trauma bond relationships; that is, the children lose their natural curiosity and spontaneity—they fear truth and avoid reality. An analogous situation exists when decisions have to be made regarding children who live with abusive parents: Leaving a child in an abusive environment is harmful, and removing the child is traumatizing. The child must be protected from harm but cannot be protected from the pain of separation. What we can provide is a holding, loving environment, but the distress for the child cannot be avoided.

Our last contributor to this chapter shares knowledge she has gleaned from child refugee work in many countries. She describes how children cope with their attachment disruptions and losses, methods that include internalizing the absent parent, who then guides and supports them. We are reminded that we must not be misled by the appearance of maturity in adolescents; they are often troubled and confused when their community cannot help them assume their natural roles in the society. The author generalizes these processes to children's emotional survival in other circumstances. Many examples of structured healing situations are given, some planned and some that occur naturally when the children are given opportunity and support by the community.

Dialogues with Resettled Refugee Children: Attachment Issues*

My work with refugee children has focused mainly on issues related to losses, separations, and psychological trauma. The fate of many of these children has been determined by overwhelming circumstances they have experienced and witnessed. Attachment and assistance also play a significant role in their coping and integrating trauma, especially when provided by parents and caregivers as well as those helping them in their homeland during their journeys and in their "refuge."

I will briefly describe Ben, who, like many other refugees from

*Contributed by Yaya de Andrade, Vancouver, British Columbia

Southeast Asia, was considered a troubled child when I first met him at school to interview him for a group support program for resettled refugee children. At the time he was living with his parents and three of his four older siblings and was attending sixth-grade classes in a public elementary school.

In my first meeting with Ben, I was impressed by his energy and his ability to maintain a conversation in English. He was curious and spontaneous, expressing positive feelings about the future activities and projects I proposed to the group (drawings and workbooks). His teacher told me he was a troublemaker in class, rejected by peers, and very aggressive. The school counselor was concerned not only about him but also about his parents, who were described as isolated and depressed.

I was told that the family had many traumatic experiences prior to their arrival in Canada. Two of their young children died of starvation while the family moved through the jungles of Cambodia toward Thailand. They were constantly forced to go from place to place and, at a very early age, Ben witnessed killings and experienced major separations and losses.

These losses and the disruption of Ben's family life are, in my view, the main cause, or at least the major stressor, of his difficulties, especially those related to insecure attachment to his family, peers, and authorities in general.

He said he couldn't make friends, trust anyone, or love people around him despite feeling close to his parents and siblings. In his view there was no one to comfort, nurture, and care for him, and he felt he was alive because of his luck, not because of his parents' efforts or his ability to survive.

At the present time, it seems that his parents and teacher have difficulties caring for him and nurturing him. He appears to them as a child who gives nothing in return. The emotional security Ben requires is not available from his parents because they are mourning their own losses. His parents' aching sadness has burdened them with ongoing suffering, and although they are genuine as they worry about Ben and the future of the children, they have not been able to resolve and integrate their emotional scars into present living. The family has many other problems besides posttraumatic stress. Their symbols of cultural attachment have been lost, and it is as if they lost themselves as they were forced to leave their homeland, to have no identity.

Ben learned as a very young child that he had to be attached to aggressors as his ticket for survival. He reported feeling increasingly fascinated and frightened by camp guards, and he was drawn to their power, making them his models. This identification with aggressors may have transformed his fears and pain into feelings of omnipotence. His drawings show a fixation on power and physical strength, in contradiction to his physical body. Unable to cling to images of parents and siblings, being vulnerable and later developing feelings of inferiority, Ben has yet to develop a healthy identity. He tries to organize his defenses against an invariable background of fear, anger, threat, and anxiety and of memories of losses, death, and hopelessness.

He plays double roles: that of an aggressor, in an attempt to master prior trauma, and that of a frightened, depressed, isolated child, despising himself for the comfort he needs from others but doesn't dare ask for or expect.

He was first described by his mother as always complaining of bad dreams, being unable to rest or stay calm, being prone to violence, and having outbursts of anger at home. Now she feels he is more calm and sleeping better, and he has been coping with his traumatic experiences in many ways. For example, once he was telling about one of his older brothers who had to hide from the Khmer Rouge, who were going to kill him. Then suddenly he told me he had played hide-and-seek that day at school. It was interesting to see how he shifted his attention from a source of distress, a memory of painful reality, to something else, more likely to be considered an adaptive experience.

Ben and his family represent one of the tragedies of war. His parents have been distressed and are only marginally capable of responding to the daily needs of themselves and their children. Like other refugee and displaced children, Ben had poor empathy, low self-esteem, and low frustration tolerance. His insecure attachments arose from experiences first with his family and then with authorities in the camp and have possibly been perpetuated by other adults who think it is difficult to accept him due to his aggression and poor appropriate emotional ties.

His teacher does not recall major concentration problems, and it seems Ben has been able to follow instructions as well as produce adequate schoolwork. Nevertheless, the school counselor remains concerned about his lack of social skills, inability to make friends, impulsivity, and violence. The counselor has also been concerned about Ben's future, which Ben had perceived as hopeless.

In my view the quality of love, care, and compassion surrounding resettled refugee children is vital. Like other refugee children, Ben has to learn that genuine caring adults will be continually available to him and that he will have opportunities through support group programs at school to express feelings about his traumatic experiences and be validated without being judged.

His uncertainties and inappropriateness will diminish, given the appropriate buffering features in his family and school contexts, and eventually he will face the past as something that is gone, even though its recollection remains possible in the present and future. In practical terms, as his social skills improve and his impulsivity and violence decrease, he will become more engaged in using his potential and will make significant attachments.

Ben suffers the impact of psychosocial trauma. He may have been too young to understand what was going on around him, and his vulnerability only increased his antisocial behavior and anger. He still gets angry with himself, especially because kids call him names, and he remains with a temper. In his own words, "When I get mad, I want to punch people. It is so hard to control." Unfortunately, people around him have been too distracted with their own pain and fear to provide nurturing and appropriate coping models. We have to help him understand that we can only care about trauma, not cure or magically make those experiences disappear. In retrospect, Ben's interactions with other refugee children have been a vital buffer for his psychosocial trauma. He could listen to their traumatic and stressful experiences, share his struggles to cope with memories of extraordinary events, discuss current demands at school and at home, and increase his trust in himself and others. He remains concerned about possibilities of revenge by individuals and gangs, and he recalls the odd nightmares where monsters with scissors and knives are chasing him.

Survival Attachment and Attachment with the Parental Identifier Project*

> I couldn't grow, Grandmother. It was as if a hand was squeezing my head.
>
> —A kidnapped girl

Every child needs to establish an adequate attachment for his or her psychophysical development. In extreme cases there are children that create an attachment for survival purposes only, regardless of the price. Normally they create the attachment with the Parental Identifier Project. We call the former Survival Attachment (SA) and the latter Attachment with the Parental Identifier Project (APIP).

As is well known, a military dictatorship in Argentina took possession of power during the years 1976 to 1983, leaving a settlement of 30,000 "missing," of which approximately 500 were children, and leaving the total population overwhelmed with terror.

Some children were kidnapped along with their parents, and some were born in clandestine jails, after their pregnant mothers were taken as prisoners. Many of them were eyewitness to the kidnapping, torture, and assassination of their own parents. A number of these children were assassinated, and others were given to kidnappers and to others alleged to have been involved with the kidnappings.

Most of these children are still missing, and some of them were found by the Grandmothers of Plaza de Mayo** and returned to their original families.

The families who took the children—"appropriating families"—registered them as their legitimate sons or daughters and concealed all information in an attempt to erase any of the past. They estab-

---

*Contributed by Julia Braun and Marcelo Bianchedi, Buenos Aires, Argentina.

The Parental Identifier Project (PIP), is the totality of the atmosphere that generates the desire of the parents for having a child, the place the child is assigned, the name he is given, the emotional bond that exists, and the feelings and personal values of the family. The overlapping of the PIP and the potential of the child will shape his development.

**The Grandmothers of Plaza de Mayo is an organization of mothers and grandmothers who are devoted to searching for children of the Disappeared who vanished during the military dictatorship in Argentina.

lished themselves as "messianic parents," saviors of the children and destroyers of the natural parents' lives and ideologies. This situation leads the child to an SA.

The SA is based on an affirmation of lies regarding the child's identity, hidden origin, true name, and other historical and familiar circumstances. The child is forced to cooperate to sustain the lie and is subjected to manipulations, such as isolating him from people and circumstances that might reveal the truth. This has resulted in bizarre prohibitions and behaviors. For example, the child is taught that he must keep his head low when among strangers. This is said to be a rule of "good education" when in fact it is a means of avoiding recognition.

The SA is both strong and fragile. Its strength stems from the children's complicity, the intensity of seeking to avoid encounters with horror and death, and the effort to keep secret the outcome of hidden crime. The attachment is fragile and subjected to dissolution because of the constant danger of the truth becoming unveiled. As a result, the child finds himself in a conflict that he attempts to resolve by developing inhibitions and becoming "superadapted."

In the first instance, he loses his natural curiosity, spontaneity, and desire to know the facts and falls into a state of apathy and disinterest. In the second, he is transformed into a model child, creating the illusion of being able to hold back the love of elders forever, attempting to avoid the likelihood of a new loss. The child pays for the right to know, the price of being loved; the requirement necessary for survival is that he is forbidden to think.

When the child is found and returned to his original family, he suffers a hypercritical experience. The child is made aware of his true history; the child's truth, as he knows it, becomes unveiled, converted to a lie. The child experiences intense anguish and feelings of great anxiety.

We believe this moment is a "rectified traumatic experience." It is traumatic because of the intensity of mental pain produced by change in the totality of his objective world. At the same time, it is a rectified experience because of the rapid breakthrough to reorganization. In all the cases we observed, the restitution to the original family began a period of surprising psychic and physical growth.

The act of returning the child to his true family takes place in the presence of a judge, who assumes the role of the absent parent and who redeems the law by making possible orders of subversion against reigning values.

The return of the child to the refuge of his true family begins a period in which the child has an intense desire to know about his own history as a member of his family. This process, which the child and family accomplish together, allows for an APIP.

The truth, like valor, forms an organized base for the construction of mental categories—good/bad, truth/lie—that are necessary for the structure of the psyche. The establishment of an attachment based on reliability results in an unfolding of curiosity and interest. These children discover psychic and physical similarities with their natural families through salvaging memories and bodily contact. This also facilitates a process of integrating past experiences into their lives and makes the bereavement process possible. At the same time, they are free of the need to sustain the lie and free of the obligation of permanent gratitude to those whose messianic actions "saved their lives."

Free from the weight of their SA, they create their own process of verification and confirmation to prove the parental attachment's worth, opening a road to research that had been prohibited.

We could say, metaphorically, that these children realize a process of rebirth within their true ecological niches.

This contribution is based on the experiences of working with the children returned to the Grandmothers of Plaza de Mayo.

For reasons of privacy we have omitted statements of personal histories.

Recognizing International Attachment Problems*

An element crucial to a child's emotional survival is the sense of security gained from having a home and family. Refugee children face the same losses and dangers as refugee adults but do not have an adult's ability to comprehend the reasons for their situation or the ability to isolate this time from memories of happier ones. As one young child recalls, "I was a child when the war began. Once the

*Contributed by Jan Williamson, Richmond, Virginia.

war started, everyplace was dangerous. No one place seemed safer than another. Still, I was not afraid, because I figured out that a man can die only once."

Much can change around children without causing a major upset, but when an event affects the child's connection to the family, it inevitably affects the child. It is the family that gives the child a sense of identity and self-worth. Remove this and you threaten the child's belief in his or her own existence or right to exist. Obviously children do learn to survive without adults. Populations of street children attest to this fact, but it is often a survival without hope or joy. It is a survival that leads to self-doubt and distrust of the world. Not all children reach the conclusion that "a man can die only once." Many reach the conclusion that they are unworthy of being in the world, a thought that will follow them for the rest of their lives.

Refugee children lost from their families often dream of visits by mothers or fathers who instruct them in what to do. It is not uncommon for children to internalize or carry a mental picture of the lost family and to feel this image speaks to them and guides them in their lives. One young boy talks about his mother's spirit, which tells him to gain knowledge and make the most of his life. Another is told his father's spirit will protect him and keep him safe from harm. So great is the child's need to belong to someone that even imagining a caring presence is preferable to the loneliness of a child without a family.

The loss of childhood, home, and family does not respect age boundaries. An abandoned infant or young child loses not only a family but a personal history as well. Where can a child find an anchor in life, a sense of belonging, and in turn a sense of self-worth when nothing is known about him and he grows to adulthood in a refugee camp or in a community without benefit of traditional activities, language, culture—without a history? Refugee teenagers often give the appearance of maturity and young adulthood but still see the world through childish eyes and with childlike understanding. They are cut adrift from the community that would normally offer them a safe haven in life and teach them how to assume their natural roles in the community. Gone are the cultural supports that would guide them to a secure adulthood. As young adults they often move through the refugee population isolated and without benefit of the most basic feelings of identity, self-worth, or belonging to the community surrounding them.

Despite this depressing picture, some refugee children protect and nurture their hope and trust in the world around them, against all reason from an adult's point of view. It may be only a happy memory, or a phrase remembered from the time they were a part of a loving, protective family. These remnants of a happier life help sustain some children through the worst of times. "Before the war the people always kept their traditions. The temples, the festivals, and the games were a part of our souls. I remember it was a happy time." Other children try not to dwell on the unknown in their lives and look to more concrete memories for their emotional anchors. "Several days after we left our village we reached the temples. I miss them very much, just as I miss the mountains near our village. Of course, I miss my parents too. I don't know whether I will find them when I go back. The temples and mountains are sure to be there. But father and mother? I'm not sure."

Mariana and her brother live with their grandparents in a small village in Central America. They have lived there as long as she can remember. Her father, her uncle, and an older cousin disappeared one night when soldiers came through the village looking for food. No one knows what happened to them; no one speaks of the disappearances. She often hears her grandparents talking in hushed tones, but no one can tell her what is known of her family for fear she will tell someone.

Her mother left shortly after her father disappeared, to try to find work and a safe place to live. She promised her daughter and son she would be back in a year. After a year and a half, the mother sent a letter with some money, saying it would take longer than she thought to join them. Mariana is happy with her grandparents but wishes someone could tell her where her parents are and why they left. She is afraid to ask and thinks maybe she does not behave well enough to be told. After all, if she were not so loud or didn't fight with her brother or did better in school, they would know she was old enough to talk with them about her father, or to join her mother. She thinks if she can just learn to be good enough, her mother will send for her, or someone in the village will tell her where to find her father and she can see him again. She often cries at night because it is harder and harder to remember what they looked like.

She is afraid she might not recognize them if they came for her and she would be left behind again.

How do we assist when such catastrophic losses occur for children? The children themselves frequently show what we can do to help and how we can do so, if we only pay attention.

Despite differences in culture and child-rearing practices, the basic needs of children do not change, whether they are in the inner cities of the United States or in a besieged apartment in Sarajevo, confined to refugee camps or in a displaced nomadic tribe. Children seek continuity and a sense of order in their lives when the world is turned upside down. Adults, whether they be social workers or emergency relief workers, can work toward restoring such order and familiarity for children in a number of ways.

While not the complete answer for soothing the pain of loss, restoring a routine and a predictable set of events can offer a large measure of comfort to children. When a child has structured activities, when he can predict the beginning, middle and ending, he gains a sense of accomplishment and mastery in a chaotic world. This was poignantly illustrated in an African camp where 15,000 adolescent boys lived following displacement due to fighting and drought. Many were on the brink of starvation, were without possessions or even clothing. Emergency workers arriving at this desolate location were greeted by a startling sight. Hundreds of boys and the few adults in the camps stood in orderly groups and conducted classes. Those who could read and write were teachers. The boys used sticks to draw their lessons in the dirt at their feet. In the face of overwhelming despair, "school" was in session.

The United Nations High Commission on Refugees developed the *UNHCR Guidelines on Refugee Children* that briefly outlines methods for working with children through the use of animators, or group leaders, from the child's community. This lends itself to a culturally appropriate approach in working with children through such methods as storytelling, drawing, dance, clay, and drama. These activities allow children to express or hear others express their feelings and concerns about events in their lives. While this approach may sound simplistic, it is the crucial element in assisting children to examine, understand to some degree, and integrate stressful events as a part of their experiences. Children are not so different from adults in this respect. When a frightening event occurs, there is a need to repeat the event and tell the story many times—a need on the part of adult and child alike, to be heard and to gain some perspective. Yet it is also important that we recognize the ways children differ from adults in expressing their distress.

Children do this in a more protected way, by utilizing an indirect form of expression, such as making drawings, telling stories about "others," or watching others act out events they themselves have witnessed. The key idea is to allow the events to be expressed. Allowing the child to choose a method for such expression and offering mediums that are culturally acceptable are a part of this approach.

Refugee children frequently choose activities incorporating traditional themes that don't vary much in the course of storytelling, music, or dance. In one refugee camp in Malawi, an elderly man came to the school each day to tell folktales to a young audience. These stories were selected not only for their comforting familiarity but for the steps taken in problem solving and the examples of how the heroes gained mastery over frightening events.

Families had barely arrived and erected crude shelters in Cambodian camps in Thailand, yet one could hear the strains of music and the stamp of feet as large crowds surrounded a hut set aside for community dance, long banned in their home country. Trained dancers, musicians, and teachers began appearing in the schools and children's centers to teach the movements and songs to those who wanted to learn. In traditional dance performances children began to practice, over and over again, the soothing movements dictated by the past. Learning these parts provided a degree of mastery and regained a small piece of the disrupted culture.

Other children prepared dramas and acted out not only the horrifying past of Pol Pot but the everyday stressful events of refugee life. These elaborate plays included caricatures of the relief workers and their "strange behavior" and were performed with humor before eager audiences. Soon adults were performing reenactments of their own experiences for large audiences. These traditional activities offered what was needed by providing the protection of an acceptable way to "tell" what had long been kept secret when other forms of treatment were not available.

Yet another group of children in Africa began incorporating into a traditional dance a reenactment of traumatic events that had happened to them. In their performance the young participants suddenly became soldiers and guns appeared; people were killed and injured in a mock attack; and at the end one child was left to pick up the guns and pile them alongside the bodies. At this point the children moved from the traumatic reenactment into completing the dance in its original form. This was done over and over again, and to the adult observers it appeared to leave children "intact."

All of these examples are obvious in their importance. Children were able to turn to what they knew and were able to call on the customs of the culture around them as a safe avenue to approach terrifying memories of overwhelming loss and grief. The need to gain a measure of safety, for telling the secrets and for obtaining release from the past, was identified by children and realized through the predictable and safe format of a traditional dance, song, or story.

16

Dynamic Play Therapy

Creating Attachments

Steve Harvey

Dynamic Play Therapy is an intervention style in which parents and children play together using art, movement, drama, and video expression. Such play often takes on a gamelike format. Some expressive activities are directed by the therapist, while others are generated by the family members themselves. Simple group activities, such as rolling a ball back and forth, running under parachutes, or finishing a mural, are extremely difficult for families who are experiencing problems, while families who trust one another and have developed a healthy expression of feelings and problem solving are able to transform any simple expressive activity into a delightful experience that forwards and promotes their good feelings for one another. Play activities are used to produce fun and exciting mutual expression in families who have problems relating to one another.

A mother recently brought four-year-old Molly, her adoptive daughter, into therapy. The girl had been knocked off her bicycle and run over by a truck. Fortunately, there were no major physical injuries, but Molly became increasingly oppositional, had nightmares, and was constantly trying to control her mother's whereabouts.

The youngster had been adopted at the age of six months following removal from her birth mother, who was unable to control her crack habit and neglected the child. Molly was born addicted to crack cocaine. The adoptive parents divorced two years prior to

Molly's treatment as a consequence of the father's uncontrollable alcoholism. Molly missed him desperately, and he was not available physically and emotionally.

Despite all her earlier difficulties, the little girl had developed relatively problem-free while living with her adoptive mother. The truck accident clearly stimulated this girl's fear of abandonment, and she developed a strong need to control her adoptive mother's behavior.

The mother and child were asked to play Follow the Leader, and the little girl immediately nominated herself as leader. In the next ten minutes, however, the game developed the quality of "chase" rather than Follow the Leader. The girl refused to allow her mother to lead, darting quickly from one part of the room to the other. Molly clearly could not or would not take her mother's movement into account to create a more organized game. The mother quickly became frustrated.

Mother and daughter were then asked to complete together, on a single piece of paper, a drawing in which they drew themselves coming out of separate houses. Molly refused to develop any story or metaphor with her mother. She drew herself going off the paper and asked for her own, second, piece. By now the mother was thoroughly frustrated and angry, and Molly continued to misbehave in response to her mother's frustration. She became increasingly oppositional, and her physical expressiveness quickened.

The youngster and her mother were able to make a house out of large pillows after several weeks of guided expressive activity. Molly invented a game in which she would dart out of the house and a large ball would try to run her over. She would then yell for her mother to rescue her or would throw her mother a stretch rope (a "saving rope") to pull Molly back into the house. She eventually changed the game, and would kick the ball/tire away from her. Molly gradually added large, Raggedy Ann–type dolls as dramatic characters who were threatened by the ball. She could stop the ball and have her mother rescue both her and the dolls. Mother and daughter experienced a great deal of excitement and delight during these rescue scenes as the mother carried the little girl back "home."

Images and the use of props and metaphors kept changing throughout the course of therapy in this example. The quality of playful interactions between mother and daughter also became significantly different, changing from frustration and anger to mutual delight. This shift in the quality of their shared mood offered an excellent opportunity for them to develop a new and trusting aspect of their relationship; each looked forward to the other's ideas to build and create new aspects of their story. Their relationship began to reflect a mutual attraction and positive feelings for each other.

Play between parents and children who are experiencing emotional difficulties, especially concerning issues of trust, can be painful and frustrating. Play between parents and children who trust each other in a more natural, bodily felt way unites them. A basic principle of Dynamic Play Therapy is that mutual expressive activities can become a window that helps families create play experiences in which feelings of attachment can grow. Dynamic Play Therapy teaches the family to incorporate several expressive forms, in a creative problem-solving process. One modality is usually insufficient. When moving back and forth between art and movement, for example, frustrating experiences generated in one activity can be played out in another, helping family members continue to experience the act of playing with, rather than being, their problems.

Natural Creativity

Play and relationship development normally go hand in hand in a natural and effortless way as parents and children establish their initial and all-important emotional ties. Examples of this connection between natural play and relationship creation are very apparent once we look for them—a young mother singing to her unborn child, a father throwing his giggling baby into the air and catching him, an infant and parent or sibling taking delight in face play, preschool children and their parents playing on a slide or swings, or a young child kicking a soccer ball to a parent. While several developmental psychologists and researchers have identified characteristics of this mutual play—the development of attunement or expressive rhythm sharing, the ability to creatively problem-solve—the most powerful aspect of such play is the natural and effortless quality of the way it can occur. A baby's first smile, for instance, can bring instant, spontaneous playful responses to her mother's face. Preschool children and their parents can naturally improvise if provided with a box of scarves and hats, producing excited, fanciful exchanges.

Such play also pulls the participants into mutually shared spontaneous moments. Intimacy and delicate feelings can be shared completely and instantaneously during the light mood of those moments. Such activity is clearly full-bodied during early childhood, when attention is physically felt and shared. Each player freely and reciprocally contributes ideas, gestures, and involvement throughout the flow of the physical play.

A final aspect of this play state that can be used therapeutically is the creative space that allows a spontaneous give-and-take adjustment of mismatches. In the example given previously, Molly first ran away from her mother in an attempt to control her; then the mother and child shifted into developing a drama in which the child ran away from a ball that was going to run over her.

Naturalness, spontaneity, physically involved expression, mutual attraction, and transformative problem solving can be used and highlighted in therapy situations, even if only for moments at a time, when confronting extremely problematic parent-child relationships.

Dynamic Play as Therapy

Dynamic Play Therapy highlights and reinforces these natural qualities of play while trying to engage parents and children in expressive, playful interactive activities. Talking, insight, and verbal understanding of problematic interactions are important and useful at times, but the main ingredient of change in Dynamic Play Therapy occurs as the parent and child themselves experience the quality of mutual play together—the experience itself offers the true moments of change and growth of attachment and trust.

The techniques of Dynamic Play Therapy encourage complete physical interactions between parents and children in order to accomplish change and facilitate natural play. Typically, movement, art, or dramatic games are set up that initially involve simple interactions and roles for the entire family. These games are either therapist-directed or occur spontaneously. Therapist games can include things like Follow the Leader, with everyone getting a chance to be leader; Tug-of-War, using stretch ropes between family members; or constructing a house out of large pillows and making up a story about a family using stuffed animals as characters. Art activities can include making murals together or having each person in the family draw a house with a person coming out of it and then creating a story about the drawing.

Families may play games in which everyone tries to outscribble one another (Scribble Wars) as a way to settle fights and disagreements. These activities can be videotaped and given movie titles, then watched with a view toward creating better or more complete conflict resolutions, or devising and taping satisfying second scenes.

The goal of these therapist-directed activities is to help the family focus on their interactions and offer them a place where natural interactive play can occur spontaneously. These initial games are likely to fall apart quite easily in families in which the children are experiencing problems related to attachment difficulties and trauma. Here the play serves a diagnostic function as barriers to positive relationship interactions are demonstrated in the play. Corrective interventions are incorporated in a new game that facilitates relationship building.

Those interventions teach families ways to improvise from their mistakes and then continue their play until their interactions become more satisfying. The family then begins to play about their difficulties, allowing their own natural ability to play creatively together to flourish.

Switching the expressive medium can be helpful when family members get involved in strong disagreements as their play occurs. If, for instance, a family disagrees over who will lead in Follow the Leader, the therapist stops the play and encourages family members to draw their versions of what happened, draw their current feelings, or even scribble their reactions to the game.

After families experience some success and enjoyment in playing together, play scenes can be focused on basic themes involving trust, fear, and abandonment.

The Playroom

The playroom contains a number of large pillows, approximately four-by-two-feet, which can be used to make houses or walls or to signify different lands in the playroom. Stuffed animals, some as large as people and others of more usual size, can be used in dramatic enactments.

Stretch bands are long pieces of surgical tubing encased in soft, colorful fabric. These promote physical interactions, such as playing Tug-of-War or throwing the bands out as "saving ropes" when young children engage in enactments where they need to be saved or rescued.

Large, brightly colored scarves can be feeling messages, letters, or costumes, or simply used to start scarf fights.

Large gymnastic balls encourage physical interactions between family members.

Pieces of art, newsprint, and butcher paper can quickly facilitate a switch from drama to art or be used to make needed props for enactments. Children often draw ghosts, monsters, or other perpetrators; cut them out; and place them into the drama.

Music can be quite helpful. The selection should include typical children's music as well as selections of widely expressive music from opera, classical, jazz, and current rock.

The room allows expressive play to go from physical interaction to drama, and back again. This is especially helpful where attachment-related problems are physically expressed. For example, children using stuffed animals may become anxious, stop their play, and distance themselves. The therapist might then use the pillows to "make" walls, boundaries, or lands and encourage the child to move away from his or her parents. The youngster is later encouraged to invade Momland or to ask to be rescued from the parents' place.

In this way the therapist helps parents and children freely use spontaneously generated movement interactions to develop therapeutic activities. The physical play can be taken into fantasy through the use of imaginative metaphor-making; play images related to emotion can be generated.

Dynamic Play Therapy assumes that all physical interaction has a potential attachment story in it, whether expressed metaphorically through traditional verbal expressions or shown by immediate interactive physical behavior. Using the family members' spontaneous interactions helps them develop a quality of natural interactive play. Moments of instantaneous joining can occur as parents and children experience the freedom of their own improvisation together, be it in drama, art, or movement expression.

Another important therapeutic element of this mutual play is best described as spontaneous choice-making. The therapist helps the family recognize that each member's expression is full of interactive choices, and each person is free to respond. One result of the natural play is that each member is free to contribute a choice on which all can build playful interaction. An example from normal mother-infant play illustrates this point: A child smiles to initiate an interaction, and the parent mirrors the smile. The child develops the smile into a laugh and giggle, with the mother then freely responding with the choice of a verbalization or physical expression.

This same responsiveness to choice-making is important in the process of mutual play. An example is the description of Molly playing "chase" with her adoptive mother. They played "fast racing" and "slow racing." In fast racing, the mother and Molly raced against each other, accommodating the youngster's choice of quick movement. The mother's preference for slow movement was then captured in slow-motion racing, in which the person who was slower was declared the winner. The mother and child played this game several times, alternately each choosing whether the race should be fast or slow. The primary intent was to highlight for each that she had a choice of speed in relation to the other. Recognition of their choices helped transform the very frustrating experience of Follow the Leader into mutual games in which both mother and daughter could feel successful at playing with each other.

Case Example: Amy and Mrs. Moore

Three vignettes from a case involving a five year old in an adoptive situation serve to illustrate how expressive, playful interaction was used to address a child's significant attachment problems.

Amy was a year and a half old when she was removed from her mother's care by the Department of Social Services due to severe neglect and physical abuse. She was placed in a series of several foster care settings over the next two and a half years. Amy became more oppositional in each placement, biting, hitting, kicking, having tantrums, and exhibiting other negative behaviors. She was sexually victimized by a foster father prior to her final placement.

Amy had significant problems with lying, stealing, and oppositionalism. She got what she wanted by first being oppositional and then resorting to strong expressions of false sadness and crying. She was manipulative and quite distressing to live with by the time she was placed with Mr. and Mrs. Moore.

Amy did not engage in significant negative behavior during her first six months with the Moores. Her new parents were alarmed when her apparently satisfactory adjustment to their home changed. They were inexperienced parents and were an easy target for Amy's antics. They became very concerned when Amy started having trouble during her kindergarten year at school.

She was constantly being caught stealing by her classroom teacher during the first few months of the school year. She got into several fights where she would push, hit, and bite her classmates and would then make up elaborate stories to explain her misbehavior to her parents. These episodes of misbehavior seemed to escalate out of control. One day might begin with an episode of stealing. The next day Amy would be caught lying or fighting. By the third day Amy and the Moores were beside themselves with anger and frustration, and these episodes led to the worst feelings between the child and her parents.

The Birth Story

Amy was brought into therapy by her adoptive mother. I set up an initial play scenario in which the room was divided into Goodland and Badland. The play instruction was that when Amy went into Badland, she would pretend to steal all the props she could that were close to her. Mrs. Moore was to throw a stretch rope to Amy in an attempt to rescue her.

This game proceeded with Amy getting excited by avoiding her adoptive mother's rope and pretending to steal more and more things. When she finally did grab the rescue rope, she developed it into a Tug-of-War, not wanting to leave Badland. Amy was clearly involved in a physical struggle with her adoptive mother, and the struggle took the full attention of both. It had the same quality as the emotional turmoil the two had described earlier, but they were now able to continue the interaction within a spirit of playfulness.

Amy finally allowed herself to be pulled into Goodland. She

came running to her mother far more quickly than she expected, bumping into Mrs. Moore's leg and slightly injuring both of them. The bump became a cue to be incorporated into the game. I had Mrs. Moore place several large pillows around her. Amy was asked to get as far away from her mother as she could and to run and jump on these pillows in an attempt to bump her adoptive mother. Amy was excited by this activity and spent the next session and a half running and jumping on the pillows surrounding Mrs. Moore. Amy began to laugh and thoroughly enjoy herself, the laughter becoming infectious and spreading to her mother.

After several jumps Amy started crawling under the pillows to "get into" her adopted mother and found several ways to crawl beneath them. She suddenly said she was now inside her mother. Mrs. Moore, Amy, and I decided it was time for Amy to be born to her adoptive mother. The enacted birth was quite moving for Mrs. Moore and Amy. At the end of the "birth," Amy lay down on her mother's lap in a very soft and vulnerable emotional state, and Mrs. Moore was able to look into her eyes for a long time. During the next year of therapy, they talked about this experience as being deeply significant for them.

Finding the Real Mom

Some months later Amy began to talk about what her "real mother" was like, and she was encouraged to draw a picture of her. She had not seen her birth mother for several years and had no clear memory. Her inability to recollect provided a clear starting point for later expression and conversations about adoption. I encouraged Amy to use the pillows to make a house in which she could place the drawing of her birth mother, while Mrs. Moore constructed her current house. Amy was encouraged to journey back and forth between these two homes. She drew a map during one of these sessions to describe what the journey was like, and she developed fantasy images of storms and forests through which she needed to travel to get from one home to the other. Amy became quite dramatic during one thirty-minute episode, crawling slowly from one home to the other, falling down and resting, showing that she was lost in a storm. She chose very dramatic classical music to accompany the enactment. Mrs. Moore used voice expression and called to her in song to help Amy find her way through the storm. This dramatic play produced a strong and engaging episode.

Touch "Innings" Scene

Amy's oppositional and manipulative behavior at school and home persisted despite the clinical activities that produced much good feeling between adoptive mother and daughter. Mrs. Moore described the relationship as being a constant struggle to have Amy complete even the simplest home behavior, such as taking a bath or going to bed. I devised a game wherein Mrs. Moore would stay on Momland and Amy either could stay with her to be held, rocked, and taken care of or could leave. Amy began by having Mrs. Moore attempt to catch her, only to move away at the last second. I then extended the game to include hard, medium, or soft touches, or to be free, in an attempt to have both Amy and Mrs. Moore participate in mutual choice-making.

In the modified game, Mrs. Moore would start by holding Amy on her lap, and Amy could choose to either stay or leave. Mrs. Moore would hold Amy in a hard, medium, or soft fashion, or free her, depending on Amy's choice, but Amy would have to control her body to match her verbal choices. If Amy chose to be hard, she could struggle to get away as hard as she wanted; if she chose medium, she would need to soften her muscle tone and slow her body down; if she chose soft, she needed to let her body be very soft and move slowly as she moved away; and if she chose free, her body needed to show free and easy movements.

They played this game for five or six sessions before they could generate much pleasure and creative interchange. During the beginning sessions, Amy consistently chose free or soft to get away from her mother, but she would move her body with strong, quick movements. Mrs. Moore would respond to these hard movements rather than to Amy's verbal choices, a response that frustrated Amy. Amy then learned to control her body by saying soft or free with her body until the very border of Momland, when she would call "hard" and attempt to beat her mom at the last minute by becoming hard and quickly darting away from her. This in turn frustrated her mother, who would grab her at the very last moment. Amy would usually cry in response, and scream quite convincingly that she was being hurt. These expressions were always manipulations and attempts to have her mother let her go so she could win by getting away.

The game was enlarged. Mrs. Moore and Amy chose how long the holding game would last, that is, thirty seconds, one minute, two minutes, five minutes. We began to keep score. Mrs. Moore was the winner if she could hold Amy on Momland for the prescribed time. Amy won if she was able to get away. Amy and her adoptive mother began to play this final game, which we now called "Innings," quite easily and with a style and quality of mutual engagement and fun. As with the play episodes described earlier, they experienced a more positive and intimate emotional quality in their relationship once they began to use each other's touch choices in a reciprocal way. Amy's behavior changed, and she became much less manipulative at home and school as mother and daughter began to experience more playful and creative exchanges in the playroom. Mrs. Moore described her feelings toward Amy as being more naturally loving and intimate around her adoptive daughter.

I saw this family for a year and a half following Amy's placement with the Moores, and in my telephone conversations with Mrs. Moore over the next several years she indicated Amy was still living successfully and happily in this adoptive placement.

The Moores needed advice in behavioral management techniques that involved the use of natural consequences to confront Amy's misbehavior. Mrs. Moore and Amy said the actual playing of the games provided the most significant experiences in their therapy. These playful experiences clearly helped form an atmosphere in which they could begin to develop a sense of trust and attachment. In the final stages of therapy, they were able to choose which game they wanted to play and to improvise their own playful interchange throughout most of the hour.

Both adoptive mother and daughter came to enjoy physical involvement with each other in a natural and enjoyable way. They learned to recognize and respond to each other's physical (touch) or dramatic ideas and they were able to begin to create spontaneously playful exchanges with each other. They could develop dramas, stories, and games about the emotional difficulties between them. The "birth" and "real mom" dramas helped this adoptive mother's and daughter's playful experience in a positive way. Innings helped them to introduce a playful aspect into their power struggles.

17

Developmental Play Therapy

Viola Brody

In 1954, I developed a treatment modality, which I now call Developmental Play Therapy, in response to the needs of severely disturbed hospitalized children who had not benefited from traditional "talking" therapy and other play therapies. The major element of my new approach was to physically touch the youngsters—hold them, carry them, bathe them, sing to them, and allow them to touch me as well. I did not permit them to run away when it was time for their session no matter how scared they might be. The children responded to this "touching" attention immediately; they began to relate to others, their appetites increased and they gained weight, they resumed their maturation process and took their appropriate places in the world. Neither my staff nor I recognized at the time that touching, body contact, initiated the attachment process in these children. I have since worked with other children in elementary schools, the Headstart program, and day care centers, and have come to appreciate and to understand that touch is the basis for all growth.

I have also come to realize that adults need to be trained to do this simple, parent-child touching. Developmental Play training focuses on changing the adult rather than changing the child by enabling the adult to experience what the child needs—to be seen and to be touched. Many trainees comment on how difficult this is to do in spite of its apparent simplicity. They soon realize that it is the quality of their presence, not what they say or do, that makes the difference.

The goal of Developmental Play Therapy is to provide an environment in which the child can develop a core self by experiencing her physical body and the pleasure of her aliveness. The child is aware that she is being touched, and by whom. She gets pleasure from being noticed and touched and preserves this inner sense of being by inviting more contact. That invitation starts the attachment process.

Developmental Play is not intended to get the child to say, do, or feel anything specific. It is not a "prescription" therapy.

The Developmental Play therapist (DPT) controls the activities but does not restrict the child unless she is destructive or is hurting herself or the therapist. The therapist initiates the session as in the following:

DPT: (to a 4-year-old child in a first session) Since I don't know you, will you tell me your name?

Child (C): Anna.

DPT: I like the sound of your name. Could you say it again?

C: Anna (a little louder).

DPT: You said it louder that time. Did you hear that? Well, as I look at you, I see you brought your hands (touching one of them lightly).

C: (Looks at hand touched, smiles and holds other hand out to be touched).

DPT: Oh, that's nice. That hand wants me to say Hello to it too (touching other hand).

If the child responds to the touch by pulling back her hand, she is simply communicating without words where she is at that time. The DPT does not respond by interpreting the avoidant behavior, but simply tries another way of helping the youngster feel seen ("I do see that you have two hands"). At this point some children will hide their hands. The interaction then begins with both child and therapist participating, the child hiding her hands and the DPT looking for them.

Some psychotic children show they don't feel anything when touched. Here the DPT might try a variety of things to help the child feel his body, such a picking the child up and holding him. If he resists, the DPT will put him down but the child's resistance itself shows he has felt something.

The child's response demonstrates that the touch has an effect on the child's inner structure. It opens the child to the presence of his own existence and to the presence of the person doing the touching. This makes it possible for the child to relate and become attached.

The following principles of DPT and the accompanying vignette are reprinted from my book with permission.*

1. *A child who experiences herself as touched develops a sense of self.*

In the context of Developmental Play Therapy, the child's experience of being touched causes her to relate to the adult who touches her. The child who is touched is enabled to recognize herself as an *I* and to recognize the Toucher as an Other toward whom she has feelings and toward whom she can take action.

Broadly speaking, the child who feels touched can either *accept* the Toucher (often shown by moving toward the Toucher) or *reject* the Toucher (often shown by turning away from the Toucher). The child who repeatedly experiences being touched cannot, however, fail to relate in some way to the adult who touches her. And relating, of course, means the interaction of separate selves. Being touched not only authors the sense of self in the touched child, it opens the child to the myriad formative influences of relationship. Through relationship the child grows.

2. *In order for a child to experience herself touched, a capable adult must touch her.*

A capable adult is one who has had the experience of being touched. Because she knows what it feels like to be touched and she knows what the Toucher did to create that being-touched feeling, she is able to be the one who touches. She knows how to provide the relationship needed for a child to feel touched, too.

---

*A. V. Brody, *The Dialogue of Touch: Developmental Play Therapy* (Treasure Island, Fla.: Developmental Play Training Associates, 1993), 7–8.

3. In order to be a Toucher, the adult must first be willing to learn to be the One Touched.

Allowing yourself to feel touched is not easy, especially if you are a therapist, a teacher, or a parent. It is often difficult because the experience of being touched opens you to childhood memories (some good, some not so good). Yet it is these being-touched experiences that make you capable of touching children.

4. In order to feel touched, a child has to allow herself to be touched.

Children who have been abused in one way or another may not allow themselves to be touched. For them, relating to an adult has been painful. Instead of responding by moving toward an adult who touches her, the abused child either turns away or remains unresponsive. Yet if the therapist is sensitive and remains quietly present without withdrawing, these children begin to experience their bodily selves. Little by little, they allow the adult to see them and eventually touch them.

5. A child feels seen first through touch.

We first experience being seen at birth. The experience comes when a parent touches us for the first time. For us humans, touch precedes more formal, more complex ways of relating. But other ways of relating do not supersede touch as we age. Throughout life, touch arouses emotions and embodies the quality of interactions between persons.

Both children and adults have reported that they feel seen and acknowledged when they are touched.

Touch as a way of being seen continues throughout the course of therapy embodied in a variety of physical contacts—those chosen by the adult as right for a particular child at each phase of the relationship that develops between them.

In Developmental Play Therapy, the right touch is the one that helps a child feel touched, to acknowledge her own body signals, to experience her relationship to the adult touching her in the moment of their live meetings.

6. To provide the relationship the child needs to feel touched, the adult controls the activities that take place in a Developmental Play session.

During a Developmental Play session, the adult creates the experiences in which a child feels touched. To this end, the adult initiates the action in Developmental Play sessions.

The adult takes charge because it is up to the adult, not the child, to act so that a therapeutic relationship between adult and child becomes possible and then grows.

The following excerpt from session six with a 4-year-old boy who did nothing but scream and run around in the beginning, illustrates how the dialogue of touch initiates the attachment relationship.

SCENE: The Developmental Play Therapist is sitting on the floor facing Alan, who is lying on the floor facing the therapist with his legs straddling her lap.

DPT: (Leans over and kisses Alan on his right cheek)

ALAN: (Looks at T, smiles, and rubs his cheek with his right hand)

DPT: (Looking surprised) What happened to that kiss?

ALAN: (Laughing) I rubbed it off.

DPT: Well, I guess I'll have to put it back on.

(Leans over and kisses him again)

ALAN: (Giggles and rubs it off again, looking at T)

DPT: Who rubbed that kiss off? Who did that?

ALAN: I did! (Giggling) *I did it*!

DPT: Then I'll have to put one on the other cheek.

(Leans over and kisses him on the left cheek)

ALAN: (Again laughs and rubs it off)

DPT: (Kisses him, then picks him up and cradles him)

ALAN: (Lies quietly in her arms; reaches up and plays with her hair.)

From the children's point of view the value of the cradling to them is expressed in their responses to the question, "Out of all the things we did (in their therapy), what did you like best?" Ninety per cent always say, "The cradling."

In conclusion, it is important that we recognize our fear of touch. It is unfortunate that our phobias and taboos against touch prevent us from providing children with the kinds of nurturing, non-seductive, and non-demanding touch illustrated in this chapter. Appropriate, caring touch changes those who give it and those who receive it.

References

Barnum, K. E., & Brazelton, T. B. (1991). *Touch: The foundation of experience*. New York: International University Press.

Brody, V. A., Fenderson, C., & Stephenson, S. (1976). *Sourcebook for developmental play*. Treasure Island, FL: Developmental Play Training Associates.

Brody, V. A. (1978). Developmental Play: A relationship-focused program for children. In *Child Welfare, 58*(9).

Buber, Martin (1958). *I and thou*. New York: Charles Scribner.

18

Playback Theatre

Children Find Their Stories

Jo Salas

Imagine a group of about sixteen children and staff members gathered together in the gym at a residential treatment center, seated on chairs curving around an open space. On the "stage" there is another group of adults. They're also staff members—a recreation worker, psychologists and creative arts therapists, a teacher's assistant. But at this moment they are in a different role: They are offering themselves as Playback Theatre performers. The leader, called the "conductor," invites the children to tell stories from their lives. A ten-year-old boy gets up. With the help of questions from the conductor, he tells about getting lost when he was five. The boy chooses actors for all the roles. "Steve can be me. Dana can be the policewoman." Without discussion the actors prepare the stage. They enact the story using dialogue, movement, music, and simple props. The boy watches from his chair beside the conductor's at the side of the stage. At the end he nods with a big grin, "Yeah, that's what happened." He returns gleefully to his seat in the audience, and another child comes to the teller's chair.

Playback Theatre is a form of theatrical improvisation in which theatre scenes are created from personal stories told by volunteers from the audience or group. Founded in upstate New York in 1975 by Jonathan Fox, Playback Theatre was conceived as a response to the human need, both individual and social, for the communication and validation of personal experience. Theatre in its earliest forms perhaps fulfilled this function when members of the tribe (we can imagine) might have gathered together to tell in action what had happened to them during the day and to honor, at times of transition, the important stories of the group. In our modern Western culture, these purposes of community gathering, healing, and artistic synthesis have become separated into quite unconnected arenas. We might appreciate theatre as entertainment or high art; we might seek personal healing through psychotherapy; we might participate in various public celebrations and rituals. Our intention in Playback Theatre has been to develop a new context that combines essential aspects of all these experiences, to re-create a community forum in which art and redressive action are equally integral.

Playback's power to affirm and heal, always implicitly present wherever it is happening, has led to its increasing use in therapeutic settings. While we all share the need to bear witness to our own stories, to find listeners who will respect what we say, and to open ourselves to the stories of others, these needs are particularly acute for people whose lives lack even the usual opportunities for story-sharing—our so-called special populations. Psychiatric patients, the institutionalized elderly, recovering substance abusers, troubled adolescents—all are likely to be hungry for the chance to tell, to be heard, to have a means of comprehending and respecting their experience.

Playback Theatre's form itself is versatile. It can readily be adapted to different conditions and purposes, always maintaining the essential ritualized framework and the fundamental respect for stories. A trained Playback leader working alone may invite the whole group to participate in the enactments—it can be as empowering for the people enacting a story as for the one telling it. In other situations it may be more therapeutic to use something close to the standard performance mode, with a team of trained actors, a conductor, and (usually) a musician.

In the Playback work with the emotionally disturbed children I described at the beginning, we use a performance style rather than a therapy group model. Almost all of the children are the survivors of grievous abuse and neglect. They have suffered the effects of the worst ills of our culture—drugs, poverty, violence, political disenfranchisement. Amazingly, the children are full of spirit and a resilient optimism. But they do not have the ego strength to successfully adopt roles in one another's stories, although they are easily able to accept adult actors playing themselves, their family members, and whoever else might appear in the story.

There's another advantage to using a performance mode—the children think of the sessions as festive events, not as therapy. They feel that they are receiving a special treat when they have a chance to attend a Playback show.

When we first brought Playback Theatre to the institution, we planned a careful introduction to ensure that the children understood what kinds of stories we were asking from them—not stories as they might be used to thinking of them, fairy stories or movie plots or books, but their own stories from their own lives. But we soon realized that explanations and demonstrations were unnecessary. All we have to say is, "We're here to listen to what really happened to you, and then we'll act it out." They understand immediately. There are always more stories than we have time to enact. And those who do tell their stories—perhaps three during a show—choose moments from their lives that are rich with meaning and resonance, for the other children as well as for themselves.

We have been offering these shows for about three years, once every month or two. There are some recurring themes: injustice, personal triumph, physical injury, mischief. Many stories are about relationships: All of these children are separated from their families, some permanently. Most of them hope to be reunited with their parents, painfully unrealistic as this hope may be for some. Others have accepted the reality of the loss of their families and focus more on the new connections they are trying to make.

Several stories have celebrated the experience of finding others who can, even briefly, substitute for the lost family. Nine-year-old Rashid tells about going to the park with his group. He wanders off by himself and makes friends with two "perfect" little boys, he says. They are both younger than Rashid. He has a happy time playing Ninja Turtles with these children, while their mother watches from a park bench.

Rashid, a sensitive, affectionate, creative child, has had no contact with his parents for years. His grandmother has told him they are dead. The truth is that they are too deeply involved with drugs to care about their child. He visits his grandmother sometimes. She complains that he is bad, and she's not sure she wants to have him.

Eventually he will be discharged to her care, if she decides she can commit herself to him. In the meantime, Rashid yearns for a family. He wants us to know about this moment in the park, his glimpse of what it might be like to be a perfect little boy playing under a mother's watchful eye.

In another show twelve-year-old Liz approached me as we were setting up. I knew that she had just returned from a stay in a children's psychiatric hospital following an emotional crisis. I knew also that for years Liz has struggled to cope with a mother whose own extreme mental instability made her daughter's world into a nightmare of unpredictability. One of Liz's responses has been to develop a facade of adultlike behaviors, trying fruitlessly to pick up the responsibilities her mother does not fulfill. She has become extremely sarcastic and intolerant of others—everyone, staff and children, tries to steer clear of Liz's sharp tongue. But, of course, she's not an adult, only a child who has not had enough childhood. Her knowing, articulate stance doesn't help at all when she is engulfed by her feelings of anger and abandonment.

Liz whispers to me that she has a story about her time at the hospital. Once the show is under way, I invite her to the teller's chair. She comes to the stage with her usual jittery impatience. But she has decided to tell a different story, one about affirmation, not crisis: about her first meeting, two years ago, with Jan and Phil, two people looking for a child to befriend.

"What was a word for you at that meeting, Liz?"

"Hyperactive!" she says, looking at me with a smile. "But they really liked me. They told Sister Margaret that they definitely wanted to get to know me. Then they came to visit that next Saturday, and now I go to their house for weekends. I'm probably going for Thanksgiving, I hope."

The actors portray the series of interactions that lead up to this moment. The enactment includes a scene that Liz hadn't actually been present for—the meeting between Sister Margaret and Jan and Phil. "She seems like a lovely child, Sister Margaret. So bright and mature—more than we expected, after what you say she's been through." The scene ends with Liz receiving her first phone call from her new volunteers. "Liz, we really enjoyed meeting you. Can we see you again soon, maybe this Saturday?"

Liz watches from the teller's chair at the side of the stage. She claps her hands to her face at one point, so excited and pleased is she to see her experience come to life in front of her eyes and to share it in this vivid way with her friends and staff in the audience. At the end she grabs my arm, shy now that the focus is back on her.

"And Liz, you're still friends with Jan and Phil?"

"Oh yes, I'm seeing them on Friday."

Sometimes a story like Liz's, focusing on a new, hopeful relationship, can open the door to a story about the other side, the losses that have led these children to be so desperately in need of Jan and Phil or whomever they can find. In a recent show that took place in a classroom, with barely enough room for a "stage" area in front of pushed-back desks and chairs, the first story was about going to town to get pizza for lunch as a reward for good classroom behavior. Accompanying Latissa on her trip was another child who had earned the reward, along with the teacher's assistant who had bestowed it. They were both present at the performance, so Latissa's story also had the effect of being a reminder and an acknowledgment to them. Underlying the lighthearted fun and pleasure of the experience itself and gently brought out in the enactment was the warm awareness of an adult's companionship and caring.

The second teller was eleven-year-old Jesse, who had played a cinnamon bun in Latissa's story, to the delight of his classmates. He had a very different story, and it took him a little while to be sure that he wanted to tell it. It was about his first foster placement. When he was seven, Jesse and his brother were taken from school, without warning, and brought to a foster home. His own mother loved them, he said, but she wasn't able to control them or herself. Mrs Reider, the foster parent, turned out to be far worse than his mother. She was cold and cruel. She beat them with wire coat hangers for crimes such as not eating dinner. "We just didn't like her food," said Jesse. Visiting their mother several months later, the boys had a chance to tell her how bad it was. She was very upset. Although she had hit the children herself, she couldn't bear to think of them being hurt by a stranger. She was able to arrange for them to be removed to a better foster home.

Sensing the other children's absorption as Jesse told this story, I asked if anyone else had been in foster care. All raised their hands.

They looked around at one another. This was something they had not known about themselves as a group. The teacher was struck too. She had never realized that she had a whole classroom of foster children.

We watched the scene—the boys carted off abruptly, the incomprehensible harshness of Mrs. Reider, the despair of the mother as she realized how her children were being treated. Jesse, who had told his story with a purposeful calmness and dignity, was very caught up in the enactment. He called out some extra information for the actors every couple of moments, and he nodded appreciatively when they incorporated what he said. The scene ended with the mother taking the boys away from Mrs Reider. "I wish I could take you home myself, but I can't, not yet." There was a silence when it was over.

"Is there anything that you would like to say to Mrs. Reider, now that you're eleven, perhaps something that seven-year-old Jesse was too young to say?" I said to Jesse after a minute. He didn't hesitate.

"I'd like to tell her that *no one* has the right to treat kids like that. Not even if they're your own kids. You just can't hurt kids. It's wrong."

The actors did one more scene, short but intense, between Jesse and the cowering Mrs. Reider. Jesse—a big boy now, not so helpless—makes his impassioned demand for justice and kindness for all children. Mrs. Reider has no choice but to hear him. Watching, the real Jesse nods in satisfaction.

We were coming to the end of this show. I invited the other children to share, if they wanted to, the thoughts and feelings they had been aware of during Jesse's story. I was moved by the readiness and honesty of their responses. Although the children are very quick to tell their stories in the teller's chair, they are usually much more reserved about sharing feelings outside of the Playback format. Jesse's courageous openness and his story itself had allowed them to feel their own stories with unusual directness.

Part of the willingness to express themselves had to do with their teacher, who had carefully developed an atmosphere of trust and respect in her classroom. She had no difficulty in recognizing the significance of Jesse's story, for the others as well as for Jesse himself. She indicated to me after the show that she would be sure to follow up with time for further talking, especially about the revelation that every child in the class had been in foster care.

This sensitivity to the need for follow-up on the part of teachers, therapists, and childcare workers is important to the success of our work. Although discussion and interpretation are out of place in Playback Theatre, the children's stories often provide an opening for a new level of sharing that might take place later in the classroom, the living unit, or a therapy session.

The regular staff have a valuable role to play at our shows, not only in terms of noticing and responding to the need for further attention but also simply in their sympathetic, supportive presence. Unfortunately, not all staff members are as alert as Jesse's teacher, or as receptive to Playback. Some are disconcerted by the focus on subjective experience in the stories, perhaps even uncomfortable with the unwavering respect given to the children. They tend to see their professional task as behavior management above all, and it is hard for them to understand why we would put so much effort into listening to the child's experience. They sense, accurately, a profound difference between our demeanor and approach to the children and theirs. What we are doing is placing ourselves and our creativity in service to the children's experience, in the belief that everyone's story is worthy of being heard and understood through the vehicle of theatre. It is essentially humble work, and it is not without vulnerability: We take considerable personal risks when we offer ourselves as Playback performers in front of our colleagues and our young clients. It is, in a way, the diametric opposite of a professional stance based on distance and authority.

What did Jesse gain from telling his story in Playback Theatre? He learned, for one thing, that he was not alone, that his experience of being a foster child was shared by every one of his classmates. He was able to convey his love and loyalty for his mother, and hers for him, despite her shortcomings as a parent. He was also able to externalize the hidden, agonizing shame of having been a beaten child. His anger was focused on Mrs. Reider, but his statement after the first version of the scene showed that he realized it was wrong too for his mother to be physically abusive.

This memory of pain and humiliation was for the first time brought out into the realm of public communication. I expect that he will need to tell his story many more times before he is through with it. But an important step was taken.

Like many of the stories we have been privileged to enact, Jesse's touched on universal themes—in this case, love, loss, and injustice. I can think of many other stories that have directly or indirectly dealt with the children's concerns about the relationships in their lives—the unfulfilled ones, the lost ones, the stuck and painful ones, the idealized ones, the fragile new ones. Seven-year-old Allan was mourning the recent death of his grandmother, who had always taken care of him. He proudly told about the time she entrusted him to go to the store for her—"Soup! She wanted soup!" he remembered halfway through the enactment. Vicky, who had lived with the most shocking violence in her home, told a story about a delicious time going to church with her volunteers, squashed between them on the pew and belting out gospel songs. Plump, pretty Danielle, long ago abandoned by her family, had to have an operation and felt touched by the kindness of everyone at the hospital, especially Arline, a childcare worker usually known for her gruffness. Manny, on his twelfth birthday, came straight to a Playback show from a disastrous birthday visit with his borderline personality mother. He told his story to bear witness to his anguish and to gain at least some sense of comprehension. Playback Theatre has served all of these children in their undaunted search for connection, meaning, and survival.

19

A Residential Care Attachment Model

Dave Ziegler

Attachment disorder is much like many other issues in our society wherein we coin a new term for a very old problem and then scare ourselves about how bad it is. Don't misunderstand—an attachment disorder is a serious problem, but it is not what it has been presented to be by sensational stories and made-for-TV books. Children with attachment disorders are just that—children. They are difficult, yes; they can be hurtful, yes again; but they are not lost causes, much less developing Ted Bundys. Our program works with these difficult children every day, and we see clear progress in nearly all of them.

There are tens of thousands of children in our systems of "care," which means we have far too many children who have not been cared for where it counts—in their families. These children often have defenses and a tough shell that few can penetrate. Without a knowledgeable and understanding care provider, this can lead to problems in reaching out and bonding.

These children have attachment themes rather than an attachment disorder. Without someone reaching them while they are still more connected to family than to peer group (usually under the age of twelve), these children may well become the delinquents and criminals of tomorrow. The halls of our prisons today are filled with the youngsters of our systems of care in the past. For these children it is either pay now—with resources for social workers, therapists, and trained foster parents—or pay later—with free room and board in our institutions. These children may well be the criminals of tomorrow, but they should not be confused with children with a true attachment disorder.

Children with a severe attachment disorder have never had a successful attachment to anyone. Children with a mild to moderate disorder have had only partial and never truly rewarding attachments in their short lives. These children start life in the first twelve to eighteen months with failure in the most basic of instincts in human beings—bonding immediately, first of all to survive and then to find a successful place in the interdependent world of other human beings. When things go badly to begin with, the instinct to bond (promoting physical survival) is overridden by avoiding the pain and neglect of attaching (emotional survival). The seeds of attachment are often sown long before the results are observed. Without a disruption in the cycle of an attachment disorder, it may grow into a lifelong and unsuccessful search for a place in the social network of our society.

I believe we are still in a phase where as a society we are not sure how to help these children. In our confusion and to some extent desperation, we have developed what appear to be desperate therapies, and some parents, professionals, and programs believe these intrusive approaches are all that can work. I suggest that we take our desperation and first work to clearly understand the problem and its causes and then commit the necessary resolve and patience to test our solutions. I would like to share with you one such patient testing ground, which is a small residential treatment program called Jasper Mountain Center.

How Jasper Mountain Started

The center was founded by three babyboomers who were raised by their own families with varying levels of health as well as dysfunction. Armed with college degrees, professional experience, and seemingly unlimited energy, the three of us set out to make a difference in the world, following the advice of Mother Theresa—one person at a time. The goal was to create a seamless integration of our home life and our professional work. This goal was quite effectively reached, and we are not clear to this day whether this has been as good for us as it has been for the program's children. The practical steps are easy enough to recount: endless meetings to determine the criteria to find the healthiest place in the United States to live, moving to the promised land in southern Oregon, and purchasing a rural ranch. After six months of acclimating and very long days fixing up the old ranch, we informed the state child protection agency that we were ready for their biggest challenges. The reaction from the state's workers was one of equal parts elation and suspicion. Elation that people interested in accepting very disturbed children into their home would also be experienced professionals with counseling backgrounds. And suspicion as to why people who had a choice would want very disturbed children in their home! Eleven years later there are those who still have suspicions.

Jasper Mountain Center was founded in 1982 on an eighty-acre ranch southeast of Eugene, Oregon. The scenery was beautiful enough, with two major rivers, heavily wooded forest, waterfalls, an artesian spring, miles of hiking trails, and sheer cliffs rising to a thousand-foot mountain, all of which were on the property. The ranch even had history as part of the second homestead in this region of Oregon and the end of the Oregon Trail for Cornelius and Jasper Hills. To this beauty and history we worked to bring hope to some very confused and abused children. From the beginning the children came to Jasper Mountain telling their stories of abuse and pain. The program quickly turned its focus to healing the scars of sexual abuse, which were present in almost all the children. We soon saw that some children healed very differently from others and that some didn't seem to heal at all. Of all the children, there were those who didn't look at you, would push away any affection, and were quick to use and abuse you as they had been themselves. In the early 1980s we began identifying children who had bonding problems, and invariably they were the most difficult of our difficult children.

How the Program Works

Jasper Mountain is based on principles of health in body, mind, and spirit. The program ensures clear air, clean water, plenty of exercise, and treatment components in a context of family where the parents are professionals. This family focus has turned out to be the most important ingredient in the therapeutic stew. Not that being in a family makes much difference to attachment-disordered children, but in the final analysis it is the ability of the family and its staying power that will make the difference in the bonding process. In the early years the three of us did everything without outside help. At this point the program has the state's highest classification for supervision and treatment which requires one staff for every three children.

The program uses four basic categories of intervention: environmental, behavioral, psychotherapeutic, and self-esteem.

- Environmental intervention creates a therapeutic Disneyland, but rather than the happiest place on earth, we strive for the healthiest place on earth. There is close scrutiny to every environmental aspect of the program, from the architecture of the buildings to diet, and from the amount of natural light to the control of violent themes that reach the children from the outside world (e.g., having no commercial TV).
- Behavioral interventions include the mundane but important behavior management systems wherein the children earn levels that determine privileges. At Jasper Mountain the children have a behavioral system for the residence and another for the on-site school. Although the level system is the most traditional part of the program, the children get up each morning and go straight for the chart to find out what level they are on for the day. Modifying behavior is an important step, but is only a beginning step in treatment. Behavioral ways to require a give-and-take framework are essential with children with an attachment disorder.
- Psychotherapeutic interventions include all the individual, group, and family therapy interventions, as well as art and play therapy. They also include occasional chemical interventions and sessions with the program's psychiatrist. Each child has two individual counselors in addition to our psychiatrist to promote skills at developing relationships with various adults.
- Self-esteem intervention is where some of the unique aspects of the program can be found. These include a variety of routes to the self-worth of the child, including biofeedback, concentration and meditation training, therapeutic recreation, an equestrian program, hiking and rock climbing, jogging, gardening, visual and performing arts, computer and CD-ROM competency, posi-

tive video feedback to enhance the self-image of the children, and many others.

But even with magical interventions like the above (and there is something that every child will find magical on this list), there is no guarantee that an attachment-disordered child will use any of these to heal his or her disposition toward others. With this backdrop of our basic residential treatment program comes the specific approaches used for these challenging children.

What Makes the Difference

At Jasper Mountain we are often asked why children with attachment disorders who can strike fear into the hearts of parents, caseworkers, and therapists are not feared in our program. And here is step one in making a difference with these children—they must not be feared or their controlling nature takes over. Relationships with these children are often initially no less than warfare. In this struggle for dominance, if the child wins, everyone loses, and if the adult wins, everyone wins. I see it as just that simple. Of course, how to win the struggle with these masters of control is not simple at all. That we do not fear these children in our program may come from the fact that no matter how good they are, so far none has been able to win the control war at Jasper Mountain. In most cases the children, who are usually very bright, realize within weeks that they may be able to control an individual staff person for a while but not the program.

Another factor critical to our success with these children is to work as a team and control all variables in the child's life producing a unified approach. In our program there is only a building change from the residence to the school; the approach and staff act in unison. We take time to work with caseworkers and family so that the methods the child has used to irritate, control, and keep others distant do not work on campus or off.

Treatment with these children not only must strip them of their remarkably intricate insulation and defenses but also must provide a real and attractive alternative. How can getting close ever look attractive to a child with an attachment disorder? The answer is as simple as the first principle of negotiation—you get some of what you want only when I get some of what I want. Despite attempting to look otherwise, these children want lots of things. They are generally extremely motivated by material belongings, although they believe that if you knew this, it would make them vulnerable, and thus they pretend to be apathetic to almost everything. Don't believe it. At the same time, they will take without giving if you let them. You must teach them reciprocity and hold them accountable. There must be a constant pressure to connect. With normal children (has anyone seen one of these lately?) coercion is not a positive or useful approach. But with these children they get dessert only after a polite request; they go to the movies only after doing a chore for you; they play fifteen minutes of Nintendo only after sharing two important events at school today. The approach is clear: You don't get something for nothing (except love).

The effectiveness of treating these children comes down to every interaction between adults and the child. This means that every contact between a program staff member and the child is a very small part of the puzzle but critical to the overall picture. Manipulative children do not change if their tricks work on anyone. If the therapist and parents work together but the school is out of the loop, the child will never change, due to intermittent variable reinforcement, the same principle that brings confident gamblers to Las Vegas to lose their money time after time. The child tells himself that he will prevail in the end.

As stated before, these children are usually quite smart, and when they understand that they must work to get what they want, here is their sequence: First they start by not doing it, to see if you get flustered; then they do it halfway and grudgingly (punishing you); then, if they must do it right, they will do it with a bad attitude; and eventually they just do it. These progressive steps occur only when they have to do their part to get what they want. When this pattern is repeated over and over for years the psychological principle of cognitive dissonance steps in, whereby if your behavior changes, eventually your attitude must change, and if your attitude changes, then your behavior must eventually change as well.

You must demand that children with attachment disorders do just what you want of them (which are progressive steps toward relationship). They need not do it with an open heart or with honesty; they just need to do it. What you begin to systematically show them is that they will not be abused when they are vulnerable and that the world where you get what you want by being close to others is far superior to using others and being emotionally and personally alone in the world.

The last factor that makes a difference is a four-letter word, *time*. Time is a four-letter word in our culture because we don't want to take the time to do most anything right. We are irritated by the traffic light that delays us three minutes; we want the flu medicine that gives us fast, fast relief; and incredibly we are impatient when we have to wait two and a half seconds to store our documents on our old model computer. Is it any wonder that we flinch at the prospect of taking years to treat an attachment disorder? This may have something to do with the do-it-quick "holding" therapies that promise some bonding after an intensive weekend, or at least after the twelve-week special. Some may believe that the pattern of withdrawal and distance in a true attachment disorder can be extinguished relatively quickly and a new pattern of interdependency and vulnerability learned soon after, but I do not believe there is any shortcut to the years of concentrated effort described above. For the *Star Trek* generation, where any galactic problem is solved within the hour, years of effort are inconceivable, but they are truly necessary.

To be fair to all of us parents who have a child with an attachment disorder in our home (I have one by adoption), we would have a better chance at putting in years of effort if only we saw some progress, even tiny successes, or at least the reassurance that we were heading in a direction other than futility and exasperation. This is precisely what our program tries to give parents—a road map. We all know that human beings take at least twelve years to raise before the onset of their teen years. Our current thinking is that the relearning process may take five to seven years. I believe parents can learn to persist if they are shown a way that works, as long as they don't get a false message that there is a quick fix.

The Jasper Mountain method works. Whether it is the place, the people, the approach, the time invested, or all of the above simultaneously. The important thing is that the program wears the child's defense down before the child wears the staff down. We do not describe the children as "cured" when they leave Jasper Mountain. Attaching is not only an instinct; it is also a skill. We should not leave children in a rather scary and indifferent world without their defenses unless they are given new tools to succeed in the game of life. It takes a very long time to learn how to bond even after the children decide they want to. This is usually a process of unlearning and then relearning. It is important that we not lead these children down this long road to healing if we are not prepared to go the distance. In residential care this means that you never completely close a case. Our program's graduates keep in touch, come by, borrow money, and bring by their fiancé to meet the family. We have invited our children into our extended family, and nearly all accept.

In adoptions we must understand that there may be no other chance for these children. Due to the time it takes to free a child for adoption, to place the child in the right home, and to invest the five to seven years with him or her, there may not be time for a "Plan B" and starting the process over with another family. This may sound like a great deal of responsibility for the adoptive family, but if real bonding doesn't happen in the first adoptive family, it may never happen.

Perhaps the ultimate abuse is to take a child who is dependent on others for her very life, thwart her survival instinct by not placing her where she can form an attachment, fail to help her connect with others during her early years, and expect her to live the rest of her life emotionally and spiritually alone and separated from friends, a spouse, her own children, and even God. It comes very close to a definition of hell, doesn't it? I hope you agree with all of us at Jasper Mountain that years of hard work are not too high a price to save the quality of life for a child with an attachment disorder.

20

Adoption and Attachment*

Dave Ziegler

The Adoption Courtship Model

Out of necessity, Jasper Mountain Center (JMC) staff have attempted to isolate why some adoptions worked during the first five years of our program and why most didn't. The result of two years of considering this question has been the development and implementation of an adoption model for children who

- are emotionally disturbed;
- are hard to place; and/or
- have single or multiple adoptive failures.

The operating principles for our Adoption Courtship Model are the following:

- Standard adoptive procedures are insufficient for special-needs children and their prospective families.
- The odds are often against a successful adoption with these children, without preparation, training, and professional support.
- The child and the family must be prepared for the *reality of this adoptive relationship*.
- The adoption commitment must be made by *both* the child and

*Reprinted with permission from SCAR/Jasper Mountain, Springfield, Oregon.

the family and can only be made based on a relationship, not on information or interest.

The model has three phases:

1. *Phase I.* The child is prepared for the adoption by understanding his or her role in making it work or not work. The child's considerable power in the situation is made clear. The family goes through the regular certification steps and is selected by the adoption committee. The family meets with the caseworker and JMC staff to learn what to expect from the initial meeting. The child is also prepared for this meeting. The two sides meet with the caseworker and family therapist. The child begins to build trust by getting to know the family as a unit, then the family members as individuals, and finally the family in the home environment.
2. *Phase II.* This is where the reality must begin to come in. Both sides have an image of what they are doing and who they are doing it with, but it must become very clear and very real. This phase is characterized by extended visits and family counseling. The process starts with a focus on the strengths and positive attributes of both sides, moves to the faults and flaws of both sides, and finally underscores the realities of the combination of strengths and weaknesses of the adoption.
3. *Phase III.* There are three necessary commitments for the adoption to work. The initial commitment on the part of both child and family is a commitment of interest, time, and effort in regard to adoption. The second is a commitment to relationships with the child, and the child to the family. The final commitment is to family for life. The last commitment is the final step in a successful adoption of special-needs children, not the first step as in regular adoptions. This commitment must be made to a person, not a concept. This is important for these children because the reality of how difficult adoption is with disturbed children must be stronger than the commitment to the adoption as a concept.

Suggestions and Techniques

PHASE I

Preparation. Phase I starts long before the family and the child meet. One of the keys here is preparation. There is an important question to ask before the specific adoption work begins: "Has everyone received some preparation for the adoption?" Too often the family receives more preparation than the child. Preparing the child for an adoptive placement should ideally begin a year prior to meeting the family, with specific counseling on the issues that will come up. Along with adoption classes, it is valuable to have the prospective parents meet with the adoption worker or counselor who will work with the transition process to prepare the family for the probable struggles that are ahead.

Initial meeting. After the adoption committee gives its blessing to a match and the Adoption Courtship Model is decided on, it is then important for the family to meet with the adoption worker(s) and the counselor who will provide the transition counseling and discuss the model, the process, and the goals. Keep in mind that most adoptive families are in a mild to huge rush to have the child. A rushed courtship is almost always problematic. Gain the family's agreement and commitment to the process or don't use this model (in general, the bigger the rush the family is in, the more concerns there are about their readiness).

The initial meeting of child and family. Again the suggestion is for the worker(s) and counselor to be actively involved. Often for this population, meeting the parents alone before children are involved is less complex and overwhelming for the adoptive child. There should be informal time between the child and the parents, as well as the worker and counselor outlining what will be happening over the next few months and why. Keep the meeting from being stuffy or too formal. Make it clear that the goal is to see if in the long run this is a good match for everyone concerned. All sides will have a voice (empower the child to influence his or her future and you will have a much better response).

Process. Start with meetings in counseling to get to know each other. Have the whole family come the second time. Use techniques to rapidly point out the different personalities in the family (who is the clown, who is grumpy in the morning, etc.). A technique here is to have the members of the family write on a sheet of paper the things they like and dislike about the family member to their left and right. The counselor reads the items and has the family guess whom it was written about. Start with afternoon visits away from the family home. Go to day-long visits and then an overnight visit, again away from the family home. This is to equalize the playing field. In the family home only the adoptive child is unfamiliar with the environment. In a park, restaurant, or motel at the beach, the focus is on the relationships, not on getting used to the family's turf. The adoptive child should have a chance to get to know all family members at least a little, both individually and together, before going to the family home.

Counseling. The initial meetings and discussions should take place in the counselor's office. After each visit there should be a session. The counselor plays the role of bringing the family and child together and facilitating the process so both sides know that the situation is organized and under control.

PHASE II

Counseling. Counseling continues to be frequent but not necessarily occurring each time. Involve foster care providers to help make the child's strengths and weaknesses clear.

Process. GET REAL! Arrange extended visits, primarily in the home environment. Get away from special events and get down to everyday life. The goal of this phase is to make it clear what this adoptive combination will really be like.

Techniques. Stress the strengths and weaknesses of the match, the family, and the child. It may be difficult or embarrassing, but it is time to air everyone's strong points as well as dirty laundry. Use techniques like having everyone answer such questions as "When I get really angry, I . . . ," "I show sadness by . . . ," "When I am grumpy, the best way to deal with me is . . . ," etc. Role-play some of this. Have children act like Mom in the morning before coffee. How do the parents fight with each other? Have the adoptive child act out some of his less impressive qualities, such as being rude, disrespectful, or hurtful. Whatever family members will see later should be talked about, even acted out, now.

PHASE III

Process. Now that everyone has met and should know a lot about one another, the emphasis shifts to commitments. There are three levels of commitment: (1) time and effort, (2) relationship, and (3) life commitment. Commitment 1 should have long since been made and operationalized. It will be important to review and evaluate how everyone has handled this commitment because it will be an indicator of the next two. How interested is everyone in a commitment to relationship? In the case of attachment-disordered children, this must be reviewed carefully to have realistic expectations. It is clearly time to begin putting out on the table the issue of lifelong commitment. Again, the commitment must be to people, not to the concept of adoption.

Counseling. Here is where the skill of the counselor is most needed. There is much complexity in commitments. There may be resistance on everyone's part to addressing this. If things are going smoothly, why upset the apple cart? No one really wants the final analysis to be halting the adoption because it is not overall a good match, but this may be the case. The counselor must be firm and willing to be the bad guy. The capacity of the child to commit himself may be problematic, and the parents may have better intentions than abilities.

Ritual. If the adoption gets a green light, then some have found a formal recognition of the adoptive commitment an important step. Consider having a ceremony: Invite friends and throw a party. Our culture does this for most important events.

A Final Thought

Adoptions can work with special-needs children, but the work is never completed (yet when is any parent's job done?). Despite an excellent placement for both the child and the family, the work has only begun. The transition into the home will set an all-important tone, but don't fool yourself that the job will get easier. Our experience is that new struggles come up with each physical and developmental stage of the child. But that just makes adoption like life—a new challenge around every corner.

Surviving and Thriving in a Difficult Adoption

Adoptions can be much like marriages: Too many dissolve with pain for everyone; others stay together but everyone is unhappy; some get by with everyone lowering his or her expectations; and too few are a wonderful experience of loving, learning, and growing for all concerned. To foster success, adoptions need as much care, thought, and skill training as marriages. Marriages and adoptions fail partly because those involved do not know what they are actually saying yes to and discover they don't have what it takes to handle the reality they find. The goal becomes not only how to survive the reality of the adoption but how to thrive with the challenges involved.

Maintaining More than Your Sanity

Maintaining a healthy adoption can be compared to maintaining an automobile. There are issues that need attention, and, as the ad goes, "You can pay me now or pay me later." Here are some comparisons:

Check the radiator	Keep it cool, don't overheat
Check the steering/brakes	Stay in control at all times
Keep the battery charged	Keep your energy
Tune up for performance	Maintain your power
Check the plugs	Keep your spark
Check wear on tires	Realize you are wearing down before you burst

Contained in each of these suggestions is all you really need to know about maintaining health in an adoption. The best truths are simple ones. A recent best-seller tells us that we learned in kindergarten everything we need for a happy, fulfilled life. Well, some of us may have gotten it all the first time, but most of us could use a refresher. If you got it all at first, then stop here. But if you need to hear a bit more, read on.

Why Do Adoptions Fail?

There are many reasons for disrupted adoptions, but they all boil down to one overall issue. Families choose to adopt for many reasons, but they want to do a good thing for all concerned. Although they know there will be struggle, they do not adopt to put everyone through great pain. Adoptions fail when a commitment to a child begins to harm commitments to other loved ones. If it gets to the point that something has to go, it will probably be the adopted child. There are two important perspectives here:

The family. There may be many reasons to adopt, but in the end a family decides it has room in its members' lives and hearts for a new family member. But what are they to do if their offers of love and affection are met with lack of interest or even hostility? The family can understand that life may have been difficult for the child but believe all that can change if the child simply accepts the loving care of this new family. After weeks and then months of a child letting the family know that he or she wants neither their home nor their heart, all that the adoption seems to be bringing everyone is pain. Maybe the child would be better off somewhere else, and clearly the family members were better off before all this started. This often becomes the final chapter, one filled with failure, guilt, and grief for everyone.

The child. All adopted children have experienced deep loss or they wouldn't need a family. Most special-needs children have experienced much more than loss. Fearful and adrift in the foster care system, the child is informed that he will soon get a new family. But do people realize what family may mean to the child—the ones that were supposed to always be there for you but weren't?

To the child, Mom and Dad may mean someone who didn't care, or worse, someone who was very abusive. The child has probably been in numerous homes and schools. Such children can't put their heart on the line again unless they know it will be safe, so they test the family. Sometimes their testing is misinterpreted by the family, and a negative cycle begins. The worse it gets, the more fear arises and then more testing occurs. The child begins to see the family stop trying and waits for the caseworker to appear and once again move the child from a home that was supposed to always be there for him or her but wasn't. This confirms again that the world is a cruel place where you have to fight to survive and avoid being vulnerable at all costs. And the world has another antisocial personality.

How can these traps be avoided? How can the process not only last but be a good experience for everyone?

What Successful Adoptions Look Like

Successful adoptions involving a child with special needs tend to have a lot of TLC. Tender loving care, you say? Absolutely not! Tender loving care, is almost always in abundant supply in failed adoptions with these children. That just may be one of the principal problems. In this case TLC means something very different:

T = **Translating** correctly what is really going on with the child in order to understand where the child really is. It is commonly known that manipulative teenagers (and aren't they all) talk in opposites. It is often a safe bet to retranslate what they are saying to get closer to the truth. Practice by retranslating the following: I don't want rules; I'm not worried about my future; I am all caught up on my schoolwork; I'll be home early tonight. This same principle works with special-needs children.

L = **Learning** from the challenges of adopting a difficult child becomes one of the indicators of success, not how smooth it's going for everyone. If you want smooth, get some Jell-O™. But adopting is not smooth—it is trouble or challenge, depending on your point of view. The more you see it as a challenge to learn from, the better the candidate you are to adopt a difficult child.

C = Stay in **control** at all times in all situations involving the child. These children did not get difficult on their own; they had lots of help from chaotic, abusive, and neglectful families that could not provide a safe or secure home. Constant control sounds pretty heavy, but if you adopt one of these children, he or she will constantly test to see just how in control you are. If the child is able to gain control, everyone loses; if the child can't, everyone wins. It's that simple.

TLC—Translating, Learning, and Control—is easier said than done. But here is part of the point—what does a difficult adoption offer you? It offers an opportunity to grow yourself, as you give a deserving child a fresh chance to be part of a family.

Seven Strategies for Success

1. Understand the real needs of the child. It is not often helpful to listen to the child's words or even to accept the child's behavior at face value because of the opposite issue. If the child has had an abusive or neglectful past, then his or her needs are pretty straightforward despite the way the child acts. These children need the following:

Safety. Will I be safe in a nonviolent environment where my basic needs will be met?

Security. I need a structured situation where a parent is in charge and I can just be a kid.

Acceptance. I need people who can accept me as a person even if they don't like or accept my behavior.

Belonging. I need to belong to someone; I need to be connected to others and learn to give and receive affection.

Trust. I need to learn to trust and be trusted; I need to be treated fairly, with honesty, respect, and firmness.

Relationship. I need to be in relationships with others in a way that no one is victimized and both sides are enhanced.

Self-awareness. I need to learn how to make changes in my personality and behavior by self-understanding.

Personal worth. The final indicator of my being a success as a person is, Do I believe in myself and my own worth?

2. Positive discipline is the quickest route to your control and to the child's personal worth. Techniques include separate the child from the behavior; don't punish—discipline (which means to teach); don't let "time-outs" become a disguised punishment; use logical consequences; don't ask the child to lie by asking questions you know the answer to; avoid power struggles; have the child fight with him- or herself, not with you; keep your sense of humor and don't let the child decide what you will feel; and allow the child to change and be more responsible by not always locking the youngster into past behaviors.

3. Learn to win the manipulation game. Don't let the child use your rules against you. Don't be completely predictable to a manipulative child; you'll become an easy target. Keep the child off balance when he or she is trying to beat you. In general, if the child is manipulating to get something, do your best to prevent the child from getting his or her way or you will get more manipulation (because it worked). Stay a couple of steps ahead by predicting what the child might do and what you will do in return. Don't respond emotionally; you won't think very creatively then. Parenting is best done by a team; talk over your next move and get advice and ideas. If the child has you on the run, the child will win the manipulation game and both of you will lose.

4. Get the help you need from the right source. Quite frankly, some counselors who don't understand these children can make the situation considerably worse. It is not much of a challenge for a manipulative child to be "perfect" an hour a week in someone's office. If the counselor starts looking at you like you must be the problem, get someone else. Ask prospective counselors about their experience with adoption, abused children, and kids with attachment problems. Or better yet, go to a counselor who comes highly recommended for his or her skills with a child just like yours.

5. The only given is that this type of adoption will be difficult; it does not have to be terrible. The difference is something you have complete control over—your feelings and sense of humor. A wise man once said, "If you lose your sense of humor, the world just isn't funny anymore," and adoption is like that.

6. Make sure you are more than a parent. If you are a parent twenty-four hours a day, you have become pretty dull. Be a wife, a student, a hiker, a volunteer, a square dancer, an artist, a husband,

or whatever, but don't get stuck in the parent role where there is a whole lot more giving than receiving. Batteries don't last long if they never get recharged.

7. Don't get in a hurry. The saddest failed adoptions are the ones where the child is desperately testing and the parents call it off. If only they could understand that the desperation is an indicator that the testing is nearly over and that they have almost passed the test. It has taken a long time for these children to be hurt; it takes time for them to be vulnerable again. But don't continue down a road that is clearly leading nowhere. Get some good help from a counselor who has a good road map—there may be a much better road to get where you want to go.

Final Thoughts

So what do you think? If it sounds like a lot more work than you thought, don't feel alone. Just consider—if parents knew all they would have to endure with their birth children, would they be so eager to go through with it? Make no mistake—parenting is the world's most complex and difficult job. It is even more challenging if you have to pick up the pieces that someone else has failed with. If all this is more than you can imagine, then get a pet. But if you want the ride of your life, if you want to be the most substantial influence in a young person's life, and if you want to learn more about yourself than you thought was possible, then boy, does CSD have a deal for you!

21

What If . . .

Newly birth'd book
The labor ended
Weary, spent, satisfied
A little warty, could use more polish
. . . A metaphor for the work perhaps

In low-gear rumination, I wonder if our whole society is suffering from trauma-related attachment disturbances. Do we, as a society, have the same concerns and the same blind spots as do the parents we're trying to help?

We respond to our children's behavior as if their problems reside entirely within *them*, or are caused by TV, or by video games, or by the schools, and we do not consider how we take care of them. We react to their frightening behavior and ignore their loneliness and pain. We call their terror, rage.

We group-chant our mantra on talk shows, in meetings, in the courts . . .

> It's awful—we're doing all we know how to do—it's awful

. . . as we unconsciously trance-dance to ancestral rhythms, passing on the moves to the yet unborn.

And where are the therapists for our society? Who will help us with identity and behavioral limits? With society's alarm-numbing response and trauma bonds? Can *we* hang in there for as long as it takes?

AND WHAT IF . . .

. . . businesses, churches, industry, government, and volunteer organizations all joined together and created enrichment programs

for families, with prizes and recognition for outstanding programs and leadership?
. . . family centers were developed in every community, and these centers focused on family activities—sports, gardens, adventure trips, neighborhood improvement, crafts, shops for woodworking, plumbing, mechanics, sculpture, ceramics, science and computer laboratories, theater, arts, dance, and classes for puppetry, stress management, yoga, cooking, money management?
. . . vulnerable and troubled families were helped, supported, and cheered on much sooner?
. . . serial placements for children were identified as the atrocities they are?
. . . enriching, playful, teaching, and therapeutic daycare centers for children and families were available as an alternative and adjunct to foster care, staffed by well-paid veteran foster care folks—the wise, loving, fun ones?
. . . children with enduring attachments to parents unable or unwilling to provide adequate care for them were permanently placed with another family while we supported them in maintaining their relationship with parents, avoiding multiple failed placements?
. . . dedicated, veteran foster parents of all colors, ages, and sizes were recruited, awarded fellowships, and trained in group work with children and parents? And what if they were then placed in neighborhood centers where they received and gave professional consultation, and researchers sought the wisdom of these elders?
. . . all schools had counselors available for children and had play and activity groups that dealt with children's life issues, such as loneliness, love, fear, joy, divorce, pride, and conflict?
. . . the world's leaders committed to a policy of cherishing all the world's children and their families?

And what would happen if we, as a society, recognized that our future lies in the dance we dance with these children who belong to us all?

Bibliography and References

Achenbach, T. & Edelbrock, C. (1979). Child Behavior Checklist.

Ainsworth, M. D. S., Blehar, M.C., Waters, E., & Wall, S. (1978). *Patterns of attachment: A psychological study of the strange situation.* Hillsdale, NJ: Lawrence Erlbaum.

Armsworth, M. W., & Holaday, M. (1993). The effects of psychological trauma on children and adolescents. *Journal of Counseling and Development*, V 72, 49–56.

Barnard, K. E. (1988). Nursing Child Assessment Satellite Training (NCAST) Assessments: Community Life Skills Scale, Difficult Life Circumstance Scale, Network Survey, My Family and Friends Scale: Teenage Version, Parent-Child Interaction Scales.

Barnum, K. E., Brazelton, T. B. (1991). *Touch: The foundation of experience.* New York: International University Press.

Basch, M. F. (1988). *Understanding psychotherapy: The science behind the art.* New York: Basic Books.

Belsky, J. (1990). Parental and non-parental child care and children's socioemotional development: A decade in review. *Journal of Marriage and the Family, 54*, 885.

Belsky, J., & Nezworski, T. (1988). *Clinical implications of attachment.* Hillsdale, NJ: Lawrence Erlbaum.

Blacher, J., & Meyers, C. E. (1983). A review of attachment formation and disorder of handicapped children. *American Journal of Mental Deficiency, 87*, 359.

Bowlby, J. (1960). Separation anxiety. *International Journal of Psychoanalysis*, 41, 89–113.

Bowlby, J. (1969). *Attachment and Loss.* Vol. 1, *Attachment.* New York: Basic Books.

Brody, V. A. (1993). *The Dialogue of Touch: Developmental play therapy.* Treasure Island, Florida: Brody and Associates.

Brody, V. A., Fenderson, C., & Stephenson, S. (1976). *Sourcebook for developmental play.* Treasure Island, FL: Developmental Play Training Associates.

Bowlby, J. (1980). *Attachment and loss.* Vol. 3, *Loss: Sadness and depression.* New York: Basic Books.

Brazelton, T. B., Koslowski, B., & Main, M. (1974). The origin of reciprocity: The early mother-infant interaction. In M. Lewis & L. A. Rosenblum (Eds.), *The effect of the infant on its caregiver* (pp. 49–76), New York: Wiley.

Buber, M. (1958). *I and thou*. New York: Charles Scribner.

Buck, J.N. (1966). House-Tree-Person (H-T-P) Projective Technique, Western Psychological Corporation.

Carlson, C., Cicchetti, D., Barnett, D., & Braunwald, K. (1989). Disorganized/disoriented attachment relationships in maltreated infants. *Developmental Psychology, 25*(4), 525–531.

Carson, M. (1989). *On the safe side*. Sacramento, CA.: California Services for Children.

Carson, M., & Goodfield, R. (1988). The Children's Garden Attachment Model. In R. W. Small & F. J. Alwon (Eds.), *Challenging the limits of care*. pp. 115–126 Needham, MA: Albert Trieschman Center.

Cicchetti, D. (1984). The emergence of developmental psychopathology. *Child Development, 55*, 1–7.

Clark, R. (1985), Early Relational Assessment, Parent-Infant Relationship Global Assessment of Functioning-Scale Diagnostic Work Group of Zero To Three, National Center for Clinical Infant Programs.

Coles, R. (1967). *Children of crisis: A study of courage and fear*. Boston: Atlantic Monthly Press.

Conners, C. K. (1973). Conners' Rating Scales, Western Psychological Corporation.

Cook, D. (1991). Shame, attachment, and addictions: Implications for family therapists. *Contemporary Family Therapy, 13*, 405.

Crittenden, P. M. (1981). Abusing, neglecting, problematic, and adequate dyad: Differentiating by patterns of interaction. *Merrill-Palmer Quarterly, 27*(3), 201–218.

Crittenden, P.M. (1987). Relationships at risk. In J. Belsky & T. Nezworski (Eds.), *Clinical implications of attachment*. Hillsdale, (pp. 136–174) NJ: Erlbaum.

Crittenden, P. M., & Ainsworth, M. D. (1989). *Child maltreatment*. In D. Cicchetti & V. Carlson (Eds.), New York: Cambridge University Press.

Crittenden, P. M. (1992). Children's strategies for coping with adverse home environments: An interpretation using attachment theory. *Child Abuse and Neglect, 16*, 329.

Derogatis, L. R. (1990), Symptom-Checklist-90-Revised (SCL-90R), National Computer System.

Derogatis, L. R. (1992), Brief Symptom Inventory, National Computer System.

de Young, M. & Lowry, J. A. (1992). Traumatic bonding: Clinical implications in incest. *Child Welfare, 71*, 165.

Donovan, D. M., & McIntyre, D. (1990). *Healing the hurt child.: A developmental-contextual approach*. New York: W. W. Norton.

Dugan, T. F., & Coles, R. (1989). *The child in our times: Studies in the development of resiliency*. New York: Bruner/Mazel.

Erikson, E. H. (1963). *Childhood and society*. New York: W. W. Norton.

Erickson, F., Korfmacher, J., & Egeland, B. (1992). Attachments past and present: Implications for therapeutic intervention with mother-infant dyads. *Development and Psychopathology, 4*, 495–507.

Eth, S., & Pynoos, (Eds.). (1985). *Post traumatic stress disorder in children*. Washington: American Psychiatric Press.

Figley, C. R. (Ed.). (1985). *Trauma and its wake*. New York: Bruner/Mazel.

Fraiberg, S. (1980). *Clinical studies in infant mental health*. New York: Basic Books.

Fraiberg, S., Adelson, F., & Shapiro, V. (1975). Ghosts in the nursery: A psychoanalytic approach to the problems of impaired mother-infant relationships. *Journal of the American Academy of Child Psychiatry*, 14, 378–421.

Garbarino, J., Kostelny, K., & Dubrow, N. (1991). *No place to be a child*. Boston: Lexington Books.

Garbarino, J., Scott, F. M., Faculty Erickson Institute (1992). *What children can tell us*. San Francisco: Jossey-Bass.

Gil, E. (1983). *Outgrowing the pain*. Rockville, MD: Launch Press.

Gil, E. (1992). *The healing power of play*. Rockville, MD: Launch Press.

Goldberg, S. (1990). Attachment in infants at risk: Theory, research, and practice. *Infants and Young Children, 2*(4), 11–20.

Harris, D. B. (1963), Goodenough-Harris Drawing Test (Draw-a-Man), Psychological Corporation.

Greenberg, M. T., Cicchetti, D., & Cummings, E. M. (Eds.). (1990). *Attachment in the preschool years: Theory, research, and intervention*. Chicago: University Chicago Press.

Greenspan, S. J., & Lieberman, A.F. (1988). A clinical approach to attachment. In J. Belsky & T. Nezworski (Eds.), *Clinical implications of attachment*. (pp. 387–424) Hillsdale, NJ: Lawrence Erlbaum.

Hacker, F. J. (1976). *Crusaders, criminals, and crazies: Terror and terrorism in our times*. New York: W. W. Norton.

Hall, D. K. (1993). *Assessing Child Trauma*. Toronto: Institute for the Prevention of Child Abuse.

Hamada, R. S. (1993). *Children of hurricane Iniki: Effects of evacuation and school intervention*. Paper presented at annual meeting of the American Academy of Child & Adolescent Psychiatry, San Antonio, Texas.

Harmon, R. J., Morgan, G. A., & Glicken, A. D. (1984). Continuities and discontinuities in affective and cognitive-motivational development. *Child Abuse and Neglect, 8*, 157–167.

Helfer, R. E., & Kempe, C. H. (Eds.). (1968). *The battered child*. Chicago: University of Chicago Press.

Herman, J.L. (1992). *Trauma and recovery*. New York: Basic Books.

Hornstein, N.L. (1989, January). *MPD and dissociation in children, adolescents, and families: Development, diagnosis, and intervention*. Paper presented at Shepard Pratt Hospital, Baltimore, MD.

Horowitz, M. J. (1976). *Stress response syndromes*. New York: J. Aronson.

Izard, C. E., Haynes, O., Chisholm, G., & Baak, K. (1991). Emotional determinants of mother-infant attachment. *Child Development, 62*, 906.

James, B. (1989). *Treating traumatized children.* Boston: Lexington Books/Macmillan.

James, B., & Nasjleti, M. (1983). *Treating sexually abused children and their families.* Palo Alto, CA: Consulting Psychologists Press.

Jernberg A. & Booth, P. (1979). Marschach Interaction Method (MIM), Theraplay Institute.

Kagan, J. *The nature of the child.* New York: Basic Books.

Katz, L. (1987). An overview of current clinical issues in separation and placement. *Child and Adolescent Social Work, 4*, 3–4.

Knoff, H. M., & Prout, H. T. (1989). Kinetic Drawing System for Family and School, Western Psychological Corporation.

Krystal, H. (1988). *Integration and self healing: Affect, trauma, alexithymia.* Hillsdale, NJ: Analytic Press.

Krystal, H., & Neiderland W. (1968). Clinical observations of the survivor syndrome. In H. Krystal (Ed.), *Massive psychic trauma.* (pp. 327–348). New York: International University Press.

Lewis, J. (1952). The humanitarian theory of punishment. *Res Judicata,* 6, 224–228.

Lifton, B. J. (1979). *Lost and Found: The adoption experience.* New York: Harper & Row.

Lifton, R. J. (1976). *The life of self.* New York: Simon & Schuster.

Lifton, R. J. (1979). *The broken connection.* New York: Simon & Schuster.

Lindemann, E., (1944). Symptomology and management of acute grief. *American Journal of Psychiatry*, 101, 141–148.

Main, M., & Solomon, J. (1986). Discovery of new insecure-disorganized/disoriented attachment pattern. In M. Yogman & T. B. Brazelton (Eds.), *Affective development in infancy.* (pp. 95–124) Norwood, NJ: Ablex.

Mc Dougal, J. (1982). Alexithymia, psychosomatosis and psychosis. *International Journal of Psychoanalytic Psychotherapy.* 9:377–388.

Milgram, S. (1974). *Obedience to authority.* New York: Harper & Row.

Miller, L. C. (1989). Louisville Behavior Checklist (LBC), Western Psychological Corporation.

Mills, J. C., & Crowley, R. J. (1986). *Therapeutic metaphors for children and the child within.* New York: Bruner/Mazel.

Monahon, C. (1993). *Children and trauma: A parent's guide to helping children heal.* Boston: Lexington Books/Macmillan.

Nathanson, D. L. (1992). *Shame and pride: Affect, sex, and the birth of self.* New York: W. W. Norton.

Perry, B. D. (1994). Neurobiological sequelae of childhood trauma: Post-traumatic stress disorders in children. In M. Murberg (Ed.), *Catecholamines in PTSD.* (pp. 233–255). Washington: American Psychiatric Press.

Perry, B. D. (1993). Medicine and psychotherapy: Neurodevelopment and the neurophysiology of trauma. *The Advisor,* 6, 1–18.

Phimister, M. (1993). Personal communication.

Plenk, A. M. (1993). *Helping young children at risk.* Westport, CT: Praeger Publishers.

Pynoos, R. S., & Eth, S. (1986). Witness to violence: The child interview. *Journal of American Academy of Child Psychiatry*, 25, 306–319.

Pynoos, R. S., & Nader, K. (1988). Psychological first aid and treatment approaches to children exposed to community violence: Research implications. *Journal of Traumatic Stress Studies*, 1, 445–473.

Reynolds, W. M. (1987). Reynolds Child Depression Scale (RCDS) and Reynolds Adolescent Depression Scale (RADS), Psychological Assessment Resources.

Robertson, J. (1957) Film: *A two year old goes to hospital.*

Rutter, M. (1980). Parent-child separation: Psychological effects on the children. In S. Harrison & J. McDermott (Eds.), *New directions in child psychotherapy.* (pp. 323–353) New York: International Universities Press.

Rutter, M. (1981). *Maternal deprivation reassessed.* Harmondsworth, England: Penguin Books.

Rutter, M., Cox, A., Tupling C., Berger, M., & Yule, W. (1975). Attainment and adjustment in two geographical areas: I. The prevalence of psychiatric disorder. *British Journal of Psychiatry, 126*, 493–509.

Sameroff, A. J., & Emde, R. N. (Eds.). (1989). *Relationship disturbances in early childhood.* New York: Basic Books.

Salas, J. (1993). *Improvising Real Life: Personal story in Playback Theatre.* Dubuque, Iowa: Kendall/Hunt.

Seligman, M. E. P. (1970). On the generality of the laws of learning. *Psychological Review, 77*, 406–418.

Solnit, A. J., Nordhaus, B. F., & Lord, R. (1992). *When home is no haven.* New Haven: Yale University Press.

Spitz, R. (1947) Film: *Grief: A peril in infancy.*

Sroufe, L. A. (1989). *Pathways to adaptation and maladaptation: Psychopathology as developmental deviation.* Paper presented at the Rochester Symposium on Developmental Psychopathology, Rochester, NY.

Sroufe, L. A., & Rutter, M. (1984). The domain of developmental psychology. *Child Development, 55*, 17–29.

Steinhauer, P. D. (1991). *The least detrimental alternative: A systematic guide to case planning and decision making for children in care.* Toronto: University of Toronto Press.

Stern, D. N. (1985). *The interpersonal world of the infant: A view from psychoanalysis and developmental psychology.* New York: Basic Books.

Straker, G., Moosa, F., Becker, R., & Nkwale, M. (1992). *Faces in the revolution.* Athens, OH: Ohio University Press.

Terr, L. (1981). Forbidden games: Post-traumatic child's play. *Journal of the American Academy of Child Psychiatry, 20*, 741–760.

Valliant, G. E. (1985). Loss as a metaphor for attachment. *American Journal of Psychoanalysis, 45*(1), 59–67.

van der Kolk, B. A. (Ed). (1984). *Post traumatic stress disorder: A psychological and biological sequelae.* Washington, DC: American Psychiatric Press.

van der Kolk, B. A. (Ed.). (1987). *Psychological trauma.* Washington, DC: American Psychiatric Press.

van der Kolk, B. A. (1989). The compulsion to repeat the trauma: Re-enactment, re-victimization, and masochism. *Psychiatric Clinics of North America, 12*(2), 389–406.

Vernberg, E. M. & Vogel, J. M. (1993). Part I: Children's psychological responses to disasters. *Journal of Clinical Child Psychology*, vol 22, No. 4, 464–484.

Vernberg, E. M. & Vogel, J. M. (1993). Part 2: Interventions with children after disasters. *Journal of Clinical Child Psychology*, vol 22, No. 4, 485–498.

Williamson, J. & Moser, A. (1988). *Unaccompanied Children in Emergencies: A field guide for their care and protection*. International Social Service: Geneva, Switzerland.

Williamson, J. G. (1989). *UNHCR Guidelines on Refugee Children*. UNHCR: Geneva, Switzerland.

Winnicott, D. (1960). *The maturational process and the facilitating environment*. New York: International Universities Press.

Index

Contributors

T. Nalani Waiholua Archibeque, Ph.D., is a clinical psychologist who devotes half her work to her private clinical practice in Maui, and half to teaching, consultation, and supervision.

Katharine Stone Ayers, D.C., is a somatic developmental psychologist who practices on the Big Island of Hawaii and provides professional training for the Bodynamics Institute of Denmark.

Blair Barone, Psy. D., is a staff psychologist in the Department of General Pediatrics at Boston Children's Hospital and at the Trauma Clinic at Massachusetts General Hospital.

Sharon K. Bauer, is a licensed professional clinical counselor and certified marriage and family therapist who specializes in trauma, attachment, adoption, and grief work.

Lani Bowman raises foster children in the same environment where she herself was raised—a rural part of Hawaii.

Marcelo Bianchedi is a psychoanalyst practicing in Buenos Aires, Argentina.

Julia Braun is a psychoanalyst practicing in Buenos Aires, Argentina.

Viola Brody, Ph.D., is a clinical psychologist, the director of Developmental Play Training Associates, and an adjunct professor at Eckerd College in St. Petersburg, Florida.

MaryLou Carson, an L.C.S.W. in Napa, California, specializes in providing training and treatment related to attachment and trauma.

Yaya de Andrade, a registered psychologist in Vancouver, British Columbia, has interned at Harvard Medical School Trauma Clinic, and is a Ph.D. candidate.

Mark D. Everson, Ph.D., is clinical associate professor and director of the Childhood Trauma and Maltreatment Program in the Department of Psychology, University of North Carolina at Chapel Hill.

Claudia Gibson provides supervision, consultation, and court testimony related to parent-child visitation.

Richard T. Gibson, M.D., is a child psychiatry fellow at the University of Hawaii.

Harriet Glass, M.A., D.T.R., is on the graduate faculty of the Department of Theater and Dance at the University of Hawaii.

Judith E. Orodenker, A.T.R., is a registered art therapist.

Eliana Gil, Ph.D., is a nationally recognized lecturer, author, and clinician.

Carolyn Han, M.A., is an author and teacher at University of Hawaii.

Steve Harvey, Ph.D., A.D.T.R., R.D.T., R.P.T./S., is a licensed psychologist in Colorado Springs and is registered by three national dance, drama, and play therapy associations.

Sandra Hewitt, Ph.D., is a child psychologist in private practice in the Twin Cities who has worked with child sexual abuse for seventeen years.

Valerie Iles, C.C.W., B.A.A. E.C.E., is an infant mental health worker at the Creche in Toronto and maintains a private clinical practice.

Joycee Kennedy, L.C.S.W., B.C.D., is the director of Hampden Academy in Aurora, Colorado and specializes in research and treatment of adolescents recovering from traumatic stress.

Louis Lehman, Ph.D., is a staff therapist at Comprehensive Mental Health Center in Tacoma, Washington, and director of a Native American counseling center.

Molly Reed, M.A., is a child and family therapist in Eugene, Oregon.

Jo Salas, M.A., C.M.T., is a founding member of the original Playback Theatre company.

For information about training please write to Jo Salas care of International Playback Theatre Network, P.O. Box 1173, New Paltz, NY 12561.

Felix Sarubbi, C.I.S.W., is a school social worker in an in-school counseling program for regular education students at the elementary level.

Ruth Sheets, R.N., M.A., is a pediatric and family nurse practitioner in San Francisco.

Bernard W. Sigg, M.D., is a practicing psychoanalyst in Paris, where he founded the Municipal Psychotherapeutic Center in 1971.

Edith Sigg-Piatt, has been a psychopedagogue in state schools in her native France since 1971.

Stuart M. Silverman, M.D., is assistant professor and clinical director of the Children's Inpatient Unit Department of Psychiatry, University of Hawaii.

Karen Sitterle, Ph.D., has a clinical practice in Dallas, Texas, is on the clinical faculty at University of Texas Southwestern Medical Center, and co-ordinates Mental Health Teams in Response to Disaster.

Peter H. Sturtevant, C.A.G.S., L.C.P.C., is a counselor in the public school system in Kittery, Maine where he also has a private practice.

Molly Romer Whitten, Ph.D., is a supervising psychologist at Michael Reese Hospital and maintains a private practice in Chicago where she specializes in the diagnosis, treatment and other issues related to infant mental health.

Jan Williamson, M.F.C.C., is a private consultant on international children's issues and is based in Richmond, Virginia.

Charlene Winger, D.C.S., is a psychotherapist whose work since 1984 has been primarily with children and adult survivors of child sexual abuse.

Dave Ziegler, M.C., N.C.C., L.P.C., L.M.F.T., is the founder and executive director of SCAR/Jasper Mountain Center.

Printed in the United States
By Bookmasters

BARRON'S

Writing for the TOEFL® iBT

5TH EDITION

Lin Lougheed
Ed.D., Teachers College
Columbia University

Published in 2014, 2011, 2008, 2004, 2000 by Barron's Educational Series, Inc.

All inquiries should be addressed to:
Barron's Educational Series, Inc.
250 Wireless Boulevard
Hauppauge, NY 11788
www.barronseduc.com

Library of Congress Catalog Card No. 2014945838

ISBN: 978-1-4380-7456-6

PRINTED IN THE UNITED STATES OF AMERICA
9 8 7 6 5 4 3 2 1

10%
POST-CONSUMER
WASTE
Paper contains a minimum of 10% post-consumer waste (PCW). Paper used in this book was derived from certified, sustainable forestlands.

CONTENTS

1

Introduction

The Writing section of the TOEFL® Internet-based Test (iBT) includes two writing tasks: an Integrated Task and an Independent Task.

INTEGRATED TASK

This task consists of a 250–300 word passage on an academic subject followed by a two-minute lecture or discussion on the same topic. The test taker is then given a question about the topic. The test taker must write a 150- to 225-word summary of the important points made in the listening passage and explain how these points relate to those in the reading passage. The test taker may write more than 225 words if time permits.

INDEPENDENT TASK

This task asks for an opinion about a topic. The test taker will use personal knowledge and experience to write an essay of at least 300 words to answer the question. The test taker may write more than 300 words if time permits.

The test taker has a total of 50 minutes to complete these two essays: 20 minutes for the Intergrated Task and 30 minutes for the Independent Task. Both essays must be written on the computer; they cannot be written by hand. The essays are then scored by two or more readers on ETS's Online Score Network. Each essay receives a score of 0–5.

HOW TO USE THIS BOOK

There are three steps in creating an essay: planning, writing, and revising. *Writing for the TOEFL iBT* provides a step-by-step guide for planning, writing, and revising your essays for both the Integrated Task and the Independent Task on the TOEFL iBT. You will learn to follow a simple three-step model and practice applying it to writing both types of essays.

STEP 1 PLAN
STEP 2 WRITE
STEP 3 REVISE

You will have 20 minutes to plan, write, and revise your essay for the Integrated Task, and you will have 30 minutes to plan, write, and revise your essay for the Independent Task. In those limited amounts of time, you must produce writing that is clear, coherent, and correct. This book will help you do that.

WARNING

Study the models carefully. Analyze them completely. Do NOT memorize them. Your writing will not be scored if it matches an essay in this book. Your writing on the TOEFL iBT must be your OWN original work.

Just as you must *plan* your essays, you also need to plan your studying. This book provides you with a plan for studying for the TOEFL iBT essays. By following the chapters in the book in order and doing all the practice exercises, you will learn a three-step method for writing your essays, and you will have many opportunities to practice writing. You will also learn writing skills that you can apply to both tasks and to your writing in general.

The best way to learn to *write* is by writing. You will do a great deal of writing when you do the practice exercises and practice tasks in this book. For additional practice, you can choose topics from the model integrated tasks and model independent essays at the back of the book.

When you are learning to write, you must, at the same time, learn to *revise*. You must make it a habit to revise the essays you write for practice in this book. Revision is as important a part of the writing process as the writing itself.

A good essay takes time—time to *plan*, time to *write*, time to *revise*. When you write your TOEFL iBT essays, you will have a limited amount of time. If you take the time now to learn how to write, you'll easily be able to write your TOEFL iBT essays in the limited time allowed.

QUESTIONS AND ANSWERS

How Much Time Do I Have to Work on Each Writing Task?

For the Integrated Task, after you read the passage for three minutes and listen to the lecture, you have 20 minutes to plan and write your essay. For the Independent Task, you have 30 minutes to plan and write your essay on the given topic.

Do I Have to Use the Computer?

Yes, you do. It is an Internet-based test. Use of the computer is required. You should learn to use the QWERTY keyboard. This keyboard is named for the first six letters on the top row of letters.

Do I Have a Choice of Topic?

No, you don't. For the Integrated Task, you will respond to a question using information from the reading passage and lecture provided. For the Independent Task, you will be given only one topic, and you must write about that topic.

Will All Test Takers Have the Same Topic?

No, not every test taker will have the same topic.

What Will Happen If I Don't Understand the Topic on the Independent Task?

If you study this book, that won't be a problem. You will understand all the possible topics. On the day of the test, you will not receive any help with the topic.

What Will Happen If I Don't Understand How to Work the Computer?

There will be test administrators in the room who can answer your questions about using the computer. They will not answer any questions about the use of English.

What Kind of Pencils Should I Bring?

None. Everything you need to write your essays will be given to you at the testing center. If you need extra pencils or paper, ask your test administrator.

Can I Bring a Clock with Me?

No. Nothing can be brought into the test room. You can wear your watch or look at the clock on the computer screen.

Can I Bring a Dictionary with Me?

No. Nothing can be brought into the test room.

Can I Bring Paper with Me?

No. Nothing can be brought into the test room. Scratch paper will be supplied.

What Happens to the Notes I Take?

You can write your notes in English or your first language. They will be collected and discarded. They will not be seen by the raters.

Is There a Spell Checker or Grammar Checker on the Computer?

No. You will have to do your own proofreading. Don't worry about a few spelling errors or a few mistakes with punctuation or grammar. A few small errors will not count against your score. Hint: If you are unsure how to spell a word, use a word you do know how to spell.

How Long Should the Writing Sample Be?

On the Integrated Task, you should write 150–225 words. You may write more if you have time. On the Independent Task, you should write around 300 words. You may write more if you have time.

What's More Important, Organization or Grammar?

Both are important. A reader judges an essay on its organization, the use of details to support the main points, and your facility with English. See the section, *Scoring the Essay*, for more information on this.

What Happens If I Don't Finish?

You do not need to have an elegantly stated conclusion. What you do write should demonstrate your facility with English. Do not end with an apology. Do not apologize to the reader for what you did not do or for what you think you should have done better.

Is There an Extra Fee for the Writing Section of the Test?

No. The test fee covers all parts of the TOEFL.

Is the Writing Section Required?

Yes. All test takers who take the TOEFL must take the writing section of the test.

How Is My Writing Scored?

Two readers will read each essay and will give a score of 0–5. Neither reader will know the score the other reader gives. If the scores are more than one point apart, a third person will read your essay. Your score will then be converted to a scaled score of 0–30.

Will I See My Scores Immediately?

No. Your scores will be available online and mailed to you approximately two weeks after the test date.

What If I Don't Like My Scores?

Sign up to take the test again after you do all the exercises in this book a few more times. You should see an improvement in your scores.

Where can I find extra help?

Visit the Learning Center on Dr. Lin Lougheed's website at *www.lougheed.com* to view sample essays.

For test tips and new vocabulary words, follow Dr. Lin Lougheed on Twitter @LinLougheed.

Want your essays posted to Facebook for feedback from others? Post them directly at http://www.facebook.com/EssaysTOEFL.IELTS or search on Facebook for "**IELTS and TOEFL Essay Writing.**"

TO THE TEACHER

Writing for the TOEFL iBT presents step-by-step methods for completing the two tasks in the writing section of the TOEFL. By following the steps in order, your students will build new skills on top of previously developed ones. Although the activities in this book are specifically aimed at the two writing tasks in the TOEFL, your students will be learning skills that they can apply to their writing in general. They will learn how to organize their thoughts, develop their essays, and use appropriate sentence structure to express their ideas. The activities in this book are well suited for classroom use. The activities are carefully structured and can easily be completed in class. They can also be done as homework and then corrected in class.

Expanding the Activities

INTEGRATED TASK

STEP 1 Plan

This book provides many opportunities for students to plan and practice taking notes on reading passages and lectures. You can provide additional practice by having the students take notes on passages that you or they supply. You can use passages from reading texts, newspapers, magazines, and other sources that are available and are of interest to the students. Encourage the students to read often and to make notes on what they read. Students can bring their notes to class to share with their classmates.

STEP 2 Write

This book provides many opportunities for practice writing summaries of reading passages and lectures. Again, you can provide additional practice by having the students write summaries of things they have read or news stories they have listened to. Encourage students to share with the class summaries of interesting articles they have read or movies or TV programs they have seen.

STEP 3 Revise

While working on Step 3, students can practice revising by checking each other's work, looking at the development, organization, grammar, punctuation, and spelling. The Writing Skills section of the book provides practice with using transition words and variety in sentence structure and can be studied in conjunction with Step 3.

INDEPENDENT TASK

STEP 1 Plan

In order to plan their responses to the writing topics, students need to be able to formulate opinions on these topics. They must get used to thinking about and describing reasons and advantages or disadvantages. In small groups, students can brainstorm and discuss their ideas on the writing topics presented throughout the book and in the Appendix. Students can then practice writing thesis statements and developing concept maps on the same subjects.

STEP 2 Write

When the class is working on Steps 2 and 3, have the students check each other's essays to make sure there is a topic sentence in each paragraph and that both the theme and all the supporting points are mentioned in the introduction. Have the students check the conclusion to make sure the theme is summarized there. The model essays in the Appendix can be used for additional practice. Have the students identify in a model essay the theme and supporting points in the introduction, topic sentences in the body of the essay, and the summarized theme in the conclusion.

STEP 3 Revise

While working on Step 3, students can practice revising by checking each other's work using the revision checklist. Again, the Writing Skills section of this book can be studied along with these steps.

Writing Skills

While working on this section of the book, you can use the model essays in the Appendix to provide additional practice. You can ask students to look in these essays for examples of transition words, different types of sentences, parallel structure, passive and active voice, or whatever aspect of sentence writing you wish to focus on.

A WORD OF CAUTION

Remind students **NOT** to memorize the essays in this book. An essay will not be rated if the reader suspects it was copied from the model essays.

OVERVIEW

Question Types

I. INTEGRATED TASK—20 MINUTES (250–300 WORDS)

1. First, you will read a 250–300 word passage on an academic subject. You will have three minutes to read.
2. Then, you will listen to a two-minute lecture or discussion on the same topic. You can take notes while you listen.
3. You will not be able to read the audio lecture during the test. You will only hear it. You will not be able to see the reading passage while you listen to the audio.

Sample Question

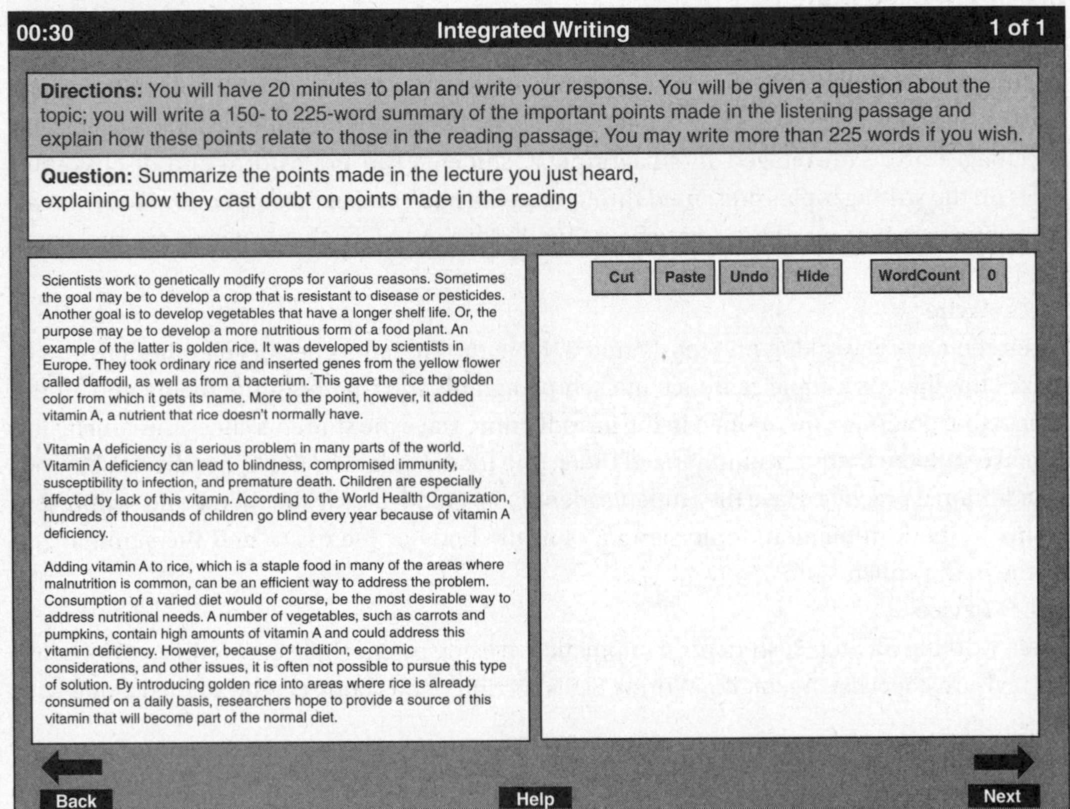

00:30
Integrated Writing
1 of 1
Directions: You will have 20 minutes to plan and write your response. You will be given a question about the topic; you will write a 150- to 225-word summary of the important points made in the listening passage and explain how these points relate to those in the reading passage. You may write more than 225 words if you wish.
Question: Summarize the points made in the lecture you just heard, explaining how they cast doubt on points made in the reading
Scientists work to genetically modify crops for various reasons. Sometimes the goal may be to develop a crop that is resistant to disease or pesticides. Another goal is to develop vegetables that have a longer shelf life. Or, the purpose may be to develop a more nutritious form of a food plant. An example of the latter is golden rice. It was developed by scientists in Europe. They took ordinary rice and inserted genes from the yellow flower called daffodil, as well as from a bacterium. This gave the rice the golden color from which it gets its name. More to the point, however, it added vitamin A, a nutrient that rice doesn't normally have.
Vitamin A deficiency is a serious problem in many parts of the world. Vitamin A deficiency can lead to blindness, compromised immunity, susceptibility to infection, and premature death. Children are especially affected by lack of this vitamin. According to the World Health Organization, hundreds of thousands of children go blind every year because of vitamin A deficiency.
Adding vitamin A to rice, which is a staple food in many of the areas where malnutrition is common, can be an efficient way to address the problem. Consumption of a varied diet would of course, be the most desirable way to address nutritional needs. A number of vegetables, such as carrots and pumpkins, contain high amounts of vitamin A and could address this vitamin deficiency. However, because of tradition, economic considerations, and other issues, it is often not possible to pursue this type of solution. By introducing golden rice into areas where rice is already consumed on a daily basis, researchers hope to provide a source of this vitamin that will become part of the normal diet.
Cut
Paste
Undo
Hide
WordCount
0
Back
Help
Next

II. INDEPENDENT TASK—30 MINUTES (AT LEAST 300 WORDS)

You will read a question that asks for your opinion on a topic.

Sample Question

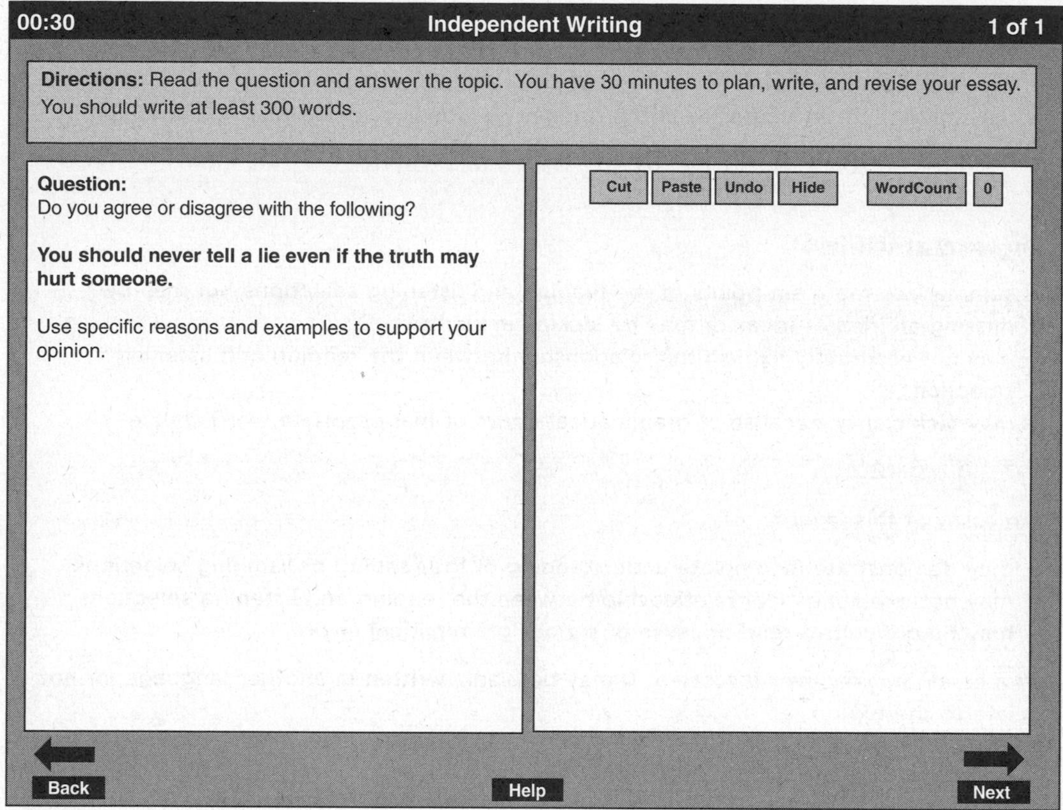

SCORING

Integrated Task

The Integrated Task essay is scored on a scale of 0 to 5. The scorers will look at how well you addressed the task of summarizing and comparing the reading selection and the listening selection. They will also look at your use of correct grammatical forms and vocabulary. The chart below provides some simple descriptions of the characteristics of essays at three levels.

RATING SCALE
4–5 GOOD
An essay at this level - clearly and concisely summarizes the main points of the reading and the listening selections - clearly and concisely explains how they support or contradict each other - uses correct grammatical forms and appropriate word choice - may have slight inaccuracies in the summary of ideas or occasional grammatical errors
2.5–3.5 FAIR
An essay at this level - summarizes the main points of the reading and listening selections but may be missing an idea or ideas or may be lacking in clarity - may not accurately explain the relationship between the reading and listening selections - may lack clarity because of grammatical errors or inappropriate word choice
1.0–2.0 LIMITED
An essay at this level - may demonstrate incomplete understanding of the reading or listening selections - may not explain a clear relationship between the reading and listening selections - may be difficult to read because of serious grammatical errors (An essay that receives a score of 0 may be blank, written in another language, or not relate to the topic.)

Sample Scored Essays

The following sample essays were written in response to the sample reading passage and lecture on pages 29–30.

SCORE: 5

The author explains that understanding learning styles can improve learning and training. The speaker, however, suggests that understanding learning styles doesn't always provide a solution.

The author states that understanding learning styles helps individuals learn better and professors and trainers instruct better. The author explains different ways to describe learning styles. Some people learn more easily by listening, others by seeing, and still others by doing. Active learners understand new information by doing something with it. Reflective learners understand information by thinking about it. Sequential learners look at information as a series of steps, but global learners prefer to look at the whole rather than the parts. The author believes that understanding learning styles can improve study skills. Sequential learners, auditory learners, and reflective learners, for example, can each choose the study methods that best suit their individual learning styles. Similarly, instructors and trainers who are aware of the various learning styles can take this into account when planning lessons.

NOTE

The samples in this book include paragraph indents, but you will not be scored down if you do not use them on the test.

The speaker presents a different point of view. First, some subjects have to be taught in certain ways. Math has to be taught sequentially. In addition, the speaker suggests that students "simply aren't interested" in information about learning styles and don't want to spend time thinking about it. Some professors aren't interested in learning styles, either. They just teach using their own style.

REVISION CHECKLIST

- ☑ Content
  - ☑ Thesis Statement
  - ☑ Topics that support the thesis
  - ☑ Main ideas
  - ☑ Supporting details
- ☑ Fluency and Cohesion
  - ☑ Transition words
  - ☑ Grammar and Spelling
  - ☑ Sentence variety

Content

This essay addresses the task by giving concise summaries of both the reading passage and the lecture and explaining clearly how the main ideas of both contrast with each other.

The first paragraph states a clear thesis, explaining that the reading and the lecture present contrasting ideas. The second paragraph supports the reading main idea by summarizing the main points of the reading. The third paragraph supports the listening main idea by summarizing the main points of the listening. The paragraphs have topic sentences and supporting details. In the body of the essay, the topic sentences of the paragraphs match the topics introduced in the first paragraph.

Fluency and Cohesion

The essay uses appropriate transition words such as *for example, first,* and *in addition*. There are no grammar or spelling errors. The essay contains a variety of sentence structures such as simple and compound sentences and adjective clauses.

SCORE: 4

The author explains that understanding learning styles can make learning and training better. The speaker says the opposite, that knowing about learning styles doesn't always help teachers and students.

In the reading passage, the author says that understanding learning styles helps students learn better and teachers teach better. The author explains the different kinds learning styles. Some students learn by listening, some by seeing, and some by doing. Also, some students are active learners. They need to do things with new information. Sequential learners see information in sequence. The author says that if you understand learning styles, can improve your study skills. Sequential learners and auditory learners, for instance, they can choose the best study methods for their learning styles.

The speaker has a different opinion. First, some things have to be taught in certain ways. Math is an example. It has to be taught sequentially. Also, the speaker says that students "simply aren't interested" in information about learning styles. Some professors don't interested in learning styles, either.

REVISION CHECKLIST

- ❑ Content
  - ☑ Thesis Statement
  - ☑ Topics that support the thesis
  - ☑ Main ideas
  - ❑ Supporting details
- ❑ Fluency and Cohesion
  - ☑ Transition words
  - ❑ Grammar and Spelling
  - ☑ Sentence variety

Content

This essay addresses the task by giving summaries of both the reading passage and the lecture and explaining how the main ideas of each contrast with each other. The writer left out a few supporting details from the summary of the reading. She mentioned active learners but not reflective learners. She mentioned sequential learners but not global learners.

The thesis is clearly stated, explaining that the reading and the lecture present contrasting ideas. The second paragraph and third paragraph support the main ideas of the reading passage and the lecture by summarizing the main points of each. In the body of the essay, the topic sentences of the paragraphs match the topics introduced in the first paragraph.

Fluency and Cohesion

The essay uses appropriate transition words such as *for instance, first,* and *in addition*. There are a few grammar errors, but they don't interfere with understanding the essay.

...the different <u>kinds learning</u> styles.
...the different kinds of learning styles.

...if you understand learning styles, <u>can</u> improve your study skills.
...if you understand learning styles, you can improve your study skills.

Sequential learners and auditory learners, for instance, <u>they</u> can choose...
Sequential learners and auditory learners, for instance, can choose...

Some professors <u>don't</u> interested in learning styles, either.
Some professors aren't interested in learning styles, either.

The essay contains a variety of sentence structures such as simple, compound, and complex sentences.

SCORE: 3

The author explains that understanding learning styles can make learning and teaching better, but the speaker says the opposite opinion. Even if teachers and students know about learning styles, doesn't always help them.

In the reading passage, it says that understanding different learning styles help students and teachers better. They can improve learning. There are different kinds of learning styles such as listening, seeing, and doing. In addition, there are active learners and reflective learners. Finally, we have sequential learners and global learners. The author says that learning styles will improve your study skills. You can to choose the best way to study for your learning style.

The speaker says the opposite. First, some things you have to teach them in certain ways. Math is an example. Also, some people don't like learning styles. Some students and some professors don't like different ways of learning. It's too bad because it can help them.

REVISION CHECKLIST

- ❑ Content
  - ☑ Thesis Statement
  - ☑ Topics that support the thesis
  - ☑ Main ideas
  - ❑ Supporting details
- ❑ Fluency and Cohesion
  - ☑ Transition words
  - ❑ Grammar and Spelling
  - ☑ Sentence variety

Content

This essay addresses the task by giving summaries of both the reading passage and the lecture and explaining how the main ideas of each contrast with each other. The writer left out some supporting details from the summary of the reading. She mentioned the names of the different learning styles but did not explain what they are or how they differ from each other. In the last paragraph, she mentioned math as an example of something that has to be taught in a certain way but did not explain how it was an example.

There are some inaccuracies in explaining the supporting details of the lecture. The essay states "Some students and some professors don't like different ways of learning." In the lecture, however, the speaker made the point that some people aren't interested in thinking about learning styles. That is somewhat different than saying that they don't like learning styles.

Fluency and Cohesion

The essay uses appropriate transition words such as *in addition, first,* and *also*. There are several grammar errors.

...<u>doesn't</u> always help them.
...it doesn't always help them.

...different learning styles help students and teachers <u>better</u>.
...different learning styles help students and teachers do their work better.

You can <u>to</u> choose the best way...
You can choose the best way...

First, <u>some things you have to teach them</u> in certain ways.
First, you have to teach some things in certain ways.

The essay contains a variety of sentence structures such as simple, compound, and complex sentences.

SCORE: 2

In the reading passage it says that it is important to understand different learning style because it can improbe teaching and learning. In the lecture, it also talks about different learning styles.

In the reading passage, it talks about different learning styles that can help students and teachers. They can learn and teach more better if they know this. Some students learn better when they listen, see, or do. Another learning style it is active and reflactiv. And finally there is sequential and global. The author says that learning styles will going to improbe your study skills. If you are an active learner, you can study one way and another way if you are reflactive. This is an example. You have to have a good style.

The speaker talks about learning styles, too. Math is a subject that you can teach sequentially, so it is good for sequential learners. There are some people they aren't interested in learning styles. But some people they are good at learning and their different learning styles can help them.

REVISION CHECKLIST

- ❑ Content
  - ❑ Thesis Statement
  - ❑ Topics that support the thesis
  - ☑ Main ideas
  - ❑ Supporting details
- ❑ Fluency and Cohesion
  - ☑ Transition words
  - ❑ Grammar and Spelling
  - ☑ Sentence variety

Content

This essay attempts to address the task by giving summaries of both the reading passage and the lecture. It fails in both the thesis statement and the summaries to show the relationship between the ideas in the reading passage and the lecture. Both talk about learning styles, but their main points contrast with each other. This essay does not mention the contrast.

The main idea of the reading passage is explained, although the supporting details are somewhat confused. The details, moreover, could be more thoroughly explained. All the learning styles are mentioned, but the differences between them are not explained. The summary of the lecture fails to explain the main idea—that understanding learning styles does not always improve learning.

Fluency and Cohesion

The essay uses some transition words such as *another* and *finally*. There are several grammar errors.

They can learn and teach more better.
They can learn and teach better.

Another learning style it is active...
Another learning style is active...

The author says that learning styles will going to improve your study skills.
The author says that learning styles will improve your study skills.

There are some people they aren't interested in learning styles.
There are some people who aren't interested in learning styles.

There are also a few spelling errors.

~~improbe~~ improve
~~reflactiv~~ reflective

The essay contains a variety of sentence structures such as simple, compound, and complex sentences.

SCORE: 1

In the reading passage it talks about different learning styles, and the lecture too.

In the reading passage, it tells you how you can learn better for what it is your own style. Then it is improve what the teachers and the students do. The different learning styles they are about listening, seeing, and doing. And so too they are actave and reflect. That means if you do something or if you think about it. They are about sequential and globule. That is mean it is step by step or the whole thing.

The speaker is also about learning styles, too. But they are not so good. Some things you need one style. Like for math. Some people aren't interest. Some students, they don't care if it is style. Their teachers, too. They just teach their own style, like the way they do best. If students can do it, good. But if not they can do it, too bad for the students.

REVISION CHECKLIST

- ❑ Content
  - ❑ Thesis Statement
  - ❑ Topics that support the thesis
  - ☑ Main ideas
  - ❑ Supporting details
- ❑ Fluency and Cohesion
  - ❑ Transition words
  - ❑ Grammar and Spelling
  - ❑ Sentence variety

Content

This essay attempts to address the task by giving summaries of both the reading passage and the lecture. The thesis statement does not mention the contrast between the ideas in the reading passage and the lecture. The summaries of the reading and the lecture both mention the main idea and the supporting details, but the details are not clearly explained, and the ideas are often difficult to follow.

Fluency and Cohesion

The essay lacks transition words. There are several grammar errors, for example:

THE STUDENT WROTE: In the reading passage it talks about different learning styles, and the lecture too.
CORRECT: The reading passage talks about different learning styles, and the lecture does, too.

THE STUDENT WROTE: Then it is improve what the teachers and the students do.
CORRECT: This improves what the teachers and the students do.

THE STUDENT WROTE: The different learning styles <u>they</u> are about listening, seeing, and doing.

CORRECT: The different learning styles are about listening, seeing, and doing.

There are also a few spelling errors.

~~actave~~ active

~~globule~~ global

The essay contains a number of awkward sentences, which make it difficult to follow the ideas.

Independent Task

The Independent Task essay is scored on a scale of 0 to 5. The scorers will look at how well you addressed the topic and developed and supported your ideas. They will also look at your use of correct grammatical forms and vocabulary. The chart below provides some simple descriptions of the characteristics of essays at three levels.

RATING SCALE

4–5 GOOD

An essay at this level

- is well organized and well developed
- uses correct grammatical forms and appropriate word choice
- may have slight weaknesses in the elaboration of ideas or occasional grammatical errors

2.5–3.5 FAIR

An essay at this level

- has a thesis that is supported by reasons, examples, and details
- may have weaknesses in the development and support of the main points
- may lack clarity because of problems with organization or poor use of transitions
- may have grammatical errors or inappropriate word choices that interfere with meaning

1.0–2.0 LIMITED

An essay at this level

- may lack sufficient detail to clarify ideas
- may not address the question asked
- may be difficult to read because of serious grammar or vocabulary errors

(An essay that receives a score of 0 may be blank, written in another language, or not relate to the topic.)

Sample Scored Essays

SCORE: 5

Topic 9

Some people prefer to eat at food stands or restaurants. Other people prefer to prepare and eat food at home. Which do you prefer? Use specific reasons and examples to support your answers.

Although many people enjoy eating home-cooked meals, my preference is to eat out whenever possible. The main reason is that I know absolutely nothing about cooking. In addition, eating out allows me to spend more time studying and less time in the kichen. And, believe it or not, eating out is often cheaper than eating meals prepared at home.

To begin with, I don't know a thing about cooking. When you don't know how to cook, there is a good chance that what you cook will not be worth eating. In addition to leaving you with an unsatisfied appetite, this also results in a waste of food as well as a waste of money and effort.

In the second place, cooking takes a lot of time. The food you prepare might not actually be on the stove for very long, but you also have to take into account the time needed for the other steps involved in cooking. In order to prepare a meal, you have to spend time shopping for the ingredients, cleaning and chopping them, and then cleaning up the kichen after the meal is over.

Finally, eating out can be surprisingly economicall. Of course it costs a lot to eat at elegant restaurants, but there are other places to enjoy a good meal. Food stands and some small, casual restaurants provides plenty of good food at very reasonable prices. Many places of this type are located near the university and therefore are very convenient for students. It doesn't cost any more to eat this way than it does to cook at home, and it may cost even less.

As my life changes, my preferences about where to eat may change, too. For now, however, while I am still a student, eating out is the most practical choice I can make.

REVISION CHECKLIST

- ❑ Content
  - ☑ Thesis Statement
  - ☑ Topics that support the thesis
  - ☑ Main ideas
  - ☑ Supporting details
- ❑ Fluency and Cohesion
  - ☑ Transition words
  - ☑ Grammar and Spelling
  - ☑ Sentence variety

Content

This essay has a clear thesis in the beginning and is also very well organized. The first two of the three body paragraphs give reasons why the writer does not want to cook at home, while the third gives reasons why eating out is better. There are sufficient details to support the main idea in each paragraph. The conclusion paraphrases the main idea rather than simply repeating it.

Fluency and Cohesion

The essay uses appropriate transition words such as *in addition, to begin with, also,* and *finally*. There is one grammar error, and it doesn't interfere with understanding the essay:

> Food stands and some small, casual restaurants provides plenty of good food...
> Food stands and some small, casual restaurants provide plenty of good food...

There are also just two minor spelling errors.

kichen	kitchen
economicall	economical

The essay contains a variety of sentence structures such as simple, compound, and complex sentences.

SCORE: 4

Topic 38

Some people think that the family is the most important influence on young adults. Other people think that friends are the most important influence on young adults. Which view do you agree with? Use examples to support your position.

We are all influence by whomever we meet. We all stand as models to everyone in this world. However, our choice of a model is important especially when choosing a career. I believe that in the case concerning our future and our career, families have more influence on us than friends.

Friends are the ones we spend time having fun, enjoying, playing and so forth. Friends also teach good things and help us. Friends advice good things about life, but not like family. Family always think that their children will become superior ones in the future. They want their children to be smarter than anyone else. However, friends are not such an influential adviser like family. Family feels that time is waste when their adult children have too much fun. However, friends influence us more to play or have fun rather than advising us about our career. Therefore, family puts their substanshil impact on their children in order to shape up their future career.

In the US, most young adults are usually influence by their friends rather than their parents. It depends on what type of influence it is. Usually, people are busier in the US. They don't have time to give important influence to their children. Therefore, the children choose their own way to catch up their careers. Whatever they see around influences them. However, this influence might not be good for their future careers.

Therefore, I'd say family influences their adult children more and better than friends.

REVISION CHECKLIST

- ❑ Content
  - ☑ Thesis Statement
  - ☑ Topics that support the thesis
  - ☑ Main ideas
  - ☑ Supporting details
- ❑ Fluency and Cohesion
  - ☑ Transition words
  - ❑ Grammar and Spelling
  - ☑ Sentence variety

Content

The thesis of this essay is very clear and easy to locate at the end of the introduction. The essay is generally well organized. The writer carefully compares and contrasts the level of influence one receives from one's parents with the influence one receives from one's friends. The thesis is well developed, and there is a conclusion that restates the thesis.

Fluency and Cohesion

The essay uses appropriate transition words such as *however, also,* and *therefore.* There are a few grammar errors, but they don't interfere with understanding the essay.

We are all influence by whomever we meet.
We are all influenced by whomever we meet.

Family feels that time is waste...
Family feels that time is wasted...

Therefore, family puts their substanshil impact on their children...
Therefore, families have a substantial impact on their children...

In the US, most young adults are usually influence by their friends...
In the US, most young adults are usually influenced by their friends...

There is one spelling error.

~~substanshil~~ substantial

The essay contains a variety of sentence structures such as simple, compound, and complex sentences.

SCORE: 3

Topic 46

Do you agree or disagree with the following statement? Playing a game is fun only when you win. Use specific reasons and examples to support your answer.

Some would like to play the game such as, basketball, tennis, swimming, and riding bike for exercises and fun. But some, they play for their achievement. I agree that playing game is fun when we win.

As a matter of fact, when I was in High school, I like to play basketball as my hobby. I was very excited when I won the game. All high schools in Cambodia, they required students to choose one kind of game, such as volleyball, soccer, basketball, tennis and swimming. By that time, I took basketball as my favorite hobby. My school gave me the best basketball coach. He had a lot of experience of training basketball players. My teams and I were trained by him everyday for two months. After two monthes of training, My coach wanted us to compete with other schools.

When the competition day came, our emotion was combined with happy and scare of losing the game. But our coach encourage us. He told us that "don't be afraid of your competitors, they are as same as you, so you have to have a confident in yourself." When time of competition of game started, our coach led us to basketball court to get to know our competitors. The result of competition was my team completely won. My coach and our team were very happy to win that game.

I believe that playing game is very difficult if we don't know a weakness of our competitors. We have to have a confident in ourselves. I agree that playing game is very fun when we win.

REVISION CHECKLIST

- ❑ Content
  - ☑ Thesis Statement
  - ❑ Topics that support the thesis
  - ❑ Main ideas
  - ❑ Supporting details
- ❑ Fluency and Cohesion
  - ❑ Transition words
  - ❑ Grammar and Spelling
  - ☑ Sentence variety

Content

This essay is adequately organized and developed. It shows development of ideas and some facility with English. In the first paragraph and in the conclusion, the writer states the opinion that playing a game is fun when one wins. However, the writer does not directly address the topic, which is more black and white: playing a game is fun ONLY when one wins. It is likely that the writer did not understand the question clearly. The writer uses a personal story to illustrate the thesis. This story seems to indicate that the writer also had a good time playing basketball even when he/she didn't win.

Fluency and Cohesion

The essay does not make use of transition words. There are a number of grammar and vocabulary errors that distract the reader from the meaning.

But some, they play for their achievement.
But some play for their achievement.

When I was... I like to play basketball as my hobby.
When I was... I liked to play basketball as my hobby.

...our emotion was combined with happy and scare of losing the game.
...our emotion was a combination of happiness and fear of losing the game.

We have to have a confident in ourselves.
We have to have confidence in ourselves.

There are some spelling and punctuation errors.

~~monthes~~ months

As a matter of fact, when I was in High school...
As a matter of fact, when I was in high school...

He told us that "don't be afraid of your competitors...
He told us, "Don't be afraid of your competitors...

There is sentence variety but there are also numerous errors in sentence structure.

SCORE: 2

Topic 37

Some people prefer to spend time with one or two close friends. Others choose to spend time with a large number of friends. Compare the advantages of each choice. Which of these two ways of spending time do you prefer? Use specific reasons to support your answer.

People need friends they include in a society. Some people try to find good people but some people just take any person around them. Which means first one is very serious to find friends and second people are not to serious to have friends. Some people prefer to spend time with one or two. Others choose to spend time with a large number of friends.

First of all, some people want to spend time with one or two friends. Those people always take care of their friends very well. For example, when they have a party they can invite everyone to their home even thow it is small. Also, they can talk with each friend before the party is over. Because they don't have many friends so they can be able to talk with everyone. Therefore, all the friends returns home very happy after party.

Secondly, some people want to spend time with a large number of friends. Those people love people also they can get a good advise from friends. For example, when they have a problem they can ask their many friends and then they can collect every answer. Therefore, they are figure it out to fix their problem very easily.

REVISION CHECKLIST

- ❑ Content
  - ❑ Thesis Statement
  - ❑ Topics that support the thesis
  - ☑ Main ideas
  - ❑ Supporting details
- ❑ Fluency and Cohesion
  - ☑ Transition words
  - ❑ Grammar and Spelling
  - ☑ Sentence variety

Content

The organization and development of the topic is not adequate. The writer talks about each choice but never accomplishes the task: to express a preference. There is a good attempt at addressing the task, discussing the topic in English, and demonstrating a basic level of competence as a writer in English.

Fluency and Cohesion

The essay uses some transition words, such as *however, first of all,* and *secondly.* There are a number of grammar and vocabulary errors that distract the reader from the meaning.

Which means first one is very serious to find friends...
This means the first one is very serious about finding friends...

Because they don't have many friends so they can be able to talk with everyone.
Because they don't have many friends, they can to talk with everyone.

Therefore, all the friends returns home very happy...
Therefore, all the friends return home very happy...

There are some punctuation errors.

Those people love <u>people also they</u> can get a good advice from friends.
Those people love people. Also, they can get good advice from friends.

For example, when they have a <u>problem they</u> can ask their many friends...
For example, when they have a problem, they can ask their many friends...

There are several spelling errors.

~~to~~ too
~~thow~~ though
~~advise~~ advice

There is sentence variety but the many grammatical errors make it difficult to follow.

SCORE: 1

Topic 43

Some people say that physical exercise should be a required part of every school day. Other people believe that students should spend the whole school day on academic studies. Which opinion do you agree with?

I agree an opinion that students should spend the hole day on academic studies. Because there are have many opportunites for students to be a very good student, like, they have a lot time to spend studies, also, they will be effected by school when they are stay in school. Because of many people staying in library to spend their study, I think that, It will advise me to follow them. More over, staying in school is good for students to enrolling to university. Because they don't have to think something of outside so they really have to think of their lerning, this is a good idea for students to stay. Besides that, if they go home to study, it is ok. But when you are studying in your home, suddenly your father or someone call you at that time, I think, you are confusing about your study. Anyway, I still like to spend the whole school day on academic studies, Because there are have enough books and have many things to use in my knowledge. So I love staying in school day to increase my knowledge.

REVISION CHECKLIST

- ❑ Content
  - ❑ Thesis Statement
  - ❑ Topics that support the thesis
  - ❑ Main ideas
  - ❑ Supporting details
- ❑ Fluency and Cohesion
  - ❑ Transition words
  - ❑ Grammar and Spelling
  - ❑ Sentence variety

Content

This essay is flawed on several levels. It is possible that the writer does not fully understand the task. The writer seems to think that the choice is between staying at home or staying in school. The writer doesn't say why one should spend the whole school day on academics and does not address why some physical education would be bad. The information is not organized into an essay, but is all one paragraph. There are insufficient details to support the author's opinion.

Fluency and Cohesion

The ideas are unclear and there are no clear transitions between them.

There are quite a number of grammar errors. In fact, there are errors in nearly every sentence.

I agree an opinion that students should spend the whole day on academic studies.
I agree with the opinion that students should spend the whole day on academic studies.

Because there are have many opportunities for students to be a very good student...
Because there are many opportunities for them to be very good students...

...they have a lot time to spend studies...
...they have a lot of time to spend on their studies...

There are a number of punctuation errors, mixed in with other errors.

I think that, It will advise me to follow them.
I think that it will be advisable for me to follow them.

There are several spelling errors.

~~hole~~	whole
~~opportunites~~	opportunities
~~effected~~	affected
~~more over~~	moreover
~~lerning~~	learning

There is very little sentence variety.

WRITING STRATEGIES

1. Understand the directions before you begin. Focus on the task not the directions.
2. In the integrated task, take notes as you read. This will help you remember the key words.
3. In the integrated task, as you read, try to guess what the lecture will be about.
4. In the integrated task, take notes as you listen to the lecture. This will help you understand the relation between the reading passage and the lecture.
5. Read the question carefully and understand what you are to do.
6. Make an idea map to help you organize your essay.
7. In the integrated task, write at least one paragraph about the reading passage and at least one paragraph about the lecture.
8. Write in English. You will not have time to translate your essay from your native language into English.
9. Use words and grammar that you are familiar with.
10. Pay attention to the time. Leave a few minutes to go over your writing so you can correct any mistakes.

Time Strategies

INTEGRATED TASK	TOTAL TIME: 25 MINUTES
Read the passage	3 minutes
Listen to the lecture	2 minutes
Plan	3 minutes
Write	14 minutes
Revise	3 minutes

INDEPENDENT TASK	TOTAL TIME: 30 MINUTES
Plan	5 minutes
Write	20 minutes
Revise	5 minutes

The time remaining is shown on the title bar of the computer screen. Check the time periodically.

Self-Test

2

Try the Self-Test for the Integrated and the Independent Tasks now. Pretend you are taking the actual TOEFL. Later, as you study this book, come back to this Self-Test and take it again. When you finish the book, take the test one last time. See how much easier it is. See how much you have learned about planning, writing, and revising.

INTEGRATED TASK

Give yourself 3 minutes to read the passage. Then listen to the lecture on the CD. The lecture will take about 2 minutes. Don't forget to take notes as you listen and read. You should begin thinking about your planning as you do this. Then write an essay in response to the question within 20 minutes. Write between 150 and 225 words.

Divide your writing time like this:

STEP 1 PLAN 3 minutes
STEP 2 WRITE 14 minutes
STEP 3 REVISE 3 minutes

Read this passage within three minutes.

Concern about the phenomenon known as global warming has been growing in recent years. Earth's temperature is rising, largely as a result of human activity. Since the Industrial Revolution, humans have added significantly to the greenhouse gases in the Earth's atmosphere through increases in activities such as cutting down forests and burning fossil fuels like coal and oil. Greenhouse gases hold heat in the atmosphere, and to a certain extent, their presence is natural. An artificial increase in the amount of these gases, however, leads to a rise in temperatures on Earth.

In the middle of the twentieth century, scientists discovered that Earth was getting warmer. Then they discovered that carbon dioxide levels in the atmosphere were increasing. They realized that there was a relationship between rising temperatures and rising levels of carbon dioxide. Most of this carbon dioxide comes from emissions from industrial activity and gasoline-powered motor vehicles.

Earth's average temperature increased almost 1.5°F during the twentieth century. Scientists predict that during the twenty-first century, temperatures will continue to increase. What changes could this bring about on our planet? We have already begun to see changes in weather patterns, snow and ice cover, and sea level.

Changes in weather patterns may lead to increased flooding and drought worldwide, as well as more frequent extreme weather conditions such as powerful hurricanes. Rising global temperatures may also result in increasing water scarcity and in extinction of numerous plant and animal species. But not just the weather will be affected. Changes in climate can lead to economic losses, particularly in the agricultural and transportation sectors. One report predicts a possible 1% drop in gross domestic product and a 20% decrease in per capita consumption worldwide.

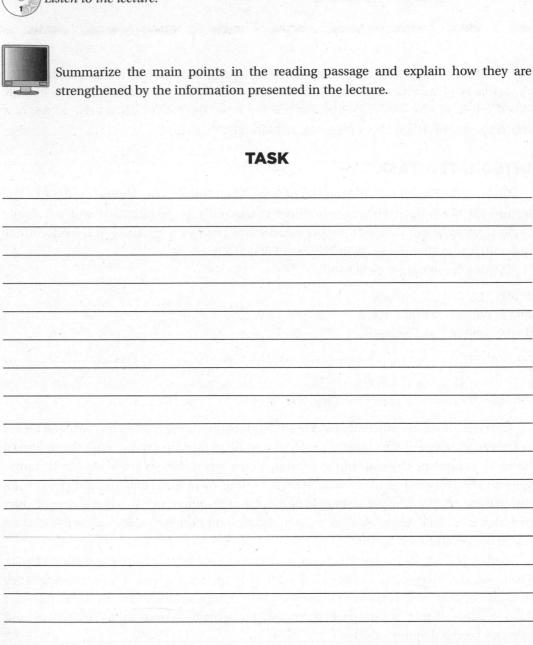

TRACK 1 *Listen to the lecture.*

Summarize the main points in the reading passage and explain how they are strengthened by the information presented in the lecture.

TASK

Revise

Use the following checklist as a guide in revising your essay. You may not be familiar with some of these items now. You will learn about them all as you study this book.

REVISION CHECKLIST

- ❑ Content
  - ❑ Thesis Statement
  - ❑ Topics that support the thesis
  - ❑ Main ideas
  - ❑ Supporting details
- ❑ Fluency and Cohesion
  - ❑ Transition words
  - ❑ Grammar and Spelling
  - ❑ Sentence variety

A model essay is on page 165. Your essay does not have to match this model. It is only one of many possible responses.

INDEPENDENT TASK

Read the topic and plan your essay. Write an essay on this topic within 30 minutes. Write at least 300 words.

Divide your writing time like this:

STEP 1 PLAN 5 minutes
STEP 2 WRITE 20 minutes
STEP 3 REVISE 5 minutes

Essay Topic 1

People attend college or university for many different reasons. Why do you think people attend college or university? Use specific reasons and details to support your answer.

TASK

Revise

Use the following checklist as a guide in revising your essay. You may not be familiar with some of these items now. You will learn about them all as you study this book.

REVISION CHECKLIST

- ❑ Content
  - ❑ Thesis Statement
  - ❑ Topics that support the thesis
  - ❑ Main ideas
  - ❑ Supporting details
- ❑ Fluency and Cohesion
  - ❑ Transition words
  - ❑ Grammar and Spelling
  - ❑ Sentence variety

A model essay is on page 170. Your essay does not have to match this model. It is only one of many possible responses.

Writing Skills: Integrated Task

3

STEP 1: PLAN

How to Take Notes

Taking good notes is an important part of planning your essay. In this section, you will learn how to take notes on the reading passage and on the lecture and you will learn different ways of organizing your notes.

READING

When you read, it is important to recognize the topic, the main ideas, and the supporting details. These will help you understand and remember what you read. Identifying these elements will also help you respond on the integrated task.

On the TOEFL iBT, the reading passage is on the computer screen. You cannot mark or highlight it as you could if you were reading a book. You must take notes on a piece of paper. You will need to summarize or paraphrase the main ideas and the supporting details. You will need to compare them to the lecture.

Look at the example below of a reading passage. The first highlighted sentence is the topic or main idea of the whole passage. The other highlighted words or phrases are the main ideas of the paragraphs. Notice that these come at or near the beginning of each paragraph.

TIP

Every passage has a *main idea*. Every paragraph should also have a main idea. *Topic* is another way of referring to the main idea of the whole passage. A *thesis statement* is what you plan to write about—it is your main idea statement for the whole essay.

Sample Reading Passage

Much research has been done into learning styles. Many educators believe that understanding learning styles can greatly improve what goes on in a classroom or training session. Individuals who are aware of their own learning styles can better focus their learning. Professors and trainers who understand different learning styles are better able to design instruction so as to reach all their students or trainees.

Learning styles have been described in different ways. People may be described as auditory learners, who learn best by listening; visual learners, who learn best by seeing; or kinesthetic learners, who learn best by doing. Another system sees some people as active learners who process new information by doing something with it or using it in some way. Other learners are seen as reflective, preferring to process new information by thinking about it rather than by using it. Similarly, learners might be described as either sequential or global. Sequential learners see new information in logically connected steps, whereas global learners understand things better by looking at the whole picture rather than focusing on the parts.

Understanding learning styles can improve study skills. Sequential learners, for example, can make a habit of outlining new information. Auditory learners can form study groups so that they can talk with others about the topics they are learning. Reflective learners can find ways to reflect on what they have learned, by asking themselves questions about the material, for example, or by writing summaries.

Professors and trainers who understand the different types of learning styles can take them into account when designing their courses. By incorporating a variety of types of activities into their teaching, professors and trainers have a better chance of reaching all their students and improving the learning experience for everyone.

LISTENING

When you listen to a lecture or discussion in an academic setting, you listen for the same information that you do when you read for the topic, main ideas, and supporting details. To help you remember what you hear, you can take notes just as you do when you read.

Usually a speaker will give the main idea or his/her opinion in the first few sentences. The supporting details usually follow. You must listen for the main ideas and the supporting details. These will help you understand and remember what you hear. They will also help you when you write your response. You will need to summarize or paraphrase the main ideas and the supporting details.

Look at the example below of part of a lecture. The first highlighted phrase is the topic or main idea of the lecture. The other highlighted phrases are supporting details.

Sample Lecture

There has been a lot of interest in learning styles over the years, but despite all the research that has been done on the topic, it doesn't present a magic solution. For one thing, there are topics that have to be presented in certain ways, no matter what the learning styles of the students may be. Mathematics, for example, needs to be taught in a logical, patterned way. It is also true that many students simply aren't interested in finding out about their learning style. They don't want to spend time reflecting on how they learn and then applying this to their study habits. They don't see a value in it. Instructors, too, aren't necessarily interested. In fact, many instructors tend to teach the way they themselves were taught. Or they present information in the way they understand it, according to their own style, with the assumption that everyone learns the way they do. So, while the research may provide us with some interesting information and food for thought, applying the results to real-life situations can be problematic.

Outlines and Idea Maps

There are two ways you can organize your notes for both the reading passage and the lecture. You can use either an outline or a graphic organizer, such as an idea map. Use whatever works best for you to organize what you read and listen to. Your notes will not be collected or graded. They are for your use only. It is important to practice taking notes so that you can learn to take them quickly. The time you have for planning and writing your essays is limited.

Good notes will make planning your essay much easier. When you take your notes, you write down the topic or main idea for the entire passage or lecture. When you plan your writing, you also write your main idea for the whole essay, and this now becomes your thesis statement.

An **outline** can look like this.

INTRODUCTION
  TOPIC/MAIN IDEA
BODY
  IDEA 1
    Detail 1
    Detail 2
    Detail 3
  IDEA 2
    Detail 1
    Detail 2
    Detail 3
  IDEA 3
    Detail 1
    Detail 2
    Detail 3
CONCLUSION
  IDEA 1, 2, and 3

An outline can also look like a simple chart. Look at these outlines and notes for the sample reading passage and the sample lecture.

READING		
Topic/Main idea	Understanding learning styles can improve learning and training.	
Paragraph 1	Main idea	Improve classrooms and training sessions
	Supporting details	(1) Individuals can study better. (2) Professors and trainers can instruct better.
Paragraph 2	Main idea	Different ways to describe learning styles
	Supporting details	(1) Auditory, visual, kinesthetic (2) Doing, reflecting (3) Sequential, global
Paragraph 3	Main idea	Improve study skills
	Supporting details	(1) Sequential—make outlines (2) Auditory—talk in study groups (3) Reflective—questions, summaries

LECTURE	
Topic/Main idea	Understanding learning styles does not always provide a solution.
Supporting details	**Idea 1** Some things have to be taught in certain ways. (1) math - sequential
	Idea 2 Some students are not interested in learning styles. (1) don't want to spend time on this
	Idea 3 Some instructors are not interested in learning styles. (1) teach in their own style (2) teach how they were taught

You can also organize your notes on idea maps. An **idea map** can look like this.

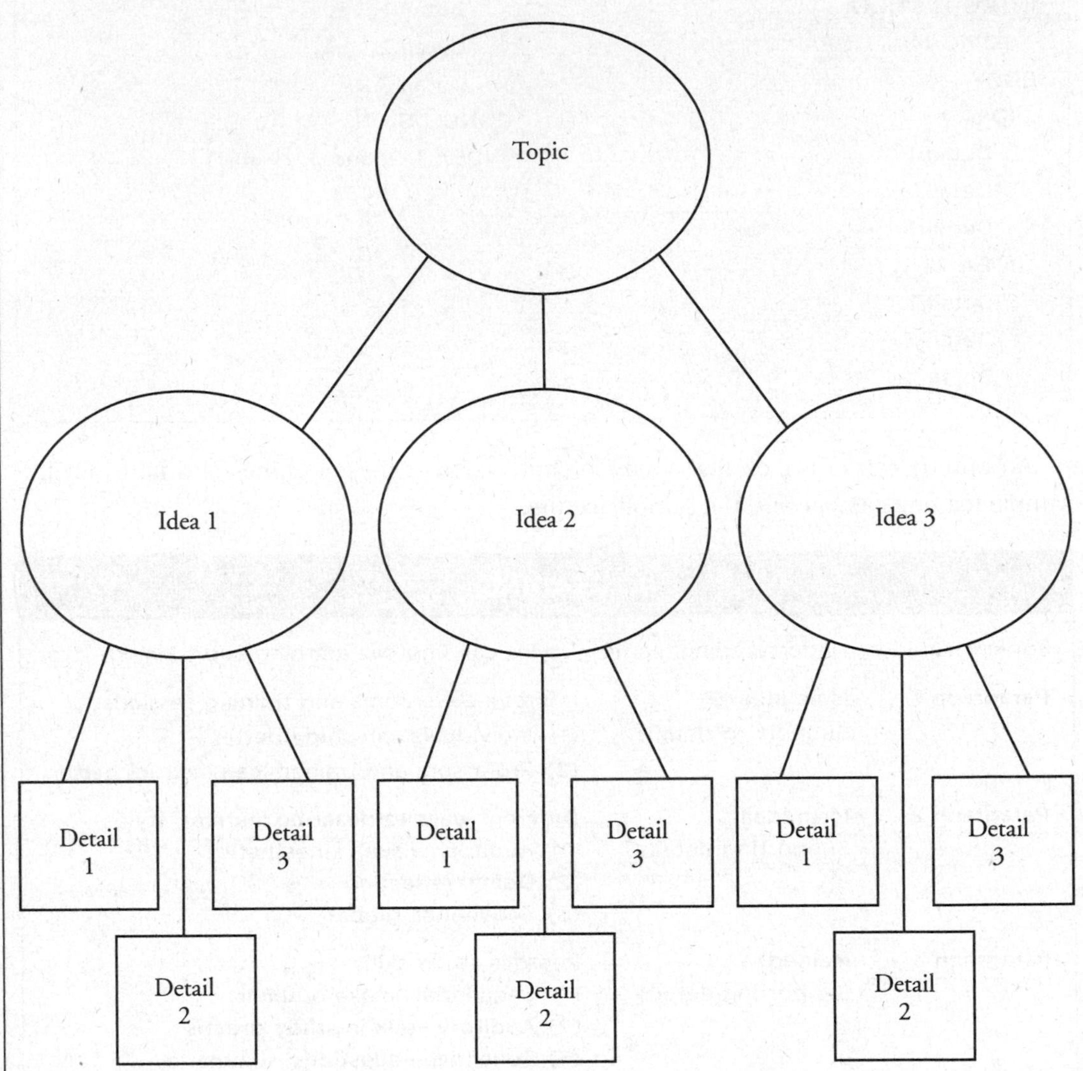

Look at these idea maps for the sample reading passage and sample lecture on pages 29–30.

IDEA MAP FOR READING

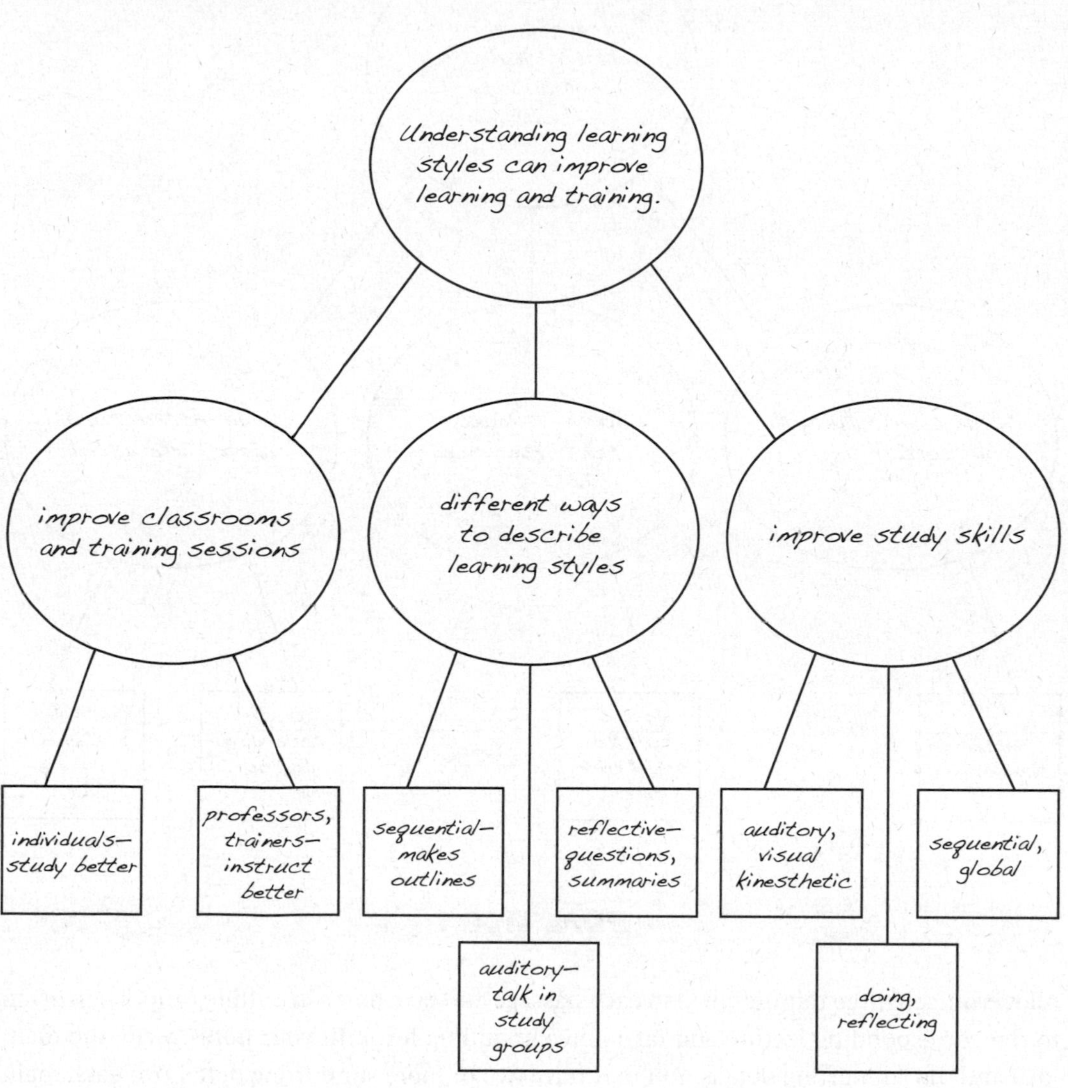

IDEA MAP FOR LECTURE

Understanding learning styles = not always a solution

- some things taught in certain ways
  - math—sequentially
- some students aren't interested
  - do not want to spend time on this
- some instructors aren't interested
  - teach according to their own style
  - teach the way they were taught

PRACTICE 1

TIP

For extra practice, do these outlines twice: once using just phrases, the second time using complete sentences.

Allow yourself three minutes to read each passage and take notes in outline form. Then listen to the corresponding lecture and take notes in outline form. In your notes, write the main idea and the supporting details. You may have two or more supporting details for each main idea. Photocopy the blank outline on this page as many times as you need and use the copies for taking your notes.

OUTLINE

Main idea

____

Supporting details (1) ______________________________

(2) ______________________________

(3) ______________________________

Reading 1

 *Read the paragraph and take notes in outline form.*

Invasive plants are a growing problem. In the United States, there are over one thousand species of nonnative plants that have been identified as a threat to native plants and animals. One way nonnative plants are introduced into an area is through gardening. In the past, gardeners cultivated nonnative species for food or medicine. Gardeners still bring in plants from other parts of the world, sometimes because they want hardy or drought-resistant plants, in other cases because of the particular beauty of some species. If the conditions are right in their new environment, these nonnative plants can escape the garden and grow wild. Many of them are very aggressive. Then we call them invasive. They take over an area, pushing out the native species. They may shade out the local plants, strangle them with vines, or deplete the soil of nutrients. The effects on the local ecology can be devastating. Native plants are reduced in number, and animals suffer loss of habitat and reduction of food supplies.

Lecture 1

Listen to the lecture and take notes in outline form.

Reading 2

 *Read the paragraph and take notes in outline form.*

Does television affect school performance? Many researchers have found that there are strong links between television viewing habits and children's performance in school. Studies have shown that children who spend a lot of time in front of the TV get lower grades than their peers who watch little or no TV. It has also been shown that children who have television sets in their bedrooms earn lower test scores than children with no television sets in their bedrooms. There are those who see TV as a potential educational tool. However, there are actually very few programs on TV that teach children important academic or thinking skills. Most programs aimed at children, such as cartoons, for example, contain little valuable content. Children who spend more time watching TV, spend less time doing homework or interacting with other people. They learn to be passive rather than active. Research supports the view that parents interested in supporting their children's success in school should keep the television turned off.

Lecture 2

Listen to the lecture and take notes in outline form.

Reading 3

Read the paragraph and take notes in outline form.

Smoking prevention campaigns, particularly those aimed at young people, have met with significant success all around the country. The current campaign to prevent tobacco use among teens in our own state, for example, has had a measurable positive impact. This program includes an advertising campaign, the implementation of no-smoking policies for places frequented by teens, and various community antismoking events. Close to 25% of teens surveyed said that they had participated in one of these events during the past year. More significantly, over 50% reported having seen the antismoking ads. The survey also found that those who had seen the ads were much less likely to start smoking than those who had not seen any of the antismoking ads. The public health department plans to continue and expand the campaign so as to reach more young people throughout the state. Clearly, such campaigns can go a long way toward addressing public health issues.

Lecture 3

Listen to the lecture and take notes in outline form.

Reading 4

Read the paragraph and take notes in outline form.

Many researchers have looked into the effect of mood on consumer behavior. It has been shown that mood affects the shopper's perception of the store, the amount of time spent shopping, and the number of items purchased. A shopper's mood, of course, may be influenced by many things. Something as uncontrollable as the weather can have a great effect on what and how much a person buys on any particular day. A person's work or personal life also influences the mood that he or she brings into the store, and, of course, retailers have no control over this, either. But retailers do have control over their store environment, and this has been shown to have a great impact on shoppers' moods and therefore on their behavior as consumers. Retailers spend a great deal of effort with such things as lighting, colors, music, and product displays in an effort to create an environment that will have a positive impact on shopper mood and thereby increase sales.

Lecture 4

Listen to the lecture and take notes in outline form.

PRACTICE 2

Allow yourself three minutes to read each passage and take notes on an idea map. Then listen to the corresponding lecture and take notes on an idea map. In your notes, write the main idea and the supporting details. You may have two or more main ideas for each topic and two or more supporting details for each main idea. Photocopy the blank idea map on the next page as many times as you need and use the copies for taking your notes.

Reading 5

Read the passage and take notes on an idea map.

Advances in technology are usually assumed to increase worker productivity, but that is not always the case. Technology has made it possible for office workers to never leave their desks, and the physical consequences of this can actually lead to lower productivity.

Remaining seated at a desk all day guarantees a level of physical discomfort that negatively impacts a worker's ability to achieve peak performance. Numerous studies have shown that sitting in one position all day leads to back and neck pain. Moreover, constant use of a computer often leads to eyestrain. A recent survey found that many office workers even remain at their desks while eating lunch so that they can answer their email or continue working on a project. This only exacerbates the situation. Even though workers may spend the entire work day at their desks, the resulting physical discomfort has been shown to lead to decreased, not increased, productivity.

What can be done about this? First, office workers need to be more aware of the need for breaks. Getting up and walking around for five minutes every hour or so will give their bodies a rest. Eating lunch away from the office and arranging face-to-face meetings rather than always relying on email both encourage time away from the desk. Second, arranging the desk space is crucial. Use of ergonomic equipment such as chairs and keyboards can greatly relieve strain on the back and neck, reducing discomfort and increasing productivity.

READING IDEA MAP

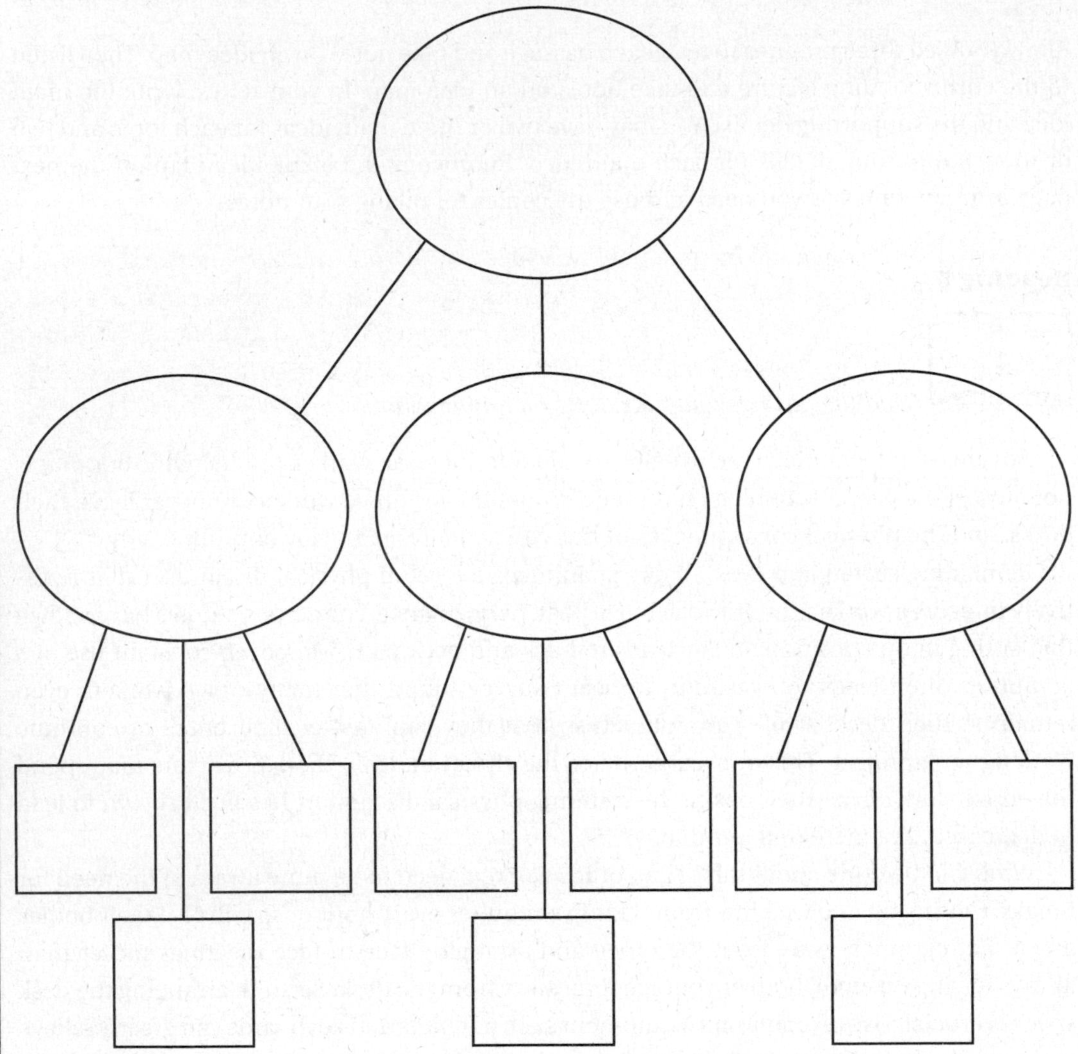

Lecture 5

Listen to the lecture and take notes on an idea map.

Reading 6

Read the passage and take notes on an idea map.

Animal-assisted therapy, or AAT, is the use of companion animals to help people improve their emotional and physical health. It is common for psychiatrists, psychologists, and physicians to recommend pets to patients struggling with emotional difficulties. Caring for pets appears to have benefits for physical health, as well.

Pets are a good source of emotional support. They are wonderful companions for people suffering from loneliness. People who feel isolated from other people may enter more easily into a relationship with a pet because it is a non-judgmental and non-threatening relationship. Caring for pets can also give focus to the lives of pet owners by establishing a need for a daily routine and by providing opportunities for hobbies and club activities. In addition, pets provide comfort and a diversion from worries. Developing a relationship of trust with a pet can help relieve people suffering from anxiety.

There is also documentation that caring for pets can improve physical health. It has been shown that petting and talking to a pet lowers blood pressure and heart rate and improves survival rates from heart disease. Pets provide the opportunity for regular physical activity. Pets also provide the opportunity to play. It is well established that animals (including humans) who play live longer, healthier lives than those who do not. In fact, pet owners make up to 20% fewer visits to doctors' offices than non-pet owners.

Pet therapy is common practice in homes for the elderly. These institutions often keep resident cats and birds as pets. Volunteers often visit the homes with dogs and other types of pets, as well. It is now becoming more widely accepted that pet therapy can provide needed emotional support to people of all ages, and that there are physical benefits, as well.

Lecture 6

Listen to the lecture and take notes on an idea map.

Reading 7

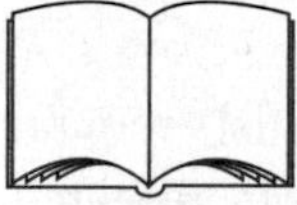
Read the passage and take notes on an idea map.

Pollution of our oceans is a serious problem. There are different sources of ocean pollution, and much of it results from activities that take place on land. In fact, 80% of ocean pollution originates on land. For example, oil is one of the major sources of ocean pollution, but only about 12% of this type of pollution results from oil spills at sea. Another 36% of it comes from waste from cities and factories which travels to the ocean through rivers and drains.

Fertilizers are another serious source of ocean pollution. Fertilizers wash off farms and lawns and eventually end up in the ocean. Once in the ocean, they allow algae to grow. The overgrowth of algae depletes the ocean of oxygen and suffocates other marine plants, resulting in dead areas. There are several large dead areas in the world's oceans, including the Gulf of Mexico and the Baltic Sea.

Garbage is another type of pollution in our oceans, and it can seriously harm marine animals. One of the worst culprits is plastic. This material does not break down easily. Animals often mistake it for food and eat it. Plastic bags can block an animal's breathing passage. The plastic rings that hold packs of cans together can choke birds and other small animals.

Toxic chemicals also cause serious pollution problems. Until the 1970s, toxic waste chemicals were freely dumped into the oceans. In the 1970s, laws were passed banning such activity. However, run-off from manufacturing and disposal sites as well as accidental leaks continue to pollute our oceans with toxic chemicals. These chemicals accumulate in the animals that ingest them and move up the food chain. They eventually end up in the seafood that we eat.

Lecture 7

Listen to the lecture and take notes on an idea map.

Reading 8

Read the passage and take notes on an idea map.

The psychological effects of color have been of interest to people for a long time. The ancient Egyptians, Chinese, and Indians all used color as part of healing therapies. The psychology of color is still of interest in modern times. Interior decorators, graphic designers, and web designers all incorporate an understanding of the relationship between color and mood into their work.

In selecting color for an interior space, the designer considers what type of mood is compatible with the activities that will be carried out in that space. At least one study has found that office workers are able to concentrate better in rooms that are painted with cool blues or dark greens. Yellow might be considered suitable for a sales office because it contributes to a positive mood. Health care centers, on the other hand, are often painted with neutral colors, as these convey a sense of cleanliness and help the healthcare workers stay clear and focused. Restaurants are often painted orange or bright red as it is believed that these colors stimulate the appetite.

There is some research indicating that color may have an effect on the body as well. Some scientists believe that blue slows the heart rate and reduces blood pressure. Red, on the other hand, is believed to increase blood pressure.

While there is a great deal of interest in the psychology of color, many scientists remain skeptical. Although the effect of color on mood has been observed in many cases, research has shown that this effect is often temporary. In addition, observed psychological effects of a particular color may not hold up across cultures.

Lecture 8

Listen to the lecture and take notes on an idea map.

STEP 2: WRITE

Write a Thesis Statement

Your thesis statement is what you plan to write about. It is your main idea statement for the whole essay. For the Integrated Task, your thesis statement must refer to the main ideas of both the reading passage and the lecture and must say whether the ideas are similar or opposite.

Point of View

In both the reading passage and the lecture, a point of view is explained. When you write your response for the Integrated Task you will have to restate these points of view. You can look at the main idea that you wrote in your notes. This should be a restatement or summary of the main point of view explained in the reading passage or the lecture.

When you restate another person's ideas, you use reporting verbs. Here are a few common reporting verbs.

REPORTING VERBS

believe	think	suggest	describe
propose	assert	tell	warn
state	say	point out	explain

Look at the following examples of restating a point of view.

EXAMPLES

Reading 1
The author explains that understanding learning styles can improve learning and training.

Lecture 1
The speaker suggests that understanding learning styles does not always provide a solution.

Tell and ***Warn***

Tell is usually followed by an object.
The author tells us *that students don't always care about learning styles.*

Warn is sometimes followed by an object, but not always.
The author warns us *that students don't always care about learning styles.*
The author warns *that students don't always care about learning styles.*

PRACTICE 1

Look at the main ideas in the notes you wrote in Step 1: Plan, Practice 1 and 2 on pages 34 and 37. Rewrite each idea as a restatement of point of view. Use reporting verbs.

Reading 1 The author states that ____________________
Lecture 1 The speaker explains that ____________________

Reading 2 The author believes that ____________________
Lecture 2 The speaker proposes that ____________________

Reading 3 The author ____________________
Lecture 3 The speaker ____________________

Reading 4	The author	________
Lecture 4	The speaker	________
Reading 5	The author	________
Lecture 5	The speaker	________
Reading 6	The author	________
Lecture 6	The speaker	________
Reading 7	The author	________
Lecture 7	The speaker	________
Reading 8	The author	________
Lecture 8	The speaker	________

Compare and Contrast

When you write your response for the Integrated Task, you will be asked to compare the ideas in the reading passage and the lecture if they are similar in some way. You may be asked how the information in the lecture adds to, supports, or explains the information in the reading passage. Here are some words you can use when you compare ideas.

COMPARE

like	similar to	also
and	similarly	likewise
in the same way	as	agree

You will be asked to contrast the ideas in the reading passage and the lecture if they are different or opposite to each other. You may be asked how the information in the lecture casts doubt on the information in the reading passage. Here are some words you can use when you contrast ideas.

CONTRAST

however	on the other hand	but
although	in contrast	disagree

In Practice 1 on page 41, you restated the main point of view of each reading passage and lecture. When you write your thesis statement, you will put these two ideas together and say whether they are similar or opposing points of view.

Look at these examples from Practice 1 on page 34.

EXAMPLES

Reading 1

The author explains that understanding learning styles can improve learning and training.

Lecture 1

The speaker suggests that understanding learning styles does not always provide a solution.

These ideas are opposite to each other. When you write the thesis statement, you will *contrast* them.

EXAMPLE

> **Thesis statement**
> **The author explains that understanding learning styles can improve learning and training. The speaker, *however*, suggests that understanding learning styles does not always provide a solution.**

This example uses the word *however* to show that the two points of view oppose each other.
See page 42 for more examples of ways to compare and contrast.

PRACTICE 2

Look at the restated points of view you wrote in Practice 1 on page 41. Write a thesis statement that combines each pair of viewpoints.

1. Compare Reading 1 and Lecture 1 points of view.

   Thesis statement: ______________________________

   ____

2. Contrast Reading 2 and Lecture 2 points of view.

   Thesis statement: ______________________________

   ____

3. Contrast Reading 3 and Lecture 3 points of view.

   Thesis statement: ______________________________

   ____

4. Compare Reading 4 and Lecture 4 points of view.

   Thesis statement: ______________________________

   ____

5. Contrast Reading 5 and Lecture 5 points of view.

   Thesis statement: ______________________________

   ____

6. Compare Reading 6 and Lecture 6 points of view.

   Thesis statement: ______________________________

   ____

7. Compare Reading 7 and Lecture 7 points of view.

   Thesis statement: ______________________________

   ____

8. Contrast Reading 8 and Lecture 8 points of view.

   Thesis statement: ______________________________

   ____

Write the Supporting Details

When you write your response for the Integrated Task, you must explain the ideas you read and heard. These are not your own, original ideas. They are your explanation or report of other people's ideas.

When you write the supporting details in your response, you should report the most important supporting details the author and speaker used. You can use **paraphrasing** and **citing** to do this.

PARAPHRASING

When you paraphrase, you use your own words to express what another person wrote or said. When you paraphrase a sentence or a group of sentences, focus on the most important points. Restate them in your own words by using synonyms, changing the word order, using active instead of passive voice, and leaving out the unimportant words.

Original

People may be described as auditory learners, who learn best by listening; visual learners, who learn best by seeing; or kinesthetic learners, who learn best by doing.

Paraphrase

Some people learn more easily by listening, others by seeing, and still others by doing.

Original

Another system sees some people as active learners who process new information by doing something with it or using it in some way. Other learners are seen as reflective, preferring to process new information by thinking about it rather than by using it.

Paraphrase

Active learners understand new information by doing something with it. Reflective learners understand information by thinking about it.

Original

Similarly, learners might be described as either sequential or global. Sequential learners see new information in logically connected steps, whereas global learners understand things better by looking at the whole picture rather than focusing on the parts.

Paraphrase

Sequential learners look at information as a series of steps, but global learners prefer to look at the whole rather than the parts.

PRACTICE 3

Read each original text. Then choose the best paraphrase.

Reading 1

1. In the past, gardeners cultivated nonnative species for food or medicine. Gardeners still bring in plants from other parts of the world, sometimes because they want hardy or drought-resistant plants, in other cases because of the particular beauty of some species.

   Paraphrase

   (A) In the past, gardeners grew nonnative plants for food and medicine. Now they do not because these plants are neither hardy, drought resistant, nor beautiful.

   (B) Gardeners from around the world introduce each other to different species of plants. Each gardener tries to find the hardiest, most drought-resistant, or most beautiful plant in the world.

   (C) Gardeners have introduced nonnative plants for food and medicine. They may also plant them because they are hardy, drought resistant, or beautiful.

2. Then we call them invasive. They take over an area, pushing out the native species. They may shade out the local plants, strangle them with vines, or deplete the soil of nutrients.

   Paraphrase

   (A) Invasive plants harm native species by shading them out, strangling them, or using up all the nutrients in the soil.

   (B) Many local plants grow on vines and invade an area with shade.

   (C) In order to grow, invasive plants require plenty of shade and soil rich in nutrients.

3. The effects on the local ecology can be devastating. Native plants are reduced in number, and animals suffer loss of habitat and reduction of food supplies.

   Paraphrase

   (A) The local ecology devastates native plants and reduces food supplies.

   (B) The local ecology suffers because there are fewer native plants and animals lose their homes and food.

   (C) Large numbers of native plants and animals suffer a devastating loss of habitat.

Reading 2

4. It has also been shown that children who have television sets in their bedrooms earn lower test scores than children with no television sets in their bedrooms.

   Paraphrase

   (A) Children who have TV sets in their bedrooms get low grades in school because they do not get enough sleep.

   (B) Children who have TV sets in their bedrooms do not do as well in school as their classmates.

   (C) Children who spend a lot of time watching TV spend less time preparing for their school tests.

5. There are those who see TV as a potential educational tool. However, there are actually very few programs on TV that teach children important academic or thinking skills. Most programs aimed at children, cartoons, for example, contain little valuable content.

   Paraphrase

   (A) Some people think of TV as educational, but most children's programs actually do not have much valuable or educational content.

   (B) TV is not a useful academic tool because educators do not believe that children should watch cartoons.

   (C) Children usually prefer to watch cartoons because the academic content of educational programs makes them think too hard.

6. Children who spend more time watching TV spend less time doing homework or interacting with other people. They learn to be passive rather than active.

   Paraphrase

   (A) TV watching is a passive activity while doing homework is active.

   (B) Children should keep the TV turned off when they are doing their homework or interacting with other people.

   (C) TV takes time away from important activities like doing homework or being with other people.

7. Research supports the view that parents interested in supporting their children's success in school should keep the television turned off.

   Paraphrase

   (A) Parents can help their children by turning off the television.

   (B) Parents should do more research about school success and television.

   (C) Parents are often interested in children's television programs.

Reading 3

8. This program includes an advertising campaign, the implementation of no-smoking policies for places frequented by teens, and various community antismoking events.

   Paraphrase

   (A) The program frequently included teens who implemented a variety of events.

   (B) The program included advertising, no-smoking policies, and antismoking events.

   (C) The program implemented advertising in a variety of places throughout the community.

9. Close to 25% of teens surveyed said that they had participated in one of these events during the past year. More significantly, over 50% reported having seen the antismoking ads.

   Paraphrase

   (A) Many teens participated in the events and many more saw the ads.

   (B) Almost 25% of teens had surveyed the program and heard about the events.

   (C) A significant number of teens participated in an advertising campaign and reported on the events.

10. The public health department plans to continue and expand the campaign so as to reach more young people throughout the state. Clearly, such campaigns can go a long way toward addressing public health issues.

Paraphrase

(A) The public health department will continue to ask young people throughout the state about public health issues that affect them.

(B) The public health department plans to address more public health issues concerning young people.

(C) The public health department will continue with this successful campaign to improve public health among young people in the state.

Reading 4

11. A shopper's mood, of course, may be influenced by many things. Something as uncontrollable as the weather can have a great effect on what and how much a person buys on any particular day. A person's work or personal life also influences the mood that he or she brings into the store, and, of course, retailers have no control over this, either.

Paraphrase

(A) A shopper may feel he or she has no control over his life when the weather is bad or when there are problems at work, and this puts retailers in a bad mood.

(B) A shopper usually does not buy much from retailers when the weather is bad or when there are problems at work or at home.

(C) A shopper's mood may be influenced by things that retailers cannot control, such as the weather or personal or work problems.

12. But retailers do have control over their store environment, and this has been shown to have a great impact on shoppers' moods and therefore on their behavior as consumers.

Paraphrase

(A) Retailers can influence shoppers' moods by controlling the store environment.

(B) Retailers feel the impact of consumers' behavior in the store environment.

(C) The behavior of moody shoppers has a great impact on the store environment.

13. Retailers spend a great deal of effort with such things as lighting, colors, music, and product displays in an effort to create an environment that will have a positive impact on shopper mood and thereby increase sales.

Paraphrase

(A) It takes a lot of effort to create a positive environment and increase sales.

(B) Shoppers buy more when retailers use lighting, color, and music to improve shopper mood.

(C) More effort is needed to determine the impact of the retail environment on shopper mood.

TIP

Some sentences include ellipses (...). These show where unnecessary words were left out. Some sentences also have words in brackets ([ ]). These words were added to help the reader understand the sentences.

PRACTICE 4

Paraphrase the following original sentences from the lectures. Some of the paraphrases have been partially written for you.

Lecture 1

1. Garlic mustard is a problem in several areas in the United States. It's a cool season plant, blooming in midspring. It's replacing several other spring-blooming species because it competes with them for light, nutrients, and space.

   Paraphrase

   ______________ in the U.S. because it threatens ______________ by taking up ______________.

2. The West Virginia white butterfly is also threatened by this invasive plant. Garlic mustard pushes out certain native species of mustard, which the butterfly relies on for a food source.

   Paraphrase

   Garlic mustard also threatens ______________. It competes with ______________ which are the butterfly's ______________.

3. Garlic mustard was first introduced to the United States in the nineteenth century as a food source. It was first recorded on Long Island but now thrives throughout the eastern and midwestern United States.

   Paraphrase

   Garlic mustard was first grown on ______________ for ______________ and has since spread to ______________.

Lecture 2

4. TV can expose children to new ideas and information that they might otherwise not have access to.

   Paraphrase

   ____

   ____

5. The key here is the amount of time spent in front of the TV.

   Paraphrase

   ____

   ____

6. Children who spend three hours a day or more in front of the TV do poorly in school, scoring lower on both math and reading tests than children who watch some, but less, TV.

   Paraphrase

   ____

   ____

Lecture 3

7. Surveys taken near the end of this campaign, in March of last year, showed that well over half of those surveyed were aware of the campaign...and that 40% reported that they were unlikely to try smoking.

   Paraphrase

   ____

   ____

8. Just three months after the campaign ended, this figure changed dramatically.

   Paraphrase

   ____

   ____

9. At the end of June, 58% of survey participants reported that they were "very likely" to smoke in the next year. At the same time, less than 30% reported awareness of the anti-smoking campaign.

   Paraphrase

   ____

   ____

Lecture 4

10. The researchers found that restaurant patrons who heard music with a slow tempo tended to remain at the restaurant longer than patrons who heard fast music.... they [also] purchased more food, which of course is the effect desired by the restaurant owner.

    Paraphrase

    ____

    ____

11. The study subjects were... college students. Some of them heard currently popular hit songs while shopping—the "familiar" music—while others heard music normally aimed at an older age group.

Paraphrase

____

____

12. [The students] who heard familiar music stayed in the store longer than those listening to unfamiliar music. They also expressed more positive opinions of the products offered for sale.

Paraphrase

____

____

QUOTING

When you paraphrase, you express another person's ideas using your own words. Sometimes you may also want to include a phrase or sentence using the exact words that were used by the source (the author or speaker). When you include the exact words written or spoken by another person, you need to put quotation marks (" ") around them. Whether you paraphrase or quote, you need to mention the source. This means that you acknowledge that you are reporting someone else's ideas or words, and that they are not your own.

EXAMPLE

Original

Sequential learners, for example, can make a habit of outlining new information.

Paraphrase with quote

The author proposes that sequential learners "make a habit of outlining new information."

Notice that the example has quotation marks around the words that were borrowed from the source, and that the source, *the author*, is mentioned.

TIP

Most of the reporting verbs are followed by a *that* clause. (*Describe* is often followed by an object and an *as* clause instead.) *Tell* and *remind* must have an object before *that*.

You will need to use a reporting verb to introduce your paraphrase or quote. Here are several reporting verbs that you can use.

REPORTING VERBS

say	tell	state	remind
suggest	claim	remark	assert
report	explain	point out	contend
note	propose	believe	think
describe	warn	confirm	deny

Look at the following examples.

EXAMPLES

Original

People may be described as auditory learners, who learn best by listening.

Paraphrase with quote

The author tells us that auditory learners "learn best by listening."

Original

Global learners understand things better by looking at the whole picture.

Paraphrase with quote

The author explains that global learners prefer to look at "the whole picture."

Original

It is also true that many students simply are not interested in finding out about their learning style.

Paraphrase with quote

The speaker suggests that students "simply aren't interested" in information about learning styles.

TIP

The topic itself and terms customarily used to discuss a topic do not need quotes. Common words do not usually need quotes unless they are used in some unusual way.

PRACTICE 5

For each paraphrase below, add an appropriate reporting verb. Then put quotation marks around the quoted word or words.

1. **Original** The effects on the local ecology can be devastating.
   Paraphrase The author ______________ that invasive plants may have devastating results.
2. **Original** Most programs aimed at children, such as cartoons, for example, contain little valuable content.
   Paraphrase The author ______________ that most children's TV programs do not have valuable content.
3. **Original** Smoking prevention campaigns, particularly those aimed at young people, have met with significant success all around the country.
   Paraphrase The author ______________ that antismoking campaigns for teens have had significant success.
4. **Original** ... office assistants can devote themselves to other tasks. Offices can operate with fewer assistants, thus spending a great deal less on salaries and benefits.
   Paraphrase The speaker ______________ that offices save money because office workers can now devote themselves to other tasks.

5. **Original** The fact is, research shows that children who watch an hour or so of TV daily...actually do better in school than children who do not watch TV at all.

   Paraphrase The speaker ______________ that when children watch TV, they actually do better in school.

6. **Original** It is well established that animals (including humans) who play live longer, healthier lives than those who do not.

   Paraphrase The author ______________ that play helps people live longer, healthier lives.

7. **Original** Health care centers, on the other hand, are often painted with neutral colors, as these convey a sense of cleanliness...

   Paraphrase The author ______________ that neutral colors are used in health care centers to convey a sense of cleanliness.

Write the Response

SUMMARIZING

A summary is a short description of the main idea and supporting information in a passage. When you write the response for the Integrated Task, you will summarize the main points of the reading passage and the lecture and compare or contrast them.

Your notes will give you the foundation to write a concise summary and comparison of the different ideas presented. You can use the notes you wrote in Step 1, and the thesis statement and rephrased sentences you have written in Step 2.

Look at the following notes for the sample reading passage and lecture on pages 29–30.

STEP 1 PLAN

Reading Notes

Topic/Main idea	Understanding learning styles can improve learning and training.	
Paragraph 1	**Main idea**	Improve classrooms and training sessions
	Supporting details	(1) Individuals can study better. (2) Professors and trainers can instruct better.
Paragraph 2	**Main idea**	Different ways to describe learning styles
	Supporting details	(1) Auditory, visual, kinesthetic (2) Doing, reflecting (3) Sequential, global
Paragraph 3	**Main idea**	Improve study skills
	Supporting details	(1) Sequential—make outlines (2) Auditory—talk in study groups (3) Reflective—questions, summaries

Lecture Notes

Topic/Main idea	Understanding learning styles does not always provide a solution.
Supporting details	(1) Some things have to be taught in certain ways. (2) Some students are not interested in learning styles. (3) Some instructors are not interested in learning styles.

Now look at the way the notes were used to write a **thesis statement** and **paraphrased sentences.**

STEP 2 WRITE

Thesis Statement

The author explains that understanding learning styles can improve learning and training. The speaker, however, suggests that understanding learning styles does not always provide a solution.

Paraphrased Sentences

Reading

- Understanding learning styles helps individuals learn better and professors and trainers instruct better.
- Some people learn more easily by listening, others by seeing, and still others by doing.
- Active learners understand new information by doing something with it. Reflective learners understand information by thinking about it.
- Sequential learners look at information as a series of steps, but global learners prefer to look at the whole rather than the parts.
- Sequential learners, auditory learners, and reflective learners, for example, can each choose the study methods that best suit their individual learning styles.

Lecture

- Some subjects have to be taught in certain ways. Math has to be taught sequentially.
- The speaker suggests that students "simply aren't interested" in information about learning styles.
- Some professors are not interested in learning styles.

Finally, read this summary, which contrasts the reading passage and the lecture.

Summary

The author explains that understanding learning styles can improve learning and training. The speaker, however, suggests that understanding learning styles does not always provide a solution. — *Thesis statement*

NOTE

Formal writing generally does not use contractions. The sample responses for the Integrated Task use contractions only in material cited from the Lecture. Contractions are, of course, natural in spoken English, even in fairly formal situations.

The author states that understanding learning styles helps individuals learn better and professors and trainers instruct better. He explains different ways to describe learning styles. Some people learn more easily by listening, others by seeing, and still others by doing. Active learners understand new information by doing something with it. Reflective learners understand information by thinking about it. Sequential learners look at information as a series of steps, but global learners prefer to look at the whole rather than the parts. The author believes that understanding learning styles can improve study skills. Sequential learners, auditory learners, and reflective learners, for example, can each choose the study methods that best suit their individual learning styles.

Rephrased sentences from Reading

The speaker presents a different point of view. First, some subjects have to be taught in certain ways. Math has to be taught sequentially. In addition, the speaker suggests that students "simply aren't interested" in information about learning styles. Some professors are not interested in learning styles, either.

Rephrased sentences from Lecture

PRACTICE 6

Look at these notes, thesis statements, and rephrased sentences from the practice exercises. Use them to write summaries comparing or contrasting the main points in the reading passage and lecture.

SUMMARY 1

(based on Reading 1 and Lecture 1, page 35)

Reading Notes

Main idea	Invasive plants harm native plants.
Supporting details	(1) They are introduced to an area through gardening.
	(2) They escape from the garden and grow wild.
	(3) They push out native species, causing devastating effects on the local ecology.

Lecture Notes

Main idea	Garlic mustard is an invasive species that causes problems.
Supporting details	(1) It competes with other spring-blooming species.
	(2) The West Virginia white butterfly is threatened by this plant.
	(3) Garlic mustard was introduced to the United States as a food source.

Thesis Statement

The author states that invasive plants harm native plants, and the speaker explains that garlic mustard is an invasive species that causes problems.

Paraphrased Sentences

Reading

- Gardeners have introduced nonnative plants for food and medicine. They may also plant them because they are hardy, drought resistant, or beautiful.
- Invasive plants harm native species by shading them out, strangling them, or using up all the nutrients in the soil.
- The local ecology suffers because there are fewer native plants and animals lose their homes and food.

Lecture

- Garlic mustard threatens other spring-blooming plants by taking up light, nutrients, and space.
- Garlic mustard also threatens the West Virginia white butterfly. It competes with other types of mustard which are the butterfly's food source.
- Garlic mustard was first grown on Long Island for food and has since spread to other areas of the country.

SUMMARY 2

(based on Reading 2 and Lecture 2, page 35)

Reading Notes

Main idea	TV viewing has negative effects on children's school performance.
Supporting details	(1) Children who watch a lot of TV get lower grades and test scores. (2) Few TV programs teach academic or thinking skills. (3) When children spend time watching TV, they spend less time on homework, with other people, and being active.

Lecture Notes

Main idea	TV watching can actually improve school performance.
Supporting details	(1) TV exposes children to new ideas and information. (2) Children should watch some TV, but not too much.

Thesis Statement

The author believes that TV viewing has negative effects on children's school performance. The speaker, on the other hand, proposes that TV watching can actually improve school performance.

Paraphrased Sentences

Reading

- Children who have TV sets in their bedrooms do not do as well in school as their classmates.
- Some people think of TV as educational, but most children's programs actually do not have much valuable or educational content.
- TV takes time away from important activities like doing homework or being with other people.
- Parents can help their children by turning off the television.

Lecture

- Children can learn new things from TV.
- The amount of time spent watching TV is important.
- More than three hours a day of TV watching results in lower reading and math test scores.

SUMMARY 3

(based on Reading 3 and Lecture 3, page 36)

Reading Notes

Main idea	A particular smoking prevention campaign aimed at young people has been successful.
Supporting details	(1) Many teens participated in antismoking events, and many saw antismoking ads.
	(2) Teens who saw the ads are less likely to start smoking.
	(3) The public health department will continue and expand the campaign.

Lecture Notes

Main idea	The initial results of public health campaigns can be misleading.
Supporting details	(1) Surveys taken near the end of an antismoking campaign showed 40% unlikely to try smoking.
	(2) Surveys taken three months later showed 58% very likely to try smoking.

Thesis Statement

The author tells us about a particular smoking prevention campaign aimed at young people that has been successful. In contrast, the speaker warns us that initial results of public health campaigns can be misleading.

Paraphrased Sentences

Reading

- The program included advertising, no smoking policies, and antismoking events.
- Many teens participated in the events and many more saw the ads.
- The public health department will continue with this successful campaign to improve public health among young people in the state.

Lecture

- Surveys made at the end of a recent antismoking campaign showed that 50% knew about the campaign and 40% would probably not smoke.
- Three months later, the numbers had changed.
- Many more said they would probably smoke and many fewer said they knew about the campaign.

SUMMARY 4

(based on Reading 4 and Lecture 4, page 36)

Reading Notes

Main idea	A good mood makes shoppers buy more.
Supporting details	(1) Mood can be affected by weather, personal life, and store environment.
	(2) Retailers create a store environment to have a positive impact on mood and therefore on sales.

Lecture Notes

Main idea	Studies show that mood can make consumers spend more time shopping.
Supporting details	(1) When listening to slow music, restaurant patrons remained longer and purchased more food.
	(2) When listening to familiar music, shoppers stayed in a store longer and expressed more positive opinions about the products.

Thesis Statement

The author proposes that a good mood makes shoppers buy more. Similarly, the speaker explains that studies show that music can make consumers spend more time shopping.

Paraphrased Sentences

Reading

- A shopper's mood may be influenced by things that retailers cannot control, such as the weather or personal or work problems.
- Retailers can influence shoppers' moods by controlling the store environment.
- Shoppers buy more when retailers use lighting, color, and music to improve shopper mood.

Lecture

- Research showed that slow music caused customers to stay at the restaurant longer and order more food.
- Some of the study subjects, college students, heard popular music in the store, and others heard older music.
- Those who heard familiar music shopped longer and said better things about the store's products.

STEP 3: REVISE

Use the Revision Checklist

Revision is an important part of the writing process. After you write your response, you need to check the content and language. You need to make sure that the content is well developed and well organized, and you need to make sure you have used correct language and punctuation. You can use the following revision checklist as a guide.

REVISION CHECKLIST

- ❑ Content
  - ❑ Thesis Statement
  - ❑ Topics that support the thesis
  - ❑ Main ideas
  - ❑ Supporting details
- ❑ Fluency and Cohesion
  - ❑ Transition words
  - ❑ Grammar and Spelling
  - ❑ Sentence variety

Read the following model task. Notice how it matches the items on the checklist.

MODEL TASK 1

Summarize the main points of the reading passage and explain how the points made in the lecture oppose them.

The author asserts that advances in technology do not always lead to increased productivity. The speaker, in contrast, suggests that investment in technology is paid back in increased productivity.

The author explains that because of technology, workers often stay at their desks all day, but this does not lead to increased productivity. It can cause back, neck, and eye pain. This is very uncomfortable and actually lowers productivity. Workers need to take breaks more often and go out for lunch. They also should have meetings in person instead of using email. In addition, companies can buy special equipment that is more comfortable to use.

The speaker has the opposite point of view. She believes that technology increases productivity. Photocopy machines, for example, can copy, collate, and staple much faster than a person. Because of this, workers can spend their time doing other things. Also an office can hire fewer people and save money on salaries. When people communicate by email, they do not have to go to so many meetings. They can spend more time working. The speaker does not mention the physical pains that using technology can cause. Clearly, technology solves some problems, but it causes others.

(based on Reading 5, page 37 and Lecture 5, page 38)

Content

REVISION CHECKLIST

- ❑ Content
  - ☑ Thesis Statement
  - ❑ Topics that support the thesis
  - ❑ Main ideas
  - ❑ Supporting details
- ❑ Fluency and Cohesion
  - ❑ Transition words
  - ❑ Grammar and Spelling
  - ❑ Sentence variety

✓ Check for Thesis Statement

The model essay has a thesis statement that shows understanding of the task. The task asks the writer to summarize points and explain how they oppose each other, that is, to contrast them. The first two sentences are the thesis statement. They summarize the main idea of the reading and of the lecture. The transition words *in contrast* let the reader know that these ideas are in opposition to each other.

Task:	Summarize points and explain how they oppose each other
Contrast words:	*in contrast*

REVISION CHECKLIST

- ❑ Content
  - ❑ Thesis Statement
  - ☑ Topics that support the thesis
  - ❑ Main ideas
  - ❑ Supporting details
- ❑ Fluency and Cohesion
  - ❑ Transition words
  - ❑ Grammar and Spelling
  - ❑ Sentence variety

✓ Check for Topics that Support the Thesis

The supporting topics are the main idea of the reading and the main idea of the lecture. They are presented in the thesis statement. The model essay summarizes the main points of the reading and of the lecture and explains how the author's ideas contrast with the speaker's ideas.

Main idea of the reading and lecture

Reading Advances in technology do not always lead to increased productivity.
Lecture Investment in technology is paid back in increased productivity.

REVISION CHECKLIST

- ❑ Content
  - ❑ Thesis Statement
  - ❑ Topics that support the thesis
  - ☑ Main ideas
  - ❑ Supporting details
- ❑ Fluency and Cohesion
  - ❑ Transition words
  - ❑ Grammar and Spelling
  - ❑ Sentence variety

✓ Check for Main Ideas

The second paragraph in the model essay supports the reading main idea by summarizing the main points of the reading. The third paragraph in the model essay supports the lecture main idea by summarizing the main points of the lecture.

MAIN IDEA OF THE READING AND LECTURE	DEVELOPED FURTHER IN...	IDEAS THAT ARE DEVELOPED
Advances in technology do not always lead to increased productivity.	Paragraph 2	Technology means workers stay at their desks all day. This causes discomfort.
Investment in technology is paid back in increased productivity.	Paragraph 3	Photocopy machines and email make work faster and more convenient.

REVISION CHECKLIST

- ❑ Content
  - ❑ Thesis Statement
  - ❑ Topics that support the thesis
  - ❑ Main ideas
  - ☑ Supporting details
- ❑ Fluency and Cohesion
  - ❑ Transition words
  - ❑ Grammar and Spelling
  - ❑ Sentence variety

✓ Check for Supporting Details

The paragraphs in the model essay have topic sentences and supporting details. In the body of the response, the topic sentences of the paragraphs match the topics introduced in the first paragraph.

Paragraph 2: *Main Idea*

...because of technology, workers often stay at their desks all day, but this does not lead to increased productivity.

SUPPORTING DETAILS

- This is very uncomfortable and actually lowers productivity.
- Workers need to take breaks more often and go out for lunch.
- They also should have meetings in person instead of using email.
- In addition, companies can buy special equipment that is more comfortable to use.

Paragraph 3: *Main Idea*

...technology increases productivity.

SUPPORTING DETAILS

- Photocopy machines, for example, can copy, collate, and staple much faster than a person.
- When people communicate by email, they do not have to go to so many meetings. They can spend more time working.

Fluency and Cohesion

REVISION CHECKLIST

- ❑ Content
  - ❑ Thesis Statement
  - ❑ Topics that support the thesis
  - ❑ Main ideas
  - ❑ Supporting details
- ❑ Fluency and Cohesion
  - ☑ Transition words
  - ❑ Grammar and Spelling
  - ❑ Sentence variety

✓ Check for Transition Words

Transition words show how the ideas fit together. The model essay includes appropriate transition words.

TRANSITION WORD	PARAGRAPH	FUNCTION
also	Paragraph 2	Adds information
In addition	Paragraph 2	Adds information
for example	Paragraph 3	Clarifies as point
Also	Paragraph 3	Adds information

REVISION CHECKLIST

- ❑ Content
  - ❑ Thesis Statement
  - ❑ Topics that support the thesis
  - ❑ Main ideas
  - ❑ Supporting details
- ❑ Fluency and Cohesion
  - ❑ Transition words
  - ☑ Grammar and Spelling
  - ❑ Sentence variety

✓ Check for Grammar and Spelling

There are no grammar or spelling errors in the model essay.

REVISION CHECKLIST

- ❑ Content
  - ❑ Thesis Statement
  - ❑ Topics that support the thesis
  - ❑ Main ideas
  - ❑ Supporting details
- ❑ Fluency and Cohesion
  - ❑ Transition words
  - ❑ Grammar and Spelling
  - ☑ Sentence variety

✓ Check for Sentence Variety

The model essay uses a variety of sentence structures.

SENTENCE TYPE	PARAGRAPH	EXMAPLE
Series	Paragraph 2	It can cause back, neck, and eye pain.
Adjective clause	Paragraph 2	In addition, companies can buy special equipment that is more comfortable to use.
Complex sentence	Paragraph 3	When people communicate by email, they do not have to go to so many meetings.
Simple sentence	Paragraph 3	They can spend more time working.
Compound sentence	Paragraph 3	Clearly, technology solves some problems, but it causes others.

PRACTICE 1

Read the following model tasks. Do the exercises that follow each one.

MODEL TASK 2

Summarize the main points of the reading passage, and explain how they are supported by the information presented in the lecture.

The author explains that animal-assisted therapy is used to improve emotional and physical health, and the speaker tells us about a study that showed positive effects of pet ownership on health.

The author explains how pets improve both emotional health and physical health. Pets are good companions for lonely people. They also give their owners things to do, like hobbies or club activities. In addition, pets are a comfort to anxious or worried people. Pets are good for physical health, as well. They help people with high blood pressure and heart problems. They help people stay physically active. They give people a chance to play. Finally, pet therapy is used with elderly people.

The speaker supports pet therapy. He describes a study where pets had a positive effect on the health of heart patients. Half the patients had a dog to take care of. The other half only got traditional treatment. After six months, the patients with pets had lower blood pressure, and they had lost more weight than the other patients. They felt happier, too. These are all things that can affect heart disease. This is a case that shows how pet therapy works to improve physical health.

(based on Reading 6, page 38 and Lecture 6, page 39)

REVISION CHECKLIST

- ❑ Content
  - ❑ Thesis Statement
  - ❑ Topics that support the thesis
  - ❑ Main ideas
  - ❑ Supporting details
- ❑ Fluency and Cohesion
  - ❑ Transition words
  - ❑ Grammar and Spelling
  - ❑ Sentence variety

EXERCISES

1. Find the thesis statement. Underline it.
2. In the first paragraph, find the topics that support the thesis. Number them.
3. Put a check (✓) next to the main idea in the second paragraph. Mark each supporting detail with a letter: A, B, C, etc.
4. Put a check (✓) next to the main idea in the third paragraph. Mark each supporting detail with a letter: A, B, C, etc.
5. Underline all transition words in the second and third paragraphs.
6. Check grammar and spelling. Correct any errors.
7. Find and mark one simple sentence (ss), one compound sentence (cm/s) and one sentence with an adjective clause (adj.c).

MODEL TASK 3

Summarize the main points in the reading passage and explain how the information presented in the lecture adds to them.

The author warns that ocean pollution is a serious problem. In the same way, the speaker explains how plastic garbage threatens sea animals.

The author explains that different things cause ocean pollution. Oil from factories and cities enters the ocean through rivers and drains. **Similarly**, fertilizers wash into the ocean, and they cause large growths of algae. Toxic chemicals continue to pollute the ocean, **as well.** There are laws against dumping these chemicals, but the chemicals still leak into the ocean. Animals eat them, and when we eat seafood, we eat these chemicals, **too**. There is **also** a lot of garbage in the ocean. Plastic is the worst kind because it does not break down quickly. Animals think it is food. They eat it and choke on it.

While the author gives an overview of ocean pollution, the speaker specifically describes the problem of plastic garbage. People produce billions of pounds of plastic a year, and a lot of this ends up in the ocean. The water and wind break large pieces of plastic into smaller pieces. **Then** animals try to eat these pieces. An animal may choke on plastic. It may starve because it does not feel hungry after eating plastic. Animals are often caught in floating plastic. They are also strangled by it. There are many types of pollution in the ocean. Plastic garbage is one of the worst examples.

(based on Reading 7, page 39, and Lecture 7, page 40)

REVISION CHECKLIST

- ❑ Content
  - ❑ Thesis Statement
  - ❑ Topics that support the thesis
  - ❑ Main ideas
  - ❑ Supporting details
- ❑ Fluency and Cohesion
  - ❑ Transition words
  - ❑ Grammar and Spelling
  - ❑ Sentence variety

EXERCISES

1. Find the thesis statement. Underline it.
2. In the first paragraph, find the topics that support the thesis. Number them.
3. Put a check (✓) next to the main idea in the second paragraph. Mark each supporting detail with a letter: A, B, C, etc.
4. Put a check (✓) next to the main idea in the third paragraph. Mark each supporting detail with a letter: A, B, C, etc.
5. Underline all transition words in the second and third paragraphs.
6. Check grammar and spelling. Correct any errors.
7. Find and mark one compound sentence (cm/s), one complex sentence (cx/s), and one simple sentence (ss).

MODEL TASK 4

Summarize the main points of the reading passage and explain how the points made in the lecture cast doubt on them.

The author explains that color has psychological effects. In contrast, the speaker tells us about a study that showed no effect of color on appetite.

The author describes different ways people have used the psychological effects of color. Ancient people used color for healing, and modern designers use color to create mood. Designers might use yellow to create a positive mood in an office. Likewise, they might use neutral colors to create a clean, clear, and focused mood in health care centers. Restaurants often use orange and red to stimulate the appetite. Some scientists say that blue lowers the heart rate and blood pressure. Red, on the other hand, raises blood pressure. Other scientists do not believe that color affects mood. They say the effect is temporary and also that it is different in every culture.

The speaker describes a study that showed no relationship between color and appetite. A fast-food restaurant chain had orange walls in half its restaurants and beige walls in the rest of its restaurants. It recorded all the food ordered for two years. There was no difference between the restaurants with orange walls and the restaurants with beige walls. People ordered the same food in both types of places. In other words, according to the company president, there is no effect of color on appetite. He said that the study proved it. In this case, at least, there was no psychological effect of color.

(based on Reading 8, page 40, and Lecture 8, page 40)

REVISION CHECKLIST

- ❑ Content
  - ❑ Thesis Statement
  - ❑ Topics that support the thesis
  - ❑ Main ideas
  - ❑ Supporting details
- ❑ Fluency and Cohesion
  - ❑ Transition words
  - ❑ Grammar and Spelling
  - ❑ Sentence variety

EXERCISES

1. Find the thesis statement. Underline it.
2. In the first paragraph, find the topics that support the thesis. Number them.
3. Put a check (✓) next to the main idea in the second paragraph. Mark each supporting detail with a letter: A, B, C, etc.
4. Put a check (✓) next to the main idea in the third paragraph. Mark each supporting detail with a letter: A, B, C, etc.
5. Underline all transition words in the second and third paragraphs.
6. Check grammar and spelling. Correct any errors.
7. Find and mark one compound sentence (cm/s), one sentence with a noun clause (nc), and one simple sentence (ss).

PRACTICE 2

Complete each essay by answering the questions that follow.

TIP

Reading ahead in the essay will help you choose the best answer.

ESSAY 1

Summarize the main points of the reading passage and explain how they are strengthened by the information presented in the lecture.

The author explains why global warming is a serious problem.

(1) ________________, the speaker explains the impact of global warming in the northeastern United States.

(2) ________________. Greenhouse gases, such as carbon dioxide, hold heat in the atmosphere and result in rising temperatures on Earth. As average temperatures rise, there are a number of effects. (3) ________________, scientists predict that weather patterns will change. In addition, snow and ice will melt and sea levels will rise. This can lead to flooding, drought, and powerful storms. It can also affect the economy, particularly agriculture and transportation. (4) ________________.

The speaker explains the effects of global warming in the northeastern part of the United States. This is a cold and snowy area. (5) ________________. There are also fewer days with snow on the ground than there used to be. This has an effect on the economy because many people in this part of the world depend on the ski industry to make a living. The predicted effects of global warming that the author described are already coming true, at least in the northeastern United States.

1. Choose the best way to complete the thesis statement.
   (A) In contrast
   (B) As a result
   (C) Likewise

2. Choose the best main idea for this paragraph.
   (A) The author explains that human activity, such as industry and cutting down forests, has resulted in an artificial increase in greenhouse gases in Earth's atmosphere, with serious results.
   (B) The author explains that it is difficult for scientists to come to agreement about whether or not global warming is actually occurring in the world today.
   (C) The author explains that some people believe that greenhouse gases are very harmful, while others are sure that global warming is not such a very serious problem.

3. Choose the best transition word for this sentence.
   (A) Nevertheless
   (B) First
   (C) However

4. Choose the missing supporting detail.
   (A) People will be better off economically, especially farmers.
   (B) Economists predict that global warming will lead to a drop in gross national product and consumer consumption in countries around the world.
   (C) Warmer temperatures will result in people using transportation more often as they will take more frequent vacations.

5. Choose the missing supporting detail.
   (A) Since 1965, many people have moved to this part of the country.
   (B) Since 1965, there has been a decrease in employment in this area.
   (C) Since 1965, temperatures in this region have risen.

ESSAY 2

Summarize the main points of the reading passage and explain how they are supported by the information presented in the lecture.

The reading passage talks about camouflage as a key survival strategy used by many animals. (6) ________________.

The author explains how camouflage helps animals survive. There are different kinds of camouflage. Some animals are similar in color to their surroundings. Deer, (7) ________________, have brown fur, which helps them blend in with their forest habitat. Some arctic animals, such as the arctic hare, change color with the seasons. (8) ________________. Striped zebras and fish with shiny scales are two examples of this. Some animals are mimics, taking on characteristics of another object or animal in their environment. The green anole, a type of lizard, looks like a leaf. The caterpillar of the hawk moth resembles a snake. Camouflage is important to both predators and prey. It helps predators to be invisible to their victims, and it helps prey animals to hide from the animals that hunt them.

The speaker talks about how camouflage helps certain animals hide in the arctic environment. Many of them are brown in the summer to match their summer environment and white in the winter when snow covers the ground. One example is the arctic fox. (9) ______________. It is also a prey animal and needs to hide from its predators. When winter approaches, the fox sheds its brown fur and grows white fur. (10) ______________ animal that does this is the lemming. It needs to be brown in the summer and white in the winter in order to hide from its main predator—the arctic fox.

6. Choose the best way to complete the thesis statement.
   (A) Additionally, the speaker discusses other survival tactics used by animals.
   (B) Similarly, the speaker talks about the way that several arctic animals use camouflage for survival.
   (C) In contrast, the speaker explains how predators attack their prey.

7. Choose the best transition word for this sentence.
   (A) for example
   (B) on the other hand
   (C) in addition

8. Choose the missing supporting detail.
   (A) Some herd animals have patterns on their fur that make it very easy to see them in any season of the year.
   (B) Some herd animals have patterns on their fur that make them very beautiful to look at.
   (C) Some herd animals have patterns on their fur that make it difficult for predators to pick out one animal from the group.

9. Choose the missing supporting detail.
   (A) It looks very nice in the winter when it plays in the snow.
   (B) It is a predator, so it needs to be invisible to its prey while it hunts.
   (C) In the summer it eats berries and other fruits and vegetation.

10. Choose the best transition word for this sentence.
   (A) Another
   (B) However
   (C) Furthermore

ESSAY 3

Summarize the main points of the reading passage and explain how the points made in the lecture oppose them.

(11) ______________. In contrast, the lecture reports evidence that girls and women do better in school than boys and men.

The author describes research done by a psychologist who claims that men have higher intelligence than women. The psychologist studied the results of intelligence tests taken by university students aged 17 and 18. (12) ______________. Furthermore, more men than

women qualify as geniuses. The psychologist suggests that the reason for men's higher intelligence is their larger brain size.

(13) ________________. In the first place, study after study has shown that girls outperform boys in elementary school. (14) ________________ in high schools all around the country there are far more girls than boys in advanced-level classes. (15) ________________. Each year, 170,000 more women than men earn college degrees. The facts presented by the lecturer completely contradict the results of the study described in the reading passage.

11. Choose the best way to complete the thesis statement.
   (A) The reading passage describes a study which claims that men are more intelligent than women.
   (B) The reading passage describes a study proving that girls are better students than boys.
   (C) The reading passage describes a study of different educational methods used in schools around the country.

12. Choose the missing supporting detail.
   (A) Some researchers believe that IQ tests are not a valid measure of an individual's intelligence.
   (B) Some schools these days use intelligence tests to evaluate their students' academic potential.
   (C) The results showed that the IQs of the men averaged four points higher than the IQs of the women.

13. Choose the missing main idea.
   (A) The lecturer agrees that among school children, girls are generally smarter than boys.
   (B) The lecturer has a contradictory viewpoint, discussing evidence that girls are better students than boys.
   (C) The lecturer contradicts the author, stating that girls take more tests in school than boys do.

14. Choose the best transition word for this sentence.
   (A) In addition
   (B) In contrast
   (C) In other words

15. Choose the missing supporting detail.
   (A) Finally, the same number of women as men attend college.
   (B) Finally, more than 60% of college students are women.
   (C) Finally, both men and women have found success in college.

ESSAY 4

Summarize the main points of the reading passage and explain how the points made in the lecture cast doubt on them.

The reading passage describes the benefits of genetically modified foods. The lecture, (16) ________________, discusses the disadvantages of these foods.

The author explains what genetically modified foods are and describes the advantages they have for food production and health. (17) _______________. Some crops are genetically modified to be resistant to disease. As a result, they are easier to cultivate and farmers can grow larger crops. Other crops are genetically modified to contain more vitamins and minerals. Golden rice, (18) _______________, has been modified to contain more vitamin A. Additionally, some genetically modified crops are used to develop new products. Scientists are currently working on a banana, for example, that can be used to produce vaccines against serious diseases.

(19) _______________. In the first place, some crops have been genetically modified to be resistant to insects, but their genes could actually be transferred to those insects. Then the insects would be resistant to insecticides, and the crops would not be protected. (20) _______________, the effects of genetically modified foods on our health are not yet known, but there are serious possibilities. Some examples are the development of allergies and of resistance to antibiotics. Finally, many people are concerned that widespread use of genetically modified foods would allow a few large companies to dominate food production. According to the speaker, genetically modified foods may cause more problems than they solve.

16. Choose the best way to complete the thesis statement.
    (A) on the other hand
    (B) therefore
    (C) similarly

17. Choose the missing supporting detail.
    (A) Genetically modified foods have a number of advantages and disadvantages.
    (B) Genetically modified foods are available for sale in most grocery stores.
    (C) Genetically modified foods come from crops that have had their genes altered by technology.

18. Choose the best transition word for this sentence.
    (A) for instance
    (B) however
    (C) likewise

19. Choose the missing main idea.
    (A) The speaker discusses some serious problems with genetically modified foods.
    (B) The speaker believes that genetically modified foods have many advantages.
    (C) The speaker mentions that corn and soybeans are crops that are often genetically modified.

20. Choose the best transition word for this sentence.
    (A) Consequently
    (B) Furthermore
    (C) Although

PRACTICE 3

Read the following essay and use the revision checklist to identify what is missing or incorrect. Then revise the essay, adding the missing parts and correcting the errors. Write the revised essay on your computer or on a piece of paper.

REVISION CHECKLIST

- ❑ **Content**
  - ❑ **Thesis Statement**
  - ❑ **Topics that support the thesis**
  - ❑ **Main ideas**
  - ❑ **Supporting details**
- ❑ **Fluency and Cohesion**
  - ❑ **Transition words**
  - ❑ **Grammar and Spelling**
  - ❑ **Sentence variety**

Summarize the main points of the reading passage and explain how they are supported by the information presented in the lecture.

The reading passage explains why farming is difficult in far northern regions in general. The lecture is similar.

In the first place, the growing season is very short. It might last three months or less, which is not enough time for most crops to mature. Additionally, few people live in northern regions because the cold weather is not attractive. Therefore, farmers have to pay to transport their crops long distances to cities where they can sell them to a larger market. Consequently, the harsh climate causes farm machinery to break down frequently. The cost to repair or replace specialized farm equipment can to be very high.

The speaker discusses farmers working in a particular northern province. He explains that many people have stopped farming in that area because they are no longer able to make a living that way. One reason is the disease affecting the rye crop, one of the few crops that can be grown so far north. Another reason is the rising cost of transportation. Fewer and fewer farmers can afford to ship their crops to cities. Although, because of the losses due to the rye disease, many farmers have difficulty paying the cost of maintaining their buildings and equipment. For reasons similar to those outlined in the reading passage, many people in this northern province is leaving their farms to look for jobs in towns and cities.

Missing items:

Paragraph 1: ______________________________

Paragraph 2: ______________________________

Paragraph 3: ______________________________

Grammar and vocabulary errors:

Paragraph 1: ______________________________

Paragraph 2: ______________________________

Paragraph 3: ______________________________

CHECK THE SPELLING AND PUNCTUATION

Spelling

Remember that there is no spell checker on the computer that you will use during the TOEFL iBT. You must work to improve your spelling before you take the test. Whenever you read in English, pay close attention to words. This will help you understand English spelling patterns. You should be able to spell the most common English words before you take the test.

Here are some hints for dealing with spelling on the Integrated Task.

- Pay special attention to how key words in the Reading passage are spelled.
- Take careful notes on the spelling of these words.
- Listen for these same words as you take notes during the Lecture.
- When you revise your essay, check your spelling against your notes.

NOTE

You will not be penalized if you use a space between paragraphs instead of indents. Also, remember that proper nouns are capitalized.

Punctuation

Also, whenever you read in English, pay attention to punctuation. This will help you when writing your response. There are three important things to remember about punctuation when you write your responses.

- **Indent each paragraph or use a space between paragraphs.**
  This will help the reader determine when you are starting a new topic.
- **Capitalize the first word of each sentence.**
  This will help the reader determine when you are starting a new sentence.
- **Put a period or question mark at the end of each sentence or question.**
  This will help the reader determine when you are ending a sentence or question.

Commas help the reader follow your ideas, but be careful not to use them where they are not needed.

Here are some other forms of punctuation that will help make your response easier to read.

COMMA

Use a comma in a list of three or more things. It is optional to put a comma before the *and*.

> Plants require sunlight, water, and soil.
> It was an educational, interesting and entertaining program.

Use a comma between a noun and a following description.

> The Baltic Sea, in northern Europe, is polluted with trash.
> The study participants, teenagers sixteen to eighteen, were asked about smoking habits.

Use a comma to separate transition words, adjectives, or participles that are not part of the sentence or were added for emphasis.

> Unfortunately, the success of the program did not last.
> The effects on the local ecology, however, can be devastating, very devastating.

Use a comma between two independent clauses.

Office workers need to take frequent breaks, and they should use ergonomic equipment.

Many teens saw the ads, but only a few quit smoking.

Use a comma to separate a non-restrictive clause.

Elderly people, who are often lonely, can benefit from pet therapy.

The study, which included all of the company's restaurants, looked at color of the walls and how this affected sales.

Use a comma after a subordinate clause at the beginning of a sentence.

If the store environment is pleasant, shoppers may spend more money.

Because we produce so much plastic, it ends up in the oceans.

SEMICOLON

Use a semicolon to separate two closely related sentences.

Some people thought the program was successful; others disagreed.

COLON OR DASH

Use a colon or dash in front of a list or explanation.

There are three things retailers can use to improve the store environment: color, lighting, and music.

Invasive vines are considered a threat for a very good reason—they strangle native plants.

PRACTICE 4

Read the following sentences. Some have misspelled words. Revise the sentences, correcting the spelling. If a sentence has no misspelled words, write "correct."

1. Garlic mustard is a problm in the U.S. because it threatens other spring-bluming plants by taking up lite, nutrients, and espace.

____

____

____

2. Garlic mustard also thretens the West Virginia wite butterfly. It compeats with another type of mustard which is the butterfly's food sourse.

____

____

____

3. Garlic mustard was first grown on Long Island for food and has since spread to other areas of the country.

4. Childrens can learn new thins from TV.

5. The amownt of time spent waching TV is important.

6. More than three hours a day of TV watching results in louer reading and mathes test scors.

7. Surveys made at the end of an antiesmoking campane showed that more than 50% new about the campane and 40% would probably not smoke.

8. Three months later, the numbers had changed.

9. More than haf said they wood probaly smoke, and fewer than one-therd said they knew about the campaign.

____

____

____

10. Reserch showd that slow music coused customers to stay at the restarant longer and order more food.

____

____

____

11. Some of the study subjecs, college students, herd popular music in the store, and others heared older music.

____

____

____

12. Those who heard familiar music shoped longer and said better things about the store's products.

____

____

____

PRACTICE 5

Read the following essays. Then revise the essays, adding punctuation. Write on your computer or on a piece of paper.

ESSAY 1

Summarize the main points of the reading passage and explain how they are strengthened by the information presented in the lecture.

the author states that invasive plants harm native plants and the speaker explains that garlic mustard is an invasive species that causes problems.

gardeners have introduced nonnative plants for food and medicine. they have also planted them because they are hardy drought resistant or beautiful. however these plants escape from the garden and cause problems. invasive plants harm native species by shading them out strangling them or using up all the nutrients in the soil. the local ecology suffers because there are fewer native plants and animals lose their homes and food.

garlic mustard is an example of an invasive plant that harms the local ecology. it threatens other spring-blooming plants by taking up light nutrients and space. it also threatens the West Virginia white butterfly by competing with another type of mustard which is the butterfly's food source. garlic mustard was first grown on long island for food and has since spread to other areas of the country.

(based on Reading 1 and Lecture 1, page 35; see Summary 1 on page 54)

ESSAY 2

Summarize the main points in the reading passage and explain how the points made in the lecture oppose them.

the author believes that TV viewing has negative effects on children's school performance. The speaker on the other hand proposes that TV watching can actually improve school performance.

according to the author children who have TV sets in their bedrooms do not do as well in school as their classmates. some people think of TV as educational but the author asserts that most children's TV programs do not have "valuable content." in addition TV takes time away from important activities like doing homework or being with other people. parents can help their children by turning off the television.

the lecturer does not agree with this point of view. it is his opinion that children actually can learn new things from watching TV. he points out however that the amount of time spent watching TV is important. he says that more than three hours a day of TV watching can result in lower reading and math scores.

(based on Reading 2 and Lecture 2, page 35; see Summary 2 on page 55)

ESSAY 3

Summarize the main points in the reading passage and explain how the points made in the lecture cast doubt on them.

the author tells us about particular smoking prevention campaign aimed at young people that has been successful. in contrast the speaker warns us that initial results of public health campaigns can be misleading.

the antismoking campaign described in the passage included advertising no-smoking policies and antismoking events. many teens participated in the events and many more saw the ads. the public health department plans to continue with this successful campaign to improve public health among young people in the state.

the speaker warns us that we can be deceived by the initial results of public health campaigns He mentioned a recent antismoking campaign as an example. surveys made at the end of the campaign showed that 50% knew about the campaign and 40% would probably not smoke. three months later however the numbers had changed. many more said they would probably smoke and many fewer said they knew about the campaign. so a public health campaign that looks successful at first can look less successful a few months later.

(based on Reading 3 and Lecture 3, page 36; see Summary 3 on page 56)

ESSAY 4

Summarize the main points of the reading passage and explain how they are supported by the information presented in the lecture.

the author proposes that a good mood makes shoppers buy more. similarly the speaker explains that studies show that music can make consumers spend more time shopping.

the reading passage explains that a shopper's mood may be influenced by things that retailers cannot control such as the weather or personal or work problems. retailers can however influence shoppers' moods by controlling the store environment. shoppers buy more when retailers use lighting color and music to improve shopper mood.

the speaker describes research about the effect of music on consumers. research showed that slow music caused customers to stay at a restaurant longer and order more food. in another study some of the subjects college students heard popular music in a store and others heard older music. those who heard familiar music shopped longer and said better things about the store's products. these two studies show that restaurant and store owners can influence shoppers' moods and encourage them to buy more.

(based on Reading 4 and Lecture 4, page 36; see Summary 4 on page 57)

EXTRA PRACTICE

Study the model tasks on pages 58, 62, 63, and 64. Circle all the punctuation.

PRACTICE INTEGRATED TASK

Read the passage for three minutes.

Many people agree that the most important invention of the late twentieth century was the cell phone. Cell phones have now become a regular part of daily life. Cell phones have made many things much more convenient, but they have also brought new dangers to our lives.

Cell phone use has risen dramatically everywhere over the past several years. In the United States alone, just fifteen years ago, there were 4.3 million cell phone users. Today more than 224 million people use cell phones in this country. Everywhere we go—restaurants, stores, buses, parks, offices, schools—people are talking on their cell phones.

Cell phones have made many things more convenient for people, but they have also raised some serious safety concerns, most notably for drivers. Talking on the phone distracts the driver's attention from the road, and cell phones have been blamed for many traffic accidents. In several cases, drivers in accidents involving cell phones have been successfully sued by the victims. Employers have also been held liable for accidents involving cell phones and caused by their employees.

In response to such concerns, laws have been passed restricting cell phone use while driving. In some places, talking on the phone while driving is completely prohibited. In other places, use of a headset is required. Some places allow talking on the phone while driving but fine drivers responsible for crashes involving phones. In other places, drivers may lose their automobile insurance if they were talking on the phone when involved in an accident. In as many as 40 countries around the world, there are laws restricting or prohibiting the use of cell phones while driving.

Listen to the lecture.

Summarize the main points of the reading passage and explain how the points made in the lecture cast doubt on them. Write on your computer or on a piece of paper. Write for no more than 20 minutes.

Writing Skills: Independent Task

4

STEP 1: PLAN

Write a Thesis Statement

The Independent Task is different from the Integrated Task because it is more personal. In the Integrated Task, you write about other people's ideas, but in the Independent Task, you write about your own ideas. In the Independent Task, you are asked to explain your opinion about a subject. Your opinion about a subject is the thesis of your essay.

A good essay has a clearly stated thesis. A thesis statement focuses the direction of the topic and helps the reader understand what you want to say. It tells the reader what your essay is about.

Look at these example topics to see how different thesis statements can come from the same topic.

NOTE

Remember that a *thesis statement* is what you plan to write about—it is your main idea statement for the whole essay.

ESSAY TOPIC 33

You have been told that dormitory rooms at your university must be shared by two students. Would you rather have the university assign a student to share a room with you, or would you rather choose your own roommate? Use specific reasons and details to explain your answer.

Thesis Statement A

Since I would like to live with a neat and organized person like myself, I prefer to choose my own roommate.

From this statement, we can infer that the writer will discuss why he or she wants a neat and organized person as a roommate.

Thesis Statement B

The opportunity to meet new people is an important benefit of a university education, so I believe it is better to let the university choose my roommate for me.

From this statement, we can presume the writer will discuss the benefits of meeting new people at a university.

A thesis statement must be on the topic. Pay close attention to what the topic asks you to do.

ESSAY TOPIC 32

Some people think governments should spend as much money as possible exploring outer space (for example, traveling to the moon and to other planets). Other people disagree and think governments should spend this money for our basic needs on Earth. Which of these two opinions do you agree with? Use specific reasons and details to support your answer.

Thesis Statement A

The moon is a better place to explore because it is nearer than the planets.

This thesis statement is NOT a good thesis statement for this topic. It takes two of the words from the topic and writes about exploration possibilities. The topic, though, is how best to spend limited resources: on space exploration or on needs on Earth. This thesis statement is off topic.

Thesis Statement B

While there is still hunger, poverty, and illiteracy on Earth, our resources should be focused here and not in outer space.

From this statement, we can presume the writer will discuss why hunger, poverty, and illiteracy on earth are more worthy of attention than space exploration.

Thesis Statement C

Gaining psychological and scientific knowledge through space exploration will benefit us more than trying to solve problems here on Earth.

From this statement, we can presume the writer will discuss in detail the psychological and scientific benefits that we receive from space exploration.

PRACTICE 1

Choose the thesis statements that are appropriate to the topic. There can be more than one possible answer.

1. What is one of the most important decisions you have made? Why was this decision important? Use specific reasons and details to explain your answer.
   (A) Decisions are important because without them nothing would get done.
   (B) Deciding to leave home to attend school in the U.S. has been so far the most important decision I've made.
   (C) It is difficult to make important decisions, especially when you are young and have your whole future ahead of you.

2. Someone who was considered an educated person in the past (for example, in your parents' or grandparents' generation) would not be considered an educated person today. Do you agree or disagree? Use specific reasons and examples to support your answer.
   (A) If you define education as earning degrees, than I would have to agree that today people are more educated then they were in the past.
   (B) It was more difficult to get an education in the past since there weren't as many schools.
   (C) Both my grandfather and my grandmother attended university, which is where they met.

3. Many people visit museums when they travel to new places. Why do you think people visit museums? Use specific reasons and examples to support your answer.
   (A) New museums are opening in almost every city in the world.
   (B) When people travel to new places, they enjoy visiting interesting sites such as museums.
   (C) Travelers want to see in person famous works of art that they have only seen in books so they head to museums when in new cities.

4. In the future, students may have the choice of studying at home by using technology such as computers or television or of studying at traditional schools. Which would you prefer? Use reasons and specific details to explain your choice.
   (A) Interaction with my fellow students is important to me so I would prefer to study in a more traditional setting.
   (B) Computers and television are two examples of technology that will change a lot in the future.
   (C) Technological advances have already made home education a real possibility for many people.

5. In general, people are living longer now. How will this change affect society? Use specific details and examples to develop your essay.
   (A) People are living longer now because of improvements in medical care.
   (B) As the majority of our population becomes older, our communities will have to shift their focus from providing services to the young, like schools, to services to aging adults, like medical care.
   (C) Society has been around a long time and it is always changing.

EXTRA PRACTICE

Do any or all of the following activities on your own or in a group. There are no answers provided.

1. Write your own thesis statement for the five topics above.
2. Write essays on the above topics. Allow yourself no more than 30 minutes to write each essay. Write about 300 words.

Make Notes About General Ideas and Specific Details

In the Integrated Task, you make notes about what you read in the reading passage and what you hear in the lecture. Your notes are about other people's ideas. In the Independent Task, you write your own ideas about your own opinion. You make notes as a way of organizing your ideas before you write. When you wrote your thesis statement, you wrote your opinion about a subject. Now you will write notes about your ideas that explain your opinion.

Just as in the Integrated Task, you can use either an outline or an idea map to organize your ideas for the Independent Task. Both outlines and idea maps help you organize your thoughts into a thesis, topics (general ideas), and details (supporting statements). Use whichever form works best for you.

As a rule, you should try to have three general ideas per essay and at least two supporting details per general idea. This will vary according to your topic and the way you choose to organize it.

OUTLINES

Look at the following examples of outlines and essays for specific topics.

ESSAY TOPIC 52

The twentieth century saw great change. In your opinion, what is one change that should be remembered about the twentieth century? Use specific reasons and details to explain your choice.

Thesis	Medical advances are the most important change.	
Paragraph 1	**Main idea**	Vaccines and antibiotics have saved lives
	Supporting details	(1) Polio vaccine
		(2) Penicillin
Paragraph 2	**Main idea**	Increased access to health care
	Supporting details	(1) More clinics and hospitals
		(2) Easier to get treatment
Paragraph 3	**Main idea**	Improved surgical techniques
	Supporting details	(1) Microscopic and laser surgery easier to perform
		(2) Patients recover faster

Compare the outline with the following essay.

Medical Advances: An Important Change of the Twentieth Century

There were many important changes, both technological and cultural, during the twentieth century. In my opinion, the most important of these are the advances that were made in medical science. The development of vaccines and antibiotics, increased access to health care, and improvements in surgical techniques are all things that improved, and saved, the lives of people all around the world.

Vaccines and antibiotics have saved the lives of many people. Until the middle of the twentieth century, many people became crippled or died from polio. Now the polio vaccine is available everywhere. In the past, people could die from even simple infections. Now penicillin and other antibiotics make it easy to cure infections.

Increased access to health care has also improved the lives of millions of people. In the past, many people lived far from hospitals and clinics. Now hospitals, clinics, and health centers have been built in many parts of the world. More people have the opportunity to visit a doctor or nurse before they become very sick. They can be treated more easily. They are sick less, and this leads to a better quality of life.

Improved surgical techniques make it easier to treat many medical problems. Microscopic and laser surgery techniques are more efficient than older methods. It is easier for the doctor to perform them, and easier for the patient to recover. Surgery patients can return to their normal lives more quickly now than they could in the past.

Everybody needs good health in order to have a good quality of life. Advances in medical science have improved the lives of people all around the world. They are improvements that are important to everyone.

SAMPLE ESSAY TOPIC

Think of the most important class you have ever had. Why did you enjoy this class so much? Use specific reasons and details to explain your answer.

Thesis	I learned a lot in Intro. to Art History, and it was inspiring.	
Paragraph 1	**Main idea**	Art History teaches you about more than art.
	Supporting details	(1) History, religion, literature, mythology
		(2) I didn't learn these things in my engineering classes
Paragraph 2	**Main idea**	I had a very good teacher.
	Supporting details	(1) Experienced and well known
		(2) Enthusiastic and inspiring
Paragraph 3	**Main idea**	I learned about the history of engineering.
	Supporting details	(1) Buildings and bridges
		(2) City planning

Compare the outline with the following essay.

Art History

Even though I am an engineer, I have to say that Introduction to Art History is the most important class I have ever taken. In this class I had the opportunity to learn new things, not only about art, but about other areas as well. I had a teacher who inspired me. And, believe it or not, it was important to my career as an engineer.

The course not only had interesting content but also a very inspiring teacher. My art history professor had a lot of enthusiasm for her subject, and she was able to convey that enthusiasm to her students. Even though I am in a different field, this professor was a sort of role model for me. It is always inspiring to see people who love their work, no matter what it is. As I pursue my career as an engineer, I often think of this professor and hope that I bring the same enthusiasm to my own work.

Art History should be a required course for everyone because it teaches you about so many things. I learned not only about art, but also about history, religion, literature, and mythology. These are subjects I didn't learn about in my engineering classes, so it was a wonderful opportunity for me.

NOTE

Because the Independent Tasks are personal in nature, the sample responses include some contractions.

Studying art history taught me some things about the history of engineering. In old paintings, I saw how buildings and bridges were built in the past. I saw how cities were planned. I realized that I could learn about my own field in different ways.

I learned a lot of things in my art history class. I learned about art, about engineering, and about other things I hadn't imagined. Both the subject and the teacher inspired me to expand my mind. I am very glad that I took this class.

PRACTICE 2

Read each essay. Then complete the missing parts of each outline.

ESSAY TOPIC 30

Some people prefer to live in places that have the same weather or climate all year long. Others like to live in areas where the weather changes several times a year. Which do you prefer? Use specific reasons and examples to support your choices.

If I could choose a place to live according to climate alone, I would definitely live in a place that has warm weather all year. It would make my life much easier and more comfortable. I would be healthier, have more fun, and save money if I lived in a warm climate.

I would always be healthy if I lived in a warm climate. Where I live now the winters are long and cold, so I get sick every winter. I often miss days of school because I get bad colds. I wouldn't have this problem in a warm climate. Also, in a warm climate I would be able to be outside all year long. I would play sports and get exercise everyday. That would make me healthier, too.

I would have more fun if I lived in a warm climate. I really enjoy outdoor activities such as going to the beach, playing soccer, and riding my bicycle. I can't do these things when the weather is cold, which means I can't do them at all during the winter in a cold climate. In a warm climate, I would be able to enjoy my favorite activities all year.

I would save money if I lived in a warm climate. It costs money to heat the house during cold winters, and this can get very expensive. In a warm climate I would not have to worry about this expense. It also costs money to buy new clothes every time the season changes. This is another expense I wouldn't have to worry about in a warm climate because I could wear the same clothes all year.

My life would be better if I lived in a warm climate. My health, my free time activities, and my bank account would all improve. In fact, I plan to move to a warm climate as soon as I finish school.

Thesis	I prefer to live in a warm climate.	
Paragraph 1	**Main idea**	(1) ____________________
	Supporting details	Now I get sick every winter
		I could be outside all year
Paragraph 2	**Main idea**	I would have more fun.
	Supporting details	(2) ____________________
		Favorite activities all year
Paragraph 3	**Main idea**	I would save money.
	Supporting details	(3) ____________________
		No need to buy new clothes

ESSAY TOPIC 34

Some people like doing work by hand. Others prefer using machines. Which do you prefer? Use specific reasons and examples to support your answer.

I prefer using machines to doing work by hand. Machines can work faster than I can work by hand. They can also work more neatly. Most of all, machines never get tired.

Machines are fast. If I want to make a dress, it would take me hours and hours working with a needle and thread to make each stitch by hand. If I use a sewing machine, however, I can make a dress in an hour or less. If I want to build something out of wood, I could cut each piece with a handsaw. That would take a very long time. But a power saw cuts much more quickly. When I bake a cake, I can stir in each ingredient by hand, or I can use an electric mixer, which makes the work go so much faster.

Machines are neat. They never make mistakes. Every line or cut is neat, straight, and in the right place. Machines don't get distracted and spill coffee all over the work or cut something the wrong size or add the wrong ingredients. Machines can do the same job over and over again, each time as neatly as the time before. I could never be as neat as a machine.

Machines never get tired. I can use my sewing machine to sew one seam or ten. The machine never gets tired of pushing the needle and thread through the fabric. The power saw doesn't slow down because it has cut too many pieces of wood. A machine keeps working with the same amount of energy until the job is done, and doesn't even need to stop for a rest break.

I can depend on machines to do the job right each time, but I can't always depend on myself to be fast, neat, and tireless.

Paragraph 1	**Main idea**	Machines are fast.
	Supporting details	Sew a dress
		Build with wood
		(4) ______
Paragraph 2	**Main idea**	(5) ______
	Supporting details	No mistakes
		Not distracted
		All jobs neat
Paragraph 3	**Main idea**	Machines don't get tired.
	Supporting details	Sewing machines
		(6) ______

NOTE

In the Independent Task essay, there is no right or wrong opinion. The task measures your ability to express your opinion in writing, to explain your opinions clearly, and to back your opinion with supporting details.

PRACTICE 3

Create an outline for each of the following topics. Photocopy the blank outline on this page as many times as you need and use the copies for writing your outlines. You may have two or more main ideas for each topic and two or more supporting details for each main idea. Then write an essay from each of your outlines. Allow yourself no more than 30 minutes to write. Write about 300 words. Compare your essays with the essays for those topics in the Model Essay section beginning on page 163.

Thesis	______	
Paragraph 1	**Main idea**	______
	Supporting details	(1) ______
		(2) ______
		(3) ______
Paragraph 2	**Main idea**	______
	Supporting details	(1) ______
		(2) ______
		(3) ______
Paragraph 3	**Main idea**	______
	Supporting details	(1) ______
		(2) ______
		(3) ______

ESSAY TOPIC 7

Do you agree or disagree with the following statement? Universities should give the same amount of money to their students' sports activities as they give to their university libraries. Use specific reasons and examples to support your opinion.

ESSAY TOPIC 6

Some people prefer to live in a small town. Others prefer to live in a big city. Which place would you prefer to live in? Use specific reasons and details to support your answer.

ESSAY TOPIC 5

How do movies or television influence people's behavior? Use reasons and specific examples to explain your answer.

ESSAY TOPIC 49

Imagine that you have received some land to use as you wish. How would you use this land? Use specific details to explain your answer.

Idea Maps

Look at the following examples of idea maps and essays for specific topics.

SAMPLE ESSAY TOPIC

When choosing a place to live, what do you consider most important—location, size, style, number of rooms, types of rooms, or other features? Use reasons and specific examples to support your answer.

Idea Map

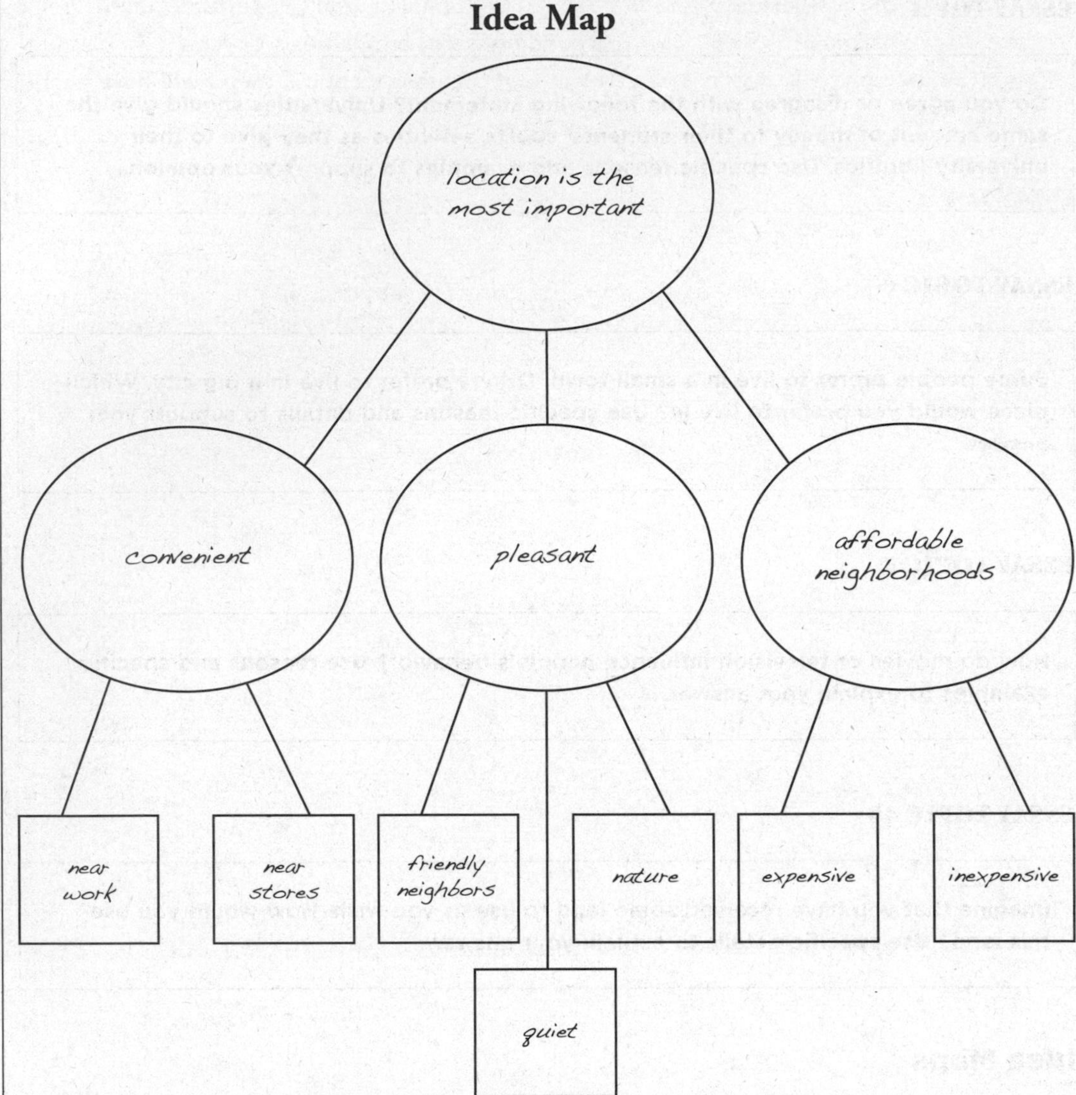

Compare the idea map with this essay.

House Hunting

When choosing a place to live, I look at several things. I need to consider price, size, and type of housing. However, the most important thing of all is location. I look for a house in a convenient and pleasant neighborhood that has rents I can afford to pay.

My apartment must be conveniently located. I don't have a car, so I want to be near my job. I want to be able to walk or take the bus to work. I don't have a lot of time for shopping, so I want to be near stores, too.

I want to live in a pleasant neighborhood. I like quiet areas with little traffic. I like to have nature around me, so I prefer a neighborhood with a lot of trees, gardens, and maybe even a park. Most of all, I want to have friendly neighbors.

Some neighborhoods are more expensive than others. I have to look for my apartment in neighborhoods that aren't too expensive. Some neighborhoods are very beautiful, but if the rents are too high, I can't afford to live there. If I only look in areas of the city that have affordable rents, I won't be disappointed.

The size of my apartment and the style of the building aren't important to me. I don't care if my apartment is small or if the building is old and in need of repair. If I can find an affordable place to live in a convenient and pleasant location, then I will have everything I need.

ESSAY TOPIC 1

People attend college or university for many different reasons. Why do you think people attend college or university? Use specific reasons and examples to support your answer.

Idea Map

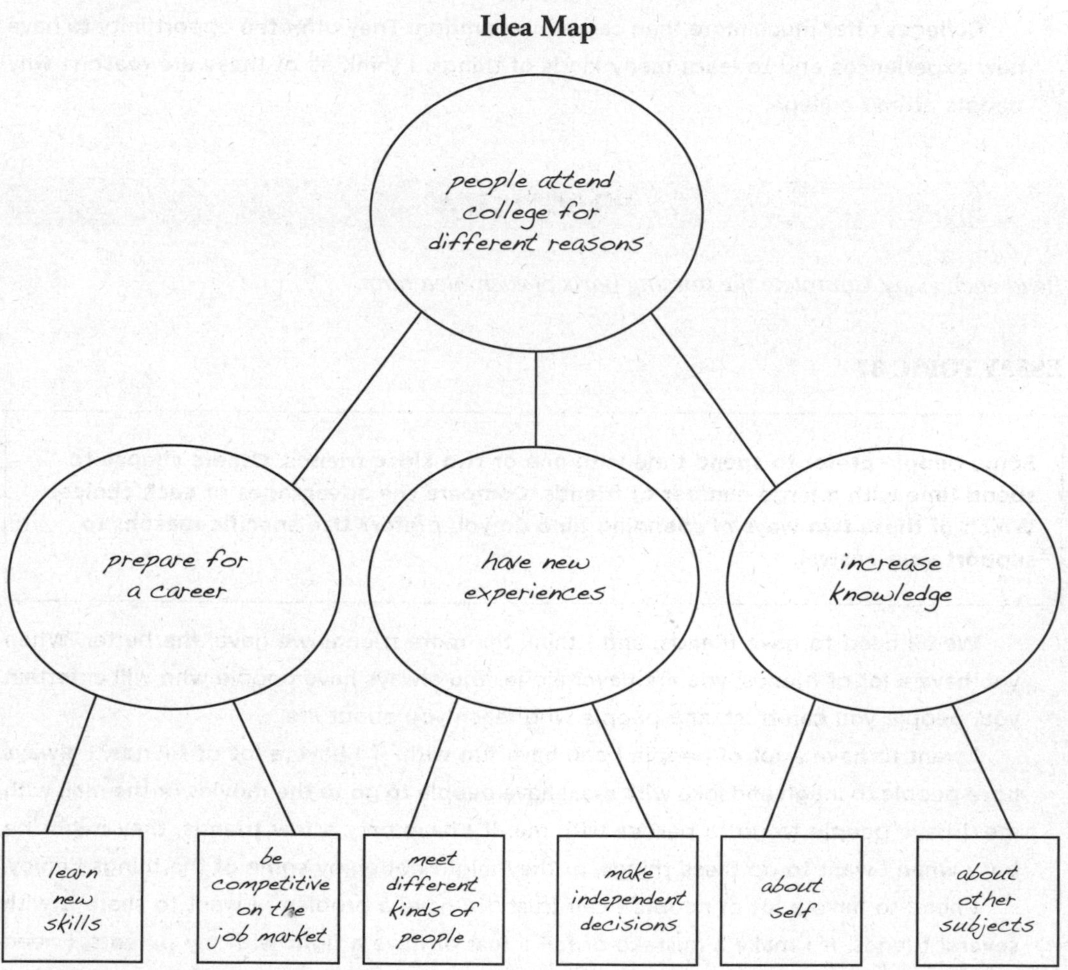

Compare the idea map with this essay.

Three Reasons People Attend College

People attend college for a lot of different reasons. I believe that the three most common reasons are to prepare for a career, to have new experiences, and to increase their knowledge of themselves and of the world around them.

Career preparation is probably the primary reason that people attend college. These days, the job market is very competitive. Careers such as information technology will need many new workers in the near future. At college, students can learn new skills for these careers and increase their opportunities for the future.

Students also go to college to have new experiences. For many, it is their first time away from home. At college, they can meet new people from many different places. They can see what life is like in a different city. They can learn to live on their own and take care of themselves without having their family always nearby.

At college, students have the opportunity to increase their knowledge. As they decide what they want to study, pursue their studies, and interact with their classmates, they learn a lot about themselves. They also, of course, have the opportunity to learn about many subjects in their classes. In addition to the skills and knowledge related to their career, college students also have the chance to take classes in other areas. For many, this will be their last chance to study different subjects.

Colleges offer much more than career preparation. They offer the opportunity to have new experiences and to learn many kinds of things. I think all of these are reasons why people attend college.

PRACTICE 4

Read each essay. Complete the missing parts of each idea map.

ESSAY TOPIC 37

Some people prefer to spend time with one or two close friends. Others choose to spend time with a large number of friends. Compare the advantages of each choice. Which of these two ways of spending time do you prefer? Use specific reasons to support your answer.

We all need to have friends, and I think the more friends we have, the better. When you have a lot of friends, you are never alone. You always have people who will entertain you, people you can trust, and people who teach you about life.

I want to have a lot of people I can have fun with. If I have a lot of friends, I always have people to laugh and joke with me. I have people to go to the movies or the mall with me. I have people to go to parties with me. If I have only a few friends, they might be busy when I want to do these things, or they might not enjoy some of the things I enjoy.

I need to have a lot of people I can trust. If I have a problem, I want to share it with several friends. If I make a mistake or fail a test or have a fight with my parents, I need my friends to help me. I want to be able to pick up the phone and know I can easily find some friends to talk with. If I have only a few friends, they might not be available when I need them.

I like to have a lot of people who teach me about life. If I have a lot of friends, I have a lot of different people to learn from. Each person has different experiences and a different point of view. I can learn a lot of things from a lot of different people. If I have only a few friends, I will see only a few points of view.

I like to have a lot of friends around me. I like to have fun with them and to learn from them and to know that I can rely on them. My life is better because of all the friends I have.

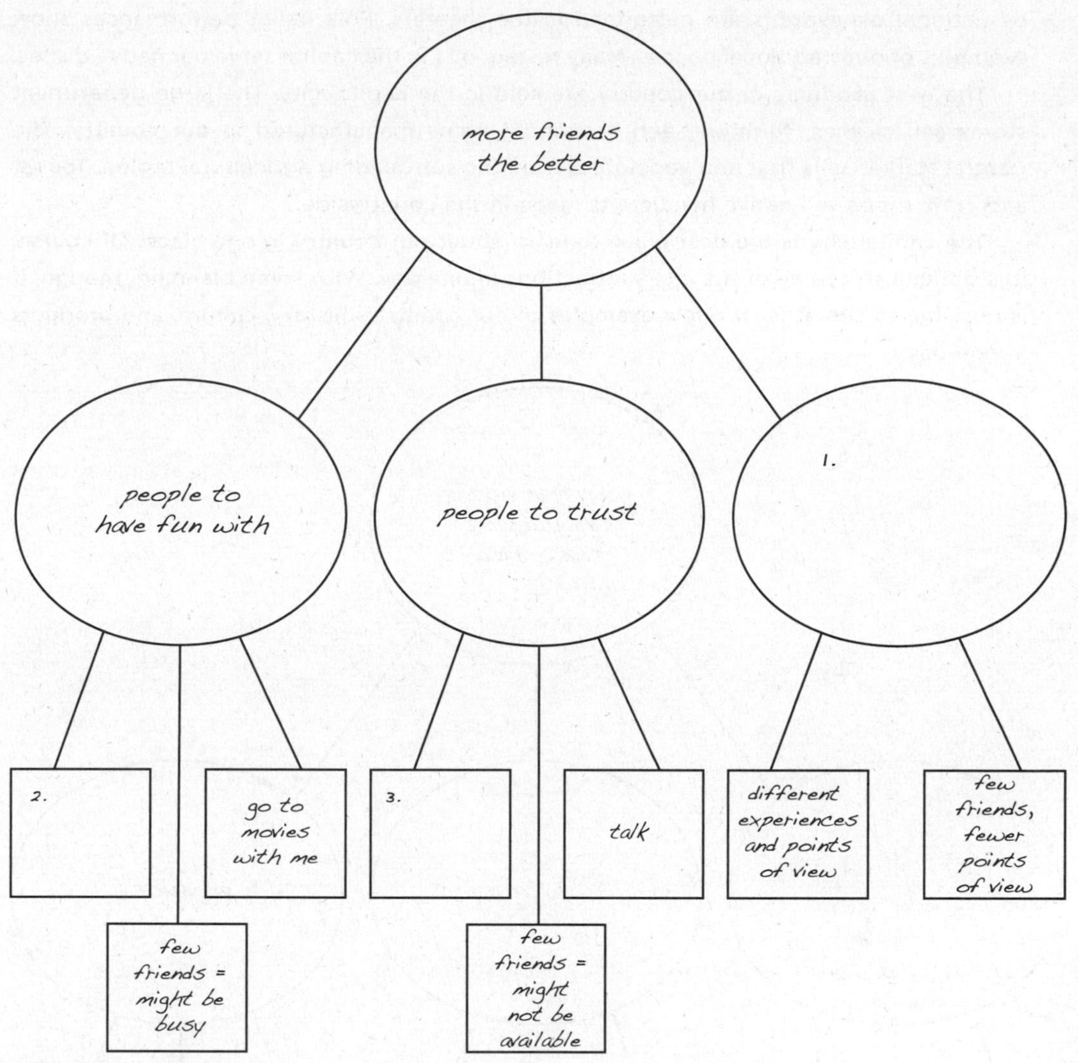

ESSAY TOPIC 29

A foreign visitor has only one day to spend in your country. Where should this visitor go on that day? Why? Use specific reasons and details to support your choice.

A foreign visitor with only one day to spend in my country should definitely spend that day in the capital. Spending time in the capital is the easiest way to see many aspects of our country in one place. In this city, the visitor can learn about our history, see examples of our culture, and buy our best products.

Our country's history is represented in several ways throughout the city. In the Government Palace, a visitor can learn about the history of our independence. In our National Museum, a visitor can see exhibits that show all the different stages of our history, from ancient times to the present. In parks all around the city, a visitor can see monuments to famous historical people and events.

It is also possible to see different representations of our culture throughout the city. Our art museums and galleries show paintings and sculptures by our artists. Plays written by national playwrights are performed in the theaters. Folk ballet performances show examples of our traditional dances. Many restaurants in the capital serve our native dishes.

The best products of our country are sold in the capital city. The large department stores sell clothes, furniture, and household items manufactured in our country. The Central Market sells fruit and vegetables from the surrounding agricultural region. Tourist and craft shops sell native handicrafts made in the countryside.

The capital city is the best place to learn about our country in one place. Of course, it is difficult to see all of the city's attractions in one day. With some planning, though, it is possible to see at least a few examples of our country's history, culture, and products in one day.

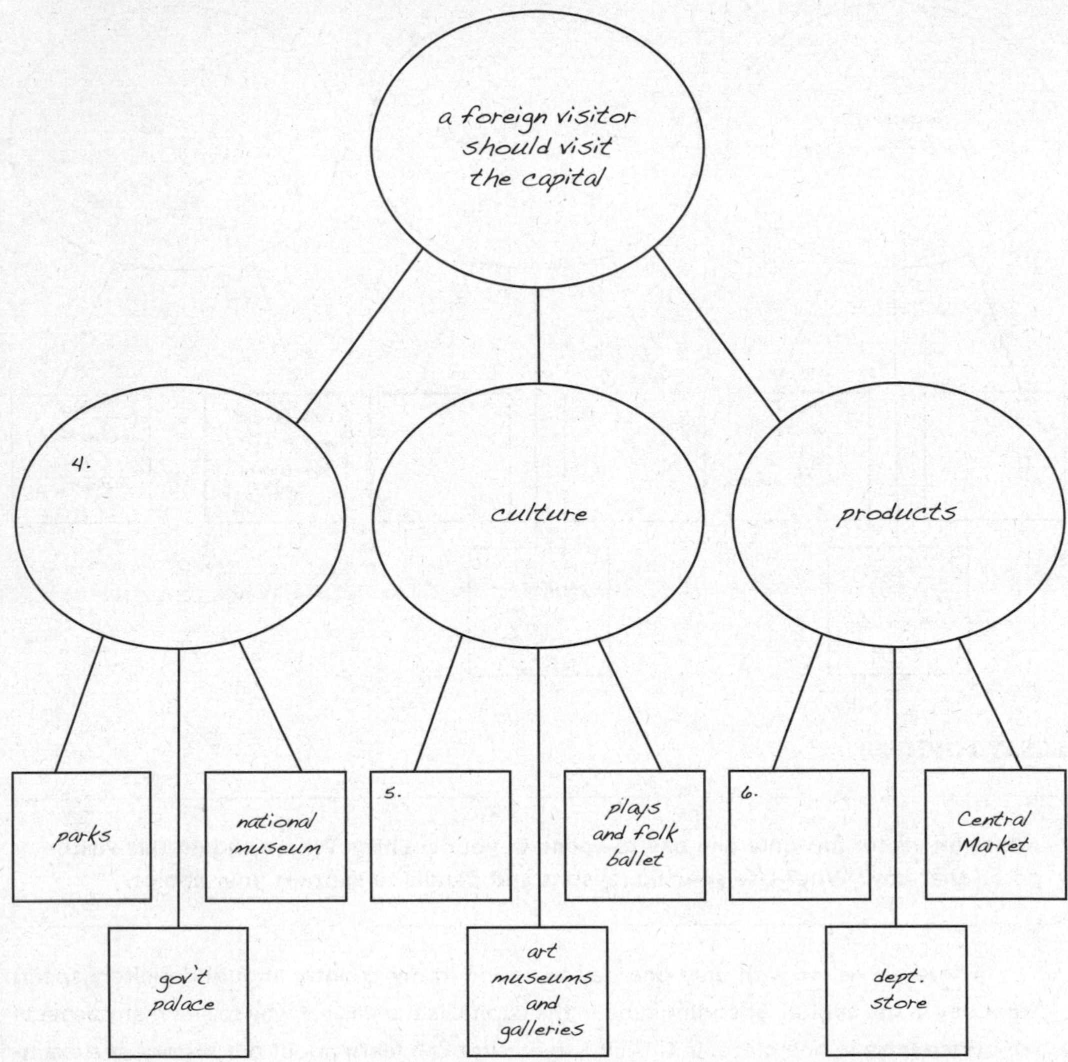

PRACTICE 5

Create an idea map for each of the following topics. Photocopy the blank idea map on this page as many times as you need and use the copies for making your idea maps. You may not need all parts of the map for every topic. Then write an essay from each of your idea maps. Allow yourself no more than 30 minutes to write. Write about 300 words. Compare your essays with the essays for those topics in the Model Essay section beginning on page 163.

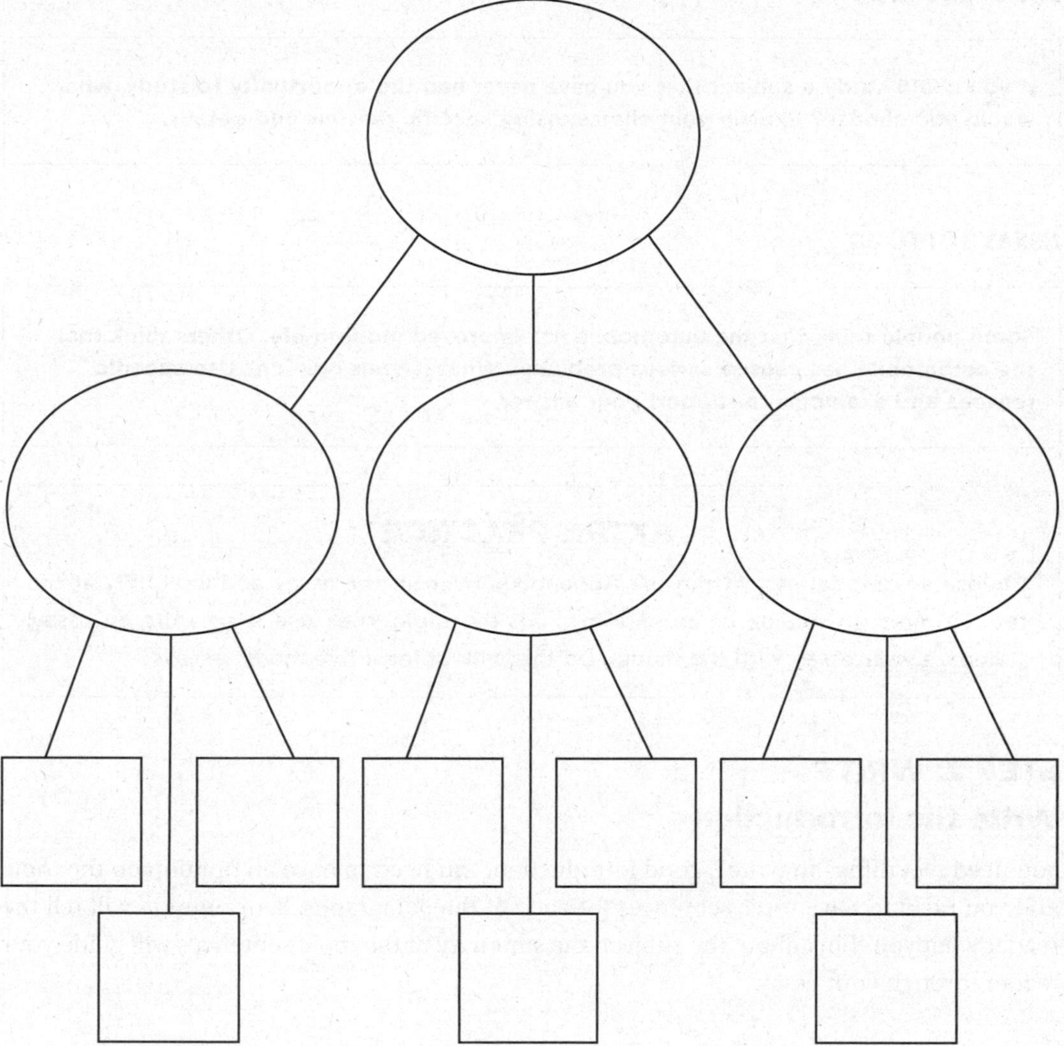

ESSAY TOPIC 42

Do you agree or disagree with the following statement? It is more important for students to study history and literature than it is for them to study science and mathematics. Use specific reasons and examples to support your opinion.

ESSAY TOPIC 50

> **In some countries, people are no longer allowed to smoke in many public places and office buildings. Do you think this is a good rule or a bad rule? Use specific reasons and details to support your position.**

ESSAY TOPIC 24

> **If you could study a subject that you have never had the opportunity to study, what would you choose? Explain your choice, using specific reasons and details.**

ESSAY TOPIC 25

> **Some people think that the automobile has improved modern life. Others think that the automobile has caused serious problems. What is your opinion? Use specific reasons and examples to support your answer.**

EXTRA PRACTICE

Choose any model essay from the Appendix. Cover up the essay and look only at the topic. Create an outline or an idea map for the topic, then use it to write an essay. Compare your essay with the model. Do this with at least five model essays.

STEP 2: WRITE

Write the Introduction

You need two things to write a good introduction. You need to have an opinion on the topic and you need to have topic sentences for each of the paragraphs. Your opinion will tell the reader what you think about the subject; the summary of the topic sentences will guide your reader through your essay.

STATE YOUR OPINION

The introduction to your essay should tell the reader what your opinion is on the topic. The Independent Task is a personal essay. Your ideas on a topic are important. The readers are interested in what you have to say. There is, however, no right or wrong opinion. The readers look to see how you express your opinion, whatever it is.

You can express your opinion by using set phrases or by varying the verbs, adjectives, and adverbs you use. On the Independent Task, you must show a variety in your vocabulary and expression as well as your sentence types to score high. This section will help you give your writing more variety.

Here are some examples of set phrases that you can use to express your opinion.

SET PHRASES

In my opinion	It is my opinion that
	I believe
To my way of thinking	I think
In my view	It seems to me that
To me	It appears that
From my point of view	To my mind

EXAMPLES

In my opinion, university students must attend classes.
From my point of view, one must change with the times.
To me, there is nothing more important than good health.

It is my opinion that one learns by example.
It seems to me that a good neighbor is one who respects your privacy.
It appears that all the information one needs is available on computer.

PRACTICE 1

Give your opinion about these topics. Use the phrases suggested.

1. People's lives (are/are not) easier today.
   In my opinion, people's lives are easier today.
2. Most people (prefer/do not prefer) to spend their leisure time outdoors.
   It seems to me that, ______________________________
3. An apartment building (is/is not) better than a house.
   To my mind, ______________________________
4. It (is/is not) good that English is becoming the world language.
   From my point of view, ______________________________

Verbs

You can use different verbs to show how strongly you feel about something. *Believe* and *think* are the most common verbs used to express a personal opinion.

agree	realize
believe	suppose
guess	think
hope	understand
imagine	

EXAMPLES

I agree that studying science is more important than studying literature.

I hope that people remember the special gifts I gave them.

I realize that most young people feel they have nothing to learn from older people.

I understand why people like to work with their hands.

PRACTICE 2

Give your opinion about these topics. Use the verbs suggested.

1. High schools (should/should not) allow students to study what they want.
   I believe that ______________________________
2. It is better to be a (leader/member) of a group.
   I guess that ______________________________
3. People (should/should not) do things they do not enjoy doing.
   I agree that ______________________________
4. I would rather have the university (assign/not assign) me a roommate.
   I suppose that ______________________________

EXTRA PRACTICE

Read the introductions to some of the model essays in the Appendix. Look for examples of the verbs in the box on page 95. Find at least ten examples.

Adjectives

You can use different adjectives to show how strongly you feel about something.

certain	positive
convinced	sure

EXAMPLES

I am certain that movies influence people's behavior.

I am convinced that having a pet can contribute to a child's development.

PRACTICE 3

Give your opinion about these topics. Use the adjectives suggested.

1. Children (should/should not) spend a great amount of time practicing sports.
   I am sure that ______________________________
2. A shopping center in my neighborhood (will/will not) be a benefit to our community.
   I am positive that ______________________________

Adverb Phrases

You can use different adverb phrases to qualify your opinion. These adverb phrases show how strongly you feel about something.

NOT VERY STRONGLY	SOMEWHAT STRONGLY	VERY STRONGLY
apparently	probably	certainly
conceivably	presumably	undoubtedly
possibly	likely	definitely
perhaps		surely
maybe		
supposedly		

EXAMPLES

Presumably, playing games can teach us about life.

Daily exercise definitely should be a part of every school day.

Undoubtedly, helping a child to learn to read is important.

Individual sports are possibly better than team sports for some students.

PRACTICE 4

Give your opinion about these topics. Use the adverb phrases suggested.

1. A zoo (has/does not have) a useful purpose.
   Maybe, ______________________________
2. The city/countryside is a better place to grow up.
   Probably, ______________________________
3. Our generation (is/is not) different from that of our parents.
   Certainly, ______________________________
4. A sense of humor can sometimes be (helpful/detrimental) in a difficult situation.
   Surely, ______________________________

You can use different adverb phrases to make a general statement about how you feel about something.

all in all	basically	generally
all things considered	by and large	in general
altogether	essentially	on the whole
as a rule	for the most part	overall

EXAMPLES

All in all, it is better to learn from a teacher than on your own.

As a rule, it is better for students to wear uniforms to school.

For the most part, countries are more alike than different.

On the whole, higher education should be available to all.

PRACTICE 5

Give your opinion about these topics. Use the adverb phrases suggested to make a general statement.

1. The family (is/is not) the most important influence on young adults.
   All things considered, ______________________________
2. Parents (are/are not) the best teachers.
   In general, ______________________________
3. People (are never/are sometimes) too old to attend college.
   By and large, ______________________________

You can use different adverb phrases to qualify your opinion. These adverb phrases show an idea is not completely true.

for all intents and purposes	to some extent
in a sense	up to a point
in a way	

EXAMPLES

Up to a point, people succeed because of hard work, not because of luck.

For all intents and purposes, television has destroyed communication among family members.

PRACTICE 6

Give your opinion about these topics. Use the adverb phrases suggested to show an idea is not completely true.

1. It is better to make a wrong decision than to make no decision.

   or

   It is better to make no decision than to make a wrong decision.

   In a way, ______________________________

2. Watching movies (is/is not) more enjoyable than reading.

   To some extent, ______________________________

3. You (can/cannot) learn as much by losing as winning.

   In a sense, ______________________________

Guide the Reader

The introduction to your essay should also tell the reader how you plan to develop your topic. The topic sentences that you develop from your outline or idea map should be summarized in the introduction.

Compare these introductions.

INTRODUCTION TO TOPIC 1

Version A

I believe that people attend college for many different reasons. These reasons are personal to them.

Version B

People attend colleges or universities for a lot of different reasons. I believe that the three most common reasons are to prepare for a career, to have new experiences, and to increase their knowledge of themselves and the world around them.

Comment

Version A starts with the writer's opinion, but it does not tell us much. What are these reasons? We need to know the basic reasons so we can prepare ourselves to find supporting details in the body of the essay.

Version B gives three specific reasons that the writer believes are the most important ones: to prepare for a career, to have new experiences, and to increase their knowledge of themselves and the world around them. From this introduction, we will expect to see one paragraph for each of these three reasons.

INTRODUCTION TO TOPIC 4

Version A

I think there are changes necessary in my hometown. It is always the same. There has to be something different.

Version B

If I could change one thing about my hometown I think it would be the fact that there's no sense of community here. People don't feel connected, they don't look out for each other, and they don't get to know their neighbors.

Comment

Version A starts with the writer's opinion but doesn't say what changes are necessary. We need some guidance.

Version B narrows in on the topic and talks about the sense of community. The writer says that "People don't feel connected, they don't look out for each other, and they don't get to know their neighbors." From this introduction, we will expect to see one paragraph for each of these three reasons.

INTRODUCTION TO TOPIC 9

Version A

I believe that some people like to eat at food stands, and some like to eat in restaurants. There are different reasons for this.

Version B

Some people like to eat out at food stands and restaurants, while others like to prepare food at home. Often it depends on the kind of lifestyle people have. Those with very busy jobs outside the house don't always have time to cook. They like the convenience of eating out. Overall, though, I think it is cheaper and healthier to eat at home.

Comment

In Version A, the writer does not share what these reasons are. There are no general statements.

In Version B, the writer tells us that the choice depends on a person's lifestyle. The writer will probably give us more details about the reasons of convenience, costs, and health.

TIP

For extra practice, choose five model essays from the Appendix and analyze the introductions in the same way: identify the writer's opinion and the focus of each paragraph.

PRACTICE 7

Read the following introductions and tell us what the writer believes and the focus of each paragraph. You might not have three paragraphs for all introductions.

1. **Introduction to Topic 37**

   We all need to have friends, and I think the more friends we have, the better. Friendship helps us learn how to trust others, it helps us know what to expect from others, and it helps us profit from experiences. I want to have a lot of friends around me so I can learn more about myself from different people.

   Opinion: I think the more friends we have, the better

   Paragraph focus: learn how to trust others

   Paragraph focus: learn what to expect from others

   Paragraph focus: helps us profit from experiences

2. **Introduction to Topic 48**

Almost everyone, whether child or adult, loves games. The types of games we like may change as we grow up, but our enjoyment of them never does. I believe that playing games is both fun and useful because it teaches us the skills we need in life. Games teach us about cause and effect relationships, teamwork, and following rules.

Opinion: ______________________________

Paragraph focus: ______________________________

Paragraph focus: ______________________________

Paragraph focus: ______________________________

3. **Introduction to Topic 38**

Although friends make an impression on your life, they do not have the same influence that your family has. Nothing is as important to me as my family. From them, I learned everything that is important. I learned about trust, ambition, and love.

Opinion: ______________________________

Paragraph focus: ______________________________

Paragraph focus: ______________________________

Paragraph focus: ______________________________

4. **Introduction to Topic 36**

There are people who say they prefer to be alone, but I cannot understand this. I always choose to spend time with friends whenever possible because friends bring so much to my life. They keep me company, they are enjoyable to talk with, and they teach me new things. I cannot imagine my life without them.

Opinion: ______________________________

Paragraph focus: ______________________________

Paragraph focus: ______________________________

Paragraph focus: ______________________________

5. **Introduction to Topic 21**

Traveling alone is the only way to travel. If you take someone with you, you take your home with you. When you travel alone, you meet new people, have new experiences, and learn more about yourself.

Opinion: ______________________________

Paragraph focus: ______________________________

Paragraph focus: ______________________________

Paragraph focus: ______________________________

EXTRA PRACTICE

Choose any model essay from the Appendix. Cover up the first paragraph and read the rest of the essay and the topic. Use these as a basis to write your own introduction for the essay. Then, uncover the first paragraph and see how it compares with yours. Do this with at least five model essays.

Write the Paragraphs

Once you have stated your opinion and shown the reader how you plan to develop your essay, the rest is easy. You simply turn the supporting details in your outline or idea map into sentences. Of course, you must make sure your sentences are written correctly, and you must show variety in your vocabulary and sentence types. (See Part 4, Writing Skills—Both Tasks for further practice with sentence writing.)

Look at these examples of how an outline and an idea map become paragraphs.

Sample 1

Paragraph 3 from Essay Topic 47

Paragraph 3	**Main idea**	The foreign language program needs well-trained instructors.
	Supporting details	(1) Current teachers don't speak well (2) Teachers make frequent errors (3) Well-trained teachers are good models

The foreign language program should be staffed with well-trained instructors. The current teachers in the program don't speak the language well enough. In our classes, teachers frequently make errors that the students repeat. If the teachers were well trained, they would be good models for the students.

Sample 2

Paragraph 2 from Essay Topic 43

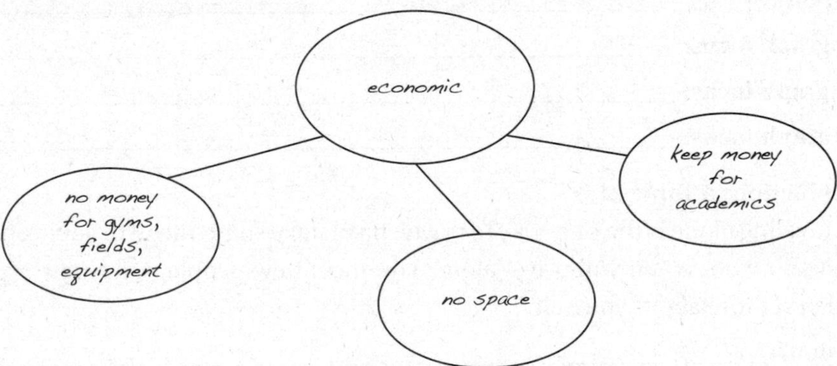

Another issue is economic. Many schools simply do not have the money to provide gym facilities, playing fields, and athletic equipment for their students. Other schools are located in cities where that kind of space just isn't available. A few schools would rather keep money for academic purposes.

PRACTICE 8

Look at the following outlines and idea maps. Use each one to write a paragraph on a separate piece of paper or on your computer. Compare your paragraphs with the cited paragraphs for those topics in the Model Essay section beginning on page 163 of the Appendix.

Paragraph 3 from Essay Topic 9

Main idea Eating at home is better than eating at restaurants.

Supporting details
(1) Restaurant meals high in fat and calories
(2) At home you control ingredients
(3) Restaurants big plates of food
(4) At home you control portion size

Paragraph 4 from Essay Topic 31

Main idea A good roommate is fun.

Supporting details
(1) invites you to parties and concerts
(2) introduces you to friends
(3) plans free time activities with you

Paragraph 3 from Essay Topic 56

Main idea Loving a pet can interfere with relationships with people.

Supporting details
(1) neglect spouse and children
(2) lose interest in making friends
(3) less complicated than relationships with people

Paragraph 2 from Essay Topic 14

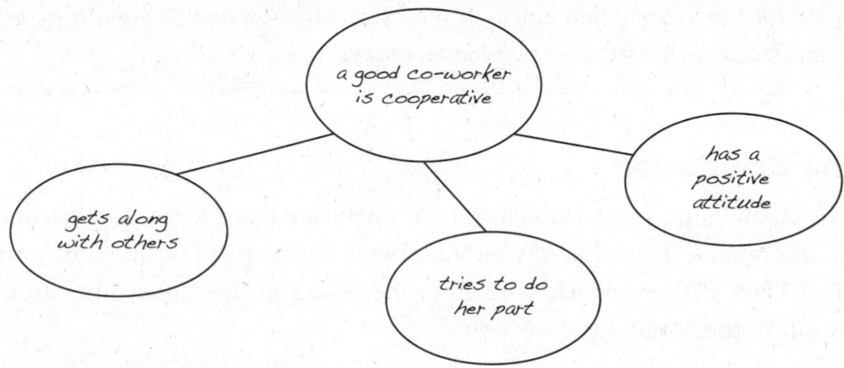

Paragraph 2 from Essay Topic 26

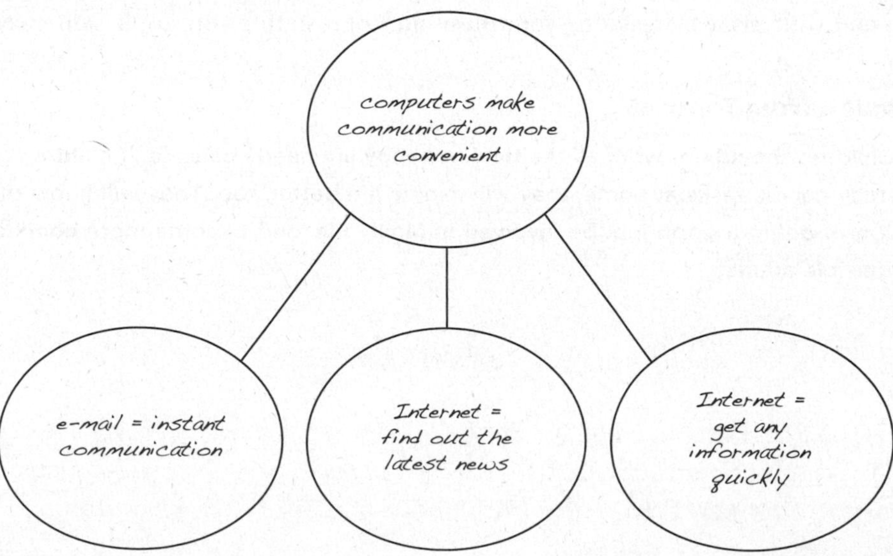

Paragraph 2 from Essay Topic 53

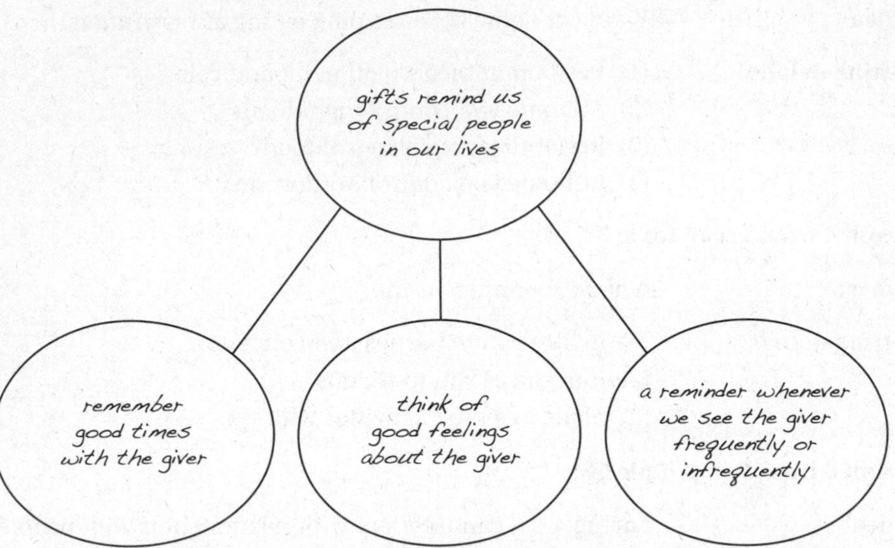

EXTRA PRACTICE

Choose any model essay from the Appendix. Cover up the main part of the essay and read only the topic and the introduction. Use these as a basis to write your own body paragraphs for the essay. Then, uncover the essay and see how it compares with your paragraphs. Do this with at least five model essays.

Write the Conclusion

A good essay should have a good conclusion. A conclusion has a few sentences that support your thesis and remind the reader of your intentions. There are a few different ways to write a conclusion. Look at these conclusions from the essays in this book. You can review the complete essay in the Model Essay section.

RESTATEMENT

You can end your essay by restating your thesis and/or restating your topic sentences.

Conclusion from Topic 45

Children should not work all the time. A happy life needs balance. If children can successfully handle tasks at home, they will handle life better, too. They will know the satisfaction of doing a good job, be involved in family life, and become more confident and responsible adults.

GENERALIZATION

You can use all the information you provided and make a generalization about it.

Conclusion from Topic 39

All things considered, I think I'd like to have a lot of acquaintances who are different and a few close friends who are similar to me. That seems to be the best of both worlds.

PREDICTION

You can summarize the information you provided and point the reader toward the next logical step.

Conclusion from Topic 16

I believe that a new movie theater is a fine idea. I support it because of the changes it will bring to our citizens and our town. I believe that the reduction in crime, the increase in employment, and the improved infrastructure will make our town a nicer place to live.

QUESTION

You can conclude with a question that does not need an answer. This is called a rhetorical question. The answer is contained in the question.

Conclusion from Topic 2

The most important thing to realize is that we all have many teachers in our lives. Where would we be without our parents, teachers, and our peers to guide us? What would we do without books, newspapers, and television to inform us? All of them are very valuable.

RECOMMENDATION

You can urge your readers to do something with the information you provided.

Conclusion from Topic 9

Both eating at restaurants and cooking at home can be satisfying. Both can taste good and be enjoyed with family and friends. I prefer cooking at home, because of the money and health issues. I encourage my friends to eat out less, but it's up to them to make the choice that fits their lifestyles best.

NOTE

Your conclusion does not have to be long. Two or three sentences may be enough for your summary.

PRACTICE 9

What kind of a conclusion is each of these sentences or paragraphs? Refer to the whole essay, in the Appendix, beginning on page 163, to help you decide.

1. Conclusion from Topic 20

If you give up, you might as well die. My advice is to always look for another opportunity, another goal, or another option. There is always something else. Don't give up.

(A) Restatement
(B) Generalization
(C) Prediction
(D) Question
(E) Recommendation

2. Conclusion from Topic 40

Clothes don't change you into a different person, but they can make you behave differently. If you are dressed inappropriately for a situation, people will react to you in a different way. This reaction can, in turn, change your behavior. If you want good reactions from people, make sure to dress appropriately for every situation.

(A) Restatement
(B) Generalization
(C) Prediction
(D) Question
(E) Recommendation

3. Conclusion from Topic 15

On the whole, though, I think my neighborhood should support having a shopping center built here. It would bring more variety to our shopping, give us the opportunity to amuse ourselves at movie theaters and restaurants, and bring more jobs into the area.

(A) Restatement
(B) Generalization
(C) Prediction
(D) Question
(E) Recommendation

4. Conclusion from Topic 41

If we all based our final opinion of others on first impressions, it would be hard to get to know anyone. We would probably miss many opportunities to make good friends. Isn't it important to give everyone the chance to show us who they really are? And don't you want other people to do the same for you?

(A) Restatement
(B) Generalization
(C) Prediction
(D) Question
(E) Recommendation

5. **Conclusion from Topic 18**

The more I moved the more I would experience change. I would meet new people in every place I lived; I could move to sample countries with four seasons or even a continent like Antarctica, which only has two. Wherever I lived, I would experience living in housing particular to that area. I would then be a citizen of the world, wouldn't I? Could you call me a foreigner if I called everyplace my home?

(A) Restatement
(B) Generalization
(C) Prediction
(D) Question
(E) Recommendation

EXTRA PRACTICE

1. Choose at least five model essays from the Appendix. Identify the type of conclusion each contains.
2. Choose any model essay from the Appendix. Cover up the conclusion. Read the essay and write your own conclusion. Then, uncover the conclusion and see how it compares with yours. Do this with at least five model essays.

STEP 3: REVISE

Use the Revision Checklist

After you write your essay, you need to check the content and language. You need to make sure that the content is well developed and well organized, and that you have used correct language and punctuation. You can use a revision checklist similar to the one for the Integrated Task.

REVISION CHECKLIST

- ❑ Content
  - ❑ Thesis Statement
  - ❑ Main ideas
  - ❑ Supporting details
- ❑ Fluency and Cohesion
  - ❑ Transition words
  - ❑ Grammar and Spelling
  - ❑ Sentence variety

Read the following model essay. Notice how it follows the items on the checklist.

ESSAY TOPIC 2

Do you agree or disagree with the following statement? Parents are the best teachers. Use specific reasons and examples to support your answer.

Parents shape their children from the beginning of their children's lives. They develop close emotional ties with their children. They share their interests with them. They teach them values. Parents can be very important teachers in their children's lives; **however**, they are not always the best teachers.

main ideas

thesis statement

Parents may be too close to their children emotionally. For example, they may limit a child's freedom in the name of safety. A teacher may organize an educational trip to a big city, but a parent may think this trip is too dangerous. A school may want to take the children camping, but a parent may be afraid of the child getting hurt.

Another problem is that parents sometimes expect their children's interests to be similar to their own. If the parents love science, they may try to force their child to love science too. **But** what if the child prefers art? If the parents enjoy sports, they may expect their child to participate on different teams. **But** what if the child prefers to read?

Finally, although parents want to pass on their values to their children, values can change. The children of today are growing up in a world different from their parents' world. Sometimes parents, especially older ones, can't keep up with rapid social or technological changes. A student who has friends of different races at school may find that his parents have narrower views. A student who loves computers may find that her parents don't understand or value the digital revolution.

Parents are important teachers in our lives, but they aren't always the best teachers. Fortunately, we have many teachers in our lives. Our parents teach us, our teachers teach us, and we learn from our peers. Books and newspapers also teach us. All of them are valuable.

Content

REVISION CHECKLIST

- ❑ Content
  - ☑ Thesis Statement
  - ❑ Main ideas
  - ❑ Supporting details
- ❑ Fluency and Cohesion
  - ❑ Transition words
  - ❑ Grammar and Spelling
  - ❑ Sentence variety

✓ Check for Thesis Statement

The task asks the writer to agree or disagree with a statement. In the first paragraph, the writer clearly expresses disagreement with the statement.

Task: Agree or disagree

Thesis: Parents . . . are not always the best teachers.

REVISION CHECKLIST

- ❑ Content
  - ❑ Thesis Statement
  - ☑ Main ideas
  - ❑ Supporting details
- ❑ Fluency and Cohesion
  - ❑ Transition words
  - ❑ Grammar and Spelling
  - ❑ Sentence variety

✓ Check for Main Ideas

The first paragraph mentions three topics that support the thesis. These will become the main ideas of the paragraphs in the body of the essay.

Thesis: Parents... are not always the best teachers.

LOCATION	MAIN IDEA
Paragraph 1, Sentence 2	...develop close emotional ties...
Paragraph 1, Sentence 3	...share their interests...
Paragraph 1, Sentence 4	...teach them values

REVISION CHECKLIST

- ❑ Content
  - ❑ Thesis Statement
  - ❑ Main ideas
  - ☑ Supporting details
- ❑ Fluency and Cohesion
  - ❑ Transition words
  - ❑ Grammar and Spelling
  - ❑ Sentence variety

✓ Check for Supporting Details

The paragraphs have topic sentences and supporting details. In the body of the essay, the topic sentences of the paragraphs match the topics introduced in the first paragraph.

Paragraph 2: *Main Idea*

Parents may be too close to their children emotionally.

SUPPORTING DETAILS

- For example, they may limit a child's freedom in the name of safety.

Paragraph 3: *Main Idea*

Another problem is that parents sometimes expect their children's interests to be similar to their own.

SUPPORTING DETAILS

- If the parents love science, they may try to force their child to love science too.
- If the parents enjoy sports, they may expect their child to participate on different teams.

Paragraph 4: *Main Idea*

Finally, although parents want to pass on their values to their children, values can change.

SUPPORTING DETAILS

- A student who has friends of different races at school may find that his parents have narrower views.
- A student who loves computers may find that her parents don't understand or value the digital revolution.

Fluency and Cohesion

REVISION CHECKLIST

- ❑ Content
  - ❑ Thesis Statement
  - ❑ Main ideas
  - ❑ Supporting details
- ❑ Fluency and Cohesion
  - ☑ Transition words
  - ❑ Grammar and Spelling
  - ❑ Sentence variety

✓ Check for Transition Words

This essay uses appropriate transition words.

TRANSITION WORD	PARAGRAPH	FUNCTION
however	Paragraph 1	Shows contrast
Another	Paragraph 3	Adds information
But	Paragraph 3	Shows contrast
Finally	Paragraph 4	Shows order of ideas

REVISION CHECKLIST

- ❑ Content
  - ❑ Thesis Statement
  - ❑ Main ideas
  - ❑ Supporting details
- ❑ Fluency and Cohesion
  - ❑ Transition words
  - ☑ Grammar and Spelling
  - ❑ Sentence variety

✓ Check for Grammar and Spelling

There are no grammar or spelling errors in this essay.

REVISION CHECKLIST

❑ Content	❑ Fluency and Cohesion
❑ Thesis Statement	❑ Transition words
❑ Main ideas	❑ Grammar and Spelling
❑ Supporting details	☑ Sentence variety

✓ Check for Sentence Variety

This essay uses a variety of sentence structures.

SENTENCE TYPE	PARAGRAPH	EXAMPLE
Simple sentence	Paragraph 1	They share their interests with them.
Compound sentence	Paragraph 2	A teacher may organize an educational trip to a big city, but a parent may think this trip is too dangerous.
Complex sentence	Paragraph 3	If the parents love science, they may try to force their child to love science too.
Adjective clause	Paragraph 4	A student who has friends of different races at school may find that his parents have narrower views.
Series	Paragraph 5	Our parents teach us, our teachers teach us, and we learn from our peers.

PRACTICE 1

Read the following model essays. Do the exercises that follow each one.

ESSAY TOPIC 9

Some people prefer to eat at food stands or restaurants. Other people prefer to prepare and eat food at home. Which do you prefer? Use specific reasons and examples to support your answer.

Although many people prefer to eat at restaurants because it is easier than cooking at home, I prefer to prepare food at home. I believe it is much cheaper and healthier to eat at home, and it can be more convenient, too.

While eating in restaurants is fast, the money you spend can add up. When I have dinner at a restaurant, the bill is usually $25 or more. I can buy a lot of groceries with that much money. Even lunch at a food stand can easily cost seven or eight dollars. That's enough to feed a whole family at home.

Eating at home is better for you, too. Meals at restaurants are often high in fat and calories. When you cook at home, however, you can control what you eat. You can cook with low-fat and low-calorie ingredients. Restaurants also often serve big plates of food. You may eat a big plate of food at a restaurant because you paid for it, while at home you can control your portion size. You can serve yourself as little as you want.

It may seem more convenient to eat at a restaurant because you don't have to shop, cook, or clean up. All you do is eat. Cooking at home, however, can actually be more convenient. There are a lot of simple meals that don't take long to prepare. In addition, when you eat at home, you don't have to drive to the restaurant, look for a parking space, wait for a table, and wait for service.

People often choose to eat at restaurants because it seems more convenient. I find, however, that cooking at home is actually easier, and it is cheaper and healthier as well.

REVISION CHECKLIST

- ❑ Content
  - ❑ Thesis Statement
  - ❑ Main ideas
  - ❑ Supporting details
- ❑ Fluency and Cohesion
  - ❑ Transition words
  - ❑ Grammar and Spelling
  - ❑ Sentence variety

EXERCISES

1. The topic asks the writer to state a preference. Look at the first paragraph of the essay. Find the thesis statement, which states a preference, and underline it.
2. In the first paragraph, find the topics that support the thesis. Number them. They will become the main ideas of the paragraphs in the body of the essay.
3. Put a check (✓) next to the main idea in the second paragraph. Mark each supporting detail with a letter: A, B, C, etc.
4. Put a check (✓) next to the main idea in the third paragraph. Mark each supporting detail with a letter: A, B, C, etc.
5. Put a check (✓) next to the main idea in the fourth paragraph. Mark each supporting detail with a letter: A, B, C, etc.
6. Underline all transition words in the second, third, fourth, and fifth paragraphs.
7. Check grammar and spelling. Correct any errors.
8. Find and mark one simple sentence (ss), one complex sentence (cx/s) and one sentence with an adjective clause (adj.c).

ESSAY TOPIC 10

It has recently been announced that a new restaurant may be built in your neighborhood. Do you support or oppose this plan? Why? Use specific reasons and details to support your answer.

I can see both advantages and disadvantages to having a new restaurant built in our neighborhood. I believe, however, that the disadvantages outweigh the advantages. A new restaurant would bring more traffic problems to the area. In addition, it could attract undesirable people. Most of all, I think there are other types of businesses that would be more beneficial to the neighborhood.

Traffic congestion is already a problem in our neighborhood, and a new restaurant would just add to the problem. Most restaurant customers would arrive by car and crowd our streets even more. In addition, they would occupy parking spaces and make it even harder for residents to find places to park near their homes.

I'm also concerned about the type of patrons that a new restaurant would bring into our neighborhood. If the restaurant serves drinks and has dancing, there could be problems. The restaurant would stay open late and people leaving the restaurant might be drunk. They could be noisy, too. That is not the kind of thing I want to see in my neighborhood.

Finally, there are other types of businesses that we need in our neighborhood more. We already have a restaurant and a couple of coffee shops. We don't have a bookstore or pharmacy, however, and we have only one small grocery store. I would prefer to see one of these businesses established here rather than another restaurant. Any one of them would be more useful to the residents and would maintain the quiet atmosphere of our streets.

A new restaurant could disrupt the quiet lifestyle of our neighborhood. It might bring jobs, but it would also bring traffic and noise. Moreover, it would use space that might be better used for another type of business. This is why I would oppose a plan for a new restaurant.

REVISION CHECKLIST

- ❑ **Content**
  - ❑ Thesis Statement
  - ❑ Main ideas
  - ❑ Supporting details
- ❑ **Fluency and Cohesion**
  - ❑ Transition words
  - ❑ Grammar and Spelling
  - ❑ Sentence variety

EXERCISES

1. The topic asks the writer to support or oppose a plan. Look at the first paragraph of the essay. Find the thesis statement, which states support for or opposition to a plan, and underline it.
2. In the first paragraph, find the topics that support the thesis. Number them. They will become the main ideas of the paragraphs in the body of the essay.
3. Put a check (✓) next to the main idea in the second paragraph. Mark each supporting detail with a letter: A, B, C, etc.
4. Put a check (✓) next to the main idea in the third paragraph. Mark each supporting detail with a letter: A, B, C, etc.
5. Put a check (✓) next to the main idea in the fourth paragraph. Mark each supporting detail with a letter: A, B, C, etc.
6. Underline all transition words in the second, third, fourth, and fifth paragraphs.

7. Check grammar and spelling. Correct any errors.
8. Find and mark one complex sentence (cx/s), one simple sentence (ss), and one compound sentence (cm/s).

ESSAY TOPIC 11

Some people think that they can learn better by themselves than with a teacher. Others think that it is always better to have a teacher. Which do you prefer? Use specific reasons to develop your essay.

Most people can learn to do something simple on their own with just a set of instructions. However, to learn something more complex, it's always best to have a teacher. Teachers help you find the way that you learn best. They help you stay focused on what you're learning. They provide you with a wider range of information than you might find on your own. In short, teachers provide you with a lot more support and knowledge than you can usually get by yourself.

Teachers can help students learn in the way that is best for each student because teachers understand that different people have different learning styles. For example, some students learn better by discussing a topic. Others learn more by writing about it. A teacher can help you follow your learning style, while a book can give you only one way of learning something.

Teachers help you focus on what you are learning. They can help you keep from becoming distracted. They can show you which are the most important points in a lesson to understand. If you have to study on your own, on the other hand, it might be difficult to keep your attention on the material or know which points are most important.

Teachers bring their own knowledge and understanding of the topic to the lesson. A book presents you with certain information, and the teacher can add more. The teacher might also have a different point of view from the book and can provide other sources of information and ideas, as well.

There is nothing wrong with studying on your own. For the best possible learning, though, a teacher is the biggest help you can have.

REVISION CHECKLIST

- ❑ Content
  - ❑ Thesis Statement
  - ❑ Main ideas
  - ❑ Supporting details
- ❑ Fluency and Cohesion
  - ❑ Transition words
  - ❑ Grammar and Spelling
  - ❑ Sentence variety

EXERCISES

1. The topic asks the writer to state a preference. Look at the first paragraph of the essay. Find the thesis statement, which states a preference, and underline it.
2. In the first paragraph, find the topics that support the thesis. Number them. They will become the main ideas of the paragraphs in the body of the essay.

3. Put a check (✓) next to the main idea in the second paragraph. Mark each supporting detail with a letter: A, B, C, etc.
4. Put a check (✓) next to the main idea in the third paragraph. Mark each supporting detail with a letter: A, B, C, etc.
5. Put a check (✓) next to the main idea in the fourth paragraph. Mark each supporting detail with a letter: A, B, C, etc.
6. Underline all transition words in the second, third, fourth, and fifth paragraphs.
7. Check grammar and spelling. Correct any errors.
8. Find and mark one complex sentence (cx/s), one simple sentence (ss), and one compound sentence (cm/s).

ESSAY TOPIC 14

We all work, or will work, in jobs with many different kinds of people. In your opinion, what are some important characteristics of a good co-worker (someone you work closely with)? Use reasons and specific examples to explain why these characteristics are important.

I've worked in several offices, and I've found there are certain characteristics that all good co-workers have in common. They tend to be cooperative people, they adapt well to changes, and they are helpful to others in the office. People who have these characteristics are easy to work with.

A good co-worker is very cooperative. She does her best to get along with others. She tries to do her work well because she knows that if one person doesn't get her work done, it affects everyone else. She also has a positive attitude that creates a pleasant working environment.

A good co-worker is adaptable. She is not stubborn about changes in schedules or routines. She doesn't object to having her job description revised. She has no problem with new procedures. In fact, she welcomes changes when they come.

A good co-worker is helpful. For instance, she lends a hand when someone falls behind in his or her work. She is willing to change her schedule to accommodate another worker's emergency. She doesn't keep track of how often she has to take on extra work.

We spend more time with our co-workers during the week than we do with our family. Thus, it's important for our co-workers to be people we can get along with. When co-workers are cooperative, adaptable, and helpful, everyone gets along better and can get their jobs done well.

REVISION CHECKLIST

- ❑ **Content**
  - ❑ Thesis Statement
  - ❑ Main ideas
  - ❑ Supporting details
- ❑ **Fluency and Cohesion**
  - ❑ Transition words
  - ❑ Grammar and Spelling
  - ❑ Sentence variety

EXERCISES

1. The topic asks the writer to describe something. Look at the first paragraph of the essay. Find the thesis statement, which tells us what the writer will describe, and underline it.
2. In the first paragraph, find the topics that support the thesis. Number them. They will become the main ideas of the paragraphs in the body of the essay.
3. Put a check (✓) next to the main idea in the second paragraph. Mark each supporting detail with a letter: A, B, C, etc.
4. Put a check (✓) next to the main idea in the third paragraph. Mark each supporting detail with a letter: A, B, C, etc.
5. Put a check (✓) next to the main idea in the fourth paragraph. Mark each supporting detail with a letter: A, B, C, etc.
6. Underline all transition words in the second, third, fourth, and fifth paragraphs.
7. Check grammar and spelling. Correct any errors.
8. Find and mark one complex sentence (cx/s), one simple sentence (ss), and one sentence with a noun clause (nc).

PRACTICE 2

Complete each essay by answering the questions that follow.

TOPIC 23

TIP

Reading ahead in the essay will help you choose the best answer.

Many teachers assign homework to students every day. Do you think that daily homework is necessary for students? Use specific reasons and details to support your answer.

(1) ________________. Students already spend most of the day in school. They need time to spend with their families, to work, and to just relax. They can learn their lessons with homework two or three times a week, but every day isn't necessary.

(2) ________________. They are still young, and they need the guidance and support their parents can give them. They need the companionship of their brothers and sisters. (3) ________________, many families rely on their older children to help out at home. They take care of the younger children and help with the cooking and cleaning. If students have too much homework, the won't have time for their families.

Many high school students have jobs. They go to their jobs after school and on weekends. Some work in order to help their families. (4) ________________. Students' jobs are important to them. If they have too much homework, they won't have time and energy to go to work.

Students need time to relax. They study hard in school all day, and many work at jobs after school. But they are still young. They need to spend time with their friends and have fun. When students relax with friends, they then have more energy for school and work. (5) ________________. Having free time is important for a child's development. If students have too much homework, they won't have time for relaxation.

Homework is important for students, but other things are important, too. Some homework is good, but daily homework can take time away from a student's family, job, and relaxation. There needs to be a balance.

1. Choose the best thesis statement.
   (A) Teachers often assign homework.
   (B) I believe that daily homework is not necessary.
   (C) Homework may involve solving math problems or writing essays.

2. Choose the best main idea for this paragraph.
   (A) All students need to spend time with their families.
   (B) Many students have to work.
   (C) Some families believe that homework is important.

3. Choose the best transition word for this sentence.
   (A) For example
   (B) Although
   (C) In addition

4. Choose the missing supporting detail.
   (A) Others work to save money for college.
   (B) Others spend time relaxing with friends.
   (C) Others do homework all evening.

5. Choose the missing supporting detail.
   (A) They should spend their energy getting a job.
   (B) They never have time for their families.
   (C) They have a chance to develop social skills or to pursue their own interests.

TOPIC 22

Do you agree or disagree with the following statement? Businesses should do anything they can to make a profit. Use specific reasons and examples to support your position.

After I get my degree, I plan to start my own business. Like any business owner, my goal is to make as much money as I can. (6) _______________. I must always keep in mind that the success of my business depends on (7)_______________, the customers I serve, and the community I live in.

My employees are a very important part of my business. Without them, my company would not be able to function. I depend on my employees to carry out the day-to-day operations of the business, and I rely on them for their advice on what to sell and how

to sell it. Naturally, I have to compensate them for their contributions to the company. I can't take a large profit without sharing it with the people who made it possible.

(8) ________________, I would not have a business without my customers. I can never forget that they could take their business somewhere else. Therefore, I have to give them good value for their money and not overcharge them just because I want to make a few more pennies. (9) ________________.

My employees and I are part of the social life of our community. We have an obligation to be active community members. (10)________________. We need to support local programs to support our neighbors, for example, summer jobs for high school students, campaigns to clean up city parks, and efforts to make the shopping area more attractive.

A business must make profits, of course, but we all—workers customers, community members—must profit from a successful business, as well.

6. Choose the best thesis statement.
   (A) To clarify, making a profit means earning money rather than losing it.
   (B) In fact, earning a profit is the most important aspect of a business.
   (C) However, I can't forget that there are more important things in life than earning a profit.

7. Choose the missing topic that supports the thesis.
   (A) the money I earn
   (B) the people I work with
   (C) the product or service I provide

8. Choose the best transition word for this sentence.
   (A) Therefore
   (B) Similarly
   (C) Otherwise

9. Choose the missing supporting detail.
   (A) I want my customers to trust me and keep coming back.
   (B) If some customers leave, I can always find others.
   (C) I should earn as much profit from my customers as possible.

10. Choose the missing supporting detail.
   (A) Taking part in community activities is an enjoyable way to spend free time.
   (B) If I am active in the community, I will get more customers and earn higher profits.
   (C) I feel it is important that some of the profits my business earns from the community be returned to the community.

TOPIC 6

Some people prefer to live in a small town. Others prefer to live in a big city. Which place would you prefer to live in? Use specific reasons and details to support your answer.

I grew up in a small town and then moved to a big city. I didn't think I would like living here, but I was wrong. (11) ________________. Transportation is much more convenient, everything is more exciting, and there is a greater variety of people. I can't imagine ever living in a small town again.

Transportation is easier in a city. In a small town, you have to have a car to get around because there isn't any kind of public transportation. In a city, (12) ________________, there are usually buses and taxis, and some cities have subways. Cities often have heavy traffic and expensive parking, but it doesn't matter because you can always take the bus. Using public transportation is usually cheaper and more convenient than driving a car, (13) ________________ you don't have this choice in a small town.

City life is more exciting than small town life. In small towns usually nothing changes. You see the same people every day, you go to the same two or three restaurants, everything is the same. (14) ________________. You see new people every day. There are many restaurants, with new ones to choose from all the time. New plays come to the theaters, and new musicians come to the concert halls.

(15) ________________. There are fewer people in a small town, and usually they are all alike. In a city you can find people from different countries, of different religions, of different races—you can find all kinds of people. This variety of people is what makes city life interesting.

Life in a city is convenient, exciting, and interesting. After experiencing city life, I could never live in a small town again.

11. Choose the best thesis statement.
    - (A) I think life is much better in a big city.
    - (B) However, I still prefer living in a small town.
    - (C) Big cities are busy and noisy, while small towns are quiet and peaceful.

12. Choose the best transition word for this sentence.
    - (A) consequently
    - (B) for example
    - (C) on the other hand

13. Choose the best transition word for this sentence.
    - (A) but
    - (B) also
    - (C) so

14. Choose the missing supporting detail.
    - (A) In a city, life can be very confusing.
    - (B) In a city, things change all the time.
    - (C) In a city, most people follow a routine.

15. Choose the best main idea for this paragraph.
    - (A) Cities have many of the same types of people that you can find in a small town.
    - (B) Cities have a larger population than small towns do.
    - (C) Cities have a diversity of people that you don't find in a small town.

TOPIC 27

Do you agree or disagree with the following statement? Boys and girls should attend separate schools. Use specific reasons and examples to support your answer.

(16) ______________. They will not be separated when they finish school and start their careers, so why should they be separated in school? When boys and girls study together, they are assured of getting equal quality of education, (17) ______________, and they learn how to become friends. It is a much better preparation for life than studying in separate schools.

When boys and girls attend the same school, they get equal education. They are in the same classrooms with the same teachers studying from the same books. (18) ______________. One school might be better than the other. By studying together, girls get the same education as boys. This helps them work toward having equality in society.

By attending the same schools, boys and girls learn how to work together. Some people say that they should study separately because they have different learning styles. I think it's better to study together, (19) ______________. It gives them the chance to learn to work together despite their differences. This will help them in the future when they have to work together professionally.

When boys and girls see each other in school every day, they have the chance to become friends. (20) ______________. If they attend separate schools, they don't know each other. It's easy to misunderstand, or even fear, each other. When boys and girls have the chance to become friends, their lives are much richer. They will have better relationships in the future.

By studying together, boys and girls get equal education, they learn to work together, and they become friends. This prepares them for adult life where men and women live and work together every day.

16. Choose the best thesis statement.
    (A) I agree that education is as important for girls as it is for boys.
    (B) I don't think it's a good idea for boys and girls to attend separate schools.
    (C) In many countries, boys and girls attend separate schools.

17. Choose the missing topic that supports the thesis.
    (A) they learn how to work together
    (B) they attend the same school
    (C) they do the same kind of homework

18. Choose the missing supporting detail.
    (A) If they attend separate schools, they could still study the same subjects.
    (B) If they attend separate schools, they will learn more.
    (C) If they attend separate schools, the quality of the schools might be different.

19. Choose the best transition word for this sentence.
    (A) however
    (B) for instance
    (C) moreover

20. Choose the missing supporting detail.
    (A) Children should have a lot of friends.
    (B) They see each other as normal people, not as strangers.
    (C) Friends can help each other with their schoolwork.

PRACTICE 3

Read the following essay and use the revision checklist to identify what is missing or incorrect. Then write your revision of the essay on a separate piece of paper or on your computer, adding the missing parts and correcting the errors.

REVISION CHECKLIST

- ❑ **Content**
  - ❑ Thesis Statement
  - ❑ Main ideas
  - ❑ Supporting details
- ❑ **Fluency and Cohesion**
  - ❑ Transition words
  - ❑ Grammar and Spelling
  - ❑ Sentence variety

TOPIC 12

It is better for children to grow up in the countryside than in a big city. Do you agree or disagree? Use specific reasons and examples to develop your essay.

Yes, I think so. When children grow up in the countryside, they have a healthier life. They also have a safer life. Children also learn to appreciate nature when they grow up in the countryside.

Life in the countryside is healthier for children than life in the city. Drinking water in the city is usually dirty. In the countryside, on the other hand, the drinking water are clean and pure.

They don't have to worry about crime because there are fewer criminals in the countryside than in the city. They don't have to worry about traffic accidents, either, because there are fewer cars in the countryside. Furthermore, they don't have to worry about strangers who might hurt them because in the countryside almost everybody knows everybody else.

Life in the countryside help children appreciate nature. There are few plants in the city. In the countryside, for instance, children see trees and flowers around them all the time. They also have opportunities to see wild animals, while in the city they can only see animals in zoos. In addition, they know where there food comes from. In the countryside children are surrounded by farms, but in the city they only see fruits and vegetables in the grocery stores.

Life in the countryside is definitely much better for children than life in the city. It is cleaner, safer, and closer to nature. When I have children, I plan to let they grow up far away from any city.

Missing items:

Paragraph 1: ______________________________

Paragraph 2: ______________________________

Paragraph 3: ______________________________

Paragraph 4: ______________________________

Paragraph 5: ______________________________

Grammar and vocabulary errors:

Paragraph 1: ______________________________

Paragraph 2: ______________________________

Paragraph 3: ______________________________

Paragraph 4: ______________________________

Paragraph 5: ______________________________

Check the Spelling and Punctuation

Just as you did in the Integrated Task, you will have to check the punctuation and spelling on the essay you write for the Independent Task.

SPELLING

Remember that there is no spell checker on the computer that you will use during the TOEFL iBT. You should be able to spell the most common English words before you take the test. On the test, try to use words that you are sure how to spell.

PUNCTUATION

There are three important things to remember about punctuation when you write your responses.

- **Indent each paragraph or use a space between paragraphs.**
  This will help the reader determine when you are starting a new topic.
- **Capitalize the first word of each sentence.**
  This will help the reader determine when you are starting a new sentence.
- **Put a period or question mark at the end of each sentence or question.**
  This will help the reader determine when you are ending a sentence or question.

Here are some other forms of punctuation that will help make your response easier to read.

NOTE

You will not be penalized if you use a space between paragraphs instead of indents. Also, remember that proper nouns are capitalized.

Comma

Use a comma in a list of three or more things. It is optional to put a comma before the *and.*

I want to have a kitchen, living room and bedroom.

I want a large, airy, inexpensive house.

Use a comma between a noun and a following description.

Central Park, the huge expanse of green space in the center of New York City, is visited by thousands of people every day.

Use a comma to separate transition words, adjectives, or participles that are not part of the sentence or were added for emphasis.

On the other hand, I think eating at home saves money.

The apartment was very, very expensive.

Excited, I signed the lease without reading the fine print.

Use a comma between two independent clauses.

It is important to get along with co-workers, and it is important to get along with bosses as well.

Use a comma to separate a non-restrictive clause.

All the neighbors, who are very friendly, get together for parties and picnics.

Use a comma after a subordinate clause at the beginning of a sentence.

After I've chosen an area, I decide whether I want to live in a house or an apartment.

NOTE

Commas help the reader follow your ideas, but be careful not to use them where they are not needed.

Semicolon

Use a semicolon to separate two closely related sentences.

I wanted a renovated townhouse; none was available.

Colon or Dash

Use a colon or dash in front of a list or explanation.

I looked at three kinds of apartments: studio, one-bedroom, and two-bedroom.

My needs are simple—a nice neighborhood and a park nearby.

PRACTICE 4

Read the following essay. Then write your revision of the essay on a separate piece of paper or on your computer, adding punctuation.

ESSAY TOPIC 13

people are living to be much older these days than ever before. the main reasons for this are greater access to health care improved health care and better nutrition.

basic health care is available to many more people now than it was in the past. when someone is ill nowadays he or she can go to a public hospital instead of having to pay for private care. there are also more clinics and more trained doctors and nurses than there used to be. years ago health care was not available to everyone. people who didn't live in big cities often did not have easy access to doctors or hospitals and many people couldn't afford to pay for the medical care they needed.

in addition to increased access to health care the quality of that health care has greatly improved over the years. doctors now know much more about diseases and how to cure them. in the past people died young because of simple things such as an infection or a virus. now we have antibiotics and other medicines to cure these diseases. furthermore advances in medical science have made it possible to cure certain types of cancer and to treat heart disease. this has prolonged the lives of many many people.

the quality of nutrition has also improved over time. because of this people tend to be healthier than they used to be. now we know how to eat more healthfully. we know that eating low fat food can prevent heart disease. we know that eating certain fruits and vegetables can prevent cancer. we have information about nutrition that can help us live longer healthier lives.

improved health care and healthy eating habits are allowing us to live longer. now we need to make sure that everyone in the world has these benefits.

EXTRA PRACTICE

Study the model essays on pages 108, 111, 113, 114, *and* 115. *Circle all the punctuation.*

PRACTICE INDEPENDENT TASK

On your computer or on a separate piece of paper, write an essay on the following topic. Take no more than 30 minutes to plan, write, and revise your essay. Use the revision checklist to guide your revision.

ESSAY TOPIC 54

Some famous athletes and entertainers earn millions of dollars every year. Do you think these people deserve such high salaries? Use specific reasons and examples to support your opinion.

REVISION CHECKLIST

- ❑ Content
  - ❑ Thesis Statement
  - ❑ Main ideas
  - ❑ Supporting details
- ❑ Fluency and Cohesion
  - ❑ Transition words
  - ❑ Grammar and Spelling
  - ❑ Sentence variety

Writing Skills—Both Tasks

5

A well-written essay has good organization of ideas. It also has well-written sentences. In a well-written essay, transition words and phrases are used to make connections between ideas. There is variety of sentence structure and vocabulary. The reader can easily follow the writer's ideas and stays interested in them.

TRANSITION: CONNECTING AND LINKING

Transition Words

Transition words and phrases will help your reader follow your ideas from sentence to sentence and from paragraph to paragraph. Without transition words and phrases, your ideas will stand alone, unrelated to the thesis of your essay.

In this section, you will learn to use transition words that show time, degree, comparison and contrast, and cause and effect. You will also learn transition words that let you add more information and transition words like pronouns that let you make connections to previously mentioned subjects.

TIP

Transition words, phrases, or clauses that begin with transition words at the beginning of a sentence are usually followed by a comma.

TIME

When you are explaining the sequence of events, you may want to use these expressions.

before	first	while	after
then	second	meanwhile	once
next	finally	at the same time	when

EXAMPLE

The school counselors should help students who are new to a school. *Before the first day* of school, they should give an orientation to the building. *When* school opens, they should introduce the students to the teachers. *After* the students have gotten used to their classes, the counselors should find out about the student's hobbies and recommend some extracurricular clubs. *At the same time*, the counselor should invite the parents to visit the school so they can meet the teachers and administrators.

DEGREE

When you are explaining why one thing is more or less important than another thing, you may want to use these expressions.

most important	even more	in the first place	primarily
more importantly	even less	to a certain extent	principally
less important	above all	to a greater/lesser degree	chiefly

EXAMPLE

A pet is one the *most important* things psychologists can recommend to patients suffering from loneliness. Pets can do many things for lonely people, but *above all* they provide companionship. To a *lesser* degree, they provide a distraction from anxieties. But *primarily*, they help isolated people stay emotionally connected with the world.

Comparison and Contrast

When you are explaining how two or more things are similar or how they are different, you may want to use these expressions.

TO COMPARE

too	likewise	similarly	by the same token
also	compared to	similar to	in a like manner
just as	by comparison	in the same way	in a similar fashion

TO CONTRAST

yet	whereas	conversely	in contrast to
but	unlike	nevertheless	on the other hand
while	however	although	otherwise

EXAMPLE

Although my friend chose to buy a car with his gift, I would have gone on vacation. He said he needed the car to go to work, *but* I think he should take the bus. He also wanted the car for convenience. *However*, a taxi is *just* as convenient and doesn't have to be serviced. We are both alike in that neither of us knows how to drive. *Otherwise*, I might have bought a car, too.

Cause and Effect

When you are explaining how something caused a change in something else, you may want to use these expressions.

so	thus	consequently	therefore
for this reason	as a result	because, because of	owing to
since	due to	accordingly	as a consequence

EXAMPLE

Effective advertising wants to change people's behaviors. Some public service ads show coffins of people who died of lung cancer; *as a result* many people have quit smoking. Other ads show glamorous people smoking; *consequently* young people start to smoke. *Owing to* the influence of advertising on youth, many cigarette ads are not allowed near schools or on TV.

Explanation

If you are explaining what something is by giving an example or if you are restating something for emphasis, you may want to use these expressions.

in other words	to clarify	to explain	for one thing
I mean	specifically	that is	for example
such as	for instance	to illustrate	namely

EXAMPLE

People are never too old to attend college. *For example*, there are many women who stayed at home to raise their families and now have time to return to school. There are other examples *such as* retired people who move to a college town just so they can take occasional classes or even working people in their sixties, *for instance*, who want to take some night classes. *In other words*, you are never too old to learn.

Adding More Information

If you are adding more information to make your point stronger, you may want to use these expressions.

in addition	besides	furthermore	as well as
moreover	in fact	also	what's more

EXAMPLE

In addition to music, retailers can use lighting to improve the store environment. *Besides* helping customers see the products better, certain types of lighting can create different moods. Soft music creates a relaxed atmosphere. *Similarly*, soft lighting helps customers feel at ease. Relaxed customers stay in the store longer. *What's more*, they make a greater number of purchases.

PRACTICE 1

Read the following paragraphs. Choose the appropriate transition words or phrases to complete each sentence.

1. If I chose my own roommate, I'd (1) ______________ pick some candidates from the list supplied by the university. (2) ______________ I'd write to them and they'd write back. Through our letters, we'd find out if we shared common interests, (3) ______________ sports or movies. (4) ______________ we'd find out if we had similar habits. (5) ______________ my investigation, I'd probably find someone compatible with me.

   next **first** **as a result of**
   in addition **such as**

2. Billions of tons of plastic are produced every year, and it takes hundreds of years for plastic to break down. (1) ______________, the ocean is filled with plastic trash. Many birds, (2) ______________ seagulls, commonly eat fish eggs. These birds eat small pieces of plastic that look like fish eggs. (3) ______________ eating a big meal of plastic, a bird might starve to death. This is because the plastic has no nutritional value. (4) ______________ many birds choke when they try to swallow plastic pieces. (5) ______________ whenever we throw plastic away, we are contributing to the threats to ocean life.

   moreover **such as** **consequently**
   in other words **after**

3. A major part of adapting to life in a new country is learning that country's language. Generally, children have an easier time with this than adults do. (1) ______________, children's young brains are ready to learn many new things, including language. (2) ______________, they spend most of the day in school using their new language in class and on the playground. Adults, (3) ______________, have many other things to fill their time and their minds. They have to find ways to make a living and take care of their families, (4) ______________. Since they aren't in school all day long, they have fewer opportunities to make new friends who speak the country's language. (5) ______________, adults may take longer learning the language of their new country.

   moreover **In the first place** **on the other hand**
   as a result **for example**

4. Decorators may choose certain colors for rooms in order to create certain moods. (1) ______________, they may use blue in a bedroom to create a relaxing atmosphere or red in a kitchen to stimulate the appetite. (2) ______________, a decorator may choose yellow for a sitting room to give it a cheerful air. Beige is a color that gives a feeling of cleanliness. (3) ______________, it is often used in doctors' offices. This neutral color helps the doctors and nurses stay clear and focused, (4) ______________. (5) ______________ many people believe that color has a strong influence on mood, scientists are skeptical.

   as well **for example** **similarly**
   because of this **although**

5. People often say that it is always important to be honest, but I don't agree with this. (1) ______________, I feel that sometimes honesty is not the best policy. You wouldn't want to tell your best friend that her expensive new dress doesn't look good on her, (2) ______________. That would only hurt her feelings and possibly damage your friendship. (3) ______________, you wouldn't tell your neighbors that you don't like the way they redecorated their house. That would just cause bad feelings between you. (4) ______________, honesty isn't always a good thing. (5) ______________, it can lead to problems that could easily be avoided by telling people what they want to hear.

so	on the contrary	by the same token
in fact	in fact	

VARIETY: WORDS AND SENTENCES

In order to be a good essay, your essay must interest the reader. One way to do this is to vary your vocabulary. Learning different ways to express similar ideas by using synonyms will help you develop semantic variety.

A good essay also has a variety of sentence structures that keep the ideas clear and interesting to the reader. You can develop variety in your prose by using parallel structures, making your paragraphs cohesive, and writing sentences that vary in type, length, subject, and voice.

Synonyms

When you are writing on one topic, you don't want to repeat the same verb or adverb, noun or adjective in every sentence. You should try to use words that are similar in meaning, and that will carry the meaning of the sentence. Synonyms are important because they help you link closely related words or ideas. Synonyms provide coherence in your essay.

Read the paragraph below. Look for these synonyms of *discuss* and *discussion*.

VERB	SYNONYMS
discuss	argue, confer, debate, dispute, elaborate, examine, explain, hash over, reason
NOUN	**SYNONYMS**
discussion	argument, conversation, discourse, explanation

EXAMPLE

Last month, I had a *dispute* with my parents. It started as a simple *conversation* that turned into an *argument*. I wanted to take a year off from school. Of course, my parents *argued* that I should stay in school. I tried to *reason* with them; I tried to *persuade* them that taking a year off from school and working would be valuable experience. My *explanation* fell on deaf ears, and they refused to let me continue the *discussion*. They felt I had not thoroughly *examined* the issue and saw no reason to *debate* the subject any longer. I *conferred* with my sister who felt we could *hash* it *over* later when my parents were in a better mood.

PRACTICE 2

Read the following topic and essay. Then revise the essay, choosing synonyms from the chart to replace the underlined words. Write your revision on your computer or on a separate piece of paper. You can find a revised version of this essay in the Model Essay section of the Appendix.

TOPIC 35

You need to travel from your home to a place 40 miles (64 kilometers) away. Compare the different kinds of transportation you could use. Describe which method you would choose. Give specific reasons for your choice.

When I think about the different methods of transportation I could choose to travel 40 miles from my home, I have three choices: bicycle, car, or public transportation. In order to choose the best method of transportation, I have to consider how much it will cost, how long it will take, and why I need to make the trip. Then I can choose the best method for the circumstances.

Bicycle is the least expensive choice. The only cost is the physical energy I need to pedal for 40 miles. This method, however, is extremely time consuming. I imagine it would take me all day to make the trip. On the other hand, biking is excellent exercise, so if my only goal is to burn calories and get stronger, then bicycle is my best choice.

Public transportation is another method that is inexpensive, since the fares in my area are low. On the other hand, you cannot depend on public transportation where I live. The schedules are inconvenient, and it might take me all day to make my 40-mile trip if I include waiting time. Public transportation is good for the environment since it causes less pollution than cars. But, I can't depend on it to get me to my destination on time, so I don't like to use it.

Private car is the most expensive way to travel. Since I don't own a car, I would need to borrow one from my parents. I would have to pay for the gasoline, which costs a lot, and I would also have to pay for parking at my destination. A car is the most dependable way to travel if you need to get somewhere fast. If convenience is my goal, I should choose to travel by car.

When I consider these points, I must confess that I am spoiled. I prefer the convenience of the car over the exercise of a bicycle and the virtues of public transportation. I like to come and go as I please without waiting, even if it costs me more.

SYNONYMS					
choose/ choice	public transportation	car	travel	expensive	depend on
pick select decide on alternative option	buses and trains mass transit	private vehicle automobile this type of transportation	go make a trip	costly	rely on count on

Pronouns

If you are describing someone or something, you may use some of these pronouns to refer to the person or thing you are describing.

Pronouns that replace a subject

he	she	it	they
this	that	those	

Pronouns that replace an object

his	her	them
this	that	those

Pronouns that replace a possessive

his	her	its	their

EXAMPLE

My community should hire a health worker. I worked in a rural area one summer with a community health worker and saw the wonderful ways she helped the people in the area. She worked with mothers teaching *them* how to keep *their* children healthy. She worked with school teachers helping *them* recognize early signs of illness. She worked with restaurant personnel showing *them* proper food handling techniques. A community needs help in many ways. *This* is one way its citizens can make it healthier.

NOTE

***This* in the last sentence refers to the whole paragraph. *This* equals *hiring a health worker*.**

Parallel Structures

Parallelism gives your essay rhythm. It makes it easier to read and understand. Your structures must be parallel. That is, the subjects, verbs, adjectives, adverbs, and gerunds, when listed in a sentence, must have the same word form.

PARALLEL SUBJECTS

Work and play should be more evenly divided in my day.

Both *work* and *play* are the same kind of nouns. The subjects are parallel.

Working and play should be more evenly divided in my day.

Here *working* is a gerund, *play* is not. The subjects are not parallel.

Working and playing should be more evenly divided in my day.

Here both *working* and *playing* are gerunds. The subjects are parallel.

PARALLEL VERBS

We press a button, wait a short time, and remove the food from the microwave.

All three verbs are in the present tense. The verbs are parallel.

We press a button, wait a short time, and can remove the food from the microwave.

The third verb uses the auxiliary *can,* while the first and second do not. The verbs are not parallel.

We can press a button, wait a short time, and remove the food from the microwave.

Here, because *can* precedes the first verb, it does not have to be repeated for the remaining verbs in the list. All the verbs are now parallel.

PARALLEL ADJECTIVES

I found the movie long and boring.

The adjectives are both parallel.

I found the movie long and it bored me.

The sentence is not wrong, but it is not parallel.

PARALLEL ADVERBS

Athletes often move gracefully, easily, and powerfully.

The three adverbs all end in *-ly*. They are all parallel.

Athletes often move with grace, easily and powerfully.

The first description is a prepositional phrase. The adverbs are not parallel.

Athletes often move gracefully, carefully, and powerfully.

The second adverb *easily* was replaced with another adverb carefully. The meanings of *easily* and *carefully* are not the same, but *carefully* could be used to describe how an athlete moves. In this sentence, *carefully* adds to the rhythm of the sentence since the suffix *-fully* is used three times.

Athletes move with grace, ease, and power.

This sentence can also be made parallel by using three prepositional phrases. The objects of the preposition *with* are all parallel nouns: *grace, ease,* and *power*.

PARALLEL GERUNDS

I enjoy shopping and keeping up with the latest styles, but not paying the bills.

Shopping, keeping up, and *paying* are gerunds. The gerunds are parallel.

I enjoy shopping and to keep up with the latest styles, but not to pay the bills.

To keep up and *to pay* not only are not parallel with *shopping,* they are incorrect. The verb *enjoy* must be followed by a gerund, not an infinitive.

PARALLEL SENTENCES

> **While there are advantages and disadvantages to both machine-made, and hand-made products, I prefer machine-made products. While hand-made products are generally high quality, I find them expensive. While I appreciate high-quality products, I can't afford them.**

These three sentences are parallel. They all begin with an adverb clause introduced by *While.* The subject of the independent clause in all three sentences is *I.* Each sentence after the first one takes an idea from the previous sentence and carries it forward using the same construction. There is a nice rhythm to these sentences. Be careful though. There is a narrow line between rhythmic parallels and boring repetitions.

> **While there are advantages and disadvantages to both, given my type of personality, I prefer machine-made products. While hand-made products are generally high quality, they are also very expensive. While I do appreciate high quality, my status as a student makes me appreciate low cost as well.**

In this version, the basic parallel construction remains. The last two sentences have been changed. In these two sentences, the parallelism is within the sentences as well as between the sentences.

> **Hand-made products are high quality.**
> **Hand-made products are very expensive.**
>
> **I appreciate high quality.**
> **I appreciate low cost.**

The writer draws a similarity between adjectives *high quality* and *very expensive,* and contrasts the products with the adjectives *high quality* and *low cost.*

PRACTICE 3

Read the sentences and decide if the underlined word or phrase should be changed. Some underlined words are incorrect; others are grammatically correct, but not well-written. If the word should be changed, rewrite it.

1. Dogs provide older people an important chance to learn or maintaining social skills.
2. My parents didn't have time to analyze their feelings or thinking about themselves.
3. I believe zoos are useful both in terms of educating and they can advance scientific research.
4. I prefer a combination of living at a small, suburban town and working in a big city.
5. Agricultural research improves individual citizen's lives, whereas successful businesses to improve a country's economy.
6. Heated debate is interesting, and interest things are easier to learn about.

7. One might think that it is a waste of time to go out to see a movie when you can watch DVDs at home.

8. Teachers can instruct tomorrow's leaders; doctors can make those leaders healthier; and engineering can guarantee that future generations have good housing.

9. I could see the house where my grandmother grew up and where my cousins still live in that house.

10. Many people want to travel abroad to see new places and things; people also want to travel abroad so that they can improve their educational opportunities.

Coherence

Transition words help the reader see the relationship between sentences and ideas. They are one way to provide coherence in an essay. There are two other ways to provide coherence: repeating words and rephrasing ideas.

REPEATING

Repeating words can provide a rhythm to a paragraph. In the example below, notice how the phrase *She worked with* is repeated three times to show ways a community health worker helped people.

EXAMPLE

She *worked with* mothers teaching them how to keep their children healthy. She *worked with* school teachers helping them recognize early signs of illness. She *worked with* restaurant personnel showing them proper food handling techniques. A community needs help in many ways.

Repeating words can also link ideas that may be several sentences apart. Look at the Pronoun example on page 131. The second sentence in the example ends with *she helped the people in the area.* The next to the last sentence, *A community needs help in many ways,* emphasizes the need of the community for help.

REPHRASING

We can rephrase words and sentences to provide coherence to the essay. Rephrasing gives the reader a second chance to understand the idea. Synonyms are one way to rephrase.

EXAMPLE

The countryside where I grew up is very *isolated*. You can drive for miles without seeing another car. It seems in all directions you look at a *breathtaking vista*. The scenery near the ocean is especially *dramatic, with giant dark* cliffs rising out of the water.

Rephrased Version

Such a *secluded, remote* environment is a perfect place to relax. The *spectacular views* bring out the artist in me. I often take my paints and a canvas and try to capture the exciting *feel of the shoreline*.

Notice the ideas that are rephrased

The countryside where I grew up is very *isolated*. You can drive for miles without seeing another car.

Such a *secluded, remote* environment is a perfect place to relax.

It seems in all directions you look at a *breathtaking* vista.

The *spectacular* views bring out the artist in me.

The *scenery near the ocean* is especially *dramatic, with giant dark* cliffs rising out of the water.

I often take my paints and a canvas and try to capture the exciting *feel of the shoreline*.

PRACTICE 4

Choose which phrase or sentence best completes the paragraph and makes the paragraph cohesive.

Paragraph 1. An effective advertisement matches images and music to its product and (1) _______________. For instance, if it's selling cars to young men, it uses the image of speed and rock music. If it's selling cars to families, it uses the image of practicality and pleasant melodies. (2) _______________.

1. (A) its market
   (B) the market it wants to reach
   (C) to those who will buy the product
2. (A) If it's trying to sell a more expensive car, it uses classical music to suggest elegance and comfort.
   (B) If the car is for the rich, advertisers will want to emphasize elegance and wealth.
   (C) If it's selling cars to wealthy executives, it uses the image of wealth and classical music.

Paragraph 2. Our parents studied grammar, a subject that a lot of schools don't teach today. They studied penmanship, a skill that today few people have mastered. (3) ______________. They didn't have to learn advanced mathematics, but (4) ______________ how to do basic math without the help of a calculator.

3. (A) A foreign language, which is optional today, was a required subject.
   (B) They were taught to communicate in a foreign language.
   (C) They studied a foreign language, something that is not a requirement in many schools today.
4. (A) they had to learn
   (B) it was important to learn
   (C) they felt they should know

Paragraph 3. The contributions scientists make to society are more obvious. The cars we drive, the computers we use at home and at work, (5) ______________—all of these come from the ideas and hard work of scientists. Because of scientific contributions, we're living longer and healthier lives. Scientists also (6) ______________ the arts. Movies are the result of science, as are television, radio, and compact discs.

5. (A) and the stove and cleaning machine
   (B) the appliances we have to help us cook our meals and clean our houses
   (C) the cooking and cleaning inventions
6. (A) contribute to
   (B) help fund
   (C) support

PRACTICE 5

Choose which sentence or phrase best completes the paragraph, rephrasing the underlined sections.

Paragraph 1. Zoos are also important for the research opportunities they provide. Because <u>zoos are controlled environments</u>, research is safer and easier to conduct. (1) ______________. They may not be as secure in the wild. For example, while conducting a medical experiment in an animal's <u>natural environment</u>, scientists have to worry about both the animals they are working with and other animals nearby (2) ______________. In zoos, however, they need only focus on the research subject.

1. (A) Scientists can feel protected in the confined area of the zoo.
   (B) Scientists are better able to manage their resources at the zoo.
   (C) Scientists carry out their work more effectively at the zoo.
2. (A) in hiding
   (B) in the bush
   (C) in proximity

Paragraph 2. Not everyone learns in the same way. For instance, some students learn better by discussing a topic while others (3) ______________ by writing about it. Teachers know this and have been trained to teach using whatever methods help their students learn the most about a subject. A textbook can only give one way of learning something, but a teacher can help students learn (4) ______________.

3. (A) study much harder
   (B) absorb more knowledge
   (C) enjoy the experience more
4. (A) using a different style
   (B) faster and more efficiently
   (C) in the ways that work best for them

Paragraph 3. Both art and music help students express themselves. Students who have never before drawn a picture or tried playing the piano may be surprised to find that they enjoy these methods of (5) ______________. It is also always satisfying to try something new. It usually takes a while to develop skills in art and music, but the process of (6) ______________ can be as satisfying as producing a perfect piece of art at the end.

5. (A) communicating their inner feelings
   (B) learning about art and music
   (C) improving their talents
6. (A) being part of a class
   (B) starting a new project
   (C) acquiring new abilities

Sentences

Both the Integrated Task and Independent Task want you to demonstrate syntactic variety. You can vary the types of sentences you use, the length of the sentences, the subject of the sentences, and the voice of the sentences.

SENTENCE TYPES

There are four types of sentences: simple, compound, complex, and compound-complex.

Simple Sentence

A simple sentence has one subject and one verb.

Television commercials (subject) are (verb) the most effective form of advertising.

Compound Sentence

A compound sentence has two or more simple sentences linked by the conjunctions *and, or,* and *but.*

Newspaper ads are often ignored (simple sentence 1), and (conjunction) radio ads are quickly forgotten (simple sentence 2).

Complex Sentence

A complex sentence is made up of a simple sentence (independent clause) and one or more subordinate clauses.

> Most people listen to radio (simple sentence) when they're driving to work (subordinate clause).

Compound-Complex Sentences

A compound-complex sentence has two or more simple sentences (independent clauses) and one or more subordinate clauses.

> Although families may listen to a radio during the day, the parents listen only for news reports, and the children use it for background noise.

SENTENCE LENGTH

Some students think they have to use compound-complex sentences to show they are very proficient in English. This makes the essay very heavy and very difficult to read. It is better to mix up the type of sentences you use. For example, a complex sentence followed by several simple sentences can be very effective.

EXAMPLE

> As the number of pets increase, the amount of money being spent on pets is also increasing. Pet owners buy special toys for their pets. They order them special clothes. They put them in day care centers. They treat them like children.

PRACTICE 6

Label the sentences by their type in the following essay.

Simple = S	Complex = Cx
Compound = C	Compound - Complex = C-Cx

TOPIC 8

Why People Visit Museums

1. S ____________
2. ____________
3. ____________
4. ____________
5. ____________

People visit museums for a number of reasons. They visit museums when traveling to new places because a museum tells them a lot about the culture of those places. They also go to museums to have fun. People also are usually interested in museums that feature unusual subjects. It's impossible to get bored in a museum.

6. ____________
7. ____________

When visiting someplace new, you can find out about the culture of that place by going to a movie or a place of worship or a nightclub. Another option is to sit in the park and listen to

the people around you. The easiest way to learn about a place, 8. ____________
though, is by visiting its museums. Museums will show you the 9. ____________
history of the place you're visiting. They will show you what art 10. ____________
the locals think is important. If there aren't any museums, that 11. ____________
tells you something, too.

Museums are fun. Even if you're not interested in art or history, 12. ____________
there is always something to get your attention. Many museums 13. ____________
now have "hands-on" exhibits. These exhibits usually involve 14. ____________
activities like pushing a button and hearing more about what 15. ____________
you're looking at, or using similar materials to create your own
work of art, or trying on clothes like those on the models in the
museum.

People also enjoy museums about unusual subjects. For 16. ____________
instance, in my hometown there's a museum devoted to the 17. ____________
potato. This museum has art made out of potatoes, it tells all 18. ____________
about the history of the potato, and it sells potato mementos, 19. ____________
like key chains and potato dolls. People enjoy this museum
because it's so unusual.

People everywhere like museums. They like learning about 20. ____________
interesting and unusual things. No matter who you are or what 21. ____________
you like, there is a museum that will amaze and interest you. 22. ____________

Subject

Not all sentences should have the same subject. You will want to vary the subjects that you use. Notice in the example in the section Sentence Length on page 138, the subject of the last four sentences is the same: *Pet owners* and the pronoun *they*. In this case, there is a rhythm to the paragraph, and the sentences do not seem monotonous. These last four sentences are essentially a list; they tell you on what four things pet owners are spending money.

Compare these two versions of the same paragraph.

TOPIC 55

Every generation of people is different in important ways. How is your generation different from your parents' generation? Use specific reasons and examples to explain your answer.

Version A

My parents' generation has strict standards about acceptable behavior. My parents' generation has a difficult time accepting other standards of behavior. My parents' generation is still very concerned about what other people think of them. My parents' generation grew up in small communities where everyone knew everybody.

Version B

My parents' generation has strict standards about acceptable behavior. Consequently, they have a difficult time accepting other standards of behavior. Since my parents' generation grew up in small communities where everyone knew everybody, they are still very concerned about what other people think of them.

By combining sentences and rearranging the order, you can provide variety to the paragraph and not repeat the same subject in every sentence.

PRACTICE 7

Choose the subject that best completes the sentence.

Paragraph 1. High school students can't decide alone what they need to study. (1) ____________ need the guidance of experts in the field of education. However, they also need the freedom to follow their curiosity and interests. (2) ____________ should have the freedom to choose some courses and should be required to take others.

1. (A) They
   (B) We
   (C) Secondary school attendees
2. (A) One
   (B) You
   (C) They

Paragraph 2. English is a difficult language to learn. Its pronunciation is erratic, and so is its spelling. Why are *though, through,* and *thought* pronounced differently? Why do many English words have two different spellings? (3) ____________ is very idiomatic, too. Everywhere you travel in an English-speaking country, (4) ____________ find different expressions for the same thing, and different pronunciations for the same word.

3. (A) Spelling
   (B) Pronunciation
   (C) English
4. (A) you'll
   (B) travelers
   (C) there'll

Paragraph 3. A good neighbor respects your property and asks your permission before doing something that might affect it. This means (5) ____________ doesn't put in a driveway that takes up part of your lawn or build a fence that cuts off part of your backyard. A good (6) ____________ works with you to decide where to put the fence, and maybe the two of you could share the cost.

5. (A) he or she
   (B) they
   (C) it
6. (A) fence builder
   (B) friend
   (C) neighbor

Voice

There are two voices in English: active and passive.

Active voice

> Parents must teach their children computer skills.
> subject action object

Passive voice

> Children must be taught computer skills by their parents.
> subject action agent

The active voice emphasizes the agent (the one who performs the action). The agent is the subject of the sentence. The passive voice emphasizes the recipient of the action or the action itself. The recipient is the subject of the sentence. Most of the time we use active voice. It is a very direct way of writing and is often clearer and easier to read than passive voice.

We use passive voice when the agent is unknown or unimportant. The passive voice is useful for changing the emphasis of a sentence or for avoiding the need to mention unknown or unimportant information.

Look at these comparisons of active and passive voice.

Active voice

> Fifty years ago, somebody built a factory in my town.

Passive voice

> Fifty years ago, a factory was built in my town.

The first sentence sounds awkward and strange. Who is "somebody?" We don't know and it doesn't matter. The important information is the building of the factory, not the person or people who built it.

Active voice

> Many people lost their jobs when the owners closed the factory last year.

Passive voice

> Many people lost their jobs when the factory was closed last year.

The first sentence is possible, but the second sentence is better. We don't need to mention the agent, "the owners," because it is obvious that it was they who closed the factory. In this case, mentioning the agent takes emphasis away from the important information: the fact that the factory was closed.

PRACTICE 8

Underline the verbs in the following essay and tell whether they are active or passive.

TOPIC 3

No Factory!

1. active
2. ______
3. ______
3. ______
4. ______
5. ______

People <u>like</u> factories because they bring new jobs to a community. In my opinion, however, the benefits of a factory are outweighed by the risks. Factories cause pollution, and they bring too much growth. In addition, they destroy the quiet lifestyle of a small town. That is why I oppose a plan to build a factory near my community.

6. ______
7. ______
7. ______
7. ______
8. ______
9. ______
10. ______
11. ______
11. ______

Factories cause smog. If we build a new factory, the air we breathe will become dirty. Everything will be covered with dust. Factories also pollute rivers and streams. Our water will be too dirty to drink. The environment will be hurt and people's health will be affected.

12. ______
12. ______
13. ______
14. ______
15. ______
16. ______
17. ______

Some people will say that more jobs will be created by a factory. However, this can have a negative result. Our population will grow quickly. Many new homes and stores will be built. There will be a lot of traffic on the roads. Fast growth can cause more harm than good.

18. ______
19. ______
20. ______
21. ______
22. ______
22. ______
23. ______

Our city will change a lot. It is a pleasant place now. It is safe and quiet. Everybody knows everybody else. If a factory brings growth to the city, all of this will change. The small-town feel will be lost.

24. ______
24. ______
25. ______
26. ______

A factory would be helpful in some ways, but the dangers outweigh the benefits. Our city would be changed too much by a factory. I cannot support a plan to build a new factory here.

PRACTICE 9

Choose the active sentence that has the same meaning as the passive sentence.

1. Our lives have been dramatically improved by changes in food preparation.
   (A) Changes in food preparation have dramatically improved our lives.
   (B) Our lives are changing dramatically and so have changes in food preparation.
   (C) Our food preparation improvements have been dramatic changes.

2. Young people will be helped to overcome the fear of aging by associating with older people.
   (A) Our fear of associating with older people can overcome young people.
   (B) Young people can associate with older people who fear aging.
   (C) Association with older people will help young people overcome the fear of aging.

3. I do not like the fact that these products are made by machines.
   (A) I do not like the fact that these are machine-made products.
   (B) Products made by machine are not liked; it's a fact.
   (C) It's not a fact that these products were made by machines.

4. Large sums of money are earned by entertainers who do little to contribute to society.
   (A) Society earns a little from entertainers' contributions.
   (B) Entertainers earn large sums of money yet contribute little to society.
   (C) Money is contributed to society by entertainers who earn a lot.

6 Model Tests

This chapter contains four model tests. Each test includes one Integrated Task and one Independent Task. After you complete a model test, you can use the revision checklist to check your work. Before you fill in the checklist, follow the suggested steps to make sure you have covered everything. Then, look for the corresponding model essay in the appendix, read it, and check it, following the same steps. See how your essay compares with the model. Remember, there is no one correct way to write any of these essays, but reading the model essays and using the revision checklists will help you see the strengths and weaknesses of your writing.

Integrated Task

STEPS

1. Find the thesis statement. Underline it.
2. In the first paragraph, find the topics that support the thesis. Number them.
3. Put a check (✓) next the main idea in the second paragraph. Mark each supporting detail with a letter: A, B, C, etc.
4. Put a check (✓) next the main idea in the third paragraph. Mark each supporting detail with a letter: A, B, C, etc.
5. Underline all transition words in the second and third paragraphs.
6. Check grammar and spelling. Correct any errors.

REVISION CHECKLIST

- ❑ Content
  - ❑ Thesis Statement
  - ❑ Topics that support the thesis
  - ❑ Main ideas
  - ❑ Supporting details
- ❑ Fluency and Cohesion
  - ❑ Transition words
  - ❑ Grammar and Spelling
  - ❑ Sentence variety

Independent Task

STEPS

1. Find the thesis statement and underline it.
2. In the first paragraph, find the topics that support the thesis. Number them. They should become the main ideas of the paragraphs in the body of the essay.
3. Put a check (✓) next to the main idea in the second paragraph. Mark each supporting detail with a letter: A, B, C, etc.

4. Put a check (✓) next to the main idea in the third paragraph. Mark each supporting detail with a letter: A, B, C, etc.
5. Put a check (✓) next to the main idea in the fourth paragraph. Mark each supporting detail with a letter: A, B, C, etc.
6. Underline all transition words in the second, third, fourth, and fifth paragraphs.
7. Check grammar and spelling. Correct any errors.

REVISION CHECKLIST

- ❑ Content
  - ❑ Thesis Statement
  - ❑ Main ideas
  - ❑ Supporting details
- ❑ Fluency and Cohesion
  - ❑ Transition words
  - ❑ Grammar and Spelling
  - ❑ Sentence variety

Model Test 1

INTEGRATED TASK

Read the passage for three minutes.

The presence of technology in schools has greatly increased over the past two decades. More and more classrooms are equipped with computers and wireless technology, with the aim of boosting academic achievement. How far has technology gone toward reaching this goal?

The perceived benefits of classroom technology are several. According to many educators, one of the greatest advantages is that it provides a variety of learning tools, making it easy to address different learning styles. It allows students to experience a topic in verbal, written, spatial, quantitative, and graphical ways. Students can take in and use information in the ways that make most sense to them. Technology also helps teachers expand the boundaries of the classroom. Through use of the Internet, students can connect with people and ideas anywhere in the world.

In order to receive these benefits, however, technology must actually be used. Surveys have found that only a low percentage of teachers use technology on a regular basis, and that as many as half of all teachers never use it at all. Many teachers who do use technology do not use it to its fullest advantage. Rather, the tendency is to use computers to do the same things that can be done with pencil and paper.

Studies have shown that, properly used, technology does boost academic achievement. It has also been shown that teacher training can make the difference. In one study, teachers who received training in classroom use of technology used it regularly and used it in ways that developed higher-order thinking skills in their students. This study also showed that students in these classrooms scored higher on math tests than their peers in other classrooms. School systems, therefore, need to focus on training teachers in addition to equipping classrooms with computers.

WARNING

Study the models carefully. Analyze them completely. Do NOT memorize them. Your writing will not be scored if it matches an essay in this book. Your writing on the TOEFL iBT must be your OWN original work.

NOTE

Models for these practice tasks can be found in the Appendix. Remember, there is no one correct response. If you follow the steps outlined in the previous chapters, you will be able to write an appropriate response that is your own, original work.

TRACK 11

Listen to the lecture.

Summarize the main points in the reading passage and explain how they are strengthened by the information presented in the lecture. Write on your computer or in the space provided below. Write for no more than 20 minutes.

INDEPENDENT TASK

Write an essay on the following topic. Write on your computer or on the lines below. Write for no more than 30 minutes.

ESSAY TOPIC 28

Is it more important to be able to work with a group of people on a team or to work independently? Use reasons and specific examples to support your answer.

Model Test 2

INTEGRATED TASK

Read the passage for three minutes.

The study of animal intelligence has long been of interest to humans. In studying the question of whether or not animals can be said to have intelligence, researchers look at such areas as emotions and self-recognition, among other things. The topic of animal intelligence has generated a great deal of controversy.

In one study designed to look at emotions, chimpanzees watched videos of other chimpanzees in different situations which might cause feelings of fear or happiness. The behavioral reactions of the chimpanzees watching the video were observed to be appropriate for each situation. Their brain activity was also shown to change according to the different emotions demonstrated on the videos.

Mirrors have been used in experiments to determine whether or not animals recognize themselves. In one study, dolphins were marked on different parts of their bodies. The fact that they raced to the mirror to look at their image as soon as they felt the markers demonstrated to researchers that the dolphins did indeed recognize themselves in their mirror images. Similar studies have been done with elephants and chimpanzees. Researchers have also looked at language, tool use, memory, and problem-solving ability in attempts to define intelligence in animals.

Research on animal intelligence raises a number of difficulties. For one, there is disagreement about what we actually mean by the word "intelligence." There is also disagreement about the correct way to interpret animal behavior observed in experiments. And, it is difficult to separate actual feelings and cognitive reasoning from instinctual behavior.

Listen to the lecture.

Summarize the main points of the reading passage and explain how they are supported by the information presented in the lecture. Write on your computer or on a piece of paper. Write for no more than 20 minutes.

INDEPENDENT TASK

Write an essay on the following topic. Write on your computer or on the lines below. Write for no more than 30 minutes.

ESSAY TOPIC 17

Do you agree or disagree with the following statement? People should sometimes do things they do not enjoy doing. Use specific reasons and examples to support your answer.

Model Test 3

INTEGRATED TASK

Read the passage for three minutes.

William Shakespeare (1564–1616) is considered to be one of the greatest writers of English literature. But did he really write *Romeo and Juliet, Hamlet, Macbeth,* and the other plays attributed to him? Scholars have long questioned the authenticity of the claim that these works were written by William Shakespeare of Stratford-on-Avon, England. There are a number of reasons why.

In the first place, William Shakespeare was a man of humble origins. He was not a wealthy aristocrat or nobleman. Rather, he was the son of a tradesman, and there is no record that he ever went to school. Yet many of his plays deal with the lives of nobility and show an understanding of politics, science, literature, and foreign languages that only an aristocrat or an educated person would have had.

In addition, very few concrete facts about Shakespeare's life are known. There are very few written records containing information about him. This seems unusual for someone who became as well known as Shakespeare did. Some scholars take this as evidence that records were destroyed to hide the true identity of the author of the plays attributed to Shakespeare.

Several contemporary writers have been suggested as the possible true author of Shakespeare's works. One of the more popular theories is that they were written by Sir Francis Bacon, a prominent scholar, diplomat, and writer. This claim is based in part on perceived similarities between some of Bacon's writing and certain phrases found in the plays attributed to Shakespeare. Other well-known writers, including playwright Christopher Marlowe and Edward de Vere, 17th Earl of Oxford, have also been put forth as possible authors of the plays.

Listen to the lecture.

Summarize the points in the reading passage and explain how they are challenged by points raised in the lecture. Write on your computer or on the following lines. Write for no more than 20 minutes.

INDEPENDENT TASK

Write an essay on the following topic. Write on your computer or on the lines below. Write for no more than 30 minutes.

ESSAY TOPIC 144

> **If you could invent something new, what product would you develop? Use specific details to explain why this invention is needed.**

Model Test 4

INTEGRATED TASK

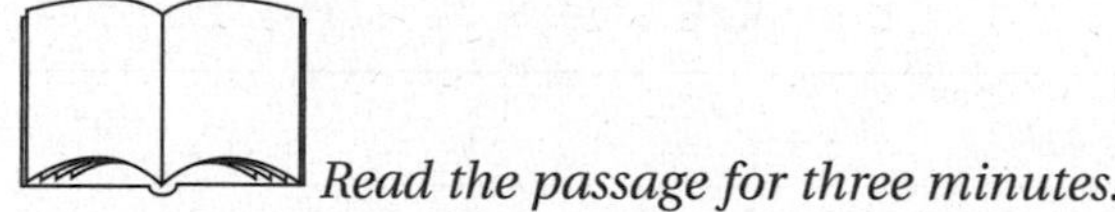

Read the passage for three minutes.

The bubonic plague, also known as the Black Plague or the Black Death, swept through the world during the Middle Ages. Originating in China, it left behind a lasting legacy.

The worst outbreak of the plague occurred in the mid-1300s. The deadly disease appeared in China in the early 1330s. Since China was a busy trading nation, the plague was soon carried from its ports to the rest of the world. The disease was transmitted to people by fleas. Rats, which infested trading ships, were the means of transporting the disease-ridden fleas throughout the world.

In 1347, several Italian trading ships returned from the Black Sea and docked in Sicily. Unbeknownst to the crew, the cargo they carried included plague-carrying rats, and a number of the sailors were dying, or already dead, from the disease. The plague spread quickly from the port to the surrounding countryside, and then throughout Italy. By the following year it had reached northern Europe. During the cold season, the plague seemed to recede, but it returned each spring with renewed vigor when fleas awakened from their winter dormancy.

It is estimated that 75 million people worldwide fell victim to the disease within the next five years. In Europe, 25 million people—one third of the continent's population—died. The widespread death led to breakdowns in the existing social order. Among other effects, the authority of the church weakened and there were peasant uprisings. There continued to be recurrences of the plague every generation or so for the next several centuries, though none as terrible as the outbreak of the 1300s. The plague finally disappeared in the 17th century.

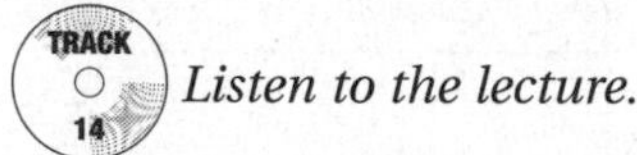

Listen to the lecture.

Summarize the points in the reading passage and explain how they are challenged by points raised in the lecture. Write on your computer or on the following lines. Write for no more than 20 minutes.

INDEPENDENT TASK

Write an essay on the following topic. Write on your computer or on the lines below. Write for no more than 30 minutes.

ESSAY TOPIC 19

You have received a gift of money. The money is enough to buy either a piece of jewelry you like or tickets to a concert you want to attend. Which would you buy? Use specific reasons and details to support your answer.

Appendix

Model Essays

The Model Essay sections of the appendix contain 10 model essays for the Integrated Task and 183 model essays for the Independent Task. They are provided as examples of ways to respond to the TOEFL essay writing tasks. There is no one correct way to respond to any of the writing task questions. These are models of well-organized essays that are clear, coherent, and address the question. These models show one possible way of responding to the particular question.

You can study these models as examples of ways to respond to the tasks. You can also use them to compare with your own writing.

For the Integrated Task essays, you can complete a practice task in the exercises or model tests, then compare your essay with the corresponding model essay in the appendix. Notice how the lecture and reading are summarized and compared in the model essay and in your own. You might not have used the exact same words, but your essay should follow the same general points as the model essay.

For the Independent Task essays, choose one of the questions and write your own response to it before looking at the model essay. Since the Independent Task asks you to express your own ideas and opinions, your essay will be very different from the model essay. The model essay, however, will show you how to develop a theme with a main idea, supporting ideas, and details. Notice how this is done in the model essay, then check your essay to make sure it follows the same type of structure.

A good practice technique is to write out the essays by hand. This will help you become familiar with the structure of a sentence, the words used, and the organization of the essay. You can write them over several times. It is important to do this by hand. There is a correlation between the hand and the brain. This will help you internalize the patterns.

You can also use the essays to practice typing. This will help you with spelling and the formatting of the essay.

MODEL ESSAYS: INTEGRATED TASKS

These model Integrated Tasks are based on reading passages and lectures used in the Self-Tests and exercises in this book. Each task is identified so that you can easily find the reading passages and lectures that correspond to each model. These are examples only so that you can see ways to respond to the Integrated Task.

MODEL 1 (SELF-TEST, pages 23–24)

The author explains why global warming is a serious problem. Likewise, the speaker explains the impact of global warming in the northeastern United States.

The author explains that human activity, such as industry and cutting down forests, has resulted in an artificial increase in greenhouse gases in Earth's atmosphere, with serious results. Greenhouse gases, such as carbon dioxide, hold heat in the atmosphere and result in rising temperatures on Earth. As average temperatures rise, there are a number of effects. First, scientists predict that weather patterns will change. In addition, snow and ice will melt and sea levels will rise. This can lead to flooding, drought, and powerful storms. It can also affect the economy, particularly agriculture and transportation. Economists predict that global warming will lead to a drop in gross national product and consumer consumption in countries around the world.

The speaker explains the effects of global warming in the northeastern part of the United States. This is a cold and snowy area. Since 1965, temperatures in this region have risen. There are also fewer days with snow on the ground than there used to be. This has had an effect on the economy for people who depend on the ski industry to make a living. The predicted effects of global warming that the author described are already coming true, at least in the northeastern United States.

MODEL 2 (TASK 1, page 58)

Summarize the main points of the reading passage and explain how the points made in the lecture oppose them.

The author asserts that advances in technology do not always lead to increased productivity. The speaker, in contrast, suggests that investment in technology is paid back in increased productivity.

The author explains that because of technology, workers often stay at their desks all day, but this does not lead to increased productivity. It can cause back, neck, and eye pain. This is very uncomfortable and actually lowers productivity. Workers need to take breaks more often and go out for lunch. They also should have meetings in person instead of using email. In addition, companies can buy special equipment that is more comfortable to use.

The speaker has the opposite point of view. She believes that technology increases productivity. Photocopy machines, for example, can copy, collate, and staple much faster than a person. Because of this, workers can spend their time doing other things. Also an office can hire fewer people and save money on salaries. Moreover, when people use email, they don't have to go to so many meetings. Instead, they can spend more time working. The speaker does not mention the physical pains that using technology can cause. Clearly, technology solves some problems, but it causes others.

MODEL 3 (TASK 2, page 62)

Summarize the main points of the reading passage and explain how they are supported by the information presented in the lecture.

The author explains that animal-assisted therapy is used to improve emotional and physical health, and the speaker tells us about a study that showed positive effects of pet ownership on health.

The author explains how pets improve both emotional health and physical health. Pets are good companions for lonely people. They also give their owners things to do, like hobbies or club activities. In addition, pets are a comfort to anxious or worried people. Pets are good for physical health, as well. They help people with high blood pressure and heart problems.

They help people stay physically active. They give people a chance to play. Finally, pet therapy is used with elderly people.

The speaker supports pet therapy. He describes a study where pets had a positive effect on the health of heart patients. Half the patients had a dog to take care of. The other half only got traditional treatment. After six months, the patients with pets had lower blood pressure, and they had lost more weight than the other patients. They felt happier, too. These are all things that can affect heart disease. This is a case that shows how pet therapy works to improve physical health.

MODEL 4 (TASK 3, page 63)

Summarize the main points in the reading passage and explain how the information presented in the lecture adds to them.

The author warns that ocean pollution is a serious problem. In the same way, the speaker explains how plastic garbage threatens sea animals.

The author explains that different things cause ocean pollution. Oil from factories and cities enters the ocean through rivers and drains. Similarly, fertilizers wash into the ocean, and they cause large growths of algae. Toxic chemicals continue to pollute the ocean, as well. There are laws against dumping these chemicals, but the chemicals still leak into the ocean. Animals eat them, and when we eat seafood, we eat these chemicals, too. There is also a lot of garbage in the ocean. Plastic is the worst kind because it does not break down quickly. Animals think it is food. They eat it and choke on it.

While the author gives an overview of ocean pollution, the speaker specifically describes the problem of plastic garbage. People produce billions of pounds of plastic a year, and a lot of this ends up in the ocean. The water and wind break large pieces of plastic into smaller pieces. Then animals try to eat these pieces. An animal may choke on plastic. It may starve because it does not feel hungry after eating plastic. Animals are often caught in floating plastic. They are also strangled by it. There are many types of pollution in the ocean. Plastic garbage is one of the worst examples.

MODEL 5 (TASK 4, page 64)

Summarize the main points of the reading passage and explain how the points made in the lecture cast doubt on them.

The author explains that color has psychological effects. In contrast, the speaker tells us about a study that showed no effect of color on appetite.

The author describes different ways people have used the psychological effects of color. Ancient people used color for healing, and modern designers use color to create mood. Designers might use yellow to create a positive mood in an office. Likewise, they might use neutral colors to create a clean, clear, and focused mood in health care centers. Restaurants often use orange and red to stimulate the appetite. Some scientists say that blue lowers the heart rate and blood pressure. Red, on the other hand, may raise blood pressure. Other scientists do not believe that color affects mood. They say the effect is temporary and also that it is different in every culture.

The speaker describes a study that showed no relationship between color and appetite. A fast-food restaurant chain had orange walls in half its restaurants and beige walls in the rest of its restaurants. It recorded all the food ordered for two years. There was no difference between the restaurants with orange walls and the restaurants with beige walls. People ordered the same food in both types of places. In other words, according to the company president, there is no effect of color on appetite. He said that the study proved it. In this case, at least, there was no psychological effect of color.

MODEL 6 (PRACTICE INTEGRATED TASK, page 76)

The author discusses the dangers of cell phone use while driving. The speaker, however, believes that cell phones are not any more dangerous to drivers than other distractions.

The author explains that talking on the phone while driving is dangerous because it distracts the driver. Because of this, drivers in accidents involving cell phones have been held responsible for the accidents. The author also discusses laws that prohibit the use of cell phones while driving.

The speaker disagrees with these laws. He points out that drivers can be distracted by things other than talking on the phone, such as eating, talking to passengers, taking care of children, putting on make up, and other things. He cites a study that found that cell phone use actually causes fewer accidents than other distractions. He mentions another study that used video tapes. The tapes showed that drivers were less distracted by their phones than by other activities. Finally, the speaker emphasizes that cell phones contribute to our safety. People use cell phones to report accidents and dangerous drivers on the road.

MODEL TASK 7 (MODEL TESTS, INTEGRATED TASK 1, page 147)

The author explains that technology in the classroom can improve academic achievement, but only when it is used properly. The speaker agrees that adequate teacher training is necessary.

The author talks about the ways that technology can improve learning, by addressing different learning styles and by connecting to the rest of the world through the Internet. Unfortunately, teachers do not always use technology in the best way possible, so their students do not benefit from it. Academic achievement can be improved through technology if teachers are trained to use it.

The speaker completely supports this point of view by discussing two studies. A survey of teachers found that they often do not receive enough training to use technology, so they feel very uncomfortable with it. The majority do not use computers in their classrooms. The speaker then mentioned a special program in one school district. The teachers received 200 hours of training. They used technology in their classrooms to help their students develop thinking skills. These students scored much higher on achievement tests than other students in the school district.

MODEL TASK 8 (MODEL TESTS, INTEGRATED TASK 2, page 151)

The author gives an overview of the study of animal intelligence and points out that there is a lot of controversy around such research. Likewise, the speaker discusses research on animal intelligence, specifically on self-recognition, and also mentions that not all scientists agree with interpretations of the results.

The author especially mentions emotions and self-recognition as two things researchers look at when studying animal intelligence. She describes a particular study with dolphins.

After scientists placed marks on the dolphins' bodies, the dolphins rushed to the mirror to look at the marks. So, scientists say, the animals recognized themselves in the mirror. The author adds that there is a lot of disagreement among scientists researching animal intelligence, including disagreement about how results should be interpreted.

The speaker describes specific research on animal intelligence. She talks in more detail about how studies are done with mirrors. Certain animals react to their reflection in a mirror. For example, they try to touch it. The only animals that do this are apes, dolphins, and elephants. In a self-recognition test, a mark is painted on the animal's face. When the animal looks in the mirror, it might try to wipe the mark off its face. This means that it recognizes itself in the mirror, scientists say. But not all scientists agree. The animal might be interested in the mark but that doesn't mean it connects the mirror image with itself.

MODEL TASK 9 (MODEL TESTS, INTEGRATED TASK 3, page 153)

The author describes reasons why scholars believe that William Shakespeare was not the true author of his plays. In contrast, the speaker says there is not evidence to support this idea.

The author explains several reasons for doubting that Shakespeare wrote the plays. First, William Shakespeare was not wealthy and was probably not educated. The plays contain a lot of information that only a wealthy or educated person would know. Second, there are not many written records about Shakespeare's life. It is possible that records about him were destroyed to hide the fact that another person actually wrote the plays. Who was that other person? There have been several suggestions. Some people think it was Francis Bacon because there are some similarities between his writing and Shakespeare's plays.

The speaker disagrees with the theory that Shakespeare did not write the plays. He explains that Shakespeare could have had the knowledge to write the plays. He may have attended a school in his town, and he actually did have contact with wealthy people because of his theater work. The lack of records is also not evidence because records may have been lost over time. He also states that Bacon could not have written the plays because his writing style is very different from Shakespeare's.

MODEL TASK 10 (MODEL TESTS, INTEGRATED TASK 4, page 157)

The author asserts that the bubonic plague originated in China during the Middle Ages and disappeared in the seventeenth century. The speaker, on the other hand, explains that the plague may actually have originated in ancient Egypt and that outbreaks still occur today.

According to the author, the worst outbreak of the bubonic plague occurred in the 1300s. The disease started in China and was transported to other parts of the world by rats. The rats carried disease-ridden fleas onto ships. The plague arrived in Europe through Italy in 1347. Over the next five years, it killed 25 million people in Europe and 75 million people worldwide. This led to a breakdown of the social order. The plague continued to recur every generation until the seventeenth century, when it disappeared.

The speaker presents a different theory of the origins of the bubonic plague. She describes the work of an archeologist who found evidence of the plague in ancient Egypt. The archeologist found the remains of fleas at the site of an ancient village. The archeologist then turned up evidence that ancient Egyptians had experienced epidemics which may have been the bubonic plague. The speaker says that rats may have carried the disease from Africa to Europe on ships. She also points out that the bubonic plague has not disappeared. There are still several thousand new cases reported around the world every year.

MODEL ESSAYS: INDEPENDENT TASKS

The essay topics on the following pages may appear on your actual TOEFL. You should become familiar with the list before you take the TOEFL. Remember that when you take the test you will NOT have a choice of topics. You must write only on the topic that is assigned to you.

The essay topics are classified according to their type. Remember this classification is not always precise. *Giving an Explanation* can also be called *Making an Argument* in some cases. Both tasks are very similar. These classifications are to guide you only.

TOEFL TOPICS			
MA	Making an Argument	PR	Stating a Preference
AD	Agreeing or Disagreeing	EX	Giving an Explanation

As you study these topics and the essays, look for the organizational patterns. Can you find the three main points and the supporting details in each essay?

1 EX

People attend college or university for many different reasons. Why do you think people attend college or university? Use specific reasons and examples to support your answer.

People attend college for a lot of different reasons. I believe that the three most common reasons are to prepare for a career, to have new experiences, and to increase their knowledge of themselves and of the world around them.

Career preparation is probably the primary reason that people attend college. These days, the job market is very competitive. Careers such as information technology will need many new workers in the near future. At college, students can learn new skills for these careers and increase their opportunities for the future.

Students also go to college to have new experiences. For many, it is their first time away from home. At college, they can meet new people from many different places. They can see what life is like in a different city. They can learn to live on their own and take care of themselves without having their family always nearby.

At college, students have the opportunity to increase their knowledge. As they decide what they want to study, pursue their studies, and interact with their classmates, they learn a lot about themselves. They also, of course, have the opportunity to learn about many subjects in their classes. In addition to the skills and knowledge related to their career, college students also have the chance to take classes in other areas. For many, this will be their last chance to study different subjects.

Colleges offer much more than career preparation. They offer the opportunity to have new experiences and to learn many kinds of things. I think all of these are reasons why people attend college.

2 AD

Do you agree or disagree with the following statement? Parents are the best teachers. Use specific reasons and examples to support your answer.

Parents shape their children from the beginning of their children's lives. They develop close emotional ties with their children. They share their interests with them. They teach them values. Parents can be very important teachers in their children's lives; however, they are not always the best teachers.

Parents may be too close to their children emotionally. For example, they may limit a child's freedom in the name of safety. A teacher may organize an educational trip to a big city, but a parent may think this trip is too dangerous. A school may want to take the children camping, but a parent may be afraid of the child getting hurt.

Another problem is that parents sometimes expect their children's interests to be similar to their own. If the parents love science, they may try to force their child to love science too. But what if the child prefers art? If the parents enjoy sports, they may expect their child to participate on different teams. But what if the child prefers to read?

Finally, although parents want to pass on their values to their children, values can change. The children of today are growing up in a world different from their parents' world. Sometimes parents, especially older ones, can't keep up with rapid social or technological changes. A student who has friends of different races at school may find that his parents have narrower views. A student who loves computers may find that her parents don't understand or value the digital revolution.

Parents are important teachers in our lives, but they aren't always the best teachers. Fortunately, we have many teachers in our lives. Our parents teach us, our teachers teach us, and we learn from our peers. Books and newspapers also teach us. All of them are valuable.

3 PR

A company has announced that it wishes to build a large factory near your community. Discuss the advantages and disadvantages of this new influence on your community. Do you support or oppose the factory? Explain your position.

People like factories because they bring new jobs to a community. In my opinion, however, the benefits of a factory are outweighed by the risks. Factories cause pollution and they bring too much growth. In addition, they destroy the quiet lifestyle of a small town. That is why I oppose a plan to build a factory near my community.

Factories cause smog. If we build a new factory, the air we breathe will become dirty. Everything will be covered with dust. Factories also pollute rivers and streams. Our water will be too dirty to drink. The environment will be hurt and people's health will be affected by a factory.

Some people will say that more jobs will be created by a factory. However, this can have a negative result. Our population will grow quickly. Many new homes and stores will be built. There will be a lot of traffic on the roads. Fast growth can cause more harm than good.

Our city will change a lot. It is a pleasant place now. It is safe and quiet. Everybody knows everybody else. If a factory brings growth to the city, all of this will change. The small-town feel will be lost.

A factory would be helpful in some ways, but the dangers outweigh the benefits. Our city would be changed too much by a factory. I cannot support a plan to build a new factory here.

4 MA

> **If you could change one important thing about your hometown, what would you change? Use reasons and specific examples to support your answer.**

If I could change one thing about my hometown, I think it would be the fact that there is no sense of community. People don't feel connected, they don't look out for each other, and they don't get to know their neighbors.

The people who live here don't feel connected to the community. Many of them have jobs in nearby towns, so they spend most of the day somewhere else and are home only in the evenings and on weekends. Also, they tend to change jobs frequently and move away. This means they don't put down roots, and they don't do things that would mean making a commitment to the community, such as joining community organizations, participating in school events, or beautifying the neighborhoods. They don't feel like community members.

People in my hometown generally don't try to support their neighbors. They don't have the habit of watching out for each other's children or checking in on the elderly or keeping an eye on the house next door when the owner is on vacation. They would have no way of knowing if a neighbor suffered an accident or lost a loved one. There just isn't much community support for individuals.

Neighbors in my hometown don't seem interested in getting to know each other. There isn't much casual visiting among neighbors, and neighborhood events such as block parties are not the custom. Also, when there is a problem, such as children riding their bikes uninvited through someone's garden, there is no casual, friendly way of working it out. A simple problem can easily become a major disagreement because there is not a sense of friendliness or trust.

My hometown is a nice place to live in many ways. It is pretty and peaceful and very safe, but it would be much nicer if we had that sense of community.

5 EX

> **How do movies or television influence people's behavior? Use reasons and specific examples to support your answer.**

Television is a big influence in most of our lives. We spend hours every week watching television programs, so of course it has effects on our behavior. Unfortunately, those effects are usually negative. Television makes people less sensitive to violence, less active, and less imaginative.

Many programs and movies on television are violent, and the more we see this violence, the less sensitive we become to it. Eventually, violence stops seeming wrong or bad. This is especially true because violence on television doesn't seem to have consequences. We might see an actor killed one week on one television program and then appear alive and well the next week on another program. Even though we know the violence and killing aren't real, if we see enough of it on television, it's easy to start confusing it with reality. It's easy to forget that violence in real life has real consequences and that killing someone is permanent.

Another effect of television is that it makes us less active, mentally as well as physically. Watching television requires almost no effort on the part of the watcher. We just push buttons to turn the television on and change the channels. In addition, all the time we spend sitting in front of the television is time we aren't spending moving around, playing a sport, or talking a walk. It's time we aren't spending reading books, conversing with our friends, or studying. It's time we aren't exercising our bodies or minds in meaningful ways.

Finally, television can stifle the imagination. On television, all the stories are told for us. We don't have to imagine what a character or place looks like, as we do when we read books, because everything is shown to us. Furthermore, since we can turn on the television so easily, we don't have to invent ways to spend leisure time. Any time we have a few free moments, we can just sit down and watch and let the television do the entertaining for us.

Television is a big influence in modern life, and it can be a valuable educational tool. The other side, however, is that it has strong negative effects on our behavior, encouraging us to accept violence and to be inactive and unimaginative.

6 PR

Some people prefer to live in a small town. Others prefer to live in a big city. Which place would you prefer to live in? Use specific reasons and details to support your answer.

I grew up in a small town and then moved to a big city. I didn't think I would like living here, but I was wrong. I think life is much better in a big city. Transportation is much more convenient, everything is more exciting, and there is a greater variety of people. I can't imagine ever living in a small town again.

Transportation is easier in a city. In a small town, you have to have a car to get around because there isn't any kind of public transportation. In a city, on the other hand, there are usually buses and taxis, and some cities have subways. Cities often have heavy traffic and expensive parking, but it doesn't matter because you can always take the bus. Using public transportation is usually cheaper and more convenient than driving a car, but you don't have this choice in a small town.

City life is more exciting than small town life. In small towns usually nothing changes. You see the same people every day, you go to the same two or three restaurants, everything is the same. In a city things change all the time. You see new people every day. There are many restaurants, with new ones to choose from all the time. New plays come to the theaters and new musicians come to the concert halls.

Cities have a diversity of people that you don't find in a small town. There are much fewer people in a small town and usually they are all alike. In a city you can find people from different countries, of different religions, of different races—you can find all kinds of people. This variety of people is what makes city life interesting.

Life in a city is convenient, exciting, and interesting. After experiencing city life, I could never live in a small town again.

7 AD

Do you agree or disagree with the following statement? Universities should give the same amount of money to their students' sports activities as they give to their university libraries. Use specific reasons and examples to support your opinion.

I disagree strongly with the idea that the same amount of money should go to university sports activities as to university libraries. Although playing sports is an important part of education, libraries are fundamental. Students cannot study without them and they require a lot of financial support to maintain up-to-date technology, to keep new books and magazines on the shelves, and to keep them operating.

Students need up-to-date library facilities to get a good education. They need computerized programs and access to Internet research databases. It costs money to have these things available, but they are fundamental to education. If a university offers its students only resources of a decade ago, it deprives those students of a tremendous amount of information.

Although we get a lot of information from computers and the Internet, university libraries still need to maintain a complete book and magazine collection. Every day new information is published on every subject, and every university wants to have this information available to its students. Again, this requires money.

It also costs money for universities to operate their libraries. University libraries are usually open for long hours and during this time they use heat and electricity. Most important, a university library needs a well-educated, knowledgeable staff. In order to be able to hire the best people, they have to be able to pay good salaries.

University students are only going to benefit from their education if they can get all the tools they need to learn. Sports are secondary to the resources that students need from university libraries. For this reason, libraries should always be better funded than sports activities.

8 EX

Many people visit museums when they travel to new places. Why do you think people visit museums? Use specific reasons and examples to support your answer.

People visit museums for a number of reasons. They visit museums when traveling to new places because a museum tells them a lot about the culture of those places. They also go to museums to have fun. People also are usually interested in museums that feature unusual subjects. It's impossible to get bored in a museum.

When visiting someplace new, you can find out about the culture of that place in many ways. The easiest way to learn about a culture, though, is by visiting its museums. Museums will show you the history of the place you're visiting. They'll show you what art the locals think is important. If there aren't any museums, that tells you something, too.

Museums are fun. Even if you're not interested in art or history, there is always something to get your attention. Many museums now have what they call "hands-on" exhibits. These exhibits have activities such as pushing a button to hear more about what you're looking at, or creating your own work of art. Everyone, from child to adult, enjoys these hands-on activities in museums.

People also enjoy visiting museums about unusual subjects. For instance, in my hometown there's a museum devoted to the potato. This museum has art made out of potatoes. It also tells the history of the potato, and sells unusual items such as potato dolls. People enjoy visiting this museum because it is so unusual. There is no other place like it.

People everywhere like museums. They like learning about interesting and unusual things. No matter who you are or what you like, there is a museum that will amaze and interest you.

9 PR

Some people prefer to eat at food stands or restaurants. Other people prefer to prepare and eat food at home. Which do you prefer? Use specific reasons and examples to support your answer.

Although many people prefer to eat at restaurants because it is easier than cooking at home, I prefer to prepare food at home. I believe it is much cheaper and healthier to eat at home, and it can be more convenient, too.

While eating in restaurants is fast, the money you spend can add up. When I have dinner at a restaurant, the bill is usually $25 or more. I can buy a lot of groceries with that much money. Even lunch at a food stand can easily cost seven or eight dollars. That's enough to feed a whole family at home.

Eating at home is better for you, too. Meals at restaurants are often high in fat and calories. When you cook at home, however, you can control what you eat. You can cook with low-fat and low-calorie ingredients. Restaurants also often serve big plates of food. You may eat a big plate of food at a restaurant because you paid for it, while at home you can control your portion size. You can serve yourself as little as you want.

It may seem more convenient to eat at a restaurant because you don't have to shop, cook, or clean up. All you do is eat. Cooking at home, however, can actually be more convenient. There are lots of simple meals that don't take long to prepare. In addition, when you eat at home, you don't have to drive to the restaurant, look for a parking space, wait for a table, and wait for service.

People often choose to eat at restaurants because it seems more convenient. I find, however, that cooking at home is actually easier, and it is cheaper and healthier as well.

10 PR

It has recently been announced that a new restaurant may be built in your neighborhood. Do you support or oppose this plan? Why? Use specific reasons and details to support your answer.

I can see both advantages and disadvantages to having a new restaurant built in our neighborhood. I believe, however, that the disadvantages outweigh the advantages. A new restaurant would bring more traffic problems to the area. In addition, it could attract undesirable people. Most of all, I think there are other types of business that would be more beneficial to the neighborhood.

Traffic congestion is already a problem in our neighborhood, and a new restaurant would just add to the problem. Most restaurant customers would arrive by car and crowd our streets even more. In addition, they would occupy parking spaces and make it even harder for residents to find places to park near their homes.

I'm also concerned about the type of patrons the new restaurant would bring into our neighborhood. If the restaurant serves drinks and has dancing, there could be problems. The restaurant would stay open late and people leaving the restaurant might be drunk. They could be noisy too. This is not the kind of thing I want to see in my neighborhood.

Finally, there are other types of businesses that we need in our neighborhood more. We already have a restaurant and a couple of coffee shops. We don't have a bookstore or a pharmacy, however, and we have only one small grocery store. I would prefer to see one of these businesses established here rather than another restaurant. Any one of them would be more useful to the residents and would maintain the quiet atmosphere of our streets.

A new restaurant could disrupt the quiet lifestyle of our neighborhood. It might bring jobs, but it would also bring traffic and noise. Moreover, it would use space that might be better used for another type of business. This is why I would oppose a plan for a new restaurant.

11 PR

Some people think that they can learn better by themselves than with a teacher. Others think that it is always better to have a teacher. Which do you prefer? Use specific reasons to develop your essay.

Most people can learn to do something simple on their own with just a set of instructions. However, to learn something more complex, it's always best to have a teacher. Teachers help you find the way that you learn best. They help you stay focused on what you're learning. They provide you with a wider range of information than you might find on your own. In short, teachers provide you with a lot more support and knowledge than you can usually get by yourself.

Teachers can help students learn in the way that is best for each student because teachers understand that different people have different learning styles. For example, some students learn better by discussing a topic. Others learn more by writing about it. A teacher can help you follow your learning style, while a book can give you only one way of learning something.

Teachers help you focus on what you are learning. They can help you keep from becoming distracted. They can show you which are the most important points in a lesson to understand. If you have to study on your own, on the other hand, it might be difficult to keep your attention on the material or know which points are most important.

Teachers bring their own knowledge and understanding of the topic to the lesson. A book presents you with certain information, and the teacher can add more. The teacher might also have a different point of view from the book and can provide other sources of information and ideas, as well.

There is nothing wrong with studying on your own. For the best possible learning, though, a teacher is the biggest help you can have.

12 AD

It is better for children to grow up in the countryside than in a big city. Do you agree or disagree? Use specific reasons and examples to develop your essay.

I have to disagree that it is better for children to grow up in the countryside. In the countryside, children have limited opportunities to see and learn about things. In the city, on the other hand, they are exposed to many different things. They see all kinds of different people every day. They have opportunities to attend many cultural events. They see people working in different kinds of jobs and therefore can make better choices for their own future. Growing up in the city is definitely better.

All different kinds of people live in the city, while in a small town in the countryside people are often all the same. City people come from other parts of the country or even from other countries. They are of different races and religions. When children grow up in this situation, they have the opportunity to learn about and understand different kinds of people. This is an important part of their education.

In the city, there are many opportunities to attend cultural events, whereas such opportunities are usually limited in the countryside. In the city there are movies and theaters, museums, zoos, and concerts. In the city children can attend cultural events every weekend, or even more often. This is also an important part of their education.

People in the city work in different kinds of jobs, while in the countryside there often isn't a variety of job opportunities. People in the city work at all different types and levels of professions, as well as in factories, in service jobs, and more. Children growing up in the city learn that there is a wide variety of jobs they can choose from when they grow up. They have a greater possibility of choosing a career that they will enjoy and do well in. This is perhaps the most important part of their education.

People usually move to the city because there are more opportunities there. Children who grow up in the city have these opportunities from the time they are small. The city is definitely a better place for children to grow up.

13 MA

In general, people are living longer now. Discuss the causes of this phenomenon. Use specific reasons and details to develop your essay.

People are living to be much older these days than ever before. The main reasons for this are greater access to health care, improved health care, and better nutrition.

Basic health care is available to many more people now than it was in the past. When someone is ill nowadays, he or she can go to a public hospital instead of having to pay for private care. There are also more clinics and more trained doctors and nurses than there used to be. Years ago, health care was not available to everyone. People who didn't live in big cities often did not have easy access to doctors or hospitals, and many people couldn't afford to pay for the medical care they needed.

In addition to increased access to health care, the quality of that health care has greatly improved over the years. Doctors know now much more about diseases and how to cure them. In the past, people died young because of simple things such as an infection or a virus. Now we have antibiotics and other medicines to cure these diseases. Furthermore, advances in medical science have made it possible to cure certain types of cancer and to treat heart disease. This has prolonged the lives of many, many people.

The quality of nutrition has also improved over time. Because of this, people tend to be healthier than they used to be. Now we know how to eat more healthfully. We know that eating low fat food can prevent heart disease. We know that eating certain fruits and vegetables can prevent cancer. We have information about nutrition that can help us live longer, healthier lives.

Improved health care and healthy eating habits are allowing us to live longer. Now we need to make sure that everyone in the world has these benefits.

14 MA

We all work or will work in jobs with many different kinds of people. In your opinion, what are some important characteristics of a good co-worker (someone you work closely with)? Use reasons and specific examples to explain why these characteristics are important.

I've worked in several offices, and I've found there are certain characteristics that all good co-workers have in common. They tend to be cooperative people, they adapt well to changes, and they are helpful to others in the office. People who have these characteristics are easy to work with.

A good co-worker is very cooperative. She does her best to get along with others. She tries to do her work well because she knows that if one person doesn't get her work done, it affects everyone else. She also has a positive attitude that creates a pleasant working environment.

A good co-worker is adaptable. She is not stubborn about changes in schedules or routines. She doesn't object to having her job description revised. She has no problem with new procedures. In fact, she welcomes changes when they come.

A good co-worker is helpful. For instance, she lends a hand when someone falls behind in his or her work. She is willing to change her schedule to accommodate another worker's emergency. She doesn't keep track of how often she has to take on extra work.

We spend more time with our co-workers during the week than we do with our family. Thus, it's important for our co-workers to be people we can get along with. When co-workers are cooperative, adaptable, and helpful, everyone gets along better and can get their jobs done well.

15 PR

> **It has recently been announced that a large shopping center may be built in your neighborhood. Do you support or oppose this plan? Why? Use specific reasons and details to support your answer.**

There would be both advantages and disadvantages to having a shopping center built in my neighborhood. Overall, however, I think the advantages are greater. The most important advantage would be convenience. In addition, a shopping center would give local residents more choices for shopping and entertainment. Finally, it would provide employment opportunities.

It would be very convenient to have a shopping center in the neighborhood. Now there are very few stores near my house, and we have to drive long distances to buy groceries and other necessities. Shopping would be much easier and faster if we had a shopping center in our own neighborhood. Also, in a shopping center all the stores are together in one place, so that would make shopping even more convenient for us.

In addition to convenience, a shopping center would give us more choices. There would be a variety of stores selling different kinds of products. There would probably also be restaurants and food courts, so we would have a greater variety of places to eat. There would likely be a movie theater, too. So, the shopping center would provide us with a range of options for both shopping and entertainment.

Having a shopping center built in the neighborhood would also bring more jobs to the community. Initially, these jobs would be in the construction of the center. In the long term, there would be jobs in the stores, theaters, and food establishments. The shopping center would provide a variety of employment opportunities, from maintenance and janitorial work to retail jobs to managerial positions.

On the whole, though, I think my neighborhood should support having a shopping center built here. It would bring more variety to our shopping, give us the opportunity to amuse ourselves at movie theaters and restaurants, and create more jobs in the area.

16 PR

> **It has recently been announced that a new movie theater may be built in your neighborhood. Do you support or oppose this plan? Why? Use specific reasons and details to support your answer.**

Some people will say that a new movie theater in our neighborhood would be a bad thing. However, I fully support the plan to build one. I feel that a movie theater would provide more opportunities for entertainment, reduce teenage delinquency, and bring more business to our town.

A movie theater would provide a much needed source of entertainment to our area. Right now, there is little to do in my town. There is almost nowhere to go in the evenings, and the nearest place that has movie theaters and restaurants is thirty minutes away. If we build a movie theater here, we can enjoy evenings right in our own neighborhood.

A movie theater would reduce juvenile delinquency. Like everywhere else, teenagers here are bored. They need activities to keep them busy and out of trouble. A movie theater would not only provide them with entertainment, it would also be a source of jobs for them. We need more businesses that want to employ young people, and a movie theater is the perfect sort of business for that.

A movie theater would attract more business to our town. People who come from other towns to use our movie theater would also shop in our stores. New stores and restaurants might open because there would be more customers for them. Our town could become more prosperous, and more interesting, too.

I believe our town would benefit greatly from a new movie theater. It would make life here more interesting and could make us more prosperous. I fully support the plan and hope that others in the neighborhood will join me to convince residents and local governments.

17 AD

Do you agree or disagree with the following statement? People should sometimes do things that they do not enjoy doing. Use specific reasons and examples to support your answer.

I agree that people should sometimes do things that they don't enjoy doing. This is a basic part of life. There are many small things we have to do in both our personal and professional lives that we may not enjoy, but that are part of our responsibilities. In addition, sometimes by doing things we don't enjoy, we actually learn to like them.

Most people's personal lives are filled with tasks that they don't enjoy doing, but they do them anyway. Who likes going to the doctor or dentist, for example? But we do this because we know that it is important to take care of our health. I don't know many people who like changing the oil in their cars or mowing the lawn. We do these things, however, because we understand that we need to maintain our personal property.

Similarly, our professional lives are filled with tasks that are not fun, but that are necessary parts of our jobs. No one likes to do boring assignments or to work with someone who no one else likes. If we're in management, we may sometimes have to fire someone. No one likes to do things like these, but if they are part of our professional responsibilities, we have to do them.

On the other hand, sometimes doing something we don't enjoy can lead to enjoyment. Simply by trying it again, we may decide we like doing it. For instance, we may think we hate to dance. We agree to go to a club only to please someone else. Yet, for some reason, this time we enjoy dancing. The same can be true of trying new foods or going to a new type of museum.

Not everything in life is fun. Unpleasant or boring tasks are a necessary part of life. We don't like them, but we do them anyway. And sometimes they surprise us and turn into something enjoyable.

18 PR

Some people spend their entire lives in one place. Others move a number of times throughout their lives, looking for a better job, house, community, or even climate. Which do you prefer: staying in one place or moving in search of another place? Use reasons and specific examples to support your opinion.

Even though I have lived in the same house, in the same neighborhood, in the same city my entire life, I know I would be happy living in a variety of places. Moving would expose me to new people, new weather, and new housing.

Even if I moved to another part of my own city, I would encounter new people. Each neighborhood has a distinct personality. If I moved to a new neighborhood, I would meet the shopkeepers and residents that shape that neighborhood's personality. It would be a new experience for me and I could become part of a new community.

If I want to experience a different kind of climate, I would have to move far from my city. Where I live now, it is the same temperature all year. I would like to go to a place where there are four seasons so I can experience really cold weather. I would like to walk in the snow and learn winter sports such as skiing.

Now I live with my parents in their house. It is a one-story house built around a courtyard where we spend a lot of time. If I could move to a different kind of house, I would like to live in an apartment on a very high floor so I could see all around me. I could also meet my neighbors on the elevator and we could get together for coffee in my apartment.

The more I moved the more I would experience change. I would meet new people in every place I lived; I could move to sample countries with four seasons or even a continent like Antarctica, which only has two. Wherever I lived, I would experience living in housing particular to that area. I would then be a citizen of the world, wouldn't I? Could you call me a foreigner if I called everyplace my home?

19 PR

You have received a gift of money. The money is enough to buy either a piece of jewelry you like or tickets to a concert you want to attend. Which would you buy? Use specific reasons and details to support your answer.

The choice between spending money on tickets to a concert or spending money on jewelry is an easy one. Given this choice, I would definitely buy jewelry. To me, the reasons are obvious. Jewelry is a good financial investment, it lasts a long time, and it is beautiful.

Buying jewelry is a good way to invest money. In fact, I believe that everyone should own some gold jewelry because its value always goes up. Then, if one day you have a financial problem, you can sell your jewelry to get the money you need. You would not be able to sell a used concert ticket, however. After the concert is over, the ticket has no value at all.

Jewelry also lasts a long time. You can wear it as often as you like, and it will give you pleasure for years and years. Each time you put it on, you can remember the day you bought it. Your jewelry may need a little cleaning from time to time or an occasional minor repair, but it never wears out. Your concert ticket, on the other hand, is no longer useful once you've attended the concert.

Jewelry is beautiful to look at. I would feel very attractive wearing a shiny gold bracelet or a sparkly diamond pin. I could use my jewelry to dress up for a fancy party, to make my business outfits look better, or just to make a boring day a little nicer. Other people would enjoy the beauty of my jewelry, too, when they saw me wearing it.

I would feel very rich with my jewelry. I would have a good investment that was long lasting and beautiful, as well. Then, when someone invited me to a concert (and paid for my ticket), I would have something nice to wear.

20 AD

The expression "Never, never give up" means keep trying and never stop working for your goals. Do you agree or disagree with this statement? Use specific reasons and examples to support your answer.

As the old saying goes, "If at first you don't succeed, try, try again." I think there is great wisdom in these words. If you give up, you lose your chance to try again for what you want. But if you keep working for your goals, you will find that there is always another opportunity, another goal, or another option.

Once I ran for president of my class. Unfortunately, I lost the election because I did little to promote myself. I looked at my mistakes and saw how I could correct them. The following year, I ran for class president again. This time I did the things I hadn't done before. I gave speeches, called voters on the phone, and handed out brochures, and this time I won the election. Instead of giving up, I waited for another opportunity to try, and I was successful the second time.

Once I thought I wanted to study medicine. Unfortunately, I found that I didn't like science, and I failed all my science courses at school. After thinking about it for a while, I realized that what attracted me to a career in medicine was the chance to help people. So, I changed my goal from healing people to helping people, and now I am studying psychology. Instead of giving up, I adjusted my goal to one where I was more likely to be successful.

Once I was going through a difficult time and I really needed to talk to my best friend. My computer was down, so I couldn't email him. I tried calling him several times, but he didn't answer the phone. Finally, I decided to get on the bus and go to his house so we could talk in person. I didn't give up when I found that I couldn't reach my friend by email or phone. I looked for another option, and I successfully reached my goal.

If you give up, you might as well die. My advice is always look for another opportunity, another goal, or another option. There is always something else. Don't give up.

21 PR

Some people like to travel with a companion. Other people prefer to travel alone. Which do you prefer? Use specific reasons and examples to support your choice.

Traveling alone is the only way to travel. If you take someone with you, you take your home with you. When you travel alone, you meet new people, have new experiences, and learn more about yourself.

When you travel with a friend, you spend all your time with that friend and do everything together. Since you have a companion, you don't make an effort to reach out to other people. When you travel alone, on the other hand, you are more motivated to look for new friends. You seek out opportunities to talk with other tourists or with local people. You might share a meal or go on an excursion with them, and then you become friends. It's much easier to meet new people when you travel alone.

When you travel with a friend, your routine is predictable. You probably act the same way that you do at home. When you travel alone, however, you have to adapt yourself to the customs of the place. You might take a nap in the afternoon and then eat dinner late at night, for example, even if that is not how you behave at home. You might be adventurous and go dancing at a club all night instead of going to bed at your usual time. You will be more open to new experiences like these when you travel alone.

When you travel with a friend, you have someone to take care of you, but when you travel alone, you have to learn to take care of yourself. If you encounter a difficult situation, you have to find a solution on your own. If you don't speak the local language, you have to figure out how to make yourself understood. If the food is unfamiliar, you have to make your own decisions about what to eat. When you travel alone, you have many opportunities to learn about how you handle yourself in new or strange situations.

I think it is always important to do things on your own. You can find new friends, have new experiences, and learn a lot about yourself, too. Isn't that the point of travel?

22 AD

Do you agree or disagree with the following statement? Businesses should do anything they can to make a profit. Use specific reasons and examples to support your position.

After I get my degree, I plan to start my own business. Like any business owner, my goal is to make as much money as I can. However, I can't forget that there are more important things in life than earning a profit. I must always keep in mind that the success of my business depends on the people I work with, the customers I serve, and the community I live in.

My employees are a very important part of my business. Without them, my company would not be able to function. I depend on my employees to carry out the day-to-day operations of the business, and I rely on them for their advice on what to sell and how to sell it. Naturally, I have to compensate them for their contributions to the company. I can't take a large profit without sharing it with the people who made it possible.

Similarly, I would not have a business without my customers. I can never forget that they could take their business somewhere else. Therefore, I have to give them good value for their money and not overcharge them just because I want to make a few more pennies. I want my customers to trust me and keep coming back.

My employees and I are part of the social life of our community. We have an obligation to be active community members. I feel it is important that some of the profits my business earns from the community be returned to the community. We need to support local programs to support our neighbors, for example, summer jobs for high school students, campaigns to clean up city parks, and efforts to make the shopping area more attractive.

A business must make profits, of course, but we all—workers, customers, community members—must profit from a successful business, as well.

23 MA

> **Many teachers assign homework to students every day. Do you think that daily homework is necessary for students? Use specific reasons and details to support your answer.**

I believe that daily homework is not necessary. Students already spend most of the day in school. They need their time outside of school to do other things. They need time to spend with their families, to work, and to just relax. They can learn their lessons with homework two or three times a week, but every day isn't necessary.

All students need to spend time with their families. They are still young and they need the guidance and support their parents can give them. They need the companionship of their brothers and sisters. In addition, many families rely on their older children to help out at home. They take care of the younger children and help with the cooking and cleaning. If students have too much homework, they won't have time for their families.

Many high school students have jobs. They go to their jobs after school and on weekends. Some work in order to help their families. Others work to save money for college. Students' jobs are important to them. If they have too much homework, they won't have time and energy to go to work.

Students need time to relax. They study hard in school all day and many work at jobs after school. But they are still young. They need to spend time with their friends and have fun. When students relax with friends, they then have more energy for school and work. They have a chance to develop social skills or to pursue their own interests. Having free time is important for a child's development. If students have too much homework, they won't have time for relaxation.

Homework is important for students, but other things are important, too. Some homework is good, but daily homework can take time away from a student's family, job, and relaxation. There needs to be a balance.

24 MA

> **If you could study a subject that you have never had the opportunity to study, what would you choose? Explain your choice, using specific reasons and details.**

I have always been interested in art and literature, so people will think my choice is strange. If I could study something I have never had the opportunity to study, I would choose calculus. If I could actually learn something as difficult as that, it would give me a lot of confidence. Besides that, I think I would like it and it could help me learn some useful skills.

The only mathematics I have studied are the required courses in high school. I finished those requirements early and since then I have chosen to study other subjects. I never liked my math classes and I didn't do well in them. I have always thought that I couldn't learn math. But now I would like to try it. I think if I made the effort, I could learn calculus. If I learned calculus, I would feel very smart.

I like art and literature because I like beauty and creativity. I never liked math because I didn't think it was beautiful and creative. I like solving problems, however. And I might actually discover something beautiful and creative about math. I think if I tried studying calculus, I would actually like it.

There are some new skills I would like to develop. There are some electrical problems in my house and I would like to learn how to fix them myself. I would like to learn how to do repair work on my CD player or even on my computer. If I learned calculus, it would help me develop the skills I need to do these things.

I think it would be really interesting to try learning something completely new. For me, calculus would be a big challenge. If I learned it, I would feel smart, I would enjoy myself, and I could develop new skills. It would be a big accomplishment for me.

25 MA

Some people think that the automobile has improved modern life. Others think that the automobile has caused serious problems. What is your opinion? Use specific reasons and examples to support your answer.

There is no question that the automobile has improved modern life. It has opened up job opportunities to people, allowed families to stay connected, and given people the chance to travel to new places. The automobile is one of the best modern inventions.

With an automobile, a person has more choices of places to work. He can work close to his home if he finds a suitable job nearby, but he can also pursue job opportunities farther away. An automobile makes it possible to take a job in another town or city without having to go there to live. Without an automobile, however, a person can only look for jobs near the place where he lives. This puts a big limit on his choices.

With an automobile, it is much easier for a person to visit his family. Many people these days live far away from their relatives. Young adults pursuing their careers often find jobs in other cities. If they have cars, it is easy for them to visit their parents and other relatives whenever they want to. They can stay connected with their families even though they live at a distance. But without an automobile, they have to spend time and money taking a bus or train. It is not easy to visit relatives as often and family ties start to loosen.

With an automobile, a person can explore new places. He can just get in the car and drive wherever he wants to go, whenever he wants to. He has many opportunities to see new places, meet new people and learn more about the world. Without an automobile, a person can only go where the bus, train, or plane takes him. It is not very convenient.

The automobile has greatly improved modern life. It has opened up new worlds and new opportunities to people. It has made many things possible. Where would we be without it?

26 MA

Some people say that computers have made life easier and more convenient. Other people say that computers have made life more complex and stressful. What is your opinion? Use specific reasons and examples to support your answer.

Almost everything these days is done with the help of a computer. Computers make communication much more convenient. They make many tasks of daily life easier. They help many people do their jobs better. Overall, computers have made life easier and more convenient for everybody.

Through the Internet, computers make communication much more convenient. Email makes it possible to communicate with people instantly at any time of day. This is important for both our work and our personal lives. The Internet makes it possible to find out the latest news right away—even if it is news that happens someplace far away. The Internet makes it possible to get almost any kind of information from anyplace quickly, right in your own home or office.

Although we may not realize it, computers make many daily tasks easier. Check-out lines at stores move faster because a computer scans the prices. The bank manages your account more easily because of computers. The weatherman reports the weather more accurately with the help of computers. A computer is involved in almost everything we do, or that is done for us.

Most people these days do their jobs with the help of a computer. Architects use computer programs to help them design buildings. Teachers use computers to write their lessons and get information for their classes. Pilots use computers to help them fly planes. With the help of computers, people can do complicated jobs more easily.

We are living in the computer age. We can now do more things and do them more easily than we could before. Our personal and professional lives have improved because of computers.

27 AD

Do you agree or disagree with the following statement? Boys and girls should attend separate schools. Use specific reasons and examples to support your answer.

I don't think it is a good idea for boys and girls to attend separate schools. They will not be separated when they finish school and start their careers, so why should they be separated in school? When boys and girls study together, they are assured of getting equal quality of education, they learn how to work together, and they learn how to become friends. It is a much better preparation for life than studying in separate schools.

When boys and girls attend the same school, they get equal education. They are in the same classrooms with the same teachers studying from the same books. If they attend separate schools, the quality of the schools might be different. One school might be better than the other. By studying together, girls get the same education as boys. This helps them work toward having equality in society.

By attending the same schools, boys and girls learn how to work together. Some people say they should study separately because they have different learning styles. I think it's better to study together, however. It gives them the chance to learn to work together despite their differences. This will help them in the future when they have to work together professionally.

When boys and girls see each other in school every day, they have the chance to become friends. They see each other as normal people, not as strangers. If they attend separate schools, they don't know each other. It's easy to misunderstand, or even fear, each other. When boys and girls have the chance to become friends, their lives are much richer. They will have better relationships in the future.

By studying together, boys and girls get equal education, they learn to work together, and they become friends. This prepares them for adult life where men and women live and work together every day.

28 MA

Is it more important to be able to work with a group of people on a team or to work independently? Use reasons and specific examples to support your answer.

The ability to work on a team is one of the most important job skills to have. It is usually necessary because most jobs involve teamwork. It is usually the best way to work because a team can get more work done than an individual. In addition, a worker on a team has a lot of support from his coworkers.

Most work is done in groups or teams. Professionals work with their professional colleagues, and they also usually have assistants and support staff. Construction workers work with other construction workers, auto mechanics work with other auto mechanics; they all have assistants, and almost nobody works alone. It is necessary for all coworkers to get along and work well together.

More work can be done by a team than by individuals working alone. On a team, each member is responsible for one part of the job. Each member has to concentrate only on her part and do it as well as possible. Then all the parts are put together and the job is done. An individual working alone has to worry about every aspect of the job. He might not do such a good job because he has to think about everything at once.

A worker on a team has the advantage of support from his coworkers. If a worker can't finish a job on time or doesn't understand a task or needs help planning, he has a group of people to help him. The team supports him and he can get the job done. An individual working alone has to solve all her problems herself. She has to stop work while she finds a solution, or do a poor job.

Most jobs involve teamwork. Teams can usually do a better job than an individual working alone. A person who cannot work well on a team will have a hard time in today's workplace.

29 MA

A foreign visitor has only one day to spend in your country. Where should this visitor go on that day? Why? Use specific reasons and details to support your choice.

A foreign visitor with only one day to spend in my country should definitely spend that day in the capital. Spending time in the capital is the easiest way to see many aspects of our country in one place. In this city, the visitor can learn about our history, see examples of our culture, and buy our best products.

Our country's history is represented in several ways throughout the city. In the Government Palace, a visitor can learn about the history of our independence. In our National Museum, a visitor can see exhibits that show all the different stages of our history, from ancient times to the present. In parks all around the city, a visitor can see monuments to famous historical people and events.

It is also possible to see different representations of our culture throughout the city. Our art museums and galleries show paintings and sculptures by our artists. Plays written by national playwrights are performed in the theaters. Folk ballet performances show examples of our traditional dances. Many restaurants in the capital serve our native dishes.

The best products of our country are sold in the capital city. The large department stores sell clothes, furniture, and household items manufactured in our country. The Central Market sells fruit and vegetables from the surrounding agricultural region. Tourist and craft shops sell native handicrafts made in the countryside.

The capital city is the best place to learn a lot about our country in one place. Of course, it is difficult to see all of the city's attractions in one day. With some planning, though, it is possible to see at least a few examples of our country's history, culture, and products in one day.

30 PR

Some people prefer to live in places that have the same weather or climate all year long. Others like to live in areas where the weather changes several times a year. Which do you prefer? Use specific reasons and examples to support your choice.

If I could choose a place to live according to climate alone, I would definitely live in a place that has warm weather all year. It would make my life much easier and more comfortable. I would be healthier, have more fun, and save money if I lived in a warm climate.

I would always be healthy if I lived in a warm climate. Where I live now the winters are long and cold, so I get sick every winter. I often miss days of school because I get bad colds. I wouldn't have this problem in a warm climate. Also, in a warm climate I would be able to be outside all year long. I would play sports and get exercise everyday. That would make me healthier, too.

I would have more fun if I lived in a warm climate. I really enjoy outdoor activities such as going to the beach, playing soccer, and riding my bicycle. I can't do these things when the weather is cold, which means I can't do them at all during the winter in a cold climate. In a warm climate, I would be able to enjoy my favorite activities all year.

I would save money if I lived in a warm climate. It costs money to heat the house during cold winters, and this can get very expensive. In a warm climate I would not have to worry about this expense. It also costs money to buy new clothes every time the season changes. This is another expense I wouldn't have to worry about in a warm climate because I could wear the same clothes all year.

My life would be better if I lived in a warm climate. My health, my free time activities, and my bank account would all improve. In fact, I plan to move to a warm climate as soon as I finish school.

31 MA

Many students have to live with a roommate while going to school or university. What are some of the important qualities of a good roommate? Use specific reasons and examples to explain why these qualities are important.

You want to feel comfortable in the place where you live, so it is very important to have a good roommate. A bad roommate can become your worst enemy, but a good roommate can end up being your best friend. In my opinion, a good roommate is one who is considerate, flexible, and fun.

A good roommate is considerate of your needs and thinks about the effects her actions might have on you. For example, she tries to be quiet when you want to sleep or study. She doesn't plan a party or use your things without asking you first. A good roommate doesn't think only about herself; she thinks about you, too.

A good roommate is flexible. She is willing to bend a little in order to make things easier for both of you. If, for example, you are neat and your roommate is messy, you can each try to change a little bit so that you will both be happy. Your roommate can try to be a little neater, and you can try to live with a little mess.

Finally, a good roommate is fun. If she is planning to go to a party or a concert, she invites you to go with her. She introduces you to her friends and includes you when she plans activities with them. She is also open to planning free time activities with you. A good roommate may be serious about her studies, but she knows that it is important to have fun, too. She also knows that when you enjoy fun activities together, your friendship is strengthened.

The best situation is to have a roommate who is also your friend. If your roommate is considerate, flexible, and fun, you are sure to get along well and have a good experience living together.

32 AD

Some people think governments should spend as much money as possible exploring outer space (for example, traveling to the moon and other planets). Other people disagree and think governments should spend this money for our basic needs on Earth. Which of these two opinions do you agree with? Use specific reasons and details to support your answer.

I believe that we should spend whatever money is required to explore outer space. It is true that we have many needs here on Earth, and many problems to solve. Exploring outer space, however, has invaluable benefits for people on Earth. It helps medical research, it leads to useful inventions, and it can help solve our overpopulation problem. I think space exploration is worth the cost.

Research carried out in space contributes a great deal to medical science. There is some research that can be conducted only in space. The research on the effects of gravity on bone marrow is one example. Research such as this will continue to contribute to advances in medicine. It benefits everybody on Earth.

Many useful inventions have happened because of space exploration. Different kinds of plastics that were developed for space travel are also now used on Earth. Things we use in our daily lives are made from "space age" materials. This is another aspect of space exploration that benefits everyone.

The search for other planets can help solve our overpopulation problem. People are living longer and healthier lives these days. That's a good thing, but it means more people on Earth. The Earth will not get bigger. Through space exploration, we may be able to find other planets where people can live. This is one more thing that will have a benefit for all people.

Space exploration results in benefits for people everywhere on Earth. It contributes to medical science, to inventions, and to a solution to overpopulation. It is expensive, but the benefits are worth the price. Space exploration is one of the best ways governments can spend our money.

33 PR

You have been told that dormitory rooms at your university must be shared by two students. Would you rather have the university assign a student to share a room with you, or would you rather choose your own roommate? Use specific reasons and details to explain your answer.

I'd rather have the university assign a roommate to share a room with me. I don't know many people at the university I plan to attend. I'm sure the university will choose a roommate who is compatible with me, and this will give me the chance to make new friends.

None of my close friends will attend the university with me. We all plan to attend different schools. I have a few acquaintances at my university, but I don't know them well. I don't think they are people I would choose to live with. At this time, I really can't choose my own roommate. I am glad the university can do it for me.

The university has a very good system for assigning roommates. All the students have to fill out information sheets. We write about our majors, our interests, our study habits, and our goals. The university uses this information to match roommates. They can match people who have similar habits and interests. I think it is a good system.

When the university assigns me a roommate, I have a chance to make new friends. For one, my roommate will be a new friend. We already know that we will have similar habits and interests, so we will probably enjoy spending time together. In addition, my roommate's friends could become my friends, too. My roommate can introduce me to new people, and I can do the same for him.

I think it's a good idea for a university to choose roommates for the students. They can match people who are compatible and give everyone a chance to make new friends. Meeting new people is an important part of a university education, and this is one way to make that happen.

34 PR

Some people like doing work by hand. Others prefer using machines. Which do you prefer? Use specific reasons and examples to support your answer.

I prefer using machines to doing work by hand. Machines can work faster than I can. They can also work more neatly. Most of all, machines never get tired.

Machines are fast. If I want to make a dress, it would take me hours and hours working with a needle and thread to make each stitch by hand. If I use a sewing machine, however, I can make a dress in an hour or less. If I want to build something out of wood, I could cut each piece with a handsaw. That would take a very long time. But a power saw cuts much more quickly. When I bake a cake, I can stir in each ingredient by hand, or I can use an electric mixer, which makes the work go so much faster.

Machines are neat. They never make mistakes. Every line or cut is neat, straight and in the right place. Machines don't get distracted and spill coffee all over the work or cut something the wrong size or add the wrong ingredients. Machines can do the same job over and over again, each time as neatly as the time before. I could never be as neat as a machine.

Machines never get tired. I can sew one seam with my sewing machine, or ten. The machine never gets tired of pushing the needle and thread through the fabric. The power saw doesn't slow down because it has cut too many pieces of wood. A machine keeps working with the same amount of energy until the job is done, and doesn't even need to stop for a rest break.

I can depend on machines to do the job right each time, but I can't always depend on myself to be fast, neat, and tireless.

35 EX

You need to travel from your home to a place 40 miles (64 kilometers) away. Compare the different kinds of transportation you could use. Describe which method of travel you would choose. Give specific reasons for your choice.

When I think about the different methods of transportation I could choose to travel 40 miles from my home, I have three options: bicycle, car, or public transportation. In order to pick the best way to travel, I have to consider how much it will cost, how long it will take, and why I need to make the trip. Then I can decide on the best method for the circumstances.

Bicycle is the least expensive alternative. The only cost is the physical energy I need to pedal for 40 miles. This method, however, is extremely time consuming. I imagine it would take me all day to make the trip. On the other hand, biking is excellent exercise, so if my only goal is to burn calories and get stronger, then bicycle is my best choice.

Public transportation is another method that is inexpensive, since the fares in my area are low. On the other hand, you cannot depend on buses and trains where I live. The schedules are inconvenient, and it might take me all day to make my 40-mile trip if I include waiting time. Mass transit is good for the environment since it causes less pollution than cars. But, I can't rely on it to get me to my destination on time, so I don't like to use it.

Private car is the most costly way to travel. Since I don't own an automobile, I would need to borrow one from my parents. I would have to pay for the gasoline, which costs a lot, and I would also have to pay for parking at my destination. A private vehicle is the most dependable way to go if you need to get somewhere fast. If convenience is my goal, I should choose to make a trip by this type of transportation.

When I consider these points, I must confess that I am spoiled. I prefer the convenience of the car over the exercise of a bicycle and the virtues of public transportation. I like to come and go as I please without waiting, even if it costs me more.

36 PR

Some people prefer to spend most of their time alone. Others like to be with friends most of the time. Do you prefer to spend your time alone or with friends? Use specific reasons to support your answer.

There are people who say they prefer to be alone, but I cannot understand this. I always choose to spend time with friends whenever possible because friends bring so much to my life. They keep me company, are enjoyable to talk with, and teach me new things. I cannot imagine my life without them.

There is nothing better than to be in the company of my friends. They keep me from feeling lonely. If I feel like doing anything, I call a friend or friends to do it with me. Whether it's going shopping, seeing a movie, or even studying at the library, it's always fun to do things with friends. It isn't fun, on the other hand, to do anything alone.

One of my greatest pleasures is talking with my friends. If I have a problem, the first thing I do is talk it over with my friends. By discussing something together, we can find the solution to just about any kind of problem. Additionally, if something good or interesting happens to me, I share that with my friends, too. My friends share their problems and experiences with me, as well, and I always enjoy hearing about them. Our lives are so much richer because we share important things with each other.

I learn a lot when I spend time with my friends. A friend might invite me to a movie that I haven't ever heard of. A friend might tell me about a trip she took or a book she read. A friend might have a different point of view about a political issue. I learn a lot of new and interesting things when I am with my friends.

Friends make our lives fuller. They keep us company, share their problems and experiences with us, and teach us many things. Life would be sad and lonely without friends.

37 PR

Some people prefer to spend time with one or two close friends. Others choose to spend time with a large number of friends. Compare the advantages of each choice. Which of these two ways of spending time do you prefer? Use specific reasons to support your answer.

We all need to have friends, and I think the more friends we have the better. When you have a lot of friends, you are never alone. You always have people who will entertain you, people you can trust, and people who teach you about life.

I want to have a lot of people I can have fun with. If I have a lot of friends, I always have people to laugh and joke with me. I have people to go to the movies or the mall with me. I have people to go to parties with me. If I have only a few friends, they might be busy when I want to do these things, or they might not enjoy some of the things I enjoy.

I need to have a lot of people I can trust. If I have a problem, I want to share it with several friends. If I make a mistake or fail a test or have a fight with my parents, I need my friends to help me. I want to be able to pick up the phone and know I can easily find some friends to talk with. If I have only a few friends, they might not be available when I need them.

I like to have a lot of people who teach me about life. If I have a lot of friends, I have a lot of different people to learn from. Each person has different experiences and a different point of view. I can learn a lot of things from a lot of different people. If I have only a few friends, I will see only a few points of view.

I like to have a lot of friends around me. I like to have fun with them and to learn from them and to know that I can rely on them. My life is better because of all the friends I have.

38 PR

Some people think that family is the most important influence on young adults. Other people think that friends are the most important influence on young adults. Which view do you agree with? Use examples to support your opinion.

Although friends make an impression on your life, they do not have the same influence that your family has. Nothing is as important to me as my family. From them I learned everything that is important. I learned about trust, ambition, and love.

Your family is with you forever. They are not going to leave you because they find another son or daughter they like better. They are not going to leave you because they think you cause too many problems. They stick by you no matter what happens because they are your family. Friends come and go, but a family is permanent. I know that my family will always be there for me. I have learned that I can always trust them.

Your parents know that they are responsible for preparing you for the future, and they want you to have the best future possible. They encourage you to do your best, to push yourself, and to improve yourself. Friends, on the other hand, may care about you, but they aren't concerned about your future. Often, they don't want you to change because they don't want to lose the friendship. My family, not my friends, have taught me to have ambitions.

A family's love is not judgmental. They love you just the way you are. Friends, on the other hand, may love you because of circumstances. They may want to spend time with you because you have a new car or know how to play soccer well. They may be interested in you because you go to the same school or share a similar interest. Then, when the circumstances change, the friendship changes, too. But your family always loves you independent of the circumstances. From my family I have learned what love really is.

I wouldn't know what to do without my family. I wouldn't feel as secure. I might not have the ambition to go to school. I probably would be afraid to love. My family is my greatest influence.

39 PR

Some people choose friends who are different from themselves. Others choose friends who are similar to themselves. Compare the advantages of having friends who are different from you with the advantages of having friends who are similar to you. Which kind of friend do you prefer for yourself? Why?

There are a lot of advantages to having friends who are different from you. They can introduce you to new food, books, and music. They can present you with a different way of looking at the world. However, there are times when you need a friend who really understands you. That is why I enjoy having all kinds of friends—both those who are different from me and those who are similar.

Someone who is different from you can show different ways of looking at things. If you tend to be a spontaneous person, a scheduled person can help you be more organized. And you can help that person loosen up a bit at times, too. If you are impatient, a patient friend can help you calm down. If you are a little bit timid, an assertive friend can help you develop more self-confidence.

Someone who has different tastes from you can introduce you to new things. A friend might persuade you to read a book that you thought you wouldn't like. A friend might get you to try new kinds of food. You can share your different tastes and interests with your friend, too. Together you can dare to try new things.

There are times, however, when you really need a friend who is similar to you. Sometimes you get tired of compromising on what you want to do. You want to be with someone who has the same tastes as you. A friend who is similar to you probably has the same reactions to situations as you do. Therefore, if you feel unhappy, a friend who is similar to you can understand just why you feel that way.

Friends who are different from you have a lot to offer. Friends who are similar offer something else. That is why it is important to know all kinds of people.

40 AD

Do you agree or disagree with the following statement? People behave differently when they wear different clothes. Do you agree that different clothes influence the way people behave? Use specific examples to support your answer.

People behave differently depending on what they are wearing. The reason is not because they have changed, but because people's reactions to them have changed. Strangers react to your appearance because it is all they know about you. A friend may be influenced by your dress also, if it is inappropriate for a situation. In addition, appearance is almost always important at work.

Strangers can judge you only by the clothes you wear. Once I was wearing an old army coat. I went into a fancy candy shop to buy some chocolates. The woman saw my coat and was very suspicious of me. Because of the woman's negative reaction to me, I acted more politely than usual. The woman reacted to my clothes and that made me behave differently.

With friends clothes are less important because friends know more about you. However, friends can also react to you because of your clothes. Imagine you arrive at a friend's party. Everyone is wearing formal clothes and you are wearing casual clothes. You might have a good reason for this mistake, but your friend will still be disappointed. You will probably feel uncomfortable all evening because you disappointed your friend and because you are dressed differently from everyone else.

Certain clothes are appropriate for certain jobs. For example, business clothes are appropriate for some jobs; uniforms are appropriate for others. If you are not dressed appropriately for your job, clients and coworkers take you less seriously. You might begin to take yourself less seriously also, and your work could suffer. On the other hand, if you are wearing the right clothes, people will have confidence that you are the right person for the job, and you will feel this way, too.

Clothes don't change you into a different person, but they can make you behave differently. If you are dressed inappropriately for a situation, people will react to you in a different way. This reaction can, in turn, change your behavior. If you want good reactions from people, make sure to dress appropriately for every situation.

41 MA

Some people trust their first impressions about a person's character because they believe these judgments are generally correct. Other people do not judge a person's character quickly because they believe first impressions are often wrong. Compare these two attitudes. Which attitude do you agree with? Support your choice with specific examples.

Some people think it is unfair to judge others based on first impressions, but I disagree. People can show us who they really are in just a few minutes. Even if someone is having an unusually bad day, it is still easy to see their true character. If I don't like someone at first, I don't want to waste time being friendly just because he or she might change later. First impressions give us valuable information.

It doesn't take long for people to show their true character. Some people think you have to see how people act in different situations and talk to them a lot to get to know them. I don't believe this is true. When you meet someone, pay attention to how the person greets you. You can see right away if the person is friendly or shy, polite or rude. See how the person tries to make conversation and you will know what topics are interesting to him or her. All of this gives us a lot of information about a person.

Even on a bad day, you can see what a person is really like. Some people think that it isn't fair to judge people quickly because they might be having a bad day. I disagree. A bad day tells you a lot about people. You can see how they react to bad situations. Do they get very angry or take it all in stride? Do they get depressed and cry or just try to forget the problem? These are important parts of a person's character.

I feel I can learn a lot about a person in a few minutes, so I don't want to waste my time if the first impression isn't good. If I don't like the way a person greets me, or if I am uncomfortable with the way a person responds to a bad situation, will my impression change later on? Probably not. If I spend more time with the person, I'll probably just see more of the same. I would prefer to spend that time looking for people who I like.

If we all based our final opinion of others on first impressions, we would save ourselves a lot of time. We would probably have more opportunities to meet other people we have more in common with. First impressions provide us with enough insight to a person's character to indicate if a further friendship is possible.

42 AD

Do you agree or disagree with the following statement? It is more important for students to study history and literature than it is for them to study science and mathematics. Use specific reasons and examples to support your opinion.

In my opinion, it is much more important for students to study science and mathematics than it is for them to study history and literature. Science and mathematics are much more practical. It is easier to get a job with science and math skills. Scientists and mathematicians have more social prestige, and they can earn higher salaries.

People who study science and mathematics get jobs more easily than people who study history and literature. There are always jobs in fields such as medicine, computer science, engineering, and other professions that require a science or math background. People who study history or literature can only become writers or college professors. It is difficult to get well-paying jobs in those fields.

Scientists and mathematicians have a lot of social prestige. Let's face it—our society values science and math. If you go to a party and say, "I am a rocket scientist," people will be interested in you. They will want to talk to you and be your friend. If you say, "I am an historian," no one will pay any attention to you.

Scientists and mathematicians also earn more money than people in other fields because society values them more. A doctor, a chemist, a medical researcher,—a person in any one of these professions usually earns a far higher salary than a literature professor, for example, or a history expert.

Our society values science and math, so it is important to develop skills in these areas. If you have a science or math background, you are sure to get a good job, have lots of social prestige, and earn a good salary. Faced with this fact, who would want to study anything else?

43 MA

Some people say that physical exercise should be a required part of every school day. Other people believe that students should spend the whole school day on academic studies. Which opinion do you agree with? Give specific reasons and details to support your answer.

While physical exercise is important, I do not believe that it is a school's responsibility to provide physical training for its students. If physical exercise is part of the school program, that means that students have to receive grades for it and that the school has to pay for the necessary space and equipment. This seems a waste of effort and resources when students can usually get enough physical exercise on their own.

If a school offers physical education classes, then students will have to be graded in them. It is not always easy to do this fairly. Some schools, especially smaller ones, may not be able to offer activities that interest everyone. Then some students might get poor grades simply because the school couldn't offer an activity they enjoy or do well in. In addition, research suggests that participation, not excellence, in physical activities is what benefits the body.

Another issue is economic. Physical education costs money and many schools do not have the money to provide gym facilities, playing fields, and athletic equipment for their students. Other schools are located in cities where that kind of space just isn't available. A few schools would rather keep money for academic purposes.

Many students get plenty of physical exercise as part of their daily life or recreation. Some students walk or ride their bicycles to schools. Some participate in soccer teams or tennis leagues outside of schools. Young people are usually active and have plenty of chances to get exercise outside of school, whether in organized activities or not.

It is important to get plenty of physical exercise, and young people usually do this. They don't need the school to focus effort and money on their physical education. It is much better to direct the school's resources toward academic achievement.

44 EX

If you could invent something *new*, what product would you develop? Use specific details to explain why this invention is needed.

If I could invent something new, I'd invent a device or pill that could put people to sleep immediately and would have no side effects. The proper amount of sleep is important for our concentration, mental health, and physical health.

When we don't get enough sleep, our concentration is strongly affected. We're easily distracted, we can't remember things, and we don't notice what's happening around us. For example, a lot of car accidents are caused by tired drivers. When we get enough sleep, our powers of concentration are sharper. We're more focused on what we're doing. We perform better.

Mental health is also affected by lack of sleep. When we don't get enough sleep we're irritable. We lose our tempers easily and overreact to situations. In fact, experiments have shown that lack of sleep over a long period of time can cause a complete mental breakdown. When we get our proper rest, we're more alert and responsive. Our outlook is positive, and we're much easier to get along with.

Sleeplessness also affects our physical health. We have less energy, and everything seems like a major effort. Over a long period of time, we become slow and unresponsive. The wear and tear on the body from lack of sleep can be a very serious health problem. Every doctor will tell you that getting enough sleep is important for your health.

Wouldn't it be great to go to bed every night knowing you'd have no problem getting to sleep? Getting enough sleep is always going to be an important part of how you respond to your situation. I think this device would be very helpful to all of us.

45 AD

Do you agree or disagree with the following statement? Children should be required to help with household tasks as soon as they are able to do so. Use specific reasons and examples to support your answer.

I believe that children should be required to help with household tasks because it facilitates their development in important ways. It helps them learn skills, develop a sense of responsibility, and contribute to family life. Sharing in household tasks benefits children of all ages.

First of all, doing household tasks builds skills. When very young children do a simple task such as picking up their toys and putting them away, they develop motor and classification skills. Older children learn skills that they will need when they grow up and have homes of their own. They learn to cook, clean, and do laundry. They learn to carry out the tasks that they will need to do in order to take care of themselves and their own families when they are adults.

Secondly, children learn about responsibility when they help with household tasks. They learn to organize their time so that they can do everything that needs to be done. They learn that duties come first and that they have to complete their chores before they can play. Children who understand that effort pays off will be more successful later in life.

When children help with household tasks, the entire family benefits. When parents come home tired from their jobs, they're faced with all the housework. But if their children help with the household chores, then everything is easier for everyone. The work gets done more quickly, and the family has more time to relax together afterwards. The children are helpers, and the parents don't feel like servants to them.

Children should not work all the time. A happy life needs balance. If children can successfully handle tasks at home, they will handle life better, too. They will know the satisfaction of doing a good job, be involved in family life, and become more confident and responsible adults.

46 AD

Do you agree or disagree with the following statement? Playing a game is fun only when you win. Use specific reasons and examples to support your answer.

I agree with the old saying, "It's not whether you win or lose, it's how you play the game." I have fun playing all games because they give me time to be with my friends, learn new things, and work as a team.

Tennis is one game that I enjoy. It's a great opportunity to socialize. First, I have to talk to my partner in order to arrange a time to play a game. We also talk about other things at the same time. We have another opportunity to talk while we are waiting for the tennis court to be free. After the game, we almost always go out for coffee and talk some more. We often don't even talk about tennis. The game is just an excuse for us to get together.

The board game Scrabble provides a good opportunity to build my language skills. It's a challenge to try to form words from the letters that are in front of me. I always learn new words from my opponents, too. Often we don't even keep score when we play the game. We just enjoy being together and improving our English.

The game of soccer gives me the chance to be on a team. I like traveling with the group when we go to other schools to play games. I like learning how to play as a team. Our coach tells us that the most important thing is to play well together. It's also important to have fun. Winning is secondary.

I play games because they are fun. Playing games gives me the opportunity to do things that I enjoy and be with people that I like. You can't win every time, but you can always have fun.

47 MA

If you could make one important change in a school that you attended, what change would you make? Use reasons and specific examples to support your answer.

A big problem at my high school is the foreign language program. The math and science programs receive a lot of attention, but foreign language instruction has been neglected. This is unfortunate because I believe that foreign languages are as important as other school subjects. The school can improve the foreign language program by offering more classes, hiring well-trained instructors, and incorporating the use of technology.

The first thing the school should do is add more levels to the foreign language program. Right now we don't have any classes above the second-year level. Two years just isn't enough time to develop skills in a foreign language. This situation is especially frustrating for those of us who want to continue language study in college because we won't be well prepared.

Next, the foreign language program should be staffed with well-trained instructors. The current teachers in the program don't speak the languages well enough. In our classes, teachers make errors that the students repeat. If the teachers were well trained, they would be good models for the students.

Finally, we need to use current technology in our language classes. Our school has a well-equipped computer laboratory, and many classrooms have computers in them. Strangely enough, however, we don't use computers in our language classes. The school needs to provide us with computer software that is made for learning languages. We also need to be able to spend class time using the Internet to search for current, real-life materials in the languages we study.

In the modern world, foreign language skills are just as important as math, science, and other skills we learn in school. Our school needs to make an investment in the foreign language program so that we can develop the language skills we will need for our future.

48 AD

Do you agree or disagree with the following statement? Playing games teaches us about life. Use specific reasons and examples to support your answer.

Almost everyone, whether child or adult, loves games. The types of games we like may change as we grow up, but our enjoyment of them never does. I believe that playing games is both fun and useful because it teaches us the skills we need in life. Games teach us about cause and effect relationships, teamwork, and following rules.

First of all, games teach us about cause and effect. If we hit a ball, for example, it will land somewhere or someone will catch it. If we hit the ball harder, it will land farther away or be more difficult to catch. If we are able to make certain combinations of cards because we have followed the action of the game, then we win points. We learn how our actions lead to certain results.

Playing games also teaches us how to deal with other people. When we play team games, for instance, we learn about teamwork. We learn how to work with others to reach a goal and how to use the strengths of each individual. When we play other sorts of games, we can still learn about interacting with other people. We learn how to negotiate rules and how to get along with others.

Finally, playing games teaches us about rules. We learn about the importance of rules and how to follow them. We find out that if we want to reach a particular goal, we need to know what the rules are for getting there. We learn how to develop strategies for working within the rules to reach our desired ends.

Games are fun to play, but they are more than just a pleasant pastime. Games provide us with important experiences, and by playing them, we develop skills that are useful in all aspects of our lives.

49 MA

Imagine that you have received some land to use as you wish. How would you use this land? Use specific details to explain your answer.

I would like to use my land for something that everyone can enjoy. Therefore, I would build a campground on it. Right now we don't have any good places for outdoor recreation in my town. A campground would be an inexpensive place for outdoor recreation and would provide activities that everybody would enjoy.

There aren't many opportunities for outdoor recreation in my town. We have only one small park and a playing field behind the high school. That really isn't enough space for our needs. In addition, the park is not well maintained so people don't like to use it. A well maintained campground would give our town a nice place to enjoy outdoor activities.

We have many opportunities for indoor recreation, but they are all expensive. We have a brand new movie theater, but the ticket prices go up every day. It is especially hard to pay for tickets if you have several children. We have a museum of local history, but that, too, is expensive. Young people like to go to the mall, but of course that just encourages more spending. A campground, on the other hand, is an inexpensive place to spend time, even for large families.

At a campground, everybody can find activities that they enjoy. People can play different kinds of games outdoors, they can go hiking or study nature, or just sit and relax. At night they can enjoy talking around a campfire. It is a nice place for families to enjoy some free time together.

A campground would provide an inexpensive and enjoyable place for families and friends to spend time together. It would be a great asset to our town. I think it would be a very good way to use land.

50 MA

In some countries people are no longer allowed to smoke in many public places and office buildings. Do you think this is a good rule or a bad rule? Use specific reasons and details to support your opinion.

I strongly believe that it is not fair to ban smoking in public places. It is not fair to take away smokers' rights, and it is not fair to impose on their ability to relax. Since it is possible to protect nonsmokers by designating special smoking and nonsmoking areas, there is no reason to ban smoking in public.

Smokers have rights just like everyone else. Just because some people don't like to be around smoking, that doesn't mean it should be banned. Some people don't like motorcycles, either. Some people don't like being around dogs. Some people don't like seeing action movies. However, there are no laws against having these things in public. People who don't like smoking have to learn to tolerate it just as they tolerate anything else they may not like.

People smoke to relax. They don't smoke to harm other people. Many people like to unwind by enjoying a cigarette after a meal, for example, but if they have to leave a restaurant to go home and smoke, then it isn't relaxing. Other relaxing activities are allowed in public, so smoking should be allowed, too.

It is easy to designate special smoking areas in public places. Smokers can sit in their own section of a restaurant, airport, bus, or any other place. Nonsmokers can sit in their own section, too, and then they won't be bothered by the smoke. In this way, both smokers and nonsmokers can enjoy their use of the public space equally.

It is true that smoking is bothersome to many people, and some people are even allergic to it. It isn't fair, however, to take away smokers' rights just because some people don't like it. It is possible for smokers and nonsmokers to share public space. It is the only fair thing to do.

51 PR

In the future, students may have the choice of studying at home by using technology such as computers or television or of studying at traditional schools. Which would you prefer? Use reasons and specific details to explain your choice.

I believe that it is better to study at school than at home. I can learn a lot if I study alone at home, but I can learn more if I study at school with other people. I can gain a lot of information from other people. I also learn a lot by interacting with them. I am motivated to study more if I don't work alone. Therefore, I believe I can learn a lot more at school.

Information comes from technology, but it also comes from people. If I study at home, I can get a lot of information from my computer, DVD player, and television. If I study at school, I can get all this information, and I can also get information from my teachers and classmates. So, I learn more.

Interaction with other people increases my knowledge. At home I have nobody to talk to. Nobody can hear my ideas. At school I have the opportunity to interact with other people. We can explain our ideas to each other. We can agree and disagree. Together we can develop our ideas and learn to understand new things.

Competition motivates me. When I am at home, nobody can see my work. Nobody can tell me that I did a good job or a bad job. When I am at school, my teacher and my classmates see my work, and I can see my classmates' work. I want to do a good job like my classmates, or even a better job. So, I want to study harder.

Some people can study very well when they are alone at home, but I can't. I need to have other people near me. When I am with other people, I have the possibility to learn more information. I have the opportunity to develop my ideas more completely. I have the motivation to do a better job. Therefore, school is the best place for me.

52 MA

The twentieth century saw great change. In your opinion, what is one change that should be remembered about the twentieth century? Use specific reasons and details to explain your choice.

There were many important changes, both technological and cultural, during the twentieth century. In my opinion, the most important of these is the advances that were made in medical science. The development of vaccines and antibiotics, increased access to health care, and improvements in surgical techniques are all things that improved, and saved, the lives of people all around the world.

Vaccines and antibiotics have saved the lives of many people. Fifty years ago, many people became crippled or died from polio. Now the polio vaccine is available everywhere. In the past, people could die from even simple infections. Now penicillin and other antibiotics make it easy to cure infections.

Increased access to health care has also improved the lives of millions of people. In the past, many people lived far from hospitals or clinics. Now hospitals, clinics, and health centers have been built in many parts of the world. More people have the opportunity to visit a doctor or nurse before they become very sick. They can be treated more easily. They are sick less and this leads to a better quality of life.

Improved surgical techniques make it easier to treat many medical problems. Microscopic and laser surgery techniques are more efficient than older methods. It is easier for the doctor to perform them, and easier for the patient to recover. Surgery patients can return to their normal life more quickly now than they could in the past.

Everybody needs good health in order to have a good quality of life. Advances in medical science have improved the lives of people all around the world. They are improvements that are important to everyone.

53 EX

People remember special gifts or presents they have received. Why? Use specific reasons and examples to support your answer.

I think we remember special gifts we've received because these gifts often hold special memories for us. They may be memories of special people, of special events, or even of ourselves as we once were in the past.

Gifts can remind us of special people in our lives. When we look at gifts, we remember the good times we have enjoyed with the giver. We think of the good feelings we have about that person. The giver may be someone we see frequently or infrequently. Either way, the gift is a special reminder of him or her.

Gifts may also bring back memories of special events in our lives. Some gifts mark special turning points in our lives such as school graduations. Some gifts may hold memories of special birthdays or anniversaries. They help us remember the special times in our lives.

Gifts can also be a symbol of our past. A gift received in childhood may remind us of games we enjoyed then. A gift received in high school makes us think of the music or clothes we loved when we were young.

Gifts are important to us because they remind us of the special people, events, and interests of our lives. They are a way of surrounding ourselves with our past.

54 MA

Some famous athletes and entertainers earn millions of dollars every year. Do you think these people deserve such high salaries? Use specific reasons and examples to support your opinion.

Famous athletes and entertainers earn a lot of money and they deserve it. They work hard to achieve fame, they provide us with good entertainment, and they give up their privacy in order to do this. I think they deserve every cent they get.

Fame doesn't just appear overnight; people have to work hard to achieve it. If someone has a lot of fame now, it means he has spent years working hard to develop his talent. He has spent a lot of time at low-paying jobs in order to get experience and recognition. He continues to work hard now in order to maintain his talent and fame. Just like anybody else, famous people deserve to be rewarded for their hard work.

Athletes, actors, and musicians provide us with entertainment. On weekends, most of us attend at least one sporting event or movie or concert. After watching a famous person perform, we might even be inspired to learn to play a sport or a musical instrument ourselves. Famous athletes and entertainers help us make good use of our free time. They deserve to be paid for this.

Famous people suffer a loss of privacy. Since we admire them, we want to feel as if we know them. We want to know how they live and what happens in their daily lives. Therefore, journalists follow them all the time in order to find out the details of their private lives. These details, true or not, are published in magazines all around the world. This is a big disadvantage to being famous. Earning a lot of money can, in part, compensate for this.

Famous people work hard to entertain us, and then they lose their privacy. They contribute a lot to our lives. They deserve to earn a lot of money.

55 EX

Every generation of people is different in important ways. How is your generation different from your parents' generation? Use specific reasons and examples to explain your answer.

The one thing that makes the difference between my parents' generation and my own is modern technology. When my parents were growing up, they had TV, radio, and cars, but they didn't have the amount of technology we have now. They didn't have personal computers, they didn't have satellite TV, and they didn't have cell phones.

My parents didn't grow up with computers, but I did. They have a computer now, but they don't use it as I do. I write all my schoolwork and keep all my files on the computer. My parents still like to use paper. I do all my research and get all my news off the Internet. My parents still use newspapers and TV. Because of computers, I am accustomed to having more access to information than my parents are. I am used to doing more work more efficiently. It is a completely different way of living.

My parents had only local TV when they were young, but I have satellite TV. I grew up seeing programs from all over the world. I am used to seeing foreign movies and cartoons. I have some ideas about things in foreign countries and a lot of interest in them. Satellite TV exposes me to things that have opened up my mind. My parents didn't have the same opportunity when they were young.

Cell phones are common now, but they didn't exist when my parents were young. They didn't even have answering machines or voice mail. They couldn't talk to people at any time or leave messages easily. I can do this. Right now it is a fun part of my social life. When I have a job it will be more important. I will be able to contact people easily and that will make my work more efficient. Cell phones have made a big difference in the way we work.

Modern technology has made a big difference in the way we work, in our understanding of the world, and in the expectations we have of friends and colleagues. It has completely changed the way we live. The world of my generation is a different place than it was for my parents' generation.

56 MA

Many people have a close relationship with their pets. These people treat their birds, cats, or other animals as members of their family. In your opinion, are such relationships good? Why or why not? Use specific reasons and examples to support your answer.

Pets are important because they provide us with companionship and even with love. It is not good, however, to have too close a relationship with a pet, or to treat it like a human being. Devoting too much attention to pets can prevent you from focusing on other activities and on relationships with people. It can also be a waste of money.

Sometimes people who love their pets don't want to become involved in other activities. If you invite such a friend out for coffee, for example, the friend might say, "I don't have time. I have to walk the dog." Sometimes people don't want to take a weekend trip because they don't want to leave their pets alone. They put their pets' interests before their own. Then they live life for their pets and not for themselves.

Loving a pet too much can interfere with good relationships with people. Sometimes people neglect their spouses and children in favor of their pets. A person who lives alone might devote all his attention to his pet. He might lose interest in making friends and being with people. A relationship with a pet is less complicated than a relationship with a person. Sometimes it seems easier to choose pets over people.

People spend thousands of dollars on their pets, but this money could have other uses. It seems strange to buy special food for a pet or take it to the doctor, when some people don't have these things. Children all around the world grow up without enough food, or never get medical care. It would be better to give a pet simple things and send the extra money to charity.

Pets give us a lot and they deserve our care and attention. It is never a good idea to go to extremes, however. It is important to balance your pet's needs with your own.

57 EX

Nowadays food has become easier to prepare. Has this change improved the way people live? Use specific reasons and examples to support your answer.

Food is a basic part of life, so it follows that improved methods of food preparation have made our lives better. Nowadays we can prepare meals much faster than we could in the past. We can also enjoy a greater variety of food and eat more healthfully, all because of modern methods of food preparation.

Microwave ovens have made it possible to prepare delicious food quickly. People these days rarely have time to shop and prepare meals the old-fashioned way. We live very fast lives. We are busy working, caring for our families, traveling, playing sports, and many other things. Because of microwave ovens, we have time to enjoy a good meal with our family and then play soccer, go to a movie, study, or do anything else we want to afterwards.

Modern methods of preserving food have made it possible to enjoy a wide variety of food. Because of refrigerators, freezers, canning, and freeze-drying, we can eat fruits and vegetables that come from far away places. We can prepare a meal one day and save the leftovers in the refrigerator or freezer to eat at another time. We can keep different kinds of food in the refrigerator or on the shelf. It's easy to always have food available and to be able to eat completely different meals every day.

Healthful eating is easier now than it ever was. Because of modern transportation methods, fresh fruits and vegetables are available all year round. Modern kitchen appliances make it easy to prepare fruits and vegetables for cooking. Bread machines make it possible to enjoy healthful, home-baked bread whenever we like. We can eat fresh and healthful food every day because modern methods have made preparation easy.

Our lifestyle is fast, but people still like good food. New food preparation methods have given us more choices. Today we can prepare food that is more convenient, healthier, and of greater variety than ever before in history.

58 PR

It has been said, "Not everything that is learned is contained in books." Compare and contrast knowledge gained from experience with knowledge gained from books. In your opinion, which source is more important? Why?

"Experience is the best teacher" is an old cliché, but I agree with it. We can learn a lot of important things from books, but the most important lessons in life come from our own experiences. Throughout the different stages of life, from primary school to university to adulthood, experience teaches us many skills we need for life.

As children in primary school, we learn facts and information from books, but that is not all we learn in school. On the playground we learn how to make friends. In our class work, we learn how it feels to succeed and what we do when we fail. We start to learn about the things we like to do and the things we don't. We don't learn these things from books, but from our experiences with our friends and classmates.

In our university classes, we learn a lot of information and skills we will need for our future careers, but we also learn a lot that is not in our textbooks. In our daily lives both in class and out of class, we learn to make decisions for ourselves. We learn to take on responsibilities. We learn to get along with our classmates, our roommates, and our workmates. Our successes and failures help us develop skills we will need in our adult lives. They are skills that no book can teach us.

Throughout our adulthood, experience remains a constant teacher. We may continue to read or take classes for professional development. However, our experiences at work, at home, and with our friends teach us more. The triumphs and disasters of our lives teach us how to improve our careers and also how to improve our relationships and how to be the person each one of us wants to be.

Books teach us a lot, but there is a limit to what they teach. They can give us information or show us another person's experiences. These are valuable things, but the lessons we learn from our own experiences, from childhood through adulthood, are the most important ones we learn.

59 AD

Do you agree or disagree with the following statement? Television has destroyed communication among friends and family. Use specific reasons and examples to support your opinions.

Some people believe that television has destroyed communication among friends and family. In my opinion, however, the opposite is true. Television can increase communication. News and other information we see on TV gives us things to discuss with our friends and family. TV also helps us understand each other better because we all have access to the same TV programs. Finally, TV can help us share our interests with other people.

Television programs give us things to think and talk about. These days it is always possible to hear up-to-the minute news every time we turn on the television. We hear about things happening all around the world that directly affect our lives. Everybody has opinions about these things and everybody wants to discuss their opinions with other people. So, TV news and information programs encourage us to discuss our ideas with our friends and family.

No matter what city you live in, you have access to the same TV programs as people in other parts of the country. When you go to a new city to work, study, or take a vacation, you will already have something in common with the people there. When you meet new people, you will probably be familiar with at least some of the same TV programs. This gives you something to talk about and a way to begin new friendships.

Most people use TV as a way to pursue their interests. People who play sports usually like to watch sports on TV. People who like to cook watch cooking shows. If your friends and family watch some of the same programs as you do, they can learn more about the things that interest you. This is an excellent form of communication that helps people understand each other better.

TV is a tool that gives us access to information, entertainment, and education. When we watch programs that interest us, we want to share this interest with other people. That is why I believe TV encourages communication among people.

60 AD

"When people succeed, it is because of hard work. Luck has nothing to do with success." Do you agree or disagree with the quotation above? Use specific reasons and examples to explain your position.

When people succeed, it is because of hard work, but luck has a lot to do with it, too. Luck is often the final factor that turns years of working hard into success. Luck has helped people invent and discover things, it has helped people become famous, and it has helped people get jobs.

Many people have discovered or invented things with the help of luck. Columbus worked hard for years to prepare for his trip around the world. Many thought he was crazy, but still he was able to get support for his endeavor. He worked hard to be able to make his trip to India, but it was because of luck that he actually found the Americas.

Luck can help people become famous. Consider movie stars. Many work hard to learn how to act. They take acting classes. They work at small, low-paying jobs in order to gain experience. Then one day a lucky actor may be given a certain part in a movie, and he gets noticed for it. Or he meets a movie director at the right time and place. Years of hard work bring him close to success, but that one lucky chance finally helps him succeed.

Because of luck, many people find jobs. A person may spend weeks writing and sending off résumés, looking at help wanted ads, and going on job interviews. But often it is because of luck that a job hunter meets the person who will give him or her a job, or hears of an opportunity that isn't advertised in the newspaper. Being in the right place at the right time is often what gets a person a job, and that is all about luck.

It is certainly difficult to be successful without hard work, but hard work also needs to be helped by a little luck. Luck has helped many people, both famous and ordinary, become successful. I think that luck and hard work go hand in hand.

61 MA

Some people believe that university students should be required to attend classes. Others believe that going to classes should be optional for students. Which point of view do you agree with? Use specific reasons and details to support your answer.

Some people believe that going to classes should be optional for university students, but I disagree with this point of view. Students learn a lot more in classes than they can from books alone. In class, they have the advantages of learning from the teacher, interacting with their classmates, and developing the responsibility it takes to be a good student.

When students attend class, they receive the benefit of the teacher's knowledge. The best teachers do more than just go over the material in the class textbook. They present their own interpretations and opinions of the material. They draw their students into discussions so that the students can develop and present their own interpretations, too. Teachers also provide supplementary information by inviting guest speakers or showing films. None of these experiences are available by reading alone.

Going to class also teaches students how to work with other people. In class, students have to present their ideas to their classmates. They have to defend their ideas if their classmates disagree with them but still remain friendly when the discussion is over. In addition, they may have to work in groups to complete class projects, so they have the opportunity to learn to work with others in order to reach a goal.

Attending classes teaches students responsibility. They have to be in class on time and ready to participate. They have to hand in their assignments by the due date. These are all skills they will need if they want to be successful in their future careers.

Anyone can get information from books, but students receive many more advantages when they attend class. They get the benefit of the teacher's knowledge and experience, and even more than that, they learn how to work with others and how to develop a sense of responsibility. These are not optional skills in life, so attending classes should not be optional at a university.

62 MA

Neighbors are the people who live near us. In your opinion, what are the qualities of a good neighbor? Use specific details and examples in your answer.

A good neighbor is always appreciated, but it takes certain qualities to be one. If you have a good neighbor, you are a lucky person. You live near someone who is respectful of your property, is helpful when those little everyday problems arise, and is supportive in times of crisis.

A good neighbor is someone who respects your property. That means she thinks about how her actions might affect you. She doesn't plant a huge tree between your houses, for instance, without first asking you how you feel about it. Or, if she wants to put up a fence that abuts your yard, she talks it over with you before finalizing her plans. In other words, when she wants to make changes to her property, she takes her neighbors' feelings into consideration.

A good neighbor is someone who is willing to lend a hand when you need a little help. She gladly lends you some butter if you run out in the middle of cooking dinner. She doesn't mind giving you a ride if your car breaks down. She watches your children for you if you have to stay late at work. She pitches in when you need a little help, and you do the same for her. Both of you help make each other's lives easier.

A good neighbor is someone who offers her support when you are going through a crisis. If there is a death or illness in your family, for example, your neighbor might offer to cook some meals for you or clean your house. She might stay by your side during the sadness of a funeral. She looks for ways, big or small, to help you get through the challenging times of life.

A neighbor might be a close friend or a more distant acquaintance. Either way, she is someone who respects you and supports you when she can. We should all be lucky enough to have good neighbors.

63 MA

What are some important qualities of a good supervisor (boss)? Use specific details and examples to explain why these qualities are important.

Whether working in a large company or a small one, a factory or an office or another setting, all good supervisors have certain qualities in common. A good supervisor treats her employees fairly, gives them clear directions and, most important of all, acts as a good role model.

A good supervisor is fair. She treats all of her employees with equal respect and doesn't have favorites. When it's time for performance evaluations, she uses the same set of criteria to assess each person. She doesn't let her personal feelings about an individual influence her treatment or evaluation of him. Instead, she is careful to conduct herself professionally in all situations.

A good supervisor gives clear and understandable directions. She doesn't get angry when an employee is confused and needs more explanation. Rather, she looks for ways to help that person understand what is required of him. She is also consistent with her instructions. She doesn't constantly change her mind about what she wants done. Therefore, her employees can feel confident that they are doing what they are supposed to be doing.

Finally, a good supervisor sets the standards for her employees by her own behavior. She works hard, acts responsibly, and gets her work done on time. She follows the company's rules and guidelines, dresses appropriately for the job, and treats everyone with respect. In short, she does what is expected of her and does it the best she can. She can only expect her employees to act professionally if she acts professionally too.

Employees are more likely to do a good job when they are treated fairly, given good directions, and have a good example to follow. This is why good supervisors are so important to the success of any type of business.

64 MA

Should governments spend more money on improving roads and highways, or should governments spend more money on improving public transportation (buses, trains, subways)? Why? Use specific reasons and details to develop your essay.

Governments should definitely spend more money on improving all forms of public transportation. The widespread use of private cars has contributed to some serious problems in society, including depletion of natural resources, increased pollution, and the loss of a sense of community. By encouraging the use of public transportation, governments can do a lot to counteract these problems.

Cars depend on oil and gasoline, which are nonrenewable resources. Once we have used them up, they are gone forever. Every time a person gets into a private car to go to work, to the store, or anywhere, gasoline is used up just to take one person to one place. The more people drive their cars, the more resources are used up. When people use public transportation, on the other hand, less oil and gasoline are used up per person.

Cars cause pollution. Every time a person drives his car somewhere, more pollution is put into the air. In many big cities, the high amount of air pollution causes health problems for the residents. Public transportation means fewer cars on the road, and that means less pollution.

Cars tend to isolate people from each other. When a person uses a private car, he is alone or only with people that he already knows. He doesn't have the opportunity to see other people or talk to them or feel that he is part of a larger community. When he uses public transportation, however, he is surrounded by neighbors and other fellow city residents. He has a chance to be with people he might not otherwise see, and maybe even to get to know them a little.

Environmental problems and increased isolation are some of the most serious problems of modern society. Encouraging the use of public transportation is one way governments can work against these problems and start creating a better world.

65 MA

In some countries, teenagers have jobs while they are still students. Do you think this is a good idea? Support your opinion by using specific reasons and details.

I don't think it is a good idea for teenagers to have jobs while they are still students. It can interfere with their studies, it can disrupt their home life, and it takes away part of their childhood that they can never replace.

A job can interfere with a teenager's schoolwork. Education today is very complex and difficult. In order to learn and get good grades, a student must work very hard and concentrate. This means attending classes for most of the day, then doing research for projects, then going home and doing homework. It is very difficult to do all this and have a job, too.

Having a job can also disrupt a teenager's home life. If a teenager has a job to go to after school, he won't be home for dinner. He won't be home after dinner either, and may not get home until late at night. This means he doesn't have much time to spend with his family. Teenagers may be almost grown up, but they still need the companionship and support they get from their families.

The main drawback of a teenager having a job is that he misses out on the fun of being young. He has a whole lifetime ahead of him in which he'll have to earn a living. This is the last free time he'll have. It's the last chance he'll have to hang out with friends and just enjoy himself. Soon enough he'll have to start worrying about paying the rent and buying food.

Jobs bring money, but money isn't everything. For a teenager it is important to concentrate on his studies, spend time with his family, and enjoy being young. A teenager with a job gives up too much.

66 EX

A person you know is planning to move to your town or city. What do you think that person would like and dislike about living in your town or city? Why? Use specific reasons and details to develop your essay.

A friend of mine from college is moving to my city. I think there are things she will like about living here, but there are also things she might dislike. I like living here because there are a lot of things to do, there are a lot of nice neighborhoods to live in, and we have beautiful parks. On the other hand, my friend might not like it because it's very crowded and expensive and we're far from beautiful places like the mountains and the beach.

Living in this city is very exciting because there are so many interesting things to do, although you pay a price for it. We have museums, art galleries, and lots of movie theaters. We have restaurants with food from all over the world. However, when you go to these places they are always very crowded. Also, there is almost always heavy traffic on the way and it is difficult to find parking once you arrive. I know my friend likes peace and quiet, so she may not enjoy the crowds in my city.

In this city we have many beautiful neighborhoods, although some of them are very expensive. We have neighborhoods of old houses with interesting architecture. We have more modern neighborhoods with new apartment buildings. We have lots of nice places to live, but it isn't always easy to find a place that you can afford. I know my friend doesn't earn a big salary, so she might not like this aspect of living here.

Even though we are far from the countryside, we have many beautiful, natural areas right here in the city. We have a big park where people go hiking and biking, and in the winter they go ice skating. We also have many small parks throughout the city and lots of trees and gardens. It is a pretty city and I know my friend will like that. However, we are far from the mountains and far from the beach. I know my friend likes to spend time in the countryside, so she might not like living far away from those places.

All in all, there are both advantages and disadvantages to living here. My friend will have to decide if she prefers excitement and crowds or quiet and nature before she makes her final decision about moving here.

67 AD

Do you agree or disagree with the following statement? Television, newspapers, magazines, and other media pay too much attention to the personal lives of famous people such as public figures and celebrities. Use specific reasons and details to explain your opinion.

I think the media pay too much attention to the private lives of famous people. They discover things that happened years ago and report them as if they still mattered. They publicize things about famous people's lives that are really private, personal matters. They put out information that could end up having a bad effect on a person's family and personal life. They do this just to entertain the public, but I don't find it entertaining at all.

The media like to dig up bad information about the past actions of famous people. They find out that a person took drugs when he was young, or that someone was a reckless driver and caused a bad accident. Then a person in her forties has to explain something that she did when she was fifteen. I don't understand how something that happened so long ago could have any interest or importance now.

The media says that the public has the right to know about the private actions of famous people. They say it is our right to know if someone had an extramarital affair or didn't pay back some money that he owed. I say these are personal matters. We respect the privacy of ordinary people and we should do the same for famous people.

The media seem to report these things without considering what might happen as a result. Reporting on a celebrity's personal affairs could have an effect on that person's family, especially the children. A celebrity's good name and credibility could be ruined before he or she can prove that the rumors are false. A person's entire career could be ruined by something that is reported in the media.

Having details of one's personal life reported in public can have all sorts of negative consequences on a person's life. Ordinary people don't have to suffer this sort of attention, and I see no reason why celebrities should either.

68 MA

Some people believe that the Earth is being harmed (damaged) by human activity. Others feel that human activity makes the Earth a better place to live. What is your opinion? Use specific reasons and examples to support your answer.

The quality of human life has improved greatly over the past few centuries, but Earth is being harmed more and more by human activity. As we develop our technology, we use more and more natural resources and cause more and more pollution. As our population grows, we destroy more and more natural areas in order to expand towns and cities. The Earth is being harmed, and this harms people as well.

We often act as if we have unlimited natural resources, but this isn't true. If we cut down too many trees to build houses and make paper, not all the trees will grow back. If we catch too many fish, the fish population will get smaller and smaller. If we aren't careful about how we use our natural resources, we will lose many of them. We are already losing some.

We don't seem to pay attention to the amount of pollution human activity can cause. Our cars pollute the air. Our factories pollute both the air and the water. We throw our waste into rivers and streams. We act as if the air and water can clean themselves up, but they can't.

As urban populations grow, the cities grow too, taking over more and more land. New houses, stores, and office buildings are built all the time. Land that was once forest or farms is now parking lots and apartment buildings. We seem to act as if we have unlimited land, but we don't. We need to plan more carefully so that we use our limited land in the best way possible.

People need to respect the Earth and try to preserve it. If we don't, we will lose all the natural resources that we depend on for life. Then what will happen?

69 PR

It has recently been announced that a new high school may be built in your neighborhood. Do you support or oppose this plan? Why? Use specific reasons and details in your answer.

I oppose having a new high school built in my neighborhood. I don't think there is a real need for one. I think it would cause traffic problems in our area, and it would mean that we would lose the use of our beautiful neighborhood park. I don't think a high school would be of any benefit to us at all.

First of all, there are very few teenagers in our neighborhood. Most of the residents here are either retired or are young couples with babies and small children. This means that most of the high school students would come from other parts of town, but that the majority of the people who live here would not benefit.

Second, a high school would cause a lot of traffic. Most of the students would live too far away to walk to school, so they would come by car or school bus. In addition to the traffic on regular school days, there would be even more traffic after school and on weekends for sports events, school drama productions, and other school activities. This would disrupt the quiet life style of our neighborhood.

Finally, everyone in the neighborhood would be upset by the loss of the park, which is the site that has been selected for the high school. Parents take their small children to the park every day to play. Older people like to walk there in the evenings after dinner. On weekends, people enjoy having picnics and playing games in the park. We would be sorry to lose our neighborhood park.

Our town may need a new high school, but our neighborhood is not the right place for it. We don't want our quiet lifestyle disrupted, and most people in this area have no need for a high school, anyway.

70 MA

Is it better to enjoy your money when you earn it, or is it better to save your money for some time in the future? Use specific reasons and examples to support your opinion.

When I have a choice between spending money and putting it in my savings account at the bank, I always choose to put it in the bank. I know I will have a lot of expenses in the near future. I need to finish my education, I would like to travel, and then there are always unforeseen emergencies. I need to set money aside so that I will be able to pay for these things.

Education is expensive. My parents aren't able to pay all my bills. My tuition, room and board, books, and incidental expenses all have to be paid for. My parents help me, but I am still responsible for paying part of it. If I spend all the money I earn now, I won't have enough to meet my expenses next semester. So, saving money now will enable me to finish my education.

Another thing that is important to me is travel. Right now I am trying to save money so that I can take a big trip as soon as I graduate. I would like to travel around the world and visit as many countries as I can. If I save money now, there's a good chance that this dream will come true. But If I spend all my money now, I doubt I will ever have enough to make such a trip.

Finally, we should always remember that emergencies can happen at any time. I might have an unexpected illness and need to pay for doctors and medicines. Or, one of my family members may need help, and I will have to send some money. We can't predict emergencies such as these, but we can be prepared. If I save money now, then I will have what I need if the unforeseen occurs.

It is better to plan ahead rather than spend money carelessly. I know I will need money for my schooling, and I would like to have some for travel. I know that I will also have unexpected expenses from time to time. I need to save money for all these things.

71 AD

Businesses should hire employees for their entire lives. Do you agree or disagree? Use specific reasons and examples to support your answer.

In some places, the common practice is to hire workers when they are young and keep them employed for the rest of their working lives. In other places, companies commonly hire people to do a particular job and then fire them when they are no longer needed. I agree with the latter position. In the modern economy, companies need to consider an employee's performance, speed, and ability to change. Loyalty is not important.

In today's competitive business climate, we need to hire workers who can help us keep up with the competition. This means we need to employ people who have the skills needed for the modern workplace and who can do the job without the need for a lot of extra training. We require employees who are suited to the job we need done, and if the job changes, we change the worker.

Because of the competitive climate, we also need to be able to produce goods and services quickly. We need young people who will push themselves to do the job faster and who are willing to work long hours when necessary. We can't accommodate workers who are unable to keep pace with the pressures of the modern workplace.

The competitive climate also means that we have to be ready to meet changing demands. If we change our workforce regularly, we can bring in new and contemporary ideas. By hiring new workers, we get fresh points of views, We don't stagnate and lose our position in the market because of sticking with outdated approaches.

Although a feeing of loyalty between a company and its workers is a noble idea, it is not practical today. A company needs to keep up with the changing forces of the economy. In order to be able to do this, it needs to be able to change its workforce as necessary.

72 AD

Do you agree or disagree with the following statement? Attending a live performance (for example, a play, concert, or sporting event) is more enjoyable than watching the same event on television. Use specific reasons and examples to support your opinion.

Some people think that attending a live performance is preferable to watching it on television. I say, however, that if you have a good TV, it is much better to watch a performance that way. It is much more convenient and comfortable, and it is cheaper, too. I almost never attend a live performance of anything.

It is much more convenient to stay home and watch a performance on TV. I don't have to go anywhere. I don't have to worry about leaving the house on time. I don't have to worry about traffic or parking. I don't have to stand on line for a ticket. I just turn on the television at the time the event begins, sit back, and enjoy myself.

It is much more comfortable to watch a performance at home. I can wear any clothes that I want to. I know I will have a good seat with a good view. I can get up and get a snack at any time. I can relax and enjoy myself in the comfort of my own home.

It is much cheaper to watch a performance on TV. I don't have to buy a ticket. I don't have to pay for parking or for dinner at a restaurant before the performance. I already own a TV, so watching a performance on it doesn't cost me anything. If it turns out I don't like the performance, I can just turn off the TV and go do something else. I haven't lost any money, or much time either.

Watching a performance on TV is so comfortable and convenient, I don't know why people attend live performances. It's much better to enjoy them at home.

73 EX

Choose one of the following transportation vehicles and explain why you think it has changed people's lives.

- **automobiles**
- **bicycles**
- **airplanes**

Use specific reasons and examples to support your answer.

Ever since the discovery of the wheel, innovations in transportation have had profound effects on the way people live. In the modern era, the airplane is a form of transportation that has changed our lives in a number of ways. Thanks to the airplane, our lives are now faster, more exciting, and more convenient than before.

It cannot be denied that airplanes are fast. A business person can leave London in the morning and arrive in New York just a few hours later, in time to begin a full day's work. The speed of airplane travel makes it possible for friends and relatives to visit each other more frequently. In both our business and personal lives, airplanes make it possible for us to travel to more places more quickly.

Trips by airplane are also exciting. When you travel by plane, you might cross time zones, oceans, and many countries. When you get off the plane, you could be in a completely different part of the world. You could be in a place where the language, food, and climate are entirely new to you. Because of airplanes, we have the possibility to experience new and exotic places.

Nothing can beat the convenience of an airplane. You can go anywhere at any time you want. You don't have to spend long hours sitting in traffic on the highway. You don't have to wait months before you can get a reservation on a boat. Airplanes leave for destinations around the world at all times of the day. You can choose the schedule that suits you best and arrive at a distant place after just a few, short, comfortable hours of travel.

No form of transportation has changed the way we work and live more than the airplane. Thanks to the speed, excitement, and convenience of the airplane, our lives are filled with more possibilities.

74 AD

Do you agree or disagree that progress is always good? Use specific reasons and examples to support your answer.

Who could disagree with the statement, "Progress is good?" Progress is a fact of life. Without it, there would be no change. We would still be living the harsh lives our ancient ancestors did. Without progress, there would be no improvements in our economy, our standard of living, or our health.

We can't keep the economy moving forward without progress. Progress means growth. It means the development of new products and the creation of new services. If we didn't have progress, the economy would stagnate. Eventually, there wouldn't be enough jobs to keep people employed or enough industries and businesses to provide us with what we need. We need progress for our economic well-being.

Progress is required to raise our standard of living. Today we live in homes that are more comfortable and have more amenities thanks to developments in home construction technology. We drive better cars and have safer highways thanks to innovations in the transportation industry. Our educational system is greatly improved thanks to the use of computers and the Internet. Progress means that our daily lives are better now than they were in the past.

We need progress to improve the health of the world's population. Without progress, there would be no vaccines against terrible diseases such as smallpox or polio. We wouldn't have treatments for conditions such as heart disease and cancer. We would have high infant mortality rates and a shorter life expectancy. Because of progress, our lives are now longer and healthier than they used to be.

Progress is a natural state. Without it, we wouldn't evolve. Without it, our economy, our standard of living, and our health would deteriorate. Who could deny the necessity of progress?

75 AD

Learning about the past has no value for those of us living in the present. Do you agree or disagree? Use specific reasons and examples to support your answer.

People often say, "Those who don't understand history will repeat the mistakes of the past." I totally disagree. I don't see any evidence that people have made smart decisions based on their knowledge of the past. To me, the present is what is important. I think that people, weather, and politics determine what happens, not the past.

People can change. People may have hated each other for years, but that doesn't mean they will continue to hate each other. Look at Turkey and Greece. When Turkey had an earthquake, Greece sent aid. When Greece had an earthquake, Turkey sent aid. These two countries are cooperating now. No doubt, if we had looked at the past, we would have believed this to be impossible. But people change.

The weather can change. Farmers plant certain crops because these crops have always grown well in their fields. But there can be a long drought. The crops that grew well in the past will die. The farmers need to try a drought-resistant crop. If we had looked at the past, we wouldn't have changed our crop. Weather changes.

Politics can change. If politicians looked only at the past, they would always do the same thing. If we looked at the past in the United States, we would see a lot of discrimination against races, women, and sexual orientation. On the whole, people now are interested in human rights, and the government protects these rights. Politics change.

As a rule, it is important to follow the mood of today. It doesn't help us to think about the past. People, the weather, and politics can change in any direction. The direction of this change, in my opinion, cannot be predicted by studying the past.

76 AD

Do you agree or disagree with the following statement? With the help of technology, students nowadays can learn more information and learn it more quickly. Use specific reasons and examples to support your answer.

It cannot be denied that technology has greatly improved the way we get information, and this has certainly had effects on the lives of students. Recent innovations in technology have made it possible for students to get more information more quickly and more conveniently than they did in the past.

An amazing amount of information is available through the Internet. It is like having all the world's libraries at your fingertips. Students can research any topic they need to learn about or answer just about any question that occurs to them. They can look up information about past events or follow current events as they unfold. Technology has made it possible to access just about any sort of information a student may need through the Internet.

Information comes through the Internet almost instantly. A student just types a few words into a search engine, and in a matter of seconds sources from all over the Internet appear on the screen. It is no longer necessary to take the time to go to the library and search the shelves there, or wait for newspapers and magazines to arrive at the store. Information is available the minute a student needs it.

A variety of electronic devices have made access to information more convenient than ever. A student can use a desktop or laptop computer to access the Internet from home or school any time of night or day. In addition, smart phones and tablet computers make it possible for students to carry around their Internet access with them. They can go online while sitting in a café or waiting for a bus. They can look for information at any time and in any place they choose.

Technology has improved the way students get information. The Internet and the devices students can use to access it have made more information available more quickly and conveniently.

77 AD

Some people think that human needs for farmland, housing, and industry are more important than saving land for endangered animals. Do you agree or disagree with this point of view? Why or why not? Use specific reasons and examples to support your answer.

Many animals are now extinct and many more are in danger of extinction. This is because their habitat is destroyed when people use land to build houses, factories, and farms. Does it matter? It certainly does. Our basic human needs, our quality of life, and the way we live are all affected when animals' habitats are destroyed.

Many animals affect our basic human needs even though we may not realize it. There is a delicate balance of nature. If one small part is removed, it will affect all the other parts. For example, if certain trees are cut down, bats will have no place to live. If there are no bats, there will be no animal to eat certain insects that destroy our crops. This will affect our basic need for food.

The loss of certain animals affects the quality of our lives. Certain flowers are pollinated by butterflies that migrate from Canada to Mexico. Some of the breeding grounds of these butterflies was destroyed. Now, these flowers are disappearing. We will no longer be able to enjoy their beauty, and we will no longer be able to enjoy the beauty of the butterflies. This is just one small example.

When animals' habitats are destroyed we may think that it only affects the animals, but it affects our way of life, too. Large parts of the Amazon rain forest have been cut down to make room for farms. This rain forest is an important part of the weather system all around the world. Weather patterns have been changing because of this. This will have a huge effect on how we live.

When animals' lives are endangered, our way of life is endangered, too. I would encourage humans to look for other alternatives for our farmlands, housing, and industries. We have alternatives; the animals do not.

78 MA

What is a very important skill a person should learn in order to be successful in the world today? Choose one skill and use specific reasons and examples to support your choice.

Although success is often defined economically, I define it socially. Therefore, a skill I would identify as being important for success is tolerance. To succeed in society, in my opinion, we need to be tolerant of one another's background, opinions, and lifestyle.

The world is filled with people from all different backgrounds. These days, the world is also becoming increasingly mobile. In the past, we tended to work only with people who grew up in the same place we did or who went to the same schools we went to. Now we often find ourselves working with people whose backgrounds are completely different from ours. This is why it is important to be tolerant of one another's differences, not only so we can work together amiably but also so we can learn from each other.

Different people have different opinions, but we cannot stop speaking to one another just because of this. We shouldn't start a fight just because someone has a different point of view. Instead, we need to look for common ground, something we can agree on. We need to respect the people we live and work with and be tolerant of their opinions. We need to look for ways to get along with everyone in our lives.

There are people living different lifestyles all around us. A woman might be living on her own, working at an important job, and supporting her family by herself. A man might choose to stay at home and raise the children while his wife earns money at a job. Social roles can change and people choose the lifestyles that suit them best. We must be tolerant of these different choices.

To succeed socially, it is important to be able to adapt to differences. It is important to be tolerant of all people regardless of their background, opinions, or lifestyle.

79 MA

Why do you think some people are attracted to dangerous sports or other dangerous activities? Use specific reasons and examples to support your answer.

Many people enjoy watching or reading about dangerous sports. Few, however, are attracted to actually participating in such sports themselves. These are usually people who love risks, seek a feeling of power, or need a way to deal with personal problems. Dangerous sports give them a way to meet these kinds of needs.

Dangerous sports are attractive to risk takers. Most people take risks in their daily lives such as risks with their money, their jobs, or their love lives. These are only ordinary risks, however, and are generally not life threatening. Risks takers, on the other hand, are people who seek the excitement of a different kind of risk—that of putting their lives in danger. Dangerous sports have that special kind of thrill that risk takers seek.

People who want a feeling of power are also attracted to dangerous sports. Climbing to the top of a remote mountain peak or learning how to sky dive successfully can give a great feeling of accomplishment. When people perform such amazing feats and survive them, they feel as though they have conquered the forces of nature. They feel more powerful than fate.

Finally, I think dangerous sports may sometimes attract unhappy people. When people are dissatisfied at work or when they have difficulties at home, they may turn to dangerous sports as a way of dealing with their problems. At the very least, this type of activity can distract them from the things that are bothering them. But even more, learning how to do something difficult can increase a person's self esteem. It can help a person feel good about himself despite any personal problems he may have.

Dangerous sports can be attractive for several reasons. They appeal to people who seek thrills, power, or a way to forget their problems. I, however, do not count myself among these people and in my opinion, dangerous sports are never worth the risk.

80 PR

Some people prefer to get up early in the morning and start the day's work. Others prefer to get up later in the day and work until late at night. Which do you prefer? Use specific reasons and examples to support your choice.

Some people have lots of energy early in the day, but I am not one of them. No one could ever accuse me of being a "morning person." I definitely prefer to get up later in the day and stay up until late at night. This routine fits my body's rhythm, my work schedule, and my social life.

I believe in following my body's natural rhythm. For me, it is natural to feel wide awake at night and sleepy in the morning. Therefore, I prefer to stay in bed until 10:00 or 11:00 every morning. When I do this, I wake up feeling energetic and ready to start the day. If I get up earlier, I feel grumpy and foggy and unable to do anything properly.

Sleeping late also suits my work schedule. I work best in the afternoon. Fortunately, I don't usually have a lot of work to do and don't need to spend all day at it. If I work from after lunch until just before dinner, that is enough time to get my work done.

My active social life is another reason I prefer to sleep late. Who gets up early in the morning to have fun? No one. If I want to go out and have a good time with my friends, I have to do it in the evening. Anything entertaining, such as parties, concerts, dances, or dinners, happens then. If I got up early in the morning, I would be too tired to enjoy myself later.

Getting up and going to bed late is the sort of schedule that suits me best. It allows me to follow my natural rhythms, get my work done, and have fun with my friends. I will probably follow this pattern for the rest of my life.

81 EX

What are the important qualities of a good son or daughter? Have these qualities changed or remained the same over time in your culture? Use specific reasons and examples to support your answer.

Most parents will tell you that they wish their children will have certain qualities. They want them to be obedient, loyal, and respectful. These are expectations that parents have had of their children for generations. These days, however, parents often find that their children demonstrate these qualities less and less.

All parents expect their children to obey them. Even when their sons and daughters grow up and have children of their own, parents still expect obedience from them. At least, that's the way it was traditionally. Nowadays, children still obey their parents when they are young. When they reach age 18 or 20, however, they start wanting to make their own decisions. They want to follow their own ideas even if these ideas are contrary to their parents' wishes.

Parents also expect their children to be loyal. They expect them to put their family first, before other relationships they may have. Also, if a dispute arises between families, parents expect their children to side with their own family. This is a quality that is still commonly valued among the younger generation. Most children today will support their family against others.

Finally, parents, quite naturally, demand respect of their children. As children become accustomed to nontraditional ways of doing things, however, this quality starts to lose strength. The world is changing rapidly, making it easy for children to view their parents as old-fashioned. They think their parents are too old to understand them and the world they live in, and they start losing respect.

The traditional virtues of obedience, loyalty, and respect are being challenged today. Children nowadays tend to show these qualities to their parents less and less.

82 PR

Some people prefer to work for a large company. Others prefer to work for a small company. Which would you prefer? Use specific reasons and details to support your choice.

While small companies and large companies each have their advantages, I am sure I would prefer to work for a large company. A large company has more to offer its employees in terms of advancement, training, and prestige.

As the employee of a large company, I could start at an entry level position and work my way up to the top. I might start working in the mailroom, for example, and get to know the company that way. Then, when there was an opening for a better position, I could apply for that. Eventually I could work my way up to a managerial job. In a small company, on the other hand, I would have fewer opportunities to advance.

If I worked for a large company, I would also have the chance to learn a variety of jobs. For instance, I might work in shipping for a while and then move on to sales. I could be trained in a variety of positions and gain valuable experience. In addition to on-the-job training, I would also probably have opportunities to take professional development classes through my company. A small company can't provide the same advantages.

In a large company, there would be more prestige. In the first place, the name of a large company would look very good on my resume. Additionally, my friends and acquaintances would be impressed when I told them where I worked. If I worked for a small company, on the other hand, few people would recognize its name and I would always have to explain what the company did.

Working for a small company would not give me the same opportunities for advancement or training as a large company would, and it would not have the same prestige. I would benefit in many ways by choosing to work for a large company over a small one.

83 EX

People work because they need money to live. What are some other reasons that people work? Discuss one or more of these reasons. Use specific examples and details to support your answer.

Although the main reason most people work is to earn a living, it is not the only reason they stay at their jobs. Working also fulfills other human needs. It provides people with the opportunity to be with other people, to contribute something to society, and to feel a sense of accomplishment.

Many people enjoy going to work because it gives them the chance to be with other people. They like interacting with their coworkers and clients. They like working with others to find ways to get a job done, and they like the chance to socialize, as well. Work provides opportunities to develop both professional and personal relationships.

People also enjoy their jobs because it gives them the chance to contribute something to society. Teachers, for example, educate our future generations. Doctors and nurses help us stay healthy. Manufacturers produce things that we need to carry out our daily lives. Through work, each individual is able to do his or her part in the world.

A lot of people like to work because it gives them a sense of accomplishment. People who work in factories, for example, can take pride in the cars they produce or the televisions they assemble. A business owner gets a sense of achievement when he sees the business he built from scratch become successful and profitable. Anybody who develops professional skills through training and experience knows the feeling of accomplishment that comes from having achieved certain levels of expertise.

Money is nice to have, but it is not the only reason people get up and go to work every day. I believe that people also value work because it allows them chances to interact with others, to make a contribution to society, and to feel that they have accomplished something. These needs may not be as fundamental as the need to have money to pay for food and shelter, but they are important needs nevertheless.

84 AD

Do you agree or disagree with the following statement? Face-to-face communication is better than other types of communication, such as letters, email, or telephone calls. Use specific reasons and details to support your answer.

I would have to agree that face-to-face communication is the best type of communication. It can eliminate misunderstandings immediately, cement relationships, and encourage continued interaction.

When you talk to someone directly, you can see right away if they don't understand you. A person's body language will tell you if they disagree or if they don't follow your line of thought. Then you can repeat yourself or paraphrase your argument. When you send an email, the receiver may misinterpret what you want to say. He or she could even be insulted. Then you have to waste time explaining yourself in another email.

When you talk face to face, you communicate with more than words. You communicate with your eyes and your hands. You communicate with your whole body. People can sense that you really want to communicate with them. This energy bonds people together. Your relationship with a person can grow much stronger when you communicate in person.

When you meet someone face to face, the interaction tends to last longer than other forms of communication. An email lasts a second; a telephone call, a few minutes. When you meet someone face to face, however, you've both made an effort to be there. You will probably spend longer talking. The longer you talk, the more you say. The more you say, the stronger your relationship will be.

In summary, if you want to establish a relationship with another human being, the best way is talking face to face. When you communicate directly, you can avoid misunderstandings that may occur in writing. You can communicate on levels other than just words and you can spend more time doing it.

85 PR

Some people like to do only what they already do well. Other people prefer to try new things and take risks. Which do you prefer? Use specific reasons and examples to support your choice.

I am not a risk taker. I like to do just those things that I am proficient at. I don't want to waste my time doing things that I don't do well. I always feel better when I do something well, and other people have a better impression of me. I don't see a good reason to try something new that I don't know how to do at all.

I don't have time to waste doing things that I don't really know how to do. For example, I don't know how to sew. I could spend a whole day trying to make a dress, and at the end of the day I still wouldn't have a dress to wear. It would be better to spend an hour buying a dress at the store. Then I could spend the rest of the day doing other things that I know I can do.

I feel good when I do a good job, but I feel terrible when I do something poorly. Once, I decided to figure my income taxes myself. But I am not an accountant and I made many mistakes. I felt very bad about it. Finally, I realized I could pay a professional accountant to do it for me. Then I could spend my time feeling good about other things that I know how to do.

When I do something well, I make a better impression on other people. If I tried to cook a meal for you, you would not have a good impression of me at all. I am a terrible cook. But I can change the oil in your car for you and I can tune up the engine. When you see me do a good job at that, you see me as a competent, accomplished mechanic instead of as a sorry cook.

Some people like to take risks and try doing new things, but I am not one of those people. When I do something that I really don't know how to do, I just end up feeling bad and I give other people a bad impression. I don't see the point of wasting my time this way.

86 EX

Some people believe that success in life comes from taking risks or chances. Others believe that success results from careful planning. In your opinion, what does success come from? Use specific reasons and examples to support your answer.

I think we must all take risks if we want to get anywhere in life, but they must be calculated risks. If we look at the great explorers and scientists of history, we see that their successes were usually a combination of both planning and risk taking. Like the great thinkers, we must plan carefully, take the risk, then be ready to change direction when necessary.

It is hard to be successful without careful planning. In his search for a new route to India, Columbus drew maps, planned his route carefully, and spent time gathering the necessary support and supplies. Madame Curie worked long hours in her laboratory setting up her experiments, then carefully recording each step she took and the results she got. Neither of these two legendary figures would have achieved what they did without this planning.

The willingness to take risks is the other important ingredient of success. Despite all his careful planning, Columbus couldn't know what would happen on his trip. He couldn't be sure he would be successful in finding a new route to India or know what he might encounter instead. Madame Curie could not be certain about the results of her experiments, of course, and the only way to find out was to actually carry the experiments out.

When things don't go according to plan, success can still be achieved if you are ready to change direction. Columbus planned to bring back spices from Asia. When he landed in America instead, he didn't just give up and go home. He didn't find spices, but he did find gold. You can reach success if you are able to make your mistakes work for you and change your plans when necessary.

You will never succeed in life if you don't take chances. But before you start, you must plan carefully so that you are ready to take advantage of every opportunity and change your plans as required.

87 MA

What change would make your hometown more appealing to people your age? Use specific reasons and examples to support your opinion.

There is almost no place in my town where young people can go to spend time with their friends after school. Therefore, I think it would be a good idea to have a teahouse that would be only for young people. We could go there to socialize, have meetings, and relax in a quiet place.

The young people in my town need a place to socialize. There are already several teahouses, but they are reserved for our fathers and their friends. Teenagers are not allowed to spend time in them. If we had a teahouse of our own, we would have a place to get together with our friends and talk about school and other things that interest us.

A teahouse of our own would also mean that we would have a place to hold meetings. Several of my friends would like to start a poetry club, but they have no place to meet. I would be interested in starting a debating society, and I know a number of young people who are interested in politics. If we had a place to hold meetings, we could form clubs to pursue these and similar interests with our friends.

Finally, it would be nice to have a place to relax away from our families. Most people in my town come from large families. This means that our homes are usually noisy and busy. Many of us have younger brothers and sisters whom we love but who can be annoying at times. Sometimes we need to get away from our hectic home lives. We need to have a quiet place where we can go to study, read, or just sit quietly.

If our town had a teahouse reserved for teenagers, it would be good for our parents. They would always know where we were. They could rest assured knowing that if we aren't at home, we are at the teahouse socializing, having a meeting, or just relaxing with our friends.

88 AD

Do you agree or disagree with the following statement? The most important aspect of a job is the money a person earns. Use specific reasons and examples to support your answer.

I strongly agree that the most important aspect of a job is the amount of money I can earn from it. When I was thinking about what kind of profession I wanted to have, I only considered professions that have a high earning potential. What is the point of working, after all, if not to make as much money as possible? If I earn a lot of money, people will know I am successful, smart, and a good marriage candidate.

Money equals success. If I earn a lot of money, I can afford to buy nice things such as fashionable clothes and a luxury car. I can also help my family and friends. I can buy a nice apartment for my parents, for instance, and lend money to my friends whenever they need it. Everyone will see that I am rich and, therefore, successful.

Earning a lot of money will show people how smart I am. Everyone knows that you need to be smart to make money. You can't move up to high positions in a company without intelligence and knowledge. No one will pay you a high salary if you are stupid.

When I earn a lot of money, my mother will be able to find a good wife for me. She will be able to tell everyone that I have a good job and a high salary. It will make it easy for her to find someone for me since all girls want to marry a rich man. They want someone who can easily take care of their material needs.

When I start working, it would be nice to get a job that is interesting to do. More important than that, however, is the amount of money I earn. Having a high-paying job will show everyone that I am successful, smart, and a good catch.

89 AD

Do you agree or disagree with the following statement? One should never judge a person by external appearances. Use specific reasons and details to support your answer.

In most cases, you shouldn't judge a person by external appearances. It is better to reserve judgment until you have had a chance to get to know the person. Judgments based on external appearances prevent you from really getting to know a person, reinforce stereotypes, and can lead you to conclusions that aren't true.

When you judge people by their external appearance, you lose the chance to get to know them. In high school I stayed away from students who were called "bad students" because they dressed a certain way. I wanted nothing to do with them. Later, I had a chance to meet a "bad student" because his mother was a friend of my mother. Then I realized that we actually had a lot in common. My impression of him was very different once I got to know him.

Judging people based on external appearances just reinforces stereotypes. You might think that a person with a tattoo, for example, is not a nice person. It's easy to start thinking that all people with tattoos are not nice people. Then you will never make friends with people who have tattoos or want to work with them or like to live near them. You will feel uncomfortable around them because all you will see about them is their tattoos.

Judgments based on external appearances can often lead you to conclusions that aren't true. Maybe you know someone who dresses in old, unfashionable clothes. If all you see are the clothes, it is easy to think that the person has bad taste or bad habits. But maybe the truth is different. Maybe that person comes from a less fortunate family than you and doesn't have money. Maybe the person is working hard to save money for school. You will never know if all you do is look at external appearance.

You should always take time to get to know new people before making judgments about them. External appearance often does not tell us anything about a person. Judging someone by their appearance is misleading, reinforces stereotypes, and doesn't lead to the truth. It can prevent you from making a true friend.

90 AD

Do you agree or disagree with the following statement? A person should never make an important decision alone. Use specific reasons and examples to support your answer.

You should never make an important decision alone. You should think out your important decisions carefully, and you need other people to help you do this. People close to you can give you good advice, give you a different perspective, and share their own experiences. It is hard to make big decisions without this kind of help.

It is very important to have advice when making decisions. When I had to decide which courses to take in high school, I talked to the school counselor. He had the knowledge and expertise to help me determine which classes were best for my goals. Without his advice, I might have chosen unsuitable courses.

Getting a friend's perspective on a situation is also usually helpful. I have always loved drama, but I thought I wasn't good enough to act in the school play. When a friend of mine found this out, she was shocked. She was able to provide me with another perspective on myself and my talents. I changed my mind and decided to audition for the school play. Imagine my surprise when I got an important part.

When other people share their experiences with you, that can help you in making your decisions. When I was trying to decide if I should study overseas, I talked with a friend. She had studied overseas the year before. She really helped me because I was very unsure about my decision. After hearing about her experiences, I decided it would be a good experience for me too. I went and it was amazing.

Whenever I am faced with an important decision, I seek advice from others so that I am well-informed and have the benefit of their experience and perspective.

91 MA

A company is going to give some money either to support the arts or to protect the environment. Which do you think the company should choose? Use specific reasons and examples to support your answer.

Deciding between supporting the arts and protecting the environment is a difficult choice to make, but I think I would choose protecting the environment. We need a healthy environment in order to survive, so we must protect it. We need to protect the environment now to help prevent health problems, to maintain the ecosystem, and to preserve the Earth for our children.

Pollution from factories and cars can cause damage to the environment. It makes the air dirty. Breathing this dirty air causes health problems, particularly for children and the elderly. We need to control the amount of pollution we produce in order to prevent health problems.

We also need to pay attention to the ecosystem. Plant life, animal life, and people all depend on each other. An unhealthy environment disturbs this ecosystem. For example, changes in the environment might cause a certain kind of plant to die. If that plant is food for a certain kind of animal, the animal will die too. If people use that animal as a food source, there could be big problems.

If we do not protect our environment now, it will continue to get worse and our children will suffer the consequences. The air and water will get dirtier, and more plants and animals will die. Our children won't have as much natural beauty to admire. Even worse, their well-being will be threatened.

Without clean air to breathe, a healthy ecosystem, and a future for our children, the human race will not survive. That's why protecting our environment is important. If we have a healthy environment, we have healthy children who can participate in and appreciate the arts.

92 PR

Some movies are serious, designed to make the audience think. Other movies are designed primarily to amuse and entertain. Which type of movie do you prefer? Use specific reasons and examples to support your answer.

Some movies make you think deeply about important issues, while others distract you from your problems. Although I sometimes enjoy watching movies that are serious, I generally prefer to see movies that amuse and entertain. These movies help me relax, laugh, and keep my perspective.

At the end of a long day, what I need to do most is relax. My classes and my job keep my mind working all day, so I am usually too tired mentally to enjoy a serious movie. An entertaining movie, however, gives my mind the rest it needs. I don't have to think while watching such a movie. I just sit back and relax. Then my mind feels renewed and I feel ready to get back to work and study.

Entertaining movies make me laugh. Laughing is important in many ways. It is good for both one's soul and one's physical health. So, laughing helps me keep feeling good. It also helps connect me with other people. When I see an amusing movie with my friends and we laugh together, it helps strengthen our friendship.

When I watch an amusing movie, it helps put my problems in perspective. Sometimes the troubles of the day can seem overwhelming. I can't stop thinking about them and they push all other thoughts out of my mind. An amusing movie can help me forget about my problems for a while. Then, when I think about them again, they don't seem so big, and solutions may be easier to find.

While I can appreciate serious movies that make you think, I prefer to be amused and entertained at the end of a hard day. Such movies allow me to take a break from the rigors of daily life by helping me relax, making me laugh, and putting my problems into perspective.

93 PR

Some people are always in a hurry to go places and get things done. Other people prefer to take their time and live life at a slower pace. Which do you prefer? Use specific reasons and examples to support your answer.

Life is short. Haste makes waste. What's your hurry? I feel there is a lot of wisdom in these words. These three sayings characterize the way I manage my daily life. I would rather take my time than rush through things just to get them done.

Life is short. You never know what may happen tomorrow, so it is important to appreciate today. By doing just a few things slowly and doing them well, you can savor the experience. You can truly enjoy what you are doing and make each minute count.

Haste makes waste. You can't just rush through your chores as if you were a machine. If you did, you might miss some steps and end up doing a poor job. Then you would have to start from the beginning and do the job all over again. It would take twice as long to get things done. But by going more slowly, you can do a chore carefully, completely, and correctly the first time around.

What's your hurry? I don't see the point of rushing through something just to get to the next experience. If you did, you would miss a lot along the way. If you are taking care of your younger brother for example, you could just keep him by your side while you work on other chores. Or, you could devote your whole attention to him, interact with him, and get to know him. There is a lot to be gained by focusing your entire attention on the task at hand rather than thinking the whole time about what you are going to do next.

I believe it is important to appreciate life by savoring each moment we have, not wasting any bit of precious time, and always slowing down enough to appreciate what is right in front of us.

94 AD

Do you agree or disagree with the following statement? Games are as important for children as they are for adults. Use specific reasons and examples to support your answers.

We usually think of games as being a significant part of childhood, but adults enjoy them, as well. In my opinion, games are important at all stages of life. They help you keep your mind sharp, they challenge you to learn new things, and they allow you to maintain social skills. These are things that are important for people of all ages.

Playing games exercises the mind. For children, this helps them develop their thinking skills. For adults, this helps them stay sharp even as they grow older. Doing things such as learning the rules of a game, working out a winning strategy, and keeping track of opponents' moves, helps both children and adults keep their brains growing and functioning. It helps them stay mentally active.

People can learn a lot from playing games. Certain types of games, for example, test the players' knowledge of geography, history, science, or current events facts. Other games require an understanding of vocabulary. Both children and adults enjoy learning and showing off the knowledge needed to play these sorts of games, so playing games can make learning fun for everyone.

Games provide an opportunity to develop and use social skills. Playing games means interacting with other people. It means learning to follow rules, playing fairly, and being considerate of others, even if they are your opponents. These are skills that are important for children to develop and for adults to maintain. Playing games also allows people to develop and maintain personal contacts. This is important for everybody because we all need friends, no matter what age we are.

Playing games is important for everyone, regardless of age. Games help you keep your mind alert, learn new things, and build friendships. These are things that matter in all phases of life.

95 AD

Do you agree or disagree with the following statement? Parents or other adult relatives should make important decisions for their older (15-18 year old) teenaged children. Use specific reasons and examples to support your opinion.

No one knows me as well as my parents, and no one cares about me like they do. It is natural that I should allow my parents to make important decisions for me. I think all older teenagers should take their parents advice on decisions that concern their education, their social life, and their future careers.

My parents are the ones who can make the best decisions about my education. They have always chosen the best schools for me to attend. They have hired tutors to make sure I understood my classes well. They have sent me to special prep classes to help me prepare for exams. When it is time to choose a college, I know they will choose the right college for me.

My parents make good decisions about my social life. When I was young, they invited children over to play with me. I became very close to these children and we are still friends. Even though I am older now, my parents still guide me in my social life. I know they don't want me to hang out with the wrong crowd. I know they want me to marry a good person who is right for me. They have more experience than I have and they can help me make decisions about my social life.

I need my parents to help me make decisions about my future career. Both my parents have successful careers of their own. My father runs a business and my mother is a well-known politician. I want to be as successful as they are, so of course I will listen to their advice about my career.

If all children follow their parents' wishes, they will be happier. They will be more successful in school, in work, and in their social life. After all, parents want only the best for their children.

96 MA

What do you want most in a friend—someone who is intelligent, or someone who has a sense of humor, or someone who is reliable? Which one of these characteristics is most important to you? Use reasons and specific examples to explain your choice.

I like people who are intelligent and I always enjoy someone with a good sense of humor. What I look for first, however, is a friend who is reliable. I need to be able to rely on my friends to provide me with companionship, to support me, and to encourage me.

I depend on my friends for companionship. If I want to see a movie or go to a concert, of course I ask some friends to accompany me. If I feel sad or lonely, I can count on my friends to spend some time with me. If I feel happy, I can invite all my friends to a party. I know they will come over to have a good time with me.

When I am having troubles, I turn to my friends for support. If I fail an exam, or have a fight with someone, I call up a friend. I rely on my friends to be willing to talk to me and help me solve my problems. I expect my friends to be there when I need them, and I do the same for them.

I need my friends to encourage me. If I am afraid to do something such as enroll in a difficult course or apply for a job to earn some extra money, my friends help me. They talk to me and give me the confidence I need to try new and difficult things. I know I can count on them to give me encouragement when I need it.

We all like to spend time with smart and entertaining people. I think the people who make the best friends, though, are people who are reliable. If someone is reliable, you know he or she will always be ready to give you companionship, support, and encouragement when you need it. That's what friends are for, isn't it?

97 AD

Do you agree or disagree with the following statement? Most experiences in our lives that seemed difficult at the time become valuable lessons for the future. Use reasons and specific examples to support your answer.

People say that experience is the best teacher, and I believe this is true. Difficult experiences, especially, can teach us valuable lessons. They can help us overcome fears, they can teach us better ways to do things, and they can show us that we have friends who are ready to help us.

Difficult experiences can help us overcome fears. I remember the first time I had to give a presentation to my classmates. I was very shy and afraid to speak in front of the whole class. I spent a long time preparing for my presentation. I was nervous and didn't sleep well the night before. I was surprised when I gave my presentation and everyone listened. No one laughed at me. They asked questions and I could answer them. Now I know I can talk in front of the class and do a good job.

Difficult experiences can teach us better ways to do things. I had a very embarrassing experience when I took the test to get my driver's license. I didn't practice for the test because I thought I was such a good driver. But I failed. I didn't really know what to expect so I got nervous and made mistakes. I was embarrassed about my failure and my parents were disappointed. Now I know that it is always better to prepare myself for something, no matter how ready I think I am.

Difficult experiences can show us that we have friends. Once I was very sick and I missed several months of school. I thought I would have to repeat the year. I didn't have to because there were a lot of people who helped me. My teachers gave me extra time to do my work. My classmates explained the homework to me. People who I didn't even know well helped me make up the work I lost. I learned that I had friends where I hadn't expected any.

Nobody looks for difficult experiences, but we all have to go through them from time to time. They help us overcome fears, learn better ways of doing things, and show us who our friends are. These are all valuable lessons for our future.

98 PR

Some people prefer to work for themselves or own a business. Others prefer to work for an employer. Would you rather be self-employed, work for someone else, or own a business? Use specific reasons to explain your choice.

Many people have dreams of becoming self-employed or starting their own business, but I don't understand this. I think it is much better to work for someone else. When I work for someone else, I don't have to take risks or make difficult decisions alone. I have someone to tell me what to do, someone to evaluate my work, and most important of all, someone to give me a regular paycheck.

As an employee, I don't have to decide what to do every day. My employer gives me work to do and she gives me deadlines for it. I don't have to worry about what needs to be done next on a project. That's my employer's job. Without this worry, I can just focus on getting the job done right.

When I have an employer, I never have to wonder if my work is good or bad. My employer tells me if I did a good job, or if I need to do something over again. I don't have to worry if a client will like my work or if a product is good enough to sell. That is my employer's concern. My employer lets me know how my work is and if necessary, I will do it again or do it better the next time.

I know I will get a paycheck every two weeks when I work for someone else. I don't have to worry if the clients have paid or if we have sold enough merchandise. If I go to work every day, I get my paycheck on a regular basis. I work so I can get paid and I want to be able to be sure of receiving my money.

Many people want to feel independent and that is why they want their own business. For me, however, it is more important to feel secure. I feel secure knowing that I have an employer to give me directions, evaluate my work, and pay me regularly. That is why I prefer to work for someone else.

99 MA

> **Should a city try to preserve its old, historic buildings or destroy them and replace them with modern buildings? Use specific reasons and examples to support your opinion.**

Of course a city should preserve its old, historic buildings. New buildings can always be built, but old ones can never be replaced. They are usually more beautiful than modern buildings, they represent the city's history, and they can even help the city by attracting tourists. Historic buildings should always be preserved.

Old buildings are usually very beautiful. Depending on when they were built, they show different periods of architecture. They have a lot of character. They were made by hand, the old-fashioned way. You can feel the personalities of the people who built them and of the people who have lived and worked in them. Modern buildings, on the other hand, are usually not so beautiful. They seem like impersonal giants that have no character.

Old buildings represent a city's history. Important things may have taken place in an old building. Maybe a peace treaty was signed there or an important meeting took place. A famous person may have lived there. Maybe it was a former president or a famous writer. When we have historic buildings around us, we learn more about our history and we appreciate it.

Old buildings attract tourists to a city. People want to see old buildings because they are beautiful or because important things happened in them. If a city has a lot of old, interesting buildings, many tourists will visit the city. That is good for the city's economy. People usually don't visit a city in order to see its modern buildings.

A city's old, historic buildings are among its greatest treasures. They are a source of beauty and a representation of history. It would be a crime to try to replace them.

100 AD

> **Do you agree or disagree with the following statement? Classmates are a more important influence than parents on a child's success in school. Use specific reasons and examples to support your answer.**

I believe that parents have more influence on a child's school success than classmates do. Classmates have an important social influence on each other, especially as they get older, but the influence of parents is stronger than this. Parents are the most important model a child has, parents love their children, and they have expectations of them. All of these things are important influences on a child's success in school.

Parents are important role models for their children. Young children like to copy other children, but they like to copy adults more. When children see their parents read, they read too. When children hear their parents talk about books or news or politics, they will think these are interesting subjects, too. Children may learn other things from their classmates, but the examples they get from their parents are stronger.

Parents are the most important people who love and care for a child. Children know how important this is, and they love their parents, too. They may have close friends in school, but their feelings for their parents are more important. If they feel loved and cared for at home, they will have the necessary confidence to do well in school.

Parents have expectations for their children. They expect them to behave well and be good people and be successful in school. Children want to please their parents so they try to fulfill their parents' expectations. They want to be nice to their classmates and get along with them, but this is not the same as fulfilling their parents' expectations.

Many people have influence on children while they are growing up, but parents are the ones who have the strongest influence. They are the most important role models their children have, they love them the most, and they have the greatest expectations of them. Nobody can influence a child more than a parent can.

101 PR

If you were an employer, which kind of worker would you prefer to hire: an inexperienced worker at a lower salary or an experienced worker at a higher salary? Use specific reasons and details to support your answer.

If I were an employer, I would prefer to hire an inexperienced worker at a lower salary. There would be several advantages to doing this. First of all, it would save me money, at least initially. I would also be able to train an inexperienced person exactly as I want, and he or she might be willing to work longer hours, as well.

As an employer, my first concern is money. In order to make a profit, I have to make sure the business brings in more money than it spends. I can save a lot of money if I spend less on salaries. I don't mean that I would pay my employees unfairly. Of course, I wouldn't want to pay them less than they expect, but I want to save on salaries when I can. Hiring inexperienced workers is one way to do this.

I like to train my employees to work according to my company's methods. Experienced people are used to doing things a certain way. If they get their experience at another company first, it is hard to change their work habits when they come to my company. It is much easier to train inexperienced people to follow my company's methods. Then I can be sure that the work is done in the way that I want it done.

I don't like to ask my employees to work overtime, but sometimes I have to. Sometimes the pressures of the market make this necessary. Inexperienced workers are usually eager to gain experience, so they more often volunteer to work extra hours. This makes the situation easier for everyone.

People may think it is not good for a company to hire inexperienced workers, but I disagree. I think everyone benefits this way. The company saves money and the workers get training and experience. I think it is the best plan all around.

102 MA

Which would you choose—a high-paying job with long hours that would give you little time with family and friends or a lower-paying job with shorter hours that would give you more time with family and friends? Explain your choice, using specific reasons and details.

At this time in my life I would definitely choose a higher-paying job even if I had to work long hours. If I want a good future, first I have to gain experience, move up in my company, and save a lot of money. I will have plenty of time for friends and family later, after I get a good start on my career.

When I finish school, I will have a lot of knowledge. I won't have any experience, however. I can get experience only by working. I want a lot of experience so that I can be among the best in my career. The only way to get experience is to work a lot of hours.

I want to have a high position in my company. I don't want to be just an employee, I want to be a supervisor, and someday, director or president. I can't do this if I work only forty hours a week. The only way to move up is to work long hours.

Living a comfortable life is important to me. I want to have a nice house, fashionable clothes, and a couple of cars. When I get married, I want my family to have nice things too. This takes money. The best time to save money is now, before I have a family. The only way to save a lot of money is to work hard and earn a high salary.

A high-paying job with long hours will give me the experience, opportunities, and money that I want. After I reach a high position in my company and have a big bank account, I can take all the free time I want to relax with friends and family.

103 AD

Do you agree or diagree with the following statement? Grades (marks) encourage students to learn. Use specific reasons and examples to support your opinion.

I believe that grades are an essential part of education. They are important for several reasons. Grades measure a student's progress in class. They give students a goal to work towards. They are something that a student can show her parents. In short, grades help students become motivated to learn.

Grades show students their progress in class. Students have a lot of required work. They have to read, work on group projects, do homework, write reports, and take tests. Without grades, students have no way of knowing how well they are doing on all this work. They have no way of knowing where they are improving and where their weak points are. Grades show students what they have learned and what they need to keep working on.

Grades also provide students with a goal. A good grade is a type of reward, and students want to work hard to receive this reward. A good grade on a test makes the student feel that his hard work was worthwhile. A bad grade motivates him to study harder so he can do better next time.

Finally, grades are something students can take home to show their parents. Students want to please their parents. They want to work hard to earn good grades so their parents will be proud of them. Conversely, parents are happy when their children bring home good grades because they know this means that their children are studying and learning. If their children bring home bad grades, then the parents know they have to give their children extra help and support.

Grades are important for students. All students want to get good grades, so they will study hard to earn them. Grades show students their progress, present them with a goal, and give them something to show their parents. They encourage students to learn.

104 AD

Do you agree or disagree with the following statement? The best way to travel is in a group led by a tour guide. Use specific reasons and examples to support your answer.

When I travel, I always prefer to go with a group led by a tour guide. The tour guide makes all the necessary arrangements for the trip. The tour guide knows the best places to visit. The tour guide is familiar with the local language and customs. When I travel with a tour guide, the only thing I have to do is relax and enjoy myself.

If I travel in a group with a tour guide, I don't have to worry about arranging the trip. I just look for a group that is going to a place I like, and I let the tour guide take care of the rest. The tour guide makes the hotel reservations and chooses the restaurants and plans the activities for each day. I don't have to worry about anything because the guide does everything for me.

If I travel in a group with a tour guide, I don't have to figure out which places to visit. The tour guide knows which are the best museums. The tour guide knows where the good beaches are and which stores have the best prices. If I had to figure this out myself, I might make the wrong choices. With a tour guide, I am sure of having the best possible experience on my trip.

If I travel in a group with a tour guide, I don't have to know the local language and customs. The tour guide knows the language and can speak for the group when necessary. The tour guide knows when the local holidays are, or how to dress appropriately for each situation. I don't have to worry about confusions with the language or customs because the tour guide can help me.

When I go on vacation, I want to relax. I don't want to worry about making hotel reservations, or learning the museum schedules, or speaking the local language. A tour guide can take care of all these things for me, and I can have a good time.

105 MA

Some universities require students to take classes in many subjects. Other universities require students to specialize in one subject. Which is better? Use specific reasons and examples to support your answer.

Universities offer opportunities to study many different subjects and university students should take advantage of this. Studying many subjects can help students better prepare for their careers. It can also help them become responsible members of society and can add to their personal enjoyment, as well.

Studying many subjects can help students be better prepared for their careers. A doctor doesn't need to know only about medicine, for example. She also needs to know how to respond to patients' emotional needs. She might need to know about accounting and legal contracts so she can run her own office. Each profession requires certain specialized skills, but all professionals also need other, more general skills in order to do their jobs well.

Studying many subjects can help students become more responsible members of society. They need to understand the economic and social issues of their communities so that they can vote responsibly. They might want to do volunteer work at a community organization. They will need to be able to educate their children, no matter what their children's abilities and interests are. They will need to know about more than just their profession in order to do these things.

Studying many subjects can add a great deal of enjoyment to a student's life. If students understand art and music, they will get a lot of enjoyment from museums and concerts. If they study literature, they will continue to read good books. Life is about more than just career. If students know about a lot of subjects, they will get a lot out of life.

Some university students think only about their careers. If the choice is left to them, they might only study courses for their future profession. They will have a much better future, however, if they study subjects in addition to their career. Therefore, universities should require students to take classes in many subjects.

106 AD

Do you agree or disagree with the following statement? Children should begin studying a foreign language as soon as they start school.

I agree with the statement that children should begin foreign language study as soon as they start school. Childhood is the best time to learn a foreign language, so it is important not to miss the opportunity. Foreign language learning is easier for younger children. It contributes to their development, and it helps them expand their knowledge.

Everybody knows that it is much easier to learn foreign languages when you are younger. Young children's minds are ready to learn many new things, including languages. When children start learning foreign languages at an early age, they learn to speak them as well as they speak their native language. If they put off language learning until they are older, it is much harder to become fluent.

Many studies have shown that learning a language helps a child's mind develop. It helps expand the intellect. Children who learn at least one foreign language tend to do better in their other school subjects as compared to children who don't study foreign languages. This effect is less apparent in children who begin foreign language study at a later age.

Learning foreign languages can help children expand their knowledge of the world. If they learn a foreign language, they will become interested in the people who speak that language. They will want to know about their country and customs. They will want to understand them instead of being afraid of them because they are different.

Learning foreign languages has benefits for all of us, no matter what our age. It contributes to our intellectual development and our understanding of the world. However, the younger a person is, the more benefits he gets from foreign language study. Therefore, it is best for children to begin learning foreign languages as soon as they start school.

107 EX

Your city has decided to build a statue or monument to honor a famous person in your country. Who would you choose? Use reasons and specific examples to support your choice.

The person I would choose to honor is not one specific famous person, but a famous type of person. I come from a small rural town. Most people here are farmers, so I would choose a farmer as the subject for a statue. The farmers of my town deserve the honor. They work hard so the rest of the country can eat, but they are not rich. They deserve to be appreciated.

The farmers in my town make an important contribution to our country. They grow the food that the rest of the country eats. Our major products are corn and milk. These things are a basic part of everyone's diet. Without our farmers, it would be harder and more expensive for people to have these things to eat.

The farmers in my town are not rich even though they work hard. A farmer's job begins at sunrise and doesn't stop until dark. A farmer rarely has a chance to take a vacation because there are always things to do on a farm. Farming is not a profitable business. If the weather is bad one year, there might be no profits at all. Still, farmers do their work because people need to eat.

The farmers in my town work hard, but they are not appreciated. People in other parts of the country don't pay much attention to my town. Nobody comes to visit because there are no tourist attractions. Nobody wants to work here because there aren't many professional jobs. Nobody thinks about the contributions our farmers make. They just buy our products in the stores without thinking about the work it takes to put them there.

Nobody thinks about the farmers in my town, but they deserve to be honored. They work hard to grow food for everyone in the country. I think we should put a big, shiny statue of a farmer in the middle of our town park. It would make everyone in town feel proud.

108 EX

Describe a custom from your country that you would like people in other countries to adopt. Explain your choice using specific reasons and examples.

In my country, many people in the towns still follow an old custom that people in the cities no longer practice. This is the custom of taking a big break at noon. In the towns, all stores and businesses close from noon until 2:00 P.M. This not only gives people a needed rest in the middle of the day, it also allows them time with their families and contributes to a slower pace of life.

In the towns, all workers get a good rest in the middle of the day. They go home, enjoy a nice meal, take a nap, and then they return to work for the rest of the afternoon. They have energy and enthusiasm for the rest of the day's work. Their afternoons can be as productive as their mornings. Without this rest, they might be tired all afternoon and not get much work done.

In the towns, most families eat their noon meal together. They have time to enjoy their food, talk about their morning activities with each other, and just be together. It is good for families to have this time together. Parents hear about their children's activities. Husbands and wives learn about each other's daily concerns. Without this opportunity, families might not be together until evening. They are usually tired then and just want to rest.

In the towns, there is a slower pace of life. Nobody can do any business at lunchtime. They have to wait until the afternoon. Because of this, people don't expect things to be done in a hurry. They have more patience. If something doesn't get done today, it doesn't matter. This is a much healthier way to live.

A big rest at noon contributes to a better quality of life. In the towns, people don't worry about getting a lot of work done fast. They are more interested in spending time with their families and enjoying their lives. I think that in the long run this actually improves work. In any case, it is a better way to live. I think everyone everywhere should follow the custom of taking a big break at noon.

109 AD

Do you agree or disagree with the following statement? Technology has made the world a better place to live. Use specific reasons and examples to support your statement.

Technology has made our lives better in many ways, but it has also made them more complicated. Technology is often expensive to buy and run, it can be difficult to use, and it often isn't easy to repair.

Technology isn't cheap. The more technology we depend on in our daily lives, the more money we have to spend. Everybody wants a modern TV, a digital camera, a DVD player, etc. Even though these things might be considered luxuries, people want them. In addition, some technology is more than a luxury. For example, teachers nowadays expect their students to have computers at home for their schoolwork. Parents have to buy the latest computers so their children can keep up with their classmates. This can be a real hardship for some families.

Technology isn't always easy to use. In fact, it is getting more and more complicated. The computers of today do many more things than the computers of even just five or ten years ago. That means a lot more things that computer users have to learn how to do. Even a simple thing like using a VCR to record a movie takes some practice and learning.

Technology isn't easy to repair. If the average person has a problem with his computer or DVD player, he probably doesn't know how to fix it himself. He'll have to spend time and money taking it to a place to get fixed. In the past, a lot of people enjoyed doing routine maintenance work on their cars. Modern technology has made today's cars more complicated. It is harder to learn how to repair and maintain them.

People think modern technology has made our lives easier. In a way this is true, but in other ways it has made our lives much less convenient. Modern technology costs us money and time and can add complications to our lives.

110 AD

Do you agree or disagree with the following statement? Advertising can tell you a lot about a country. Use specific reasons and examples to support your answer.

Advertising is like a window onto the life of a country. It tells a lot about the people there. Advertisements show what kinds of things the people in a country like to buy. It shows what kinds of situations are attractive to them. It even shows whether or not the people tend to be affluent. You can learn a lot by looking at advertisements.

By looking at advertisements, you can see what kinds of things people like to buy. Are there more advertisements for soda or for juice? For movies or for music? For vacations or for furniture? You can see what kinds of food people prefer, how they like to spend their free time, or what they save their money for. You can learn just about anything about the average lifestyle in a country.

By looking at advertisements, you can see what kinds of situations are attractive to people. If an ad shows someone driving a car freely down an open highway in beautiful scenery, you can see that people value feeling free. If an ad shows a professional-looking person in an expensive car in front of an elegant house or office building, you will know that people value success.

By looking at advertisements, you can know whether or not a country is affluent. If ads are usually about food, clothes, and other necessities of life, the people in the country may not have a lot of money. If more ads are for luxury items and expensive, high-quality products, then you know that more people in that country have money.

Advertisements can tell you a lot about a country. They show how the people there live. They show what the people want to buy and can buy. Ads give a picture of a country's daily life.

111 AD

Do you agree or disagree with the following statement? Modern technology is creating a single world culture. Use specific reasons and examples to support your answer.

Modern technology is creating a single world culture. This is because it is now much easier to communicate with people who are far away. Satellite TV, modern transportation, and the Internet have all brought people closer together. People the world over share the same sources of information and this leads to the creation of a single world culture.

Because TV is broadcast by satellite, TV programs can be received anywhere in the world. Now people in every part of the world can have access to all the same TV programs. Everybody knows that TV is one of the biggest cultúral influences there is. When people everywhere see the same news, educational, and entertainment programs, they move toward the development of a single world culture.

Because modern methods of transportation are fast, a trip to a faraway place becomes easy. People from all different places are together more now than they ever were before. They can see how people in other countries dress, eat, and spend their time. People have more exposure to customs from other countries and might start to adopt some of those customs. This also contributes to the development of a single world culture.

Because of the Internet, people have access to information and news from all over the world. They can communicate easily with people far away and share sources of information. This can do a lot toward international understanding but it can also have another result. When people share sources of information on the Internet, they come more and more under the same cultural influence. They move toward the creation of a single world culture.

Modern communications technology has brought people from all around the world closer together. People these days have more and more opportunities to share ideas and information. In this way they are coming more and more under the same cultural influence. A single world culture is being created.

112 MA

Some people think the Internet provides people with a lot of valuable information. Others think access to so much information creates problems. Which view do you agree with? Use specific reasons and examples to support your opinion.

The Internet provides us with a lot of valuable information. This is important because it keeps us informed about the world today, contributes to children's education, and even helps us shop better. It helps improve our lives in many ways.

When we want to know the latest news, we can just go to the Internet and get it right away. We don't have to wait for a news program on TV or the radio. We also don't have to listen to just one source of news. On the Internet we can get news from different newspapers and different countries. We can get information from different points of view. This greatly contributes to our understanding of current events.

When children need information for their schoolwork, they can find it on the Internet. Most schoolchildren these days do their research online. They have access to more information than they could probably find in their school libraries, and they can get the information more easily. In addition, any time a child wants to know something or needs the answer to a question, he can probably find it online.

When we want to buy something, we can usually get the information we need for our purchase online. Of course you can order almost anything you want on the Internet, but this isn't the most important part. On the Internet it is easy to find information about the quality of different products and to compare prices. This really matters if you plan to buy something expensive.

The ability to get information from the Internet has improved our lives in many ways. We can learn more about the news, improve our children's education, and become more informed shoppers. The Internet is one of the most important tools we have in modern society.

113 MA

If you could go back to some time and place in the past, when and where would you go? Why? Use specific reasons and details to support your choice.

If I could go back to a time and place in the past, I would go back to ancient Egypt. The reason is that I would like to find out how the pyramids were built. This is a great mystery to us today. We in the modern world cannot understand how the ancient Egyptians cut the stones so precisely, moved them to the building site, and lifted the heavy blocks to build the pyramid walls, all without the aid of the type of technology we have today. I would like to solve this mystery.

The stones that were used to build the pyramids were cut very precisely. All of them fit together exactly, without any space between them. How were the ancient Egyptians able to cut the stones so well without the aid of modern equipment? Nobody knows.

The stones are also very heavy, weighing several tons each. The ancient Egyptians didn't have any kind of motorized machinery to move the stones around. Yet they found those heavy stones in one place and moved them to another place to build the pyramids. How did they do this? Nobody today can figure it out.

The pyramids are very tall. They were built by placing stone blocks on top of each other. The ancient Egyptians didn't have any cranes or other type of lifting equipment such as the ones we have today. Yet they built huge pyramids out of heavy stone blocks. How did they do this? We still aren't able to understand.

The Egyptian pyramids are among the great mysteries of the ancient world. Nobody knows how the stones were cut, transported, and lifted to build the great pyramids. If I could go back in time to visit ancient Egypt, I could find this out. Then I would return to the modern world and tell everyone the answer.

114 MA

What discovery in the last 100 years has been most beneficial for people in your country? Use specific reasons and examples to support your choice.

A discovery that has been beneficial to people in my country and everywhere is the use of electricity. Electricity has made the development of modern technology possible. Without electricity we wouldn't have modern communications technology, we wouldn't have computers, we wouldn't even have electric light. Almost everything about modern life depends on electricity.

Electricity has made modern communications technology possible. Telephones, television, and radio all depend on electricity. Because we have these things, we can communicate with friends and business associates instantly. We can hear the latest news almost as soon as it happens. We can follow the newest developments in music. Both our personal and professional lives are completely different now from what they were 100 years ago.

If we didn't have electricity, we wouldn't have computers. We use computers in almost every aspect of our lives. We use them to get information in school. We use them to make our jobs easier. Computers help people fly airplanes and design buildings. We couldn't do many of the things we do today without computers. And we couldn't use computers without electricity.

Because of electricity, it is easier to light up buildings and streets at night. This seems so simple that sometimes we forget it. Before electricity, people used candles. It was hard to read at night, to go anywhere, or to do any work. Now we can live our lives as fully at night as we do during the day. We can work or play at any hour we choose. It really is an amazing thing.

Electricity has made many things possible in modern life. We wouldn't have any modern technology without it. It is the most important discovery of the modern world.

115 AD

Do you agree or disagree with the following statement? Telephone and email have made communications between people less personal. Use specific reasons and examples to support your opinion.

Some people think that telephone and email have made communication between people less personal, but I disagree. If anything, they have made communication more personal. This is because these types of communication are easy, informal, and inexpensive.

It is easy to communicate with someone by phone or email. You just pick up the phone or turn on the computer, and that's it. Email is especially easy because you can send your message at any time. If the receiver isn't available when you send the message, it doesn't matter. The message will be there when she's ready to answer. Because this sort of communication is so easy, people communicate more frequently. This brings them closer together, so it becomes a more personal form of communication.

Communication by phone or by email is informal. On the phone you converse with someone as informally as you do in person. When you write email messages, you usually use less formal styles of writing. Traditional letters, on the other hand, have formal conventions that the writer must follow. Even friendly letters have certain rules to follow. Communication that is informal is more personal than formal communication.

Telephones and email are inexpensive to use. Nowadays even long distance phone calls are cheap, and local ones are free. Email costs nothing if you already own a computer. Letters are cheap, but seeing someone in person isn't always. Even if the person lives nearby, it still costs something for the bus or gasoline to go meet them somewhere, and it takes time, too. Since email and telephone are cheap, people communicate more frequently and, therefore, more personally.

Some people think you have to meet face to face in order to have personal communication, but this isn't so. Telephones and email make frequent communication convenient. They help maintain personal relationships.

116 MA

If you could travel back in time to meet a famous person from history, what person would you like to meet? Use specific reasons and examples to support your choice.

If I could travel back in time to meet a famous person from history, I would go to Renaissance Italy to see Leonardo da Vinci. There has probably been no other person like him in all of history. I would like to meet someone who was so talented an artist and so imaginative an inventor. He was a rare genius, and I would like to know what it felt like to be so unique a person.

Da Vinci's artistic talents are well known. The Mona Lisa is, of course, his most famous painting. Its exquisite beauty has been admired all around the world. Da Vinci drew and painted many other beautiful works of art, as well. I like to draw and paint, too. Of course, my talent will never approach Da Vinci's, but because of my interest in art, it would be inspiring to meet him.

Da Vinci invented many things that were well ahead of his time. For example, he made drawings of a flying machine centuries before anyone else ever thought of building an airplane. Perhaps his inventions never got beyond the drawing board during his lifetime, but he was still able to imagine them. He came up with ideas that no one around him was thinking about. It would be amazing and inspiring to talk with a person with such a creative mind.

Da Vinci was unusually smart and talented. There was no one else like him around. In fact, throughout history there have been few others like him. I wonder what it felt like to be so different from his friends and neighbors. It must have been difficult at least some of the time. If I could meet him, I could ask him about this.

To tell the truth, I don't know a great deal about Da Vinci. I would like to learn more about him, however, because of his unique talents and ideas. It would be an inspiring experience to meet him.

117 MA

If you could meet a famous entertainer or athlete, who would that be, and why? Use specific reasons and examples to support your choice.

There are many famous entertainers that would be interesting to meet. If I could choose only one, however, I would choose Paul Newman. I realize I've missed my chance since he died several years ago, but I still think it would be interesting to know him. On top of being famous for his good looks, he was a talented actor, and a generous businessman as well. I'm sure it would be fun to spend a little time talking with him.

Paul Newman was legendary for his good looks. His most famous feature was his piercing blue eyes. He attracted a lot of attention because he was so handsome, and he could have gotten by on his good looks alone. He didn't do this, however, and that is one thing that makes him interesting.

Newman was also a talented actor. He played many different kinds of characters, and he did all of them well. He didn't just walk on screen and stand there looking handsome. He portrayed each character believably. I would enjoy talking with him about his work in movies because I really admire his talent.

Newman didn't just sit around living off the money and fame from his acting career. He and a friend started a food business. It became very successful, but Newman didn't use that as an opportunity to become wealthier than he already was. He donated one hundred percent of his profits to charitable causes. He supported educational programs, conservation projects, and other work that he believed in. He lived according to his values, and I think that is an inspiration to us all.

Paul Newman is a Hollywood legend because of his looks and acting talents. He is also a good role model for business people. I think I could learn a lot from talking with him, if only I had ever had the chance.

118 EX

If you could ask a famous person one question, what would you ask? Why? Use specific reasons and details to support your answer.

If I could ask a famous person one question, I would ask Neil Armstrong what it felt like to walk on the moon. Sometimes I think it would be scary; sometimes I think it would be fun. On the other hand, maybe Neil Armstrong was too busy to feel scared or have fun while he was walking on the moon.

I think it could be very scary to go to walk on the moon. Neil Armstrong was the first person to do it. He was well prepared for the event, but he still couldn't be sure what he would find. Also, maybe he worried that something might happen. What if he had a problem with his oxygen or couldn't get back to the spaceship on time? I wonder if he thought about these things, or if he just did his job.

On the other hand, maybe Neil Armstrong had fun walking on the moon. The gravity is different so just taking steps would feel different. I think that would be fun. If I went to the moon, I would want to run and jump and shout, "Hurray! I am on the moon!" I wonder if Armstrong felt that way.

Maybe Armstrong didn't have time to feel scared or happy or anything else. He had a very important job to do. The whole world was watching him. He had to be serious and focus on his work. His time was short. He probably didn't have time for anything except to get his job done.

It can be a scary thing or a fun adventure to do something for the first time. Being the first person to walk on the moon is one of the most incredible adventures of all time. I would like to meet Neil Armstrong so I could ask him how it felt.

119 AD

Do you agree or disagree with the following statement? Dancing plays an important role in a culture. Use specific reasons and examples to support your answer.

I agree with the statement that dancing plays an important role in a culture. Dancing meets several human needs. It keeps us connected with our traditions, brings people together, and helps us release energy. These are all things that help keep a culture alive and strong.

Folk dances keep us connected with our traditions. Folk dances were developed hundreds, if not thousands, of years ago. In the past, whole villages used to dance together to celebrate important events such as harvests or weddings. Even though our lives are different now, people still enjoy folk dances. When we dance them, we feel connected to our ancestors. We do the same dances they did and remember the things that were important to them.

Dancing brings people together. When we dance at an event such as a birthday or graduation party, we celebrate a happy occasion together. Sometimes we enjoy going out dancing with friends on weekends. It is a way of spending time and enjoying life together. Whether at a formal or spontaneous occasion, dancing helps us enjoy good times with each other.

When we dance, we release energy. After working hard all week at school or at our jobs, we feel tired and stressed. We need a change of activity and a chance to relax. Dancing is a good way to do this. When we dance, we release all our built up energy and any anger or frustrations we've been carrying around. We relax and have fun. Then we can feel ready to start a new week of school and work.

Dancing keeps us connected to our traditions and to each other. Furthermore, it helps us release energy so we can perform our daily responsibilities. These are important roles that dancing plays in our culture.

120 MA

People have different ways of escaping the stress of modern life. Some read, some exercise, others work in their gardens. What do you think are the best ways of reducing stress? Use specific details and examples in your answer.

Stress is one of our biggest enemies. It affects all aspects of our lives. I find that in order to manage stress in my life, first I have to identify the cause. Then I can decide the best way to deal with it. The most common causes of stress in my life are work, friends, and myself.

Stress at work is the easiest to combat. If I feel tense or pressured, I simply stop working for a while. I might get up from my desk and go down the hall to talk with a colleague (about topics unrelated to work, of course). Or I might go outside and take a short walk around the block to give my mind a rest. Work-related stress can be cured just by getting away from work.

Stress caused by my friends is a little more difficult to manage. It feels very stressful when a friend is angry with me. Or, if a friend is feeling anxious about something, that usually makes me anxious, too. The best way to deal with this kind of stress is to talk about the problem with my friends and to spend some time with them. Unlike work, you can't walk away from friends.

Stress I cause myself is the most difficult to deal with. If I feel anxious about an upcoming exam or worried about my future, there isn't much I can do. I just have to tell myself that I can only do my best and leave the rest up to fate.

It is important to try to lead a life with as little stress as possible. If you can reduce stress by walking away from it (as at work), talking about it (as with friends), or facing it head on (as with yourself), you will benefit in all aspects of your life.

121 AD

Do you agree or disagree with the following statement? Teachers should be paid according to how much their students learn. Give specific reasons and examples to support your opinion.

It is a bad idea to pay teachers according to how much their students learn. It just encourages teachers to teach only the material on a test. It discourages them from paying attention to slow students. It is unfair because teachers can't decide which students will be in their class. Instead of improving teaching, it keeps teachers from doing the best job they can.

If a teacher is paid according to how well his students do on a test, then he will teach only what is on the test. He will spend time teaching his students to memorize facts. He won't be able to teach them other things. The students will miss the opportunity to gain a wider variety of knowledge. They won't have the chance to develop skills besides memorization. They will learn less, not more, in this way.

Another problem is that teachers may ignore the slower students. Some students learn more quickly and easily than others. The teacher won't want to spend time with the few slowest students. She will prefer to focus on the average and fast students to make sure they get high scores on tests. She can't waste time with the students who can get only mediocre scores. These students, who need the most help in school, will get very little help at all.

Finally, a teacher has no control over which students are placed in his class. One teacher may get all the best students in a school. Another may get several of the worst. If the teacher has some average students, a few below average, and no students who are above average, then of course the class will get lower test scores on their tests. People will think those students didn't learn much. It is not fair to base a teacher's salary on something over which he has no control.

Most teachers, like other professionals, want to do the best job possible. They want to teach their students useful skills and knowledge and they want to help the students who need help. Teachers need encouragement and support, but basing their salary on their students' performance is not a good way to provide this.

122 MA

> **If you were asked to send one thing representing your country to an international exhibition, what would you choose? Why? Use specific reasons and details to explain your choice.**

When asked to send something representative of their country to an international exhibition, most people tend to think of specific objects. I would send something completely different, however: one week's worth of television programming. I feel that TV programs are a good representation of my country because they show how we live, what we value, and what we teach our children.

TV programs show how we live in my country. For example, they show the different ways we make our livings, the different kinds of houses we live in, the different types of relationships we have, and the different sorts of activities that fill our days. In short, they give a broad representation of daily life in my country.

TV programs also show what we value in my country. Comedy programs, for instance, demonstrate what we think is funny, while documentaries show what issues we are concerned about and how we want to resolve them. Sports programs show which sports are more and less popular as well as how we approach competition. In general, the range of programs that appear on TV demonstrate what we think is important and interesting and worth our while to spend time on.

Children's programs show what we think is important to teach our children. Some programs are designed to specifically teach reading and math skills. Others expose children to classic stories from literature or to traditional folktales. And some programs, such as cartoons, are simply meant to be enjoyed, which is also something we teach our children to do.

You can learn a good deal about a country by watching its television programs. You can learn about daily life, values, and education. That is why I would send a week's worth of TV programs from my country to an international exhibition.

123 PR

Some people think that governments should spend as much money as possible on developing or buying computer technology. Other people disagree and think that this money should be spent on more basic needs. Which one of these opinions do you agree with? Use specific reasons and details to support your answer.

Developing computer technology is important for the development of the country as a whole. However, we have some basic needs and issues in our country that are even more important than technology. Our children need to get a good education. Our transportation system needs to be improved. We need to develop new sources of energy. We need to work on these issues before we put a lot of money into computers.

Our children need to get a good education. We need to make sure that every child in the country has the opportunity to learn to read and write. In addition, they all need to learn skills for the modern world. They need to learn how to use computers. It costs money to buy computers for schools and train teachers to use them. If children don't learn basic computer skills in school, who will be able to use modern computer technology?

We need to improve our transportation system. In big cities, the roads are very crowded and it is hard to get around. It takes a long time for people just to get to work every day. We need to spend money developing a good public transportation system. We need to get cars off the road and have more buses and trains. Computer technology helps people at work. If it is difficult for people just to get to work, computer technology won't help them much.

We need to develop new sources of energy. Our current methods of generating energy cause a lot of pollution. We need to develop the use of solar energy and other nonpolluting energy technology. Energy research and development costs a lot of money, but it is necessary. If we don't have clean, cheap sources of energy, what will we use to run our computers?

Computer technology is important. However, we can't take advantage of it if we don't solve some problems first. We need well-educated children, good public transportation, and clean sources of energy before we can spend money on computers.

124 AD

Schools should ask students to evaluate their teachers. Do you agree or disagree? Use specific reasons and examples to support your answer.

I think it is a good idea for schools to ask students to evaluate their teachers. It is good for the teachers, good for the school administrators, and good for the students themselves.

Teachers can get a lot of useful information from student evaluations. They can find out what the students like about the class and what they don't like. They can learn what the students think is easy or difficult. They can discover which kinds of activities the students prefer. Generally, they can find out the ways they reach the students and the ways they don't. All of these things can help teachers improve their classes.

Student evaluations are also helpful for school administrators. Student evaluations help administrators learn which teachers are most effective. They give an idea of how students are satisfied or dissatisfied with their school program. With this kind of information, administrators can work better with the teachers. They can work together to improve the school program where necessary.

Evaluating teachers is a good exercise for students. They have to organize their thoughts about their teacher. They have to think about how they themselves learn best and what kind of help they need. This can help them do better in class. Evaluations also give students a chance to develop honesty and responsibility. Evaluations with real and useful information are valuable to the school. Evaluations that are used as a way of being mean or getting favors aren't worthwhile.

Student evaluations can provide a lot of useful information to a school. They help the teachers, the school administrators, and the students. I think they are a very good idea.

125 MA

In your opinion, what is the most important characteristic (for example, honesty, intelligence, a sense of humor) that a person can have to be successful in life? Use specific reasons and examples from your experience to explain your answer. When you write your answer, you are not limited to the examples listed in the question.

Although honesty, intelligence, and a sense of humor are all worthwhile characteristics, I feel the most important one to have is sensitivity. A sensitive person is aware of the way his or her actions affect others. A sensitive person knows the place of honesty, intelligence, and a sense of humor.

Honesty is not always the best policy. There is such a thing as a white lie. You don't want to tell someone that her expensive new dress doesn't look good on her. You wouldn't tell your friends that you don't like their house. Sensitive people know when it is necessary to tell the truth and when it is better to tell a white lie.

Intelligence is a wonderful thing to have, but not all intelligent people use their intelligence sensitively. It isn't good to show off your intelligence and make other people feel dumb. Sometimes you might have to say, "My answer might be wrong. We should check it." Sensitive people know when to use their intelligence and when to step back and let others answer.

A sense of humor is always valued. Different people, however, laugh at different things. A joke that is funny to you might be offensive to someone else. Some people can laugh at their mistakes but others are uncomfortable about them. A sensitive person knows when it's o.k. to laugh or tease, and when it's better to be sympathetic or just quiet.

A sensitive person can make everyone feel comfortable. A sensitive person knows that people are different and that honesty, intelligence, and humor need to be applied to each situation differently.

126 EX

It is generally agreed that society benefits from the work of its members. Compare the contributions of artists to society with the contributions of scientists to society. Which type of contribution do you think is more valued by your society? Give specific reasons to support your answer.

Artists and scientists make very different types of contributions to our society, and the contributions of both are valuable. Although the contributions of both are important, however, our society seems to value the contributions of scientists more.

Artists lift our spirits and show us who we are. A painter or writer shows us in pictures and words what we're like as a people. Performing artists entertain us. Artists take our minds off our troubles and remind us of the beauty of life. Artists also help keep society mentally and emotionally healthy, because they provide us with a means of expression. Art of all types is necessary to the human spirit.

Scientists make contributions to our material lives. The cars we drive, the computers we use at school and work, the appliances we use to clean our houses, are all results of the hard work of scientists. We can grow more food, and cure more diseases, and live healthier lives thanks to scientific research. Scientists have helped improve our material lives in many ways.

Artists make valuable contributions to society, but society seems to value scientists more. Scientists are more often rewarded with money than artists are. They generally earn higher salaries, and it is easier for them to get government funding for their work. They have more social prestige and are generally considered to be smarter people than artists. There are always exceptions, of course. Some scientists struggle to earn money. Some artists are very rich and have a great deal of prestige, but they are few. Overall, scientists have a better position in society.

The contributions of both artists and scientists are valuable to our society. They each contribute to different aspects of our lives. Unfortunately, artists don't always get the recognition they deserve.

127 PR

Students at universities often have a choice of places to live. They may choose to live in university dormitories, or they may choose to live in apartments in the community. Compare the advantages of living in university housing with the advantages of living in an apartment in the community. Where would you prefer to live? Give reasons for your preference.

I think it is better for university students to live in a dormitory. It makes their lives much easier, it gives them more opportunities to make friends, and it helps them become more involved in the university community.

Dormitory life is much easier than apartment life for a university student. If a student rents an apartment, that means she has to buy furniture and kitchen utensils. She has to shop and cook for herself every day. She has to spend time keeping the apartment clean. A dormitory room, on the other hand, already has furniture, and meals are served in the dormitory dining room. The student doesn't have to spend time taking care of household things and can just concentrate on her studies.

A student living in a dormitory has potential friends living all around her. First she'll make friends with her roommate, then with the other students living on her floor. She can make friends in the dormitory dining room and the lounge. If she feels lonely, if she needs help with her classwork, if she misses her family, there is always someone to turn to. If she lives in an apartment, she won't have all this support. She might have a roommate, but otherwise she will be alone. She'll have to put more effort into making friends in her classes.

By living in a dormitory a student is right in the middle of the university community. She is close to all the university activities and it is easy to participate in them. She can become involved in clubs, sports, or the student government. If she lives in an apartment, she is farther from all these activities. It takes more time to get to club meetings. It is harder to find out what activities are going on. It's more difficult to be part of the community.

Living in an apartment has advantages for some people, but for me dormitory life is much better. It makes daily tasks, meeting new friends, and being involved in university activities much easier. It is a convenient and fun way to live.

128 MA

Some people believe that a college or university education should be available to all students. Others believe that higher education should be available to only good students. Discuss these views. Which view do you agree with? Explain why.

Some people believe that only the best students should go to a college or university, but I don't. Academics are not the only purpose of a university education. Another important goal is to learn about yourself. When you are separated from your parents, you have to learn to be independent and make decisions about your future. I believe every student should have the opportunity to have this kind of experience.

I can understand why some people think that a college or university education should be available to only good students. Higher education is very expensive. It might seem like a waste of money to send a mediocre student to college. If a better student will learn more, why not send only the better student to college? Higher education is also a big investment of time. Maybe a mediocre student could spend his or her time in a better way, by getting a job or going to trade school.

I don't agree with this position. I think higher education should be available to all students. It is true that it is expensive and takes a lot of time, but I think every student deserves the opportunity to try it. People change. A student who didn't like school as a teenager may start to like it as a young adult. Also, having the opportunity to make independent decisions is part of a good education. A student may try college for a while and then decide that trade school is a better place for him or her. Or a student may decide, "I will work hard now because I want a good future." At a college or university students have the opportunity to make changes and decisions for themselves.

All students who want to should be given the chance to go to a college or university. In college they will have the opportunity to learn independence and to make adult decisions about their future. This is a basic part of education and an experience every student should have.

129 PR

Some people believe that the best way of learning about life is by listening to the advice of family and friends. Other people believe that the best way of learning about life is through personal experience. Compare the advantages of these two different ways of learning about life. Which do you think is preferable? Use specific examples to support your preference.

Both learning through personal experience and learning through the advice of others can help you a lot in life. I think learning through personal experience comes first, however. No one can teach you how to get along with other people, how to judge your own abilities, or how to understand who you are. You can learn this only through experience.

When we are small children, adults tell us, "Play nicely with the other children. Don't fight. Don't hit." In this way, we learn that it is important to get along with others. Only through our own experience, however, can we learn how to do this. If another child hits us, we learn that hitting isn't a nice thing. If we fight with other children, we learn that fighting doesn't always get us what we want and maybe there are other solutions. Through our own experiences, we begin to learn about ourselves and we carry this learning into our adult lives.

Friends and relatives might say to us, "You are good at science. You should become a doctor." Or, "You are a talented artist. You should study painting." Our friends and relatives can observe our abilities and point them out to us. But they can't know everything about us. Maybe you get good grades in science but you think its boring. Maybe you are a talented artist, but you like sports better. Through our daily experiences we have the chance to learn about our abilities and our tastes. If we value these experiences, we pay attention to them and use them to make decisions for our future.

The people who know us might say, "You are so hardworking." Or, "You are too shy and quiet." They can point out our good qualities to us and that is good. We need our own experience, however, to tell us who we really are. Maybe you really are shy, or maybe it just looks that way to another person. Your own experience will tell you if this is true and if it is important to you or not. When we pay attention to our own experiences, we learn a lot about who we are and who we want to be.

The advice of other people can be very helpful. It isn't much good, however, if we don't have our own experiences to compare it to. I like to ask other people for advice, but I always pay attention to my own experience first.

130 PR

When people move to another country, some of them decide to follow the customs of the new country. Others prefer to keep their own customs. Compare these two choices. Which one do you prefer? Support your answer with specific details.

When you move to another country, you have to change some of your customs of daily living. For example, you will have to make some changes in your language, your food, and your work habits. It is also important, however, to maintain some of your old customs because they are part of your identity.

The most important thing to do in a new country is learn the language. Daily life will be very difficult without it. You will need the language to find things in stores, to understand TV programs, to go to school, and for many other things. You don't have to stop speaking your own language, though. You can continue to speak it with family and friends. You need your language to maintain your connection with your own country and origins.

It is a good idea to learn to eat the food in a new country. It will make your life easier. You can't always find stores and restaurants that sell your country's food. Eating the new country's food also helps you get to know something about the country and the people. If you shop and eat only in places that sell your country's food, you will get to know only people from your country. You should also eat your country's food sometimes. You will probably prefer it on holidays, for example. It is also a good thing to share with new friends from your new country.

When you get a job, it is important to learn your new country's work habits. If the custom in the country is to arrive at work on time, you must do it. If the custom is to be friendly with clients, invite them to restaurants, and so on, then you must do that. You will not be successful in your job if you don't adapt to the work habits. You might also have some useful customs from your own culture. Maybe you have more efficient methods of organizing work. Share your ideas with your coworkers. They might appreciate it.

If you want to be successful in a new country, you have to adapt to its customs. You also need to maintain some of your own customs because they are part of who you are. The important thing is to find a good balance between the two.

131 AD

> **Some people think that children should begin their formal education at a very early age and should spend most of their time on their school studies. Others believe that young children should spend most of their time playing. Compare these two views. Which view do you agree with? Why?**

Should young children spend more time on school studies or more time playing? The answer to this question depends on several things. It depends on the quality of the school, on the quality of the play, and, most of all, on whether the children are active participants or passive observers in whichever situation they find themselves.

Not all schools are the same. In some schools children must sit still all day and memorize information. Quiet behavior and correct repetition of facts are encouraged. There is a limit to the types of skills a child can develop in such a setting. In other schools, children are encouraged to participate in a variety of activities. They are encouraged to ask questions, interact with other children, and experience things. The range of skills they can develop in this type of setting is very broad.

Not all play is the same. Sometimes it involves little more than sitting quietly in front of the TV doing nothing but watching. Other times it involves lively and imaginative activities and interaction with other children. This type of play facilitates the development of a variety of physical and intellectual skills.

Not all children are the same, but all children have the same requirements for learning. They learn when their minds and bodies are active. They learn when they socialize with other children. They can do these things during school time or play time. It doesn't matter when or where they do these things. It only matters that they do them.

Both formal education and unstructured play can be valuable learning experiences for children. What matters is that the time they spend in either of these settings is quality time, that both their minds and their bodies are actively engaged. Whenever that is the case, then children are sure to have the experiences that they need to learn and grow.

132 MA

> **The government has announced that it plans to build a new university. Some people think that your community would be a good place to locate the university. Compare the advantages and disadvantages of establishing a new university in your community. Use specific details in your discussion.**

A university can contribute a lot of good things to a city, but it also brings some disadvantages. If we built a university here, it would bring jobs, culture, and interesting new people to our town. On the other hand, it would also destroy land, cause traffic problems, and be a burden on city services. There are two sides to every story.

A university would bring jobs, but it would also destroy land. During construction, the university would have to hire carpenters, electricians, plumbers, etc. After the building is finished, they would hire people to help run and maintain the campus. We need jobs in our community, so this is a big advantage. On the other hand, the university needs land to build on. Would they take over one of our city parks, or tear down some of our houses? Either way, they would destroy things that we use and enjoy now.

The university would bring culture to our community, but it would also bring crowds. The community could take advantage of events at the university such as concerts, lectures, and art exhibits. But a lot of people from all over would also attend these events. They would fill our streets with traffic and cause parking problems. Our community would no longer be a quiet place.

The university would bring interesting people, but it would also cause a burden on our city services. People such as professors, researchers, and visiting lecturers would work at the university. They are sure to contribute a lot to our community life. However, they are also sure to have families. They will need houses, schools, and transportation. How can our city suddenly provide services for a lot of new residents?

A university would bring many advantages to our city, but it would also have some big disadvantages. The fact is, we already have two universities here and I don't think we need any more.

133 PR

> **Some people prefer to plan activities for their free time very carefully. Others choose not to make any plans at all for their free time. Compare the benefits of planning free-time activities with the benefits of not making plans. Which do you prefer—planning or not planning for your leisure time? Use specific reasons and examples to explain your choice.**

My free time is very valuable. I don't have a lot of free time, so I want to be sure to spend every minute of it well. Therefore, I always try to make plans ahead of time. In this way I don't waste any of my free time, I have a chance to make any necessary preparations, and I can invite my friends to join me.

If I make a plan for the weekend ahead of time, I don't waste any of my free time trying to decide what to do. If I don't have a plan, I might spend all morning thinking about the different things I could do. Before I knew it, half the day would be gone. I would lose half my free time making decisions and it would be too late to start a lot of activities.

If I make a plan for the weekend ahead of time, I can also make my preparations ahead of time. Then I can spend the whole weekend just enjoying myself. For example, if I want to go on a picnic, I can have my food all prepared beforehand. If I want to go to a concert, I can get my tickets ahead of time. By making plans ahead of time, I am sure I will be ready to do just what I want to do.

If I make a plan for the weekend ahead of time, it's easier to invite friends to join me. If I wait until the last minute, my friends might already have plans to do something else. If I make plans ahead of time, I can invite any friends I want to. And even if those particular friends are already busy, I still have time to invite somebody else.

It's always best to plan anything ahead of time. I think it is especially important to plan free time, because my free time is my best time. I want to enjoy every minute of it.

134 PR

People learn in different ways. Some people learn by doing things; other people learn by reading about things; others learn by listening to people talk about things. Which of these methods of learning is best for you? Use specific examples to support your choice.

I have never been able to learn well from reading or from listening to someone talk. My mind wanders and I can't grasp the situation. The best way for me to learn is by doing things. It helps me understand and remember information better, and it is much more interesting for me than reading and listening.

Doing things helps me understand. Someone may explain to me how a musical instrument works, for example. I don't really understand this, however, until I try to play the instrument myself. Then I can hear and see and feel how the sound is made. I can feel how hard I have to push a key or pluck a string to make the sound I want. Or I could read a recipe in a cookbook. But I don't really understand how to prepare the food until I try to make it myself.

Doing things helps me remember. A teacher could explain some grammar rules to me, but it's hard for me to remember them. However, when I practice using the grammar rules by speaking the language, then I will remember them better. The more I speak the language, the better I remember the rules. I could also read about math formulas in a book. But I can't remember them unless I use them to try to solve some math problems.

Doing things holds my attention. When I listen to a lecture, my thoughts wander to other things and I don't hear the information at all. When I read something, it is hard for me to follow the ideas unless I concentrate really hard. When I do something, on the other hand, I am always interested in it. I have to pay attention because I am the one who is doing it.

We all have our own learning styles. For me, it is clear that I learn best by doing things. It is the only way I can really focus my attention on information, understand it, and remember it.

135 PR

Some people enjoy change and they look forward to new experiences. Others like their lives to stay the same, and they do not change their usual habits. Compare these two approaches to life. Which approach do you prefer? Why?

Some people seem to thrive on the uncertainty of change while others prefer things to always stay the same. Change is exciting and interesting, but there is a certain security that comes when things stay the same. The approach I prefer has changed with the circumstances of my life.

People who like change are people who look for excitement. Moving to a new place, for example, or starting a new job can be risky, but these things can also be fun. There is a certain sort of thrill that comes when entering a new situation. What will it be like? Who will I meet? It is interesting to wonder and guess about what will happen next, while it can be boring to always know what tomorrow will bring.

People who prefer things to stay the same, on the other hand, tend to feel more comfortable when they know they can count on certain things to always happen. Maybe they like to know what time they will leave the office every day, for instance, and what they will have for dinner when they get home. Then they don't have to worry about making plans or solving problems. They can just relax and enjoy their quiet routines.

My preferences about these two approaches have changed as I've grown older. When I was younger, I frequently sought change. I liked to travel a lot and usually made my plans at the last minute. I liked going to new places and meeting new people and even trying out different kinds of jobs. It was fun and exciting, and I learned a lot. Now I have two small children, so routine is important. Doing things the same way everyday makes it easier for me to care for my children. It also helps my children feel more secure. I don't miss the excitement of my youth because my life is different now.

Change brings excitement and routine brings security. Whichever choice you prefer may depend somewhat on your personality, but I believe it depends even more on the circumstances of your life.

136 AD

Decisions can be made quickly, or they can be made after careful thought. Do you agree or disagree with the following statement? The decisions that people make quickly are always wrong. Use specific reasons and examples to support your opinion.

I don't agree that quick decisions are always wrong. Sometimes they can be the best decisions we make. A quick decision made about a familiar situation is usually correct. Quick decisions based on a gut feeling, or instinct, can usually be relied on. It's the decisions made out of fear or desperation that we need to watch.

In familiar circumstances you can usually trust yourself to make a good decision quickly. For example, your boss might offer you the opportunity to do a certain job. She doesn't have time to explain the details right away but needs an immediate decision from you. It is probably safe for you to accept the assignment. You know your boss and your boss knows you. You can trust that if your boss thinks this is a good assignment for you, she is probably right.

We can also usually rely on our instinct. You might be looking for a new apartment, for example. You look and look, but none of the apartments you see are right. Then you walk into one and right away you know it is the place for you. You don't know anything about the neighborhood or the landlord and you aren't sure about the rent, but you immediately sign the lease. Some people might think this is crazy. I think you will probably be very happy in that apartment because you listened to your instinct. Your instinct doesn't need a lot of information to make good decisions.

On the other hand, we can get into trouble when we make decisions out of desperation. Let's say you are on a lonely road late at night and your car breaks down. Another driver arrives and offers you a ride. There is something strange about this person. You accept the ride, however, because you are tired and cold. This is not a good decision; in fact, it is a very dangerous decision. It would be better to wait in your own car, all night if necessary, for the police to arrive. You would realize this if you made the decision more carefully.

Not all decisions need to be made carefully. We can usually rely on familiar situations and instinct to guide us in making quick decisions. We need to stop and think more carefully, however, when we make decisions in more difficult circumstances.

137 AD

Do you agree or disagree with the following statement? People are never satisfied with what they have; they always want something more or something different. Use specific reasons to support your answer.

I believe that it is part of human nature to never be completely satisfied with what we have. This is true throughout our entire lives, from the time we are small children, through adolescence, and on into adulthood. We are always trying to have something more or better or different than what we already have.

The desire for something different begins in early childhood. Give a small child a toy to play with, and she's happy—until she sees another toy. Then she wants to play with the other toy. Give her a cookie and give another cookie to her brother. She'll probably think that her brother's cookie is bigger than hers, or somehow different, and cry for it.

The dissatisfaction with what we already have continues into adolescence. A teenager may buy some new clothes. Then he sees his friend has shoes in a different style or pants of a different color. All of a sudden his new clothes are no good; he wants what his friend has. Being like their friends is very important to teens and they constantly change their desires in order to match their friends.

Even in adulthood, we are not free from dissatisfaction. A young adult may be excited to get her first job, but right away she starts thinking about moving up and getting a better job. A young couple is finally able to buy a new house after saving for several years. But soon they start thinking about buying another, bigger house. A man may finally reach a high position in his company after years of hard work. Not long after that, he starts thinking about retirement. We are never satisfied.

It is part of the cycle of life to never be entirely satisfied with what we have. This is actually a good human quality because it pushes us on to each new stage of life. Without dissatisfactions, we would probably always stay in the same place.

138 AD

Do you agree or disagree with the following statement? People should read only those books that are about real events, real people, and established facts. Use specific reasons and details to support your opinion.

Some people read only nonfiction because they say they only want to read about real things. I think this is a big mistake. There is a lot to be gained from reading fiction. In the first place, it actually can teach us about real things. In addition, it allows us develop our creativity, and it helps us express our emotions, as well. These things are just as important as learning about facts.

Even though fiction is about made-up stories, it can teach us about real things and give us a deeper understanding of them. Nonfiction tells us only facts. Novels, on the other hand, can present facts in a way that helps us understand what those facts mean or meant to real people. The novels by Charles Dickens, for example, help us really understand the consequences of poverty in Victorian England.

Fiction also encourages us to develop our creativity. When we read stories, we try to imagine what the places and characters look like. We try to imagine what it would feel like to live the characters' lives. Well-developed creativity is something that is important to have in all areas of our lives, including learning to understand real facts.

Fiction helps us understand and express our emotions. Whether we read romances, tragedies, comedies, or some of each, we read about feelings that we ourselves have. The stories may be invented, but the feelings they express are real. Reading helps us explore these feelings and gives us a mirror for our emotional lives.

It is important to learn facts, but it is also important to develop creativity and explore feelings. Reading fiction as well as nonfiction helps us do this. We should all read a wide range of things to deepen our understanding of ourselves and the world around us.

139 AD

Do you agree or disagree with the following statement? All students should be required to study art and music in secondary school. Use specific reasons to support your answer.

I agree that all students should be required to study art and music in high school. These things are just as important as any other subject a student may learn. Art and music can teach young people many important things. They help students learn about themselves, their society, and the world they live in.

By studying art and music, students can learn a great deal about themselves. Both are natural forms of self expression. Just as our ancestors drew on walls in caves and made music with drums, people today use art and music to explore emotions. Students also explore their likes and dislikes when they choose the music they want to learn to play or when they decide which subjects they want to draw. The process of making music or art is a process of self exploration.

Studying art and music means more than drawing or playing an instrument, however. Students go to museums and concerts, too, in order to have the chance to experience works produced by others. By studying pictures in museums or listening to selections in a musical program, students learn about their own culture. They learn about what their society values. They also learn about the history of their society and how lifestyles and values have changed over time.

The study of art and music from other cultures gives students the opportunity to learn about other people around the world. They learn about what is important in other societies. They learn about similarities and differences between cultures and about the history and lifestyles of other places. New worlds are opened up to them.

By studying art and music in high school, students begin to understand themselves, their own culture, and other cultures, as well. What could have more value than that?

140 AD

Do you agree or disagree with the following statement? There is nothing young people can teach older people. Use specific reasons and examples to support your position.

Many of us believe that young people have nothing valuable to teach older people. However, that is not always the case. Young people can teach older people about technology, popular culture, and current social issues.

Young people are usually better than older people at using new forms of technology. For example, children these days become familiar with computers at an early age. Older people can learn to use computers from young people. Many older people have difficulty learning to use a DVD player, while for young people this is usually easy. I taught my grandparents how to use a DVD player when I was thirteen, and now they use it regularly.

Older people are usually not familiar with popular culture, and younger people can help here too. For example, most older people don't know much about popular music. When young people teach them about it, however, they may come to enjoy it. I introduced my grandmother to some of my favorite music, and now she and I listen to it together often. I plan to teach her about a popular sport—rollerblading—very soon!

There are also more serious things that younger people can teach older people about. Today's children have grown up knowing about AIDS and school violence. These are serious social issues, but older people don't always understand them. Talking about them with younger people can help the older people learn more.

I know there are people who say, "You can't teach an old dog new tricks." However, it is plain to me that the young have plenty to teach the old if they take the time to try. When they do, I think both gain a new appreciation for each other.

141 AD

> **Do you agree or disagree with the following statement? Reading fiction (such as novels and short stories) is more enjoyable than watching movies. Use specific reasons and examples to explain your position.**

I strongly agree that reading fiction is more enjoyable than watching movies. In the first place, novels and short stories have more depth than movies. In addition, reading requires you to be more actively involved in the stories. Furthermore, reading is very convenient because you can pick up a book at any time and place you choose. I often choose books over movies.

Most novels and stories have more depth than movies. Of course there are bad books and excellent movies, but usually books contain more than movies. They explain more about the characters and show more details about the action. Part of the reason for this is that most movies have to be close to two hours long. Books, on the other hand, can be as long as the author wants.

Readers are more actively involved in a story than movie watchers are. A movie watcher just has to sit and watch. A reader, on the other hand, has to think and imagine. The reader can't see the scenes like a movie watcher can. He has to picture them in his mind and understand what they are about.

The most enjoyable thing about books is that you can read them at any time and place. You don't have to go to the movie theater or rent a video or wait for a movie to appear on TV. If you want to enjoy a story for a few minutes before dinner or while riding the bus, you can. If you want to relax for a while before going to sleep, there is always a book ready for your enjoyment. Books are the most convenient form of entertainment there is.

Movies are fun, but books are better. Books keep the reader involved and entertained. Books can be read at any time or place. I never go anywhere without a book.

142 MA

> **A university plans to develop a new research center in your country. Some people want a center for business research. Other people want a center for research in agriculture (farming). Which of these two kinds of research centers do you recommend for your country? Use specific reasons in your recommendation.**

Business research and education is already well developed in my country, so I recommend an agricultural research center. Farmers in my country still follow old-fashioned methods. We need to do research to learn how to grow more crops, grow disease-resistant crops, and educate farmers in modern methods so they can raise their standard of living.

We need to increase agricultural production for several reasons. One is that the population of my country is growing so we need to produce more food. In addition, if we could export more crops, it would be good for our economy. An agricultural research center could develop methods for growing more crops.

We also need to develop disease-resistant crops. Farmers spend a lot of time trying to protect their crops from disease. Often, they lose their crops anyway, so a lot of money and effort are lost. Some farmers end up losing their entire farms because disease kills their crops. An agricultural research center could develop methods to save crops from disease.

Farmers need to learn modern farming methods. They need to learn how to grow more and better crops and they need to learn more efficient work methods. This would benefit the country as a whole and it would also make things better for farmers. Their work would be easier and they would earn more money. An agricultural research center could develop better farming methods and teach them to farmers.

An agricultural research center would benefit everybody. We would all have more food to eat, agricultural exports would help our economy, and the farmers' standard of living would improve.

143 MA

Some young children spend a great amount of their time practicing sports. Discuss the advantages and disadvantages of this. Use specific reasons and examples to support your answer.

Participating in sports is good for children. It helps them stay in good physical shape, it helps them learn teamwork, and helps them learn to develop excellence. However, too much of a good thing is never good, and children need to balance sports with other types of activities.

It is important to stay in shape, and participating in sports is a good way to do this. In sports, children get a chance to run and jump, to develop their muscles and lungs. This is especially important after spending most of the day sitting at a desk doing schoolwork. However, if children focus too much on sports, they might neglect their homework. They might also be too tired to pay attention in school.

Participating in sports helps children learn to work on a team. They have to pay attention and cooperate and do what is best for the team. This is an important skill that will help them throughout their lives. If children always play on a team, however, they don't have the chance to learn to do things alone. They don't learn to enjoy solitary activities such as reading or drawing, and they don't learn how to play with just one or two other children and no adult supervision. These activities also help develop important skills.

Learning to play sports helps children learn to develop excellence. They want to be really good in the sports they choose. Each one wants to be the best ball player or gymnast possible. While it is good to learn to work toward goals, it is also good to participate in other types of activities. Children need activities that are just for relaxation and enjoyment. They need activities that don't involve competition. If they focus too much on sports, they might not get a chance to do these other activities.

Playing sports is an important part of a child's development. Other activities, however, are equally important. Adults should encourage children to find a balance between different types of activities in their lives.

144 AD

Do you agree or disagree with the following statement? *Only* people who earn a lot of money are successful. Use specific reasons and examples to support your answer.

Many people believe that a large income equals success. I believe, however, that success is more than how much money you make. Some of those measures of success include fame, respect, and knowledge.

Most people assume that famous people are rich people, but that isn't always true. For example, some day I would like to be a famous researcher. Few scientists are rich by today's standards. Still, I will feel myself successful if I am well known. Additionally, there are many famous humanitarians who are not rich. Mother Theresa was one. Certainly no one would say she was not successful.

I also believe that being respected by coworkers indicates success. Without that respect, money means very little. For example, I once did some work for a top attorney in a law firm. He made a very good salary, but he wasn't a nice man. No one ever did work for him willingly. He ordered everyone around, and we didn't respect him. In contrast, however, I had a wonderful band director in high school. He had to take extra jobs just to make enough money to support his family. However, his students had great respect for him and always listened to what he said. As a result, we were a very good band. In my opinion, my band director was more successful than the attorney was.

Finally, I think one of the most important indicators of success is knowledge. Wealthy people don't know all the answers. For example, in the movie *Good Will Hunting*, the only person who could solve complex problems was the janitor. He knew a lot and decided what he wanted to do with that knowledge rather than just think about money. In my opinion, he was extremely successful.

When we think of history, there are few people we remember simply because they were rich. Overall, we remember people who did something with their lives—they were influential in politics, or contributed to science or art or religion. If history is the ultimate judge of success, then money surely isn't everything.

145 AD

Do you agree or disagree with the following statement? A person's childhood years (the time from birth to twelve years of age) are the most important years of a person's life. Use specific reasons and examples to support your answer.

I think I would have to agree that the childhood years are the most important ones of a person's life. These are the years that form us. It is during this period of life that we learn about relationships with other people, begin our formal education, and develop our moral sense of right and wrong.

No doubt, the early years are the time when we learn about relationships, first with our family, then with the rest of the world. We learn how to respond to others based on the way others treat us. If we're loved, then we learn how to love. If we're treated harshly, then we learn to treat others in the same way. We also form our ideas about self-worth based on the way others treat us during these years. They can teach us that we're worthless, or they can show us that we deserve love and respect.

These are the years when we begin our formal education. In school we learn the basic skills of reading, writing, and working with numbers. These are skills that we will use throughout our lives. We also learn how to analyze and use information. This is perhaps the most important thing we learn during these years. Presumably, these are skills that will always be useful.

Most important, from my point of view, we develop our moral sense of right and wrong during these years. At first others teach us about good and bad. As we grow, we begin to decide for ourselves. During this time we also begin to develop self-discipline to live according to our morals.

I believe a person grows and changes throughout the many stages of life. However, the foundation is laid, by and large, in those first few years of life.

146 MA

Some high schools require all students to wear school uniforms. Other high schools permit students to decide what to wear to school. Which of these two school policies do you think is better? Use specific reasons and examples to support your opinion.

Some high schools require students to wear uniforms while others don't. In my opinion, requiring uniforms is a good policy because uniforms make things equal for all students. When all students dress alike, no one is treated differently because of economic level, personal looks, or social group.

Uniforms make all students look equal regardless of their economic level. All students dress the same whether they come from rich families or poor ones. They aren't focused on trying to dress stylishly or worrying about whether they have enough money to do so. This eliminates problems of envy and rejection based on clothes. It also encourages students to form friendships based on personality rather than on stylishness.

Another advantage of uniforms is that they reduce unequal treatment by teachers. Research suggests that teachers tend to have higher expectations of students who have a more attractive appearance, and appearance depends largely on clothes. When all students wear uniforms, no one appears more obviously attractive. Teachers can make fairer judgments of students' strengths and weaknesses when they aren't distracted by the appearance of the students' clothes.

Uniforms also encourage individual students to feel like part of the bigger group. It is natural for students to have their groups of friends, but it is also important for them to remember that they are all part of the school and should not isolate themselves within their own social groups. Uniforms remind students that they all have something in common, that they are part of a larger group—the school. Then students are less likely to be left out because they belong to the "wrong crowd."

Uniforms have many benefits for students, and I believe that all schools should have a policy requiring them. Uniforms give every student an equal chance in all aspects of school life.

147 AD

Do you agree or disagree with the following statement? High schools should allow students to study the courses that students want to study. Use specific reasons and examples to support your opinion.

I think the basic subjects, such as mathematics, literature, and science, should be required for all students. However, I also believe it is important to allow high school students to choose some of the subjects they study. In this way, they get to explore subjects they might want to study in college. They also get a chance to learn responsibility and to take some subjects just because they like them.

Students can start exploring possible career interests when they are allowed to choose some of their own subjects. If they have the chance to take a journalism class, for example, they may discover that field as a possible career. Or, students who like science may have the chance to learn about different branches of science. Then they can make better choices about a course of study when they go to college.

When students choose some of their own subjects, they have the chance to learn responsibility. They have to decide which courses are most compatible with their goals and interests. They have to think about what is the best way to spend their time in school. They will have to make decisions and choices for themselves throughout life. They should begin to get some experience with this in high school.

Students should also have a chance to enjoy themselves in school. If they can choose some of their own subjects, they can choose subjects they are interested in. A class such as international cooking may not be the start of a brilliant professional career, but it can be an enjoyable learning experience. Students should be able to spend some of their time exploring their interests and doing things they enjoy.

When students are allowed to choose some of their subjects, they get a chance to explore their interests and goals and take responsibility for themselves. This is an important part of education.

148 AD

Do you agree or disagree with the following statement? It is better to be a member of a group than the leader of a group. Use specific reasons and examples to support your answer.

It is always better to be a leader than a follower. It is a much more interesting role to have. Leaders have skills and a chance to use them, they are constantly challenged to do the best job possible, and they are responsible for their actions. Followers, on the other hand, only have to follow and do what they are told.

It takes skills to be a good leader. Not everyone can do it. Leaders have to assess situations and decide how to approach them. A job supervisor, for example, has to decide the best way to get a project done, organize the work, and assign tasks to each worker. The workers only have to do their assignments. In fact any one worker may have to do the same job over and over again on each new project, while the leader's job is different every time.

Being a leader is a challenging position to be in. Any time there is a problem, the leader has to decide how to solve it. If a job supervisor assigns tasks to the workers, then one or two workers get sick, the supervisor has to reorganize the work. If some workers aren't getting along with each other or need support or if supplies start to run out, it is the supervisor's job to figure out how to get the job done and keep everyone happy. The leader must do his or her job as well as possible so that everyone's work gets done well.

Leaders have responsibility. Each follower is responsible for his or her part, but the leader is responsible for the whole. If a project succeeds or fails, the leader is the one who gets the credit or the blame. This motivates the leader to do the best job possible. A follower with less responsibility is not as motivated.

It is better to be a leader because a leader has a more interesting and challenging role than a follower. A leader will always strive to do his or her best, while a follower may not be motivated to do this. I like to be challenged and I want to do my best, so I prefer being a leader.

149 EX

What do you consider to be the most important room in a house? Why is this room more important to you than any other room? Use specific reasons and examples to support your opinion.

My favorite room in a house is the kitchen. I love kitchens because they are the place where the family gathers and where food is prepared, and I have many happy memories of kitchens.

In my family, we have always had the custom of gathering in the kitchen. When my brother and I come home from school, we go straight to the kitchen for a snack. We usually do our homework at the kitchen table. Often, we are still there when my parents come home from work. Then we might help them prepare dinner. A lot of our time together is spent in the kitchen. When relatives come to visit, they also spend time in the kitchen. We usually all end up there, drinking tea while we talk.

I like eating, and I enjoy cooking too, so of course I like the kitchen. I especially love holidays when I spend all day in the kitchen with my cousins preparing special holiday food. The cooking is fun and sharing the work is even more fun. Sometimes our meals turn out well and other times not so well, but the fun of preparation is the most important part.

I have many happy memories of kitchens. I remember visiting my grandmother when I was small. Following family custom, those visits usually took place in the kitchen. I watched my grandmother cook and listened to her and my mother talk. I learned a lot about cooking and a lot about life. Now my grandmother is dead, but I always feel her near me when I am in the kitchen.

For me, many happy things happen and have happened in kitchens. When I have my own house, I will be sure that the kitchen is the biggest and most beautiful room in it.

150 PR

Some items (such as clothes or furniture) can be made by hand or by machine. Which do you prefer—items made by hand or items made by machine? Use reasons and specific examples to explain your choice.

Some people prefer to buy handmade items because of their beauty. I don't think this is important, however. I prefer machine-made items. Machine-made items are cheaper, more available, and easier to dispose of.

It is much cheaper to buy machine-made items than handmade items. A lot of time and effort goes into making things by hand, while a machine can turn out hundreds of copies of an item in just minutes. They're easier to make, so cheaper to buy. I can afford to have twenty or thirty machine-made dresses. If I bought only handmade clothes, on the other hand, I could buy only very few.

It is much easier to find machine-made items than handmade items. Go to any store in your neighborhood. How many sell handmade items? Very few, if any. Usually only specialty shops sell handmade items. If I wanted to buy a handmade chair, for example, I might spend days or weeks looking for a store that sold one I liked. If I buy machine-made chairs, I have lots of choices right in my own neighborhood.

It is much easier to dispose of machine-made items than handmade items. If I break a handmade plate, I feel I must make the effort to repair it, and repair it nicely. This is not only because of the cost of buying a new one, but also because of its beauty. People don't like to throw away handmade things because they feel that they are throwing away beauty. However, if I break a machine-made plate, I can just throw it in the trash without a second thought. Then I can go to the store and buy a dozen new ones if I wish.

Handmade items look nice, but they aren't at all practical. Machine-made items are easier to buy and to dispose of when you are finished with them. I always choose machine-made items.

151 MA

A gift (such as a camera, soccer ball, or an animal) can contribute to a child's development. What gift would you give to help a child develop? Why? Use reasons and specific examples to support your choice.

When I was a child, my favorite possession was my bicycle. My older sister gave it to me when I was ten years old. I got a great deal of pleasure from that gift, and it was an important part of my growing up years. Because of that bicycle, I got a lot of necessary exercise, had a means of transportation, and gained a sort of independence. Therefore, if I were going to give a gift to a child now, I would give a bicycle.

Bicycles are a wonderful way for a child to get physical exercise. They encourage children to spend time outdoors moving around. These days, children often want to spend their free time inside in front of the TV or computer, but a bicycle can compete with these pastimes.

Children enjoy bicycle riding as much as indoor activities, if not more. So bicycles are good for their health and physical development.

Bicycles are also a convenient form of transportation for a child. Riding a bicycle is much faster than walking, so a child can easily get to a friend's house, the library, or other nearby locations. She doesn't have to wait around for an adult to drive her places. She can make her own plans and go whenever she wants.

Finally, bicycles give children a sense of independence. They can go wherever they want whenever they want, and they can also do what they want on the way. A child on a bicycle can stop at the store or choose a more interesting road or explore new neighborhoods. He can stop to look at anything he wants. The bicycle gives him plenty of opportunities to explore the world on his own.

I remember how important my bicycle was to me while I was growing up. It gave me fun exercise, easy transportation, and freedom. For all these reasons, I think that a bicycle is a good gift that can help a child develop.

152 MA

Some people believe that students should be given one long vacation each year. Others believe that students should have several short vacations throughout the year. Which viewpoint do you agree with? Use specific reasons and examples to support your choice.

I think several short vacations throughout the year are better than one long vacation. Students can concentrate on their studies better if they have more frequent breaks. Frequent breaks also make it easier to get a fresh start when necessary. Finally, I think students can make better use of their vacation time if it is shorter.

More frequent vacations make it easier for students to concentrate on their work. Students often get tired near the end of a long school year. Time seems to drag on during the last two months of school and nobody gets much work done. If the school sessions were shorter, they would be over before students had a chance to get tired. Then students could have a break, get rested, and return for the next school session with plenty of energy to start studying again.

With more frequent vacations, students can more easily get a fresh start when they need one. Sometimes a school year just starts out badly for some students, and no matter what they do, it's hard to change. They have to wait for a new school year to begin so they can start again. If the school year is long, a lot of time is wasted. With more frequent breaks, a student who is having a bad time doesn't need to wait a whole year to be able to start anew. That opportunity will come more quickly.

If students have more frequent, shorter vacations, they can actually make better use of that vacation time. A student may start a long vacation with plans, but those plans are soon used up. He becomes bored and just sits around doing nothing. With shorter vacations, a student can plan an interesting trip or project or take a job. Before he has time to get bored with those activities, it's time for school to start again. Then he has time to make fresh, new plans before the next break comes up.

I think shorter, more frequent vacations help students make better use of both their school time and their vacation time. It is a plan that every school should adopt.

153 PR

Would you prefer to live in a traditional house or in a more modern apartment building? Use specific reasons and details to support your choice.

Some people prefer to live in a traditional house, but I believe that a modern apartment building is the best kind of place to live. It has every advantage. Everything in it is new, everything works, and it is much easier to maintain than a traditional house.

Everything in a modern apartment building is new and in good condition. There aren't any holes in the walls or roof, the floors are clean, the paint is fresh, and the kitchen appliances are modern and convenient. Furthermore, the electrical outlets are all in the right place, and the lighting fixtures are modern and light the space well. There is no need to worry about constant repairs or major renovations. It is a very comfortable way to live.

Since everything in a modern apartment is new, you can count on it to work right. You can rely on the heating system to keep you warm in the winter and on the air conditioner to keep you cool all summer, even on days of extreme temperatures. You never have to make a frantic call to a repair company because your dishwasher breaks down on the day you are planning a big party. You can feel sure that all your systems and appliances will work whenever you need them.

A modern apartment is much easier to maintain than a traditional house. A house has a garden that needs attention, a basement that needs cleaning, and a furnace that needs to be maintained. In an apartment, however, you have none of these worries. You just have to do your housecleaning, and even that is easier because an apartment is usually smaller than a house.

It is obvious that it is much easier and more comfortable to live in a modern apartment. I don't know why anyone would choose to live in a traditional house instead.

154 MA

Some people say that advertising encourages us to buy things that we really do not need. Others say that advertisements tell us about new products that may improve our lives. Which viewpoint do you agree with? Use specific reasons and examples to support your answer.

The purpose of advertising is to let people know what products are on the market. We need it so that we can make good decisions when we go shopping. Advertising tells us when new and improved products become available and lets us know which ones have the best price.

Through advertising we learn about new products. For example, many grocery stores now sell prepackaged lunches. These are very convenient for busy parents. They can give these lunches to their children to take to school. Busy parents don't have time to look at every item on the store shelf, so without advertising they might not know about such a convenient new product.

Even products we are familiar with may be improved, and advertising lets us know about this. Most people use cell phones, but new types of cell phone service become available all the time. There are different plans that give you more hours to talk on the phone, you can send text messages and photos, and next week probably some even-newer type of service will be available. By watching advertisements on TV it is easy to find out about new improvements to all kinds of products.

Advertisements keep us informed about prices. Prices change all the time, but anyone can look at the ads in the newspaper and see what the latest prices are. Advertisements also inform us about sales. In fact, some people buy the newspaper only in order to check the prices and plan their weekly shopping.

Advertisements improve our lives by keeping us informed about the latest product developments and the best prices. Advertisements serve a useful purpose.

155 PR

Some people prefer to spend their free time outdoors. Other people prefer to spend their leisure time indoors. Would you prefer to be outside or would you prefer to be inside for your leisure activities? Use specific reasons and examples to support your choice.

I prefer to spend my leisure time outdoors whenever possible. It is more interesting and relaxing than staying indoors. Being outdoors gives me the opportunity to see new sights, try new things, and meet new people.

When I am outdoors, I have the opportunity to see new sights. I might go to a new park. I could go swimming at a beach I have never visited before or take a hike in a new place. The scenery is always different, too. Indoors I always look at the same four walls. Outdoors the scene is constantly changing. The flowers change with the seasons, the birds come and go, plants grow, trees fall down, nothing ever stays the same. It is fascinating to watch nature change.

When I am outdoors, I have the opportunity to try new things. I can learn how to sail a boat or climb rocks or swim farther and faster than before. I can also study nature and learn about the different kinds of plants and animals. There is always something new to learn, and some of these things are very challenging.

When I am outdoors, I have the opportunity to meet new people. I might meet someone casually while I am taking a walk or sitting on the beach. I can also meet people in a sailing class or a hiking club. Most of the people I meet during outdoor activities are interesting people. They enjoy the same activities that I enjoy. I think becoming involved in outdoor activities is actually one of the best ways to make new friends.

I am usually bored indoors, but I always enjoy the things I do and the people I meet when I am outdoors. Doing things outdoors is the most interesting way for me to spend my time.

156 MA

Your school has received a gift of money. What do you think is the best way for your school to spend this money? Use specific reasons and details to support your choice.

Our school has many needs, but I think the best way to spend a gift of money is on new classroom equipment. Our school is old. We don't have enough desks and chairs for all the students and our classroom furniture is out of repair. If we buy new equipment, the students will feel better and want to work hard. The community will take pride in our school. New equipment will last a long time, so we will feel the benefit of the gift for many years.

It is hard for students to study when there aren't enough chairs in the classroom. It is hard for them to use old, broken blackboards. It is hard when there aren't good bookshelves and cabinets to organize the classroom supplies. With new equipment, students will feel like school is a nice place to be. They will feel like the teachers care about them. They will be motivated to study harder and do the best job they can.

It is hard for the community to feel proud of a school that looks old and broken. If members of the community visit the school and see new classroom equipment, they might feel better about the school. They might say, "This school has improved, and we can improve it more." They might be motivated to contribute money and volunteer time to further improve the school. Every school is better when community members become involved. New equipment can help motivate them.

We could spend the gift money on educational trips for the students. We could spend it on supplies such as paper and pencils or on books. All these things are important for education, but they don't last. Students this year will benefit, but students five years from now won't. Classroom equipment, on the other hand, lasts many years. If we spend the money on equipment, students will benefit for many years to come.

New classroom equipment will motivate both students and community members to improve their participation in school. Everyone will benefit from new equipment now and in the future as well. Therefore, I think this is one of the best ways we can spend a gift of money to our school.

157 AD

Do you agree or disagree with the following statement? Watching television is bad for children. Use specific details and examples to support your answer.

I think television is very bad for children. It is bad for their health, it is bad for their minds, and it is bad for their values. They should rarely be allowed to watch it.

When children watch a lot of television, they don't get a lot of physical exercise. They just sit and watch all day. Often, they eat snacks while they watch TV. The snacks are probably cookies and potato chips and other food that is bad for their health. Children need to get a lot of exercise. They need to play active games. They also need to eat healthful food. Television watching does not encourage any of this.

When children watch a lot of television, they are exposed to a lot of information and ideas. Some of this is educational, but a lot of it is not. Children don't always know the difference. There is a lot of violence, sex, and other things on TV that children shouldn't see. If children learn about adult topics from TV, they will have a distorted view of the world.

When children watch a lot of television, they are encouraged to be materialistic. Advertising teaches children that having a lot of things is important. It teaches children that they must always have the newest, biggest, or most expensive thing. In addition, the characters on TV shows drive new cars, have fashionable clothes, and live in big houses. This also encourages children to want things.

Television can educate and entertain, but it also gives a distorted view of the world. It generally does not encourage healthful, intelligent, or moral living. It should not be a big part of any child's life.

158 MA

What is the most important animal in your country? Why is this animal important? Use reasons and specific details to explain your answer.

The most important animal in my country is the dog. Almost everybody in my country has a dog or has had one at some time in his or her life. Dogs provide us with companionship, assistance, and protection. Most people like having them around.

The most common reason people have dogs is for companionship. Dogs are friendly animals, and they make life less lonely for people who live alone. People also like to have dogs to accompany them on certain activities such as walking or hunting. Dogs make good playmates for children, too. People often consider their pet dog as another member of the family. In general, dogs are good companions because they like being with people.

Another reason people have dogs is to assist with certain kinds of tasks. Seeing eye dogs, for example, help blind people get around so they can live independent lives. Sheep dogs and other kinds of herding dogs guard animals on farms. Police dogs are trained to find illegal drugs and explosives. The intelligence of dogs together with their desire to please people make them ideal for all kinds of work.

People also keep dogs as a protection from danger. A barking dog can scare strangers away from a family's home. Business owners, as well, often use specially-trained guard dogs to protect their property from trespassers. Dogs can also help find people who are lost, or they might alert their owners to fires and other dangers. Dogs are always ready to keep their owners from harm.

Most people in my country love dogs and appreciate the ways in which they can help us. They enjoy the companionship of dogs and value the assistance and protection these animals can provide. This is why I think the dog is the most important animal in my country.

159 MA

Many parts of the world are losing important natural resources, such as forests, animals, or clean water. Choose one resource that is disappearing and explain why it needs to be saved. Use specific reasons and examples to support your opinion.

We are losing many of our natural resources, but one that I feel is particularly important is trees. Thousands of acres of forest are lost every year. They are cut down to get fuel and to make room for construction of new buildings. People don't seem to realize how important trees are for us. They help us breathe, provide us with medicine, and protect our soil. Without trees, we couldn't survive.

Trees are essential to our survival because they help us breathe. They are a major player in the process of photosynthesis. Through their leaves they take in carbon dioxide from the air, then they release oxygen as a byproduct. The fewer trees there are, the less oxygen there is for us. We need trees so we can keep breathing.

Trees are also important in the development of many medicines. The bark, leaves, and seeds of different trees have been used for centuries as cures for various diseases and conditions. These days, medical researchers are learning more about the value of these types of traditional medicines made from trees and other plants. Without trees we would lose this valuable resource for our health.

Finally, trees are a key part of soil conservation. The roots of trees hold soil in place and are also an important factor in underground water distribution. Without trees, rain would wash the soil away, and then we wouldn't be able to grow our food. The whole face of the landscape would change.

Trees are important to our lives in many ways. Without trees, we wouldn't be able to breathe, we wouldn't have certain medicines, and we wouldn't be able to grow food. You could say that our very existence depends on them.

160 AD

Do you agree or disagree with the following statement? A zoo has no useful purpose. Use specific reasons and examples to explain your answer.

Many people believe that zoos are unnecessary, harmful, and even cruel. They view these institutions as nothing more than a sort of jail for wild animals. I feel, however, that zoos can have a lot of value if they are properly managed. They are educational, contribute to scientific research, and generate interest in environmental concerns.

Zoos can be wonderfully educational places. They provide people with opportunities to see animals up close. Zoo visitors can learn about animals' habits—how they eat, bathe, play, and fight—through their own observation. They can also learn about the different kinds of environments animals live in. They can even discover new kinds of animals they hadn't heard of before. A zoo is the best place to learn about animal life.

In addition, zoos provide scientists with greater opportunities for research. It is safer and easier to conduct research at a zoo than it is in the wild. The researchers have better access to animals and can more easily set up controlled experiments. It is also generally less expensive to set up research in a zoo than to transport an entire research team and its equipment to remote places in the wild.

Perhaps most important of all, zoos are a way of getting people interested in environmental issues. When people have the opportunity to see animals up close at a zoo, they are more likely to care about them. When they learn about how animals live, they can understand how animals become endangered. Then they are more likely to become concerned about protecting animals and their habitats.

It is true that there are zoos where the animals are not properly cared for, but things don't have to be that way. A zoo that provides animals with safe, clean, and comfortable homes is a good place for us to become educated about animals, do research about them, and learn how to protect them in their natural habitats.

161 MA

Plants can provide food, shelter, clothing, or medicine. What is one kind of plant that is important to you or the people in your country? Use specific reasons and details to support your choice.

I come from a tropical part of the world where the coconut tree grows in abundance, so naturally it is an important plant for us in several ways. More than just a picturesque part of the landscape, this tree is useful to us as a source of revenue, food, and shelter.

The coconut tree is a source of wealth for my country. We earn a lot of money from exporting the products of this tree such as whole coconuts, copra, coconut oil, and coconut milk. In fact, coconuts and coconut products have been our main source of foreign exchange for well over a century. The coconut plantations that were originally planted by various colonial powers have been run by our own citizens since we gained our independence. They are a major part of our national economy.

The products of the coconut tree are not only for export, however. We also use them ourselves. The coconut is the basis of much of our national cuisine. Our famous curries are made rich by the addition of coconut milk, many of our desserts and other dishes are based on the meat of the nut, and we use the oil for frying meats and vegetables. We also use the oil in beauty products, to add shine to our hair and skin.

In addition to using the fruit of the tree for food and beauty, we also use the leaves to provide ourselves with shelter. We cover the walls and roofs of our houses with the tree's large fronds because they are the perfect building material for our climate. They allow breezes to pass through, cooling our houses during the heat of the day, but keeping out the heavy rains that fall daily during the rainy season.

The coconut tree is a versatile and useful plant that is abundant in our region of the world. It is a tree that has served my country well, providing us with some of the basic necessities of life.

162 EX

You have the opportunity to visit a foreign country for two weeks. Which country would you like to visit? Use specific reasons and details to explain your choice.

If I could visit any foreign country, I would go to Iceland. Because of its far northern location, it must be unlike anyplace I have seen before. The sun never sets in the middle of the summer and I think the scenery would be spectacular. Also, I would like to learn more about the country's history.

Where I live, nighttime is always dark, so it would be a new experience for me to visit a place where the sun doesn't set all night. Of course, I would have to go to Iceland in June to have this experience because in the winter the opposite is true. The sun doesn't rise then. But I think it would be interesting to see the sun in the sky all night.

I imagine that Iceland's scenery must be very beautiful. I have seen it in photos, but I am sure it would be truly impressive to see it in real life. I would like to look at volcanoes and walk on glaciers. I would like to see the places where steam rises from the ground, and I know

I would enjoy swimming in natural hot springs. I don't think there is any other place on Earth that has scenery like Iceland's.

I think the history of Iceland is interesting, and I would like to learn more about it. I know that Vikings from Norway went there over 1,000 years ago. Why did they want to live in that strange, cold place? How did they begin their lives there? How were they able to grow food and survive? I am sure Iceland has museums that explain these things. I would like to visit them and learn everything I can.

Iceland is a unique place. It would be wonderful to visit there, see the unusual sights, and learn about the history. Maybe someday I really will be able to go.

163 MA

When famous people such as actors, athletes, and rock stars give their opinions, many people listen. Do you think we should pay attention to these opinions? Use specific reasons and examples to support your answer.

Many people pay attention to the opinions of actors, athletes, and rock stars just because they are famous. Clearly this isn't a good idea. The opinions of famous people are not any better than those of ordinary people, and are certainly not as important as an expert's opinion. In addition, if we pay too much attention to fame, we might not hear what someone is really saying.

For some reason, people tend to think that famous people's opinions are better, but this isn't true. A rock star may know a lot about music, but why should she understand politics better than you do? An athlete may understand a lot or a little about a social issue, but you might, too, and so might your neighbors. It is better to discuss issues with people you really know than to listen to the opinions of someone you will never meet.

If we are going to listen to other people's opinions, we should listen to the experts. A political scientist will have an opinion on politics that is worth listening to. You might not agree with this opinion, but at least you know it is based on knowledge and experience. You don't know where a celebrity's opinion comes from.

Sometimes all we see is a person's fame, but we don't really hear what they say. You might admire a certain actor, for example. When that actor supports a certain political candidate, you might vote for that person just because you like the actor. You don't bother to learn something about the candidate and form your own opinion. You don't take the time to make sure that this candidate represents your beliefs. This is a dangerous thing to do.

We admire famous people for their achievements in their fields. This doesn't mean, however, that we should listen to their opinions about everything. We have the opinions of experts, of our friends and relatives, and of ourselves to examine, also. Often, these are the more important opinions to pay attention to.

164 PR

When people need to complain about a product or poor service, some prefer to complain in writing and others prefer to complain in person. Which do you prefer? Use specific reasons and examples to support your answer.

Sometimes we buy a defective product or receive poor service. Then we might choose to make a complaint. When I make a complaint of this sort, I usually prefer to do it in writing. It is easier to organize my thoughts this way, and it is easier, as well, to control my emotions. Most important, it gives me written proof, just in case I need it.

When I write, I have a chance to organize my thoughts. I can take all the time I need, and I can write two or three or more versions, if necessary. In this way, I am sure of expressing my thoughts clearly. If I speak to someone in person, on the other hand, I might become confused and nervous. I can't take time to organize my thoughts. I can't erase my words and express my idea again in a different way.

When I write, I also have the chance to control my emotions. If I am making a complaint, I am probably angry. I can express this anger in writing in any way I want. Then I can throw out the letter and rewrite it in a more courteous way. I can express my anger without offending anyone because no one will see the first letter.

When I write a letter, I have written proof of my complaint. This might be important if we can't come to a friendly agreement. If we have to go to a lawyer, I will need to show documentation. A letter of complaint is one document the lawyer will need to prove my case.

Writing a letter gives me a chance to organize my thoughts and control my emotions. It also provides me with documentation. This is why I prefer to make complaints in writing.

165 MA

Is the ability to read and write more important today than in the past? Why or why not? Use specific reasons and examples to support your answer.

Today more than at any time in the history of the world it is important to be able to read and write. This change has been brought about by the Internet, which we use to communicate with one another, to get our news, and to buy products.

Millions of people today communicate through email using the Internet. In the past, people had face-to-face meetings or called one another on the phone. Today they use email and chat rooms. Of course it is necessary to be able to read and write in order to use the Internet for communication.

Today, one can subscribe to news and information on the Internet. When you turn on your computer in the morning, you see the headlines, financial news, sports scores, or social events that you requested. In the past, people got news and information from television or radio, and many still do. More and more people, however, get news from the Internet because they can subscribe to just the type of news that interests them. Again, reading skills are required to do this.

These days it is becoming more and more common to buy products on the Internet. People like this because it is more convenient than going to the store, and because it is easier to find certain products. In the past, people bought everything in stores. At a store one can just pick items off the shelf and ask the store employees any questions about the products. On the Internet, however, reading and writing skills are required to select products and order them. Buying things on the Internet will become even more common in the future.

The Internet will force us all to be literate not only in reading and writing, but also with computers. Today, we must be skilled readers and writers to be successful in the high-tech world.

166 EX

People do many different things to stay healthy. What do you do for good health? Use specific reasons and examples to support your answer.

Good health is the only thing we really have in the world. You could lose your money, your house, or your clothes and still survive. If you lost your good health, however, you would die. This is why I eat healthfully, exercise regularly, and maintain an active social life. These are the best ways I know to stay healthy.

Eating well is probably the most important thing anyone can do to maintain good health. For me, this means avoiding foods that are high in fat or sugar, such as fried food, rich desserts, and sugary soft drinks. I also rarely eat meat. I do, however, eat a lot of fresh fruits and vegetables because they are are high in vitamins and other important nutrients. I also try to cook foods properly to preserve their nutritional quality.

Exercise is another important part of staying healthy. Walking is the type of exercise I prefer, and I try to do this daily. I also work out at the gym several times a week, and on weekends I play tennis with my friends. These are all activities I enjoy, so getting exercise is fun and easy for me. It helps keep me strong, and it is good for my heart, too.

Social relationships, believe it or not, also play a role in physical health. Friends help keep you happy, and they help you deal with stress. Having good relationships with other people supports your emotional health, and studies have shown that emotional health has direct effects on physical health. So I pay attention to my friendships and make sure to allow plenty of space for them in my life.

By eating healthfully, exercising regularly, and spending time with my friends, I can keep both my mind and my body healthy. Fortunately, I like to do all these things, so I am a very healthy person.

167 EX

You have decided to give several hours of your time each month to improve the community where you live. What is one thing you will do to improve your community? Why? Use specific reasons and details to explain your choice.

Volunteering a few hours each week is an important way of contributing to the future of our society. I think the best way I can make such a contribution is by tutoring children who have poor reading skills. If I can help such children improve their reading, they will be able to keep up with their classmates, gain access to new ideas, and have a better chance at success in life.

Students who are not good readers fall behind their classmates. They don't understand the lessons, and they come to school unprepared. This sort of pattern usually starts early in a child's school career and gets worse and worse as time goes on. But with extra help, these children have a chance to improve their reading skills. Then they can keep up with their classmates, learn their lessons, and be active participants in class.

When students get better at reading, then they have access to whole new worlds of ideas. Through reading, they can travel to different places, meet different kinds of people, and have new kinds of experiences, all without ever leaving their classroom or home. They have thousands of chances to expand their minds.

Good reading skills are the basis for many other things, so they are important for success in life. Students who don't develop good reading skills are doomed to working at only the most menial jobs. Students who can overcome this handicap by improving their reading have many opportunities opened up to them. They can choose from different career possibilities because they have the basis they need for further education and training.

Our society is better off when most, if not all, of us are educated, and good reading skills are the basis of education. If I tutor children in reading, I will contribute to their education by helping them keep pace with their peers, have exposure to new ideas, and be successful in life. This will be a gain for both the individual children and society as a whole.

168 MA

People recognize a difference between children and adults. What events (experiences or ceremonies) make a person an adult? Use specific reasons and examples to explain your answer.

Reaching adulthood is more than just a matter of age. Being an adult also means having had certain experiences. A person who has graduated from school, entered the workforce, and gotten married is generally considered to be an adult by the rest of the world.

Young people often feel that when they graduate from college, they graduate into adulthood. They are no longer in school, the place of childhood, and no longer need to be economically dependent on their parents. They have spent all their lives preparing for the real world of adults, and now they are ready to enter it, make their own decisions, and take care of themselves.

A big part of becoming an adult is getting a job. A person with a job supports himself financially and manages his expenses himself. He has responsibilities at work that he must fulfill. Unlike a child, he can't cry or complain to his parents if he doesn't like something about his job. He has to work it out with his boss and coworkers or learn to tolerate it. He is expected to act like a responsible adult.

Marriage is seen by many as the final step into adulthood. When a person gets married, he is no longer responsible only for himself. He now has to consider his spouse and children, as well. He has to support them both emotionally and materially and be ready to make sacrifices when necessary. He has to be able to make decisions that will affect others as well as himself. A married person is also considered mature enough to take care of his parents when they need it.

People are seen as adults when they have had certain experiences. Experiences, such as finishing school, entering a career, and starting a family, put the person in a position of both independence and responsibility.

169 EX

Many students choose to attend schools or universities outside their home countries. Why do some students study abroad? Use specific reasons and details to explain your answer.

Many students choose to study abroad for at least part of their university years even when they can get a good education in their home countries. I believe this is because it allows them to broaden their learning experience in ways they can't at home. By studying abroad, students have the chance to learn a new language, become familiar with another culture, and grow in new ways.

People who have foreign language skills have a great advantage in today's world. The world is shrinking and international communication has become a fact of daily life. Foreign language skills are important for businesses. They are also important for taking advantage of all the information that is available through the Internet and satellite TV. By studying abroad, students can develop fluency in one or more foreign languages.

Familiarity with other cultures is also important in today's shrinking world. Expertise with different cultures is as important for successful communication as expertise with languages is. The global economy means we have more opportunities to interact with people from other countries. It also means there is more potential for conflicts and wars. Students who spend time studying in another country learn to understand and respect other cultures. They learn to communicate with people who may have a different understanding of the world than they do.

Finally, living abroad gives students the chance to grow in new ways. They have to learn to get by in a completely new environment, away from their family and friends. They have to learn to feel comfortable trying out completely new ways of doing things. This is an opportunity for personal growth that they might not get by staying home in their familiar environment.

Study abroad is enriching in many ways. It is an opportunity to learn a new language and experience a different culture. It is also a special experience that allows for personal growth. These things are all an important part of education.

170 EX

People listen to music for different reasons and at different times. Why is music important to many people? Use specific reasons and examples to support your choice.

From beating on ancient drums to twanging on modern electric guitars, people have enjoyed playing and listening to music for thousands of years. Music has been a part of our lives since civilization began. I think music has always been important because it helps us express our emotions, helps us feel connected to others, and brings beauty into our lives.

People are attracted to music because it is an expression of emotion. Music can be happy or sad, calming or agitating, angry or contented. It can touch emotions we have deep inside ourselves and allow us to feel them. In fact, people often choose to listen to a particular piece of music because they want to feel a certain way. Music is a sort of reflection of our emotional lives.

Music also helps us feel connected with one another. When we play music together or perform it for an audience, we share the emotions that the music expresses. We feel the joy of connecting with others who share our musical tastes. In addition, music has always played an important role in ceremonies and rituals because of the power it has to make people feel connected.

Finally, people enjoy music because of its beauty. It can be as beautiful as anything nature gives us. Listening to good music can be like looking at a lovely flower or a spectacular sunset. Music can also be as beautiful as any other art form. It can gives us as much joy as an exquisite painting or a magnificent sculpture.

Music has a lot to offer of us in terms of emotions, connections, and beauty. I believe this has why it has been an important part of our lives from the beginning of human history.

171 EX

Groups or organizations are an important part of some people's lives. Why are groups or organizations important to people? Use specific reasons and examples to explain your answer.

Groups and organizations are an important part of our lives because we are social beings. We have a natural need to be with others who are similar to us and to get the social and emotional support that comes from being part of a group. Therefore, most people are involved with some sort of group or organization. The most common and important ones are families, religious organizations, and political organizations.

Family is obviously the most important group a person can belong to. In fact, when we are very young, our survival depends on our family. But family is still important as we grow older. Our relatives are the people we can always count on to be there for us when we need any kind of support, whether material or emotional.

Religious organizations connect us to a larger sort of family. This is a family of people who share our beliefs. It is confirming to be with other people who believe the same things we believe and who will be with us when we need moral support. Religious organizations are a source of comfort in times of stress and a source of guidance when we aren't sure how to act or respond to a situation.

Political organizations connect us to people who share our ideas. Whatever our political philosophy—liberal, conservative, or something in between—we can find a group that matches. Political organizations help us express our ideas and fight for what we believe in. They help us be part of the larger community.

As human beings, we have a need to be with others. Different sorts of groups can meet this need to belong, but the ones people seem to rely on most often are family, religious, and political groups. They provide us with the support we need to get through life.

172 MA

Imagine you are preparing for a trip. You plan to be away from your home for a year. In addition to clothing and personal care items, you can take one additional thing. What would you take and why? Use specific reasons and details to support your choice.

If I had to leave home for a year, the one thing I would definitely take with me would be my cell phone because it allows me to stay connected with important people. With my cell phone, I can call my friends and family whenever I feel lonely, need advice, or just want to talk. It may be a small item, but it provides me with these essential things.

If I spent an entire year away from home, I would feel very lonely. I would feel a lot better if I could call my family regularly. Just hearing the voices of my parents and my brothers and sisters would take my loneliness away. Talking to my friends by phone would also make me feel less alone.

My cell phone would also allow me to call a trusted person whenever I needed advice. I have never been away from home by myself, so there are many things I don't know how to do. I don't know how to cook my own meals or drive a car or open a bank account. I think I would need a lot of advice if I were living away from home. I would probably want to call my family and friends daily for help.

I like to talk a lot. When I have new experiences, I always feel the need to talk about them. That helps me process everything I am going through. If I were away from home for a year, I would be having many new experiences. My cell phone would allow me to talk them over comfortably with familiar people.

For me, a cell phone is a necessity because staying connected is essential to my happiness. The cell phone would make my experience away from home much easier because I could connect with friends and family whenever I needed support. Of course, the phone bill would be sent to my parents.

173 EX

When students move to a new school, they sometimes face problems. How can schools help these students with their problems? Use specific reasons and examples to explain your answer.

When students go to a new school, they often have a problem fitting in. They don't know how the school operates and they don't have any friends. The school administrators, the school counselors, and the teachers can do a lot to help new students become part of the community.

School administrators can help orient new students to their school. They can take the new students on a tour of the school, showing them classrooms, the gym, the cafeteria, the computer labs, and other school facilities. They can explain the school program and tell the students about what is expected of them.

The school counselors can talk to new students about their goals and interests. They should explain the school schedule and help the students choose the appropriate classes.

They should also talk about extracurricular activities such as the school newspaper, sports teams, band, and language clubs. They should encourage new students to participate in such activities because it is a good way to make friends.

Teachers can help new students the most. They explain their coursework to them, of course. They can also encourage old students to be friendly with the new students and help them learn the school system. They are with the students all day, so they are aware if a student is having difficulties. Then they can try to help the student themselves, or ask for assistance from the counselors or administrators.

School administrators, counselors, and teachers can do a lot to help students adjust to their new school. It isn't easy, but it pays off with happier, more successful students in the end.

174 AD

It is sometimes said that borrowing money from a friend can harm or damage the friendship. Do you agree? Why or why not? Use reasons and specific examples to explain your answer.

It is not a good idea to ask to borrow money from a friend. It can damage the friendship because it places the friend in an unfair position. It is hard for a friend to say no when asked for help, to admit that she can't spare any money, or to ask for her money back when she needs it.

If you ask a friend for money, it is hard for her to say no. Friends generally want to do favors for each other, but lending money isn't always an easy or comfortable favor to do. However, saying no to a request from a friend isn't easy or comfortable either. So, asking to borrow money puts the friend in an unfair position.

Your friend may not have enough money to lend you but may be unable to admit this. She might be embarrassed to tell you the truth about her financial situation, or she may feel that she doesn't want to disappoint you. So, she ends up giving you money that she really needs for herself, and you might never know this. Again, this is not fair to the friend.

When your friend needs you to pay the money back, she may feel awkward about asking for it. Anything can happen after you receive the loan. You might quite innocently forget to pay it back, or you might have difficulty getting the money you need to repay it. Your friend could easily feel uncomfortable asking for the money because she doesn't want to pressure you or make you angry. This is also unfair to her.

Different people, even close friends, can have very different ideas about money. Therefore, it is better to borrow money from people you don't know well, such as bankers. Then, any problems that arise will not affect a friendship that you value.

175 PR

Some students like classes where teachers lecture (do all of the talking) in class. Other students prefer classes where the students do some of the talking. Which type of class do you prefer? Give specific reasons and details to support your choice.

In my country, most classes are run according to the lecture system, and this is the way of teaching and learning that I prefer. It works well for me because I am used to it, I feel it is efficient, and I am a shy and quiet student.

My classes have always been lecture classes from the day I started school, so I am used to this system. I am used to sitting quietly at my desk and listening to the teacher talk. I am used to taking notes about what the teacher says and never asking questions. When test time comes, I know exactly what to do. If I can repeat on the test everything the teacher said in class, then I will get a good grade.

From my point of view, the lecture system is an efficient one. The teacher, not the students, is the one who knows the subject. It makes sense, therefore, to spend the entire class time listening to the teacher talk. That way, we learn all the information we can in the time we spend in class. It would be a waste of time, on the other hand, to listen to students talk since they don't really understand the material.

I am a very shy person so I wouldn't get any benefit from a class where students talk. I wouldn't dare to open my mouth because I wouldn't want the other students to laugh at me and make fun of my ideas. I am much more comfortable just listening to the teacher talk. That way I can focus on the information without worrying about having to speak myself.

I hope that I can always study at a school that uses the lecture system. I feel more comfortable studying in this type of situation.

176 EX

Holidays honor people or events. If you could create a new holiday, what person or event would it honor and how would you want people to celebrate it? Use specific reasons and details to support your answer.

October 24 is United Nations Day. This day is noted on calendars but is not generally observed as a holiday around the world. I think it should be. I think the entire world should celebrate the birth of the United Nations because it has done so much for people everywhere. This organization has worked to promote peace, take care of basic human needs, and bring people together.

The most important mission of the United Nations is to promote peace. It sends peacekeeping groups to areas of conflict and works to promote human rights. It supports negotiations between opposing sides. The UN has lead peace efforts in many parts of the world and has done much to prevent or end conflicts.

The United Nations also works hard to provide basic needs to people around the world. The World Health Organization, for example, has done much to improve health conditions by doing such things as fighting disease and improving health care delivery in areas where these things are needed most. Other UN organizations support education, help economic development projects, or give aid to refugees.

The United Nations brings people together to work towards common goals. The members of the United Nations are different countries around the world. This means that on any UN project, people of different nationalities are working together. They have to learn to get along and respect and understand one another despite their cultural and language differences. The UN provides many opportunities for developing cross cultural understanding.

The United Nations has done a lot for the world, and I think people should be aware of this. It helps countries and people in need and brings different cultures together. Making United Nations Day a major holiday everywhere would do a lot to educate people about the important work of this organization.

177 MA

A friend of yours has received some money and plans to use all of it either

- **to go on vacation**
- **to buy a car**

Your friend has asked you for advice. Compare your friend's two choices and explain which one you think your friend should choose. Use specific reasons and details to support your choice.

A friend of mine has some money and has asked me whether he should spend it on a vacation or on a car. My advice is to spend it on a car because this is a much better investment. A car is useful, it lasts a long time, and, most of all, it is something my friend can share with me.

A car is a very useful thing to have. If my friend buys one, it will be easier for him to get to school and work. He can even get a job farther from home if he wants. He will also be able to help his parents by running errands for them and taking them shopping. A vacation, on the other hand, has no practical use at all. It is not something my friend can use in his daily life. It is just a luxury.

Another advantage of a car is that it lasts a long time. If my friend buys a good quality car and takes care of it, he can drive it for years. A vacation, however, is short. It lasts only a few days or weeks. When that time is over, my friend will be left with nothing but memories.

Finally, if my friend gets a car, I will benefit from it, too. My friend will be able to drive me places with him. It will be easier for us to go out together, to the movies or to restaurants or to visit our other friends. My friend might even be nice enough to drive me around while I do errands. He wouldn't be able to share his vacation with me, however. I don't think he has received enough money to invite me along.

To me it is clear that a vacation would be a waste of my friend's money when he could buy a car instead. That way he will have something that is practical and long lasting and that he can share with me. It is the best use for his money.

178 EX

What are some of the qualities of a good parent? Use specific details and examples to explain your answer.

I am fortunate to have good parents so it is easy for me to identify the qualities that make them good. I believe that good parents are those who love their children unconditionally, who trust their children, and who treat their children with respect.

All parents love their children, but not all of them love unconditionally. For some parents, their feeling of love might change in some way if their children don't meet their expectations.

Many parents have a hard time accepting a child's marriage to someone of a different religion or ethnic group, for example. Some parents reject a child who chooses a different sort of lifestyle. They find it hard to keep loving a child who does something they don't understand. Good parents, however, love their children no matter what choices they make for themselves.

Parents who love their children unconditionally also know how to trust them. They don't hover over their children and try to manage their every move. They trust their children to make the choices that are right for them. They trust them enough to let them make their own mistakes and then learn from their experiences.

Parents who love and trust their children also respect them. They treat their children as individuals with their own rights, not as extensions of themselves. They give their children guidance, of course, but do not require their children to be just like they are. Instead of telling their children exactly what to do, they talk with them, listen to them, and try to understand the choices they make for themselves.

I know that both my mother and father love me unconditionally and that they trust and respect me. Without this, I wouldn't feel confidence in myself or comfortable in the world. I feel fortunate to have such wonderful parents.

179 EX

Movies are popular all over the world. Explain why movies are so popular. Use reasons and specific examples to support your answer.

Almost everyone enjoys watching movies. Some people like romantic movies, which others prefer action movies. Still others choose westerns, adventure stories, or science fiction. But everyone likes a good movie. I think we enjoy movies so much because they add certain things to our lives. They bring us excitement, they reflect our emotions, and allow us to imagine ourselves as someone else.

Most of us live fairly ordinary lives. We get up, go to work or school, go home, go to bed, and get up the next day to begin all over again. There is nothing glamorous or adventurous in our daily routines. When we go to the movies, however, we can feel a little excitement in our lives. A movie can turn a boring afternoon into an adventure.

We humans are very emotional beings. Our lives are filled with happy times and sad times, feelings of anger and feelings of joy. Movies reflect all these emotions back to us. We can feel the characters' feelings along with them because they are feelings we experience ourselves. Movies confirm our emotional lives.

Movies give us the opportunity to imagine ourselves as different people. If a movie is about a pilot, for example, we can imagine flying a plane along with the character. A movie about a ballet dancer allows us to dance on stage, at least in our minds. Whatever the movie is about, we can imagine ourselves in those places and as those people. It is an opportunity to live fantasy lives, doing things we couldn't actually do in our real lives.

Movies allow us to have a little excitement in our lives, to feel our emotions, and to live our fantasies. Given all that, it is hard to imagine a person who doesn't enjoy watching at least some movies.

180 MA

In your country, is there more need for land to be left in its natural condition or is there more need for land to be developed for housing and industry? Use specific reasons and examples to support your answer.

In my country there is a lot of open land. It is a nice idea to leave this land in its natural condition, but we can't afford to leave all of it that way. Our economy is growing rapidly, so we need to use a lot of this land for building. We need land for factories, for housing for the people who will work in the factories, and for stores to serve the people who will live in the houses.

Our industrial sector has developed a lot over the past decade, and it continues to grow. We have built many factories, but there is still a need to build more. Using land for these factories is important because they are an essential part of our economy. They provide us with goods for our own use and for export, and they provide many jobs for our workforce.

Building factories means that we also need to build more houses. People have been moving to the cities to get jobs in the factories, and this trend will continue. Right now we have a serious housing shortage, and it will just get worse as we build more factories. Therefore, we have to be sure to build enough houses for the workers near the factories.

When we build houses, we will have to build stores, as well. The factory workers will need someplace to go shopping. They will need to buy food, clothes, and other necessities. Our cities already have stores, of course, but their population will grow as more and more factory workers arrive. Stores will be needed in the new neighborhoods that will grow up around the new factories.

Our economy is developing rapidly, and that means we need to use land for building. The construction of new factories, houses, and stores is part of our growing economy.

181 EX

Films can tell us a lot about the country where they were made. What have you learned about a country from watching its movies? Use specific examples and details to support your response.

Foreign movies can show us a lot about life in other countries that may be different from what we are accustomed to in our own country. But they also show us something else. They show us the ways that we are the same. By watching foreign movies, I have learned some things that we all have in common despite language and cultural differences. We all want to get an education, need to make a living, and like to have fun.

Once I saw a movie made in China. It showed parents helping their children with their homework. My parents helped me the same way. Another time I saw a movie from Argentina. It showed schoolchildren playing a game during recess. My friends and I used to play the same game at school. Seeing these films showed me that education is a common goal in every country. Children go to school and their parents help them with their work and want them to do the best they can. Education is something we all have in common.

By watching foreign movies, I see the different ways people earn a living. In some countries, people choose their careers according to their interests and talents. In other countries, their parents choose their careers for them. But in every country, finding a way to earn a living is a major concern, and working hard is respected. Earning a living is another common goal.

Movies often show how people have fun. People everywhere want to be entertained and want to spend time with family and friends. Different cultures may enjoy different types of activities, but all cultures enjoy some form of sports, music, and dancing. Everybody likes to have fun.

The movies I've seen make it clear to me that no matter what the cultural differences are between countries, people everywhere have the same basic needs and goals.

182 PR

Some students prefer to study alone. Others prefer to study with a group of students. Which do you prefer? Use specific reasons and examples to support your answer.

Some students like to study alone, but I am not one of them. I almost always prefer to study with a group of students because I have a much better experience that way. Working with other students helps me learn the material better, it keeps me focused, and it's a lot more fun than studying on my own.

I learn more when I study with a group because we can all help each other out. If I missed something in class, the other students in the group can give me the information I missed. If there is something I don't understand, the other group members can explain it to me. In addition, when we discuss topics together, we develop our ideas and understand the material better. When I study alone, however, I don't get any help like this.

Studying in a group also helps me stay focused on my work. When I am with friends who are studying, then I study, too. Together we choose a time and a place to study. We meet and spend the allotted time on our schoolwork. We help each other stay focused on the task. When I study alone, on the other hand, I get easily distracted. I might leave my books to watch TV or call a friend. It's hard to stay focused by myself.

Another reason I prefer to study in a group is that it's much more fun than studying alone. I feel happy when I'm with my friends even when we are working hard. After we finish studying, we often go to a movie together. That makes studying something to look forward to. I never look forward to studying when I have to do it alone, however.

It's hard for me to study alone. I learn much better when I study with my friends, I stay focused, and I enjoy it. Studying with a group is the best way for me.

183 MA

You have enough money to purchase either a house or a business. Which would you choose to buy? Give specific reasons to explain your choice.

If I had enough money, I would buy a business rather than a house. A house is only a place to live, but a business is so much more. A successful business makes many things possible. If I did well with my business, I would be able to buy a house with the money I earned, and I could do other things, as well. I would be able to travel, for example, and I could help my family, too.

I have always wanted to buy a house, and a business would make this possible. With a business I would earn enough money to buy a house. It might not happen right away, but after a few years in the business, I am sure I would have enough money. Then I would have both a business and a house.

After I buy my house, I could use my money to travel. I would like to visit other countries. With a business, I could earn enough money to do this. I might also travel for business. I might have to go to other countries to attend conferences or meet clients. One way or another, a business would give me the chance to travel.

One of my goals is to help my family. My parents don't own a house. With a business, I could help them buy one. I could also take care of them when they get older. I would also like to be able to send them on a trip. If I had a good business, I could help my parents in all these ways.

A house is just one thing, but a business is so much more. A good business would give me the opportunity to buy a house, travel, and help my parents. Buying a business is an investment for the future.

Answer Key

INTEGRATED TASKS
Step 1: Plan

PRACTICE 1 (Page 34)

Possible answers:

READING 1

Main idea — Invasive plants harm native plants.

Supporting details
(1) They are introduced to an area through gardening.
(2) They escape from the garden and grow wild.
(3) They push out native species, causing devastating effects on the local ecology.

LECTURE 1

Main idea — Garlic mustard is an invasive species that causes problems.

Supporting details
(1) It competes with other spring-blooming species.
(2) The West Virginia white butterfly is threatened by this plant.
(3) Garlic mustard was introduced to the United States as a food source.

READING 2

Main idea — TV viewing has negative effects on children's school performance.

Supporting details
(1) Children who watch a lot of TV get lower grades and test scores.
(2) Few TV programs teach academic or thinking skills.
(3) When children spend time watching TV, they spend less time on homework, with other people, and being active.

LECTURE 2

Main idea — TV watching can actually improve school performance.

Supporting details
(1) TV exposes children to new ideas and information.
(2) Children should watch some TV, but not too much.

READING 3

Main idea	A particular smoking prevention campaign aimed at young people has been successful.
Supporting details	(1) Many teens participated in antismoking events, and many saw antismoking ads. (2) Teens who saw the ads were less likely to start smoking. (3) The public health department will continue and expand the campaign.

LECTURE 3

Main idea	The initial results of public health campaigns can be misleading.
Supporting details	(1) Over half of the teens had seen the ads and participated in workshops and meetings. (2) Surveys taken near the end of an antismoking campaign showed 40% unlikely to try smoking. (3) Surveys taken three months later showed 58% very likely to try smoking.

READING 4

Main idea	A good mood makes shoppers buy more.
Supporting details	(1) Mood can be affected by weather, personal life, and store environment. (2) Retailers create a store environment to have a positive impact on mood and therefore on sales.

LECTURE 4

Main idea	Studies show that mood can affect customers' behaviors and attitudes.
Supporting details	(1) When listening to slow music, restaurant patrons remained longer and purchased more food. (2) When listening to familiar music, shoppers stayed in a store longer and expressed more positive opinions about the products.

PRACTICE 2 (Page 37)

Possible answers:

READING 5

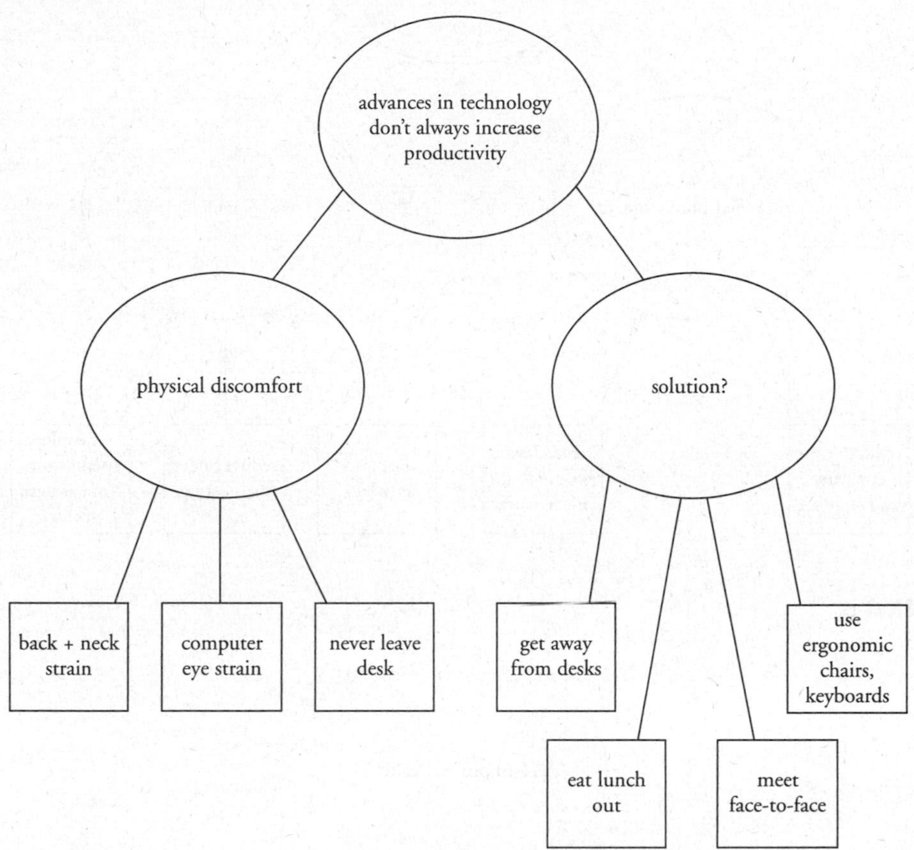

LECTURE 5

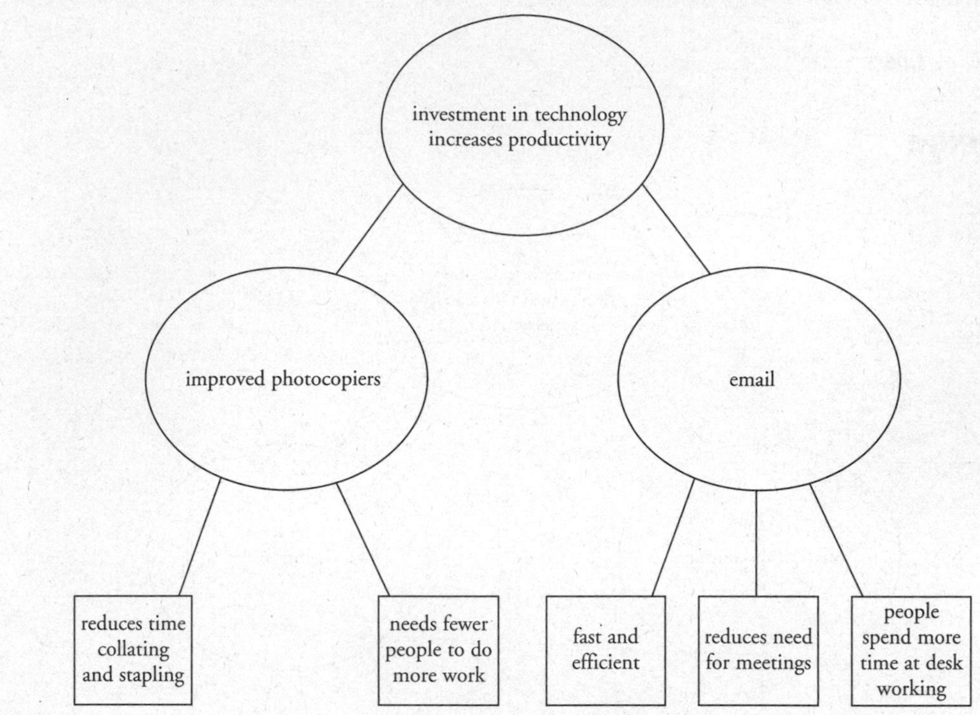

READING 6

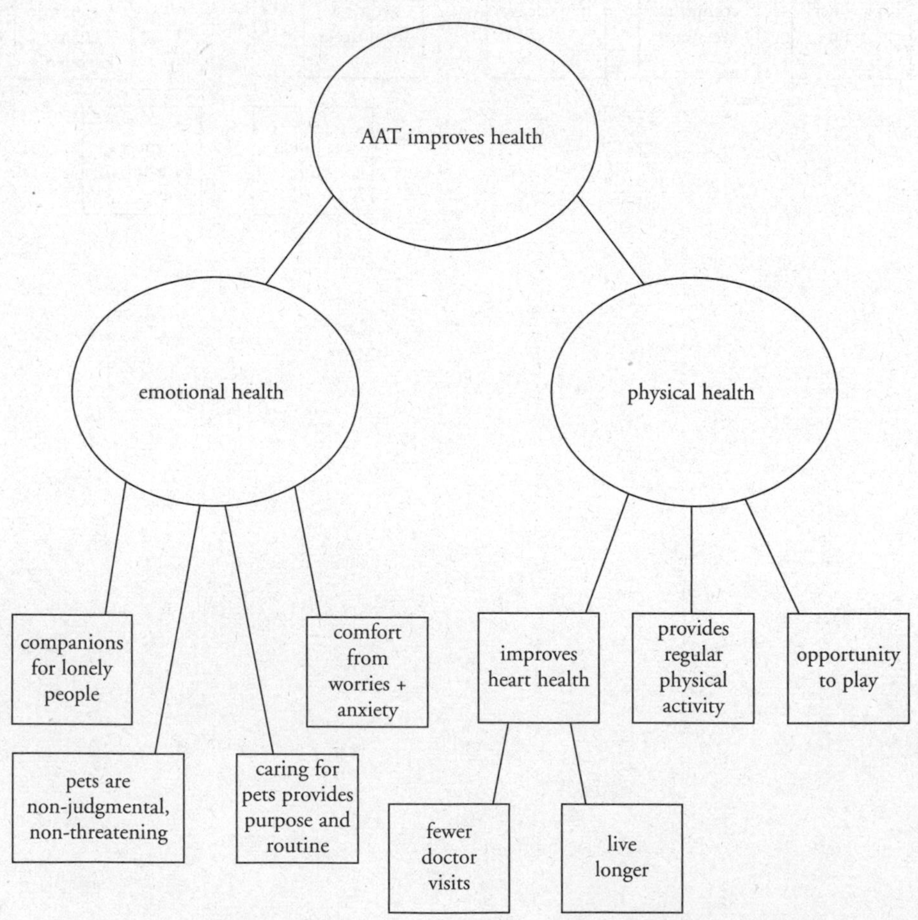

LECTURE 6

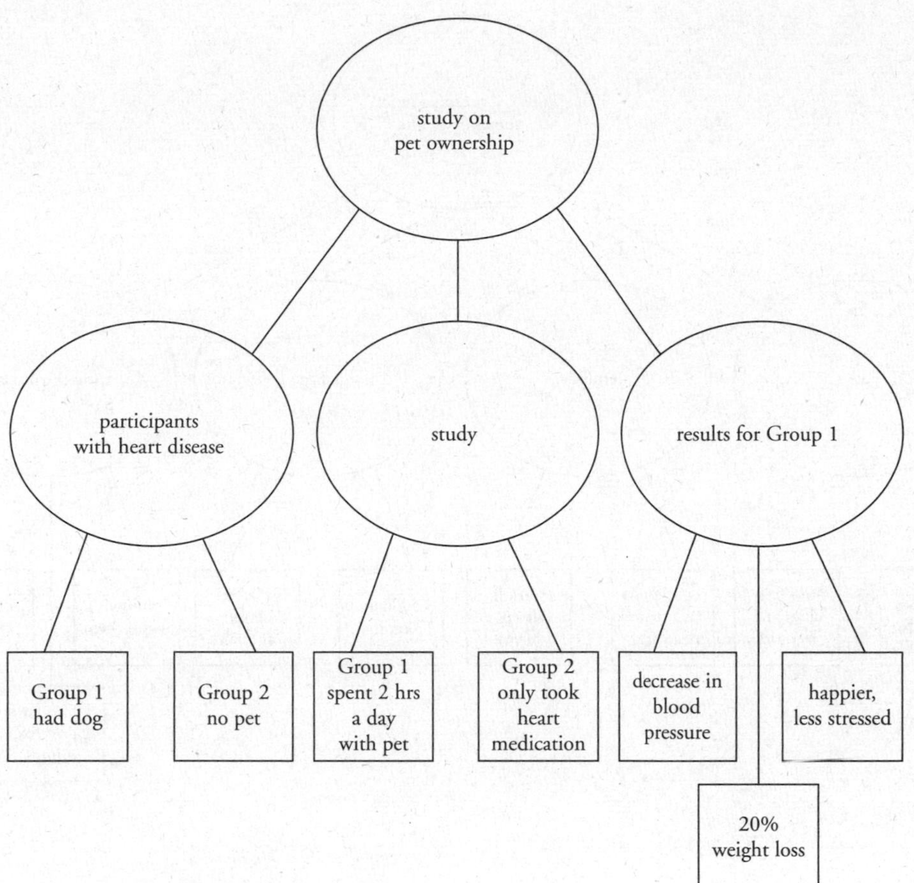

study on
pet ownership
participants
with heart disease
study
results for Group 1
Group 1
had dog
Group 2
no pet
Group 1
spent 2 hrs
a day
with pet
Group 2
only took
heart
medication
decrease in
blood
pressure
happier,
less stressed
20%
weight loss

READING 7

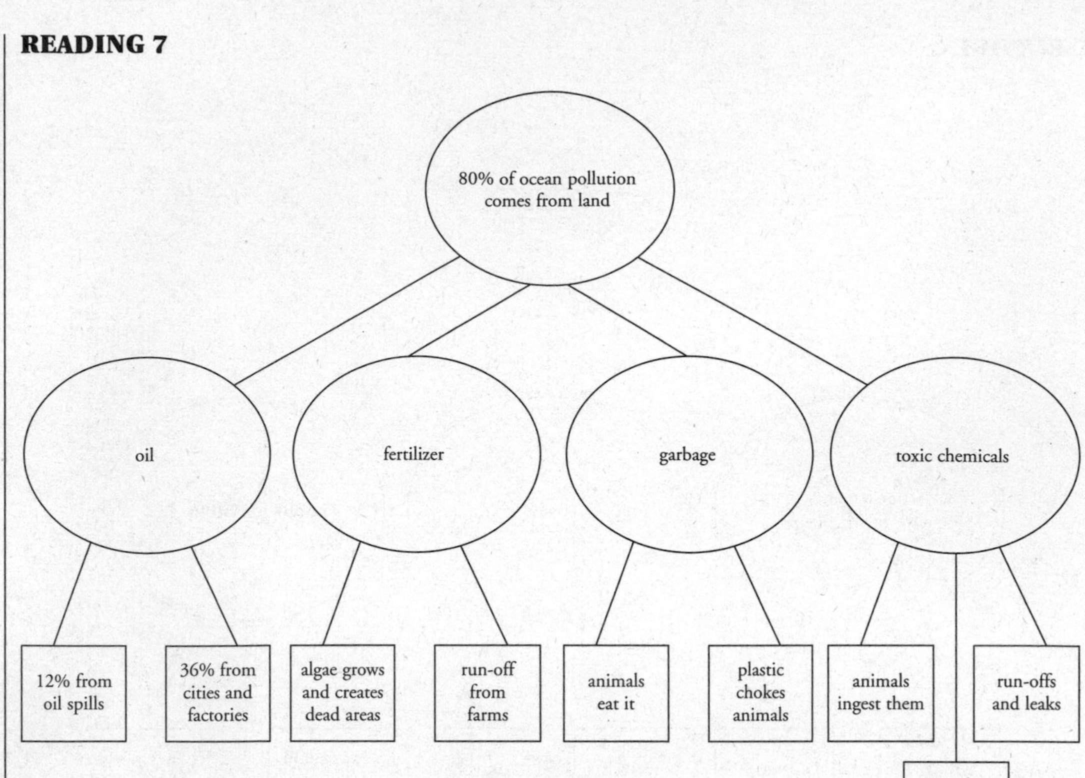

80% of ocean pollution comes from land
oil
fertilizer
garbage
toxic chemicals
12% from oil spills
36% from cities and factories
algae grows and creates dead areas
run-off from farms
animals eat it
plastic chokes animals
animals ingest them
1970s laws against toxic dumps
run-offs and leaks

LECTURE 7

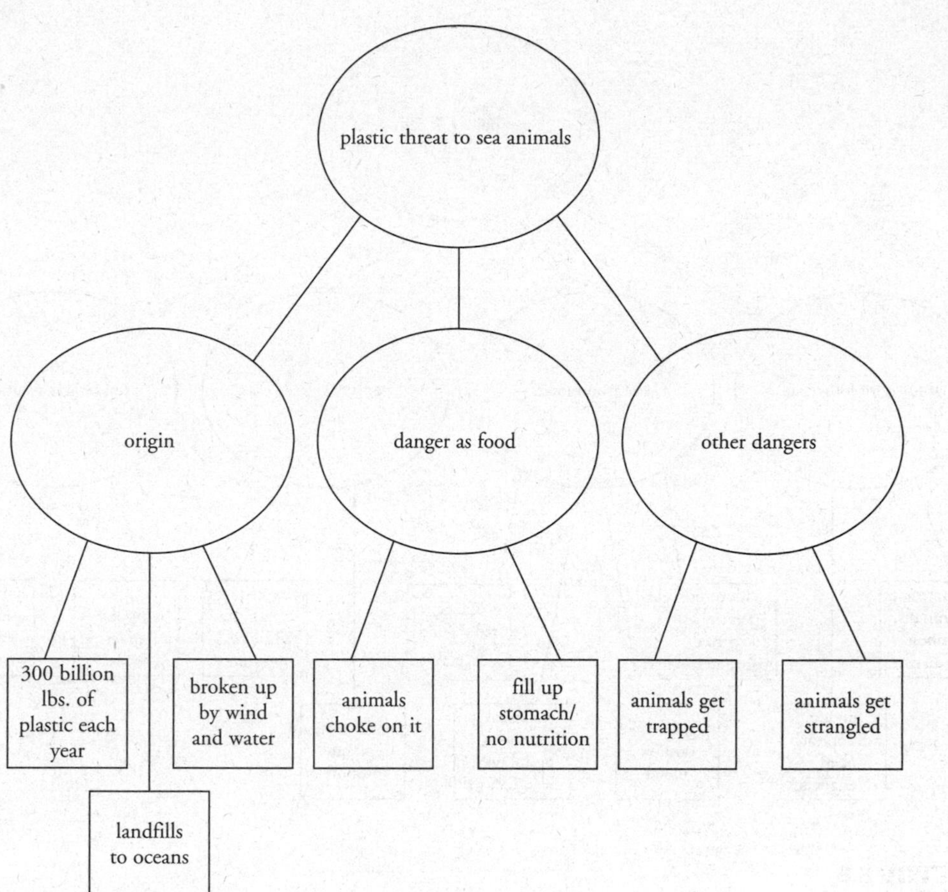
plastic threat to sea animals
origin
danger as food
other dangers
300 billion lbs. of plastic each year
landfills to oceans
broken up by wind and water
animals choke on it
fill up stomach/ no nutrition
animals get trapped
animals get strangled

READING 8

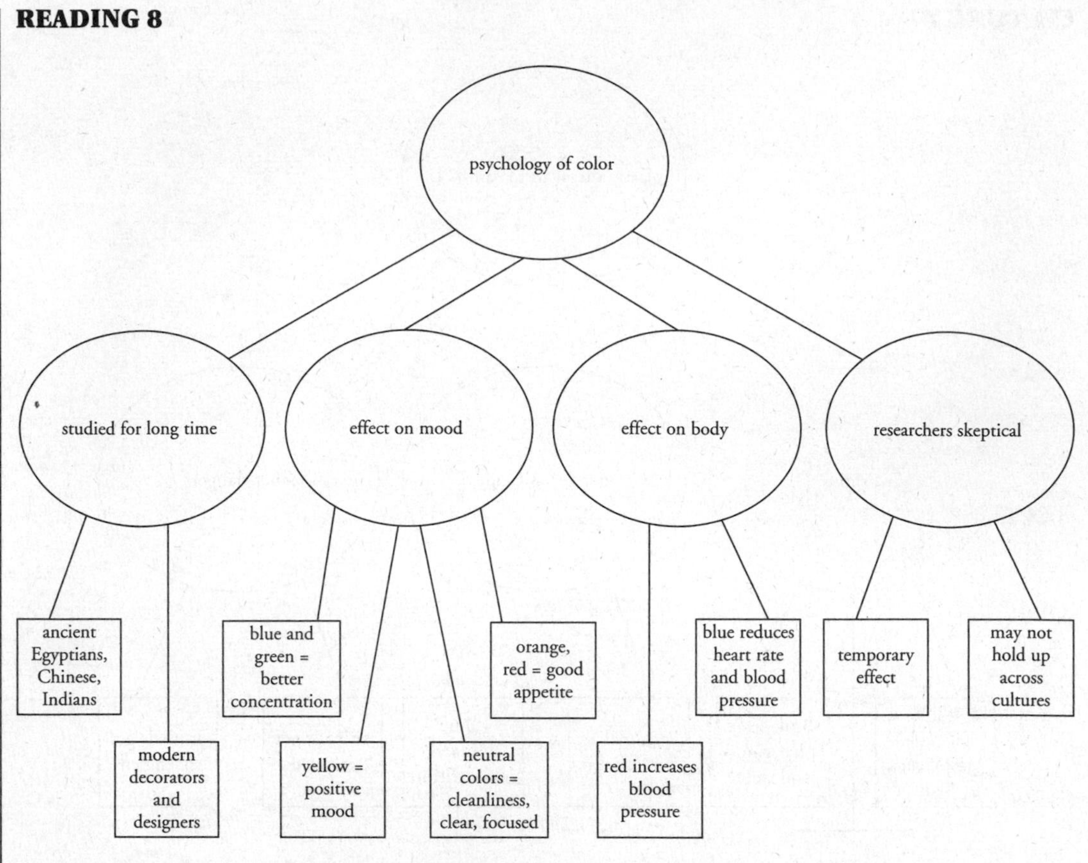
psychology of color
studied for long time
effect on mood
effect on body
researchers skeptical
ancient Egyptians, Chinese, Indians
modern decorators and designers
blue and green = better concentration
yellow = positive mood
neutral colors = cleanliness, clear, focused
orange, red = good appetite
red increases blood pressure
blue reduces heart rate and blood pressure
temporary effect
may not hold up across cultures

LECTURE 8

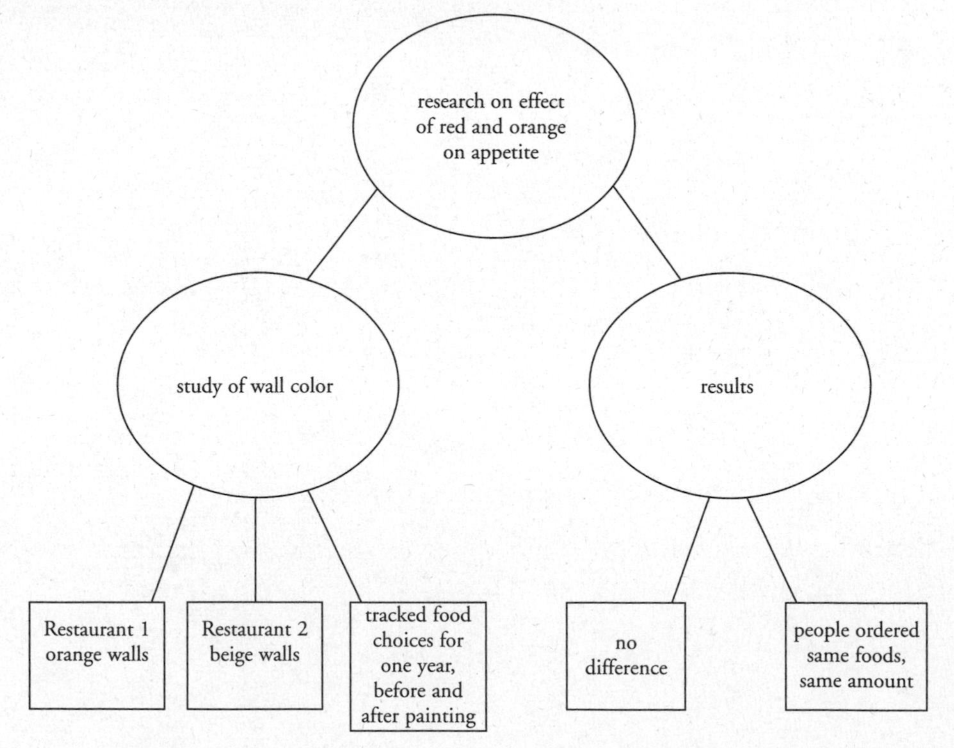
research on effect of red and orange on appetite
study of wall color
results
Restaurant 1 orange walls
Restaurant 2 beige walls
tracked food choices for one year, before and after painting
no difference
people ordered same foods, same amount

Step 2: Write

PRACTICE 1 (Page 41)

Possible answers:

READING 1 The author states that invasive plants harm native plants.

LECTURE 1 The speaker explains that garlic mustard is an invasive species that causes problems.

READING 2 The author believes that TV viewing has negative effects on children's school performance.

LECTURE 2 The speaker proposes that TV watching can actually improve school performance.

READING 3 The author tells us about a particular smoking prevention campaign aimed at young people that has been successful.

LECTURE 3 The speaker warns us that initial results of public health campaigns can be deceptive.

READING 4 The author proposes that a good mood makes shoppers buy more.

LECTURE 4 The speaker explains that studies show that music can affect consumers' behavior and attitude.

READING 5 The author asserts that advances in technology don't always lead to increased productivity.

LECTURE 5 The speaker suggests that investment in technology is paid back in increased productivity.

READING 6 The author explains that animal-assisted therapy is used to improve emotional and physical health.

LECTURE 6 The speaker tells us about a study that showed positive effects of pet ownership on health.

READING 7 The author warns that ocean pollution is a serious problem.

LECTURE 7 The speaker explains how plastic garbage threatens sea animals.

READING 8 The author describes psychological effects of color.

LECTURE 8 The speaker tells us about a study that showed no effect of color on appetite.

PRACTICE 2 (Page 43)

Possible answers:

1. The author states that invasive plants harm native plants, and the speaker explains that garlic mustard is an invasive species that causes problems.
2. The author believes that TV viewing has negative effects on children's school performance. The speaker, on the other hand, proposes that TV watching can actually improve school performance.
3. The author tells us about a particular smoking prevention campaign aimed at young people that has been successful. In contrast, the speaker warns us that initial results of public health campaigns can be misleading.
4. The author proposes that a good mood makes shoppers buy more. Similarly, the speaker explains that studies show that music can make consumers spend more time shopping.
5. The author asserts that advances in technology don't always lead to increased productivity. The speaker, in contrast, suggests that investment in technology is paid back in increased productivity.
6. The author explains that animal-assisted therapy is used to improve emotional and physical health, and the speaker tells us about a study that showed positive effects of pet ownership on health.
7. The author warns that ocean pollution is a serious problem. In the same way, the speaker explains how plastic garbage threatens sea animals.
8. The author describes psychological effects of color. In contrast, the speaker tells us about a study that showed no effect of color on appetite.

PRACTICE 3 (Page 45)

1. C
2. A
3. B
4. B
5. A
6. C
7. A
8. B
9. A
10. C
11. C
12. A
13. B

PRACTICE 4 (Page 48)

Possible answers:

1. Garlic mustard is a problem in the U.S. because it threatens other spring-blooming plants by taking up light, nutrients, and space.
2. Garlic mustard also threatens the West Virginia white butterfly. It competes with other types of mustard which are the butterfly's food source.
3. Garlic mustard was first grown on Long Island for food and has since spread to other areas of the country.
4. Children can learn new things from TV.
5. The amount of time spent watching TV is important.

6. More than three hours a day of TV watching results in lower reading and math test scores.
7. Surveys made at the end of an antismoking campaign showed that 50% knew about the campaign and 40% would probably not smoke.
8. Three months later, the numbers had changed.
9. More than half said they would probably smoke, and fewer than one-third said they knew about the campaign.
10. Research showed that slow music caused customers to stay at the restaurant longer and order more food.
11. Some of the study subjects, college students, heard popular music in the store, and others heard older music.
12. Those who heard familiar music shopped longer and said better things about the store's products.

PRACTICE 5 (Page 51)

Possible verbs; the quotes are shown where needed.

1. The author explains that invasive plants may have "devastating" results.
2. The author asserts that most children's TV programs don't have "valuable content."
3. The author reports that antismoking campaigns for teens have had "significant success."
4. The speaker claims that offices save money because office workers "can now devote themselves to other tasks."
5. The speaker states that when children watch TV, they "actually do better in school."
6. The author points out that play helps people "live longer, healthier lives."
7. The author remarks that neutral colors are used in health care centers to "convey a sense of cleanliness."

PRACTICE 6 (Page 54)

Possible summaries:

SUMMARY 1

The author states that invasive plants harm native plants. Likewise, the speaker explains that garlic mustard is an invasive species that causes problems.

Gardeners have introduced nonnative plants for food and medicine. They have also planted them because they are hardy, drought resistant, or beautiful. However, these plants escape from the garden and cause problems. Invasive plants harm native species by shading them out, strangling them, or using up all the nutrients in the soil. The local ecology suffers because there are fewer native plants and animals lose their homes and food.

The speaker mentions garlic mustard as an example of an invasive plant that harms the local ecology. It threatens other spring-blooming plants by taking up light, nutrients, and space. It also threatens the West Virginia white butterfly by competing with other types of mustard which are the butterfly's food source. Garlic mustard was first grown on Long Island for food and has since spread to other areas of the country.

SUMMARY 2

The author believes that TV viewing has negative effects on children's school performance. The speaker, on the other hand, proposes that TV watching can actually improve school performance.

According to the author, children who have TV sets in their bedrooms don't do as well in school as their classmates. Some people think of TV as educational, but the author asserts that most children's TV programs don't have "valuable content." In addition, TV takes time away from important activities like doing homework or being with other people. Parents can help their children by turning off the television.

The lecturer does not agree with this point of view. It is his opinion that children actually can learn new things from watching TV. The lecturer points out, however, that the amount of time spent watching TV is important. The speaker says that more than three hours a day of TV watching can result in lower reading and math scores.

SUMMARY 3

The author tells us about a particular smoking prevention campaign aimed at young people that has been successful. In contrast, the speaker warns us that initial results of public health campaigns can be misleading.

The antismoking campaign described in the passage included advertising, no-smoking policies, and antismoking events. Many teens participated in the events and many more saw the ads. The public health department plans to continue with this successful campaign to improve public health among young people in the state.

The speaker warns us that we can be deceived by the initial results of public health campaigns. She mentioned a recent antismoking campaign as an example. Surveys made at the end of the campaign showed that more than 50% knew about the campaign and 40% would probably not smoke. Three months later, however, the numbers had changed. Many more said they would probably smoke and many fewer said they knew about the campaign. So, a public health campaign that looks successful at first can look less successful a few months later.

SUMMARY 4

The author proposes that a good mood makes shoppers buy more. Similarly, the speaker explains that studies show that music can affect customers' behavior and attitude.

The reading passage explains that a shopper's mood may be influenced by things that retailers cannot control, such as the weather or personal or work problems. Retailers can, however, influence shoppers' moods by controlling the store environment. Shoppers buy more when retailers use lighting, color, and music to improve shopper mood.

The speaker describes research about the effect of music on consumers. Research showed that slow music caused customers to stay at a restaurant longer and order more food. In another study, some of the subjects, college students, heard popular music in a store, and others heard older music. Those who heard familiar music shopped longer and said better things about the store's products. These two studies show that restaurant and store owners can influence shoppers' moods and encourage shoppers to buy more.

Step 3: Revise

PRACTICE 1 (Page 62)

MODEL TASK 2

1–5

The author explains that (1) animal-assisted therapy is used to improve emotional and physical health, and the speaker tells us about a (2) study that showed positive effects of pet ownership on health.

The author explains how pets improve both emotional health and physical health. (A) Pets are good companions for lonely people. (B) They also give their owners things to do, like hobbies or club activities. (C) In addition, pets are a comfort to anxious or worried people. Pets are good for physical health, as well. (D) They help people with high blood pressure and heart problems. (E) They help people stay physically active. (F) They give people a chance to play. (G) Finally, pet therapy is used with elderly people.

The speaker supports pet therapy. He describes a study where pets had a positive effect on the health of heart patients. (A) Half the patients had a dog to take care of. The other half only got traditional treatment. (B) After six months, the patients with pets had lower blood pressure, and (C) they had lost more weight than the other patients. (D) They felt happier, too. (E) These are all things that can effect heart disease. This is a case that shows how pet therapy works to improve physical health.

6. There are no grammar or spelling errors.

7. (possible answers)

simple sentence:	Pets are good companions for lonely people. (para. 2)
compound sentence:	After six months, the patients with pets had lower blood pressure, and they had lost more weight than the other patients. (para. 3)
adjective clause:	He describes a study where pets had a positive effect on the health of heart patients.

MODEL TASK 3

1–5

The author warns that (1) ocean pollution is a serious problem. In the same way, the speaker explains how (2) plastic garbage threatens sea animals.

The author explains that different things cause ocean pollution. (A) Oil from factories and cities enters the ocean through rivers and drains. (B) Similarly, fertilizers wash into the ocean, and they cause large growths of algae. (C) Toxic chemicals continue to pollute the ocean, as well. There are laws against dumping these chemicals, but they still leak into the ocean. Animals eat them, and when we eat seafood, we eat these chemicals, too. (C) There is also a lot of garbage in the ocean. Plastic is the worst kind because it doesn't break down quickly. Animals think it is food. They eat it and choke on it.

While the author gives an overview of ocean pollution, the speaker specifically describes the problem of plastic garbage. (A) People produce more than 300 billion pounds of plastic a year, and a lot of this ends up in the ocean. The water and wind break large pieces of plastic into smaller pieces. (B) Then animals try to eat these pieces. An animal may choke on plastic. It may starve because it doesn't feel hungry after eating plastic. (C) Animals are often caught in floating plastic. (D) They are also strangled by it. There are many types of pollution in the ocean. Plastic garbage is one of the worst examples.

6. There are no grammar or spelling errors.

7. (possible answers)

compound sentence: Similarly, fertilizers wash into the ocean, and they cause large growths of algae. (para. 2)

complex sentence: Plastic is the worst kind because it does not break down quickly. (para. 2)

simple sentence: An animal may choke on plastic. (para. 3)

MODEL TASK 4

1–5

The author explains that (1) color has psychological effects. In contrast, the speaker tells us about (2) a study that showed no effect of color on appetite.

The author describes different ways people have used the psychological effects of color. (A) Ancient people used color for healing, and modern designers use color to create mood. (B) They might use yellow to create a positive mood in an office. (C) Likewise, they might use neutral colors to create a clean, clear, and focused mood in health care centers. (D) Restaurants often use orange and red to stimulate the appetite. (E) Some scientists say that blue lowers the heart rate and blood pressure. Red, on the other hand, raises blood pressure. Other scientists don't believe that color affects mood. They say the effect is temporary and also that it is different in every culture.

The speaker describes a study that showed no relationship between color and mood. (A) A fast food restaurant chain had orange walls in half its restaurants and beige walls in the rest of its restaurants. (B) It recorded all the food ordered for two years. (C) There was no difference between the restaurants with orange walls and the restaurants with beige walls. People ordered the same food in both types of places. In other words, according to the company president, there is no effect of color on appetite. He said that he proved it. In this case, at least, there was no psychological effect of color.

6. There are no grammar or spelling errors.

7. (possible answers)

compound sentence: Ancient people used color for healing and modern designers use color to create mood. (para. 2)

noun clause: Other scientists do not believe that color affects mood. (para. 2)

simple sentence: People ordered the same food in both types of places. (para. 3)

PRACTICE 2 (Page 65)

1. C	5. C	9. B	13. B	17. C
2. A	6. B	10. A	14. A	18. A
3. B	7. A	11. A	15. B	19. A
4. B	8. C	12. C	16. A	20. B

PRACTICE 3 (Page 70)

Missing items:
Paragraph 1: Incomplete thesis statement
Paragraph 2: Main idea
Paragraph 3: none

Grammar and vocabulary errors:
Paragraph 1: none
Paragraph 2: Consequently, the harsh climate…; …can to be very high…
Paragraph 3: Although, because of the losses…; …many people in this northern province is…

Rewritten essay.
Possible added and corrected parts are underlined.

The reading passage explains why farming is difficult in far northern regions in general. In a similar way, the lecture describes difficulties faced by farmers in a particular northern province.

According to the author, the cold climate of far northern regions makes it very difficult for farmers to make a living. In the first place, the growing season is very short. It might last three months or less, which is not enough time for most crops to mature. Additionally, few people live in northern regions because the cold weather is not attractive. Therefore, farmers have to pay to transport their crops long distances to cities where they can sell them to a larger market. Finally, the harsh climate causes farm machinery to break down frequently. The cost to repair or replace specialized farm equipment can be very high.

The speaker discusses farmers working in a particular northern province. He explains that many people have stopped farming in that area because they are no longer able to make a living that way. One reason is the disease affecting the rye crop, one of the few crops that can be grown so far north. Another reason is the rising cost of transportation. Fewer and fewer farmers can afford to ship their crops to cities. Furthermore, because of the losses due to the rye disease, many farmers have difficulty paying the cost of maintaining their buildings and equipment. For reasons similar to those outlined in the reading passage, many people in this northern province are leaving their farms to look for jobs in towns and cities.

PRACTICE 4 (Page 72)

Corrected words are underlined.

1. Garlic mustard is a problem in the U.S. because it threatens other spring-blooming plants by taking up light, nutrients, and space.
2. Garlic mustard also threatens the West Virginia white butterfly. It competes with another type of mustard which is the butterfly's food source.
3. *correct*
4. Children can learn new things from TV.
5. The amount of time spent watching TV is important.
6. More than three hours a day of TV watching results in lower reading and math test scores.
7. Surveys made at the end of an antismoking campaign showed that more than 50% knew about the campaign and 40% would probably not smoke.
8. *correct*
9. More than half said they would probably smoke, and fewer than one-third said they knew about the campaign.
10. Research showed that slow music caused customers to stay at the restaurant longer and order more food.
11. Some of the study subjects, college students, heard popular music in the store, and others heard older music.
12. Those who heard familiar music shopped longer and said better things about the store's products.

PRACTICE 5, INTEGRATED TASK (Page 74)

See Step 2, Practice 6 answers for correctly punctuated versions of these essays.

PRACTICE INTEGRATED TASK (Page 76)

Possible response:

The author discusses the dangers of cell phone use while driving. The speaker, however, believes that cell phones are not any more dangerous to drivers than other distractions.

The author explains that talking on the phone while driving is dangerous because it distracts the driver. Because of this, drivers in accidents involving cell phones have been held responsible for the accidents. The author also discusses laws that prohibit the use of cell phones while driving.

The speaker disagrees that using cell phones while driving is so dangerous. She points out that drivers can be distracted by things other than talking on the phone, such as eating, talking to passengers, taking care of children, putting on makeup, and other things. She cites a study that found that cell phone use actually causes fewer accidents than other distractions. She mentions another study that used video. The video showed that drivers were less distracted by their phones than by other activities. Finally, the speaker emphasizes that cell phones contribute to our safety. People use cell phones to report accidents and dangerous drivers on the road.

INDEPENDENT TASKS

Step 1: Plan

PRACTICE 1 (Page 80)

1. B It mentions a specific decision.
2. A It answers the question *Do you agree or disagree?*
3. C It mentions reasons why people visit museums.
4. A It states a preference.
5. B It states an opinion.

PRACTICE 2 (Page 84)

Possible answers:

1. I would be healthy.
2. Beach, soccer, bicycle
3. No need to heat the house
4. Bake a cake
5. Machines are neat.
6. Power saw

PRACTICE 3 (Page 86)

Answers will vary.

PRACTICE 4 (Page 90)

Possible answers:

1. people to teach me about life
2. laugh and joke with me
3. problems
4. history
5. restaurants
6. tourist and craft shops

PRACTICE 5 (Page 93)

Answers will vary.

Step 2: Write

PRACTICE 1 (Page 95)

1. In my opinion, people's lives are (or are not) easier today.
2. It seems to me that most people prefer (or do not prefer) to spend their leisure time outdoors.
3. To my mind, an apartment building is (or is not) better than a house.
4. From my point of view, it is (or is not) good that English is becoming the world language.

PRACTICE 2 (Page 96)

1. I believe that high schools should (or should not) allow students to study what they want.
2. I guess that it is better to be a leader (or member) of a group.
3. I agree that people should (or should not) do things they do not enjoy doing.
4. I suppose that I would rather have the university assign (or not assign) me a roommate.

PRACTICE 3 (Page 97)

1. I am sure that children should (or should not) spend a great amount of time practicing sports.
2. I am positive that a shopping center in my neighborhood will (or will not) be a benefit to our community.

PRACTICE 4 (Page 97)

1. Maybe a zoo has (or does not have) a useful purpose.
2. Probably, the city (or countryside) is a better place to grow up.
3. Certainly, our generation is (or is not) different from that of our parents.
4. Surely, a sense of humor can sometimes be helpful (or detrimental) in a difficult situation.

PRACTICE 5 (Page 98)

1. All things considered, the family is (or is not) the most important influence on young adults.
2. In general, parents are (or are not) the best teachers.
3. By and large, people are never (or are sometimes) too old to attend college.

PRACTICE 6 (Page 99)

1. In a way, it is better to make a wrong decision than to make no decision. **Or,** In a way, it is better to make no decision than to make a wrong decision.
2. To some extent, watching movies is (or is not) more enjoyable than reading.
3. In a sense, you can (or cannot) learn as much by losing as by winning.

PRACTICE 7 (Page 100)

Possible answers:

1. Opinion: I think the more friends we have, the better.
   Paragraph focus: learn how to trust others
   Paragraph focus: learn what to expect from others
   Paragraph focus: help us profit from experiences
2. Opinion: I believe that playing games is both fun and useful.
   Paragraph focus: teaches cause-effect relationship
   Paragraph focus: teaches us about teamwork
   Paragraph focus: teaches us to follow rules
3. Opinion: Nothing is as important to me as my family.
   Paragraph focus: learned about trust
   Paragraph focus: learned about ambition
   Paragraph focus: learned about love
4. Opinion: I prefer to spend time with friends.
   Paragraph focus: keep me company
   Paragraph focus: are enjoyable to talk with
   Paragraph focus: teach me things
5. Opinion: Traveling alone is the only way to travel.
   Paragraph focus: meet new people
   Paragraph focus: have new experiences
   Paragraph focus: learn more about yourself

PRACTICE 8 (Page 102)

Answers will vary.

PRACTICE 9 (Page 106)

1. E—gives advice (*look for another opportunity; don't give up*)
2. E—gives advice (*make sure to dress appropriately for every situation*)
3. C—explains what could happen (*it would bring more variety…, give us the opportunity to amuse ourselves…, bring more jobs…*)
4. D—ends with questions (*Isn't it important…? Don't you want…?*)
5. D—ends with questions (*…wouldn't I? Could you call me…?*)

Step 3: Revise

PRACTICE 1 (Page 111)

ESSAY TOPIC 9

1. I prefer to prepare food at home.
2. Main ideas: (1) cheaper
   (2) healthier
   (3) more convenient
3. Main idea: While eating in restaurants is fast, the money you spend can add up.
   Supporting details: (A) When I have dinner in a restaurant, the bill is usually $25 or more.
   (B) Even lunch at a food stand can easily cost seven or eight dollars.
4. Main idea: Eating at home is better for you, too.
   Supporting details: (A) When you cook at home, however, you can control what you eat.
   (B) …at home you can control your portion size.
5. Main idea: Cooking at home, however, can actually be more convenient.
   Supporting details: (A) There are a lot of simple meals that don't take long to prepare.
   (B) In addition, when you eat at home, you don't have to drive to the restaurant, look for a parking space, wait for a table, and wait for service.
6. Para. 3 too
   Para. 3,4,5 however
   Para. 4 In addition
7. There are no grammar or spelling errors.

8. (possible answers)

   ss: Eating at home is better for you, too. (para. 3)

   cx/s: When I have dinner in a restaurant, the bill is usually $25 or more. (para. 2)

   adj.c: There are a lot of simple meals that don't take long to prepare. (para.4)

ESSAY TOPIC 10

1. I believe, however, that the disadvantages outweigh the advantages.
2. Main ideas: (1) ...bring more traffic problems to the area.

   (2) ...attract undesirable people.

   (3) ...other types of businesses...would be more beneficial to the neighborhood.
3. Main idea: Traffic congestion is already a problem in our neighborhood and a new restaurant would just add to the problem.

   Supporting details: (A) Most restaurant customers would arrive by car and crowd our streets even more.

   (B) In addition, they would occupy parking spaces and make it even harder for residents to find places to park near their homes.
4. Main idea: I'm also concerned about the type of patrons a new restaurant would bring into our neighborhood.

   Supporting details: (A) The restaurant would stay open late and people leaving the restaurant might be drunk.

   (B) They could be noisy, too.
5. Main idea: Finally, there are other types of businesses that we need in our neighborhood more.

   Supporting details: (A) We already have a restaurant and a couple of coffee shops.

   (B) We don't have a bookstore or a pharmacy, however, and we have only one small grocery store.
6. Para. 2 in addition

   Para. 3 also

   Para. 4 Finally, however

   Para. 5 but, Moreover
7. There are no grammar or spelling errors.
8. (possible answers)

   cx/s: If the restaurant serves drinks and has dancing, there could be problems. (para. 3)

   ss: We already have a restaurant and a couple of coffee shops. (para. 4)

   cm/s: It might bring jobs, but it would also bring traffic and noise. (para. 5)

ESSAY TOPIC 11

1. In short, teachers provide you with a lot more support and knowledge than you can usually get by yourself.
2. Main ideas: (1) ...help you find the way that you learn best.

   (2) ...help you stay focused...

   (3) ...provide you with a wider range of information...

3. Main idea: Teachers can help students learn in the way that is best for each student because teachers understand that different people have different learning styles.
   Supporting details: (A) For example, some students learn better by discussing a topic.
   (B) Others learn more by writing about it.
   (C) A teacher can help you follow your learning style, while a book can give you only one way of learning something.
4. Main idea: Teachers help you focus on what you are learning.
   Supporting details: (A) They can help you keep from becoming distracted.
   (B) They can show you which are the most important points in a lesson to understand.
   (C) If you have to study on your own, on the other hand, it might be difficult to keep your attention on the material or know which points are most important.
5. Main idea: Teachers bring their own knowledge and understanding of the topic to the lesson.
   Supporting details: (A) A book presents you with certain information, and the teacher can add more.
   (B) The teacher might also have a different point of view from the book and can provide other sources of information and ideas, as well.
6. Para. 2 For example
   Para. 3 on the other hand
   Para. 4 also
   Para. 5 though
7. There are no grammar or spelling errors.
8. (possible answers)
   cx/s: Teachers can help students learn in the way that is best for each student because teachers understand that different people have different learning styles. (para. 2)
   ss: Others learn more by writing about it. (para. 2)
   cm/s: A book presents you with certain information, and the teacher can add more. (para. 4)

ESSAY TOPIC 24

1. … there are certain characteristics that all good co-workers have in common.
2. Main ideas: (1) cooperative
   (2) adapt well to changes
   (3) helpful
3. Main idea: A good co-worker is very cooperative.
   Supporting details: (A) She does her best to get along with others.
   (B) She tries to do her work well because she knows that if one person doesn't get her work done, it affects everyone else.
   (C) She also has a positive attitude that creates a pleasant working environment.

4. Main idea: A good co-worker is adaptable.

   Supporting details:
   (A) She is not stubborn about changes in schedules or routines.
   (B) She doesn't object to having her job description revised.
   (C) She has no problem with new procedures.
   (D) In fact, she welcomes changes when they come.

5. Main idea: A good co-worker is helpful.

   Supporting details:
   (A) For instance, she lends a hand when someone falls behind in his or her work.
   (B) She is willing to change her schedule to accommodate another worker's emergency.
   (C) She doesn't keep track of how often she has to take on extra work.

6. Para. 2 also
   Para. 3 In fact
   Para. 4 For instance
   Para. 5 Thus
7. There are no grammar or spelling errors.
8. (possible answers)

   cx/s: She tries to do her work well because she knows that if one person doesn't get her work done, it affects everyone else. (para. 2)

   ss: A good co-worker is adaptable. (para. 3)

   nc: She doesn't keep track of how often she has to take on extra work. (para. 4)

PRACTICE 2 (Page 116)

1. B	5. C	9. A	13. A	17. A
2. A	6. C	10. C	14. B	18. C
3. C	7. B	11. A	15. C	19. A
4. A	8. B	12. C	16. B	20. B

PRACTICE 3 (Page 121)

Missing items:

Paragraph 1: thesis statement
Paragraph 2: supporting ideas
Paragraph 3: main idea
Paragraph 4: none
Paragraph 5: none

Grammar and vocabulary errors:

Paragraph 1: none
Paragraph 2: . . . the drinking water <u>are</u> . . .
Paragraph 3: none

Paragraph 4: Life in the countryside help...; In the countryside, for instance...;...they know where there food comes from.
Paragraph 5:...I plan to let they grow up...

Revised Essay

Added and corrected parts are underlined.

I agree that it is better for children to grow up in the countryside. When children grow up in the countryside, they have a healthier life. They also have a safer life. Children also learn to appreciate nature when they grow up in the countryside.

Life in the countryside is healthier for children than life in the city. Drinking water in the city is usually dirty. In the countryside, on the other hand, the drinking water is clean and pure. Also, the air in the countryside is much cleaner and fresher than city air. In addition, in the countryside children can play outside often, but in the city they have to spend most of their time indoors.

Life in the countryside is safer for children than city life. They don't have to worry about crime because there are fewer criminals in the countryside than in the city. They don't have to worry about traffic accidents, either, because there are fewer cars in the countryside. Furthermore, they don't have to worry about strangers who might hurt them because in the countryside almost everybody knows everybody else.

Life in the countryside helps children appreciate nature. There are few plants in the city. In the countryside, on the other hand, children see trees and flowers around them all the time. They also have opportunities to see wild animals, while in the city they can only see animals in zoos. In addition, they know where their food comes from. In the countryside children are surrounded by farms, but in the city they only see fruits and vegetables in the grocery stores.

Life in the countryside is definitely much better for children than life in the city. It is cleaner, safer, and closer to nature. When I have children, I plan to let them grow up far away from any city.

PRACTICE 4 (Page 123)

Why People Are Living Longer

People are living to be much older these days than ever before. The main reasons for this are greater access to health care, improved health care, and better nutrition.

Basic health care is available to many more people now than it was in the past. When someone is ill nowadays, he or she can go to a public hospital instead of having to pay for private care. There are also more clinics and more trained doctors and nurses than there used to be. Years ago, health care was not available to everyone. People who didn't live in big cities often did not have easy access to doctors or hospitals, and many people couldn't afford to pay for the medical care they needed.

In addition to increased access to health care, the quality of that health care has greatly improved over the years. Doctors know now much more about diseases and how to cure them. In the past, people died young because of simple things such as an infection or a virus. Now we have antibiotics and other medicines to cure these diseases. Furthermore, advances in medical science have made it possible to cure certain types of cancer and to treat heart disease. This has prolonged the lives of many, many people.

The quality of nutrition has also improved over time. Because of this, people tend to be healthier than they used to be. Now we know how to eat more healthfully. We know that eating low fat food can prevent heart disease. We know that eating certain fruits and vegetables can prevent cancer. We have information about nutrition that can help us live longer, healthier lives.

Improved health care and healthy eating habits are allowing us to live longer. Now we need to make sure that everyone in the world has these benefits.

BOTH TASKS

PRACTICE 1 (Page 128)

Paragraph 1:

1. first
2. Next
3. such as
4. In addition
5. As a result of

Paragraph 2:

1. Consequently
2. such as
3. After
4. Moreover
5. In other words

Paragraph 3:

1. In the first place
2. Moreover
3. on the other hand
4. for example
5. As a result

Paragraph 4:

1. For example
2. Similarly
3. Because of this
4. as well
5. Although

Paragraph 5:

1. On the contrary
2. for instance
3. By the same token
4. So
5. In fact

PRACTICE 2 (Page 130)

See Essay 106 on page 234 in the Model Essays Section of the Appendix for a model response.

PRACTICE 3 (Page 133)

1. maintain
2. think
3. advancing
4. in
5. improve
6. interesting
7. You
8. engineers
9. where my cousins still live
10. to

PRACTICE 4 (Page 135)

1. A   2. C   3. C   4. A   5. B   6. A

PRACTICE 5 (Page 136)

1. A   2. B   3. B   4. C   5. A   6. C

PRACTICE 6 (Page 138)

Paragraph 1:
1. S   2. Cx   3. S   4. Cx   5. S

Paragraph 2:
6. Cx   7. Cx   8. S   9. S   10. Cx   11. Cx

Paragraph 3:
12. S   13. Cx   14. S   15. Cx

Paragraph 4:
16. S   17. S   18. C   19. Cx

Paragraph 5:
20. S   21. S   22. C-Cx

PRACTICE 7 (Page 140)

1. A   2. C   3. C   4. A   5. A   6. C

PRACTICE 8 (Page 142)

Paragraph 1:
1. like (active), bring (active)
2. are outweighed (passive)
3. cause (active), bring (active)
4. destroy (active)
5. is (active), oppose (active)

Paragraph 2:
6. cause (active)
7. build (active), breathe (active), will become (active)
8. will be covered (passive)
9. pollute (active)
10. will be (active)
11. will be hurt (passive), will be affected (passive)

Paragraph 3:
12. will say (active), will be created (passive)
13. can have (active)
14. will grow (active)
15. will be built (passive)
16. will be (active)
17. can cause (active)

Paragraph 4:

18. will change (active)
19. is (active)
20. is (active)
21. knows (active)
22. brings (active), will change (active)
23. will be lost (active)

Paragraph 5:

24. would be helpful (active), outweigh (active)
25. would be changed (passive)
26. cannot support (active)

PRACTICE 9 (Page 143)

1. A
2. C
3. A
4. B

Audioscripts

INTEGRATED TASK

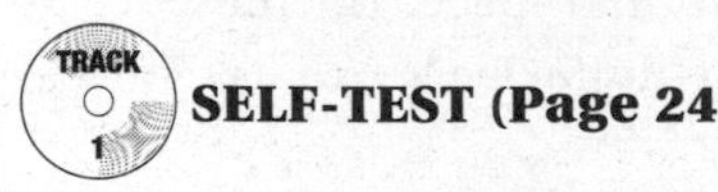

SELF-TEST (Page 24)

(male speaker)

After years of warnings from scientists, it has finally become widely accepted that average temperatures on our planet are rising, with many potentially serious consequences. And just in case anyone still has doubts about the actuality of global warming, a recent report on changing conditions in the northeastern United States should help dispel them. Data collected by weather stations throughout the Northeast shows that there has been a definite warming trend in that region over the past half century. The greatest warming has occurred in the winter season. Average temperatures in the December to March period increased between 1965 and 2005. In addition, yearly snowfall totals dropped, while the number of days with at least an inch of snow on the ground fell by an average of nine days. This is a significant change in a region that is traditionally known for its cold and snowy winters.

One sector of the economy that has taken a direct hit from this warming trend is the ski industry. The local economy in many rural areas is dependent on recreational ski centers. Less snowfall means fewer days that ski centers can be open for business. There are also increased expenses from making artificial snow to compensate for the lack of natural snow. The economic impact reaches far beyond the owners of ski resorts. Local hotels, restaurants, ski rental centers, and gift shops all suffer from the decrease in tourism that results from a poor ski season. Warm autumns also have a negative impact on local economies. Brilliant fall foliage brings tourists, and their dollars, to many remote rural areas in the Northeast. A hot summer and warm autumn mean that the fall foliage season is less colorful and less attractive to tourists.

Leading scientists have predicted that average temperatures in the Northeast will increase by several degrees Fahrenheit before the end of this century. In addition, the number of days with snow on the ground will be reduced by 25 to 50 percent. With much of the economy of the Northeast dependent on the tourism that skiing and autumn foliage bring, changes in weather patterns can have a serious effect on the economy of that region.

PRACTICE 1 (Page 34)

LECTURE 1 (Page 35)

(female speaker)

Let's take a look at some invasive species that are causing problems locally. Garlic mustard, a European native, has become a problem in several areas in the United States. It's a cool season plant, blooming in midspring. It prefers moist, shady areas at the edge of woods or along roadsides. It thrives in the same habitat as a number of native midspring bloomers, such as spring beauty, wild ginger, and trillium. Garlic mustard threatens these native species because it aggressively competes with them for light, nutrients, and space. The presence of garlic mustard also threatens many local animals that depend on the leaves, roots, flowers, and pollen of the threatened native plants as a food source.

The West Virginia white butterfly is particularly vulnerable to invasion by garlic mustard. The plant pushes out certain native species of mustard which constitute the major food source for the caterpillar stage of this rare butterfly. In addition, garlic mustard may contain chemicals which are toxic to the butterfly's eggs. It has been observed that eggs laid on garlic mustard leaves do not hatch. Garlic mustard was introduced to the United States in the nineteenth century as a food source and may have had medicinal uses as well. It was first recorded on Long Island but now thrives throughout the eastern and midwestern United States.

LECTURE 2 (Page 35)

(male speaker)

TV has been blamed for a lot of things, most particularly for poor school performance. However, we can't blame the mere fact of TV-watching for low achievement in school. For one thing, not all TV watchers are low achievers. Japanese children, who as a whole have higher test scores than American children, watch more hours of TV than their American counterparts. For another thing, in the past two decades, the amount of time American children spend watching TV has declined, but overall test scores have not risen. The fact is, research shows that children who watch an hour or so of TV daily, but not more, actually do better in school than children who don't watch TV at all.

Why is this? TV can expose children to new ideas and information that they might otherwise not have access to. Children who watch TV occasionally are probably discriminating in the programs they choose to view. Research suggests that an important point is the amount of time spent in front of the TV. Children who spend three hours a day or more in front of the TV do poorly in school, scoring lower on both math and reading tests than children who watch some, but less, TV. Guidelines for parents include: limiting children's TV-watching time to no more than two hours a day; guiding children in their choice of programs to watch; discouraging eating while watching TV; and encouraging children to participate in other sorts of activities such as reading, playing outside, or visiting zoos and museums.

LECTURE 3 (Page 36)

(female speaker)

How effective are public health campaigns? They must be evaluated with care because initial results can be deceptive. Evaluations of the effectiveness of a public health campaign too often take place close to the end of the campaign only. To truly understand the impact a public health campaign may—or may not—have had, we have to look at where we stand several months after the campaign has ended. Unfortunately, this piece is often neglected.

To illustrate the point, let's take a look at a recent campaign to reduce smoking among teens in the Midwestern region. Teens in this area were inundated with antismoking information for the better part of a year. There were ads all over the local communities, representatives went into high schools to offer workshops, literature was distributed, antismoking clubs were formed, in short, all the usual activities of a campaign of this sort were instigated. Surveys taken near the end of this campaign, in March of last year, showed that well over half of those surveyed were aware of the campaign. This means they reported that they had seen the ads, participated in workshops, attended a meeting, and so on. At the same time, forty percent of those surveyed reported that they were unlikely to try smoking in the next year. It sounds like a great success, doesn't it? Just three months after the campaign ended, however, this last figure changed dramatically. At the end of June, fifty-eight percent of survey participants reported that they were "very likely" to smoke in the next year. At the same time, less than thirty percent reported awareness of the antismoking campaign, so it seems a number of them had already forgotten the ads they had seen just a few months earlier.

This information puts the whole effort in a completely different light. Naturally, no public health official likes to see such poor numbers resulting from such a huge effort. If we truly aim for effectiveness in our public health work, however, we need to take an honest look at all the figures.

LECTURE 4 (Page 36)

(male speaker)

Retailers may find that investment in a good music system for their retail space will bring them a worthwhile return on the money. Several very interesting studies have been published recently which show positive—for the retailer, anyhow—effects of music on shopping behavior.

One study was actually done in a restaurant and compared the effects of fast and slow music on restaurant patrons. The researchers found that patrons who heard music with a slow tempo tended to remain at the restaurant longer than patrons who heard fast music. As they lingered over their meals, they purchased more food and beverages, which of course is the effect desired by the restaurant owner. When restaurant patrons heard fast music, they ate more quickly and tended not to order extras such as appetizers, desserts, and beverages. The average length of time spent in the restaurant when fast music was playing was fifteen minutes less than it was when slow music was playing. In addition, each patron spent on average four dollars less for the meal when fast music was playing.

Another study looked at the effects of familiar and unfamiliar music on shoppers in a clothing store. The study subjects were mostly college students shopping in a store that catered to their age group. Some of them heard currently popular hit songs while shopping—the "familiar" music—while others heard music normally aimed at an older age group. The students who heard familiar music stayed in the store longer than those listening to unfamiliar music. They also expressed more positive opinions of the products offered for sale. This study did not report on how many products study subjects purchased nor on how much money they spent. Retailers reading about such a study would, of course, want to know this type of information. Nevertheless, this study does give us some interesting general information on the effects of music on shopping behavior. Clearly, music has an impact, and retailers need to take this into account.

PRACTICE 2 (Page 37)

LECTURE 5 (Page 38)

(female speaker)

Purchasing new office technology and getting office staff trained to use it involves a significant investment of time and money. Quite understandably, companies are often reluctant to keep spending money in this way. Study after study, however, has shown that the investment is almost always paid back many times over in increased worker productivity. For example, in the past, an office assistant could spend a large percentage of the day photocopying documents, then collating and stapling them. It wasn't unusual for busy offices to hire assistants whose main duties involved photocopying. Now, the newest photocopiers not only copy much faster than the old ones, they also fold, collate, and staple. The work is done quickly and accurately, and office assistants can devote themselves to other tasks. Offices can operate with fewer assistants, thus spending a great deal less on salaries and benefits.

Email is another example of how technology has improved office procedures. Communication by email is fast and convenient. It's also cheap. It costs no more to send an email to a colleague in an overseas office than it does to send one to someone sitting at the next desk. Email can help projects run more smoothly. Many times, a matter can be resolved quickly through email, thus eliminating the need for frequent meetings. Important updates can be communicated to staff members in a timely manner, allowing everyone to work more efficiently. All of this means workers can spend more time at their desks producing. Hiring trained staff to keep email, websites, and Internet access running smoothly does require some investment of company resources, but the payback more than makes up for it. No doubt about it—investment in office technology is a sound business choice.

LECTURE 6 (Page 39)

(male speaker)

University Hospital, a leader in the field of cardiac disease research, recently conducted a study of the effects of pet ownership on health, more specifically, on heart health. The results showed overwhelmingly that pets can contribute to improving the health of heart patients. Participants in the study were being treated for heart disease at the hospital's Powell

Memorial Heart Clinic. Most were in recovery from cardiac bypass surgery. Half the participants were given a dog to care for at home during the course of the study. They were asked to spend one to two hours a day caring for the pet, including walking it twice a day, playing with it, feeding and bathing it, and petting it. The dogs chosen for the study came from a local animal shelter and were all considered to be mild-tempered, well trained, friendly, and easy to care for. The remaining study participants continued with traditional heart disease treatments only, which included both drug and physical therapy and dietary recommendations, but did not involve any specific exercise program to follow at home.

At the end of six months, it was found that those who had been caring for dogs had a decrease in blood pressure as compared to the patients who had received traditional treatment only. They also had an average weight loss 20 percent greater than the traditional patients. Many also reported feeling much happier and less stressed. High blood pressure, weight gain, and stress are factors contributing to heart disease. If you're wondering what happened to the dogs, put your mind at rest. The majority of dog caretakers in the study elected to keep their pets after the study was over. Several of the study participants who had been on traditional treatment only also expressed interest in the dogs. Other research hospitals in the country are looking to carry out similar studies with hopes of replicating the results. It looks like dogs may truly turn out to be man's best friend.

LECTURE 7 (Page 40)

(female speaker)

Plastic garbage poses a serious threat to ocean animals. Every year, billions of pounds of plastic are produced. Much of this plastic is in the form of bags, bottles, and other sorts of packaging, which is used once, then thrown away. Where does all this plastic garbage go? Some of it ends up in landfills, but significant amounts make their way into our oceans. Rainstorms wash all sorts of garbage into storm drains and rivers, and from there, sooner or later it reaches the ocean.

Plastic decomposes very slowly. In the ocean, large pieces eventually get broken up into smaller pieces by the movement of the water and wind. Those smaller pieces can end up floating around in the ocean's waters for decades or even centuries. Sea animals often mistake these pieces of plastic for food. A floating plastic bag could look like a tasty jellyfish to a sea turtle. Sea birds can confuse small bits of plastic with the fish eggs they usually dine on. An animal that tries to swallow plastic may choke on it. Other animals starve to death after filling their stomachs with plastic. Plastic has no nutrition, but the animal doesn't look for more food since it feels full.

Plastic bags, balloons, bottle tops, and other sorts of plastic trash have been found blocking the breathing passages and stomachs of many sea animals, but plastic can be dangerous even if an animal doesn't try to eat it. Animals frequently get caught in the middle of large accumulations of plastic garbage that float around our oceans. Others get strangled by plastic straps or plastic rings. The death toll from plastic in the oceans is high. It has been estimated that tens of thousands of sea turtles and other marine animals are killed each year by plastic garbage in the ocean. For birds the figures are much higher. As many as one million sea birds a year may fall victim to plastic garbage.

LECTURE 8 (Page 40)

(male speaker)

Have you ever noticed that many restaurants have red or orange walls? This fashion comes from the widely held belief that these two colors stimulate the appetite. Restaurateurs hope that by stimulating the appetites of their customers in this way, they can encourage them to order more food.

A large fast-food chain recently decided to test the notion that the color of the decor affects how much food their customers order. This company has restaurants in major cities across the country and caters to customers of all ages, including small children. The traditional décor of this restaurant chain includes beige paint on the walls. Several years ago, the company painted the walls in half of its restaurants orange, leaving the other half of its restaurants with their original beige walls. In order to compensate for the possible influence of cultural differences between cities, the company made sure that in every city where its restaurants are located, there were both restaurants with orange walls and restaurants with beige walls.

The restaurant chain kept track of exactly what foods were ordered in each restaurant for one year before the walls were painted, and then again for one year after the walls had been painted. They found no difference. On average, customers in each restaurant, whether it had beige or orange walls, ordered the same types and quantities of food. "It's a myth that the color of walls has an effect on appetite, a complete myth," the president of the company said. "We have proven it." The walls of all the restaurants in the chain have been restored to their original beige color. The company president explained that this color is part of the company's image. Now that the study is over, people might be confused if they walked into a restaurant expecting beige walls and got orange instead, so the company president explained.

Practice Integrated Task (Page 76)

(female speaker)

Cell phones have been accused by many of making the highways dangerous, but it's time to take a hard look at the facts. What's really behind the majority of traffic accidents? A recent study found that close to eighty percent of automobile crashes were caused by driver inattention. Of course, talking on the phone is a common cause of driver inattention, but it's certainly not the only one. Other causes found in the study were drowsiness, talking with passengers, eating or drinking, and reaching for a falling object. In fact, the study found that while drivers talking on a cell phone increased their risk of an accident, those other distractions increased the risk even more. Another study looked at driver behavior, using video cameras installed in the cars of 70 drivers. The videos showed that drivers were much less distracted by their cell phones than they were by other activities such as reaching for items or talking to passengers. The Department of Transportation lists a number of common causes of inattentive driving in addition to cell phone use. These include eating, talking, putting on make-up, changing the radio, and attending to children. It even includes things like watching videos or reading while driving! The latest distraction is, of course, using GPS.

Discussions about the dangers of cell phone use while driving tend to overlook an important fact about cell phones, which is that they actually contribute to our safety on the road. Drivers place over 100,000 emergency calls on their cell phones every day. They report accidents, road hazards, and problem drivers, thus helping keep the roads safe for everyone. Drivers' use of cell phones to report emergencies has greatly reduced response times and helped save lives. Individual drivers' own security is protected by using cell phones to contact help when they experience mechanical problems while on the road.

We cannot, of course, say that cell phones are completely innocent. Certainly, cell phone use has contributed to traffic accidents, but so have many other things. It is better to be clear-headed about the facts and look at all sides of the issue.

Model Test 1—Integrated Task (Page 148)

(male speaker)

School systems across the country are devoting resources to equipping their classrooms with computers and training teachers to use them. In reality, how well prepared are teachers to use computers with their students? The government recently conducted a survey to find out, gathering information from over one hundred schools across the country. Ninety-six percent of the teachers surveyed reported that their training consisted mainly of developing basic computer skills, which they already had prior to training. Skills and knowledge that would help them incorporate the use of computers more fully into their lessons were not addressed in most training programs. Seventy-eight percent reported that the training they received was too brief, averaging less than five hours in total. Sixty-five percent said they were not comfortable using technology and rarely or never made use of computers in their classrooms. Of those who did use computers, the majority used them for skill and drill exercises and did not feel that the use of computers had changed their approach to teaching in any significant way. School administrators are wondering whether money invested in educational technology might yield better results if used to support other educational needs.

This is a bleak picture indeed. However, there is hope. Let's look at a success story that shows how technology can support education. Five years ago, the Riverdale School District implemented a program to train teachers to integrate technology into their lessons. Teachers who participated in the program received two hundred hours of training on using technology with their students to develop critical-thinking and problem-solving skills. The training occurred over a two-year period. In addition, teachers were assigned mentors who could assist them in implementing computer-based activities in the classroom. As a result of this, computers were fully integrated into the lesson plans of these teachers. Rather than the skill and drill software so commonly used, these teachers had their students working with simulation software to solve problems. When their students took the statewide achievement tests at the end of the first year of the program, they scored significantly higher than students who were not participating in the program.

Clearly, a commitment to filling schools with computers is not enough. An equal, if not greater, commitment must be made to training teachers to use this technology in ways that enrich the learning experience of their students.

Model Test 2—Integrated Task (Page 151)

(female speaker)

The subject of animal intelligence has long been of interest to scientists. One issue is how do we define or describe intelligence? The ability to feel empathy for fellow creatures is often considered as one mark of intelligence, and has been the subject of a number of research studies. This brings up the question of how do we measure empathy? Scientists believe that an animal must be able to perceive itself as an individual in order to empathize with another. Therefore, an important step in researching the ability to empathize is to test self-recognition. The most common way to do this is to use mirrors. Elephants, dolphins, and great apes are the only animals in addition to humans that demonstrate recognition of self in a mirror. When presented with a mirror, these animals often react to their image, touching it, displaying their teeth, or preening.

There is another test that scientists commonly use to test self recognition. In this test, a mark is painted on the animal, somewhere on or near its face. The animal is then shown a mirror. If the animal tries to wipe the mark off its face while looking at its image in the mirror, this shows, scientists say, that the animal recognizes the mirror image as a reflection of itself. In a study done with dolphins, some dolphins received marks on their bodies, others were touched with a marker but no mark was made, and still other dolphins were left completely alone. A mirror was placed in the dolphins' tank. All those that had felt the marker on their body rushed to the mirror to look. Those that actually had marks used the mirror to look at them closely. In similar experiments, elephants, chimpanzees, and orangutans have responded to marks in a like way. Not all scientists agree that such a test proves self recognition. Showing interest in the painted mark does not necessarily mean that the animal makes a connection between the mirror image and the self, they say. There are still many controversies surrounding research on animal intelligence.

Model Test 3—Integrated Task (Page 153)

(male speaker)

There is a popular idea going around that William Shakespeare did not actually write his own plays. Although attempts have been made to cast doubt on the authorship of these plays, no one has yet produced any real evidence that they were not written by William Shakespeare, humble resident of Stratford-on-Avon, himself. Proponents of the theory that Shakespeare did not write the plays claim that he was too poor, too obscure, and too uneducated to have written them himself. Poor and obscure though he may have been, it is not certain that he was uneducated. There was a school in Stratford-on-Avon, and the young Shakespeare may well have attended it along with other boys of his social class. As a student at the local school, he would have gained the knowledge of literature and the classics that the author of the plays certainly had. And although he was not an aristocrat himself, through his work at the theater he had plenty of opportunity to come into contact with the aristocratic classes that he often wrote about. He could easily have observed in this way the aristocratic manners and customs that he gave characters in his plays.

The lack of records about Shakespeare's life is also not evidence that he did not write the plays. As a commoner, there would not have been many records kept about him, and any records that may have existed could easily have been lost over the course of time. Neither has there been convincing evidence that another person actually authored the plays. One of the more popular theories is that Francis Bacon was the one who actually wrote the Shakespeare plays, but it does not hold up. Some claim as proof a similarity between Bacon's writings and those attributed to Shakespeare. Even a quick comparison of works by the two authors, however, clearly shows that the writing styles of the two men are completely different.

Model Test 4—Integrated Task (Page 157)

(female speaker)

It's widely accepted that the bubonic plague, which devastated the world in the fourteenth century, originated in Asia. There is new evidence, however, that suggests that it may actually have started in North Africa. Outbreaks of the plague still occur in Africa today.

An archeologist discovered evidence of the plague in ancient Egypt accidentally. She was studying insect fossils at the site of an ancient village when she came across human and cat flea remains. According to the archeologist, insect remains can tell us a great deal about how people lived in the past. For example, the remains can give clues about what kinds of animals people kept. In the case of the flea remains, she knew this meant that the plague could have been present in the ancient village. Previous research had turned up evidence of rats living along the Nile River as long ago as the sixteenth and seventeenth centuries B.C. Those rats are known carriers of the type of flea that carries the bubonic plague. Many ancient towns and cities were built along the Nile River. Periodic flooding in the area would have driven rats out of their natural homes and into human settlements—an ideal scenario for spreading plague among human communities. Further research brought up evidence that ancient Egyptians had suffered epidemics of a disease that seemed remarkably similar to the bubonic plague. The archeologist suggests that the plague was transported to Europe by rats that carried plague-ridden fleas onto ships crossing the Mediterranean Sea.

The bubonic plague is not only a disease of the ancient world or the Middle Ages. Contrary to popular belief, it did not disappear in the seventeenth century, but still occurs today. In Madagascar, for example, between 500 and 2,000 new cases of the disease are reported each year. According to the World Health Organization, every year there are as many as 3,000 new cases of the plague worldwide. Scientists continue to study the disease. Research on epidemics both past and present help scientists understand how epidemics spread and may help predict when new outbreaks will occur. There are still many mysteries surrounding the bubonic plague. It can disappear for years, or even centuries, then reappear suddenly, and just as suddenly disappear again. Scientists have a great deal to learn about this disease.

NOTES

NOTES

NOTES

NOTES

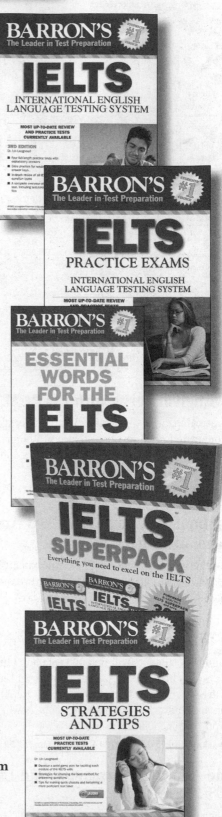